Make Your Own Electric Guitar

Make Your Own Electric Guitar

Second Edition

Melvyn Hiscock

Foreword by Brian May

NBS PUBLICATIONS

© Melvyn Hiscock 1986, 1998
Foreword © Brian May 1998

First edition published by Blandford Press 1986

This edition published 1998
Reprinted 1999, 2000, 2002

NBS

PO Box 6292
Basingstoke
Hampshire
RG21 5YX
United Kingdom

A catalogue record for this book is available from the British Library.

ISBN 0 9531049 0 7

Typeset by NBS Publications

Printed and bound in Great Britain by Antony Rowe Ltd.

Contents

Foreword

by Brian May

My dad and I joyfully (for the most part!) laboured for two years to design and construct my 'Red Special' electric guitar. Ever since the day when I first realised that our home-made electric guitar actually worked, I have intended to write a book very much like the one which you hold in your hand. I never made it, up to now – there was always too much in the in-tray, for which, I guess, I should be profoundly grateful.

Happily, however, Melvyn Hiscock has had the time, talent and infinite patience to produce this fine work, just the very thing I could have done with had it been available 30 years ago! Herein you will find a wealth of answers to questions which crop up at every stage in the design and creation of your own instrument, something which may eventually fit you more comfortably than your favourite slippers, or any commercially available guitar.

So please feel well advised to buy (or borrow – shhh . . .) this excellent companion for your days of construction. Maybe you'll join Bo Diddley and myself as living proof of the fact that, just sometimes, it's better to do it yourself.

Introduction

When I first started writing this book over fifteen years ago, I would not have believed that it would have been so popular or have lasted so long. The idea behind it came from someone asking me how to make a guitar. I simply told him to go to the library and get the relevant book. He told me that there was no such book, which took me by surprise since there had been nothing when I had started making guitars ten years before and I found it hard to believe there was still nothing suitable. At his suggestion I started writing and the end result was released in May 1986.

Since that time a lot has changed. Many of the parts that were available then have been superseded, some of the companies referred to no longer exist and, as much as anything else, I have learned a lot more. The continued sales of the book have shown that many more people are building their own guitars now than ten years ago; over the years I have met a number of them, which has been a real pleasure. It is also heartening to hear that many schools use the book and that many students have gone on to submit the instruments they have made for examinations.

Some of the methods I used in making the guitars for the book have been altered but I still feel the mix of designs I made was a good grounding in most of the areas that needed to be covered. For this edition I have added wherever necessary and included new photos and descriptions, but the message remains the same.

The electric guitar as we know it today is almost 50 years old and has changed little over the years. Apart from differing circuitry and some manufacturers' excursions into metal, carbon fibre and graphite necks, the construction of these instruments is very similar to how it was originally, and mass production has not changed these methods drastically.

Most good-quality electric guitars are still made with a combination of hand and machine wood-work, and these methods are not too difficult to translate into a form that can be used in a home workshop. However, there is still a lot of mystique surrounding guitars and I am constantly surprised by the number of people I meet who would like to make their own guitar but are apprehensive as they do not fully understand the basic principles and are confused by some of the things that have been written about guitars in recent years.

The intention of this book is to examine, using words and pictures, the various methods that are used both by individual makers and by large manu-facturers, and present them in such a way that the principles are easy to understand and the methods easy to follow. It is then up to you to design and build a guitar that is suited to your needs using the methods that you are most comfortable with. It is also my intention that if you are just interested in guitars, and have no intention of making one, you will find this book interesting and informative and that it will give you a better insight into the work-ing of your guitar, and the effort that went into its construction.

It is not difficult to make a guitar but it can be made so by lack of prior planning and preparation, or by using the wrong tools or materials. When I started making guitars, the information that I needed was not readily available and, as a result, I made a lot of mistakes through ignorance and stupidity. I hope that by understanding where the pitfalls lie you will be able to avoid them and save yourself a lot of unnecessary effort.

A BRIEF WORD ABOUT MEASURING THINGS

Since most of the history of the electric guitar stems from the United States of America it is inevitable that guitars were made using imperial measurements, those 'old-fashioned' inches and

1

fractions of inches that some of us (English people) remember from our youth. Since parts of this book describe those instruments in minute terms, the imperial measurements are used with their metric equivalents noted in brackets.

Part of the genius of Leo Fender was his use of prepared timber in easy sizes, such as one inch. Of course you can build guitars entirely by metric measurement and there is a faint chance that I might have done this in my past but I am the sort of person who makes true engineers shudder – I have been known to use both imperial and metric measurements on the same guitar, or even on the same piece of guitar! In some cases this is down to ease of application. For example, many Fender and Gibson guitars have a top nut that is $1\frac{11}{16}$ in wide. If you want to divide this in two to find the centre you need to be able to think and come up with a figure of $\frac{27}{32}$ of an inch. If you are under 40 it is sometimes easier to use 42 mm and divide that by two to give 21 mm. There is no point in making it difficult for yourself – you get no extra points for showing off – so use whatever system you are more comfortable with. I will endeavour to convert where I can.

COPYRIGHT, TRADENAMES AND COPYING

I must make it very clear that this is a book about making your *own* electric guitar, not about making one of Mr Gibson's, Mr Fender's, Mr Rickenbacker's, Mr Charvel's or even one of Mr Hiscock's. In recent years the major manufacturers have been taking action against companies and individuals who infringe their copyright on designs and names. When the first edition of this book was written, many of the guitars that have prompted these actions were not on the market. Huge amounts of money are put into designing and marketing guitars and to have someone come along and rip off your design is guaranteed to make anyone a mite angry. If you want a Fender Stratocaster, or any other off-the-shelf guitar, *go and buy one*. You will probably get it cheaper than you would if you made it yourself and never, but never, put a company logo on the guitar to fool your friends. You are only fooling one person. Do yourself a favour and design something of your own.

I am very pleased and honoured that Brian May has readily agreed to write a few words for this edition. This is partly because it was an interview with Brian in a magazine published in 1973 that fired my imagination, but mostly because his guitar is a fine example of how to go about the task correctly. Despite the lack of information and available component parts at that time, his guitar was *his* design and it contained the features that *he* decided *he* wanted. If this meant that he had to design and build a roller bridge and a tremolo system then so be it. Brian May could have had a fine career as a guitar-maker but chose to play in a band.

Throughout this book various guitars from various well-known companies are referred to. Most if not all of their easily-recognisable names are registered trademarks. They are used in this book to illustrate the various methods used in their manufacture and because most of them can be considered benchmarks for all that is good in guitar-making. I can make guitars that I am happy to play but there is always room for a good Les Paul, Strat, Tele or Gretsch or . . .

This book is dedicated to the memory of Leo Fender, who inspired at least three generations of guitarists, yet hardly played a note.

1 First Steps

Designing and building your own guitar can be both interesting and rewarding, but before you start it is worth asking yourself why you want to go to all the trouble of hacking up poor, innocent trees and brutally forcing them to become a musical instrument when you can go out and buy a decent guitar in a lot less time, with a lot less aggravation (depending on the music shop), and, in most cases, for a lot less money.

It might be true that the component parts of the guitar that you wish to build can be bought more cheaply than a similar guitar 'off the shelf', but the prices of these soon mount up and you do not just have to buy the component parts. It may be necessary to buy or rent some specialist tools and it is quite possible that you may make mistakes that could well cost you money whilst making your first guitar. Guitar-making is a skill, and like all skills will have to be learnt and cannot be successfully mastered without a lot of hard work and a few mishaps.

There is no point whatsoever in trying to make a guitar without having a basic knowledge of woodworking. If you cannot cut or plane in a straight line then making a guitar is not, at this stage, for you.

It is also a complete waste of time to try to make a guitar without the proper tools. There is a bare minimum of tools that will, at a pinch, be just sufficient to complete the work. Most of these will be found in a reasonably well equipped home workshop and others can be borrowed or rented but, again, there is no point starting to make a guitar with a few blunt tools on the kitchen table, as all you will do is waste money, wreck the kitchen table and probably chop off a few fingers in the process. The tools required are described in Chapter 4.

Do not get disheartened if you do not have the experience or the equipment to start your dream guitar immediately. Everyone has to start somewhere. Most public libraries will have a selection of books on the subject of woodworking and many further education colleges run evening classes. Any experience gained in this way will save time, effort, money and perhaps some swearing.

DESIGN OR REDESIGN?

Some people who choose to make guitars seem to want to radically redesign the instrument, or to build their dream guitar that will do everything they have always thought a guitar should do, including play itself. This attitude is fine if you have some experience already, but it can lead to problems if you just jump in at the deep end. Nine times out of ten these guitars do not work very well as they try to do too much. Start by making something straightforward to learn the basics and then go on to plan your instrument that will change the face of popular music as we know it today. There are many people who have tried to produce revolutionary guitars in the past, and most of these have quickly fallen by the wayside. The principal reason for this is that the early guitar designers got it right by keeping it simple.

Added to this, the styles of guitar-playing that have developed over the years, from country-and-western to mind-crunching heavy metal, have done so as a direct result of the instrument they are played on. If the electric guitar had been designed differently in some way at the outset, then the styles of playing would have probably evolved differently. Those styles that are used now evolved because they were comfortable to play and sounded good on the chosen instrument. If the guitar had been different, rock-'n'-roll might never have happened – what a thought!

MAKING GUITARS FOR A LIVING

I have never met a rich guitar-maker. There is a well-known saying used in yachting and aviation that can be used to describe the situation: the best way of making a small fortune in guitar-making is to start with a big one.

Over the years several people have approached me for advice on getting into guitar-making as a profession. For most it is a nice dream and a bad idea. One person turned up on my doorstep one day and, to my horror, I found that he had decided to 'be a guitar-maker as it sounded like a good job'. I was appalled that he thought it was that simple and I told him so. To make guitars successfully you need to produce a certain volume of instruments, which may not be possible on your own. Many people get by, but the competition – the big American and Far-Eastern companies – have got a huge advantage as they have the capital to produce a large number of instruments and so keep unit costs below what you or I would pay for the parts. These companies also have a double-edged marketing arrangement: not only do they have glossy advertisements in magazines but they sell their guitars through shops, where people go and browse and get influenced by salespeople. If you are building all day you are not actually selling and if you are not selling you have nothing to build.

There may come a time when, after years of hard work, your guitars gain a reputation that will let them sell themselves, but this is rare and, as I said, takes a lot of time. If having made and sold a few guitars you feel that it could be a wise move to set yourself up in business, then good luck, as it is an interesting occupation but it is not one that I would recommend.

The best attitude to have when attempting anything from making a guitar to scaling Mount Everest is to regard it as a challenge. In both cases, the exercise is hardly likely to make you rich but will definitely give you a sense of achievement. One big advantage of guitar-making over scaling Mount Everest is that very few people get frostbite while making a guitar. It is also fair to say that the view from the top of Everest is much better than the view from the top of a workbench. However, people who scale Mount Everest rarely want to do it again right away. This is not the case with guitar-making, as, no matter how good your first guitar is, there will be a feeling that if you make another, and another, they will get even better.

Making one guitar could get you hooked.

2 What is a Guitar?

It would be logical to assume that if you have made the decision to make your own guitar you should know, and be conversant with, the various parts of the guitar and their names. However, as with many subjects, it is often the most basic details that are easiest to overlook and so I shall describe, in simplistic detail, the parts and functions of the electric guitar so that nothing is taken for granted.

I asked several people, when originally writing this book, what they thought was the most important part of the electric guitar. Their answers ranged from the pick-ups through the choice of woods to the shape of the neck. All of these answers are a little wide of the mark, as the most important part of any guitar, acoustic or electric, is the *string*. This is very easily proven; if you take the strings off, the guitar does not work.

The guitar is quite simply a means of amplifying, and altering the pitch of, a set of strings. On an acoustic guitar the string is amplified by attaching it to a soundboard. The vibrating string excites the board which moves a larger volume of air than the string on its own. The air is reflected by the body out of the soundhole, and this produces a noise that is louder than the string, or even just the string and the soundboard together, could manage.

In the case of an electric guitar, in virtually all of its many forms, the string is suspended over a form of *pick-up*. This pick-up electro-mechanically converts the vibration of the string into a small electric current which is then fed into the collection of valves and wires that the guitarist keeps in a black box sitting somewhere behind him, and is amplified so it is slightly louder than the acoustic guitar.

Most electric guitars have six strings, although twelve-string guitars are made and even some seven-string guitars with a low B-string for more bass notes. Bass guitars have either four, five, six or, in extreme cases, eight strings in octaved pairs. These are anchored at one end and are fed into small geared devices called *machine-heads*, or *tuning-machines*, at the other, so that the string can be tensioned in order that it vibrates at the correct pitch. Between the anchor and the tuning-machines, the string passes over two points which determine the length that will give the correct pitch. At one end of the string is the *bridge* and at the other end is the *top nut*. These also serve to keep the string clear of the playing area of the guitar. The distance between these two points is known as the *scale length*.

The pitch of each string can be varied by pressing it against a small raised metal bar called a *fret*, which shortens the vibration of the string and, therefore, raises its pitch. These frets are placed at predetermined points along the playing area of the guitar so that each one alters the pitch of the string by one semitone.

The playing area of the guitar is called the *neck*, and on the face of this is a board into which the frets are fitted, called, not surprisingly, the *fretboard*, or *fingerboard*. In order that the guitar can be played successfully, the strings must pass over the fretboard at a height at which they can be comfortably pressed down to the fret, but not so close that they rattle against other frets along the neck. This distance between the fret and the string is called the *action*; and, in order for it to be adjustable, most electric guitar bridges are made to be moved up or down.

The neck of the guitar has to be rounded at the back so that the player's hand is able to reach round to fret the strings. This shaping has to be done so that the neck is not so slim as to make it weak, but not so cumbersome as to hinder the player's hand as he or she attempts to move up and down the neck whilst playing the guitar. Since removing any wood from the neck will make it weaker and more susceptible to bending under the pull of the strings, the neck is usually fitted with an adjustable

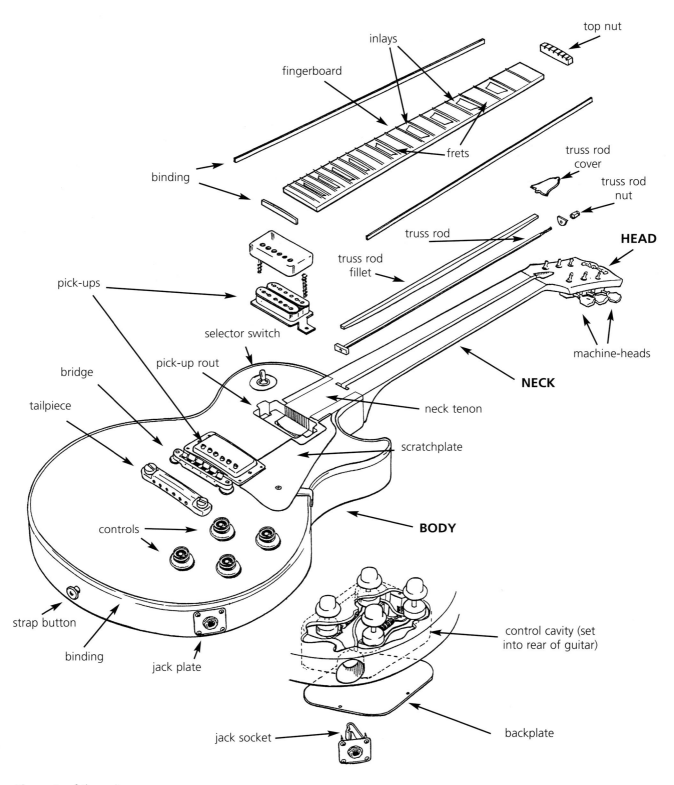

The parts of the guitar.

tensioning device which compensates for this and keeps the neck straight. This is called a *truss rod* and is adjustable at one end of the neck.

The *body* of the guitar must be of a size that is small enough to hold comfortably whilst still being big enough to balance properly when the guitar is on a strap. In order that the top frets of the neck are accessible, the body of the guitar is often cut away at one or both sides of the fingerboard to enable the player to reach these frets without having to stretch over the front of the guitar's body.

The electric guitar also has to be rigid enough not to dampen the vibration of the string without being too heavy to hold. In 1973 a granite-bodied guitar was submitted to Fender's research and development department for testing. It was found to have excellent sustain, as virtually none of the strings' vibration was absorbed by the body – although, as we will find, this is not necessarily a good thing. It was also excruciatingly heavy, and in order that it could be played was built on a stand.

Finally, the component parts of the guitar must fit together in a way that enables each to perform its correct function without impeding the function of any other part of the instrument, and without obstructing the player. I once saw a Fender Precision Bass that had been repaired by a complete idiot. A second pick-up had been fitted to the guitar along with another set of controls; and, in order to utilise the space inside the guitar to maximum effect, the idiot had fitted the jack socket on the rear of the guitar where it fouled the player's leg and ruined the look of an otherwise good instrument. The player was not very pleased.

All of this may seem very obvious, but ask yourself if there is even the smallest detail in the last few paragraphs that you had forgotten, or never really thought about; if this is the case, you will have learnt or remembered something that may make the job a little easier.

The next stage is to use this knowledge to design your own guitar.

3 Designing Your Own Guitar

The main reason that I started to make my first guitar was that, in order for me to be the greatest rock star in the history of the known universe, I simply had to be seen with a Flying V and, for this particular sixteen year-old, buying one was out of the question. So I tried to make one. Since I had no access to the real thing, and the nearest I had even been to one was halfway back in the crowd at a Wishbone Ash* gig, I had to guess the measurements and angles from looking at pictures. Of course it is theoretically possible to do a reasonable job using even this method if a little common sense is applied, but that too was sadly lacking. Not surprisingly it was awful, and I soon learnt that trying to copy an existing guitar was a course beset with problems, especially when trying to work cheaply. A Flying V can be a complicated guitar to make. I found that I got much better results when I tried designing my own guitar; it was more challenging, more rewarding and, above all, more fun.

This same approach had been adopted by another teenager a few years before. When Brian May of Queen was about sixteen, he too wanted a guitar that he could not afford – in his case a Fender Stratocaster – and so he also decided that the best course of action was to make his own. Rather than slavishly copy the Stratocaster, he took the trouble to design his own guitar that would give him the sounds he required. The result was the guitar he still uses today, which has been produced commercially by the Guild company.

Before getting down to designing your own guitar, it is worth looking at the early history of the electric guitar to help you understand why it came about and why there are several quite distinct styles of construction. In the last few years there have been some very good books and magazine articles that have covered the early days of the electric guitar in more detail than I will be able to do here, and these are often worth reading as the subject can be very interesting but sometimes rather confusing.

A SHORT HISTORY OF THE ELECTRIC GUITAR

The solid electric guitar evolved out of the earlier semi-acoustic guitar as an answer to the problem of feedback. Semi-acoustic guitars, or, as they were known at first, electric Spanish guitars, first came about in the early 1930s. At that time many guitar players were experiencing difficulty in making their acoustic instruments heard above the ever-increasing size and volume of some of the larger bands and the audience noise in small clubs. The first solution was to fit contact microphones that picked up the vibration of the guitar's top and fed the signal into the public address system. This was better than no volume at all but it could cause terrible feedback problems.

Feedback is caused when the noise coming from speakers causes the guitar's string or body to resonate. This in turn is picked up by the contact mike or pick-up, and is fed back into the amplifier where the whole process starts again. It is a vicious circle, although some have been known to use it to advantage, starting with the Beatles in the intro to the 1964 single *I Feel Fine*, and reaching a peak with the late Jimi Hendrix and his subsequent imitators.

String feedback can be stopped by simply stopping the string's vibration, or damping it. It is not so easy when it is the body that is feeding back. This happens when the noise coming from the speaker is the same as the resonant frequency of the guitar. As a result, it is the guitar body itself that is vibrating in unison with the amplified note. This is picked up especially well with a contact mike and again you get a howling sound that, in this case, could damage the guitar.

Clearly, a different type of pick-up was needed to combat the problem, and in 1931 the Rowe DeArmond company released an electro-magnetic pick-up which was very similar to the ones we know

The guitar that caused a book to be written: a good example of a 1958 Gibson Flying V.

today. This was offered as an add-on unit to fix to existing guitars, and it certainly eased, if not cured, the feedback problem. At least it was a step in the right direction.

A 'Charlie Christian' pick-up fitted, in this case, to a Gibson L5. Beneath the front of the guitar is a massive iron magnet and this is held in place by three massive bolts, two of which can be seen here.

Shortly after the introduction of the Rowe DeArmond pick-up, a few manufacturers introduced guitars with factory-fitted pick-ups. Perhaps the best known of these is the Gibson ES150, the ES standing for Electric Spanish. This guitar was introduced in 1935 and became well known as the guitar that was used by the late Charlie Christian. Since then the pick-up used on the ES150 has been known as the Charlie Christian pick-up.

These early pick-ups are crude by today's standards, although the principle of their operation is the same. They used a fairly large iron magnet wound with copper wire. As the string, which itself was made of a magnetically attractable alloy, vibrated over the pick-up it caused a small electric current to be generated in the coil which was amplified and then sent to the speaker. Strictly speaking, these should be known as electro-magnetic transducers, but pick-up is an easier term to remember.

However, as amplification got louder to cope with making the guitar heard above the noise of even noisier bands and venues, the problem of feedback returned. Several companies tackled this problem by making the tops of their guitars thicker. This helped by damping some of the vibration of the top but was not the final answer and it obviously had an effect on the acoustic properties of the guitar.

In the early 1940s several people began to seriously tackle the problem. The most notable of these were Leo Fender, Paul Bigsby and Les Paul. There will always be some debate as to who it was that actually invented the electric guitar as we know it today, but this discussion is outside the scope of this book. It is easier and perhaps more historically accurate to say that these three people at least were following broadly similar lines of enquiry at much the same time and that all three came up with similar conclusions. Exactly who did what and on which day is not too important. All three had decided that the only way to eliminate feedback was to dispense with the hollow body of the guitar. The idea was to mount the pick-ups and the neck onto a solid body so there was nothing to vibrate and cause feedback.

Solid instruments were not new. The Rickenbacker company had released a solid Hawaiian guitar as early as 1931. Other makers, including Gibson, had followed suit to cash in on the popularity that Hawaiian music was enjoying at the time and Leo Fender frequently saw these instruments in his amplifier repair shop. These guitars were simple in the extreme, being basically a plank of wood with strings suspended over it and a single bar magnet pick-up. They were played on the lap in much the same way as today's pedalsteel guitars, the steel being a short metal bar that is held across the strings as a sort of moveable fret, rather like a bottleneck, giving the distinctive Hawaiian sound.

With the benefit of hindsight, it is easy to see that the solid body was the obvious answer, but at the time it was quite revolutionary. The new guitars would, of course, be heavier than the semi-acoustics but their size could be reduced to compensate for this and to make them easier to reach around. Another advantage of the solid guitar being smaller was that it was easier to play on a strap.

The solid body of the guitar did alter the sound; after all, removing the guitar's traditional method of producing sound is rather like curing a car's mechanical problems by removing the engine. Any semi-acoustic guitar's sound, even one with a very thick top, is influenced to some degree by the hollow body; and, since the solid guitar has no sound box, the sound is theoretically purely electric in origin, making it sound a little harsher than a semi-acoustic. This was considered to be a price worth paying since the benefits outweighed the disadvantages, as the solid body of the guitar greatly increases the guitar's natural sustain, or the time taken for the note played to die away. Feedback, too, is almost eliminated.

This is a good example of early electric guitar technology. This Bakelite lap steel was made in 1936 by the Selmer company in England under licence from Rickenbacker and comes complete with its own amplifier in the case. It also has a rounded neck but Bakelite frets.

Of the three people mentioned, both Leo Fender and Les Paul have become almost household names. Paul Bigsby is, perhaps, a little less known as a guitar-maker, his name being more readily identified with the development of the tremolo arms that bear his name. The guitar that Paul Bigsby made in 1947 was commissioned by the country star Merle Travis and, if not the first solid electric guitar, was one of the first custom-made solid electrics. The guitar was very similar in looks to some later Fender guitars. It featured a single cutaway body with a single pick-up near the bridge. It also had a single-sided headstock, with all six machine-heads on one side, the shape of which was very similar to the later Fender Stratocaster. By today's standards the guitar looks a little dated, but it should be remembered that in 1947 it was high tech. The guitar still exists and is on show in the Country Music Hall of Fame in Nashville, USA.

The other two guitars produced at around this time are more significant in regard to this book as they each set a trend in guitar-making styles, and each guitar is still in production today.

Leo Fender ran a small radio repair shop in southern California and he was often called to repair amplifiers for the many local musicians. As a result, he came to appreciate the problems that these musicians faced with regard to feedback, and so he set about looking for a solution. He found time to experiment with pick-ups and amplifiers and by the early 1940s he had come to the conclusion that a solid instrument was the only answer. Several prototypes were built and rented out to local musicians whose comments were noted. As a result, in 1947, the Fender Broadcaster was ready and production began soon after. The Broadcaster, later to become better known as the Telecaster, is a twin pick-up guitar with a detachable one-piece maple neck with 21 frets. The body of the guitar is made out of a piece of ash or alder, 1¾ in (44.5 mm) thick, with a single cutaway that enables the hand to reach the highest frets. Like the Bigsby, it too has a single-sided headstock. The controls for the pick-ups are mounted on a metal plate that is let into the front of the guitar, and the circuitry is designed to give maximum possible tonal variation.

The only major changes to the standard Telecaster over the last 50-odd years have been the

A 1950 Fender Broadcaster. The simple elegance of the design is obvious. Half a century of development has hardly altered it.

change from maple to rosewood fingerboards in the late 1950s, with maple being reintroduced as an option in 1966, and a change in the tone circuit in the mid-1950s. The earliest Telecasters had the three-position selector switch wired so that in the rear position, the rear or bridge pick-up was connected; in the middle position, the front or neck pick-up was connected; and in the forward position, the front pick-up was connected through a large capacitor in the tone circuit to give a deep boomy sound. This was required because, at this point, Leo Fender had not had time to invent the bass guitar. It was not possible to get both pick-ups on together, and so this was changed to the circuit which is still in use today and gives either or both pick-ups. The Telecaster soon became popular and is still the favourite instrument of many musicians and guitar book authors.

'I wish Leo Fender would hurry up and invent the bass guitar so that Charlie has something to play!'

Les Paul is not only a talented musician but also a talented inventor. In the 1940s he was first to use the now indispensable technique of multi-track recording and, in order to further his own experiments, he designed and built the world's first eight-track recording machine which is now in the Smithsonian Institute.

Les Paul had been experimenting with ways of curing feedback and of getting more sustain out of his instruments for some years. One of his early experimental pieces was known as the Log. This was a guitar neck bolted to a 4 x 4 in (101 x 101 mm) length of railway sleeper, with the two halves of a guitar body fixed on for looks. This gave the correct sound but was a little impractical as an instrument.

Further experiments followed, and in the early 1950s Les Paul began negotiating with Gibson for the production of a solid guitar. Exactly how the sequence of events happened depends upon whose story you read but the end result was that in 1952 the Gibson Les Paul reached the market.

The Les Paul guitar is in some ways very similar, and in others quite different, to the Telecaster. Both guitars have two pick-ups and a single cutaway, but the design of the Les Paul is more like a conventional cello guitar only smaller and, of course, solid. It has a mahogany neck with an inlaid and bound rosewood fingerboard which is fitted with 22 frets. The head is of conventional design, angled back and with three machine-heads fitted per side. The body of the guitar is 1¾ in (44.5 mm) mahogany faced with ½ in (12.7 mm) maple that was added to give extra sustain. This is carved in the same way as the Gibson semi-acoustic and acoustic jazz guitars, and is bound, like the fingerboard, in cream plastic. Each pick-up has its own tone and volume controls and the selector switch gives either or both pick-ups. The guitar was, and some models still are, finished in gold and the Les Paul looks like a scaled-down version of Gibson's ES295 semi. Apart from a break in production between 1960 and 1966, the guitar has remained popular and virtually unchanged.

The Telecaster and Les Paul are made using very different production methods and the differences in style are so noticeable that, over the years, the terms 'Gibson-style' or 'Fender-style' have been used to describe other makers' guitars. Neither style of construction is better or worse than the other; they were simply reached from different directions. The differences came about as a result of the approach to the problem of designing a new instrument.

Gibson had been making quality guitars for years. They had started out by using traditional guitar-making methods and this involved doing most, if not all, of the work by hand. As production increased, methods of doing the same jobs faster, but to the same standard, were required, and some machines were adapted or designed to do the jobs. To put this another way, the mass production methods were designed around the guitar.

Fender's approach was the complete opposite. He designed the Telecaster so that it could be made easily, on fairly standard woodworking machines. Both the body and the neck of the Telecaster were designed to be built on a series of jigs using a conventional pin router and to be produced from fairly standard timber sizes. The machines are described later in the book and the advantages of using one on a guitar like the Telecaster will be readily apparent. The neck is joined to the body

The 1952 Gibson Les Paul. Note the trapeze tail-piece and the relative complexity of the instrument compared with the Broadcaster. (Courtesy of Ward Meeker, Vintage Guitar *Magazine.)*

More Fender design and a 34 inch scale length on this mid-1960s Fender Precision Bass. The earliest examples had a non-contoured body and a single-coil pick-up.

using four large screws to hold it in a simple slot in the body of the guitar. This not only eased production but meant that the neck could be replaced easily if broken or warped. The design is not the most complicated in the world, but because of this it has not only stood the test of time but has also been imitated by other manufacturers. In this book I shall cover the design and construction of both of these styles.

The whole point about the design of these instruments is that although they evolved differently and are made using slightly different methods, they were both obviously well thought-out before being placed into production and this, as much as anything else, is the key to their success.

DESIGNING YOUR GUITAR

The most important design aspect of anything, be it a simple lever or a time-travelling warp-drive interstellar vehicle, is the planning. This obviously applies, as we have seen, to the guitar. Careful planning at the design stage of the guitar will save a lot of time effort and, more importantly, money. It can be tempting to try to include everything you have ever liked about a number of different guitars into one instrument but you should ask yourself whether you are likely to want to use all of the features often enough to warrant their inclusion on your guitar.

Too many controls on the front of an instrument is a common fault with badly thought-out guitars. I have often seen guitars with any number of knobs and switches which are largely redundant since the player simply leaves the bridge pick-up turned up to 11 and plays with the one sound all night. The important thing to do is to decide what style of guitar you want, how you want it to sound and then stick to it.

As we have already decided that the most important part of the guitar is the string it seems logical to use this as the starting point in the design of a new instrument. I will presume that the minor point of deciding whether a guitar or bass is to be made has already been dealt with, and the following notes are largely applicable to both.

Scale length

The first stage is to decide on the length of string or *scale length* of the new instrument. A longer

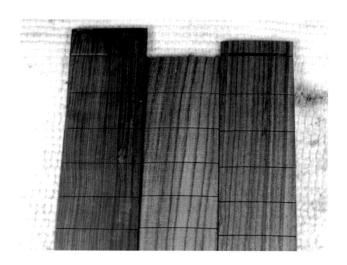

Three different length boards showing the change in fret positions. On the left is a 24¾ in scale board, the centre is a Gibson replacement from Stewart Macdonald's Guitar Shop Supply at 24⁹⁄₁₆ in and the final is a Fender replacement 25½ in scale. The changes in fret position are already noticeable by the fourth fret. Not deciding the scale length at the very start can have a marked effect on bridge position.

scale length will, to a point, give better sustain. The reason for this is that the tighter a string is stretched, within the limits of guitar design, the longer it will sustain. A string of any given thickness will have to be tensioned less over a shorter scale length than a string of the same thickness over a longer scale length in order to sound at the same pitch. The disadvantage of the longer scale length is the distances between the frets are longer and so the fingers have to stretch further in order to reach the chord positions. The Gibson Byrdland semi-acoustic guitar, designed for the jazz players Billy Byrd and Hank Garland, has a short scale length of 23½ in (597 mm) that makes fingering complex jazz chords easier and, since most jazz guitarists use fairly heavy strings, it still manages reasonable sustain. However, if you were to put a set of extra light gauge rock-'n'-roll strings onto the same guitar, it would feel and sound fairly dull and lifeless in comparison with similar guitars as the scale length would be too short. Having said this, it is a perfectly usable scale length and can be pleasant to play on, as well as being suitable for people with smaller hands.

Most guitar scale lengths vary between 24 and 26 in (610 and 661 mm). Many makers stick to the scale lengths that are used on the Les Paul and

Telecaster which are published as being 25½ in (648 mm) for the Fender and 24¾ in (629 mm) for the Gibson. In actual fact, the Gibson Les Paul has a slightly shorter scale length as the published measurement refers to the string length, which is slightly longer than the scale length since the bridge is moved away from the nut by a small amount to allow for the stretch in the string when it is fretted. This is known as *compensation* and is described later in the book. Therefore, if you try to replace the fingerboard of a Les Paul with one cut to allow a scale length of 24¾ in, it will be too long and the fret positions will not match. The actual scale length is 24⁹⁄₁₆ in (625 mm)*.

In recent years some makers have tried to combine the benefits of one with the other, and companies such as Paul Reed Smith use a 25 in (635 mm) scale length. Most basses vary between 30 and 34 in (762 and 864 mm). Fender's Jazz and Precision basses use a 34 in (864 mm) scale length. Rickenbacker's 4000 and 4001 use a 32½ in (825 mm) scale length and many of Gibson's basses use a 30½ in (775 mm) scale, as do some of Fender's cheaper instruments, while some six-string basses have as much as a 36 in (914 mm) scale.

Scale Lengths

These are based on the published scale lengths of various guitars and are to serve as a guide only.

	in	mm
Fender Guitar		
Strat/Tele	25½	648
Mustang	24	610
Duo Sonic	22¾	579
Gibson Guitar		
Les Paul, 335, SG	24¾	629
Byrdland	23½	597
RD	25½	648
PRS	25	635
Basses		
Gibson EBO	30½	775
Fender Precision	34	864
Rickenbacker 4001	32½	825
Some six-string basses	36	914

* For more details of compensation, see page 199

Longest neck award goes to the Danelectro Guitarlin, a cross between a mandolin and a guitar. Its lyre-like shape is the result of providing access to the topmost frets which are close enough together to be almost impossible to play. Keeping a neck this long straight can cause problems. Since the pick-ups are so close together they are filtered through capacitors to make the neck pick-up bassier and the bridge pick-up treblier.

With basses, the problem of sustain for a given scale length seems more acute than it is with guitars. A short scale length with any thickness of string can sound dull and lifeless and, even if it is easier to play, may still come in second place to a longer scale length when choosing a new instrument. My own preferences are 24¾ in (629 mm) on a guitar, for the simple reason that I am lazy and it is slightly easier to play, and 34 in (864 mm) on a bass as it seems to give a more even sustain across all four strings and, since I cannot play bass, the stretches do not bother me.

Frets

Once a scale length has been chosen, the next step is to decide on how many frets the new guitar will have. There are usually between 20 and 24 frets on most instruments. Some have slightly less and others have slightly more. The Danelectro Guitarlin, also known as the Longhorn, of the mid-1960s had 31 frets.

There is, in theory, no reason why you should not try to fit as many frets as possible into the instrument, but in practice there is little point in trying for too many. As the frets get further up the neck, the spaces between them get smaller to a point where they are impossible to play as there is no room for the finger to get between them to fret the note effectively. This, however, is not the only consideration.

The more frets that are fitted to the guitar the less space there is between the end of the fingerboard and the bridge. Clearly, if the guitar is to have a mass of frets it cannot have multiple pick-ups; there simply would not be space to fit them.

Too many frets would also be difficult to play as the fingerboard would extend quite a way across the face of the guitar and would be difficult to get to, as the hand would not only have to reach around the neck but would also have to stretch across the guitar body. Compensating for this by making the neck longer and the body shorter would give a badly balanced guitar with a weak neck, as the longer neck would be much more difficult to keep straight.

If you do happen to decide that you want a large number of frets on your guitar it is worth asking yourself why. The Danelectro Guitarlin was marketed as a cross between the guitar and the mandolin, hence the name and the extra frets at the top end. They may come in handy for the occasional note in the occasional song, but does the amount they are likely to be used justify their inclusion with all of the extra work, and thought, needed to fit them into the guitar?

The Les Paul has 22 frets, in common with most Gibson guitars that preceded it, and the Telecaster has 21. Both Gibson's and Fender's basses have 20 frets. In recent years guitars with 24 frets, or a full two-octave fingerboard, have become fashionable. In practice these frets are seldom used, and in certain designs, especially basses, the extra length in the neck can lead to stability problems although careful design can minimise this.

Another point to keep in mind is that both the Les Paul and the Telecaster, and indeed the Stratocaster, have their front pick-up at about the point where the 24th fret would be. This has a very great effect on the tone that will come from that pick-up. Positioning pick-ups is covered later in this chapter but if you want to get a Stratocaster-type tone from the front pick-up of your 'I-made-this-myself-o-caster' you will not be able to have 24 frets.

Neck depth

The depth of the neck must also be decided. Overall depths are usually 1 in (25.4 mm) at the body end of the neck and between ⅝ and ⅞ in (15.8 and 22.2 mm) at the nut, with the average being about ¾ in (19 mm). Fingerboards usually account for about ¼ in (6.3 mm) of this total. It must be remembered that the thinner the neck is made the more difficult it will be to keep straight.

Body shape

The next stage is to decide on the body shape of your new guitar. When making a first guitar it is worth avoiding any outlandish designs in favour of a simple one- or two-cutaway body. If you really must have a Flying V, an Explorer or a guitar in the shape of a contour map of Tierra Del Fuego, make it as a second guitar but start on something straightforward.

All sorts of weird and wonderful guitar designs have come off the drawing boards of many manufacturers over the years, from Gibson's Flying V and Explorer of 1957 through the Gretsch Bikini, which had interchangeable necks, to the pistol-shaped guitar that was marketed in England in the mid-1970s.

The Rickenbacker 4000 series bass was an innovative shape and an early through-neck design. With interesting looks, stereo output and a punchy sound, it gained a lot of popularity in the 1960s and 1970s. (Courtesy of The Guitar ReRanch/Bill Lester)

There was even a guitar made in the shape of the Live Aid logo, built in the very workshops used later in this book.

One thing that most of these designs had in common was the fact that even though they may have been very interesting as design exercises they flopped as guitars. Even the Flying V and the Explorer, which are currently enjoying popularity, hardly sold when they were first introduced. There is a story that says that some were even used as shop signs!

The Live Aid guitar: this now adorns a restaurant wall somewhere at the end of the universe.

It must be remembered that an electric guitar is, first and foremost, a musical instrument that has to be played successfully if it is to be of any use. It is no good if all that you can do with it is pose, not that there is anything wrong with posing, but most people cannot make a career out of it.

The body of the guitar serves several purposes. Not least is the need to place the hardware, the

A 1970 reissue of the Gibson Firebird 5 guitar. Not the best balanced guitar but a great sound. The Thunderbird Bass was the same shape with a very long neck.

pick-ups, the bridge and other fittings in positions where they can perform best. It also needs to contain the controls for the pick-ups and it needs to look good.

One of the main failings with many of the more outrageous guitar designs is that they do not balance. This is a very important point as if the guitar is too neck-heavy then the hand that should be fretting notes on the neck is also engaged in supporting the weight of the instrument, which is hardly ideal. This situation is more common when playing standing up with the guitar on a strap, although on some guitars it can also happen when in the seated position. When the guitar is on a strap, the point of balance is the foremost strap connection. If the guitar had a heavy set of machine-heads and a long neck then having a point of balance way towards the body is not a good idea.

One such offender is the Gibson Thunderbird range of basses, and to a slightly lesser extent the Firebird range of guitars that were first introduced in 1963. The Thunderbird has a very long neck, fitted with a large set of Kluson Bass machines, and a very small body. The Firebird has a shorter neck but is often fitted with very heavy banjo-style tuners which add to the problem. The body of the guitar is small and relatively lightweight and there are no 'horns' on the top half of the body to move the balance point nearer the head. This has not stopped both the Firebird and the Thunderbird becoming very popular over the last 30 years.

There are many people who think that the look of the instrument justifies the extra effort needed in playing it especially since, in the case of the Firebird, the pick-ups were different to anything else Gibson made and had a sound all of their own. A good 'rule of thumb' is that if the strap button on the top horn is close to the 12th fret, the guitar will probably balance.

Of course, it is all different when you have no extra weight at the head end of the instrument. The headless guitar, with its tuning-machines on the body, has been around for a long time but gained a lot of popularity in the early 1980s when the Steinberger company started marketing a range of guitars and basses that could be described as minimalist. The body was made just big enough to hold the pick-ups and controls and the bridge was a combined unit that also held the tuning-machines. The strings for these guitars and basses were made a fixed length with a ball-end at each end. The ball-end at

The Wal 5-string Bass is a fine example of a well thought-out design. The body shape is balanced, access to all 24 frets is easy, controls are well positioned and the bass is comfortable to hold and play. It also sounds good. (Courtesy of Pete Stephens, Electric Wood.)

Proof that new designs can happen, the Parker Fly is a good shape and has a pick-up built into the bridge for acoustic sounds. (Courtesy of Future Publishing/Guitarist Magazine.)

the body of the guitar fitted into the tuning-machine and was tensioned by means of a knurled nut; at the nut end it fitted into a cleverly designed top nut.

The system was successful enough for several people to imitate and develop it. For those who did not like the look of these guitars, the company also offered a more traditional double cutaway design and other manufacturers too offered guitars of varying designs that featured the same body-end tuning system. It is interesting to note that although the system is perfectly suited to minimalist designs, such as the original Steinbergers, many players prefer the look of something more traditional.

If you do decide to have a long neck with loads of frets you can use the method employed by Danelectro on the Guitarlin whose horns were made very long to keep the instrument balanced, giving it a look similar to the lyre and its nickname of the Longhorn. Bearing all this in mind, it is no surprise that many guitars have a simple one- or two-cutaway design, as they are easier to design and build, will probably balance well and will not look too unusual.

A common problem with many first-time guitar designs is that they are too big. Certainly the guitar needs to be big enough to contain all its working parts but if it is too big it can be awkward to play. It is best to plan out your new guitar full-size onto a large sheet of paper. This can then be used to check all of your measurements before committing yourself to cutting pieces of wood. However, there are other features to be chosen whose positions and style will influence the final design of your guitar, so these too must be decided on.

The neck-to-body join

The position along the neck at which the neck-to-body join will be made should also be considered, along with the method that will be used to fix the two parts together.

We have already discussed how the length of the neck can have a marked effect on its stability, and how too much fingerboard over the body will be difficult to reach. Both the Les Paul and the Telecaster have the neck-to-body join at the 16th fret; this is also true of the Stratocaster. The cutaways are then designed to allow access to the top frets without weakening the join.

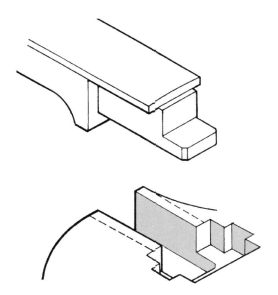

A Les Paul neck join. Here the tenon is supported on both sides by the body. Later Les Pauls have shorter neck tenons that do not extend into the pick-up cavity but are still more than adequate.

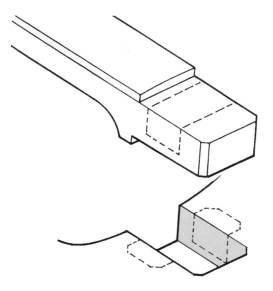

Later double-cutaway Les Paul Juniors and Specials had the tenon extended into the body. This was still tapered, following the line of the fingerboard edge. Some Specials had the front pick-up positioned very close to the join which weakened the neck.

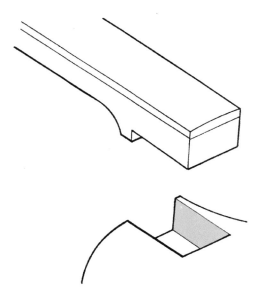

The single-cutaway Les Paul Junior's and Special's neck tenon was the full width of the fingerboard and fitted into a tapered slot in the body. In order for this to be supported the shape of the cutaway was changed slightly, giving a ledge on the outside of the neck.

A single-cutaway Les Paul Junior showing how the neck is supported by the additional wood on the inside of the cutaway and how the fingerboard is raised above the front of the guitar slightly, giving only a small neck angle.

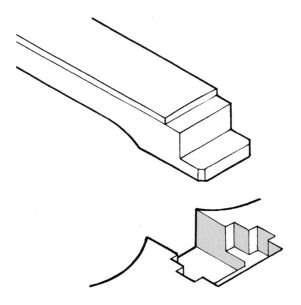

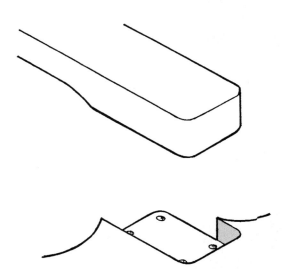

The SG neck join was also extended into the body of the guitar and varies depending on which design period the guitar comes from. The extension into the pick-up cavity helped the strength of the join. The pick-up position weakened the join a little but not as much as on some Les Paul Specials.

The Stratocaster and Telecaster bolt-on necks are well supported on one side and adequately on the other. Some guitars built in the late 1970s had a three-bolt fixing which tended to be a little less firm than the earlier four-bolt system now reinstated.

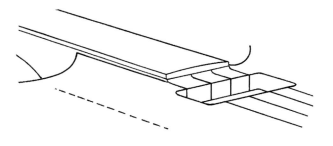

This Gibson SG from the mid-1960s shows the tenon about three-quarters of the way across the neck pick-up cavity.

Even a straight-through neck is not without potential pitfalls. By placing the front pick-up too close to the join in a double-cutaway guitar, the neck can be left without sufficient support especially if the guitar has a thin body and deep pick-up recesses. In the example above the asymmetric cutaways give additional support on the bass side of the neck.

The neck join on the Wal is a true bolt-on. The neck is fitted with inserts that are reverse threaded so they try to claw their way into the neck as they are tightened. The five bolts on this five-string neck are tightened by allen key. It is seen here on the tastefully carpeted assembly table at the factory.

Bridge heights

The following are rough guide heights. Actual bridges may vary. Whilst these figures are a good guide, careful measurement of the chosen bridge is essential.

	in	mm
Vintage Strat Trem	½	12.7
Fender Telecaster	½	12.7
Gibson Tunomatic	¾	19
Fender Bass	⅝	15.8
Gibson Stop	¾	19
Fender Jaguar	⅝	15.8
Floyd Rose	¾	19
Wilkinson	½	12.7
Musicman Stingray bass	⅝	15.8
Epiphone Rivoli bass	1	25.4

If a glued-in neck is chosen for the guitar there should be sufficient area available for gluing to give a strong glue joint. This should, ideally, be supported either side as this will give a greater gluing area and will prevent the neck moving from side to side and straining the glue joint. This also applies to bolt-on necks, as enough area is required for the fixing plate and its screws that hold the neck in place, and this too must be supported to stop it moving.

The alternative to gluing or bolting the neck is to carry it straight through the body. This does away with the need for a bulky neck joint, and the neck is held from moving side to side by the body. This style of construction has some very good advantages but also some pitfalls.

Neck angle and bridge height

In order for the strings to be carried over the fingerboard at the correct height it should be decided what, if any, neck angle is required. There are two ways of solving this problem and both have quite a marked effect on how the guitar will feel to play. The deciding factor is the height of the bridge.

Most electric guitar bridges are about the same height, around ⅜ to ½ in (9.5 to 12.7 mm) with Fender-style bridges generally being a little lower

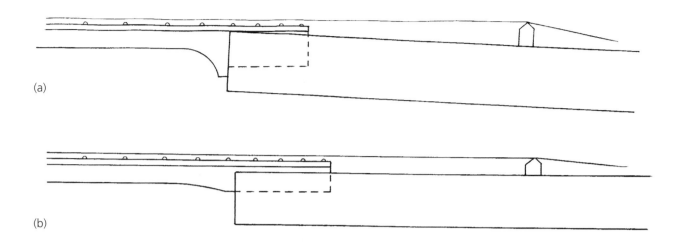

(a)

(b)

than the offerings from Gibson. Most Fender guitars have no neck angle. The fingerboard sits slightly proud of the top surface of the body and so the strings are presented to the fingerboard at the correct height. The Les Paul and many of Gibson's subsequent guitars have the fingerboards closer to the top surface of the guitar's body. In order that the string is presented to the fingerboard in a way that will keep the guitar playable the neck has to be angled back very slightly. This angle is very small. On the Les Paul it is about 4 degrees, and on some other guitars, for example double-cutaway Les Paul Juniors and Specials, it is as little as 2 degrees.

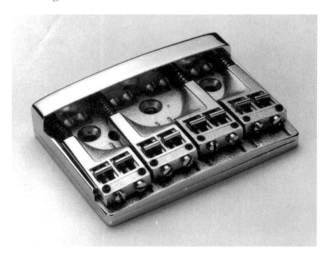

The Schaller range of bass bridges are available with a spacer that raises the bridge by either 3 or 4 mm. This eight-string bridge is used on the bass in Chapter 11.

Two ways of approaching the problem; in both cases the bridge height is the same. In (a) the bridge height has been allowed for by angling the neck backwards and the fingerboard is flush with the face of the guitar. In (b) the fingerboard is raised and the neck has no angle.

This not only gives the guitar the required low action but also brings the head of the guitar back towards the player. This makes the low positions on the fingerboard a little easier to reach as the arm does not have to reach forward as well as out to play the bottom notes. It is not much of a difference; being able to play on one style does not mean that playing the other will be impossible or even difficult, but it is a noticeable difference that may make one style a little more comfortable.

Gibson have made one or two guitars with no neck angle; the SGs made between 1972 and 1974 and many of the reissue Flying Vs are examples. On these guitars the correct string height is obtained by raising the neck to the correct height. The fingerboard stands quite proud of the face of the guitar. This gives the right action but leaves the strings a long way off the front of the instrument and pick-ups need to be raised higher in their mountings to be the correct distance from the strings. The strings being a long way off the front of the instrument can also make it feel unpleasant to play but equally it may not be a good idea to have them too close.

On some basses, having the strings quite close to the body can make playing slap styles quite difficult as the fingers need to get underneath the strings to pull them with the right amount of force.

An early-1970s Gibson SG with its fingerboard raised above the body and no neck angle. Some reissue Flying Vs were made in this way.

The height of the bridge is a deciding factor in the choice of neck angle and the make and model of bridge should be decided early on. I once had a customer who wanted a guitar made using, among other things, a genuine Gibson tunomatic bridge and tailpiece on a straight-through necked guitar. The guitar was started and a short time later he came to me saying that he had changed his mind and wanted a Fender-style tremolo unit on the guitar. By this time the guitar was well advanced and had been made with a small neck angle suitable for the Gibson bridge. There was no way that I could alter the guitar, especially since it was a straight-through neck design, so I had to politely point out that it was tough luck and he was too late.

One advantage of the bolt-on neck design is that the angle of the neck can be subtly altered by inserting small veneer shims or, in the case of some of the later Fender instruments, their patented neck tilt system. This is sufficient to make very slight adjustments (for example to give the required action on a guitar when the screws on the adjustable bridge pieces are at the top of their travel, leaving none to protrude to lacerate the hand) but will not do in the event of a serious design error. Too much of a shim can make the neck joint a little weak. This feature is also useful if a replacement trem system is fitted. While the new system may fit into the same body routs, it may not be the same height and several of the high-

tech systems on the market are slightly higher than the standard Fender unit – a point worth bearing in mind when designing any guitar.

The position of your neck–body join will decide where your bridge will be on the face of the guitar. Using the fretting tables that are worked out in Chapter 7 or those printed in Appendix 1, the distance from this fret to the bridge is easily found. The amount of fingerboard that will overhang the body can also be calculated by working out the distance from the end of the fingerboard to the bridge and subtracting it from the distance between the body–neck join and the bridge. You must allow for a little fretboard after the last fret, usually about ⅜ in (9.5 mm) will be fine. If the end of the board is too close to the last fret slot the wood might break when the last fret is inserted. For example, the last fret on a Gibson Les Paul is slightly under 7 in (178 mm) from the bridge but the fingerboard ends about 6⅝ in (168 mm) from the bridge.

If you intend to use a Fender-style bridge with a bolt-on or glued-in neck, it will probably be worth making the guitar without a neck angle and fitting the neck so that the fingerboard sits slightly proud of the face of the guitar, using the same dimensions as for bolt-on neck Fender-style guitars.

Over the years I have seen several guitars that have been completed with the fingerboard flush with the top of the body, as on many Gibson guitars, but with no neck angle. Some of these were fitted

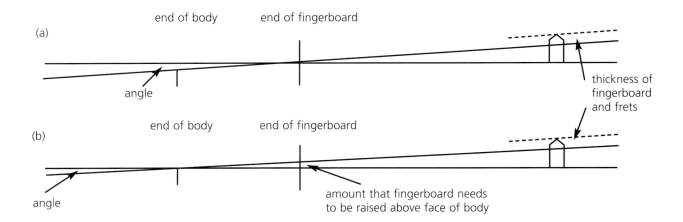

(a)   end of body   end of fingerboard   thickness of fingerboard and frets   angle

(b)   end of body   end of fingerboard   thickness of fingerboard and frets   angle   amount that fingerboard needs to be raised above face of body

with Fender Stratocaster style tremolo units which could not be lowered enough to get a reasonable action. The assumption had been made that since the Fender had no neck angle the new guitar would not need one either; the fact that the neck sits proud of the body, in order to give the right action, was completely overlooked until it was too late. In at least one case the guitar was simply discarded, but others then have the bridge set into the face of the guitar to make up for the mistake.

It is even more severe when using some of the high-tech tremolo systems which are often fractionally higher than the standard Fender units they replace. Of course, the fix may not always be possible since the block and springs in the back of the guitar need a certain amount of space and if the body is only just thick enough to contain them, lowering the bridge into the body will push them out the back. If the guitar to be made is to have a Fender-style bridge and the fingerboard flush with the top of the body then a small neck angle will have to be calculated.

Most guitar bridges are made so that they are adjustable up or down. All calculations regarding the height of the bridge should assume that when the bridge is at its lowest point the strings should be just touching the fingerboard so that the bridge can be raised to give the guitar its correct action. It is easier to raise the strings to their lower limit, which is the point at which they stop rattling against the other frets on the neck, than it is to try to lower the bridge further than the top of the guitar!

The amount of angle needed can be found by drawing some of the guitar's dimensions full-size onto a large piece of paper. Firstly a line is drawn across the paper. This is to represent the front face

These diagrams, if drawn full-size, can be used to calculate the neck angle needed if the fingerboard is to be flush with the face of the body (diagram a) or raised above as on a Gibson SG (diagram b).

of the guitar body. At one end of this line a point is marked to represent the bridge position. The distance from the bridge to the end of the fingerboard is marked, as is the position of the fret at the point where the neck and body join. The height of the bridge is calculated and this is marked perpendicular to the first line at its correct position. The height of the fingerboard together with frets is decided and this measurement is subtracted from the height of the bridge. For example if the bridge were ½ in (12.7 mm) and the fingerboard were to be ³⁄₁₆ in (4.8 mm) a mark should be made ⁵⁄₁₆ in (7.9 mm) above the position of the bridge. A second line is drawn to link this point with the point representing the end of the fingerboard. The angle that this gives is measured and this is the angle at which the neck will have to be set into the body. Once the neck angle has been decided, its effect on the guitar body will need to be dealt with.

If the fingerboard starts at the edge of the body, as it does on some late 1950s Les Paul Juniors with double cutaways, angling the neck back from the body presents no problems. If, on the other hand, the fingerboard extends over the body there are two ways of dealing with the angle. The fingerboard can either be elevated at an angle over the front of the body, as on Gibson's single-cutaway Les Paul Juniors and Specials, or the top of the guitar can be angled back with the fingerboard. Look closely at a Gibson Les Paul Standard or Deluxe. The neck angle starts at the end of the fingerboard and the angle that this

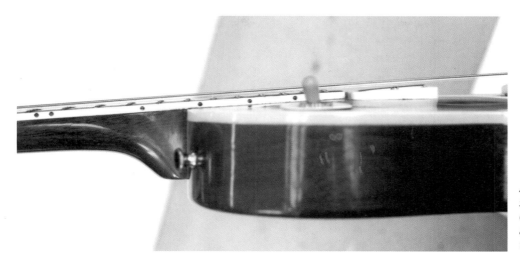

A Les Paul neck joint showing how the contouring hides the angle across the front of the body.

would normally leave across the face of the guitar is hidden by the contouring on the top. The amount that the fingerboard would have to be raised, if suspended above the body, or the amount that the body would have to be lowered is shown on the drawing as the distance between the two lines at the point representing the neck-to-body join.

Body thickness

The thickness of the body can also be decided. A quick study of other guitars will help in working out the right size for you. The guitar must not be too thin, as fitting the pick-ups and their controls could be troublesome, and it must not be too thick as it will be overly heavy and a two-hour concert will

Body thickness		in	mm
Fender Strat/Tele/bass		1¾	44.4
Fender Duo Sonic		1½	38.1
Gibson Les Paul	(centre)	2¼	57.1
	(edge)	2	50.8
Gibson SG		1½	38.1
Yamaha Pacifica		1¾	44.4
PRS	(centre)	1¾	44.4
	(edge)	1½	38.1
Ibanez S540	(centre)	1½	38.1
	(edge)	⅜	9.5

take on the feel of a six-hour workout. Since most of Fender's guitars were designed around readily available standard-sized pieces of timber, they are 1¾ in (44.4 mm) deep which is 2 in (50.8 mm) cut timber planed to remove the saw marks.

Head angle and shape

The head of many guitars is angled back. This is to make the strings pass over the top nut at an angle in order to stop the strings vibrating. Fender's guitars generally do not have an angle as their necks are made from one 1 in (25.4 mm) piece of wood. The angle of the strings over the nut (caused by them being wound down onto the machine-heads) is enough on the bottom strings but the top two strings on most guitars, and top four on some others, are held down into the nut by small metal string-retainers.

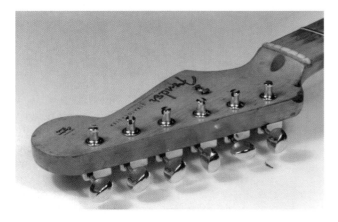

A mid-1950s Fender Stratocaster head showing the straight string pull and the small retainer that holds the first- and second-strings (if they were fitted) in the nut.

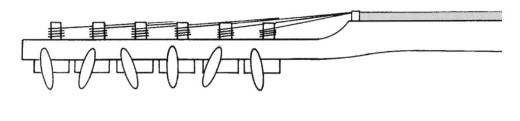

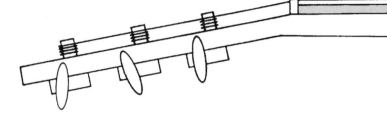

It can be seen from these diagrams that the angle of the head affects the string tension over the top nut.

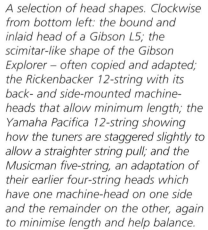

A selection of head shapes. Clockwise from bottom left: the bound and inlaid head of a Gibson L5; the scimitar-like shape of the Gibson Explorer – often copied and adapted; the Rickenbacker 12-string with its back- and side-mounted machine-heads that allow minimum length; the Yamaha Pacifica 12-string showing how the tuners are staggered slightly to allow a straighter string pull; and the Musicman five-string, an adaptation of their earlier four-string heads which have one machine-head on one side and the remainder on the other, again to minimise length and help balance.

The head angle on most guitars is between 10 and 15 degrees, although Gibson did use an angle of 17 degrees for some time. Too shallow an angle will mean that the strings may not sit in the nut as they should; too great an angle can result in the area around the nut being weak since there will be less wood actually holding the head on. One reason that Gibson changed the angle from 17 degrees was that fewer guitars then lost their heads in what could have been relatively minor accidents.

Guitars with angled heads usually have their machine-heads fitted three per side, or two per side on bass guitars. This is the traditional way of doing things and it keeps the length of the head down to an acceptable limit. The longer the head is, the more it will lay back and the deeper the piece of wood needed to make it will be. On many 12-string guitars the angle of the head is lessened to compensate for the extra length. Fender's six-a-side head is made easier and stronger because of the lack of head angle. Six-a-side heads have been made with an angle and Gibson's Explorer is one example, but the design of the head must be carefully thought out so that it is not made too weak.

The head is another part that can be almost any shape, providing that one or two simple rules are followed. If the head is too large it can adversely affect the balance of the instrument. Also the holes for the machine-heads must be positioned so that the string leaving one does not foul another. This can cause tuning problems. Head thickness is usually ½ in (12.7 mm) but this may vary slightly depending on the machine-heads fitted.

Wood

The wood that the guitar will be made from must also be decided and this is dealt with in greater detail in Chapter 5.

Pick-ups and controls

The amount of, and positioning of, the pick-ups can have a marked effect on the guitar's design. The actual point at which the pick-up is mounted under the string will determine the tone that is picked up. The nearer the pick-up is to the bridge the more trebly the tone will be, and at different points along the string differing amounts of fundamental and harmonic will be picked up which will alter the tone colour of the note.

Many guitar companies place their front pick-up at the point that would be the octave above the 12th fret, that is to say the 24th fret position. Clearly if the guitar is to have 24 or even 31 frets this is not possible and a compromise will have to be made.

Bridge pick-up positions can also vary. A good friend of mine has several old Gibsons, including a pair of Les Paul Juniors. The pick-up on one, a 1956 single cutaway is right next to the bridge; the other, a 1959 double cutaway, has the pick-up slightly further forward. Both sound great but different. Both guitars are as they left the factory and a good example of how guitars of the same model can vary.

1956 (left) and 1959 (right) Les Paul Juniors. The pick-up is approximately ¼ in (6.3 mm) nearer the bridge on the single-cutaway model.

Bridge pick-ups are also often placed under a harmonic position. There is a strong harmonic to be found just about a third of the way between the first and second frets on a guitar. On a Telecaster, this is approximately two inches from the nut and is the same distance as the bass side of the Telecaster bridge pick-up is from the bridge and the equivalent of the 43rd fret position. It is a straightforward job to work out the 'best' pick-up positions by working out where the strongest harmonics lie.

The main pitfall to avoid when placing the front pick-up is weakening the neck joint. I made this mistake on one of my early guitars and moving the guitar from side to side while playing had the same effect as a tremolo arm. The same

This Les Paul Special, seen here being refinished, shows how the front pick-up position affects the stability of the neck joint.

Keep it simple, If proof were needed, here is one of the greatest guitars of all time, the Gibson Les Paul Junior. This one dates from 1955. One pick-up, great sound, good guitar.

problem occurred on some early Gibson Les Paul Specials. These were changed in the late 1950s from a single- to a double-cutaway design. The first few guitars had the front pick-up positioned very close to the end of the fingerboard, and since the fingerboard started at the edge of the body there was very little wood holding the neck and body together. The mistake was noticed very quickly and the guitar was changed, with the front pick-up being moved closer to the bridge by about ½ in (12.7 mm). This was sufficient to strengthen the joint. The same problem is sometimes found on some double-cutaway Les Paul Juniors that have had a second pick-up fitted. Fitting the pick-up too close to the end of the fingerboard ruins an otherwise excellent guitar.

The amount of pick-ups and controls that you fit into your guitar is entirely a matter for you to decide but, as we have seen, it must be remembered that the guitar will have to be played and too many controls can complicate this unnecessarily.

To digress a little, one of my favourite guitars now is the aforementioned Les Paul Junior, which has just one pick-up, one tone and one volume control. All you do is plug it in and play it and it always sounds great (and I rarely use tone controls). It is always worth keeping the controls simple as in the heat of the battle they will be easier to find and use.

Remember also that for every control you fit there has to be a similar-sized cavity cut into the guitar to fit it into. Too many controls are going to require a very big control cavity that, depending on the method you use to cut it out, could prove very difficult to make. These will also need to be linked together with the pick-up holes. Again, keep it simple. Adding an extra pick-up and its controls to an existing guitar is a lot easier than trying to remove one that is no longer required.

"Only four more pick ups to programme and he can take his solo"

Nut width

The width of the nut should also be decided. For many years, Fender guitars came with a choice of three different width nuts. These are known as A, B and C necks. Most guitars have the B neck which is 1⅝ in (41.3 mm) at the nut, but they could be ordered in any of the three widths. The Jazz Bass usually has the A neck which is 1½ in (38 mm) at the nut, and many Precision Basses made during the 1960s had C necks which are 1¾ in (44.4 mm) wide. Most Gibsons have a 1⅝ in (41.3 mm) nut although some early SGs were slightly wider and some later guitars narrower. This of course is the overall width of the fingerboard at the nut, and the strings have to be spaced evenly from the sides of the board. The width of the fingerboard at the body end can also be calculated. This is another job that can be planned out full-size on a large piece of paper.

Firstly a line is drawn on the paper to represent the scale length. At one end, the width of the nut and the width of the string spacing at the nut can be marked perpendicular to the first line. The distance

The Fender Jazz Bass showing its 'A' width neck and the early dual concentric controls that gave volume and tone for each pick-up. Also of note is the offset body design, patented by Fender, that was said to make the bass more comfortable to play.

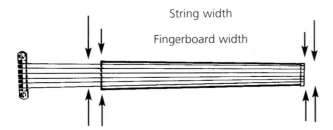

String width

Fingerboard width

The width of the fingerboard at the body end of the neck can be calculated by planning the string width at the nut and the bridge, marking the overall neck width at the nut and extending the lines along the string length parallel to the outer strings.

As can be seen on this MIghty Mite neck, the string positions are roughly ⅛ in from the edge of the fingerboard.

between the centres of the outer string saddles on the bridge can be measured and this is marked onto the drawing at the other end of the scale length line. The positions of the outer strings on the bridge end can be joined to their relative positions on the nut end, and then it is a simple job to measure along the scale length from the nut to where the end of the fingerboard will be and measure the distance between the lines representing the top and bottom strings. This is the string spacing, and all that is needed to find the fingerboard width is to add a small amount either side so that the strings do not fall off the edge of the neck when being fretted. About ⅛ in (2–3 mm) should be enough in most cases.

Some guitars have a string spacing that is almost parallel. The Rickenbacker 4000 series of basses and those of Wal have relatively narrow bridges so the fingerboard barely tapers at all. This also means that stretches are similar at both ends of the neck

The truss rod

If the neck is to have an adjustable truss rod, the position of its adjustment recess should be decided. The truss-rod adjustment can be at the head of the instrument or at the body but if there is to be a neck pick-up fitted to the guitar, a body-end adjustment could prove difficult to get at. Many of Fender's guitars have the truss-rod adjustment at the body end of the neck. This means that the neck has to be removed from the guitar in order to adjust the rod. Clearly this

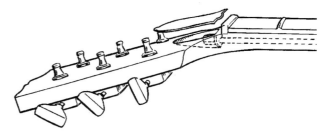

The truss-rod adjustment recess can seriously weaken the head.

A typical Gibson truss-rod adjustment nut and recess.

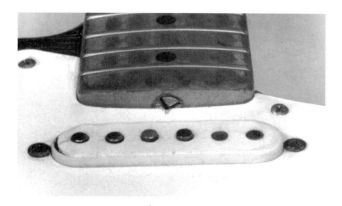

A Fender body-end adjustment, in this case on a rare purple glitter non-trem Stratocaster from the 1950s. The scratchplate mounted pick-ups are also clearly visible.

The Wal bass solves the problem of having channels drilled or routed into the body by arranging the routs so that the control cavity and pick-up positions meet. This makes construction simpler and allows enough room for the multiple wires on the pick-up and their connectors to be fed through and connected.

is difficult on a fixed-neck or through-neck guitar. Many guitars, including some Fenders, have the adjustment at the head of the instrument. This requires a certain amount of wood to be removed from the head in order to leave enough room for means of adjustment, be it spanner or allen key, but if too much wood is taken away the head of the guitar can be seriously weakened.

Mounting the controls

There are two main ways of mounting the controls onto the guitar. They can either be mounted on a

scratchplate and let into the front of the guitar, or be fitted through the face of the guitar from a recess in the back. Either way, a cavity and a cover will have to be made. On a guitar with a scratchplate the channels for the hook-up wire between the pick-ups and the controls can be cut into the top of the body, as the scratchplate will hide them when the guitar is complete. Fender use this method on most of their guitars and basses. On guitars and basses with the controls fitted through from the rear, the pick-up

The body routs on a Stratocaster. The pick-up holes have a linking channel between them and are joined to the control cavity, which is considerably deeper to take the pots and switch. The jackplate has its own hole.

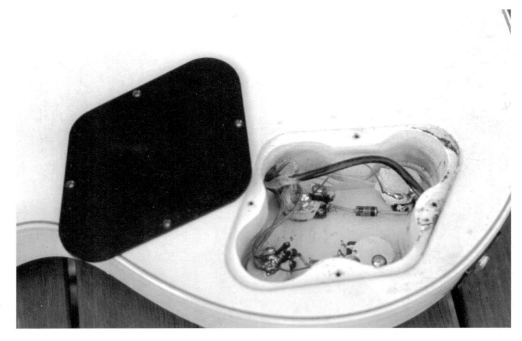

The Gibson Les Paul cavity and cover.

cavities and the control cavities are joined by drilling long holes between them. Long drill bits are required if you choose this method. Also on these guitars the cover plate at the back of the guitar is usually recessed into the wood so that it is flush with the back of the guitar. This stops it catching on the player's clothing. Most of Gibson's solids are made in this way.

Scratchplate plastic is available from guitar parts suppliers, both in solid colours and as laminates. This is PVC material and differs from the acetate used many years ago as it is not as dangerously flammable. As can be seen here, rough cutting can cause the edges to chip. The pearloid on the left is often known as Mother-of-Toilet-Seat.

Binding

Another thing to consider is whether the fingerboard or the body will have binding. Binding on electric guitars is largely ornamental although its use on acoustic and semi-acoustic guitars is a lot more functional. On these the binding prevents moisture seeping into the end grain of the guitar's top and

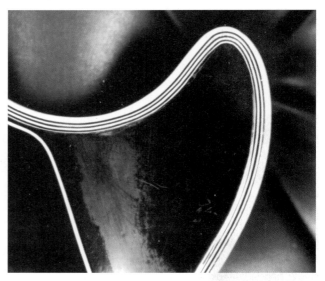

Multiple binding on a Gibson Les Paul Custom.

(above) Binding materials are available ready-prepared in a variety of colours and materials, ranging from coloured plastics to dyed and natural wood. This is just part of the selection available at Luthiers Mercantile International in Healdsburg, California.

(right) The bound and inlaid head of a Gibson Les Paul Custom.

back and ruining the wood. On fingerboards of all guitars binding seals the fret into the board and prevents moisture getting under the fret and causing it to lift.

Contoured bodies

On many Fender guitars, most notably the Stratocaster, the body is contoured. The front and back are dressed away so that the body sits snugly against the body of the player. The tops of Gibson's Les Pauls and some other guitars are carved. This, on a solid, is decorative and does make the guitar a little more comfortable to hold, and must be consid-ered carefully as it can make a difference to how well the pick-up controls fit into the guitar.

The contouring on a Stratocaster, in this case a left-handed example from Tokai.

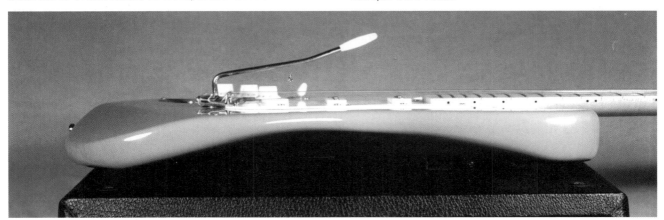

Fingerboard markers

The style of markers for the fingerboard can now be chosen. The easiest to fit are simple dots but, if you are feeling really flash, any design from simple rectangles to your name, or a carefully-inlaid Roman orgy scene, can be used. Materials such as mother-of-pearl, plastic and acetate, abalone and even gold and silver wire are frequently used on high-priced guitars. Some of the finest fingerboard inlays are to be seen on Alembic basses but the amount of work required is reflected in the high price of the instrument.

(below) Inlay does not have to be restricted to simple dots. This tree of life was inlaid by Dave King of Hampshire, England, into one of his fine acoustics.

Other parts can be inlaid too. This young lady adorns the head of a guitar and is made of 18ct gold.

A selection of inlay materials: dots in abalone and mother-of-pearl, blocks of mother-of-pearl and crown inlays in plastic.

Fretwire

Final things to decide are the style of fretwire you want and the finish. There are many ways of finishing the guitar and these are covered in Chapter 13.

Fretwire is a matter of personal taste. Some people prefer large fat frets as found on most recent Gibsons; others prefer the thinner wire used on many Fenders. Even larger and fatter wire than the Gibson frets is available and there is no real reason why this cannot be used, but a larger fret can lead to some tuning problems. These occur when light strings are used on a guitar with heavy frets. As the string is pressed down onto the fret it is stretched and this can put the guitar out of tune. The answer is to use a heavier string or simply not to press as hard. In practice it is sometimes easier to re-fret the guitar with a smaller fretwire.

Basses, in general, require larger frets than a six-string guitar. Light fretwire can be used but round-wound bass strings are very abrasive and the frets would wear out very quickly.

Choosing fretwire is far more difficult now than it was when I first started making guitars. In those days there was simply no choice, you had to use whatever you could find on sale. Now companies offer a wide range of styles and sizes and materials. Brass fretwire is still available and should be avoided but most fretwire for sale is a nickel-silver alloy and will vary in hardness. The fret does not want to be so hard that it is difficult to bend and fit but also not too soft so that it is too flexible when fitting and liable to wear quickly.

The following chart shows the main dimensions of the Jim Dunlop range in both inches and millimetres. From this range they recommend certain wires for certain jobs:

Maximum height, narrow	6105
Fender guitars	6230
Gibson 'Jumbo' wire	6130
Martin guitars	6230
Maximum mass	6000, 6100, 6110

The dimensions shown in the following chart refer to the diagram on the right.

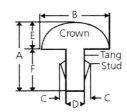

JIM DUNLOP FRETWIRE SIZES

No		A	B	C	D	E
6000	mm	3.250	2.990	0.910	0.530	1.470
	in	0.128	0.118	0.036	0.021	0.058
6100	mm	3.180	2.790	0.810	0.530	1.400
	in	0.125	0.110	0.032	0.021	0.055
6105	mm	2.990	2.290	0.790	0.530	1.400
	in	0.118	0.090	0.031	0.021	0.055
6110	mm	2.640	2.920	0.910	0.510	1.270
	in	0.104	0.115	0.036	0.020	0.050
6120	mm	3.000	2.900	0.950	0.600	1.300
	in	0.118	0.114	0.037	0.024	0.051
6130	mm	2.790	2.692	0.914	0.508	0.914
	in	0.110	0.106	0.036	0.020	0.036
6140	mm	2.800	2.700	0.950	0.600	1.000
	in	0.110	0.106	0.037	0.024	0.039
6150	mm	2.743	2.591	0.787	0.510	1.067
	in	0.108	0.102	0.031	0.020	0.042
6155	mm	2.870	2.616	0.787	0.533	1.168
	in	0.113	0.103	0.031	0.021	0.046
6160	mm	2.800	2.700	0.950	0.600	1.000
	in	0.110	0.106	0.037	0.024	0.039
6170	mm	3.280	2.500	1.220	0.600	1.100
	in	0.129	0.099	0.048	0.024	0.043
6180	mm	2.570	2.720	0.890	0.500	1.100
	in	0.101	0.107	0.035	0.020	0.043
6190	mm	2.390	2.130	0.740	0.510	0.990
	in	0.094	0.084	0.029	0.020	0.039
6200	mm	2.540	2.000	1.140	0.600	1.100
	in	0.100	0.079	0.045	0.024	0.043
6210	mm	2.540	2.000	0.860	0.500	1.100
	in	0.100	0.079	0.034	0.020	0.043
6220	mm	2.400	2.000	0.960	0.500	1.100
	in	0.097	0.079	0.038	0.020	0.043
6230	mm	2.480	1.990	0.900	0.520	1.080
	in	0.098	0.078	0.035	0.020	0.043
6240	mm	2.388	2.032	0.787	0.483	0.940
	in	0.094	0.080	0.031	0.019	0.037
6250	mm	2.413	1.905	0.914	0.508	0.762
	in	0.095	0.075	0.036	0.020	0.030
6260	mm	2.800	2.000	0.950	0.600	1.000
	in	0.110	0.079	0.037	0.024	0.039
6265	mm	2.800	2.000	0.950	0.600	1.000
	in	0.110	0.079	0.037	0.024	0.039
6270	mm	2.540	1.905	0.914	0.508	0.762
	in	0.100	0.075	0.036	0.020	0.030
6290	mm	2.337	1.981	0.787	0.508	1.016
	in	0.092	0.078	0.031	0.020	0.040
6300	mm	1.940	1.600	0.960	0.600	0.640
	in	0.076	0.063	0.038	0.024	0.025
6310	mm	2.311	1.346	0.940	0.559	0.787
	in	0.091	0.053	0.037	0.022	0.031
6320	mm	2.159	1.194	0.711	0.533	0.737
	in	0.085	0.047	0.028	0.021	0.029
6330	mm	2.388	1.092	0.787	0.508	0.787
	in	0.094	0.043	0.031	0.020	0.031
6340	mm	2.235	1.829	0.838	0.508	0.889
	in	0.088	0.072	0.033	0.020	0.035

Note: 6340 flat topped, 6180 brass

Used with permission from Dunlop Manufacturing, Inc.

You should, by now, have a pretty good idea of what your guitar will look like and how you will go about constructing it, but in order to clarify any points I have prepared the two following design exercises. Firstly I have run through the design of a well-known guitar in the ways that I have described during this chapter. Secondly, I have designed a guitar from scratch, the making of which is detailed in Chapter 9.

DESIGN EXERCISE NO.1

The intention in designing this guitar is to make an easily producible three pick-up guitar.

The first stage is to choose the scale length, which in this case will be 25½ in (648 mm) as sustain is important, and the fingerboard will have 21 frets. In order to use less wood and to ease manufacture, the neck of the guitar will be made of one piece of maple 1 in (25.4 mm) thick. The width at the nut will be 1⅝ in (41.2 mm) and at the body end of the neck it will be 2¼ in (57.1 mm) wide. The neck will be bolted to a double-cutaway body and this will extend 3 in (76.2 mm) into the guitar to stop the neck moving from side to side and to give enough room to fit the small metal fixing-plate on the back. The lower of the two cutaways will be deeper than the other, to give better access to the topmost frets, and the top cutaway horn will be longer than the bottom to help the balance of the guitar. The neck will join the body at the 16th fret.

There will be no angle on the head as the neck is to be made from one piece of wood; the machine-heads will all be fitted to one side of the head to pull the strings over the nut in a straight line, and small string-retainers will be used to pull the strings down onto the nut in the absence of the head angle. The neck will not be angled away from the body but raised slightly in its slot as the bridge to be used on this guitar is relatively low.

The bridge will be of a tremolo design that will pivot on six screws at the front of its mounting plate and be held in position against the pull of the strings by five springs in a cavity at the rear of the guitar.

The pick-ups and their controls will be mounted on a scratchplate that will cover the control cavities and the wiring channels. A separate cover plate on the rear of the guitar will cover the tremolo springs which can be adjusted to alter the tension.

The body, to be made of ash or alder, will be 1¾ in (44.4 mm) thick and will be dressed away on the front and at the rear to make it more comfortable to hold.

Simple black dot markers will be fitted into the front and sides of the neck, which will be fitted with fairly light frets. The body will be sprayed in a simple sunburst pattern and the neck, including the fingerboard, will be sprayed with clear lacquer.

You should have guessed by now that the guitar in question is the Fender Stratocaster. Although I am not going to claim that the reasons I have given for the inclusion of any of the design details are the same as those that Leo Fender and his team had decided, it should be apparent why certain features are as they are and that it is the way that these features combine which makes the guitar such a success.

A fine 1965 Fender Stratocaster.

DESIGN EXERCISE NO. 2

The scale length of the guitar will be 24⁹⁄₁₆ in (625 mm) and the guitar will have 24 frets. It will also be fitted with a Stratocaster-style tremolo unit, in this case a Schaller version of the Floyd Rose.

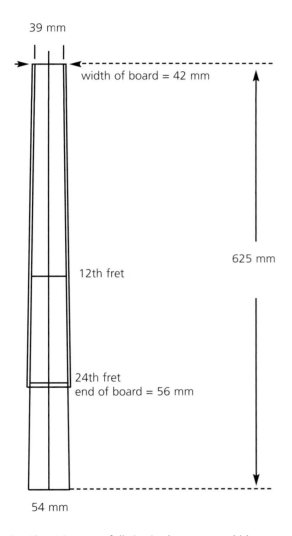

Planning the string area full-size is always a good idea.

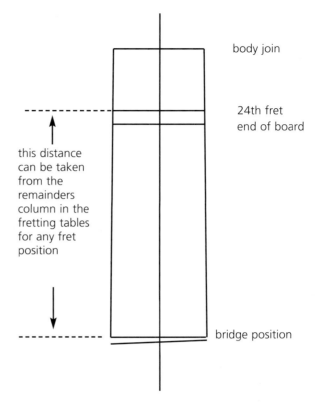

The positions of the end of the fingerboard, neck join and bridge can be transferred to the body drawing. The pick-ups will have to fit within this area and yet not be too close to the cutaways so as to weaken the neck join.

The neck–body join will be at the 20th fret, the neck being glued in, although the area around the neck join will be smoothed to make playing in the top areas more comfortable. Adequate gluing area will be needed in the tenon and there should be sufficient support for the neck so that the front pick-up cavity does not make it unstable. The bridge used will mean the guitar will need a small neck angle which will be incorporated into the top carving so the fingerboard lies flat where it passes over the body.

The neck of the guitar will be made from a laminate of three pieces of mahogany and will be slightly angled back from the body to allow for the height of the bridge with the fingerboard flush with the body. The ebony fingerboard will be inlaid with Gibson-style crown inlays and will be bound in maple for the simple reason that I like the look of it (remember, this is my guitar . . .). It will be 42 mm (1¹¹⁄₁₆ in) wide at the nut and 56 mm (2³⁄₁₆ in) at the 24th fret, ⁹⁄₁₆ in (14.5 mm) deep at the nut and 1 in (25.45 mm) at the 19th fret.

The 1⅞ in (47 mm) deep body will be a double cutaway with fairly long horns, the upper one being longer than the lower. It will be smaller than most guitars, to be more comfortable to play. It will be

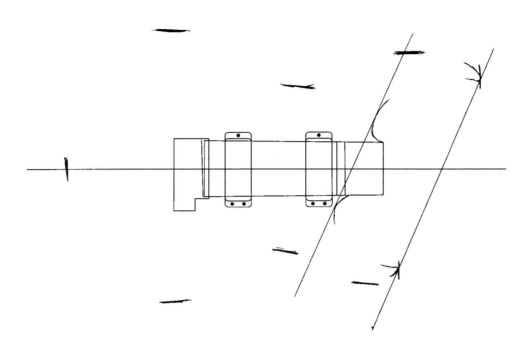

The positions of the pick-ups can be marked so that the design does not interfere with their positions. The bridge, in this case a Fender-style trem unit, is also sketched in. The basic dimensions of the body can also be sketched. For this guitar, the dimensions are simply chosen to be smaller than other guitars! The line between the points of the top and bottom horns are reflected in the position of the cutaways to give a slightly offset and asymmetric look to the guitar. The beginnings of the horn shapes are also sketched and the control positions marked. The jack socket will fit into the side of the guitar.

Once the rough shape has been decided it is not difficult to refine it and smooth out the contours to make the whole guitar look like it was designed, and not the result of a toddlers' scribbling contest. From these drawings it is then possible to start building the body.

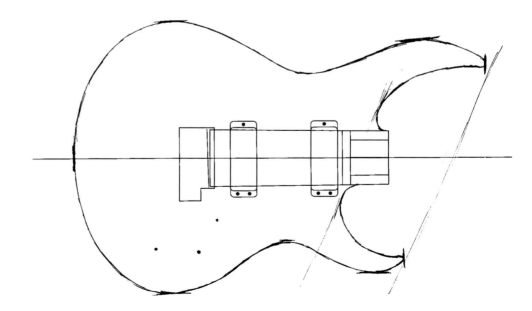

DESIGN CHECKLIST

Scale length	Guitar or bass? Long or short?
No. of frets	Will influence pick-up positioning
Neck dimensions	Depth at nut and body. Should be sufficient to install your chosen truss rod
Body shape	The **fun** part of the process
Neck-to-body join	Glued-in? Bolt-on? Straight-through?
Bridge height and position	It is essential to know the height of your bridge before you finalise the neck angle
Neck angle	Determined by bridge height and neck-to-body join type and position. One of the easiest things to get wrong on a guitar and most difficult to put right. Draw it out full-size and check carefully
Head angle	No angle may require string retainers; a big angle could make a weak head
Head shape	Another area of personal choice but there should be room for the machine-heads and they should not foul other strings
Body thickness	Must be thick enough to contain all the parts but not so large that it becomes too heavy or unwieldy
Materials	See Chapter 5
Pick-ups and controls	Choose type and number of pick-ups, type of mounting, position of pick-ups and the number and type of controls to be fitted. Remember each control needs a cutout and will need to be accessible while playing
Nut width	A matter of personal preference
Truss rod	Choose the type and installation method. Plan adjustment for neck or body end of neck
Control mounting	On a scratchplate and dropped in from the front or inserted through the wood from the rear
Binding	For body, fingerboard, head, or all three
Inlays	Either dots or something more elaborate
Contouring	Body dressed as on a Stratocaster, or carved as on a Les Paul
Fretwire	High and wide frets and light strings can cause tuning problems. Smaller frets can make bending notes more difficult
Finishing	Type and colour

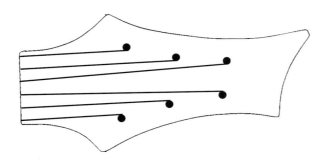

The headstock is designed to mirror, to some degree, the shape of the body. The machine-head positions have also been marked, following the line of, and ½ in (12.7 mm) in from the edge of the head. Plotting the line from each string position to the machine-head position will also show if any are likely to foul.

made of poplar with a carved top and will have the controls for the pick-up selector, etc., inserted from the rear. Poplar is chosen because it is easy to work and sounds good. The top carving will be ¼ in (6.3 mm) deep giving a depth of 1⅝ (41.3 in) at the edge of the guitar. There will be no binding

on the body but it will be contoured at the rear.

Because it has a 24-fret neck and two deep cut-aways it will not be possible to fit normal-sized humbuckers into the guitar as they would take up too much space and be rather too near the neck joint for comfort and stability. Instead, two specially designed mini humbuckers will be used and they will be fitted directly into the front of the guitar at a fixed height and wired into a circuit that gives the maximum tonal variation with the minimum of controls. There will be one volume pot and one tone pot, each with a push–pull to allow coil-tapping and a choice of tone range. They will have a standard three-position toggle switch to select either or both.

The frets will be fat Gibson-style on a small radius board. The double-action truss rod will be fitted beneath the separate ebony fingerboard and adjusted from the head end.

The headstock of the guitar will be a three-a-side unit angled back 10 degrees and fitted with Sperzel locking mini machine-heads. As with the body, the headstock will be made smaller than is normal and its design will reflect that of the body.

Finally, the guitar will be finished in (s)lime green. There is no logical reason for this but then, who needs logical reasons?

4 The Tools for the Job

Unit costs for factory-finished guitars are probably lower now than they have ever been. When one considers that in 1954, the Fender Stratocaster retailed at $249.50 (case extra) and compares this with what they cost now, it is easy to see that inflation has been beaten somehow.

There are two ways to keep unit costs down: one is to cheapen the manufacture, using cheaper parts and being less concerned about quality; the other way is to increase the volume of sales by automating the machinery that builds the guitars and purchasing parts in bulk. Differing manufacturers have gone in different directions, and some have even followed both courses, but the amount of computer-controlled machinery that is now being used means that some guitars go from being a plank of wood to a finished instrument almost without ever seeing a human being.

Further descriptions of these very expensive and complicated machines will only result in frustration if you have to do a simliar job by hand, but since many of these machines are designed to do jobs that were originally done by skilled craftsmen, it is safe to assume that electric, and indeed acoustic, guitars can be made successfully with ordinary woodworking tools. It will take longer than if you had access to some expensive machinery but it should be more satisfying and cheaper.

Some of the more specialised tools that will make the job easier can quite easily be borrowed or rented if you know where to go. What is most important for the success of your venture is not the amount of wonderful labour-saving power tools you can lay your hands on, but how you go about looking after and using whatever tools, hand or power, that you have at your disposal.

Some power tools can make certain jobs very simple but they need to be set up and used properly and, in some cases, jigs will need to be made. They can

also injure quite badly if not used correctly. If you are not used to dealing with woodworking tools, I would again urge you to take a little time to learn about them, how to use them, and how to keep them in good condition, as it cannot be overstated how much easier, and safer, this will make your chosen task, whether it is making a guitar or putting up a shelf.

The most important part of the guitar-maker's arsenal is the *workbench*. Ideally, this is situated in a warm and dry workshop with ample room and plenty of storage space, all tools easily to hand and tidy, and within easy reach of a means of making coffee or tea and sandwiches. In practice, this is highly unlikely to be the case, but the nearer you can get to this ideal the easier the job will be. In any case, the workbench needs to be firm and rigid. There is no point in even trying to cut or plane in a straight line if the workbench resembles a nervous jelly. A good *woodworking vice* is also essential. This is not only used to hold the wood or the complete guitar while it is being worked on, but it can also be used to hold such things as the fretting jig or workboard. Stewart Macdonald's Guitar Shop Supply in the United States now markets plans for a bench that has been specifically designed for guitar-making. It even has a rotatable top so that a standard woodworking area, and a soft surface for assembling finished guitars when the instrument needs to be protected from damage, are available in half the space that would normally be needed.

Using your chosen tool properly is absolutely essential, as is using the right tool for the job. Some of my earliest efforts were made with what was available. I have, in the distant past, cut guitar bodies from 2 in (50.8 mm) mahogany with a coping saw. This is stupid. It is not only hard work but also not very accurate. There is no chance of working

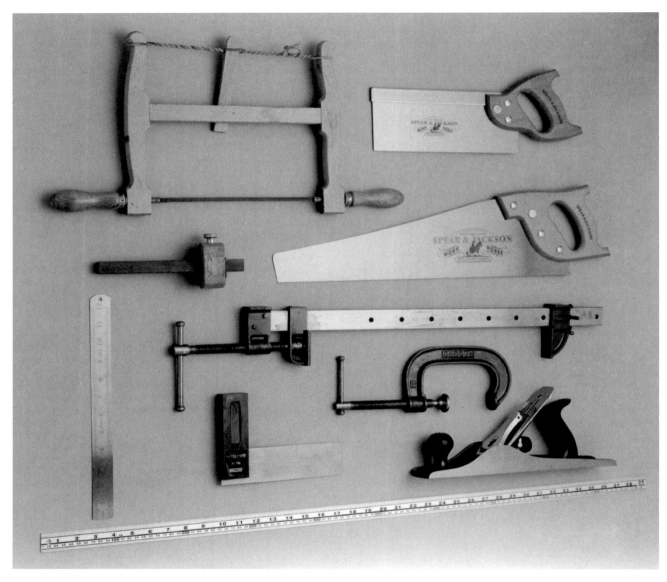

*From top left: bow saw, tenon saw, marking gauge,
rip saw, 12 in steel ruler, sash clamp, marking square,
G-clamp, shooting plane, long ruler.*

close to a line, so I had to work rough and tidy up
using spokeshaves.

I have seen some examples of how using the
wrong tool can damage a perfectly good instrument.
One case was a man who used an electric drill for all
tasks. Using a ¹⁄₁₆ in drill bit he tried to drill the head
off a damaged screw. There was far too much torque
for the drill bit to handle and the bit broke sending
half of it spinning away, and the other half, still in

the drill chuck, went straight through the top of the
guitar he was working on. You do not get enough
control over an electric drill to use it in this way.
They are very good for a number of jobs but they
must be treated with care.

Apart from the standard joinery tools such as
plane, chisels, saws and *knives*, there are some specialised tools that are relatively easy to get hold of.
For example, there are two ways of cutting out pick-
up cavities. You can either remove as much of the
waste as is possible with a drill and then tidy up
using chisels, or you can use a router. Routers are
the electric guitar-maker's friend; they are basically
an electric gouge, and can be used for any number

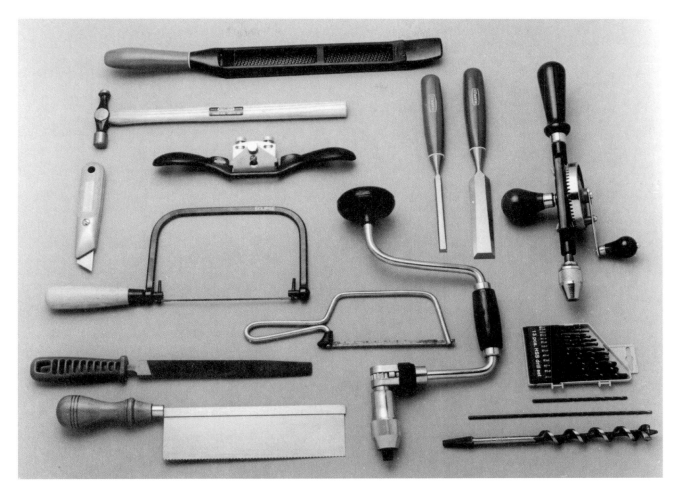

From top left: surform, pin hammer, chisels, hand drill, craft knife, spokeshave, coping saw, drill brace, junior hacksaw, drill bits, file, gent's saw.

of jobs. The problem is that they are expensive. Buying even a second-hand one will push the cost of your guitar up very steeply. The answer is to rent one. There are plenty of hire (that's rental in the USA!) shops around and the rates are not excessive.

Cutting the body of the guitar can be done by hand, although you would have to be really dumb to use a coping saw, but either way this is time-consuming. It is easier to use a *band saw*, but a good band saw is even further out of reach than a good router. It is the same with a *power planer*. There are times when machine-planing a piece of wood could save hours of hard work. The answer in these cases is to try what I used to do before I got labour-saving goodies for myself. I found that by a little polite talking I could get the guys at a local joinery company to cut out a shape or machine-plane a piece of wood. All that was needed was to ask very nicely and make a small donation to the workers'

tea and coffee fund. Of course, they would not have been too happy if I had been there every day using their machines while I turned out loads of guitars for a massive profit, but for the small amount that I was doing it was acceptable. I found that the guys who worked for the company became interested in what I was doing as, while it was all woodwork, it was in an entirely different field to them. They were also a great help as they offered advice on aspects of woodworking that I either had not learned yet or was simply too stupid to realise. You can learn from anyone, not just those in the same line as you.

The basic woodworking tools that you will need are as follows. For marking out and planning your guitar you will need a good *straight edge*, at least 18 in (458 mm) long, and a *steel rule* marked in both feet and inches and millimetres. As well as *pencils* you will need a *marking knife* and a *square*, and probably a *protractor* for marking out the angle of the guitar's head and neck if the guitar is designed in this way.

To prepare your chosen hunk of tree you will need a *bow saw*, for cutting out the basic shape of the guitar if you do not have access to a band saw, a *rip saw* and a *tenon saw*. For planing the wood flat you will need the longest *jack plane* you can lay your hands on. The longer the plane you use, the easier it is to plane a straight line. For smaller jobs and for squaring the ends of wood you will need a *shooting plane*.

G-clamps, in a selection of sizes from 1 to 8 in, will be needed when gluing up the component parts of the guitar or the laminates that make them. Clamps can prove to be expensive and so borrowing is advisable, especially as they are only used when something is being glued and when the glue is set they can be removed. If, however, you do buy them it is worth looking in army surplus stores as they can often be bought cheaply.

At least two *sash clamps* of about 18 in in length will be needed if the body of the guitar has to be laminated as in Chapter 12. These too are expensive to buy but can often be rented.

For the preparation of the guitar's body and neck a *router* will save a lot of time. It will be useful not only for cutting out the holes for the pick-ups, but also for cutting the truss rod channel, control cavities and binding channels.

For shaping the neck you will need *spokeshaves*, both concave and convex, and *wood rasps* or *surforms*. Surforms come in a variety of shapes and make carving necks and body tops a lot easier. They can also be used to carve out the contours on Stratocaster-style bodies.

A selection of chisels will be useful for a number of jobs, from tidying up the tenon on a glued-in neck to finishing off roughly cut pick-up holes, and a small *gouge* will be needed if the guitar is to be fitted with a Gibson-style head and truss rod, for cutting the adjustment recess. A *coping saw* is essential for a number of jobs, as is a *junior hacksaw*.

A *pillar drill*, or access to one, will take any of the sloppiness out of drilling machine-head holes and bridge-mounting holes but, if one cannot be scrounged, a *domestic electric drill* in one of the drill stands that are often sold as accessories will suffice. A domestic electric drill can be used for drilling all sorts of holes, although not with a 1/16 in bit, and a small *wheel brace* will pay for itself many times over as you can control the drill very easily. A good selection of drill bits from 1/16 to 1 in (1.5 to 25.45 mm) will see a lot of use.

For preparing the fingerboard you will need the jack plane and the square as well as a small *dovetail* or *gentleman's saw* for cutting the fret slots. If the fingerboard is to be inlaid then a small router will be very helpful and small sharp chisels will be needed to tidy up the recess. One of the most useful tools is one of the easiest to make. A good heavy piece of wood, approximately 3 in x 2 in by 15 in (75 x 50 x

One of the simplest but most useful tools is a sanding stick. This one is made from the remains of an old laminated neck blank and is covered with 120 grit paper on one side.

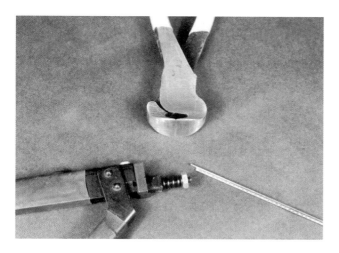

Fretting tools: specially ground endcutters for removing and trimming frets and a tang cutter for removing the small piece of fret tag when fretting inside binding. The small piece of fretwire shows the result.

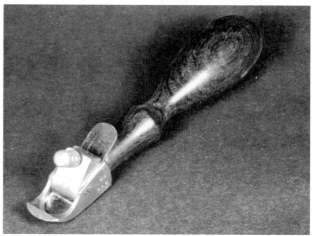

Carving guitar tops can be made much easier if using special tools. The curved spokeshave (top) belongs to English luthier Dave King but is frequently borrowed by me – sometimes for months on end – and is excellent for carving guitar tops quickly. The smaller palm plane (above) is good for fine work and where smaller radii are needed. This is quite frequently borrowed by Dave King!

380 mm) with one of the 3 in sides planed totally flat and then covered in sandpaper, will be very useful in preparing the fingerboard.

The frets are fitted using a pair of *pliers* to gently bend them to shape and a small *hammer* to fit them into the board. The ends are then cut flush with a pair of *endcutters*. These need to be fairly heavy duty as fretwire is quite tough. I used to have to buy a pair that almost fitted the bill and get a friend, who worked in the engineering shop of the local railway depot, to grind them to the shape that I needed.

Now I simply call one of the specialist guitar-makers' suppliers and order them from stock. They are quite expensive but usually last a long time.

After the frets are fitted they are levelled using an *oilstone* and recontoured using a *fretfile*. Oilstones come in a variety of sizes and are made from different compounds. Some are very soft and useful only as presents for people you do not like very much. A good oilstone will cost about five times the price of the cheapest. It should be flat and they usually have two grades of abrasive. Choose one that is not too coarse but has a very fine abrasive on the other side. The fretfile is another of the specialised tools that can be bought from guitar parts suppliers. These are concave files that are made in a variety of widths to suit the different sizes of fretwire

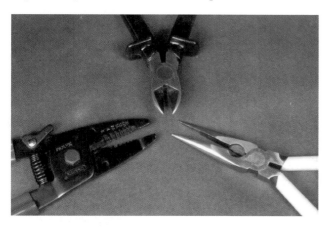

Wiring tools: long-nose pliers (essential in avoiding burnt fingers), wire strippers and side cutters.

that are available. They are used to round the fret over and remove the flat top that is left after the frets have been stoned level. This is covered in Chapter 14.

The tools used for painting the guitar are covered in Chapter 13.

For the final assembly of the guitar, *screwdrivers*, both *blade* and *crosshead*, a *socket set*, or a collection of *spanners*, will be used to install the pick-ups and machine-heads into their respective places. A *soldering iron* of about 25 watts is required to connect everything inside the guitar. A smaller iron will not be powerful enough for some jobs. A pair of *wire cutters*, *wire strippers* and a pair of *long-nosed pliers* will also see a lot of use. Other small tools that will be used for any number of jobs throughout the making of your guitar will be a sharp *craft knife* and a selection of *files*, and, if you intend to make your own truss rod, a *tap* and *die* of the right size should be bought or borrowed.

Lastly, *sandpaper* or *production paper* will be needed in all grades from 120 through to 1000 wet-and-dry

for finishing the wood and the paintwork, together with different-shaped *cork blocks* to back the sandpaper while it is being used. Also needed will be some *scrap wood* or *plywood* to use as clamping cauls, and ⅜ or ½ in (10 or 12 mm) plywood can be used to make up jigs that will take a lot of the hard work out of the job in hand. A *fretsaw* will also come in very handy for some small jobs, most notably cutting out scratch or back plates.

This list of tools is quite long and, if they were all to be bought from new, it would prove to be very expensive; however, I would imagine that, if someone has taken the decision to take on something as large as making a guitar, then they would be in possession of at least some of the tools required, if not most of them. As for the rest, it is always worth trying to borrow them as the worst anyone will say when asked is a simple 'no'.

This is, of course, far from being a definitive list as there are plenty of other tools that can be used or adapted to do various tasks. Some of these will be seen in forthcoming chapters.

5 Woods

Over the last ten years or so a lot has been written about the massive destruction of the world's rainforests. Areas the size of whole countries have been chopped down either to raise a cash crop from the timber or to produce land for farming. The political, social and economic arguments about this are way outside the scope of this book, but the original edition recommended the use of some woods that are now considered, by some, to be too exotic and hardly 'politically correct'. Certainly the quality of some of the woods that I have used in the past has been declining; evidence perhaps of a lack of supply caused by over felling. Other woods are now almost impossible to find in sizes big enough for guitar-making. However, many of the woods that are used commercially in guitar-making are not from the affected areas and are not considered to be on the danger list. Woods such as ash and alder, as used on Fender's bodies, and maple, used on the fronts of Les Pauls and for Fender necks, are easily obtained and other woods from more managed stocks are available.

It would be easy to feel that as an occasional user of exotic timber I am in part responsible for the state of the rainforest. This would actually be quite unfair. Eating some South American produced beef products could easily have had more effect since much of the land used for beef-farming is cleared by fire. In my entire career I have made relatively few guitars and I doubt if I have used more than a couple of square metres of rainforest. Of course if everyone in the world consumed the same area, the situation would have reached the critical point years ago, but the real causes of the problem need to be addressed, not the limited amount of use that has gone on for many years. As long as the stocks are managed correctly and the supply maintained at a sensible level then we should still be using good wood in years to come.

Having said this, I should also point out that some companies now offer alternative woods from species of tree that are similar to those we are more used to. As long as the wood is stable and of the right strength there is no reason why it cannot be used in place of something that might be getting a little scarce.

For those of us in the UK, there is no need to concentrate on foreign woods as we have plenty of interesting hardwoods that are perfectly suitable for guitar-making, such as sycamore and walnut. The same also applies in the United States which has an abundant supply of sustainable woods.

However, some people will invariably want to stay with what has become the standard. Many Gibson and similar guitars are made from mahogany, some, such as the Les Paul, having a maple top. The Les Paul Studio and Lite were made from alder and The Paul, a guitar from the late 1970s, was made of walnut. Fenders often have ash bodies or, occasionally, alder with maple necks. Fingerboards for most makes are usually rosewood or ebony although Fender do use maple.

Some woods used in guitar-making are purely structural and not particularly pretty to look at. Others are chosen just for their looks and may only be used as a thin veneer. The tops on many Les Pauls, Paul Reed Smiths and others are maple which is up to ½ in (12.7 mm) thick to give a harder edge to the sound of the guitar and also to look good. The best examples use a finely figured piece of wood, which itself is becoming expensive, proof perhaps of its over-use.

The use of different woods to adjust the natural sound of the guitar is something that has been discussed and argued about over the years. There are people who will claim that using a lighter or denser wood has no effect on the sound of the guitar and that the sound of the guitar is entirely due to the

The guitar that could be credited with the upsurge in pretty wood guitars. This is a 1959 Gibson Les Paul showing the curly maple top, not in this case bookmatched, that launched a thousand imitations.

A selection of various sizes and types of instrument-makers' wood at Luthier's Supplies in England. There are several companies that specialise in supplying wood to instrument-makers who will often cut wood to individual requirements. The curved piece of maple in the centre found its way into the wings of the eight-string in Chapter 11.

choice of pick-ups and hardware. Others will tell you that the final sound of a guitar can be estimated before it is built just by careful choice of wood and that the finish of the guitar will have an effect on its sound. The truth lies somewhere between the two. If one goes back to the guitar magazines that were published in the early 1970s, the general consensus was that a heavy-bodied guitar, for example one made entirely of maple, would sustain longer than one that was made of a lighter wood. This is certainly not the case. A friend of mine once owned a pair of 1962 Fender Stratocasters. One had an alder body, the other had ash. In all other respects, such as hardware, neck and even strings, they were the same. They certainly sounded different and the lighter alder-bodied guitar sustained longer than the heavier ash guitar.

To further emphasise this, during the late 1980s, the luthier Roger Giffin made several guitars with bodies made of jelutong. This is a very lightweight but sturdy wood that is often used for pattern-making. It is easy to work and takes a finish well. It is pretty boring to look at but this does not matter if it is painted. The end results were very impressive. The guitars had a lot of natural sustain and sounded very bright. They also did not wear you out if you had to have one on a strap for a two-hour concert!

Some oriental manufacturers use basswood which is also known as American lime, and the English company Shergold made obeché-bodied guitars in the early 1970s.

The only conclusion that can be drawn from this is that different woods absorb different frequencies in differing amounts but since there has been little, if any, scientific research done on this the only way of choosing is by trial and error. It should also be noted that woods can vary enormously in quality, weight and density depending on where they were grown and names used in one country might signify a markedly different wood when used in another country. Ash is a fine example of this; the ash grown in Europe is heavier than some grown in the United States. There has been much talk of the use of so-called 'swamp' ash. This is said to be much lighter in weight and grows in the swamps of the Mississippi delta in the southern states of America. The wood that grows in the very wettest areas is certainly lighter in weight and makes a good wood for building guitar bodies but trees from only a few hundred feet away may have completely different characteristics having grown in a drier area. The problem is that all of this wood is expensive, regardless of what it actually weighs. It is wise to choose carefully.

The necks and indeed the bodies on some guitars are laminated from several pieces of wood. These can be the same wood or woods of different types and colours. Companies such as Alembic have been laminating guitars from all sorts of exotic woods for years. Their necks are often made from a lot of very thin strips of wood. This serves three purposes: it is decorative, it is less wasteful than using one big piece of one wood and it is generally stronger. If just one piece on a laminated neck wants to move or warp, it will often be held in place by the other pieces. Reversing the grain on one or more pieces in

Laminated neck blanks beneath an almost finished neck. In all three cases the main wood is mahogany, with maple veneer and mahogany laminates on the blanks, and maple and an unidentified hardwood on the almost completed neck.

a multiple laminate neck is also said to help. There is no limit to how many laminates you can use or how small they can be, although the more you use, the more difficult and messy gluing them will be.

For the eight-string bass made in Chapter 12 the neck is three pieces of maple with a veneer of walnut between them. This veneer is purely decorative and serves to break up the single colour of the maple for the neck. To have used two pieces of walnut veneer and one of maple in between each piece would have been even prettier but would have meant using twice the amount of glue and each surface would have tried to slip away from the others as it was clamped which could have been a nightmare.

I rarely use a single piece of wood for a guitar neck. Because of the quality of wood that is available and the extra strength that is gained from laminating I usually use this method. If the guitar is to be painted in a block colour, I will use three laminates of the same wood. If it is to rely more on the colouring of its wood, I will use two outer pieces of the same wood either side of a sandwich of either three or five pieces of contrasting woods, sometimes with a veneer or two in there as well. For bodies, again it depends on whether the finished guitar is going to be painted. It is a waste of time to laminate a body up from all sorts of pretty wood and then go and paint it purple. Alternatively, not everyone wants a guitar looking like a veneer merchant's catalogue. Subtlety is the key to good design.

It is also possible to laminate a neck with an angled headstock from a single piece of thinner wood, or from a thinner laminate. It is possible to splice on the headstock and heel and, with care, matching the laminates together as you clamp, this can look very effective and give a stronger headstock. This is covered in more detail in Chapter 9. Alembic and some other makers take this one stage further and make the head up from a central core of wood with veneer facings both sides. When this is glued onto the angled end of the neck it shows as stripes running all around the neck.

The one other important source of wood that must be mentioned is reclaimed wood (or should I call it pre-owned?). I do not mean that you should go out and rip apart expensive antique furniture, but there are sources of wood that are perfectly suitable for guitar-making. I have used wood from old Royal Navy tables (the Royal Navy only used the best wood and it was about the best mahogany I have ever seen), some old crew bunk sides from the RMS *Queen Mary*, a bar from a London pub and old draining boards from demolished houses. The last wood was also very good. It was very close grained and, once I had cleaned off the various layers of varnish and grime, was very stable.

The most important aspect of reclaimed timber is that it must be free from nails, pins, screws and anything else that might produce a nasty surprise when it is being worked on. If you are unsure, go over it with a metal detector. If it does have items

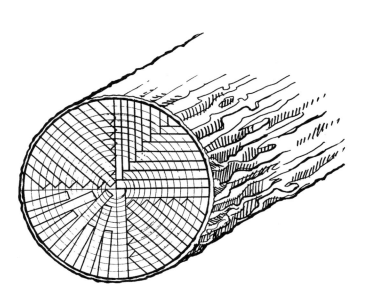
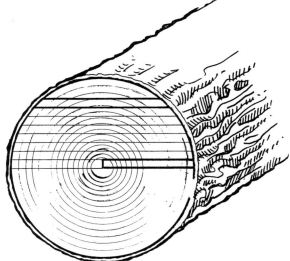

Quarter-sawn wood (left) is ideally cut so the planks are cut as radially as possible. This is both wasteful and uneconomic. Cutting the log into four quarters and slicing off each side in turn will give planks that are nearer to the ideal but slab-sawing (right) is clearly easier. It can be seen that those planks cut near the centre of the log are effectively quarter-sawn.

embedded in it you are best advised to leave it alone as removing the piece may damage the wood and not removing it may damage you.

As important as the type of wood you use for the guitar is the state the wood is in. In an ideal world, all guitar-making wood should be straight-grained, quarter-sawn and air-dried. Ideal worlds are not too common in any galaxy.

Quarter-sawn timber is not found very often, the term 'quarter-sawn' referring to the way in which the planks are cut from the log. This is done so that the planks are cut as radially as possible with the grain then running perpendicular to the widest face of the plank. Quarter-sawn wood is around 25 per cent stronger than the alternative slab-sawn wood and will shrink up to 30 per cent less across its width. However, the method of cutting quarter-sawn wood is very wasteful; many woodyards will not even consider it, and so the wood is cut in slabs through the plank. This produces some planks which have grain angled through them, but others which have a nice

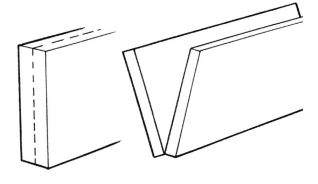

Bookmatching, by splitting the wood down the centre and opening out, gives a mirror-image grain pattern.

even and straight grain running through as one would expect on a quarter-sawn piece. The art is choosing the right piece.

Some planks will also show a certain amount of grain run-out. This is where the long fibres of the wood are cut across at an angle as the plank is sawn. This is more noticeable on quarter-sawn planks and will show as the grain will be diagonal across the plank.

Air-drying ash at Tyler Hardwoods in Wiltshire, England.

Splits, or shakes, in a piece of Douglas fir.

Air-drying the wood, as opposed to kiln-drying, is also unusual. Here the wood is stored for 20 or 30 years in the open air, slowly drying all of the time. Clearly this is uneconomic. Although air-dried wood is a little stronger than kiln-dried, it is almost impossible to find and since most wood is kiln-dried very carefully to retain just the right amount of moisture, there is less to worry about when buying.

The answer, therefore, is to use the best of what is available.

When buying the wood for your guitar I would recommend looking at the wood and not buying it unseen, and if you do not know enough to trust yourself doing this then ask the advice of someone who does have some experience. Generally most musical instrument suppliers will be very helpful, but it is still well worth taking a little time and trouble to find a piece that will not let you down by warping or splitting.

Firstly the plank should be inspected for checks and cracks. These are often known as shakes, and are small splits along the grain of the wood. Any wood in this condition should be avoided.

Since it is unlikely that you will be able to find any truly quarter-sawn wood, it is worth looking at the growth rings at the end of the plank to find a piece of wood that most closely resembles it. The growth rings should be, as near as possible, parallel to one face of the plank, and the wood will be strongest if the load is taken by the rings when on edge. So for neck wood, the rings should be perpendicular to the fingerboard when viewed from the end of the neck. If the growth rings on a plank are clearly semi-circular, the wood may well curve across the plank and split. Wood like this should also be avoided.

It is an unfortunate fact that quarter-sawn wood is generally not as pretty as slab-sawn wood, for the simple reason that it is cut so that the grain is as straight as possible. If intending to use figured wood in your guitar, it would be a good idea to use wood that is as near as possible quarter-sawn for the neck and a pretty slab-sawn (with the grain running parallel to the face) piece for the body.

Figured woods are often, as a result of their figuring, much less stable than straight-grained pieces. This is for the simple reason that the wood would probably prefer to grow straight and something prevents this, causing some figuring in the wood. Clearly this must have a detrimental effect on the wood's strength to a greater or lesser degree, depending on the figuring. The flame in curly maple is one example. This wood can be very attractive but, even when quarter-sawn, can be quite unstable. A curly

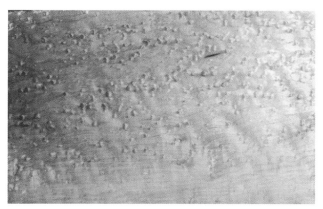

Bird's eyes in a nicely figured, but very warped, piece of maple.

maple neck on a guitar is very pretty, but I prefer to use a straight-grained piece. Bird's eyes in wood are caused by an infection in the tree and whilst they too can be very pretty, I would not recommend making necks out of bird's-eye maple. It is expensive to buy and therefore, if it does warp, you lose more money.*

Wal basses, regardless of how pretty the wood on the body is, always use straight-grained maple for the outer laminates on their necks as they do not trust figured wood and are not prepared to risk it for their customers. They also use hornbeam for the centre laminates of the neck. This is a very strong but rather boring wood which is ideal for guitar necks.

Fingerboards are generally made from ebony, rosewood or maple. Rosewood and ebony is left unfinished but maple has a clear finish applied to keep it from getting very dirty with the sort of grime that seems to emerge from all guitarists' fingertips. This gives the fingerboard a very different feel although maple still feels good if you can live with the grime and play on a sealed or oil and wax-finished neck.

The reason that maple has become popular for fingerboards has little to do with anything other than economics. When Leo Fender designed his Broadcaster/Telecaster in the late 1940s, he designed a one-piece neck. This had no separate fingerboard and so needed less manufacturing than a neck that required a board to be glued on. The choice of wood for the whole neck was based on suitability and it happened that maple was equally suitable for taking frets and, in practice, is often easier and therefore cheaper to fret. To prevent

Substitute woods are often very good. This 1960s Burns is made of European maple which is a little softer and lighter in colour than its American relative but still a good instrument-making wood. It was, after all, used by European violin-makers for centuries. This guitar is also notable for its rotary tone switch that has a setting marked 'Wild Dog'.

the board from getting dirty, as we have already mentioned, it was lacquered but this also meant that it did not have to be masked before the neck was sprayed – another economy. It is just this economy that has led to the look of maple necks becoming fashionable. Anyone who can look at a Fender guitar of the 1950s and not see a masterpiece of economic design needs their head examined!

Rosewood is often regarded as a cheap alternative for ebony but is a perfectly good wood in its own right and has long been a favourite of furniture-makers. All of the rosewood species are members of the genus *Dalbergia* and those which are marketed as rosewood come from Central and South America, Africa, India, Burma and Thailand. Perhaps the most widely sought after is Brazilian rosewood (*Dalbergia nigra*). This has been subject to export embargoes and limited supplies are sometimes available. Most guitar-makers now use Indian rosewood (*Dalbergia latifolia*) which is a different colour, being more purple than the brown of the Brazilian variety. Other members of the family which are less used but often very suitable include kingwood, Brazilian tulipwood, cocobolo, Honduras rosewood, African blackwood, Burma tulipwood, Thailand rosewood (also known as chin chan) and Mexican rosewood. All of these differ in size, colour and grain and some will make perfectly suitable fingerboards.

Ebony occurs across Africa and Asia and similar, more distantly related, woods occur in Central and South America. Some ebony is black with very little figuring and a close, almost invisible grain. Other types are far more figured. The heartwood is used for instrument-making and the outer parts of the tree are often a boring grey wood. However, this is also quite hard. Ceylon or African ebony are black and others, such as Macassar ebony, Coromandel ebony and Borneo ebony are streaked or mottled, often with brown or grey. Other related woods, include zebra wood (also known as zebrano), king marble and queen marble, both of which are

Nigerian woods. Ebony can be quite difficult to work and is not as easy to fret as rosewood as it is harder and has less 'give'.

Another wood that has been used as an alternative to both ebony and rosewood is wenge. This is a dark wood with darker stripes and is very hard. Many years ago, the range of Eko acoustic guitars made in Italy featured wenge fingerboards, and more recently it has been seen on many custom instruments as well as commercially-made guitars such as those made by the Warwick company. The variance in the grain does make it a little more difficult to work and it does not take a finish very well as it is quite open pored but it has been used and appears quite suitable.

Obviously there are no hard and fast rules as to what you can and cannot use on guitars. Some woods are quite unsuitable, such as elm which is very flexible, and oak which is far too heavy and better suited to the building of replica warships of the 17th and 18th centuries. However, advice is available both from wood suppliers and from a variety of books which can be found in public libraries or even bought.

One final and very important point is that not all woods are benign and friendly. Some are quite nasty. Certain woods have a tendency to produce irritating dust. Wenge, rosewood and ebony are examples, and it can be safely assumed that if the dust is irritating, it is probably doing you no good at all. Some woods are quite simply poisonous. Limited exposure to the dust will be relatively harmless but prolonged exposure can lead to breathing problems. Sanding also produces a mixture of dust and residue from the sanding medium. This can be quite an irritating mixture and not good for the body. Most countries have research centres looking into the effects of these dusts and it is wise to ask for advice. It is even wiser to ensure that working areas are properly ventilated and that masks are worn to protect the lungs from the effects. You only have one pair of lungs. Look after them.

---

* In a conversation with the author in August 2000 Ken Warmoth of Warmoth guitars stated: "As the manufacturer who has probably the most experience in the whole world with Birdseye, I can confidently say that there is absolutely no higher incidence of neck problems with this material than there is with plain maple. The key here that has given this wood some bad publicity is that some makers have ignored the basic underlying wood grain while simply going for the Birdseye figure. I have seen such necks where, if the Birdseye was removed and someone looked at just the remaining piece of wood, they would have never used it for a neck! Beauty can be so distracting and deceiving, but be only skin deep"

6 Truss Rods

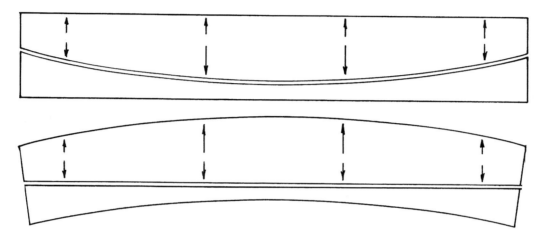

The simple mechanics of the truss rod. As the rod is tensioned it tries to straighten. In doing so it bends the neck in the opposite direction.

The theory and workings of the truss rod were the one aspect of guitar-making that I found most difficulty in obtaining any information about when I first started making guitars.

Truss rods seemed shrouded in mystique, with their secrets known only to a privileged few, and I had heard all sorts of stories about them both from unenlightened friends and from ill-informed magazine articles. For example, I had heard, and in fact still sometimes hear, that a truss rod should be used to raise and lower the guitar's action, or to remove a twist on a neck and that any attempt of adjustment by a person not in possession of the divine knowledge would result in instant disintegration of the guitar's neck and the end of civilisation in the known universe. In reality, a truss rod is much simpler.

As we have already discussed, the neck of the guitar has to be thick enough to withstand the pull of the strings whilst still being thin enough to be easily playable. The amount of pull exerted by the strings is dependent on their thickness. A light-gauge set will pull less than a medium- or heavy-gauge set when tuned to the same pitch. It is possible that a guitar strung with ultra light-gauge strings may need no adjustment on the truss

rod at all as the neck may be rigid enough to withstand the pull of the strings on its own.

Until the mid-1920s, when of course there was no such thing as a light-gauge guitar string, necks were made much thicker to withstand the string pull, which, on a set of medium-gauge strings, could be as much as 180 pounds (80 kilos). In order that guitar necks could be made thinner, a Gibson employee by the name of Ted McHugh invented a simple device for holding the neck steady. This was named the truss rod.

The string would pull the neck of the guitar away from the player and it was the truss rod's job to counteract this by pulling the neck back. Ted McHugh's truss rod, like all good ideas, was very simple. A curved rod was embedded into the neck beneath the fingerboard so that it was at its deepest in the centre of the neck. At the body end the rod was firmly anchored by a metal plate, and at the head end there was a small recess containing the adjustment nut that, when tightened, tensioned the

Rickenbacker's double truss rods. Note the large adjustment recess in the head that could cause problems if the head of the guitar was knocked.

rod. Any curved rod, when tensioned, will try to straighten and as the truss rod tries to straighten it bends the neck back in the opposite direction to which the strings are pulling it.

The introduction of the truss rod revolutionised the design of guitar necks. Almost overnight guitars were made with much thinner and more comfortable necks that were a lot easier to play, and since then it has become the accepted norm to have a truss rod in most guitar necks, the exceptions being some steel-

strung acoustics that have a steel reinforcing bar glued into the neck, which is a system that can be used on an electric guitar (although it is better to have some adjustment rather than none), and most classical guitars that do not need a rod due to the nylon or gut strings not being as highly tensioned.

There are some slightly different designs of truss rods that have developed over the years. The Rickenbacker company use twin rods in their guitars. These work on a different principle to the Gibson style of rod. They are fitted into a flat-bottomed channel cut into the neck. The rods themselves are formed of two pieces of steel bar that are joined at one end and staggered at the other. The longer of the free ends is threaded and the adjustment nut butts up against the end of the other. When tightened the whole assembly bends, taking the neck with it. The advantages of this style of truss rod are that since the rod is not permanently fixed into the neck it can be removed and replaced should it break, and that since the rod is flat and relatively shallow, necks can be made thinner still. It has the disadvantage that if the rod is over-tightened, which can happen if the neck is made very thin, the truss rod can split the fingerboard from the neck,

The general arrangement of a Gibson-style truss rod (below) with the rod installed from the front of the neck and a separate fingerboard glued on top, and a Fender-style truss rod (bottom) with the rod installed from the rear of the neck and covered by a contrasting walnut strip.

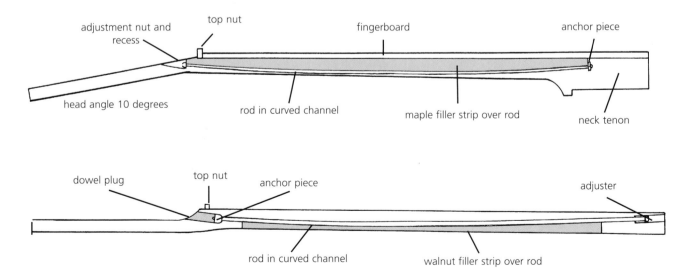

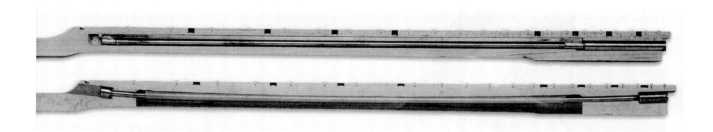

A side elevation of necks fitted with a standard curved rod and with a double-acting flat rod. (Courtesy of Warmoth Products.)

and the adjustment recess, if made large enough to remove a potentially damaged truss rod, might weaken the head.

Double-acting rods can also be made in a similar way and fitted to a flat channel. These will give either a back bow in the neck to counter the tension of the strings or a forward bow if the neck is too straight or has warped. One of these is fitted to the guitar made in Chapter 9.

Another variation on the theme is the system that was used on almost all Japanese guitars for many years. In this case, the rod is fitted not into the neck but into an inverted U-section aluminium channel and it is this channel that is fitted into the neck, just under the fingerboard. When the truss rod is tightened the aluminium channel bends towards its open side and, since this is glued into the neck, the neck bends too.

One advantage of all of these styles of rod is that, since the channel required is flat-bottomed, it is much easier to cut. For many years, and possibly in print, I have said that this style of rod has major disadvantages compared to the curved rod in a channel as invented by Mr McHugh. As with all things it is easy to be proved wrong and I have seen, and made, some guitars using this system and they have worked perfectly well and sounded good. As long as the rest of the guitar is put together well there is no reason not to use these rods. Certainly for a first guitar I would recommend using them as they are cheap and so easy to install.

Having said that, I often use the original style out of choice but this could be because I am something of a traditionalist. This can be difficult to install and if you fit it wrongly it can refuse to work at all.

A selection of truss rods. From top to bottom: a Rickenbacker-style rod, two different length box-section rods and a Gibson-style rod. All of these were bought ready made from a parts supplier.

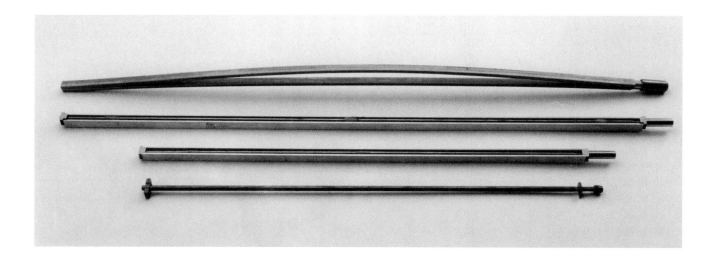

However, it is a simple system and if care is taken can work very well. Gibson still use this system and it is almost unaltered since it was first introduced. Fender, too, use this method although they fit their rods from the rear of the neck and so can use one-piece necks without a separate fingerboard. Installing the Gibson-style rod is reasonably straightforward if a router is used but the Fender-style of rear-mounted truss rod is much trickier and borders on precision engineering, although it is not impossible with a little care and preparation.

INSTALLING THE TRUSS ROD

All three styles of truss rod are installed while the piece, or pieces, of wood that make up the neck are still parallel. There are two reasons for this. The first is that if a router is used to cut the channel an edge guide can be used, and the second is that the wood will be easier to hold in the vice if the shaping has not been started.

Both the Japanese box-section rod and the Rickenbacker-style are very easy to install and both are available from guitar-makers' suppliers in a variety of lengths. The channel in the neck that will accept these rods can be cut with drills and chisels, but this will never be as accurate as using a router and its edge guide; and, even though I would use a router every time, it is not impossible to make a reasonable job by hand. The channel could also be cut with a table saw.

The position of the rod is marked on the guitar neck's centre line and the channel is cut making several passes with the router to get the correct depth and width for the channel. If the guitar is made with an angled head the channel can be extended out of the face of the head to give space for the rod's adjustment. If the guitar does not have an angled head the channel must stop on the head giving just enough room for the adjustment spanner.

When cutting the adjustment space on any guitar with the adjustment at the head end of the neck, care must be taken not to remove too much wood from around the rod as this can seriously weaken the head which is the most vulnerable part of the guitar. With both of these styles of rod the channel is cut so that the rod, when fitted, is flush with the top surface of the neck.

In the case of the Japanese box-section rod the aluminium channel is glued into the channel, taking care not to get any glue onto the adjustment nut. To glue this in I would recommend epoxy resin glue. Any excess glue should be cleaned off the face of the neck before it sets, using whatever the manufacturer of the glue recommends.

The Rickenbacker style of rod does not need to be glued into the neck, but care must be taken when gluing the fingerboard onto the neck that glue does not get into the channel and stop the rod working. Do not be too free with the glue, but use enough to fix the fingerboard securely.

The truss rod, as Ted McHugh invented it, is a little more difficult to fit but, with a little preparation and care, a good job can be made. These rods can also be bought in a variety of lengths from some guitar-makers' suppliers but I find it just as easy to make my own. An alternative is to ask your local light engineering works to make one up for you. If you are not used to metal-working this will probably save you time and money as the truss rod would not be an expensive item to have made. The rod is made up from a length of ³⁄₁₆ in (or 4.7 mm) mild steel rod. The length of rod needed will depend on the scale length of the instrument that is being made. The rod should be about 2 in (50.8 mm) longer than the distance from the nut to the point where the neck joins the body.

At the body end of the rod a small plate ½ x ¾ in (12.7 x 19 mm) is made and drilled and riveted to the rod. At the adjustment end the rod is threaded for 1 in (25.4 mm) and a suitable nut fitted. Fender

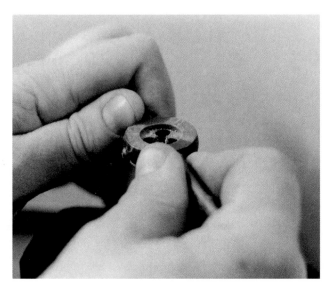

Cutting the thread.

Cutting the truss rod channel using a router and edge guide on top of a pair of curved rails that give a corresponding curved channel in the neck.

and Gibson rods are cut with a 10/32 thread and their adjustment nuts can be bought from guitar supply houses. Metric-sized rods would need the appropriate fine thread.

Another small plate is needed at this end to spread the force of the adjustment nut over a wider area and to stop the adjustment nut from just digging into the wood. This is cut to fit the recess in the head and so is curved on one side and flat on the other. This is drilled so that the rod is free to pass through.

As the channel that the rod sits in is curved, a router is the only way of successfully cutting it, and a jig that will enable the router to cut a curved slot must also be made. The simplest way of doing this is to make up a pair of curved rails that can be fixed to the top of the guitar's neck and on which the router can run while it cuts an identically curved channel in the neck. These rails must be cut carefully so that the curve is identical on each.

The amount of curve needed is not great. If there is too much the rod may be very sensitive and the

The double-acting rod fitted to the guitar made in Chapter 9 seen here before fitting. The channel is routed and the extension of the slot that will form the basis of the truss-rod adjustment cavity can be seen, as can the marked position of the threaded block. It is important to lightly lubricate the threads on a system such as this before fitting the rod as access afterwards is difficult.

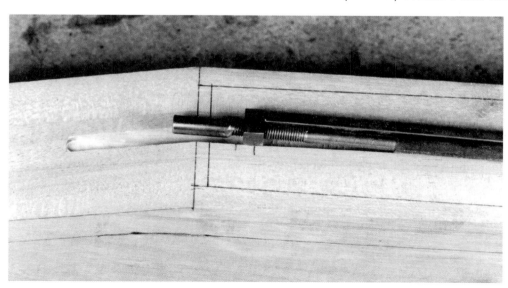

Cutting the anchor-nut slot using a small router. This is for the eight-string bass in Chapter 11.

The anchor on a 1970s Fender Jazz Bass. This is a piece of ⅜ in (10 mm) rod threaded onto the end of the truss rod.

ends. The rod should also be as close to the back of the neck as is practicably possible without running the risk of emerging from the back of the neck.

The two rails are temporarily fixed to the top of the neck using double-sided tape. The jig could be screwed in place as the fingerboard, when fitted, will hide the screw holes.

The router edge guide is set so that the cutter is in the centre of the neck and the router, fitted with a ¼ in (6.3 mm) bit, is set for a shallow cut. The first couple of passes will only remove wood from the centre of the channel but as the channel gets deeper it extends towards each end. It is important not to

neck will need to be thicker to contain it. Fender necks tend to have more curve than Gibson necks and some are very sensitive, to the point of being annoying, when being adjusted. As a guide, the Wal company use about ¼ in (6.3 mm) dip in the centre of the rod. It could be argued that more curve is needed at the head end of the neck as the neck here is thinner and more subject to the bending forces of the strings. It could also be argued that the tension of the strings will have less effect on the thicker parts of the neck but since the tension on the neck from the strings is uniform along the length of the neck, the tension of the rod should remain constant too as it will naturally have more effect on the thinner part of the neck than the thicker. I am not sure if much serious research has ever been done into the subject. Fender tend to use a very even curve but Gibsons are often flatter at the body end. Wal too use a curve that is flatter at the body end of the neck and their system works very well. I tend to use a quite even curve and the centre of the channel is about ⅛ in to 3⁄16 (3.1 to 4.2 mm) deeper than the

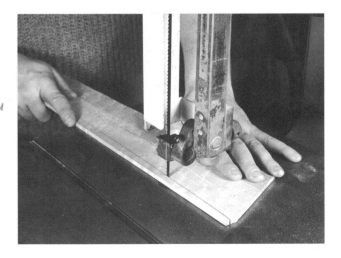

Cutting the fillet.

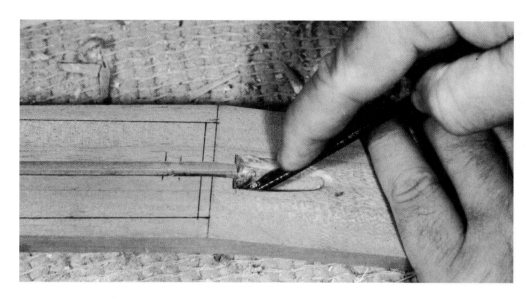

Cutting the adjustment recess using a small gouge.

The adjustment on many 1970s Fender guitars and basses was designed to minimise the weakening of the head yet still give a means of adjustment without having to remove the neck. Also notable in this view is the string retainer on the head and the bound and inlaid maple fingerboard.

try to remove too much wood in each pass as the router could wander to one side of the channel.

The channel is cut to ⁹⁄₁₆ in (14.3 mm) at the centre and so that it stops about 1½ in (38 mm) on the body side of the point where the neck and body join. The body end of the channel must be opened out slightly to accept the anchor piece. At the head end the channel is extended out over the face of the head and the adjustment hole is cut. This is started about ⅜ in (9.5 mm) from the head side of the nut using a craft knife and small gouge. It can then be cleaned up with sandpaper before the rod is fitted.

In order to work correctly the rod needs to be able to move a little but must not be so free that it will rattle in the neck. Also, since the rod is fitted into a channel that is wider than itself, it needs to be packed out. If some plastic tube of the right internal and external diameters is available the rod can be threaded into it before being installed. If this is not available, and often it is not, the rod can be wrapped in a couple of layers of tape or encased in a plastic drinks straw. In either case the rod can be rubbed with soap or candle wax to prevent it from sticking in the neck. A stuck rod will not work, so it needs to be free enough to move a little.

The rod is held in place in the neck by a wooden fillet that matches the curve of the channel. This fillet is glued and clamped just firmly enough to hold the rod in the channel but not so tightly as to jam the rod completely. When the fillet is dry it is planed down level with the top surface of the guitar neck.

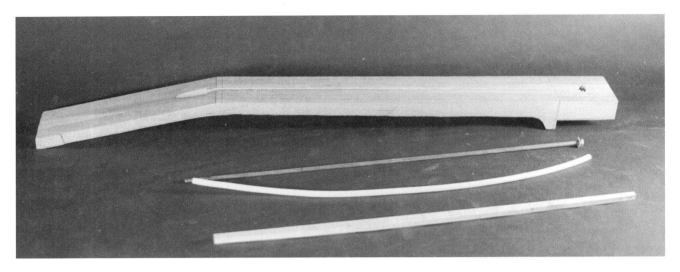

The component parts of a Gibson-style truss rod. The neck has the curved channel, anchor slot and adjustment recess; the rod has a thread cut onto one end and the anchor firmly fixed to the other. Plastic sleeving can be used to surround the rod but tape can also be used. It is a good idea to lubricate the rod with soap or paraffin wax after the tape or plastic has been added to stop it sticking in the slot. Finally the curved fillet will be glued down onto the rod.

On Fender guitars, which have the rod fitted from the rear, the channel is cut using rails that have their lowest point at either end so that the centre of the rod is still furthest away from the fingerboard. The channel stops 2½ in (63.5 mm) from the body end of the neck and 1¼ in (32 mm) from where the nut will be, and the adjustment and anchor positions are joined to the channel by holes drilled through the wood. This style of rod is covered in more detail in Chapter 10.

In the three main examples I have shown here the rod is adjusted at the head of the instrument. Since the head of the guitar is the weakest part of the instrument, removing even a small amount of wood from this area can seriously weaken the head still further. Adjusting the rod from the body end of the rod would leave the head free, but this is impractical on a lot of guitars since they have a pick-up right next to the end of the fingerboard which would get in the way of the adjustment. This is a minor problem on Fender-style guitars and basses that have the adjustment at the body end of the neck, as the neck is detachable, but clearly this is unworkable on guitars with glued-in or straight-through necks. The disadvantage of these Fenders is

The body-end adjustment is easier on basses where the front pick-up is not close to the end of the neck.

that the strings have to be slackened off for the rod to be adjusted, and so the adjustment is always a matter of trial and error.

For many other basses it is a simple matter to provide a recess at the end of the neck to give access to the truss-rod adjustment. I much prefer a body-end adjustment, if it is at all possible, and I fit it to all of my basses, as do companies such as Wal.

When the guitar is finished and strung up, the rod will need to be adjusted to take the strain of the strings, and this is covered in Chapter 15.

Whichever style of rod you choose to fit, it must not be tensioned at all until the guitar is strung as, if it bends the neck during construction, gluing up and fretting the board could be made difficult.

7 Frets and Fretting

The fingerboard and frets are the heart of the instrument. If all else on the guitar is perfect and the fretting is duff then the guitar will be useless.

One of the most common questions I am asked about guitar-making is how the distances between the frets are calculated. The answer lies in a simple mathematical formula that can be used to give the correct distances for any given scale length. The formula is traditionally known as the '18 rule', although the actual figure is slightly less than 18 at 17.817.

If you can work out these figures in your head it may be time to think about giving up guitar-making and cashing in on your incredible mental ability. On the other hand, if you are a mere mortal like me, you will need to find an easier way of doing this. By far the easiest way is to set up a small spreadsheet program on a home (or your workplace) computer.

'This fret is almost 0.0000000064 mm out of position . . .'

There will be a small error in the calculation but this is so small as to be irrelevant. It will be in the region of a thousandth of a millimetre, or 25 thousandths of an inch, which is a degree of accuracy way outside of what is achievable on a guitar. Even if it were possible to work this accurately the manufacturing process for fretwire, the finishing of the fret cannot be this accurate; the amount of stretch and shrinkage of the neck due to temperature, the flexibility of the neck and the pressure used to fret each string will change the tuning more than a thousandth of a millimetre of misplaced fret.

The features of each spreadsheet program will vary but I have used two different programs, and the procedure is very similar for both. You will need four columns and as many rows as frets plus one or two for headings, etc.

Enter the numbers 1 to whatever you choose as your last fret into cells A3 and downwards. Column B is headed 'fret' for the fret-to-fret distances, column C 'nut' for the nut-to-fret distances and column D 'remainder'. In cell C2 enter the scale length you wish to use in whatever measurement system you are most happy with, either metric or imperial. In cell B3 enter the sum of C2 divided by 17.817. This will give the distance from the top nut to the first fret. In cell C3 enter the sum C2 minus B3 and this will give you the remainder from the first fret to the bridge. In cell D4 enter the sum C3 divided by 17.817. This will give the distance from the first to the second fret.

This set of calculations can be duplicated down these two columns so that all fret positions are calculated. Changing the number of decimal places that the software gives you will also make your life easier as there is no way that you can work to millionths of a millimetre by hand so why bother having the extra numbers there?

It is not essential that you cut your own board. Ready-slotted fingerboards are available from a number of sources: these – in a variety of woods and scale lengths – are at Luthier's Mercantile International in Healdsburg, California.

This has long been the standard way of calculating fret positions but it has one major flaw. If a mistake is made in the marking, all subsequent frets will be out by the same amount compounding the error. The answer is to measure all positions from the nut and so the third column is used for this. In cell C3 enter the sum of B3 on its own. This simply duplicates the first fret distance from cell B3 in the new cell. In cell C4 enter the sum of C3 plus B4. This will give the distance from the nut to the second fret. These calculations can also be duplicated for all fret positions.

Having the individual fret measurements may not be absolutely necessary but can be useful for further double-checking since, when cutting a fingerboard, you can never be too sure of your accuracy. The second column of remainders is also very useful when working out positions of parts and components such as the neck-to-body join. For example, if your body join is at the 22nd fret on a 25½ in scale guitar, the bridge will be 7.156 in from the neck join (see Appendix 1).

There will be tiny errors. For example, on the spreadsheet I set up to remind myself how to do this while I am writing this very passage, I entered the scale length of 650 (mm). My 12th fret remainder should have read 325 but reads 324.998. As we have seen, an error of two thousandths of a millimetre is not going to ruin one of my guitars!

As a guide, this very spreadsheet took well under five minutes to set up. Calculating the positions on a simple calculator for the first edition of this book, in those far-off days before home computers, took many, many times longer as minor mistakes had to be found and checked.

Of course if you do not have access to a spreadsheet and a computer, you may well have to resort to working out your positions in the old-fashioned way, with a calculator and a piece of paper. Or you could use the tables I have included in Appendix 1.

PREPARING THE FINGERBOARD

The marking and preparation of the fingerboard must be of the highest possible standard. It is essential that the fingerboard is totally flat along its length; it can have a camber, or curve, across its width and this will be dealt with in due course. To check that the fingerboard is flat a good straight edge of at least 18 in (450 mm) is required.

The fret slots must be perpendicular to the centre line of the neck and accurately placed at the correct point along the fingerboard. It is also essential that the fret slots are vertical, as if they slant the effective position of the fret could move as the board is cambered, making the fret more difficult to fit.

You could attempt to cut the slots into the board free-hand but the marking-out and cutting of the

Roger Giffin's food-mixer powered fret slot cutting machine.

board must be extremely accurate as any mistakes will not only ruin the board but will cost you money.

Commercially-produced guitars obviously do not have each individual fingerboard marked out and cut separately by hand. A large and very expensive machine cuts several boards at once and all fret slots together. The machine has a saw blade for each fret and these are arranged along a centre spindle in the correct position for their fret. This spindle is passed across the fingerboards cutting all of the slots simultaneously. These machines are obviously very complicated and costly, and they would have to be used on many hundreds of fingerboards to be cost-effective; and if the scale length is changed each blade has to be reset individually.

I have seen some very ingenious machines in use with individual guitar-makers. One was the machine that Roger Giffin, then of Giffin Guitars in London, used. Roger's machine was a lovely example of ingenuity brought about by necessity. The motor that powered the machine was from an electric food-mixer and this spun a 4 in circular saw blade. The motor was mounted on rails that ran the width of the baseboard, and this, in turn, was mounted on rails that ran the length of the base, enabling the saw to be moved in straight lines across two planes. Two steel bars were bolted down either side of the baseboard and in these were drilled locating holes for pins that lined up the crossways member in the

correct place for scale lengths from 19 in, for short-scale travel guitars, up to 34 in bass scales, and these had been machined very accurately. The baseboard was also adjustable for height so that the depth of the fret slot could be varied. The result was a very accurate and easy-to-use machine that could cut up to three fingerboards, or even one-piece Fender-style necks, with the minimum of fuss. When Roger moved to the United States this machine was snapped up by another guitar-maker, sadly not me, and is still giving sterling service.

Roger's machine was designed to be as adaptable as possible since he was making many different styles and sizes of fingerboard. The Wal bass company, based at High Wycombe in England, can also teach a few things about ingenuity. Since all of their necks are the same size, they have a machine where the blade stays in one place, to be pulled across the board as on a cross-cut saw, but the base of the machine, on which the neck is fixed, moves along underneath it to be pinned into place for each fret position. Not only is this machine very simple but it produces some of the most accurately cut finger-boards on any guitars.

It is now possible to buy ready-slotted finger-boards from some of the guitar parts suppliers listed in the back of this book. Many of these are also available ready-cambered. Buying a fingerboard is by far the easiest way of guaranteeing that your guitar

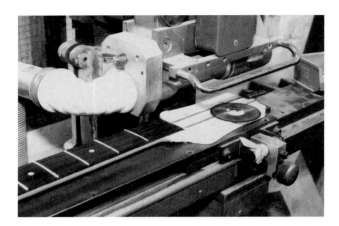

The equally clever Wal fret slot cutting machine. The metal base with neck attached slides beneath the saw. Since all Wal necks are the same basic dimensions, the depth of the saw cut and the scale length remains constant. The thicker saw blade, seen on the head, cuts the nut slot. The small knob (lower right) pulls the locating pin out of the hole, allowing the neck to be moved along to the next position.

Using the fret slot cutting jig. The square is held hard against the raised bar and, in this case, the saw is fitted with a depth stop to keep all slots uniform.

will play in tune. However, if you choose to have a 37 in (940 mm) scale bass guitar, or you want to have your fingerboard made from lignum vitae and no one sells pre-cut boards of this, you will have to cut it yourself.

If you do have to cut the board yourself it must be done to the highest possible standard of accuracy and I guarantee that this will be impossible if the wood you are working on is not held as rigidly as is possible. A good way to do this is to set up a jig for the cutting. This can also be designed to make marking the board easier.

To make sure that the fret positions are parallel you need to have a reliable point of reference. It could be that your fingerboard will be prepared as a rectangular piece with nice straight sides that can be used to ensure that the fret positions are square to the edge. This can then be tapered down afterwards to its final shape. However, if the fingerboard blank is not parallel, or is already tapered, then some sort of datum needs to be used so that the fret positions can be marked accurately.

One way is to use the jig shown in the photograph and diagram. This, if made and used with a little care, is very accurate and can be used for any scale length.

The jig is made as follows. The baseboard is a length of ⅜ in (9.5 mm) plywood, 30 in long by 8 in wide (762 x 203 mm). A centre line is marked onto this and a second line is drawn parallel to this 3 in (76 mm) to one side. A strip of hard wood is prepared 30 in (762 mm) long, ¾ in (19 mm) wide and 1 in (25.4 mm) deep. This must be accurately cut so that the sides are both dead straight and square. The strip is then carefully screwed and glued onto the baseboard so that it edges onto the second of the marked lines.

A centre line is marked onto the fingerboard and is extended over each end. Since most fingerboards are made of a dark wood it is worth scribing this line onto the wood (it will be removed when the board is cambered) and rubbing chalk into the scribed line to make it more visible.

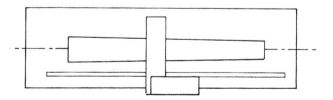

The fret slot cutting jig.

Luthiers Mercantile International offer this jig to cut fret slots. The board is fixed to a plexiglass jig (shown here with its protective covering still in place) which slides within the wooden box. The jig is held in place with the metal pin seen protruding from the side of the box on the right of the saw. The saw itself is guided between plastic blocks that also determine the depth of cut available. The board in this case is a ready-slotted 34 in board positioned for the photograph.

The fingerboard is positioned on the jig over the centre line with a little space left at either end. The board can be held in place with double-sided tape which, providing the fingerboard is properly flat, will be more than adequate for the job. The jig itself can then be held down onto the workbench either with screws or by the vice so that it is not going to move and ruin your work.

Using the scriber, the position of the nut is marked onto the centre line of the fingerboard. The fret positions are also marked with the scriber and are double-checked to ensure that they are in the correct position, and finally the end of the fingerboard is marked.

The fret positions can then be scribed across the fingerboard using a marking knife or scribe, holding the marking square firmly against the raised bar, checking carefully as you go. The slots too can be cut using the marking square as a guide, although I personally find it easier to do this by hand, allowing the scribed line to guide the saw blade as it starts cutting. It must be remembered that the saw cut will have to be centred on the marked fret position and normally the saw will tend to do this automatically; however, if using the marking square to help line the saw up, a little must be allowed for half of the width of the saw. Providing that this is done accurately and uniformly, and the saw cuts remain vertical, a reasonably accurate board will be cut. The fret slots

must only be cut deep enough to accept the tang of the fretwire; if they are cut too deep the board can be weakened and possibly damaged when removing it from the jig.

The width of the fret slots is another area that needs to be checked. The tang of different fretwires will vary in width. The Martin company have always maintained that their necks can be bowed back if they have pulled forwards by using fretwire with different sized tangs; their older guitars had no truss rods and the oversize frets would force a back-bend in the neck. In practice this apparently works very well and Martin sell their fretwire according to the size of its tang and expect their repairers to be fully aware of how to use this correctly. I have never found this to happen to any great extent on the guitars that I have made and can usually tell by feel if the fretwire is too loose or tight in its slot. A practice on a small piece of spare wood should give a good idea if the slot is the right size for the wire you have. Alternatively you could measure your fretwire and choose a saw appropriately, allowing for the slot to be very slightly narrower than the tang of the wire. Some companies that provide ready-slotted fingerboards cut these to suit specific fretwire types.

Yet another way would be to match the fretwire to the slot, which is the best method if a pre-slotted board is bought. Since there are so many different makes and types of fretwire it is impossible to state exactly which saw should be used, but I generally use a small gents saw which matches well with the Jim Dunlop fretwire I usually use. The necessity to match the frets with the slot also makes it imperative that the saw does not wander, widening the slot as it cuts.

Planing the camber onto the fingerboard after the fret slots are cut can cause problems with pieces of fretboard breaking away. It is preferable to plane the camber before cutting the fret slots, but clearly if you are attempting this at home, cutting the slots onto a cambered board will present problems of its own. The best course of action is time-consuming, messy (in terms of the sawdust it generates) but far kinder on your new board.

You can camber the board either before or after it is glued onto the neck. If doing so while it is on the guitar special care must be taken to keep the neck straight. This may also be a little cumbersome but there are times when this cannot be avoided. It is better to camber the board, at least roughly, before it is fixed to the neck if at all possible, remembering that curved clamping cauls will be needed to ensure that the edges and centre join properly.

The amount of camber that the board has can affect the playability of the guitar. Too little can make the board feel a little hard as the hand naturally curves. Too much camber will make the neck feel more comfortable but will prevent the bending of strings as they will choke against the next fret along, killing the note. Gibson guitars generally have between a 10 and 12 in (254 to 305 mm) radius camber to their necks, older Fenders generally use a 7 in (178 mm) camber and newer models a 9 in (229 mm). None are better or worse than the others; Fenders are a little more comfortable to play but the

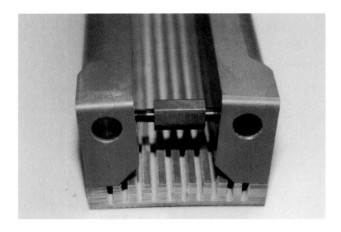

This variation on the sanding stick is available from Luthiers Mercantile International. The base can be arched to make sanding a camber easier by adjusting the nut at either end.

action on Gibson guitars can often be taken lower than on the Fender before the note chokes when the string is bent. It is a simple job to make jigs of a curve out of thin card or plastic which can be used as templates.

If you do plane the board at all, the plane must be very sharp and the cut very shallow. The best alternative is to use a sanding stick. 'Sanding stick' may not be the best description as it is far from being a stick. Using it with different grades of sandpaper it is possible to camber a board quite quickly and quite accurately enough.

The marks made by a sanding stick can be used to show if there are high or low spots. The stick can be used along the board and across, with successively finer grades of paper removing the scratches.

Both sides of the fingerboard should be worked alternately to keep the board symmetrical. The stick should be used over the whole length of the board which should be checked at frequent intervals with the straight edge. Any bumps or dips will make themselves readily apparent and should even out as work progresses.

The stick can also be used across the board to even out the camber. Although this will scratch the fingerboard across the grain, this is a good way of spotting which areas are too high or low and these marks can be removed when finer grades of paper are used to smooth the board.

I would start using nothing coarser than 80 grit paper to get the majority of the waste off, going on to 120, 240 and finally 320 grit paper to remove the marks of the other grades. The stick can be used across the board and across the grain to remove the marks made by the previous lengthways sanding as it was to even out the camber, although it is best not to go across the grain with anything coarser than 120 grit. As each grade of paper is used it should remove the marks made by the previous grade completely and the crossways sanding will always show up where the board needs more attention. The final polishing should be along the grain with a very fine grade, perhaps 600 or even 1200.

When the camber is even and the board is straight the position dots can be installed or block

markers fitted. These position markers are fitted at the main harmonic points along the string, that is to say the third, fifth, seventh, ninth, 12th, 15th, 17th, 19th, 21st and, if required, 24th fret positions.

Dots are by far the easiest to install. Guitar parts suppliers can provide dots in a number of sizes and materials. The most common material for the dots is mother-of-pearl, but often abalone and even plastic are used; for example, the dots on maple-neck Fenders are made from ¼ in (6.3 mm) black plastic rod.

Installing the dots is simplicity itself. Firstly their positions are marked. In all positions except the 12th and 24th the dot is found in the centre of the board in the space before the numbered fret, for example, between the second and third frets, or 14th and 15th frets.

Since the scribed line on the fingerboard would have been removed when the board was cambered, a centre line must be drawn onto the board in pencil. The positions of the dots can be found by halving the distance between the frets and they can be marked with the point of the scriber or a centre-punch. In the case of the 12th and 24th frets two dots are used to signify that the division of the string is an octave. Here the easiest way to mark the positions is to divide the space between the fret into two boxes either side of the centre line. Diagonal lines can then be drawn in the boxes and the point that the lines cross can be marked.

The simplest and cheapest dots are made from plastic rod. The three stages of installation are shown here. First a hole is drilled, then the rod inserted, then cut off to length before being sanded level with the board. It really is that simple . . .

The locating holes for the dots are cut using the same size of woodworking bit in the hand drill. Do not be tempted to use a power drill for this; a hand drill is easier to control and will give a cleaner cut. It is important that the holes are not drilled too deep; the dots need to be very slightly proud of the surface of the board. After carefully cutting the hole the dot can be glued into place with epoxy resin. When this has dried the dots can be levelled with the fingerboard using the sanding stick. Finally the board is sanded with 240 and then 320 grit sand-paper to remove any marks, and is finally polished using 600 or 1000 grit paper or 0000 grade wire wool.

The installation of block markers is a little more complex and this is covered in Chapter 9.

The fingerboard can be fretted before it is glued to the neck but I would not recommend this. The reason for this is that, if the board is glued down, and the neck has any small irregularities, then they could well be transferred to the fingerboard. If the board had been fretted before gluing and this was the case it would have to be defretted, the board levelled and then refretted. In theory this should never happen as the neck should be perfectly straight before the fingerboard is fitted and the board should have been made accurately, but it is better to be safe than out of pocket. As we have already seen, fretting can cause a complete neck to bow backwards so a board on its own is very likely not to remain straight and it is best to fret the board when it is safely glued onto the neck.

FRETTING

For ease of continuity I shall cover the basic rules and techniques of fretting now rather than wait until the chapters on building guitars. Fretting is very easy to do badly although with a little care it is not difficult to do properly. The general idea is to bang the frets into the fingerboard with a hammer or push them into the board by another means so that they stay there without popping out of their slots or falling out. In order that the guitar will stand any chance of being playable these have to be bedded down into the wood properly and must be the same height.

It is well worth making a false fingerboard to practise on before launching headlong into fretting your dream guitar. Cut some fret slots, using the gen-tleman's saw, into any piece of hardwood that is

A practice fretting piece.

roughly the same size as a fingerboard and planed on a camber. The positioning of the slots on the practice piece does not matter and you can cut as many as you like.

A piece of fretwire is cut so that it is about ¼ in (6.3 mm) longer than the slot that it is intended to fill. Pliers are used to gently curve the wire so that the curve is slightly tighter than the camber on the board, or practice piece, and this curve must be even and without sudden kinks. Care must be taken to bend it only in one direction and not put in any twist.

The fret can be hammered gently but firmly into the slot starting at either end. After knocking in each end the hammer can be moved from side to side across the fret knocking each end more into the wood, working towards the centre and taking care to keep the ends in place. If the middle regions of the fret are hammered too hard they will cause the ends to jump out of the wood. This can be very frustrat-ing but with practice the fret can be made to stay in place and it will also become clear if the size ratio between the fretwire and slot is correct. Moving from side to side across the fret will ensure that each end gets its fair share of attention and the fret should bed down into the fingerboard with its tang fully embedded across its length. If the ends of the fret are sticking out slightly when the centre is prop-erly embedded then the fret will have to come out and be fitted again.

If the fret is slightly proud all along it could be that the slot has not been cut deep enough. If the fret is gently undulating along its length then the

Wal use a cleverly thought-out press to install their frets. This uses a common base to the slot cutting machine shown on page 67. The slotted neck is slid along under this press which is operated by a foot treadle. The frets are lightly hammered in at each end and the press does the rest, seating them perfectly.

slot may be too narrow for the fretwire, in which case a saw with a wider cut must be used, or it is possible that you may have been a little heavy-handed with the hammer. In this case try fitting the frets when not thinking of somebody that you intensely dislike.

Commercial guitar companies will use expensive presses to convince the fret to lay in its slot. Other, smaller companies often adapt these ideas. Electric Wood, the company that produces the excellent Wal bass, have a press that is made up from parts of other machines and this installs one fret at a time. Since all the frets on Wal instruments are the same, the slots that accept them are all uniform width. Frets are cut to length and cambered slightly more than the board. Each end is then gently tapped into the board and when all are done, the neck is passed beneath the press and each fret, in turn, is pushed firmly, and accurately into its slot. It is not the most sophisticated machine in the world, but it saves a considerable amount of time (and noise) and the results are excellent.

Another alternative is to use the excellent tool developed by Stewart Macdonald's Guitar Shop Supply which is known as 'Jaws'. This is a variation on the standard mole grip and has a padded support for the back of the neck and a curved metal piece that pushes the fret into the board. The fret is put into place in the same way as on the Wal machine

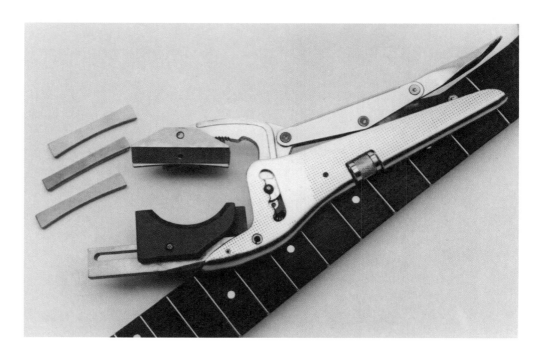

Jaws, the simple but effective fret press developed and sold by Stewart Macdonald's Guitar Shop Supply.

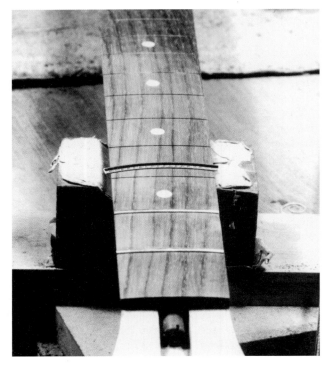 

 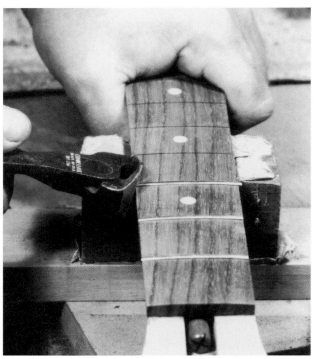

The four stages of fretting. Top left: the fretwire is curved slightly more than the radius of the fingerboard and cut about ¼ in longer. Top right: the ends of the fret are hammered into place. Bottom left: the fret is gently hammered into place taking care to keep each end bedded down. Bottom right: finally the ends are cut flush before being filed at a 45 degree angle.

and the Jaws is held over the fret and the handle squeezed. This beds the fret down firmly. Of course this cannot be used on all necks as some positions, such as the fingerboard extensions over the front of a guitar body, would be difficult to reach.

If, after you have been hammering away, the fret will not sit down into its slot properly, it is possible that the slot is too wide. You should have spotted this earlier but if not, the tang of the fret will then need to be widened. Hold the fret upside down against something hard but which will not damage the top of the bead and gently splay the bottom of the tang using either the side of an old file or the thin pin-hammering side of a pin hammer. You do not need to flatten the tang too much and it is surprising how small a splaying will work. Once this is done the fret can be recambered and rehammered home into the board. This time it should go in perfectly. If it is still causing problems it might be time to cheat. Dribble a little superglue under the fret end and hold it down with the face to the hammer for a minute or two until the glue dries. This should work, and if it does not then the chances are that your original fret slot was a real turkey so fill it with some veneer strips and cut again, taking more care next time.

An alternative to bashing frets in, which, if nothing else, does create a fair amount of noise (see Chapter 8), is to glue them into place. Now, at this point some of the more traditional guitar-makers reading this will have choked on their cola. To some people, gluing frets in is a big no-no. It is almost sacrilegious. If God had meant frets to be glued in why did he invent the hammer? In fact, there has been a lot of talk in recent years among guitar-makers about the benefits of gluing frets into place. Much of this has centred around the 'Luthier's Tips' section in the Stewart Macdonald's Guitar Shop Supply catalogues. Even in their pages, opinion seems to be polarised, with people coming out firmly in favour or against and few sitting on the fence. However, people have been gluing frets into place for years and the system does have advantages.

Many years ago, glues were not really up to the job of holding a fret (metal) into wood (generally wooden). The advent of epoxy resin glues, especially the quick-setting varieties, changed all that and even good old superglue can have a role to play here.

The disadvantage of gluing frets into place is that since the fret slot needs to be made slightly wider, there is no going back to the old system if you decide to glue. Also, since the glue will ooze out of the fret slot it can be a messy job which can make a mess out of your fingerboard and other parts of your guitar.

The plus side of gluing is that it is a little easier to make the fret stay in its slot and it can make refretting, when this is required, easier too since the fret slot is a little wider so there is less temptation for the barbs on the tang to tear the fingerboard as they come out. The fact that the fret is glued does not seem to make getting it out of the slot any harder. If you do have to de-fret your guitar for any reason, either while you are building it, perhaps to rectify a fault, or when it is showing signs of age after the odd thousand gigs or so, the fret should be heated with a soldering iron before it is pulled out of its slot. This will cause the oils in the fretboard to moisten and any glue on the fret to soften, and make getting the fret out much easier and damage to the board far less likely. However, a word of warning: heating old superglue can cause potentially dangerous gases to emerge from your fingerboard which can injure. Be prepared, be careful and protect yourself (see Chapter 8).

As already mentioned, the fret slots will have to be slightly wider than would be the case if they were being hammered into place. Ideally it should be a push fit with only a small amount of resistance. The fret will have to be cambered to the same curve as the fingerboard. The glue should be used carefully, be it superglue or epoxy, and only enough to hold the fret should be laid into the slot. The fret can then be pushed into the slot and the excess glue removed. In order to get the fret to lay properly into its slot, it will need to be held under some pressure for a while as the glue begins to harden. One way of doing this is to make up some firm, concave cauls that can be clamped over two or three frets at a time to hold them down. Cutting the curve to match that of the fingerboard will not be easy. Another way of doing this is to use a Jaws. Jaws also has the advantage of being lockable, and so there is no need to hold until the glue sets.

Fretting in this way can be easier but it is more time-consuming if you cannot hold all the frets down firmly in one go. Using superglue should be a little easier as it dries so much quicker, but several minutes' pressure should still be needed to hold each fret down. However, yet another word of warning: if using superglue, do not in any event hammer the fret at all. The glue can splash out and if it comes

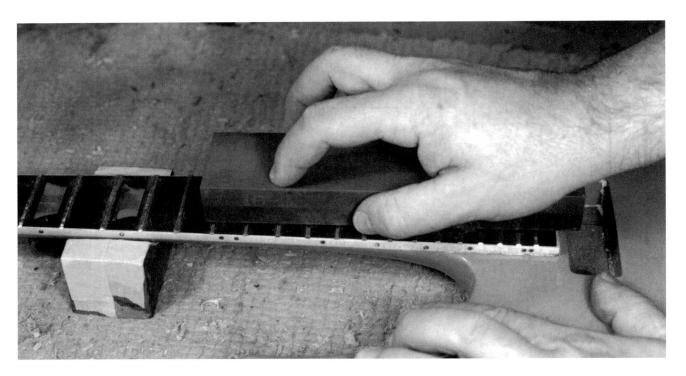

The frets are levelled using a good quality oilstone.

into contact with your, or anyone else's, eye can cause serious problems (see Chapter 8).

Fretting a guitar with a bound fingerboard is a little more complicated and is covered in Chapter 9.

When fretting your guitar be very careful to ensure that the neck is supported underneath where you are fretting and that this is padded.

When all of the frets have been successfully fitted the ends can be cut and then filed flush with the edge of the fingerboard. A file can then be used against the edge of the neck at an angle of about 45 degrees to the top surface of the board, to angle the last millimetre or so of the frets so that they do not foul the fingers.

Lastly, wear some eye protection when snipping off the end of the frets as they can be very sharp and it is odds-on that if you wear no protection one will hit your eye.

Whichever system you use, do not worry if fretting the guitar does not come straight away. It is well worth taking time to practise to ensure that the guitar is playable and it is not the end of the world if you have to pull them all out and do it again. It is character-forming.

LEVELLING THE FRETS

Another job that can be described here, although it is a little out of sequence, is the levelling of the frets. This should be done after the guitar has been finished and the lacquer or paint is totally dry, and in the case of a removable neck, before it is fitted to the body. The procedure will generate an amount of good old-fashioned grime and this can have a detrimental effect on the bare wood of any guitar. It also uses abrasives which can mark the surface of the guitar and can damage any hardware that has already been fitted.

Ideally, all of the frets should have been fitted into the fingerboard so that the tang fits snugly in its slot, with the bead resting properly against the fingerboard at all fret positions on a perfectly level board. Unfortunately this is not a perfect world and it rarely happens like this. There will be some small, uneven spots which can cause all sorts of rattles, buzzes and dead spots when the guitar is strung.

The cure for this is to remove the very top portion of the fret and then reprofile its top so that the unevenness disappears. The actual amount of fret to be removed is very small; if it were not, the rest of the fingerboard would be at fault and no amount of fret work will cure it. The procedure is sometimes

Using the fretfile to recontour the crown of the fret after stoning.

referred to as 'filing frets' but the practice of using a file on a fretboard is asking for trouble. To start with, most files are not totally flat and they can easily remove too much of the fret. The job should be done with an oilstone.

The oilstone to be used should preferably be new, or one that is used only on frets, and should be as flat as possible. Some cheap oilstones are as bad as files and can be very uneven and very soft, but there is no reason why a good stone cannot be bought if you look around hard enough. Most stones have two different grades of abrasive, one on either side. It is best to find one that is very fine on one side and slightly more abrasive on the other instead of a fierce stone that could remove an entire fret in one pass. Many new stones will need to be soaked in light oil to temper their cut before they are used on the guitar.

The whole point of stoning the frets on a guitar is to ensure that they are of uniform height and so, therefore, the neck must be adjusted so that it is as straight as possible before commencing. Guitars with varnished fingerboards, such as the Telecaster made in Chapter 10, may need to have their fingerboards masked to protect the finish, but most guitars will not need this providing the frets are not super low, and as long as the board is cleaned and polished after the job is finished.

The process is very similar in many ways to preparing the board with a sanding stick but instead of removing a large amount of wood to give the board its shape only a small amount of fret is being removed to ensure that all are level. The guitar should be supported while the work is being done so that the neck does not move around and there is no pressure on the head of the instrument that may cause the neck of the guitar to bend.

The first stage is to lightly mark all of the frets with 600 grade wet'n'dry paper used around a block across the neck, or, if you prefer, along the length of the fret. These scratches are used to show where any problems on the neck may lie. A good alternative to this, which is rather more visible, is to use a marker pen along the very top of the fret which will leave a coloured line. The fine side of the stone is then used along the neck very lightly, taking care not to tip it over the end of the frets and to keep it moving in straight lines. Any low points will show up as the scratches made by the stone will not have removed the light scratching made by the paper or the ink from the pen. Since the scratches are perpendicular to each other they will reflect light differently, and it will be very easy to spot areas where the frets are low.

The high and low spots are removed in much the same way using the rough side of the stone, firstly

Rounding over the ends of the frets before the final polish.

along the length of the neck and then across, so that each time the previous scratches are removed. The rough side of the stone can, if not used carefully, remove a substantial amount of fret and ruin the guitar, so this part of the operation must be done with care. It is also doubly important that the stone does not tip over the edge of the neck as it will round off the ends of the frets and cause the strings to fall off the edge of the fingerboard, effectively strangling not only the note being played, but also any hope of remaining aloof and superior while on stage.

Once all of the high points are even the smooth side of the stone can be used, firstly along the length of the neck and then across to remove the scratches caused by the rough side. This should leave the guitar with perfectly even frets. It all sounds very simple but takes care and practice to perfect.

When this has been done, the frets will be flat along their length and the camber of the fret should be the same as the camber of the fingerboard, but the frets will have lost their nicely rounded shape and will have sharp edges and so the shape of the fret needs to be restored and someone, somewhere has invented the right tool for the job.

The fretfile was invented for just this purpose, to recamber the top of a fret. Do not listen to anyone who tells you that they can be used to lower high

frets and stop a board buzzing. Their single purpose in life is to restore the camber of the fret. They come from a number of sources and in sizes that vary along with the size of fretwire. One thing that they have in common is that they are almost always hand-made and are, therefore, temperamental to use and quite expensive to buy.

The last lengthways stoning of the frets will leave small scratches across their width. These can be used to judge how well the fretfile is doing its job. As the file goes along the fret, it will recamber the edges of the flat that has been ground onto the top of the fret by the stoning. Light will reflect differently from the cross fret scratches and the filing marks along the fret. The idea is to leave the very centre of the fret untouched as the fretfile recambers the rest. If the scratches are difficult to see, a marker pen can be used across the top of the fret and the ink used as a guide. Recamber the frets until just a tiny ink line remains across the centre of the fret crown.

After filing the curve back onto the top of the fret the ends of the fret can be gently rounded using a needle file, taking care not to mark the edge of the fingerboard.

When all of the frets have resumed their former shape the finish can be restored on them. All of this work will have left them scratched, and so these marks must be removed with careful use of 600 and 1000 grade wet'n'dry paper used dry. Finally they can be polished with metal polish to restore the shine so that the frets will be smooth to play on. This will leave some residue on the fingerboard and this can be removed, and the fingerboard treated, with a little raw linseed oil, lemon oil, or one of the several products sold for just this purpose such as Boogie Juice. This will help prevent the fingerboard from drying out and can be used periodically throughout the life of any guitar, but the residue must be wiped clean and the fingerboard must be left to dry thoroughly before the strings are fitted as otherwise they will go very dead and all of the money spent on them will be wasted. For guitars with varnished fingerboards, the areas between the frets can be flatted back and buffed at the same time as the frets are polished after stoning.

8 Safety

One common denominator with most succesful guitarists is the use of their fingers. These are used to play the guitar and generally a full set of ten is vastly preferable to a lesser number. There are exceptions, such as Django Rheinhard, but Jimi Hendrix, Jimmy Page, Eric Clapton, George Harrison, Dan Stanley, Mark King, Stanley Clarke, Carlos Santana and many more excellent guitarists were fully stacked with digits. Most people will want to make a guitar because they want to play it. Therefore keeping the same amount of fingers when the guitar is finished as you had when the guitar was being planned is highly advisable.

I must make it very clear that working with sharp hand tools and power tools is potentially very dangerous. Probably the best piece of advice I can offer about safety is to ask you to remember that there is no such thing as a workshop accident. There is not a power tool on earth that will hurt you if you leave it alone. No woodworking tool has a mind of its own or a psychopathic streak. All injuries require at least two elements: a power tool and a human being. If, therefore, you consider that the tools are quite safe if left alone then the deciding, and dangerous, factor in all injuries is the human being. If you hurt yourself in a workshop, in all but a few cases, it will be your own fault. If you are careless you will hurt yourself.

Many of you reading this will have met people with missing fingers and far too many of them lost them in woodworking accidents. Power saws, routers and especially spindle moulders have produced some horrific injuries. If you are not fully confident in your ability to use a particular tool correctly and safely, do not use it; get someone else to do the job for you.

If you do decide to go ahead and use power tools then you, and you alone, will have made a decision to accept the risks. I can recommend ways of doing a job with a power tool but it is the responsibility of the operator to ensure the safe use of the machine, both in terms of its operation and its condition.

The spindle moulder is a particularly nasty tool. Many woodworkers have lost fingers and suffered other injuries due to contact with these machines. This one is used to rough carve necks at the Wal factory. The spindle runs on the jig as the neck is pushed past and the cutter removes a considerable amount of wood. The damage these blades could do to an unfortunate pair of hands is only too clear.

Paints, lacquers, glues and solvents can all cause problems. Again, if you leave them in a container and go and buy a guitar they will not hurt you. Superglue is particularly sticky, especially with organic material, such as your fingers, or worse still, your eyes. You can hurt yourself trying to prise apart digits that have become stuck together with superglue. There are ways of doing this which are safe and which do not injure. Learn them. If you do use superglue keep it away from your eyes. Read the manufacturer's warnings on all products and heed them, and if you have any doubts, take up knitting instead. The chart below might help focus your mind.

If you are sensible in the workshop, you should find that when you have finished your guitar you will still have enough fingers to play it properly.

Be sensible. Be safe. Be careful. It is your choice.

1)	**Always** use the tools in the correct manner.
2)	**Always** keep the working area tidy.
3)	**Always** keep your tools in good condition.
4)	**Always** unplug and put away any power tool as soon as you have finished using it.
5)	**Always** wear eye protection when using a power tool.
6)	**Always** cut away from your body.
7)	**Always** observe manufacturers' safety recommendations when using lacquers, paints and glues.
8)	**Never** adjust or change the cutting bit of any tool while it is still plugged in.
9)	**Never** fool around in a workshop.
10)	**Never** operate power tools whilst under the influence of drink or drugs.
11)	**Always** wear a face mask when sanding.
12)	**Do not** spray paints or lacquers without adequate protection.
12a)	Wear ear defenders when fretting a guitar – the noise of the hammer will affect your hearing.

9 The First Guitar

The first guitar to be built is the one designed in Chapter 3. By making a small selection of guitars I hope to be able to demonstrate most of the design features and most of the building methods that are used on pretty well all guitars and so each of the following guitars differ.

The following elements are covered: bolt-on, glued-in and straight-through necks with the truss rods installed from the front and from the rear with their adjustment at the head or body end of the neck; one-piece necks, as found on many of Fender's guitars, and guitars with separate fingerboards, both bound and unbound, and with dot and block markers; bodies made from one type of wood and laminated bodies either made up of multiple pieces or just faced with pretty wood and then bound; flat-topped and carved-topped bodies; bodies with Fender-style contouring and with Fender-style trem units; and a final section covering the assembly of guitars from commercially available component parts which also covers fretless basses. The finishes used include block colour finishes, sunbursts, an oil and wax finish and oil finishes.

Finally, I have devoted some time (in Chapter 13) to show how the various styles and methods can be mixed in order that you can build a successful guitar of any design using any combination of the methods that I have outlined.

The first edition of this book featured a twin humbucking, fairly normal, double-cutaway guitar which, for the sake of the book, was built left-handed. This new edition features a rather more complicated guitar so that I can cover the installation of tremolo systems as well as bound fingerboards and carved tops.

THE NECK

The neck of this guitar is a three-ply laminate of mahogany with each laminate being 25 x 2¼ x ¾ in (635 x 57 x 19 mm). This allows for the full depth of the neck, and its angled headstock, to be cut from one block. The wood chosen for the neck needs to be straight-grained and as close to quarter sawn as possible. Some people will tell you to reverse the grain of one piece of the timber so that if it has a tendency to warp, it is held by the other two. In practice, if it is going to warp and all three pieces come from the same plank, then it is all likely to warp and reversing one piece of grain just makes it more difficult to plane.

Many, many years ago when I was just starting out and dinosaurs still ruled the earth, I did not have a band saw and so used to cut out the three laminates roughly to shape with an electric jig saw before gluing them together, as the saw was unable to get through more than ¾ in. Cutting the laminates out to their side elevation before they are glued together should, in theory, give less waste but in practice this is rarely the case. Cutting out the laminates first also means that gluing up the pieces is more difficult as they are inclined to slip, the neck is less easy to hold in the vice while the front face is planed flat and it will also be less rigid than the larger block, making planing the front less accurate.

The added depth at the sides of the neck also makes it easier to check that the surface is square to the sides as there is more wood to rest the square against. Cutting the neck out after all the laminates have been glued also produces a lot of waste wood but this is not a problem for me as I will often use this waste for something else. I have even made complete acoustic guitar necks from the waste piece of a laminated neck for a guitar exactly like this one. It just needs careful cutting.

If you do have problems cutting out a neck shape from a 2¼ in block then it might be wise to laminate the neck from a much smaller piece of wood. To do this, a piece about 2¼ in (57 mm) across by ¾ in (19 mm) deep by 30 in (762 mm) long can be selected so that the grain is perpendicular to the face of what will be the neck. The headstock can

(above) Laminating a neck. The glue oozing out of the joins is a good sign as it shows that all the surfaces inside have been coated.

(below) Laminating a neck with a spliced head can be done in two ways. Both are suitable and give a strong join.

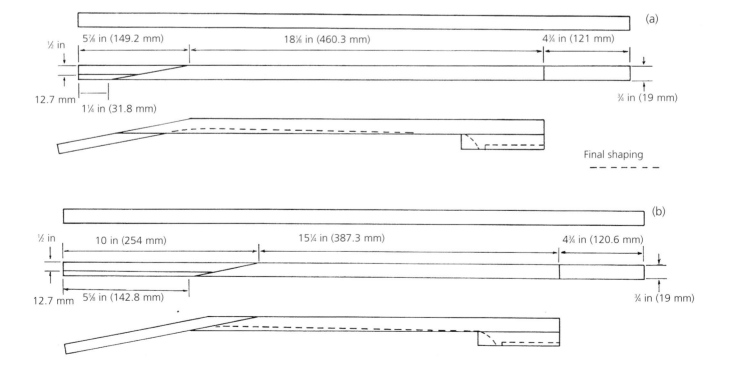

(a)

½ in

5⅞ in (149.2 mm)　18⅛ in (460.3 mm)　4¾ in (121 mm)

12.7 mm

1¼ in (31.8 mm)

¾ in (19 mm)

Final shaping

- - - - - - -

(b)

½ in

10 in (254 mm)　15¼ in (387.3 mm)　4¾ in (120.6 mm)

12.7 mm　5⅝ in (142.8 mm)

¾ in (19 mm)

A neck blank ready to be spliced as in drawing a) opposite.

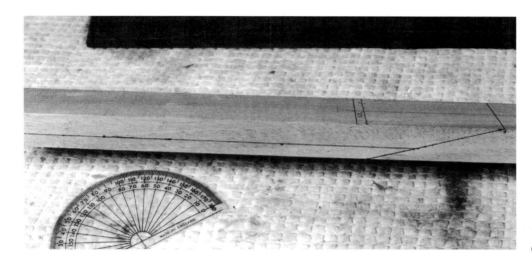

The neck blank marked as drawing b) opposite.

then be cut at an angle and spliced on. This not only saves wood but produces a stronger headstock as the grain is always running parallel to the face of the wood and there is no cross-grain on the head.

There are several ways of laminating this and there is some extra planing to do as the headstock piece will need to be just ½ in (12.7 mm) thick rather than the ¾ in (19 mm) of the rest of the neck. The heel end of the neck will also need to be laminated to give some extra thickness where the neck joins the body.

A good quality woodworking glue will be sufficient to join the three laminates and these come in a variety of types. Epoxy resins have the advantage of added strength but can be time-consuming to mix and apply. In practice, the slightly lesser strength of white PVA-based or aliphatic resin

glues is not a problem as the wood will still be weaker than the join.

As many clamps as possible are used to hold the three pieces together and enough glue should be used so that some seeps out when the pieces are clamped. This is a good indication that glue is getting where it should. If it does not seep, then there may be none in the join. It is also important that the clamps are not overtightened as this can force the glue out of the joint altogether.

Gluing is also subject to weather conditions and temperature. If it is too cold the glue can become useless and if it is too warm it can start to dry before the job is finished. Epoxy resins, especially the two-pack variety are particularly sensitive to temperature. When it is very cold they can be almost

Once the head piece is sawn it can be reversed and clamped to the rest of the wood. Planing the angle for the join in this way will keep both pieces the same and gives more surface on which to work.

With the angle planed the head piece can be planed to its correct depth and glued on as in the diagram on page 82.

impossible to mix successfully and will be very stiff, making application difficult. Some of these are designed to harden in a short space of time and if it is too hot, they can start to harden before the joint is assembled, with obvious consequences.

Another argument put forward for epoxy glues is that they are waterproof. This, again, is of no real importance since any glue join needs to be thoroughly soaked in order to start to fail and this is unlikely to happen in most cases. Having had to

Planing the front face of the neck so that it is square to the sides and totally flat.

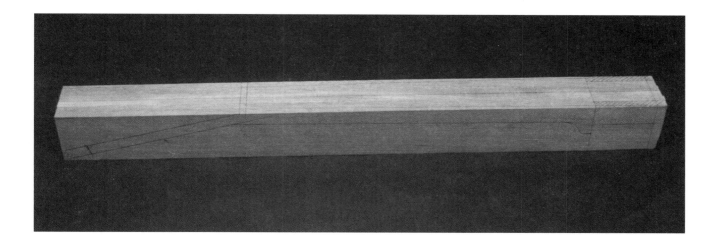

A neck blank glued, planed and marked.

remove fingerboards and other parts from guitars over the years, I have been glad they were fitted with water-soluble glue but it still does not make them easy to get off.

The excellent acoustic guitar-maker David Russell Young recommends using epoxy glues and his argument is very sound. He states that you should not need to take a guitar apart if it was put together properly to begin with. This is true but for many people making a guitar for the first time, the fact that a recently-glued join can be persuaded to part if something has been assembled wrong is a bonus.

Once glued, the neck is left overnight to dry out thoroughly before the clamps are removed.

When the neck block has dried, the clamps are removed and the top surface of the neck is planed flat and square to the sides. It is essential that this is

done well as almost all measurements and angles that are subsequently drawn onto the neck depend on this.

The next stage is to draw on the plan view and side elevation of the neck. Firstly the centre line is drawn onto the top of the wood. The end of the fingerboard and the position and width of the nut are measured, checked, and the marks are extended across the face of the neck with the marking square. The width of the fingerboard at the nut and at the end of the fingerboard is measured and marked, as is the width and length of the neck tenon. The fingerboard is a total of 42 mm (1^{11}⁄₁₆ in) wide at the nut and 56 mm (2³⁄₁₆ in) at the body; the tenon is 70 mm (2¾ in) long and 40 mm (1⁹⁄₁₆ in) wide. This is a good case for using metric measurements as they are easier to divide up! The side elevation is then drawn onto the neck starting with the angle, depth and length of the head, the depth and length of the neck tenon and finally the depth of the neck and shape of the heel. Since the neck will lay back by about 2 degrees, the tenon needs to be marked to allow for this. The position of the truss rod is also marked.

When the neck has been fully marked and all of the dimensions checked, the face of the head is sawn and planed flat and the truss rod installed as shown in Chapter 6. The truss rod chosen for this guitar is a double-acting one, which can impart forward bow as well as back bow into a neck. This is fitted into a ¼ in (6.3 mm) wide, ½ in deep (12.7 mm) flat-bottomed channel routed using the edge guide.

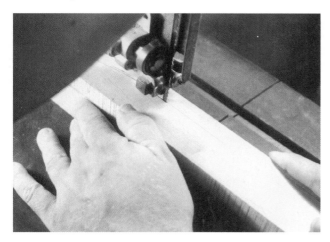

Band-sawing the neck.

The side elevation of the neck can then be carefully cut out on the band saw. For this type of rod, no fillet is needed and so the neck is put to one side while work on the body is started. There is little point at this stage in cutting the sides of the neck or the neck tenon as it is easier to cut the tenon to fit the slot than the other way round.

THE BODY

The body of this guitar could be cut from one piece of poplar 18 x 12½ x 2 in (457 x 317 x 50.8 mm). Finding a piece of wood this wide could prove to be a problem and is more expensive so I have chosen to make the body from two pieces. These are planed to give good joining surfaces and then clamped using sash clamps. Small G-clamps can be used across the joins to help stop the pieces from slipping as they are glued.

Once these laminations have been given time to dry, the surface can be planed level and the body shape is marked onto the wood. This will include the all-important centre line from which pretty well everything is marked or measured. In a two-piece body, the centre line is automatic as it is the line between the two pieces. Ideally this join should not show too much evidence of glue!

The shape is then cut out. It is at this stage that if you do not have access to a band saw, and you intend to do a similar job by hand, you will begin to appreciate just how useful a band saw can be! You may also be grateful you chose a softer wood.

The sharpness of the curves around the cutaways can be a problem and several goes might be needed with the band saw, removing a little more each time, until the correct shape is made. For this guitar I have not got too heavily involved with working with jigs and so the body is cut out carefully, as close as possible to the drawn line, so that it is easily sanded to shape.

The band saw cuts the sides of the guitar vertically, but leaves saw marks on the wood that have to be sanded away, using firstly 120 grade sandpaper, then 240 grade and finally 320 grade on a block, taking care to keep the sides square and all curves flowing. If the body had not been cut out on the band saw but on a bow saw, the sides would need a little more work to bring them up to the required standard as the saw is highly unlikely to cut as square as the band saw. It may be possible that sandpaper alone will not be enough and spokeshaves may have to be used to remove most of the waste wood. Cutting out and shaping the body in this way is hard work, even on poplar. It is not too bad in winter when physical activity is helpful in preventing hypothermia, but during the heat of summer it can be a little tiresome.

An alternative to hand sanding is to use a drum sander. These are, as their name suggests, a drum

Band-sawing out the body shape.

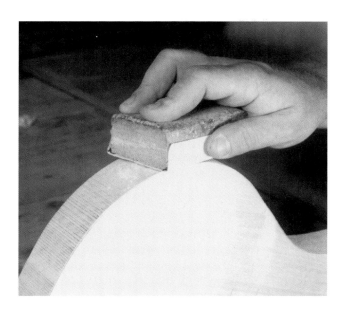

Hand sanding the sides of the body using paper over a cork block.

covered in sandpaper. They are fitted into a pillar drill and the piece to be sanded is laid on the bed of the drill and moved against the rotating drum. Of course if you have not got access to a band saw you may well not have access to a pillar drill either!

Drum sanders are very good for a number of jobs, as will be described in the following chapters, and come in a variety of sizes, but should be used with care as they are not as benign as they look. They can dig in and remove far more wood than you either want or think they are capable of. The trick is to keep the pressure against the drum relatively light and do not be tempted to get the job done too quickly. It is best to keep the wood you are sanding moving all the time and, with care, you will not get a series of undulations (which will happen if you hurry) but a smooth sanded surface.

Once the body is cut out the positions of the pick-ups, bridge and controls can all be marked, as can

The body.

Using a drum sander in a pillar drill.

the position of the neck tenon. On some designs this can be cut at this stage.

In order to use the chosen tremolo bridge the neck needs to be angled back by about two degrees. On many guitars it is possible to plane this angle onto the front of the guitar and use this angle as a base for the router to cut the slot in the body. This would then give a slot with an angle, and therefore make it possible to have a straight-bottomed neck tenon, which is a little easier to make.

This is the case in guitars where the cutaway horns do not extend much past the neck tenon, as on a Les Paul for example. The angle can be planed safe in the knowledge that it will not go deeper than the final depth the sides will need to be after carving. The carving will also remove any evidence of the angle everywhere except where the fingerboard sits on the body.

On guitars such as this with extended horns, the angle would continue a long way past the tenon so the depth at the tenon would be more than at the end of the cutaway horn, which is unacceptable. In this case, the easiest alternative would be to cut the slot with a flat bottom and angle the tenon as shown in diagram b) on page 94. Needless to say, I have gone the difficult route and will cut the tenon after the top is carved which will require quite careful work.

Even if using a flat-bottomed slot, the top surface of the body would still need to be shaped carefully to conform to the underside of the fingerboard where it fits over the top of the body.

The depth of the body at the edges should also be marked. On this guitar this is ¼ in (6.3 mm) lower than the top of the guitar. This line is drawn on using a marking gauge and made visible with a pencil.

If the guitar design is simple enough (always a good course of action), the angle can be planed at this time and the all-important centre line reinstated.

The next stage is to cut the pick-up holes. There is a school of thought which says this should be done before the body is cut out, making the workpiece easier to deal with. This is sound advice. Once again, I am doing it the difficult way.

It is possible to cut the cavities with drills and chisels. If this is done a fair amount of waste wood will need to be removed. It is important not to drill too deep so some form of depth stop on the drill, even if only a piece of tape wrapped around the bit, is essential.

The corners of the cavity should be drilled first and then as much as possible of the wood inside the lines should be drilled out. The remainder can then be removed with sharp chisels, taking care to keep the sides vertical. Doing this just once will convince you of the value of a router and a simple jig.

Some jigs are available from parts suppliers for standard-size routs. Since the pick-ups on this guitar are custom-made, a jig is made from plywood. This

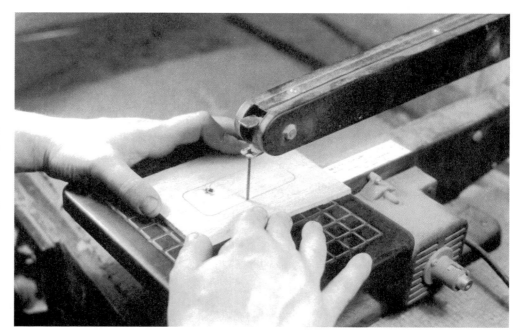

Making a pick-up jig from plywood, in this case one for the eight-string bass in Chapter 11. This is marked carefully on a sheet of ⅜ in (10 mm) plywood and carefully cut, in this case, with an electric jigsaw although they could be cut by hand and tidied with files and sandpaper. Time spent making jigs is time well spent. Mistakes on a small piece of plywood are easy and cheap to rectify. Mistakes on the guitar are not!

Preparing the router to cut the front pick-up position using a routing jig. Note the router bit has quite a depth of cut and so will need to be used inside the edges of the jig until sufficient depth has been reached to allow the shank to run against the edge of the jig.

workpiece. They do, however, have their uses and this is explained in later chapters.

Using a router bit with a bearing on the shank is possible but often the amount of cutter on the bit means that the bit will have to go quite deep into the work before the bearing runs on the jig. These bits can prove to be quite expensive and it is possible to use a normal straight bit with the shortest depth of cut available and to let the bare shank of this run against the jig. As long as the diameter of cut is exactly the same as the diameter of the shank, and as long as it is kept moving and you do not try to cut against the jig before the full depth of the cutter is past the jig, they can work very well.

The first few cuts with the router are made leaving about ⅛ in (3.2 mm) inside the jig. When enough depth has been reached the excess can be removed up to the jig, leaving the slot flush.

These pick-ups are to be screwed into the wood at a set height under the strings as I will not need to adjust them. This depth can be worked out using the known height of the bridge and the end of the fingerboard as the pick-ups will not need to be higher than this. They can be packed if they are a little too low.

The position of the bridge will have been marked already and the cavity that accepts the workings of the tremolo needs to be cut. The dimensions of this can be taken from a Stratocaster, which could almost be termed the industry standard for the job.

jig is held onto the guitar using double-sided tape. This might not seem the ideal material but if the top of the guitar is flat, not too dusty and the jig not warped, then a good contact can be made. Double-sided tape is usually pressure-sensitive so the harder you press, the stronger the join. In practice it is quite up to the job but it is well worth double-checking the jig will not slip as mistakes such as this can be costly.

There are various sorts of follower bit available for routers, some of which are available from guitar parts suppliers and others from tool dealers. Many of these have roller bearings attached to the shank of the router bit which prevent it from cutting past the jig, which the bearing will run against. These rollers can be either at the base of the bit or on the shank. Using one with the roller on the base is not suitable here as the jig would need to be underneath the

A follower bit. This is a laminate cutter, designed to cut a facing flush with what is underneath. Cutters with the bearing above are more useful for such things as pick-up cavities. Laminate cutters can be used with undersized bearings so they cut a binding channel.

Drilling the mounting holes for the claw that holds the tremolo springs. The back of the guitar is being protected with a piece of off-cut from an acoustic guitar top.

The block on the tremolo goes through the front of the guitar and is attached to springs that are in a recess on the rear of the guitar body. The first job is to cut out the area that takes the block. You will notice this is asymmetric and so needs to be marked with care.

The dimensions are 3⅛ in (80 mm) with the centre being 1⅜ in (35 mm) from the bass side. This will need to be cut ⅛ in (3.2 mm) behind the position of the treble side of the bridge, as already marked on the front and will go all the way through the guitar.

Needless to say, this is not an altogether straight-forward operation if you are not using a router but, with care, can be done by hand; the best way would be to drill all the way through and tidy with a chisel. If routing, great care must be taken not to continue the cavity into the worktop you are using.

Once the first part of the cavity is done, the rear part needs to be cut. The main part of this measures ⅝ x 2¼ x 4 in (15.8 x 57 x 101 mm) and, as stated above, is where the springs are fitted. This recess is centred on the guitar's centre line which will need to be extended around the guitar body. At the rear of this area, more wood needs to be removed to allow the block to move backwards when the tremolo arm is depressed. This space should go through the guitar to within ¼ in (6.3 mm) of the face of the guitar. Since the area immediately around the bridge will

not be contoured there is no danger of the carving cutting through into this open space.

The springs are held in the back of the body by a small claw that is fixed in place with two screws (incidentally, the same type as Fender would have used for fixing necks – another cost saving!). The claw can be held in place and the centre of the holes marked with a centre-punch. The holes need to be drilled with a ⅛ in (3.2 mm) extra-long series drill and this must be used carefully so that neither the drill bit nor the drill marks the back of the guitar. The dimensions of the cavity, together with some of the more commonly used pick-ups, are in Appendix 3.

Next the control cavity at the rear of the guitar is cut out. For this guitar the cavity has to be large enough to accept the volume and tone controls and the three-way selector switch.

Again, it is possible to cut the cavity using drills and chisels but cutting the recess for the cavity cover plate would be difficult to do in this way. If using drills and chisels it would probably be a good idea to leave the cover plate proud of the guitar back, as this will look less untidy than a bad attempt at a recess.

For this exercise I have chosen not to use a jig but to predrill the holes and use drills and a router free-hand to cut the main cavity.

The positions of the controls have been marked onto the front of the guitar body in pencil and the

The control positions have been drilled through the body using the correct diameter drill in the pillar drill. The photograph also shows the rear pick-up position and the hole that extends through the body to take the tremolo block.

proposed centres of the potentiometers are centre-punched. These positions are then drilled all the way through the body on the pillar drill, the volume and tone positions to ⁵⁄₁₆ in (7.9 mm) and the selector switch to ½ in (12.7 mm). The body is then turned over for the cavity to be cut.

The pots are roughly 1 in (25.4 mm) diameter, and so to give adequate clearance a drill of 1¼ in (31 mm) is used in the pillar drill to cut down about 1 in (25.4 mm) into the body. The position of the switch also receives this treatment, but with the 1 in (25.4 mm) drill. This leaves three holes in the positions

The control positions are drilled out at the rear using a 1¼ in (31 mm) drill for the pots and a 1 in (25.4 mm) drill for the switch. The overall shape of the cavity is marked allowing some space for the screws that will hold the cover in place.

The cavity is carefully routed freehand until it is within ¼ in (6.3 mm) of the edge of the body depth marked on the side of the guitar. This ensures the carving will not break through. It is a simple job to deepen the cavity after the top is carved but not so easy to put wood back. The position of the jack-hole is also marked on the side of the guitar. This is not drilled until after the back has been rounded over.

The finished cover plate, with some of its protective plastic cover in place, and the finished recess. The jack socket mounting hole can be seen in this view which was drilled after the back was rounded over and before the top was carved.

of the controls. The edges of these holes are joined with a pencil line. This is slightly curved so that an area is left for the cover plate to rest against without having to make the cover and its recess vastly oversize. These pencil lines are used as a guide when routing to join the holes together. About ⅛ in (3.2 mm) is removed in each pass and when the depth of the predrilled holes is reached the cavity should be deep enough for the router bit to be used against the edge of the cavity in the way that it would be used with a jig.

Whichever way the cavity is cut it should be taken to ¼ in (6.3 mm) below the line drawn around the edge of the guitar that will show the extent to which the top is carved. It is always possible to take a little more out of the cavity after the top has been carved, test-fitting the pots until they are fitted correctly, but impossible to put some back if you go too deep.

When the cavity is finished the cover plate is made and fitted. This is cut out of thin PVC sheet and is available from most guitar-makers' suppliers. It can be cut with either a fret saw or a small electric jig saw so that it overlaps the cavity by just enough for the small fixing screws to be fitted.

I have chosen to cut this freehand. The cover is first cut out of the plastic sheet. Since the plastic is black it is easier to cover it in masking tape, which

not only makes the lines easier to see but helps protect the surface. Once cut to shape on a fret saw it can be cleaned up using scrapers and sandpaper.

Cutting the recess freehand takes some care and a steady hand. Firstly the cover is positioned and scribed around. This must be done carefully so that the scriber does not slip and gouge the guitar back.

The router is set to the depth of the PVC sheet and the excess wood is carefully removed up to the scribed line. The torque from the router motor will cause it to want to wander, hence a firm hand and a good scribed line are important. The recess can then be tidied with careful use of a sharp knife or chisel and, if necessary, the cover can be trimmed to fit slightly.

The last job before carving the top is to drill the locating hole for the jack socket. This is best done before the top is contoured as the body has to be held in the vice. The hole is drilled midway between the bottom of the body and the line that shows where the contouring will end on the side. A ⅞ in (22.2 mm) bit is used and the hole is drilled so that the bit reaches the control cavity but does not fully emerge into it. A smaller drill can then be used to link the two pieces together.

Contouring tops on guitars has evolved out of violin-making practice. For violins, the way to maximise the internal space of the instrument without making the sides deeper or the overall shape, which is dictated by tradition as much as anything else, larger is to balloon the top and the back. These are raised by as much as ½ in (12.7 mm), increasing the internal volume of the soundbox as well as imparting a lot of strength to the top. This technique was used on guitars by Orville Gibson, founder of the company that bears his name. He used to hand carve the tops and backs of his guitars and mandolins in order to achieve maximum volume. He even went one stage further and partially hollowed out the necks of his guitars. It was from these instruments that the cello-bodied jazz guitar we know today emerged.

The story of why Gibson used this method on the first Les Pauls is told in several versions depending on whose account you read. What is most likely is that Gibson contoured the top so that the new guitar would not look as radical as it was in fact. It looked just like a very small bodied jazz guitar. The method also allowed the Les Paul to be much thicker in the centre of the body than would have been practical if it had not been contoured; this was considered desirable to help the sustain.

The use of carving has now gone beyond purely practical reasons and contouring tops is now done as much for aesthetics as for anything else. It does make the guitar a little more comfortable to play and if the top is made from a highly-figured wood it can make the figuring stand out even more. On this guitar it is done to demonstrate the method as much as anything else.

The area either side of the neck slot that will be covered by the fingerboard is marked, as this will not be contoured, and the top of the body is gently carved down to the line around the edge using surforms, spokeshaves and, if available, small violin-makers' planes. These are very small planes, sometimes attached to long wooden handles, and are domed on the bottom. They are used with a relatively fine cut both along and across the grain to remove the worst of the excess wood. It is important when doing this with whatever tool to keep all of the lines flowing.

When the main bulk of the work has been done the final shaping is achieved with cabinet scrapers and progressively finer grades of sandpaper. As the top reaches its final shape you can find high or low spots by gently running your fingertips over the work and these can be sanded out. Another interesting feature is that the top horn needs to have its contouring extended quite a long way back as otherwise it tends to look very clubby.

Using a violin-makers' plane to carve the top of the guitar. If kept sharp this can be used across the grain although grain tear-out can sometimes be a problem. Final shaping is done with scrapers and sandpaper.

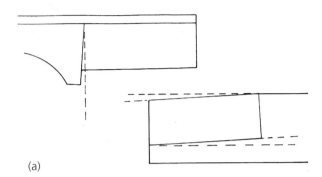

(a)

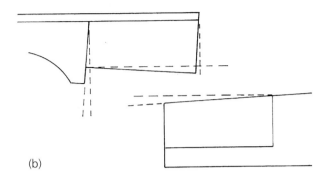

(b)

Carving a top is a time-consuming thing to do by hand and, halfway through, I always contemplate going out and buying an extremely expensive machine to do it for me. Companies that mass-produce guitars have machines that can cut as many as eight bodies in one go. Do not even think about this while you are carving a top by hand. It can ruin your day.

The slot in the body that takes the neck can now be marked and cut. The tenon on this guitar is 70 mm long and 40 mm wide (2¾ x 1⁹⁄₁₆ in). This is slightly smaller than I would normally use – a larger tenon could be exposed when carving the neck and body join, as will be seen later – but is still perfectly adequate for the job. The slot in the body must have an angled bottom to take the flat-bottomed tenon on the neck. The first stage is to cut the angle onto the area where the neck will sit. The angle is set on an angle gauge and a small amount removed so that the area remains flat across its length and width while the angle is created.

If the body slot was to be cut by hand, for example with drills and chisels, it would be easier to cut the slot with a flat bottom and then angle the bottom surface of the tenon. Since I am cheating and using the router it is just as easy for me to use the angled surface that has just been planed onto the guitar as a base for the router while it cuts a correspondingly angled slot into the front of the guitar. For this job I have made up a simple routing jig that will sit on the front of the body. It will be held in place with small screws as there is

The neck tenon can be made in two ways. If the front of the guitar is angled, as on a Gibson Les Paul, the slot can be made so the bottom is parallel to the face of the guitar (diagram a). This way the tenon can be made the same depth all the way along. If the guitar has a flat top and a flat-bottomed slot is cut, any neck angle will have to be produced by tapering the depth of the neck tenon. This may mean one end of the tenon is proud of the guitar front. In this case small inserts may need to be fitted to tidy this up. This method is used on Gibson SGs and some other guitars (diagram b).

not much area to hold the jig with double-sided tape. With care the screw holes can be positioned so that they are hidden by the guitar fingerboard when the guitar is complete.

The slot is cut to 30 mm (1³⁄₁₆ in) deep and, if necessary, the sides are tidied with a 1 in (25.4 mm) chisel.

The tenon on the neck can now be cut. Firstly the angle that enables the end of the neck to butt against the end of the body is cut into the sides of the neck. The sides of the tenon are then cut down to meet this first cut, and the depth of the tenon is cut to size. If this has been done correctly the tenon will be square and evenly dimensioned, with the heel of the neck at the correct angle and each of the three cuts that has produced it meeting perfectly. In the real world they might need a little tidying with a chisel and it is worth spending the time to make sure that the join is as accurate as

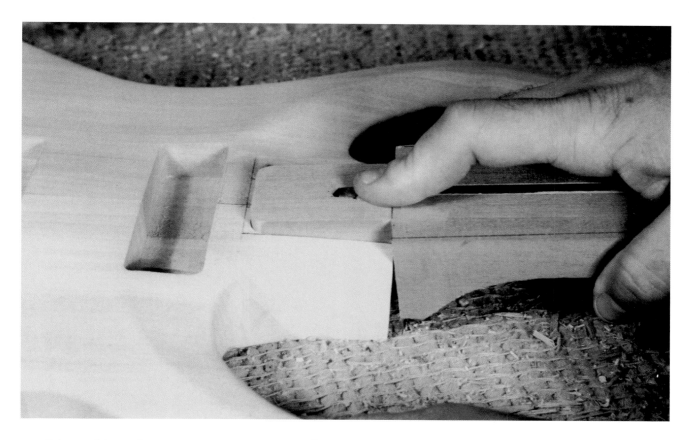

Test-fitting the neck. It should be tight enough not to move around but not so tight that all the glue will get forced from the join.

possible as this is the most important join on the guitar.

The neck can then be test-fitted into the body slot. Care must be taken to ensure that the centre lines of the neck and body line up correctly as, if there is any slight discrepancy, it may be necessary to pare away one side of the tenon and build the other side up with small pieces of veneer. This is not the ideal way of doing things but, since I have seen some very expensive factory-produced guitars with veneer-shimmed necks, I see no reason why it cannot be done on a first home-built guitar!

The neck is not fixed at this stage but is put to one side while work on the body is finished.

The back of the guitar is not contoured like the front although it will have a recess as on the Stratocaster. This was originally called 'comfort contouring' but has been nicknamed the 'beer-belly recess'. Before this is cut, the edges of the guitar at the rear can be rounded over using either a spoke-shave and sandpaper or a half-round router bit. If using the router great care should be taken around the area where the jack socket hole is as the router bit can slip into the hole causing all sorts of damage.

It is best to rout almost to the hole and finish the rounding-over by hand at that point. The cutaway can then be cut out using a band saw to remove most of the waste but would need to be jigged; holding the wood at an angle while it is being cut would not be sensible. Instead, half-round surforms can be used to remove most of the waste and the area cleaned up with spokeshaves and sandpaper.

The holes for the bridge-mounting studs are drilled on a pillar drill. These holes must be drilled accurately and so the use of a pillar drill for these is advisable. The pick-up cavities are joined to the control cavity using extra-long drills. These can be bought from engineering suppliers, although they may have to be ordered, and a ¼ in (6.3 mm) drill is used. The hole linking the front pick-up starts in the neck slot so that the drill does not have to go through the wood at an excessive angle, but great care must be taken with both holes to ensure that

Drilling the connecting holes for the wires from the front pick-up to the back pick-up. The back pick-up will be joined to the control cavity by another hole. The rear cavity that takes the tremolo springs will also need a small hole (⅛ in or 3 mm) to take the earth wire that connects the back of the pots to the spring claw. Also visible in this view is the carved ridge along the top horn and the bridge mounting holes that have already been drilled.

the drill bit does not wander and either miss the control cavity or emerge from the front, rear or side of the guitar. Each hole should be centre-punched before drilling as this helps the bit bite into the correct place on the wood. A small hole is also drilled from the spring cavity to the control cavity to take the earth wire. A ⅛ in (3.2 mm) extra-long drill is used for this.

The potentiometers and switch can also be test-fitted and if there is still too much wood on the face of the guitar the body can be held firmly onto the workbench and the cavity routed a little deeper where it is needed.

Attention can now return to the neck. If the intended head shape is wider than the existing wood it will need to be built up either side with small strips of wood of the same type as used for the neck. These must be left to dry out thoroughly before the head shape is cut.

The head shape can be cut using a band saw. The shape will need to be marked on the back of the head and the face of the head held firmly flat against the base of the saw. Alternatively the neck can be held in a vice and the shape cut using a coping saw, the cuts being cleaned up using sandpaper.

Marking the head shape from a plywood jig. The comments on the jig are dedicated to anyone who knows the true story of the first edition of this book! Note the extra pieces glued onto the neck blank to make up the full width of the head.

Drilling the machine-head holes on the pillar drill. The diameter is usually about ⅜ in or 10 mm depending whether you use American or European heads. The best position is about ½ in (12.7 mm) in from the edge of the head for the centres of the holes. It is best to drill these using scrap underneath the head as drilling through into the scrap will help stop the rear of the head splintering.

Scribing around the inlays. Notice the chalk used to fill in the line to make it more visible.

The sides of the neck can be cut down on the band saw or with a coping saw or a bow saw. Since none of these implements were designed to cut straight lines a lot of care is needed.

The fingerboard is next to be made and fitted. This is made of ebony and would be prepared in the way described in Chapter 7, except that it is made 2 mm (³⁄₃₂ in) narrower than needed as the binding will bring it up to the correct width, and it has been bought preslotted but not cambered.

The inlays are fitted in the same places as the dots would normally be and are made of mother-of-pearl, although they can be acetate or plastic. Way back at Giffin Guitars we used to call this 'mother-of-plastic'. I have since heard it referred to as 'mother-of-toilet seat'. The inlays can be bought ready-cut from many guitar parts' suppliers. They are held in their correct positions on the fingerboard and are scribed around. The scribed lines are then filled with chalk to make them stand out from the dark background of the ebony.

A small router is used with a ¹⁄₁₆ in (1.5 mm) bit to cut away most of the waste wood. This is done in two passes as the router is not powerful enough to deal with the full depth of the inlay recess and is much easier to control on small depth cuts.

Ideally the block markers would be installed before the board is cambered so the small router that cuts most of the waste has a firm, flat base on which

Using the small Dremel router to remove most of the waste wood.

Tidying up the recesses with a small chisel.

(below) The two ways that fingerboards are bound. In (a) the binding is glued into place and the tang of the fret is cut back so that it fits between the binding. In (b) the frets are fitted first and the binding is fitted around the end of the fret.

to stand. Since some precut fingerboards are also cambered, the fingerboard would need to be fixed to a plywood base and the router supported on small pieces of plywood, either side of the board, which are the same height as the centre of the board.

After the router has removed most of the waste the recesses are tidied up using a small and very

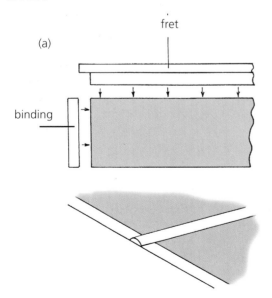

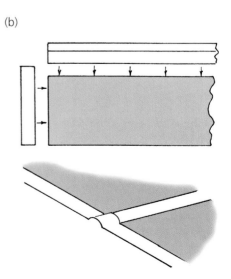

sharp chisel. The inlays are then epoxied into place and any small gaps around them can be filled with black filler. If a commercial black filler is not available one can be made up using glue and ebony dust. (An old woodworking adage goes: In glue and dust I put my trust, if that doesn't work then filler must!)

When this has set thoroughly the board is cambered using a sanding stick as a plane will not appreciate being used on the inlays and they would almost certainly break or chip. There should be enough thickness in the inlays to allow for quite a lot of camber but it is worth proceeding with caution so as not to make the edges of the inlays too thin.

There are two ways that binding is fitted to a guitar fingerboard. Both ways are similar and both stop moisture entering the fingerboard, which could cause the fret to lift, as well as to be decorative.

The first way is to fret the board before the binding is fitted. The frets are not filed off at a 45-degree angle at the edge of the board but are filed flush. The binding is then glued on so that it is slightly higher than the board and the frets. It is then filed and scraped down to the level of the board between the fret positions and the shape of the fret end. This is the method that Gibson use.

The other way is to fit the binding first and then to install the frets. The tang of the fretwire has to be cut back slightly so that the bead of the fret is carried over the binding. This method has the advantage of giving slightly more fret across the fingerboard allowing a slightly wider spacing of the strings. This is also the method that should be used when re-fretting a guitar with binding but all too often I have seen guitars refretted by supposedly professional repairers who have cut through the binding to make fitting the fret easier. The binding is fitted for a reason and cutting the binding ruins the effect and the looks.

The binding is glued to the board using epoxy or superglue (cyanoacrylate). Plastic bindings can be fixed using acetone and wooden bindings can be glued using white glue but care must be taken not to fill the fret slots with the excess. This also applies to epoxying plastic binding.

Superglue has many applications in guitar-making. If used carefully and according to the manufacturer's instructions it can be very effective. If using it on plastic binding, the surface of the binding that is to take the glue should be scraped slightly to remove the sheen. The wood of the fingerboard should then be dampened as the glue will not work on a porous surface that is dry. This also applies to wooden binding when being superglued. The glue needs to be applied generously but not so that it drowns the work. In this instance I am using one of the gel glues that are a little easier to control.

Once the two pieces are brought together the glue will need to remain under some pressure for a minute or two until it sets. Any glue that oozes out can cause the poor guitar-maker to become attached to his/her work. Have the correct solvent for the glue on hand and if you get stuck, do not panic and follow the correct procedure to get yourself free (see Chapter 8). The only downside to using superglue is that if it does not stick first time, for example if the join is not kept under pressure long enough, the join will need to come apart and be thoroughly cleaned up before regluing.

The next stage is to glue the board to the neck. Great care must be taken to ensure that it does not slip about while the clamps are being tightened, as if the board goes onto the neck crooked it will have to be removed and a new one fitted. It is also necessary to ensure that the surface of the board is not marked by the clamps. To stop this a clamping caul is used to protect the fingerboard, which will also help to even out the force of the clamps. To stop the fingerboard sliding around small double-ended pins can be used to locate it. These can be small panel pins knocked part way into the face of the neck and cut off about $\frac{1}{16}$ in (1.5 mm) above the surface and filed to a point. The board can then be positioned correctly and clamped before any glue is applied so that the pins make their own locating holes in the underside of the board. The glue is then applied, the board repositioned and the clamps tightened. All being well the board should not have moved.

When using this method it should be remembered that the pins are a) there and b) quite sharp. The best glue-spreaders are fingers and if you forget that several sharp pins are sticking out of what you are busy spreading glue over, some of that glue could go a little redder than it is meant to be!

You should use enough clamps to keep the whole length and width of the board down as firmly as possible. Again, if the glue is oozing out of the join it is a good sign but it is important to remove any glue from the area of the neck tenon before it sets so that when the time comes to fit the neck this excess dry glue will not make life difficult. Since the glue that

You do not need to use quite this many clamps. This is the laminated neck made earlier in the chapter which found its way onto another guitar. There was a slight warp in the fingerboard – not enough to worry about but it did need careful clamping. The important thing to remember if using a lot of clamps is not to overtighten and force the glue from the join. This neck is seen drying in the famous English sunshine.

I am using is water-soluble it is removed with the aid of a slightly damp cloth.

The side dots will also need to be fitted. These are made up of short lengths of black plastic rod ¹⁄₁₆ in (1.5 mm) diameter that is bought in a longer piece and inserted into a predrilled hole and cut off to length. When filed flush it will be a simple back spot.

After the glue has set and the clamps have been removed the neck can be shaped. This is done before the neck is fitted to the body as the carved top of the guitar will make it difficult to fit into the vice while the neck is carved.

The neck shaping is done with surforms and spoke-shaves, finishing off with scrapers and sandpaper.

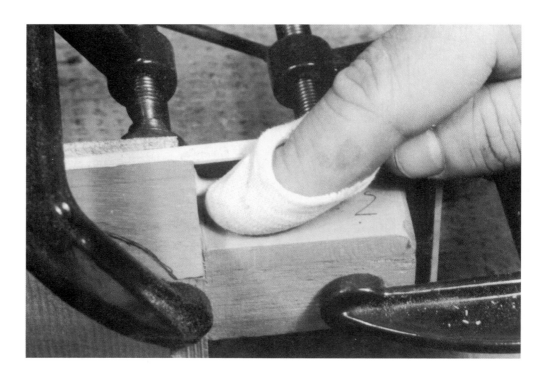

Cleaning the glue from around the neck tenon with a damp cloth. The plywood clamping caul that protects the face of the fingerboard can be seen under the left clamp.

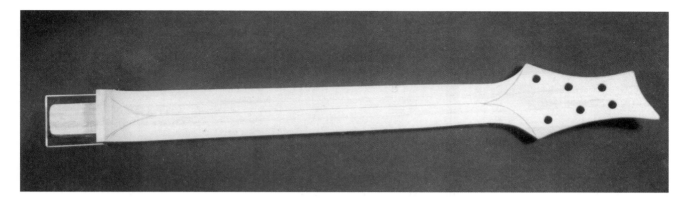

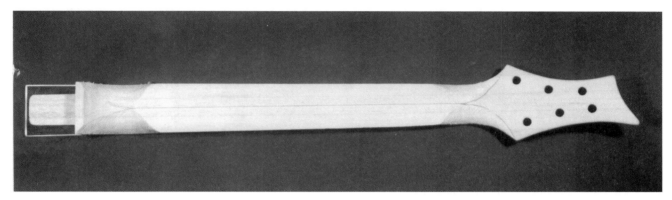

Firstly the shape at each end of the neck is carved roughly with round and half-round surforms. At this stage it is important not to remove too much wood as it is always possible to remove more later but impossible to put any back. Using a surform or spokeshave the corresponding points on the two curves are joined along the neck in a series of

(top) The first stage of carving the neck is to mark the centre line and the areas to be shaped at each end. The centre line is useful as, providing you keep it untouched, you cannot expose the truss rod.

(above) The shape at each end can be carved with surforms, rasps or spokeshaves.

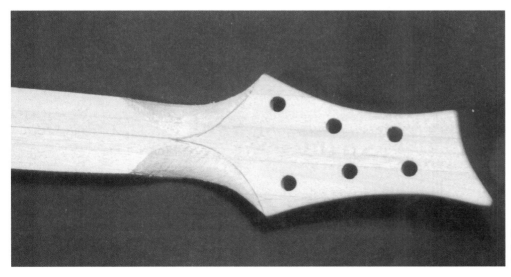

The head end of the neck showing how the shaping is made over the first portion of the neck.

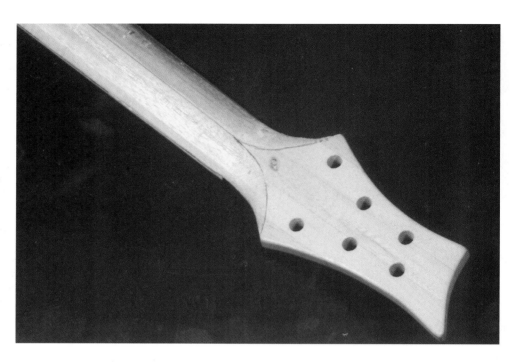

(right) The corresponding points at either end of the neck can be joined to extend the shape along the whole neck. The idea is that these lines should remain straight along the neck so that the neck is not thinner in the centre than it is at either end. It is normal to have the head end slightly shallower than the body.

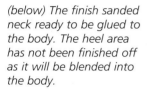

(below) The finish sanded neck ready to be glued to the body. The heel area has not been finished off as it will be blended into the body.

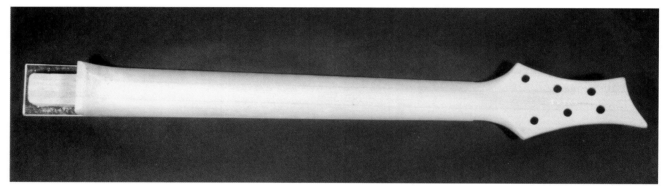

straight lines. When this has been done the neck has its rough shape and this can be refined with careful use of spokeshaves and surforms before finishing off with progressively finer grades of sandpaper.

The choice of neck contour is a matter of personal taste which, on a first guitar, can be difficult to judge. Removing too much wood will result in a neck that is too flexible and, therefore, difficult to keep straight, and there is a danger when removing too much wood that the truss rod can be exposed; although not removing enough wood will result in a neck that is fat and difficult to play. The heel end of the neck only has minimal shaping at this stage since it will be completed, for reasons that

will become apparent, when the neck is attached to the guitar.

When the neck has been sanded it can be glued to the body. The care put into checking this earlier will be apparent now as the utmost care must be taken to ensure that the neck lines up correctly with the body before the glue sets. It will be impossible to change this if it is wrong except by removing the neck and making a new one. It is well worth attempting a dry run of the neck fit, including clamping and fitting of any veneers, to iron out any problems that could occur before the glue is applied; when gluing, the whole lot will want to move as the glue will make everything slip and if you do not practise you can guarantee the clamps will be in the

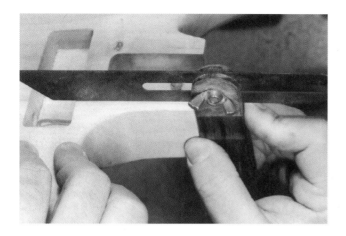

Checking the neck angle is correct before gluing.

The neck glued in. Note the first drops of glue seeping from the join – these will need to be cleaned off. The front pick-up hole also has tape sealing the hole that was drilled from the neck tenon to link the pick-up positions.

wrong part of the workshop and set to the wrong size.

After the gluing has been successfully completed the excess glue can be removed and any filling that may be needed around the neck joint attended to. The heel can also be completed at this time. On this guitar I have chosen to blend the neck shape into the body as much as I can so not only the neck heel but also part of the body is removed with the surform. This makes the guitar much more comfortable

to play in the higher areas of the fingerboard and this is the reason for using the smaller neck tenon. Even if the tenon were exposed this is not a big problem as there is plenty holding the neck in place and the guitar is to be finished in a block colour but if it were to be natural it is better to use a smaller tenon. Once the carving has been completed, the area can be sanded smooth.

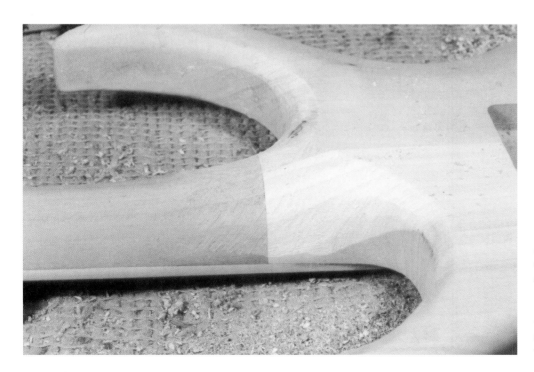

The join between the neck and body is cut away to allow the neck shape to continue into the body. This is done with surforms and spokeshaves so that all parts blend together smoothly.

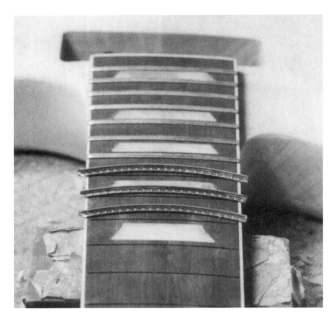

The frets are cut to be a little longer than the slot, as normal, but the tang is cut back using the tool shown on page 47. It can be seen here that the fret slots do not extend through the binding.

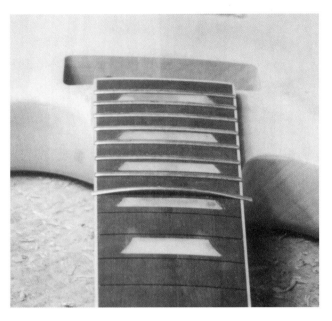

The frets are inserted as shown in Chapter 7. The binding can be damaged if the small part of fret that sits above it is hammered too hard.

The guitar is then ready to be fretted. First the neck should be double-checked for straightness, using a long straight edge. The frets have to be fitted between the binding, and so a small amount of the tang has to be removed. This can be done with a file, or with careful use of end nippers and tidying up with a file, but there is a tool available from some guitar parts suppliers that makes the job very simple. The fret is fitted in the normal way and the small length of bead that overhangs the binding is sealed in place with a small drop of superglue. This is to stop it rising up and catching any unsuspecting finger. When the glue has dried the end of the fret can be shaped in the normal way.

The final job after fitting the frets is to install the nut. The make of tremolo system used on this guitar has a lockable nut but I prefer not to use this type as if the strings are fitted properly and the guitar top nut and machine-heads set up correctly it should not be needed. Conversely, if the guitar is not set up correctly even a lockable nut will not stop it going out of tune.

The top nut is often made of a small piece of prepared bone, which is available from guitar-makers' suppliers, or one of the many plastic- or resin-based

Once the fret is safely in, the ends can be cut back as in Chapter 7. It helps if the ends of the fret are sealed with a little cyanoacrylate to stop them catching and to seal them from moisture.

Some companies offer good alternatives to elephant nasal adornment. Tusq is a synthetic ivory substitute sold by Graph Tech Systems. It is seen here on the laminated neck made earlier in the chapter. The additional sides of the head and the glue line from the spliced head are clearly visible.

An elephant busy proving to a passing safari that ivory looks best in its natural habitat.

substitutes that are now sold. Ivory used to be the standard but it does look much nicer if still attached to the business end of an elephant and is now illegal in many countries. Bone is used as a substitute on cheaper instruments and, as this is a by-product of the food industry, it is nicer than ivory for which an elephant has to be killed especially, something they generally do not take kindly to. In recent years some manufacturers have used brass, plastic compounds and materials such as graphite, and the use of these is a matter of personal taste. Some of these have even been developed to imitate the characteristics of ivory which is good news for elephants everywhere. Plain plastic nuts should not be used as they are too soft and the strings stick in the grooves making tuning difficult.

The nut is prepared with a junior hacksaw and files, and is held in place by either superglue or epoxy. The string positions are marked but not, at this stage, cut.

Construction is now essentially finished and only needs finish-sanding prior to being sprayed. All marks from the tools used should be sanded away and the marks from the coarser grades of sandpaper are removed with finer grades, finishing with 320 grade. During this procedure the fluffiness of poplar will become apparent. It can be difficult to sand as the fibres tend to want to lift but, if using the right grades and taking care, a good finish is not difficult.

The finishing of this guitar is covered in Chapter 13 and so I will not repeat it here, but after the lacquer has set and has been buffed the guitar can be assembled.

The tone and volume controls are part-wired before installation. This is easier than trying to do all of the wiring when the controls are in their positions inside the cavity. I find it easier to drill a couple of small holes in a block of wood which can hold the components steady and help avoid burnt fingers.

The pick-ups are fitted with their hook-up wire which is fed through to the control cavity and they

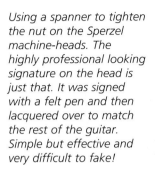

Using a spanner to tighten the nut on the Sperzel machine-heads. The highly professional looking signature on the head is just that. It was signed with a felt pen and then lacquered over to match the rest of the guitar. Simple but effective and very difficult to fake!

are screwed into the guitar. It is worth fitting the front one and wiring it into the circuit before fitting the other as the connecting wires could get confused and trying to feed a long wire through a half-completed guitar is not simple.

The machine-heads, in this case lockable Sperzels, are fitted. These are held by the nut that extends through the head to the casing of the unit and this is tightened with a small box spanner. The head is prevented from turning by a pin that fits into a predrilled hole on the rear of the head.

Installing the tremolo bridge is almost an art in itself. The claw will need to be screwed into the cavity and the tremolo unit dropped through the front of the guitar and located on its mounting studs. The springs can then be stretched onto the locating lugs on the claw and holes in the tremolo block. This is one of those jobs that requires three hands but can be done, at a push, with normally-built guitar-makers and a little thought.

Once the tremolo bridge is installed, the other parts, such as the strap buttons, jack-socket mounting-plate and control cover are also fitted and it is a good idea to have predrilled these holes before finishing the guitar.

When all of the parts have been added the guitar can be set up ready for playing. This is covered in detail in Chapter 15.

The final job is to fit the truss rod cover which, for me, always has some special significance. There is a particular feeling that I get whenever I finish a guitar. It is a mixture of achievement and concern. A lot of work goes into each guitar and it is the first notes that are played on the guitar after it has been set up that give the initial impression. If there have

been niggling problems during the making of the guitar, the moment that it is finished can be one of great relief.

On the other hand, I always get a lingering doubt that I may have forgotten something important. This is probably quite a normal paranoia, the same as you get when you arrive at your chosen holiday destination and cannot remember if you turned off the gas stove before you left, or arranged for the pet Iguana to be fed. However, all being well the guitar will be wonderful and the sense of achievement that you feel should beat that which Sir Edmund Hillary and Sherpa Tensing felt when they climbed that little hill.

This guitar has used only some of the skills that can be applied in guitar-making. There may be others that you wish to use on your guitar, and so rather than rest on my laurels I will attempt to demonstrate these by making another guitar or two.

The final, almost symbolic fitting of the truss rod cover.

10   The Second Guitar

The second guitar that I am making is a variation on the standard Fender Telecaster. The Telecaster is, of course, an excellent instrument (if anyone has a nice mid-50s Telecaster or Esquire that is surplus to requirements, it can be sent to me via the publishers!) and so there is little point in making an exact copy.

Over the past ten or fifteen years companies such as ESP, Schechter, Mighty Mite, Warmoth, Double Eagle and others have produced whole ranges of replacement parts of a number of guitars. Some of these makers also sold complete guitars that were often the same shape as existing guitars, but were made of different woods and fitted with different parts.

The guitar that I am making is an example of this approach. It has a one-piece maple neck, in common with many Fenders, but has a maple-fronted mahogany body and it is fitted with two humbucking pick-ups. The top is bound and the controls are fitted through the wood from the rear, doing away with the need for a scratchplate.

Since the original Broadcaster and Telecaster were designed around a series of jigs, much of the work on this guitar follows this approach although I will, where possible, explain how a similar job could be done at home. A commercially-bought neck could also be used on a guitar such as this, but since this is a book about guitar-making I will do it the difficult way!

THE BODY

The body of this guitar is made of one piece of mahogany 1⅝ x 16 x 13 in (41.3 x 406 x 330 mm) and two pieces of bookmatched curly maple ¼ x 16 x 6½ in (6.3 x 406 x 165 mm).

The maple is first to be prepared. This has been machine-planed to thickness by the guitar parts supplier who normally sells such pieces as acoustic guitar backs. The normal way of preparing the top

Planing the edges of the front. It sometimes helps to use some small 1 in clamps at each end of the top to hold the two pieces together.

would be to join the two halves before they are fixed to the mahogany.

Firstly the two edges to be joined should be planed flat and square. Since the pieces to be glued are quite thin there is no way that they could be clamped in the normal way using sash clamps as the wood would distort badly and so a workboard is prepared that is slightly larger than the two pieces. This is lightly waxed along its centre to avoid gluing the maple to the workboard, and the two pieces to be joined are placed on the board with a ½ in or ¼ in (12.7 or 6.3 mm) batten beneath the join. The two pieces are then held together either with small pieces of wood clamped, screwed or glued along either edge, or, more simply, by nails hammered into the board against the edge of the maple. Glue is then applied to the join and the batten is removed. A weight is then used to hold the wood down onto the board taking care that the join is flat along its length. There is enough pressure exerted by the nails

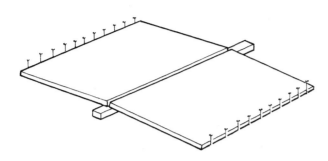

A simple method of joining the bookmatched front prior to fixing to the main body wood.

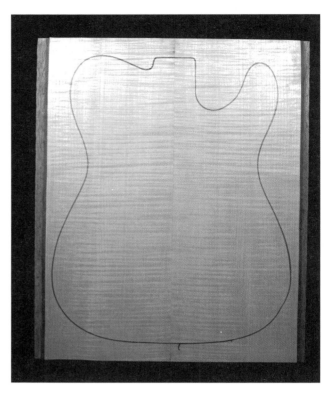

The body blank glued and ready to be cut out.

or cauls to make a good join without distorting the wood, and as long as glue can be seen to be seeping all along the join, it should be OK. Again too much pressure will force all of the glue out of the join but this would certainly also distort the maple.

In the past I have had very good results using this method but I was unable to use it on the guitar in the photographs.

The pieces of maple that I used are a good example of just how frustrating wood can be. In Chapter 5 I stated that curly maple can be unstable. The wood that I bought for this guitar was perfectly flat when I bought it and was fine until I started to work on it. As soon as the edges were planed it started to warp. The warp was not bad enough to warrant scrapping the wood, especially as it was so nicely figured, but it meant that I could not join the wood in the way described. Instead the two pieces were clamped down onto the mahogany whilst also being clamped across their width. This has held them down onto the top of the guitar but has left them with a slightly more visible glue line between the two halves. This is not unacceptable but is not as good as it could have been if the above method had been employed.

If using the first method the maple will need to be cleaned up slightly and glued down onto the mahogany using clamps and clamping cauls to distribute the force all across the front of the guitar. When this has dried out the basic shape can be cut out.

The body shape is first marked onto the wood using the routing jig, made from ⅜ in (9.5 mm)

marine plywood, as a pattern and the join between the two pieces of maple as the centre line. A felt-tip marker is used to draw the shape to give a good visible line.

The basic shape of the guitar can then be cut out on the band saw. The felt-tip pen line is of course quite thick but does allow for a bit of leeway when cutting out the shape. It does not matter if you cut into the line as long as you do not cut through it. Using a pencil line for this would require more accurate band-sawing as one would not want to cut through the line nor leave too much excess wood as this would make the next step a little more difficult.

The sides of this guitar are routed to match the shape of the jig; this guarantees that the jig and the body are exactly the same dimensions. Since a pin router is unlikely to be available, a hand-held router can be used. For this guitar I used a hand-held router mounted beneath a table so that the bit protruded in much the same fashion as a spindle moulder. Its height was adjustable and, since follower bits are rarely long enough to cope with the full depth of a guitar body, a special bit was made up

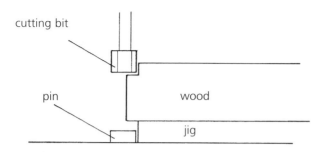

cutting bit

pin   wood

jig

(above) The principle of the pin router.

(right) A close-up of the pin router. The jig runs against the pin and the bit would cut the work flush – if there were any in this photograph.

with a short length of cutter on the end of a long shank. The bit is adjusted so that the blade is high enough out of the table to cut the wood while the shank of the router bit runs against the jig leaving the guitar body flush. This is far from an ideal arrangement and could be quite dangerous if used carelessly (see Chapter 8) but in practice, as long as

The table-mounted router. It can be seen that the shank of the bit runs against the plywood jig.

the work is kept moving so that the friction of the router bit does not burn into the jig and the guitar body, it works well. The bit was still not quite long enough to do the whole job and for the last pass the jig was removed, leaving the bit running on just the guitar body.

An alternative method would be to use a hand-held router with a similar bit on top of the work as shown in the photograph. The body, or whatever is being routed, would need to be securely fixed to the workbench so that it does not move. This could mean clamping down the guitar and jig and only half of the body could be worked on at any one time. Care would also need to be taken to stop the router toppling off the side of the jig and cutting into the work where it is not needed. I have actually used this method on far more guitars that I can remember and have rarely had any trouble with it.

Even if the table-mounted router is used, it is not possible to cut the pick-up holes or control cavity, and these are done using the router above the work, as described above and used in the last chapter.

Both of these methods are rather unkind to the plywood jigs but since relatively few guitars are made on them they are perfectly adequate.

An additional advantage of the second of these methods is that both hands are needed on the router which keeps them well away from direct, and painful, contact with the bit. As with all routing the wood must always be presented to the bit in the right direction for the cutter to work properly.

The alternative method of using the router, on top of the workpiece. The jig is attached to the body with double-sided tape or by discreet screws. Tilting the router when working in this way can badly damage the guitar sides.

The reason for cutting out the body fairly close to the line and not having too much excess wood to remove will become apparent as you work. If there is too much excess wood, or the router bit is a little blunt, it can sometimes snatch and pull out a large chunk of the body. This is very annoying if the guitar is to be finished natural and it is not unknown for guitar-makers (and book authors) to try and find the chunk of wood that has been torn out and try to glue it back into place.

The neck slot is cut using the same jig that would be used if a standard Telecaster body was being made. The size of this is the same for all Telecasters and most of Fender's other guitars. It is 3 in (76 mm) long and ⅝ in (15.8 mm) deep. The jig for this is held in place with double-sided tape. If a standard Telecaster was made the jig could be screwed to the front of the body using the positions of the screws in the guitar's scratchplate. Since no scratchplate is to

be fitted to this guitar an alternative method, in this case that wonderful invention, double-sided tape, is used.

The pick-up cavities are next to be cut. The front pick-up is positioned so that its front edge is ½ in (12.7 mm) from the end of the neck and the bridge pick-up is positioned so that its front edge is 4¾ in (121 mm) from the end of the neck. Care must be taken to ensure that the pick-ups will be perpendicular to the centre line of the guitar body. The holes are ⅝ in (15.8 mm) deep and the piece at either end that accommodates the height adjustment screws is 1¼ in (31.7 mm) deep.

The control cavity is the same size as the standard Telecaster but is cut from the rear and covered with a plate. The main body jig can be used to cut this, although it has to be turned upside down and used on the rear of the guitar. The cavity is cut 1½ in (38.1 mm) deep leaving ¼ in (6.3 mm) to mount the controls. In practice, with a ¼ in top, the cavity could be routed until the maple was seen. The cover plate is also jigged and it is a simple job to cut this.

So far the work that has been done on the body is much the same as it was in the previous chapter, and the same methods that were used on the carved-top guitar could have been used on the Telecaster body. The binding, however, has to be fitted with the aid of a router. It would be almost impossible to cut an accurate channel for the binding using any hand tool. Instead the router is fitted with an adjustable device that runs against the side of the body to prevent the bit cutting into the body more than is needed. This is useful as it can be adjusted to

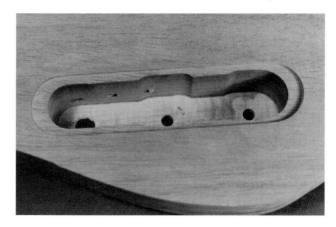

The control cavity. Note how the body is routed through to the maple facing.

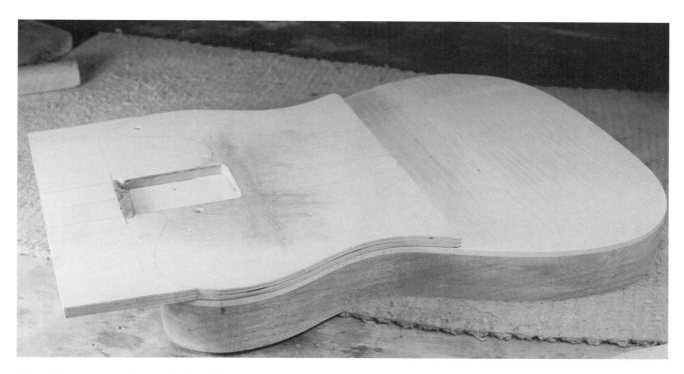

(above) The neck slot jig, made from ⅜ in (9.5 mm) marine plywood. It extends over the end of the guitar for a clean cut.

(below) The pick-up jig being taped into place.

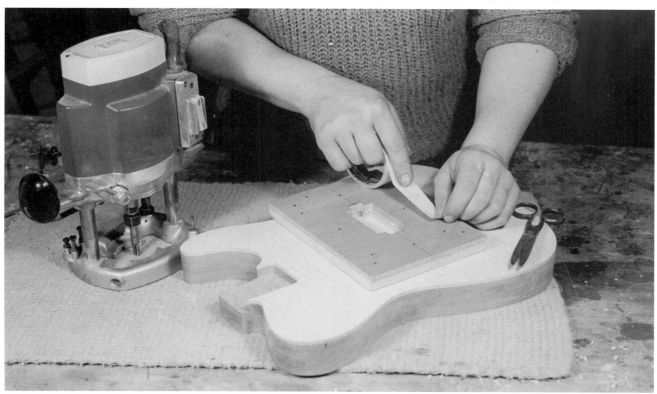

(above) The router with an attachment for cutting binding channels. There are several commercially-available attachments for routers to do this job and it can also be done by using a large diameter router bit with a smaller roller bearing, as mentioned in the last chapter.

(below) The finished binding channel.

account for any size of binding but a follower bit, with the bearing beneath the cutter, could be used. If a ⅜ in diameter bit was used with a ¼ in bearing, the bit would cut ¹⁄₁₆ in into the wood. Similar metric sizes would give the same result. Bearings are available in any number of sizes and a combination of the right size bit and right size bearing should be possible for most binding sizes. Buying a huge selection, however, can be expensive.

The binding that I am using for this guitar is a cream plastic that is bought in ready-cut lengths from a guitar-makers' suppliers. Its dimensions are ³⁄₃₂ in (2 mm) x ¼ in (6.3 mm) by about 4 feet (1200 mm), which is adequate to go right round the top edge of a Telecaster.

The channel is cut so that it is very fractionally smaller than the binding, so that when the binding is fitted it will protrude slightly. It can then be scraped back so that it is flush with the top and sides of the guitar, and this generally gives a better result than trying to fit the binding into an exact size channel.

The binding used on this guitar is quite small but if a larger binding was fitted, such as the eight-ply black and white binding found on Gibson Les Paul customs, several passes of the router might be needed to stop the bit tearing the wood and it might be difficult to find a follower bit/bearing combination that would allow a cut this wide. These bindings are also made in different depths as shown in the diagram.

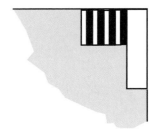

(above) The binding on a Les Paul Custom is made up from a piece of white and an eight-ply black and white of two different depths which needs a stepped binding channel.

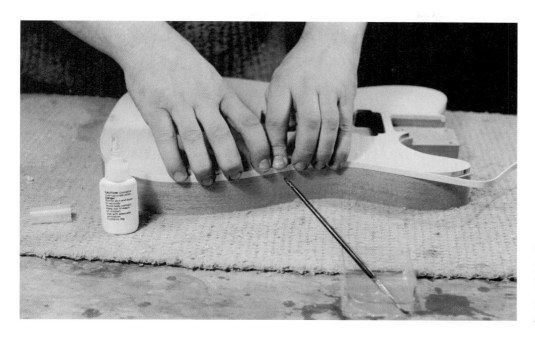

The binding is glued in using cyanoacrylate. This works best if the binding has its sheen removed with a scraper and the wood is dampened slightly before gluing.

As with all routing, the body should be held down firmly onto the bench while the channel is being cut. At the end of the cutaway horn there is only a very small area for the router to sit on and this part of the channel must be cut very carefully to stop the router toppling over the edge of the body which could damage the side of the guitar.

The binding is fixed to the guitar using superglue or acetone as was used for the fingerboard binding in

the last chapter. In either case the binding is glued on in stages, making sure that it is firmly fixed before progressing to the next stage.

When the binding is completed it can be tidied up using scrapers and fine wet-and-dry paper, used dry. If using superglue follow the manufacturer's instructions and wear some finger protection. It is not the end of the world if you glue yourself to the guitar, although you might leave a little skin behind, but I guarantee that if you do stick yourself to the guitar you will either remove yourself before the binding is set and have to clean it up and do it again, or the telephone will ring as you grimly hang on to the guitar until the glue dries.

The holes through the body that take the strings from their ferrules on the back through to the bridge are now marked and drilled. The six locating holes for the strings are marked using the main body jig and a smaller jig is used to give the positions of the four neck-fixing screws. All of these holes should be drilled on a pillar drill to ensure they go through the body straight. Trying to do this by hand might work but will probably be a disaster. The string locating holes are drilled to ⅛ in (3.2 mm) and the neck screw holes to ³⁄₁₆ in (4.7 mm); all of these should be centre-punched first.

At the rear of the guitar the strings are prevented from pulling through the wood by six small inserts, or ferrules. On some guitars these are left a little proud of the guitar back. On this guitar I am inserting

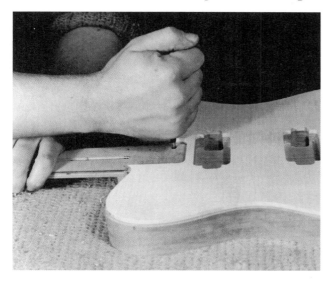

Marking the positions of the neck-fixing holes using a centre-punch and the neck jig.

A close-up of the rounding-over bit. The lack of a roller-bearing running along the guitar side means that the bit must be kept moving or the friction can burn the side of the guitar. It also means that you should not drill the jack-socket mounting hole before rounding over as the guide can fall into the hole and cause the bit to go into the front of the guitar.

them so that they are flush. The main part of the insert is ⁵⁄₁₆ in (7.9 mm) diameter, and this is drilled ⅜ in (9.5 mm) into the rear of the body using the ⅛ in (3.2 mm) hole that has already been drilled to locate the drill in the correct place. The outside lip of the insert is ⅜ in (9.5 mm) in diameter, and this too is carefully drilled so that it is just deep enough to take the insert.

The holes that link the pick-up cavities and the control cavity are also drilled. As with the previous guitar, they are drilled using a ¼ in (6.3 mm) extra-long series drill. The hole from the front pick-up cavity starts in the neck slot as in Chapter 9 so that it does not have to be drilled at an angle.

The mounting holes for the controls can also be drilled. The two potentiometers are fitted into ⅜ in (9.5 mm) holes and the toggle switch to ½ in (12.7 mm).

A hole also needs to be drilled from under the bridge plate into the control cavity to take the earth wire. A ⅛ in (3.2 mm) extra-long series drill is used for this.

The last major hole to be drilled is the jack-socket locating hole on the side of the instrument. The body is held in the vice and the hole is drilled to ⅞ in (22.2 mm). This hole has to be drilled carefully, as if the drill bit wanders to one side the hole can end up oval or the drill could split the body or emerge unexpectedly from the front of your guitar. The hole is drilled so that it is 1¼ in (31.7 mm) deep and it is linked to the control cavity with a ¼ in (6.3 mm) hole. It is important that this is not drilled before the binding channel is cut as the router guide, be it fixed

as on this guitar or a follower bit, can drop into the socket hole and the bit will obligingly cut across the face of the guitar. I will own up: this is stupid but I have done it in the past. Not surprisingly it is not something that is done twice!

The guitar body is now finished and ready for finish sanding.

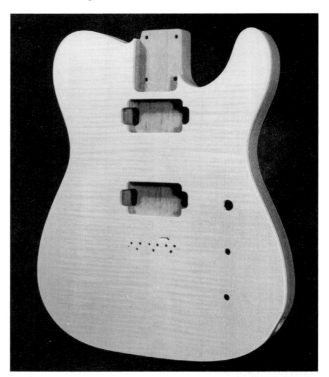

The body ready for finishing.

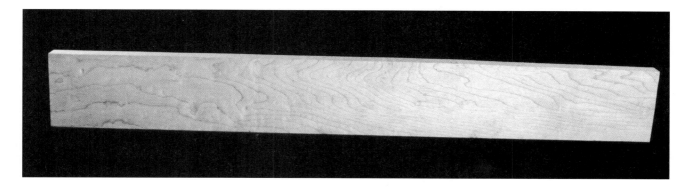

THE NECK

The neck blank.

The neck of this guitar is to be made up from one piece of maple 27 x 3½ x 1 in (686 x 89 x 25.4 mm). The construction of a one-piece neck is rather more complicated than one with a separate fingerboard and much of the work is again done on jigs. If a one-piece neck is a little too complicated for you to attempt at home, a two-piece neck can be made. Fender have, in the past, made both one- and two-piece necks. Their early rosewood neck and some of their maple necks made in the mid-1960s were two-piece, and these can be distinguished by the lack of the contrasting walnut strip at the rear and the egg-shaped insert near the nut on the face of the head.

The methods that I am using here differ only slightly from those used by the major manufacturers. Some aspects of the construction may be a little crude by their standards but they are perfectly adequate for the limited number of guitars made, and providing a little care is taken the results can be of equal quality.

Firstly one edge of the neck blank is planed straight and square and this side is used as a base for all measurements. A centre line for the neck is drawn parallel to this and 2 in (50.8 mm) into the wood. Over this the main neck jig is laid. This is put on upside down as the truss-rod channel on this guitar is cut before the neck is cut out and since this is installed from the rear there is little point in marking the front of the neck. The jig is drawn around and removed while the truss rod dimensions are marked. The channel starts 2 in (50.8 mm) from the body end of the neck and stops 14⅝ in (371.4 mm) from this point. Both of these points are marked with heavy pencil lines so that they are clearly visible.

Since the truss rod is fitted from the rear of the neck the rails that the router will run along to cut the channel have their highest point in the centre. The neck blank is clamped to the workbench and the channel is cut, using the edge guide of the router against the planed edge of the wood, until it is ¾ in

The neck blank marked ready for cutting with the plywood jig. The jig has the truss-rod channel position routed in to save having to measure each neck.

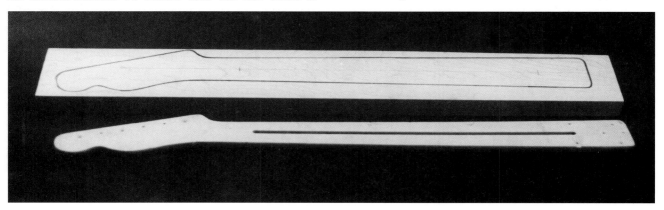

Placing the truss-rod rails onto the neck. Each end of the channel has been clearly marked.

(19 mm) deep at either end. The basic neck shape is then band-sawn out close to the line, the jig attached, and the table or pin router is used to give the final shape.

While the jig is still attached to the neck the positions of the six machine-head holes can be marked and centre-punched. The jig is then removed and the depth of the head is marked using a marking gauge set at ½ in (12.7 mm). The scribed line is easier to see if it is filled with pencil.

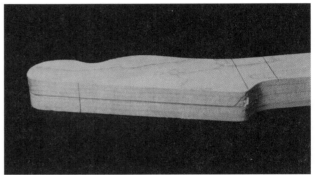

The head with the depth, centre line and nut position marked. Some router damage is visible on the edge of the neck but fortunately this is on the part that will be removed and does not affect the neck.

Drilling the machine-head holes.

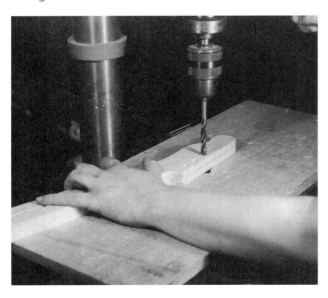

The nut position, taken from the jig, is marked onto the front of the guitar neck and a line is marked, perpendicular to the centre line of the neck, 1 in (25.4 mm) from the nut on the head side. The edges of this line are then taken down, at a slight angle, to meet the line showing the head depth. The machine-head holes are then drilled, using in the pillar drill whatever size drill is suitable for your chosen machine-heads, so that the hole passes the line showing the head depth but so that it does not emerge from the other side of the head. This will leave them much cleaner than if they are cut after the head is finished.

The head depth is then cut. A cut is made from the line that is 1 in (25.4 mm) from the nut down, at the slight angle drawn, to the line showing the head depth. The waste is then removed on the band

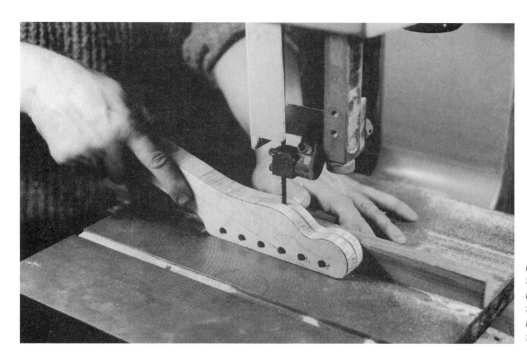

Band-sawing the depth of the head. By drilling the machine-head holes first the saw cut will ensure the hole is cleaner on the front face of the head.

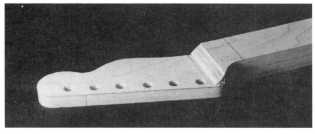

The head cut to depth showing the angle into which the anchor piece hole and covering dowel will be drilled.

saw taking care not to stray over the line. This must be done carefully, as the head must first be pushed through the band saw with the flat side of the head on the band saw table, but it should be angled during the cut so that both ends of the first line are met together.

The truss-rod channel is then joined to the anchor position at one end, and the adjustment position at the other. Four sizes of extra-long drill are used for this.

The body-end jig for joining the truss-rod channel to the neck-end adjustment point.

The head-end drilling jig has to sit over the face of the
head and is used to join the channel to the anchor
position and to drill a hole to take the dowel that seals
the anchor in place.

This part of the operation could be attempted by
hand but the chances of getting the drill to go
through the wood at the right angle and exactly
along the centre line are fairly small. Instead a jig
that holds the drill bits at exactly the right angle
and on line is used. The neck is clamped into the jig
and the two holes at the body end are drilled. The
first of these is to take the adjustment nut and this is
drilled into the end of the neck to a depth of 1⅛ in
(28.6 mm) using a ²⁵⁄₆₄ in (9.9 mm) diameter drill.
The drill bits are held at the correct angle in small
blocks of wood that have been fitted with inserts to
stop the drills damaging them.

The block is changed and the adjustment hole is
linked to the channel using a drill ¹³⁄₆₄ in (5.1 mm)
diameter. Ideally this should emerge in the channel
approximately ¹⁄₃₂ in (0.79 mm) clear of the bottom
(or top, depending upon which way you look at it)
of the channel. This allows enough space for a
plastic sleeve, or whatever else you have used to
encase the rod in the channel.

At the head end the first hole to be drilled is for
the small wooden dowel that seals the truss-rod
anchor in place. This is drilled to ⅜ in (9.5 mm)
diameter and for 1¼ (31.7 mm) into the neck. The
second hole is drilled in for a further ¼ in (6.3 mm),
¹⁹⁄₆₄ in (7.5 mm) diameter and this takes the small

The anchor piece is screwed onto the shorter thread and
the small amount that is exposed can be repeatedly centre-
punched to splay the end to stop the anchor rotating itself
off the rod.

knurled anchor. The last hole is again drilled to
¹³⁄₆₄ in (5.1 mm) and this links the anchor position
with the channel. It is at this point that you can
appreciate that trying to work with metric compar-
isons does cause some problems!

The rod itself is then made and fitted. This is
made up from a 17⅝ in (448 mm) length of mild
steel rod. It is tapped at one end for 1 in (25.4 mm)
to take the adjustment nut and for ¼ in (6.3 mm) at
the other end to take the anchor. When the anchor
is fitted the rod is permanently fixed to it by centre-
punching the end of the rod to open it out – also
known as peening – and this stops it moving in the
anchor.

Gluing the truss-rod fillet into place.

The rod is fed into the channel from the head end and the plastic sleeve or tape is fitted or wound over the length that is in the channel. The adjustment end is fed into the hole that links to the channel and the whole rod is firmly pushed into place from the head end so that the anchor is in its proper position. The walnut fillet that fills the channel, and gives Fender necks their distinctive stripe, is epoxied into place and the end of the rod is sealed with a small walnut dowel of ⅜ in (9.5 mm) diameter.

When the glue has dried thoroughly the fillet is planed down flush with the back of the neck and the face of the head can be cut to its final shape. From a point ⅛ in (3.2 mm) on the head side of the nut, a curving cut is made to meet the face of the head.

The dowel that was inserted is, of course, also cut, and this gives the familiar egg-shape on the curve.

Fitting the truss rod to a two-piece neck is much easier as it can be fitted in much the same way as was described in Chapter 6, with the exception that the holes at the adjustment end of the rod would still need to be drilled. As an alternative it is possible to fit a Japanese box-section rod. The channel could be cut to emerge at the body end of the neck. The circular adjusting nut would then be a little untidy in its rectangular hole, but the rod would work and most of the hole at the body end would be hidden by the guitar body. Alternatively the channel could be cut slightly shorter and the neck drilled to take the adjuster.

The rod, anchor and dowel.

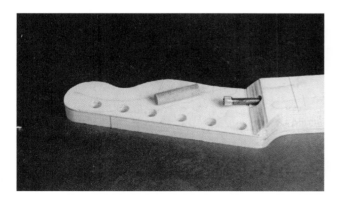

The final shape of the head.

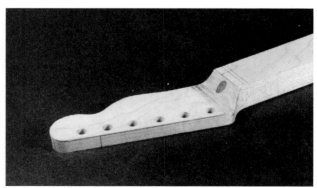

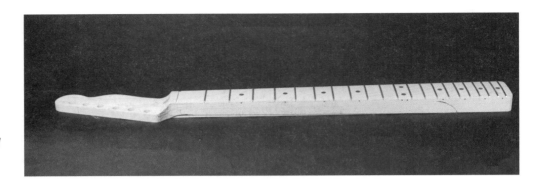

The first stage in shaping the neck is to mark the depth at the nut.

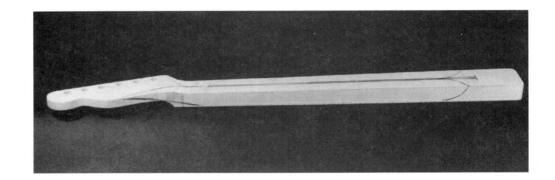

Stage two is to cut the depth of the neck and mark the approximate shape at either end.

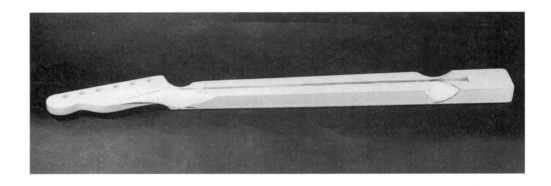

Each end can then be shaped using a surform and spokeshaves.

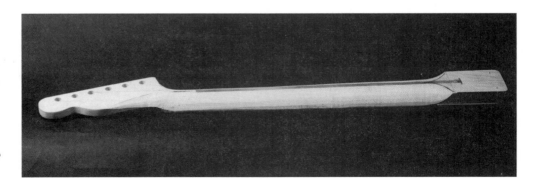

The corresponding points at either end can then be joined in straight lines along the neck. The neck only needs final sanding and scraping to remove the marks and finalise the shape.

Fitting the pick-ups into the body. The controls were part-wired before installation and only require the connection of the pick-ups.

Fender-style bass necks are made in much the same way as the neck that I have made, with the exception that the rod is, quite obviously, longer, at 22½ in (571.5 mm). The channel still starts 2½ in (63.5 mm) from the body end and the dimensions of the anchor end are the same also. The channel in the neck is 19½ in (495.3 mm) long. The neck slot is also different on a Fender bass, being 3⅞ in (98.4 mm) long, but, in common with all other Fenders, it is still ⅝ in (15.8 mm) deep.

The fret slots are next to be cut. I used Roger Giffin's food-mixer-powered special, but an alternative would be to use an adaptation of the jig shown in Chapter 7. The bar needed to rest the square against would need to be higher to allow for the full 1 in (25.4 mm) depth of the neck, and an alternative method of fixing the neck to the board might be needed to allow for the neck's extra mass.

After the fret slots have been cut the dots are fitted. These are made up from black plastic rod ¼ in (6.3 mm) in diameter. The end of the rod is fitted into the hole drilled into the fingerboard and the excess is cut off. When all have been fitted they can be sanded level with the board.

The side dots are also fitted. The diameter of these dots, in this case, is ¹⁄₁₆ in (1.5 mm). Fender use dots that are slightly bigger but I have been unable to locate a similar-sized plastic rod, and so the dots on my necks stay at ¹⁄₁₆ in.

The fingerboard camber is decided upon, in this case 12 in (305 mm), and the board is cambered and prepared for fretting. It is much easier to fret a Fender-style neck before it is carved as the underneath is fully supported all the time, making fitting the frets a lot easier. The frets also serve to protect the fingerboard while the neck is held in the vice to be shaped. This guitar is fretted with Fender's standard wire, and when the frets are securely fitted and the ends have been tidied the neck is shaped.

The depth of the neck tapers from its full 1 in (25.4 mm) at the body end to between ⅞ in and ¾ in (19 and 22 mm) at a point between the nut and the first fret. This taper is marked and cut using either surforms or the band saw.

Since the slot in the body that accepts the neck is 3 in (76 mm) long the first 3 in of the neck are not shaped. The approximate curve of the neck is drawn onto this point to act as a rough guide. Similar curves are drawn at the head end.

The neck is carved in much the same way as with the previous guitar. Firstly the approximate shape at each end is cut and the corresponding points on the curves are joined in a series of straight lines along the neck. This is then tidied with spokeshaves and sandpaper before the whole neck is finish-sanded.

Commercially-produced guitars have their necks shaped on a very sophisticated machine. This has one master neck shape which is copied onto the other necks by follower bits. Each neck is then the same shape as the master. The Wal bass company use a spindle moulder with a bit that has been made to the shape they require for their necks. It is a very quick way of doing the job but not being mechanised to that extent, I have to rely on memory to carve one neck the same shape as any other.

The last job before spraying the neck is to fit the nut. The material used on this guitar is phenolic resin. This is not an exceptionally hard substance, in common with most alternative nut materials, but it is very slippery and so the strings tend to slide over the nut rather than wear it out. It also prevents the strings sticking when they are being tuned. Its only disadvantage is that it smells even worse than bone.

After the whole guitar has been finish-sanded it is grain-filled where necessary and sprayed. This is covered in greater detail in Chapter 13.

After the guitar has dried thoroughly it can be buffed and then assembled. Buffing the finish is also covered in Chapter 13.

As with the last guitar, the controls are part-wired before being inserted and the pick-ups are fitted to their surrounds. Their connecting wires are cut to length after having been fed through their channels to avoid any unnecessary mistakes and can be soldered to the controls before they too are fitted. The wire from the bridge plate to the control cavity is installed and the bridge screwed on. The full details of the wiring of this and the other two guitars is covered in Chapter 14.

After the final details have been added to the body, for example the strap buttons, knobs and the control cavity cover, the neck is fitted. The positions of the four neck screw holes are found from the jig and are marked with a centre-punch. These are drilled to ⅛ in (3.2 mm) to accept the screws, being careful not to emerge from the front of the neck. The four fixing screws are put through their metal plate and the neck is screwed on. This can be made a little easier if a little soap or candle wax is put onto the threads. The screws should be tightened progressively so that they do not distort the mounting plate. Winding one up to full tension before fitting the others is not the way to go.

Fitting the neck.

The machine-heads, in this case Schallers, are fitted taking care not to overtighten the small fixing screws, which are intended to stop the unit from turning rather than hold it in place. Each machine-head is held by the nut that extends through the head to the casing of the unit. This nut is tightened with a small box spanner.

When all is satisfactory the guitar can be set up as covered in Chapter 15.

The final job, after the strings have been fitted and the nut slots cut, is to fit the small retainer that holds the top two strings down into their slots in the nut.

11   The Third Guitar

The third and last guitar that I am making is a through-necked eight-string bass using some exotic wood.

Through-necked guitars are not new. Both Gibson and Rickenbacker made through-necked basses in the early 1960s. The idea of a through-necked guitar is very sound. The top frets on an electric guitar are used more often than the top frets on an acoustic guitar. If the bulky neck joint of the bolt-on or glued-in neck is removed then it should be easier to reach these top frets. (I used to make through-necked instruments as I did not like making neck tenons!)

For the book I have chosen to make an eight-string bass as they sound very impressive, but the extra strain on the neck from having twice as many strings as a standard bass means that the neck has to have twin truss rods. Again this is not a new idea. Rickenbacker put twin rods into most, if not all, of their guitars and the Guild company use twin rods in their 12-string guitars.

Another reason for making this guitar with eight strings is that I have a very nice eight-string bass

bridge that is just waiting to be used. It could be argued that this is an example of how to justify spending money on a bass bridge by spending many times the amount building a guitar around it but it serves a purpose. The methods used here, in particular the double truss rod, could equally be applied to five- or six-string basses.

THE NECK

The neck and central core of the body is made up from three pieces of maple 42 x 2½ x ¾ in (1066 x 63.5 x 19 mm). These are glued together with a contrasting layer of veneer between them which, when the guitar is finished, will give a thin line along the length of the neck. I am using a walnut veneer for this as it will roughly match the facings on the body.

The three laminates could be cut roughly to shape in the way described in Chapter 9, but gluing these with the veneer between them would be difficult as there would be twice as many glued surfaces that could slip when clamped and this would be difficult

The body laminates. Note the face of the hedua is marked to indicate which pieces are bookmatched.

Marking the body depth onto the centre section of the neck prior to band-sawing out the side elevation.

to line up properly. So, for this guitar, I am gluing them first and band-sawing the shape as I did on the carved-top guitar.

The three laminates and their veneers are glued using a good woodworking glue and as many clamps as possible. While this is drying out I have been fortunate in being able to glue up the body side laminates as I have access to enough clamps to do both jobs at once. Each side has a core of 1¼ in (31.7 mm) of maple and this is faced either side with ¼ in (6.3 mm) of a wood called hedua. This is

a highly-figured brown wood that is very hard. It is also quite boring to look at until it is sanded and either oiled or lacquered, when it becomes very pretty. It sometimes sold as Shedua or Ovankol.

When both the sides and the neck laminates have dried the clamps are removed.

The top surface of the neck is planed flat and square to the sides and the side elevation is drawn on. Firstly the angle of the head is drawn, which in this case is ten degrees, and length, which is 8¾ in (222.2 mm), and the depth, at ½ in (12.7 mm).

Checking the sides are square.

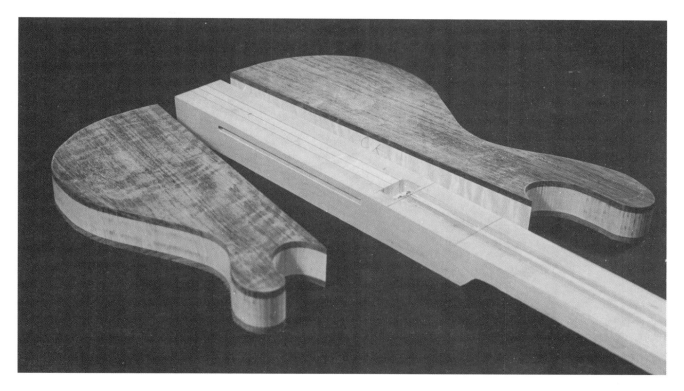

The length of the fingerboard, including the nut and the space after the last fret, is worked out, checked, and drawn on. The scale length of this guitar is 32½ in (825.5 mm). I would normally use a 34 in (863.6 mm) scale on a bass but I think that this would be a little too long on an eight-string instrument and shortening the scale length will lower the tension on an already overburdened neck.

As on the carved-top guitar, the neck needs to be angled back slightly from the body. This angle is smaller than on the carved-top guitar as the bridge is lower and the distance from the end of the fingerboard to the bridge is greater. This is calculated and the angle is drawn onto the wood starting at the end of the fingerboard. Even though the fingerboard is to cover a small area of the guitar's front, I am starting the angle at the end of the fingerboard as the neck angle is very shallow and the sides of the body can be brought down to the level of the fingerboard without looking strange.

The thickness of the body and the depth of the neck can be marked and the position and shape of the neck-to-body join can be decided and marked.

All dimensions are then double-checked before the neck and centre section are cut out on the band saw.

The body sides ready to be glued to the central core. The twin truss rods and their body-end adjustment are visible as well as the channel routed into the side of the central core to take the wires from the front pick-up. Just visible is a pencilled note on the upper body half showing that the builder thinks the join is OK.

The face of the head and the front of the body are planed flat and square and the centre line that is marked onto the face of the neck is extended along the face of the head and the front of the body centre.

The truss-rod channels are then cut. These are cut in the same way as on the carved-top guitar but are, of course, longer. They are cut with their centres 7/16 in (11 mm) apart, which will leave just enough room for a standard L-shaped truss-rod spanner to get at the adjustment nuts.

Instead of extending the truss-rod channels onto the face of the head for the adjustment hole to be cut they are extended onto the face of the body for ½ in (12.7 mm) after the end of the fingerboard, and a recess is cut for their adjustment, leaving just enough room to get the spanner on and off the nuts.

When both rods and their fillets have been fitted and left to dry they can be planed level with the front of the neck.

The sides being glued to the central core. The body is packed with the scrap which was removed when the sides were cut out.

The channel that links the front pick-up hole to the control cavity will be difficult to drill when the guitar is completed, and so a channel is cut into one side of the body centre so that the wires can be fed from the front pick-up to the control cavity through the rear pick-up cavity.

The body sides and the central core are planed square ready to be joined and the edge of the body shape can be marked onto each side, allowing for the width of the central core piece. Each side is roughly cut out, and when it is certain that the edges of the body sides and of the central core are square, the sides can be glued. It is worth using small locating pins to stop the sides slipping while they are being glued. These are made in the same way as described to stop the carved-top guitar's fingerboard slipping, although great care must be taken to ensure that none of the pins are in the pick-up positions, as

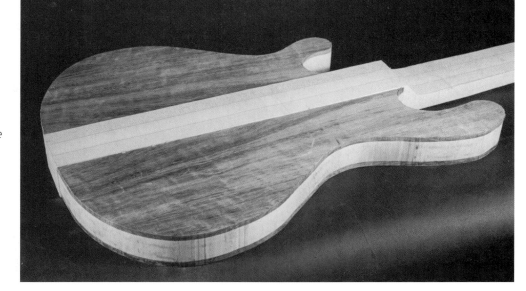

The body after gluing. The next stage is to plane the central core level with the back. It is at this time that the wisdom of pinning the sides while they are glued makes itself evident. Any slippage of the sides while being glued could be disasterous.

Using the drum sander. This one is fixed, unlike the one used in Chapter 9 which was fitted to a pillar drill.

The rounding-over bit. This one has a roller bearing that stops it burning the sides of the guitar.

when the pick-up holes are routed the pin could be thrown out, damaging the router bit and any eye that happened to be within the immediate vicinity. Clamping the sides is made a little easier if the pieces left over after cutting the body sides are used as clamping cauls to prevent the guitar sides being damaged by the sash clamps.

When the glue has dried the guitar is placed face downwards on the workbench and the central core is planed level with the sides.

Since this guitar is a one-off it is not worth making up a jig for the body shape and so this is cut to its final shape in much the same way as the carved-top guitar. A jig could be made and the guitar tidied on the pin router or table router but I have decided to do this by hand with the aid of a small drum sander. The edges of the guitar are then rounded over using a ½ in (12.7 mm) radius follower bit, taking care not to remove any wood from the area that will be covered by the fingerboard.

The very small amount of neck angle can be seen in this photograph. This can be blended in to the top of the guitar without being too obvious. A greater angle might require a different approach, such as stepping the end of the neck above the face of the body.

(above) The sides of the head are built up with small pieces of maple with more walnut veneer between them.

(below) Using a coping saw to cut out the shape of the head.

The body is blended into the neck and the contouring on the front and rear of the body are cut with surforms and spokeshaves.

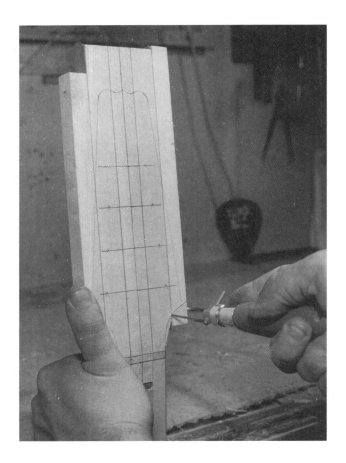

The guitar can now have the pick-up holes and control cavity routed. Even though it was not worth going to the trouble of making a full body jig it is worth making a jig up for the pick-up holes. This is made as described before. The control cavity is also jigged and a jig is made for the cover plate and its recess.

As the guitar has a slight neck angle the body sides will be a little proud of the central core in the area in which the fingerboard is situated, and so they are pared down. Since this shaping takes place in the area of the cutaways and the angle is small it is not readily noticeable when the guitar is completed.

The sides of the head are built up to their full width with small strips of maple. These are glued with a strip of veneer between them and the rest of

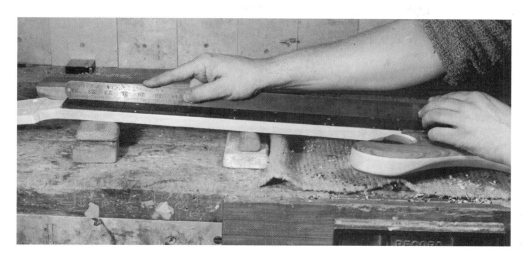

Checking the fingerboard is straight before fitting the frets. Note how the neck is supported.

the neck to match the other laminates. When these are dry the head shape is cut with a coping saw and is cleaned up with sandpaper.

The fingerboard is next to be prepared and when ready is glued onto the face of the neck. When dry the clamps are removed, the board is checked to make sure that it is level, and the frets are fitted.

Carving the neck using surforms and spokeshaves.

Shaping the neck is not as straightforward as it was on the other two guitars as the body did not get in the way as it does here. However, the order of work is the same. Firstly the head end of the neck is rough carved, and then the shape at the body end. The body end is a little more complicated as the neck shape is carried on into the body for a short way, and so not only the neck but a certain amount of the body needs to be carved. This is marked onto

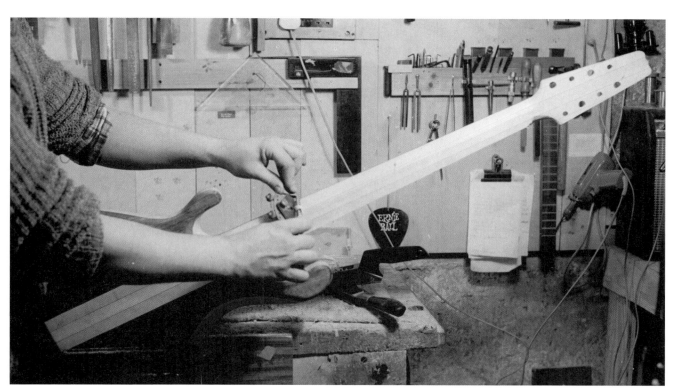

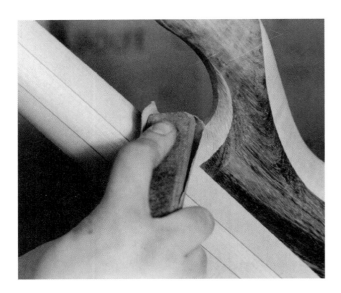

Sanding the cutaways using the sandpaper over a shaped cork block.

the back of the body in chalk. When this has been done the shape at either end can be joined using the surform in straight lines before cleaning the neck up with spokeshaves and sandpaper. Carving a neck such as this is made easier if the guitar is held in a vice or clamped to the workbench. Before doing this the vice and workbench must be checked for any hard or sharp objects that could damage the surface of the guitar.

Wet-sanding the guitar with Danish oil.

After the neck has been carved the machine-head holes are drilled. With a guitar this size it is a two-handed job. One person holds the guitar body steady while the other positions the head and drills the holes.

The final jobs on the body can now be attended to. The largest of these is the contouring of the front and the rear of the body so that it is more comfortable to hold. The positions of these recesses are marked in chalk and the waste is removed with surforms and spokeshaves before the whole lot is cleaned up using sandpaper. It is important that these contours blend in with the rest of the shaping of the guitar, such as the rounding over of the edge of the body.

The control positions are drilled, as is the hole that will accept the socket. Finally, the small hole that takes the earth wire from the control cavity to under the bridge is drilled with a ⅛ in (3 mm) extra-long drill.

The last job is to fit the nut and the guitar is ready for finish-sanding.

I have decided to finish this guitar in oil and wax, a finish that has become popular over the last few years. There are a variety of products that are suitable for use in this way and several ways of applying the finish. Since first writing this book I have found a far easier way of doing this and this is the method which is described here.

The oil used is known as Danish oil and this sets in the wood. Firstly the fingerboard is masked and the guitar is hung in a well-ventilated space. The guitar is liberally coated in oil. It is at this stage that any defects in the sanding of the guitar will show up, and slight scratches not removed will be readily apparent and will need to be dealt with. On the plus side, the oil will bring out the full beauty of the grain.

When the oil has soaked into the guitar and started to dry, the excess can be wiped off and the guitar left to dry out completely. This may take a day or two depending on the temperature.

The next stage is to wet-sand the entire guitar using 000 or 0000 grade wire wool and some more of the oil. This is a messy job but gives a very smooth surface. When all of the residue from the first oiling is removed and the surface is as smooth as a used-car salesman, the guitar should be wiped completely clean and again left to dry, at least overnight.

The wax to be used is beeswax. This is available in a variety of forms, both prepared and raw.

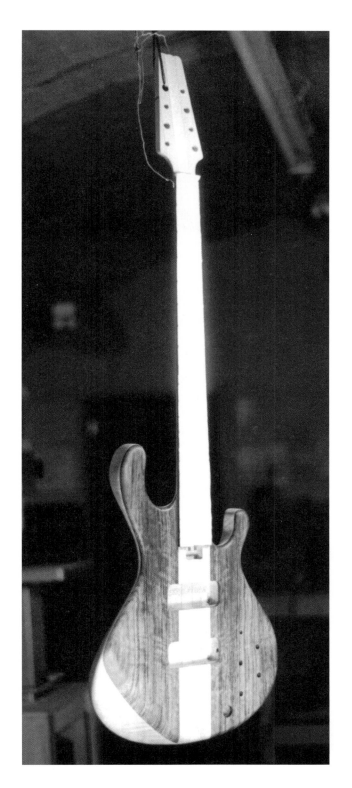

The controls are part-wired before fitting as access is easier.

Beeswax is very hard and if used raw will need to be softened with turpentine. It is far easier to use a ready-prepared beeswax, such as Briwax, which is already soft.

The wax is applied to the guitar using yet more 0000 grade wire wool. It will dry out relatively quickly – you will be able to tell by how sticky your fingers become – and a thin film can be built up. After two or three applications the wax can be allowed to dry out completely.

The final job is to buff the guitar with a stiff brush. This evens out the finish and can produce a good shine.

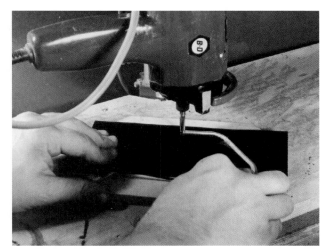

The guitar hanging in the workshop while drying out.

Making a control plate on a small pin router.

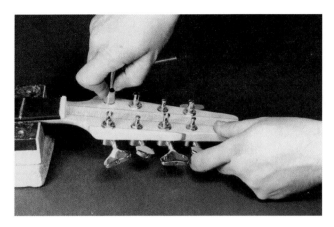

Fitting the machine-heads.

Finally stringing the new guitar.

The advantage of oil and wax as a finish is that, if the first attempt is not too good, it is little trouble to add another coat of wax. It is also very easy to maintain, and any bumps or scratches can be easily repaired.

The guitar can now be put together. This is done in much the same order as the previous two guitars. The tone circuit and the pick-ups are wired and fitted. The bridge is the Schaller eight-string unit and the machine-heads are made up from a set of Schaller M4s and two-thirds of a set of Schaller M6s. The remaining two machine-heads will be useful as spares, or I may add them to another set and build a mandocello – another example of saving money by spending more which, over fifteen years after the first edition was published, is still waiting to be made.

The final details are added: the strap buttons, knobs, control cover and a wooden truss-rod cover – made from a small leftover piece of the centre laminate so that it matches – are fitted, as is the connector. I have used a Canon audio-connector on this guitar as they are more robust than the normal jack sockets.

Finally the guitar is strung, using a set of eight-string bass strings sold by Rotosound, and set up. Not all manufacturers sell prepared sets of eight strings, but most sell custom gauge strings individually that could be used to make up an eight-string set.

The sound of the finished instrument is very impressive and it is surprisingly easy to play. Even for a non-bass player such as myself.

Fitting the truss-rod cover, made from a section laminate.

12   Mixing the Styles

In the last three chapters I have attempted to show as many of the possible styles and variations in guitar-making with just three guitars.

However, if you have taken the trouble to design a guitar of your own it is unlikely that it will include all of the same features as any one of the guitars that I have made. Providing that the construction of the guitar is attempted in the right order and is properly planned out beforehand, this should not prove to be much of a problem.

Most guitar designs will fall into one of the categories that I have covered, but as a rough guide to what is possible I shall now include a few notes on how these guitars could have been made differently or how other features could be added to the designs. Differences in finish or electrics are easily dealt with and so the notes here only apply to the construction.

THE FIRST GUITAR

There are a number of differences that can easily be incorporated into this design. The guitar that I have made is a carved-top guitar similar in style to the Gibson Les Paul, Yamaha SG series or Paul Reed Smiths. These have maple tops to increase the sustain and it would be a simple job to fit a maple top to this guitar and to make it the same thickness, which on both the Yamaha and the Les Paul is ½ in (12.7 mm) deeper than the guitar that I made at 2¼ in (57.1 mm). The prettiest-looking, and subsequently most valuable, Les Pauls had book-matched flame maple tops as I used on the Telecaster, but others, made at different times, had up to seven pieces of maple on the top.

Maple tops are usually bound to hide the join between the two different types of body wood. The

A different approach to mounting controls on a carved-top guitar can be seen on this bass by Roger Giffin. The area around the controls has been left uncontoured.

The binding channel on many early Gibson Les Pauls followed the top contour of the body so that part of the maple facing was visible inside the cutaway. Later Les Pauls had the binding channel parallel with the back of the guitar so the binding at this point in the cutaway was quite deep.

poplar top too could easily be bound. The binding channel could be cut in the same way as on the Telecaster-style guitar but would have to be done before the top was carved and the angle of the neck planed. Since the binding channel would be quite deep to allow for ¼ in (6.3 mm) of carving, the channel would have to be cut in several passes to stop the wood splitting. The binding would be fitted after the top had been carved as otherwise it could be damaged or pulled off accidentally.

The binding channel could be cut after the top is bound but a jig would need to be made up to allow the router to cut the channel without the router

Side elevation and 3D of a glued-in neck raised above the top surface of a flat-topped guitar, as fitted to many Gibson SGs.

base fouling the guitar top. Stewart Macdonald sell an attachment for a Dremel router for just this job which is usually used by makers of arch-top jazz guitars and carved mandolins.

The top of the guitar need not be carved. It is simpler to make a guitar with a flat top, but the neck would have to be fitted in a different way. It is possible, since the guitar has two cutaways, to hide the neck angle in the same way as was done on the eight-string, by carving the inside of the cutaways (see page 127), but as the neck angle on the six-string is a little steeper, this might not be as inconspicuous as it is on the eight-string. The most common way of dealing with the problem is to raise the end of the fingerboard over the body. This means that the neck angle is starting from the edge of the body, not the end of the fingerboard, and so it may be slightly shallower. This extension above the front of the guitar is used on many of Gibson's flat-topped guitars, from the early 1950s Les Paul Juniors with one cutaway to today's SGs.

Cutting the neck slot in the body on a flat-topped guitar is not as straightforward as on the carved-top guitar as the bottom of the slot may still need to be sloped. The simplest way is to make up an angled jig so that the router will cut the channel at the correct angle so that a straight-bottomed tenon could be cut onto the neck. The neck angle could also be achieved by keeping the slot flat-bottomed and cutting the tenon at the end of the neck with all of the relevant angles.

The heads on some guitars are bound and this is done in the same way as the Telecaster body, cutting carefully around the head with the router, taking care not to slip off the sides of the head. Complex head shapes may be difficult to bind as the router will have difficulty in getting into any awkward

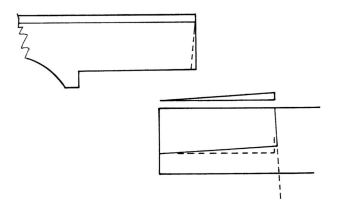

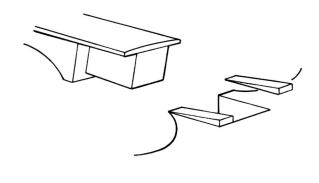

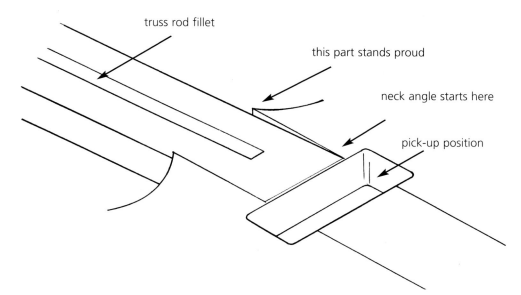

truss rod fillet

this part stands proud

neck angle starts here

pick-up position

Some carved-top guitars fitted with a straight-through neck would have the sides of the body very proud of the face of the neck. This might be difficult to hide in the way that was done on the eight-string. However, binding would be easy to fit at this stage.

shapes. These may have to be carefully finished off by hand. It is an interesting point that many Gibson guitars with bound headstocks have a head facing made of fibreboard which is prebound before being fitted to the head. The head is then cut to match.

Making the guitar with a straight-through neck and a carved top is fairly straightforward. The centre section would be made in much the same way as the eight-string, firstly glued together and then cut out and planed. The sides would then be cut to their full depth and, when square, glued to the centre section. They would stand proud of the neck where the neck angle starts and this would be carved down when the top was carved. If binding was fitted it would be an easy enough job to cut the channel in the same way as has been described for the glued-in neck guitar, either before or after the body is carved but before the fingerboard is fitted.

To make the guitar with a bolt-on neck the slot in the body could still be cut at an angle as was done for the glued-in neck. The only difference would be that the neck, at the body end, would remain the same width as the fingerboard. Nothing would need to be removed to make the tenon, and so the slot in the body would be the same shape as the end of the neck, that is to say slightly tapered. When making a bolt-on neck guitar whose dimensions are not exactly the same as a Fender, it should be remembered that Fender neck screws are quite long and could emerge from the front of the fingerboard with disastrous results if the body is thinner; if the body is thicker, the screws need to be

checked to ensure there is enough thread available to get a good join.

THE SECOND GUITAR

This guitar is already an example of what can be done to change an existing design. It would be a very simple job to have made this guitar as a standard Telecaster with standard pick-ups and fittings and no binding on an ash or alder body. However, that would have missed the point of Chapter 3 entirely and this sort of activity is quite rightly frowned upon by Fender. Even so, other alternatives are still possible. The fingerboard could be bound to match the body. Cream binding on a maple neck would not show up very well, so black could be used, depending on the circumstances. The binding channel would have to be cut into the neck while the fingerboard was still flat and before the fret slots were cut. The binding itself would be fitted after the fret slots were cut, but before the neck was fretted.

The guitar could also just as easily have a rosewood or ebony fingerboard. Many Fender necks were made with rosewood fingerboards. Early necks have the truss rod fitted from the front, as on a Gibson, with the board glued on top. Later Fender necks had the fingerboard fitted in a slightly different way and the truss rod was fitted from the rear as on a one-piece maple neck.

A rosewood fingerboard could be bound using the same procedure as above or could be bound before fitting. Cream binding and fancy inlays would not

The Giffin bass showing how the neck has no angle but is stepped above the front slightly (see page 25). This is made easier by the neck laminate being the same width as the end of the fingerboard. If it were any wider some carving would be required to blend the top and neck together.

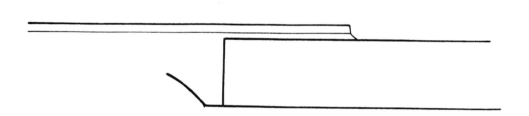

Side elevation showing the stepped end of the fingerboard.

look out of place. Several Fenders were made in the mid-1960s with bound rosewood fingerboards with block inlays and these are now worth quite a lot of money, depending on condition and model.

There would be little point in carving the top of this guitar in the same way as was done on the first guitar – although the Fender Custom Shop have produced some carved-top, fixed-neck Telecasters – but if the body was not faced it could be contoured in the same way as a Stratocaster to make it a little more comfortable to play.

The guitar could have been made with a glued-in neck by simply adjusting the size of the neck slot and tenon but the truss rod would have to be fitted from the front with a separate fingerboard and the adjustment would be easier to fit at the head end of

the neck. However, it is one of the nice advantages of the bolt-on neck that if a neck should warp or get broken it is a simple job to replace it.

The Telecaster could be made with a straight-through neck but again the truss rod would have to be fitted from the front and a separate fingerboard fitted. There is no way that a neck angle could be hidden as it was on the eight-string as the Telecaster only has one cutaway. It would be just as easy to make the guitar with no neck angle with the board raised a little above the top surface of the body. The centre section would be made in the same way as described already and the truss-rod channel cut while it is still parallel. The face of the neck that would accept the fingerboard would be planed flat and the side elevation marked. The small step down

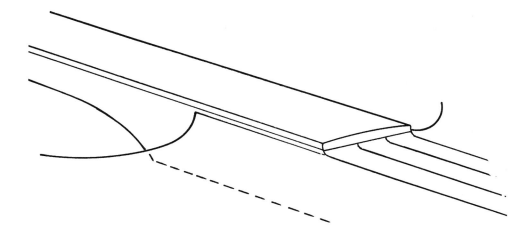

If the guitar was to have a straight-through neck and no facing the centre section would show through the body as on the eight-string bass.

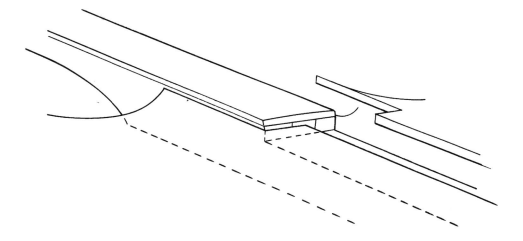

Facing a straight-through neck can be done but requires some careful fitting of the facings around the end of the neck.

on the front of the body would be cut down almost to the line on the band saw and the sides glued on before tidying up the front. This would leave the centre section visible through the body as it was on the eight-string.

The body could be faced in the same way as I have done, with a straight-through neck, but the work could be a little tricky. The centre section through the body would need to be stepped down further than it would if it was going to show, and the facing would have to be fitted closely around the end of the neck. This style is used on some of Paul Hamer's guitars and some of Yamaha's SG series of the late 1970s.

By far the easiest modification to a basic Fender-style neck is the addition of an extra fret on a fingerboard extension.

THE THIRD GUITAR

The design of the eight-string is easily convertible to a bolt-on or glued-in neck design using the pointers that I have given in the last two sections of this chapter. In both cases it would be easier to dispense with the neck angle and fit the neck so that the fingerboard is slightly proud of the body using similar dimensions to a Fender bass.

The top of the guitar could be carved but the carving would need to take into account the relatively small neck angle.

Fingerboard and body binding could easily be incorporated regardless of the style of neck join and in all cases it would be fitted before the fingerboard was glued to the guitar. Other styles of truss rod could be used but would have to be long enough to work over the whole length of the neck.

Using the same basic design it would have been just as easy to make the guitar with four, five or six strings, a wider neck and different hardware.

Some people choose to make these instruments with a longer scale length but this can cause problems in finding strings. Wal guitars are built to a standard 34 in scale and have few problems, providing suitable gauges of string are fitted. If a standard four-string bass was made only one truss rod would be needed. For the five- or six-string options a stronger neck laminate or multiple rods might be needed. It would

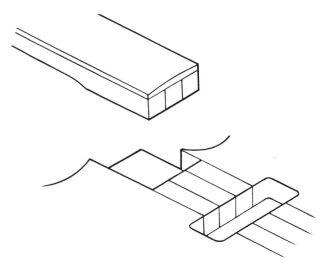

Converting the eight-string design to bolt-on or glued-in neck construction would be straightforward. The laminates could be kept through the centre of the body to give the impression of a straight-through design.

not be necessary to change the pick-ups to specific five- or six-string models as the ones used have a bar magnet that picks up everything along its width.

Making a four-, five- or six-string fretless would be simple too. It could be made with or without fret position markers, and only the adjustment after assembly would be different.

A Wal five-string bass showing the typically well thought-out design. It features the bolt-on neck (see page 23), a full two-octave neck and a neat body-end truss-rod adjustment. The string spacing has been carefully worked out and the pick-ups and bridge designed around these measurements. The end result is a fine bass that even looks good when placed on their tastelessly carpeted assembly table.

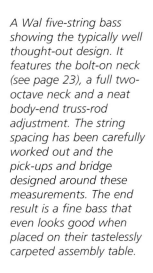

SEMI-ACOUSTICS

Of course, you could choose to make a semi-acoustic guitar. These can be either very complicated or quite simple to make. A Gibson 335-type would be very difficult as the top and back would need to be carved inside and out and the central core either left or built in afterwards. On the other hand, Fender made a thinline version of the Telecaster which had all of the same fittings as a standard

This pair of photographs from the Warmoth catalogue shows the construction features of a replacement Telecaster Thinline body. (Courtesy of Warmoth Products.)

Telecaster but the body was hollowed out. The bridge remained solid so the strings were still fitted through the body. The area around the pick-ups also remained solid but the rest of the guitar was routed and a separate top glued on.

The author's carved-top semi-acoustic. A great sound – but a lot of work.

This system can be adapted for many designs. When Brian May built his Red Special he built acoustic pockets into the body to help it feedback. Similarly, it would have been very simple to have routed out cavities in the top of the mahogany used on the sunburst Telecaster in Chapter 10 before fitting the maple top. Even something like a Stratocaster could be adapted for this method but careful thought would need to go into the design if the tremolo system was still to be used and if the body was to have the contouring found on normal Strats.

I have built semi-acoustic guitars with carved tops, similar to the guitar in Chapter 9, with the body routed hollow and the top carved both inside and out. (Note that the area around the neck tenon needs to be left with enough wood to support the neck.) These guitars sound somewhere in between a typical hollow-bodied semi-acoustic and a solid, with a lot of attack from the string, owing to the fact they are pulled through the body, a lot of sustain and a more rounded quality to the tone. They are, however, quite difficult to make and require a lot of planning. The guitar in the photograph also had some contouring on the rear of the body which was carved on the inside. This was an interesting exercise since access to it was difficult and great care had to be taken to ensure the thickness of what remained was sufficient. I chose to make this guitar without any soundhole but 'f' holes could easily have been added.

This, I think, just about covers the ways that the styles can be mixed or adapted. While I have attempted to show as many of the options as possible, there may be something I have missed. Even if I have not managed to show everything I hope that I have given enough information for you to attempt your chosen design with the minimum of fuss and that you will avoid some of the pitfalls and potential disasters that lurk around every corner.

Of course, you do not have to make guitars. This semi-acoustic electric mandolin owes its inspiration to the Gibson Les Paul Junior and is made using many of the techniques discussed in this book.

13 Finishing

The finish on the guitar is the icing on the cake. A good guitar does not need to have a super finish but it will give a better impression if it has. It could be argued that a guitar does not need to have a finish at all as it is a cosmetic job but this is not true. The finish on the guitar will protect the wood from damage and moisture, and since a finish is going to be applied it might as well look good.

Most old acoustic guitars, and many of today's finest hand-made classical guitars, are French-polished. This gives a very good shine while allegedly retaining the acoustic properties of the guitar. In recent years most guitars, both acoustic and electric, have been sprayed with one or two finishes that are much easier and quicker to apply, but if you have problems spraying or finding some of the materials, French polishing, although hard work, will give an excellent finish, especially on a guitar with pretty woods. There are other finishes that may be easier to apply but the end result might not be as glossy.

Finishing is entirely a matter of personal taste. There was a time when guitars came in sunburst. Gibson introduced a gold finish in the early 1950s and Fender used car colours. Today anything is possible, as this line up of Epiphone Les Pauls shows. These range from pink to green and ownership should be licensed.

LACQUERS

One of the most common finishes used on guitars is nitro-cellulose lacquer (also known as cellulose) and this can be sprayed clear, stained, sunburst or solid-coloured. This was used by most manufacturers until the mid-1960s when two-pack lacquers took over with some manufacturers.

Various chemical two-pack epoxy-based finishes are available in the same range of colours as cellulose but, whereas cellulose is air-dried, meaning that the solvents in the lacquer gradually evaporate into the atmosphere, the two-pack chemically cures. This enables it to be applied more thickly than cellulose, and as it sets quicker it is more economic when large amounts of guitars are being produced, as the guitars do not have to sit around waiting for the lacquer to dry. Admittedly, cellulose does seem to feel a litte nicer to play on as there is perhaps a little more friction between the hand and polyester.

In recent years, the advent of stricter environmental controls in some areas, most notably California, has meant that some of the West Coast guitar manufacturers have had to find alternatives to both of the above. Some of these have been less successful than others but the need for development has produced some finishes that are now very suitable for guitars. Many of these newer finishes are water-based and the techniques used to apply them are similar to those used for cellulose. They can be obtained from guitar parts supply companies who will often be able to supply technical notes on how best to apply them.

There are some companies that will spray a guitar for you; however this can be an expensive business. The alternative is to finish the guitar yourself in a spraybooth of some kind.

Spraying any form of paint is going to require a certain amount of equipment and will release a lot of small particles of paint and solvent, be it water or one of the cellulose thinners, into the atmosphere. These particles will not do your health any good at all and so spraying should always be done in a proper spraybooth with efficient extractor fans removing the nasties and filtering it before releasing the air back into the atmosphere.

Having said this, I am guilty in the past of using spray equipment in areas that were not really suitable or properly ventilated. The problems are not only those of health, but many lacquers and their solvents are highly flammable and therefore a considerable fire hazard. The solvents in cellulose have a debilitating effect on the human body and two-pack lacquers, such as polyesters and polyurethanes, are positively dangerous. All manufacturers' recommendations regarding the use of these materials must be followed to the letter.

Clearly if you have chosen to finish your guitar sunburst, access to a good spraygun is essential. You could attempt to do the job with a small airbrush but this would be rather like trying to bale out the *Titanic* with a teaspoon. The airbrush, quite simply, would not be up to the job and, unlike with the *Titanic*, there would be no band to listen to.

Sprayguns and compressors can be hired from most good hire centres and this is worth looking into if you intend to do the job at home but there are things that must be considered.

If you really must do the job without a spraybooth, which is not advised for the reasons given above, a well-ventilated area should be used and a face mask worn, and if any ill feelings are experienced whilst spraying you should cease immediately to allow time for the body to recover. During the Second World War, to protect workers in aeroplane factories which used cellulose dope on fabric surfaces, extra milk was allowed as it helped combat the effects of the dope. It is worth trying the same thing if spraying at home.

Any area used for spraying, either at home or in a spraybooth, should be fairly warm and dry as cold and wet conditions do not suit cellulose or most other lacquers at all. If at all possible this area should be dust-free. It should also be remembered that there will be a lot of mess from oversprayed paint settling on all surfaces.

A good finish can be achieved with careful use of car spray or some of the commercially-available spray lacquers, providing they are applied and buffed properly, as many are cellulose based and similar to what would be used anyway. Car spray is ideal if a block colour finish is chosen as there are hundreds to choose from, but avoid the metallics for a first guitar.

Obviously cans cannot be used to give a sunburst or stained finish but there are some clear lacquers in spray cans that can be used to give a very good natural finish. Not all clear lacquers sold in cans are thick enough to build up into a coat that can be buffed, but some are perfectly usable. Some are sold by companies such as Stewart Macdonald and Luthier's Mercantile, but remember if you are outside the US companies such as these cannot send certain substances to you through the post.

Spraying a complete guitar in one of these lacquers would be very expensive but for small areas, such as Fender-style necks, they are very useful.

COATING BY BRUSH

If you really must have a tinted finish and you cannot or do not want to go to all the trouble of spraying the guitar, then a brushed-on finish is an alternative. Some products are better for this than others; for example, do not even consider using tinned polyurethane or yacht varnish on a guitar as they are too soft to give a good finish.

Proper brushing cellulose can be used, although it can be difficult to apply, as well as some plastic coatings. When Brian May made his guitar he used a product called Rustins Plastic Coating. This is still available and is sold in some good craft shops; the address of the company is included in the rear of this book and they will be only too willing to supply the name of your local stockist.

The Plastic Coating is a two-pack finish that comes in clear, black and white. Other block colours are not available as the hardener used is acid-based, and this can interfere with some pigments, but the coating is compatible with a whole range of wood dyes sold by Rustins, hence the red finish on Brian May's guitar.

With any brushed-on finish the final coat will never be as smooth as one that can be achieved by spraying and so the finish needs to be slightly thicker to allow for the amount of rubbing down that will be needed before the final polishing. Again, the manufacturer's own literature is a good starting point to find the best way of using and polishing the finish.

PREPARATION

The most important aspect of the finishing is not the type of finish used or the way that the finish is applied but the care taken to prepare the wood beforehand.

Firstly, the guitar should be finish-sanded correctly. The harsher grades of sandpaper used in the making of the guitar will smooth out any unevenness in the wood, so that all curves are gradual, without bumps or dips, and the flat surfaces of the guitar are not pitted or undulating. They will, however, leave scratch marks on the wood and these will have to be removed. With finish-sanding there is no substitute for hard work; the better you do it the more your arms ache, and the more effort that is put into removing all of the scratches caused by the tools and the sandpaper, the easier it will be to finish the guitar.

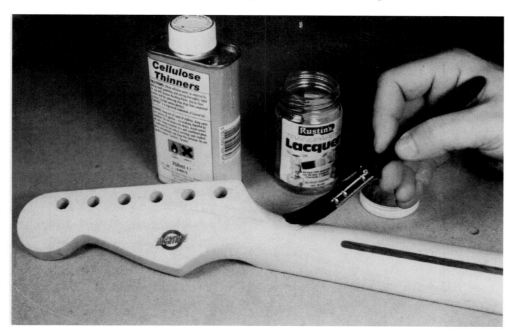

Coating by brush. This is using a clear cellulose sold in the UK by Rustins on a Mighty Mite Stratocaster-style neck. The problems with coating in this way are that brush marks are hard to remove and drips can be a problem. It is also harder to achieve an even finish. This is not recommended for tinted finishes.

Rubbing grainfiller into the pores of the wood using a soft cloth.

Wiping the excess grainfiller across the grain.

The worst marks on the body are sanded first with 120 grade paper, then 240 grade and finally 320 grade before rubbing the whole guitar down with 0000 grade wire wool. The wire wool will not only remove any remaining small scratches but will remove the dust from any places that it may have accumulated, hiding any blemishes in the wood. If a blemish appears after the guitar has been wire-wooled it is because the sanding was not done well enough and some of it will have to be done again.

When all of the marks have been removed from the guitar it should have one last check before the grain is filled.

Most woods require a grainfiller to stop the lacquer sinking into the wood. Exceptions include maple and alder as they are very close-grained and only need finish-sanding before spraying.

The grainfiller that is used should be compatible with the finish that is to be applied. The technical staff at Rustins say that no grainfiller is needed with their Plastic Coating as the finish is thick enough not to need one, and since the hardener is acid-based the grainfiller would tend to lift if one was used.

However, when using cellulose on a wood such as mahogany or ash a grainfiller is essential. The filler used should be the right colour for the wood if a clear or tinted finish is to be used. Most are available in white as well as a selection of wood colours.

The grainfiller is applied to the wood with a soft cloth (the cloth in the photograph is the mortal remains of an advertising T-shirt), along the grain, and the excess should be removed across the grain with another cloth, or piece of T-shirt. Care must be taken to ensure that the filler does not lift out of the pores when doing this as if it does a second application may be required.

When the filler is dry (two or three hours should be sufficient), it should be lightly sanded with 320 grade sandpaper.

The next stage will depend upon which finish is chosen. If the finish is to be clear cellulose, applied with either a spraygun or a brush, a sanding-sealer is often used before the lacquer. This is a clear substance that builds up quite quickly to fill the remainder of the grain and to provide a base for the subsequent clear coats.

Several coats are sprayed or brushed on and the guitar is left to dry. It is then wet-sanded with 320 grade wet-and-dry paper. Flat areas are sanded using the paper over a cork sanding block and rounded areas are sanded carefully by hand. The better the finish on the sanding-sealer the easier it will be to get a good finish on the lacquer.

APPLYING THE FINISH

As I have mentioned previously, manufacturers are often a good source of advice. Most types of finish will require slightly different application processes. For example, it is possible to spray different consistencies of lacquer, depending on the pressure used in the gun.

For many years I thinned lacquer by about 40 per cent before spraying and then sprayed anything up to 20 coats. A good friend, with whom I shared a sprayshop, had a conversation with the representative of the company that supplied our lacquer and

Masking the fingerboard of the carved-top guitar prior to spraying. The board is masked twice, once to cover just the front and again to cover the binding. That way when the colour is applied just the binding can be uncovered. Note also the bridge mounting holes have been plugged with tape to stop paint build up.

Spraying clear lacquer onto the Telecaster neck using a spray can. Not all clear lacquers in cans are thick enough to build up for a good shine. Most guitar-makers' suppliers will be able to recommend a good brand.

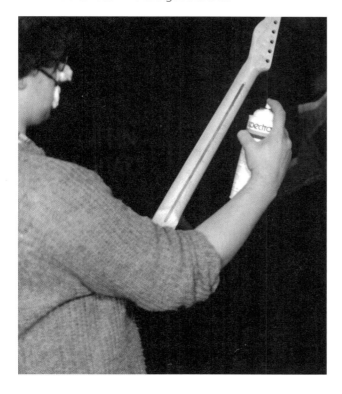

was told to spray it much thicker. The thinner the lacquer is, the less solids are contained in it and the more thinner has to escape before it can dry. By thickening up the lacquer we were able to get more onto the guitar with each coat and by careful spraying were able to get a good finish without the 'orange peel' effect that often happens when lacquer is too thick. With careful grainfilling I have managed to get a good finish onto a guitar with just four coats. This is about the same as at least one major manufacturer uses. They finish a complete guitar in just four coats in around one hour using a lacquer rather than a two-pack. The guitars are grainfilled and then given a sealer coat, colour coat and two clear coats. Between each coat the finish is flattened down, and after each coat the guitar passes through a graduated oven that helps harden the lacquer which has been sprayed on using a chemical retarder to stop it drying until it hits the guitar. After the final coat the guitar is buffed to a fine shine.

As already mentioned, if spraying a clear finish onto maple it is not entirely necessary to even sanding-seal the wood. The neck made in Chapter 10 was sprayed with clear lacquer from a can. This was applied directly to the wood and about 15 coats were needed before the neck was left to dry out.

After the final coat of lacquer the guitar is left in a warm area for at least a week for the lacquer to dry out thoroughly before it is buffed to its final finish.

It is possible to apply too much lacquer. This will

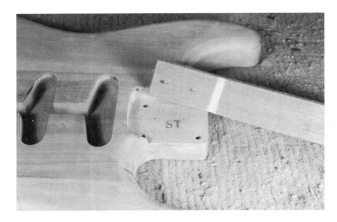

This handle is screwed into the neck recess of Fender-style guitars so the guitar can be held safely during spraying. A ridge has been cut into the area where the edge of the neck socket would be so that paint does not build up and join the guitar body and handle together.

Applying the sunburst onto the Telecaster body. The tinted lacquer is sprayed from the centre outwards so that more builds up around the edge. The centre remains predominantly yellow.

produce drips or curtaining, when a whole area of the finish decides to succumb to the effects of gravity. A rule of thumb that might help is to spray the lacquer onto the guitar so that it is just beginning to look wet. Any less and the finish will look a little like orange peel, and will need slightly more work to buff; and any more and the finish will run.

A tinted finish is applied in much the same way. I prefer not to stain the wood of the guitar body as the end grain will soak up more of the stain and will appear darker. However, on the front of guitars (for example the guitar made in Chapter 10) the yellow of the sunburst does not continue onto the back and sides of the guitar and so can be applied directly to the wood. If doing a complete guitar I prefer to suspend the dye in the lacquer and to spray it after the sanding-sealer has been applied and sanded. Several thin coats of the dye and lacquer mixture will build up to quite an even colour but beware of drips, which will mean stripping the guitar and starting again as you will never get rid of them.

Attempting a tinted finish by brush with cellulose may not be a good idea as the brush could make the colour very streaky. For a tinted finish with the Plastic Coating using one of Rustins' own wood dyes, one also has to beware of streaking, but several carefully applied thin coats would help keep the colour even.

Sunburst finishes come in a variety of colours. The most common are the so-called cherry sunburst, often used on Gibson Les Pauls, and a three-colour

black, red and yellow sunburst often found on Fenders. Many early Fender Stratocasters were finished in a two-tone sunburst of a yellow base and deep brown shading, which was actually a black dye which looked brown where it partially covered the yellow beneath.

The Telecaster body made in Chapter 10 is finished in Gibson-style cherry sunburst. Firstly, after finish-sanding and grainfilling of the mahogany back, the yellow stain is applied to the front of the guitar. This is applied directly onto the wood using a soft cloth, or old advertising T-shirt, and is left to dry for an hour or so.

Before the cherry stain can be sprayed onto the guitar the binding needs to be masked. The top edge of the binding is impossible to mask, but the sides are covered with masking tape. The guitar body is fixed to a small wooden handle, screwed into the neck slot, that is used to hold the body while it is being sprayed and this has a hole drilled in the other

Lightly sanding the guitar between coats.

end that can be used to hang the body on a hook while it dries out.

The cherry stain is mixed with lacquer and is thinned to make it suitable for the spraygun. The sunburst is sprayed on in a series of thin coats that extend further into the centre of the body to begin with and gradually move out so that extra coats are sprayed onto the edges which need to be a deeper colour. The back of the guitar is sprayed solid cherry. Early sunburst Les Pauls made until 1960 were sprayed in this way. Later reissues had sunburst backs and necks.

When the body has had time to dry the masking is removed from the binding. This is then cleaned up using a scalpel blade very carefully as a scraper. The top edge of the binding, which was left unmasked, is also scraped clean. After scraping the binding is given a gentle sanding with 320 grade wet-and-dry, used dry, to remove any marks.

The whole body is then clear lacquered. The first few coats of lacquer must be sprayed on very carefully to avoid any drips which, at this stage, will soften the finish beneath and cause the cherry stain to run, ruining the sunburst. This would then have to be stripped off and resprayed. After the final coat of lacquer the guitar is left for at least a week before it is buffed.

It has become fashionable to have some sort of artwork on guitars. This is fine but can cause all sorts of problems. Firstly, the materials used on the actual painting must be compatible with whatever will cover them. Putting cellulose over oil paints will ruin the painting. Secondly, great care must be taken not to get any runs on the guitar as these will be impossible to remove and may make the picture beneath run too.

There are two ways of spraying a guitar in a block colour. Which method is best depends upon whether a complete guitar is being sprayed or just a guitar body, whether the guitar is a simple block colour or a metallic and whether the guitar or guitar body is bound.

Many Fender guitars that are sprayed in a block colour have the colour coat itself buffed and polished to give the shine. This method is very easy to duplicate using either a spraygun or aerosol car spray. The alternative is to use the method that Gibson and many other makers employ. In this case the guitar is sprayed with its colour coats and then oversprayed with clear lacquer. This method is not very easy if you intend to use spray cans but it is quite straightforward if using a spraygun. Metallic colours are probably the most difficult to spray and are probably best attempted after some experience has been gained elsewhere. These are oversprayed with clear lacquer as buffing a metallic paint is not possible. Even more difficult are the glitter finishes that require a large amount of lacquer over the top to get a good finish.

To simply spray and buff the colour coat on a complete guitar would not be a good idea as the paint would build up in a ridge along the bottom edge of the fingerboard which would have had to have been masked to stop the paint obscuring the side position dots. It is much neater, in this case, to spray a thin colour coat, unmask the sides of the fingerboard, leaving the face of it still covered, and then spray the clear coats so that they cover the sides of the fingerboard. This method should always be used when the guitar fingerboard is bound as on the carved-top guitar made in Chapter 9.

This guitar is grainfilled, after having been finish-sanded, and the front and sides of the fingerboard masked. The guitar is then given several coats of pink and these are left to dry. The masking is then removed from the binding and the neck binding is scraped clean in the same way as the binding on the Telecaster body, with the exception that it is easier to keep to the straight line if something, in this case a straight edge, is placed over the frets.

After the binding has been scraped the whole guitar is lightly sanded using 320 grade paper to give the subsequent clear coats something to cling to, and the binding is given its final clean-up. The face of the fingerboard is then masked and the guitar is given its clear coats.

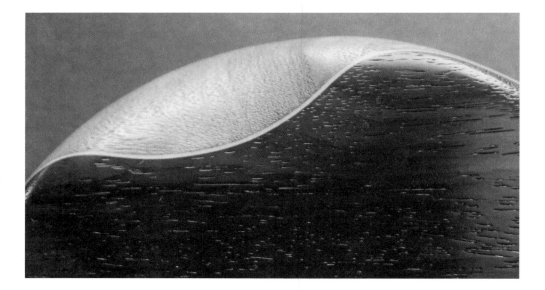

Not all guitars are gloss finished. Although some Wal basses are finished in a gloss acrylic (see picture on page 33) others are given just two coats of a very hard acrylic. This seals the wood but leaves the grain showing, giving a much more natural feel to the instrument.

During spraying the guitar is hung in the spray-booth on a suitably bent metal coat-hanger placed through one of the machine-head holes, and the guitar is sprayed carefully around this so that it does not mask any part of the head. This method of spraying not only does away with a ridge along the bottom edge of the fingerboard but can also be buffed to a deeper finish.

The Fender method is fine if spraying a separate body and a car spray can give a very good finish providing that it is used carefully.

Using spray cans on a guitar body

After finish-sanding, the guitar body is given several coats of a filler primer. This is usually a grey paint that builds up quickly, in much the same way as the sanding-sealer. The colour makes finding any bumps or dips in the surface very easy and these should be filled or sanded and the guitar is given several more coats of primer if necessary.

When the primer is dry it is lightly sanded to give the colour coats a key, and the colour is applied. The more coats that are sprayed at this stage the easier it will be to get a good finish on the guitar. About ten coats is the minimum which, if using car spray, amounts to between six and eight 6-oz cans.

Using car spray in this way can prove to be a little expensive but in the absence of a spraygun, spray-booth and a supply of paint it is an easy alternative to brush finishing which can be very time-consuming.

BUFFING THE FINISH

It is not enough simply to spray or brush your chosen finish and hope that it will be nice and shiny. The guitar needs to be buffed and polished.

The big guitar-making companies use powerful machines with lambswool wheels which, when using the right polishing compounds, should give a finish that looks like glass. At home the best results are to be had with a small cork sanding block, a supply of 600 and 1000 grit wet-and-dry paper, a little soapy water, a good polishing compound recommended for use on your chosen finish, a soft cloth or two and a large amount of armwork.

It is most important that the finish has been given time to dry out thoroughly. This will take longer in a cooler climate but at least a week should be allowed for cellulose and two to three days for a two-pack. If you can still smell the thinners, wait.

The first stage is to remove any unevenness caused by the spraying. For this the flat surfaces of the guitar are wet-sanded with 600 grit wet-and-dry, using the soapy water as a lubricant, over a cork block. The curved parts of the guitar are sanded in the same way except that the paper is used carefully over the fingers.

When the surface is smooth all of the marks left by the 600 grit paper are removed using the 1000 grit paper in the same way. This will leave the guitar

Wet-sanding the guitar using 1200 grit wet-and-dry paper over a cork block. This is lubricated with household soap to stop the paper clogging.

Wet-sanding the paint finish on a Stratocaster-style body. It is better to sand the flat areas with the aid of a cork block but the edges – and there are a lot of those on a Stratocaster – will need careful use of 1200 grit paper over the fingers. It is on the edges where the paint is thinnest and great care is needed not to rub through.

Using domestic brass polish and automotive colour restorer on a spraycan painted body. Both of these materials are a little coarser than buffing cream but are perfectly satisfactory for getting a good shine. It can be seen that buffing the paint is a good deal more messy than buffing lacquer.

with a slight sheen but still lightly scratched. These scratches are removed as the final shine is added to the guitar.

Using a soft cloth a small amount of the polishing compound is rubbed over an area of the finish. If the cloth begins to feel dry a little more of the compound is added. By working slowly over the guitar a little piece at a time, all of the scratches left by the

wet-and-dry paper can be removed. It may take quite a long time to remove all of the scratches from the guitar, especially on the plastic coating which is very hard, but the effort is worthwhile.

This will leave the guitar with its final shine that can be further improved with a domestic wax furniture polish. Many specialist guitar polishes are available but these are little different to ordinary

Final buffing of the Telecaster body using a very fine buffing cream and a soft cloth. The longer the lacquer has had to harden, the easier this job will be.

household polish and more expensive. Never use a silicon-based polish. These can affect the finish on the guitar and if they get onto any area of bare wood they will make refinishing a nightmare.

If producing a high-gloss shine does not appeal then it is not too different to produce a semi-gloss finish. After flatting the guitar with 1000 grit wet-n-

dry it can be polished using 0000 grade wire wool and a good quality wax polish. This will leave some very light scratches on the guitar but these will not be visible when the guitar is more than a few inches away.

One other finish that can be used is Tru-Oil. This is sold as a preparation for gunstocks but is very good

A very good gloss finish can be obtained using Tru-Oil. It is important to prepare the wood properly and Tru-Oil's own sealer is useful for this. This is applied with a soft cloth in thin coats. The Tru-Oil itself comes in similar pots, one of which should cover a guitar. The trick is to keep the coats as thin as possible and lightly sand in between. Tru-Oil has the advantage of drying quickly so in good weather several coats can be applied in one day.

Although Tru-Oil can give a high gloss if applied carefully, certain guitar-makers have been known to cheat and finish it semi-gloss. This can also be used on lacquer. The final coats are left to harden and the guitar is polished with a beeswax cream polish and very fine wire wool.

for guitars as it is resin-based and therefore dries faster than an oil-based product. The secret is to apply only very thin coats having prepared the surface to the highest possible standard. Each coat should be lightly flatted before the next is applied and the final coats can be lightly polished using a good wax polish.

Very high gloss finishes can be obtained in this way but require almost as much skill as French polishing. It is easier, and almost as effective, to produce a semi-gloss finish using wire wool and wax polish.

I have not attempted to cover all of the finishes that are possible, but to describe how I finished the guitars that I have made for the purposes of this book. The subject of finishing guitars could fill a book on its own. The most important thing that you

need to obtain a good finish is patience. Take your time preparing the guitar and applying the finish and do not try to buff the guitar or assemble it before it is ready.

The materials needed, such as the lacquers and spray equipment, vary considerably and so there is little point in trying to lay down hard and fast rules for their use. You are more likely to get specific information about the make and type of finish that you use from the suppliers of the finish. Most suppliers have a technical staff whose job it is to answer questions, or at least somebody working for them who has a great amount of experience in working with the products. It is always worth asking questions.

If, however, all of this seems a little confusing you could always oil and wax the guitar in the way that I did to the eight-string bass.

14   Electrickery

The choice of pick-ups and the wiring options available to any guitarist or bassist could fill an entire book its own, and probably has. In the Dark Ages, when I first started making guitars, there was really no choice; the only pick-ups available were those from the large manufacturers – which were very expensive – or cheap Japanese copies which were *very* cheap and did not sound that good. The only other alternative was to use the pick-ups from another guitar and cannibalise it, but you had to find a broken guitar first. This is the reason why Brian May's Red Special has Burns TriSonics.

All this changed in the early 1970s. Players had been experimenting for years by adding different pick-ups to their guitars, an early example being Eddie Cochrane who had a Gibson P90 in the front position of his Gretsch 6120. Others had experimented with rewinding pick-ups and making their own.

One of the first companies to market replacement pick-ups that offered a different range of sounds were Di Marzio whose first offerings were either re-creations of vintage styles or more powerful versions of the originals. These were designed to be direct replacements, needing no surgery on the guitar to fit. It was not long before other companies followed and the range of what was available increased dramatically. It was also at about this time that the Far-Eastern companies started making guitars and basses of much better quality, the forerunners of some of the excellent instruments produced today, and spare parts became an option for those too.

It was at about this time that Gibson's patent on the humbucker ran out and other companies could then produce very similar pick-ups, for example the Ibanez 'Super 70' humbucker of about 1974 is virtually indistinguishable from the Gibson of the same period.

The bolt-on goodies market peaked around the late 1970s and some companies went out of business but others have sprung up and the range of parts and the possible options to the guitarist are as wide now as they have ever been.

With so much being available, choosing one or two pick-ups for your instrument can be a daunting process. Each manufacturer will claim that they offer something more than the competition; while this may be the case, the choice of individual models is really down to the player. However, there are guidelines of what may or may not be the best and particular styles of pick-up will have particular features. To illustrate this we will start with . . .

A BRIEF HISTORY OF THE GUITAR PICK-UP

Early guitar pick-ups were quite crude by today's standards but often no less appealing because of that. The principle of the pick-up is simplicity itself. A magnet is wound with many thousands of turns of fine, insulated, copper wire. As the string, made of a ferrous alloy, vibrates it cause disturbances in the magnetic field which generate small currents in the windings. Early pick-ups were simple bar magnets and the windings were of a gauge that is a little thicker than is used today. As people began to appreciate the limitations of this design, they began to experiment to alter the sound.

Within limits, the stronger the magnet, the more current is generated within the coil, making the pick-up a little louder. Again within limits, the more windings around the magnet, the more sensitive it will be and therefore more efficient, or louder. It will also have a more middly sound and will not be as bright. The physics behind all of this is that more turns of wire mean greater resistance. The higher the resistance, within reason, the more output you will get. There is a physical limit to how much wire you can fit around the magnet. This is a factor of the size of the magnet and the available space to fit the copper wire. The more windings you have, the more space they take up. There are two

Fender Stratocaster, Gibson P90 and Fender Telecaster style pick-ups showing the wide variety of coil widths.

directions you can go, either make a tall coil with a correspondingly tall magnet, or make a wide coil that is quite squat. Both of these options may well result in the same number of windings but will sound different as they will be covering a different area of the magnetic field.

It was also found that it was difficult to get magnets that were the ideal size to be wound. The answer was to position the magnet underneath the coils and have a separate 'pole piece', from one of the magnet's poles, through the coil.

Having a bar magnet beneath the strings was not ideal. A pole piece for each string seems to 'focus' the magnetic field around it. If pole pieces could be made adjustable for height the differences in the volume of the wound and unwound strings, as they vibrated differently, could be evened out.

One of the earliest pick-ups, the Gibson P90, was built with a squat, wide coil and a set of six

In some people's view the finest pick-up ever: the Gibson P90.

adjustable pole pieces in the centre. Underneath the pick-up were two magnets, with the like poles butting up against the pole pieces. This had not only the magnetic field around the pole pieces on the top of the pick-up, but also a quite complex magnetic field affecting the lower windings in the coil. The pick-up naturally has a warm tone that comes from the wide coil and remains one of my favourites.

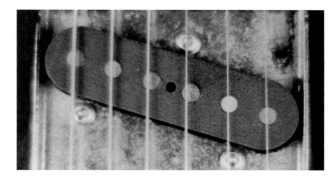

The Telecaster pick-up.

Leo Fender approached the problem differently. He had a lot of experience having dealt with musicians for many years. His Broadcaster/Telecaster pick-up was designed to be easily manufactured and featured six individual magnets as the pole pieces. These were wound with a coil that was not as flat as a P90 but not as tall and skinny as his later

Stratocaster. This, as much as anything, is the reason that Telecasters sound a little more middly than a Strat. Later versions of the Telecaster pick-up had pole pieces that differed in height to account for the difference in output from the strings and this was also done on the Stratocaster.

Leo Fender's earliest bass pick-up was similar to the Telecaster but this evolved into the Precision Bass pick-up that we know today. It has two magnets for each string to allow for the greater movement in the vibrating bass string, and two wide, flat coils. These work together and were the result of the work that had been done at Gibson on their guitar pick-ups.

An end-on view of a Gibson-style humbucker. The number of component parts is obvious.

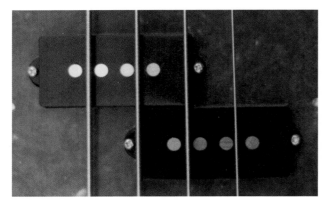

The Fender Precision Bass pick-up: two wide coils with two pole pieces per string.

On the other hand, the Jazz Bass had two pick-ups, each with two magnets per string and tall thin coils. These sound much treblier than a Precision, partly because of the position of the rear pick-up but mostly because of the coil design.

One big problem with pick-ups having just one coil is that they not only pick up the vibration of the string, they can also pick up a lot of background interference from electrical equipment. This can range from amplifiers to air-conditioning systems and lighting. The resultant hum can be disconcerting and annoying, especially when recording.

In the mid-1950s a Gibson employee called Seth Lover was working on a solution to this problem. He reasoned that if two coils were connected in series with the magnetic fields reversed, the hum would be cancelled. The result was the Gibson Humbucker.

The new pick-up was expensive to make as it had twice as many coils and three times as many component parts than a Stratocaster pick-up. However, it

removed – or bucked – the hum and gave a thick middly sound with a lot of highs and lows that players loved. The first examples were released before the patent had been granted and so were labelled 'patent applied for' on a small black label on the base. These early pick-ups are now worth a vast amount of money as they are regarded as the finest examples of the pick-up maker's art. In actual fact they do sound good but are sometimes of differing quality and can be quite prone to microphonic feedback – of which more will follow.

Later versions, with the patent number were, for a while, exactly the same but it is the earliest that make the big money and which are copied by several other manufacturers.

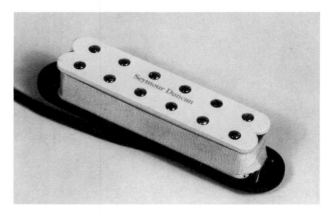

The popularity of the humbucker is such that it has been redesigned to fit into a Fender Stratocaster. This is a Seymour Duncan JB Jr.

Fender noted this new development but was not about to re-jig his whole production just to get rid of some hum that many players simply ignored. He did, as we have seen, use the principle on the Precision Bass pick-up that has two coils each for two strings. He also managed to do this without infringing Gibson's patent and having to pay royalties.

Leo Fender, being someone who loved to experiment, made many different versions of his basic designs and some of these were quite interesting.

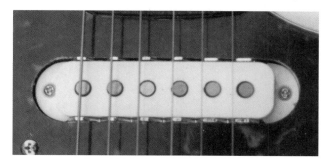

The Fender Jaguar pick-up.

The Jaguar pick-up was very similar to the Stratocaster but had extensions of the pole pieces running up the outside of the coil to increase the magnetic field. The Jazzmaster had a wide and flat coil that made the Gibson P90 look almost emaciated. Fender even made guitar pick-ups in the same manner as the Precision Bass. His 12-string had split pick-ups and his five-string bass had one coil for two strings and another for three.

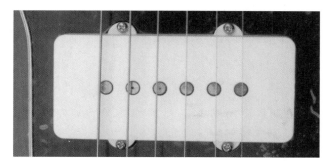

A Jazzmaster pick-up.

It was also found that the type of magnet had a bearing on the sound. The composition of the alloy making up the magnet affects its properties. Seth Lover had known this and one of his earlier pick-ups

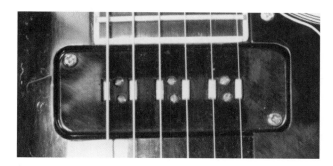

A Gibson Alnico pick-up in the neck position of a Les Paul Black Beauty reissue. The similarity to the P90 can be seen – they fit a similar-sized rout – but it is a far more complicated design. It does sound very good.

featured a magnet made of Alnico – a compound of aluminium, nickel and cobalt. This produced a strong magnet to which Mr Lover attached six oblong pole pieces and a coil similar to a P90. The result was in production for a relatively short time as some people considered it too powerful as it distorted amplifiers (oh how times have changed!) and the Humbucker was available shortly afterwards. The Gibson Alnico was used in the front position of the very first Les Paul Custom guitars and is still available on reissues.

Fender also had a humbucker in the early 1970s. This was designed by none other than Mr Seth Lover.

Most pick-ups that are available today are variations on these basic types and simply feature a differing and bewildering array of magnet types, winding types and wiring options.

The only type of pick-up that is not covered above is the active pick-up. This is something of a misnomer since the pick-up part is no more active than on any other pick-up. It is actually a pick-up with a small amplifier either built into the pick-up case or into the guitar.

Active pick-ups go back quite a long way. In the 1960s, Gibson produced the Les Paul Personal and Professional. These were based on experiments by Les Paul himself. The pick-ups used were low impedance and were boosted by a small amplifier and tone circuit in the guitar. This gave a wider range of sounds and a better mix of frequencies but was not to everyone's taste. Early pre-amps fitted to these instruments could also be quite noisy.

Other manufacturers have also tried similar paths. Ovation's strangely shaped and named Breadwinner had active pick-ups and several makes

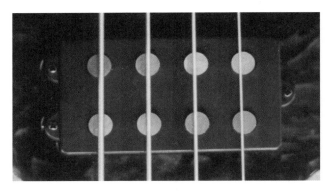

The Musicman Stingray Bass caused something of a sensation when first released as it featured an excellent pick-up and a superb pre-amp.

Jimi Hendrix using a standard Fender Stratocaster (and using it very well) at the Royal Albert Hall, London in February 1969. (Courtesy of Caesar Glebbeek, UniVibes Magazine.)

are now for sale, from companies such as EMG, offering a wide range of tones. One of the better examples of this approach was also by Leo Fender. His Musicman Stingray Bass had an excellent pre-amp that had virtually no background noise and the bass sounded very good. The matching guitar did not do so well perhaps partly because most sounds that players tend to like were produced with good old-fashioned pick-ups and valve amplifiers, and I have always found that it is easier to get bass players to look at new ideas than it is guitarists.

PICK-UP CHOICE

There are, of course, many factors governing your choice of pick-ups. It could be that you have chosen to make a guitar just to get your personal favourite mix of pick-ups into one guitar. As long as the guidelines in Chapter 3 are followed, it should be possible, within reason, to get what you are after. On the other hand you might just be a total hooligan who wants to have the nastiest, meanest and loudest guitar in the history of heavy metal. Now, I have nothing against hooligans, in fact some of my best friends qualify perfectly, but getting the most powerful pick-up does not mean that you will get the loudest guitar, and if you do, it still might not match with your chosen amplifier.

Generally, loud pick-ups are quite woolly sounding. There are exceptions but even then it is not the pick-up that is providing the volume; that is the amplifier's job. The pick-up will determine the level at which the input of the amplifier starts to distort. Once it is distorting it will not affect the

output of the amplifier, only the tone. Many of the finest heavy metal players play variations on the Fender Stratocaster and manage to get a good tone with a relatively low powered pick-up. Of course, some of these are using modified guitars but the Master of Loudness, Jimi Hendrix, used bog-standard Stratocasters.

It is a mistake to think that if you choose the same pick-up combinations and amplification as your hero you will sound the same. This is not the case as their sound comes from their talent and originality and so should yours.

Some manufacturers offer a chance to try their pick-ups. Providing that you do not drastically cut the hook-up wires and do not mark or damage the goods, they will exchange your pick-up for another in their range.

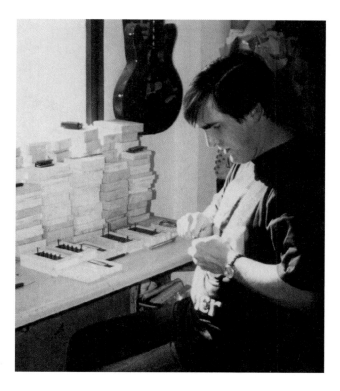

Pick-up manufacturer Kent Armstrong proving that humanoids can build pick-ups if they are prepared to wind thousands of turns of wire onto tiny bobbins, assemble these together and then mould them in epoxy.

MAKING YOUR OWN PICK-UPS

By this point in the book you will have probably learned that making a guitar is more complicated than you had originally thought. Deciding now to make your own pick-ups will make everything so far look easy. People do make their own pick-ups, and some are even quite good, but the problems of getting hold of the right materials in small quantities, the choice of types of material, managing to wind thousands of turns of wire as thin as a human hair onto the bobbin without taking forever and breaking the wire as you go, put many people off.

The windings of the pick-up need to be quite tightly packed. If they are not, they can move about and they will make a squealing sound, known as microphonic feedback, which is particularly unpleasant. Some commercially-available pick-ups suffer from this as a result of being made to a price, and many original Gibson 'Patent Applied For' pick-ups squeal.

The higher tension that is used on the wire, the more breakages you get, and therefore the more time-consuming and expensive the pick-ups are to produce. Lowering the tension means less breakages but softer coils. These will have a greater tendency to squeal. This can be cured but it is messy and with all of the problems associated with making your own pick-ups it is far simpler, and probably just as cheap, to go out and buy some.

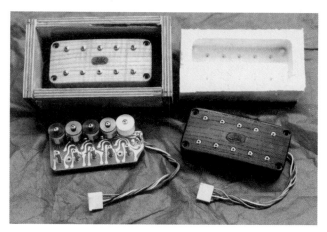

Wal make their own pick-ups. Each string has its own set of humbucking coils. These are assembled on a printed circuit board and and finally moulded in epoxy. Note that the pick-ups are connected to the guitar by push-fit connectors. Upper right is the former for the rubber mould that is top right. The half-assembled pick-up is bottom left with the completed article bottom right. This is clearly a complicated process.

ACOUSTIC SOUNDS

In the bad old days, as we have already seen, guitarists were forced to use cheap contact microphones to pick up the sound of their guitars. A common source of those was from the throat microphones used in Second World War tanks and some aircraft. These were in plentiful supply in the early 1950s and were very cheap. They also sounded pretty awful. The advent of the guitar pick-up we know today pushed the contact microphone out of the scene for many years. It re-emerged when acoustic guitarists wanted to amplify their instruments without having to use a magnetic pick-up.

The basic contact microphone is a piezo crystal that produces a current when it vibrates. Attach it to the vibrating guitar top and amplify the current and, in theory, you should get the sound of the guitar top. In practice you often get a very scratchy sound and the old problem of acoustic feedback returns. Companies such as Barcus Berry and Ovation in the United States experimented and managed to produce some workable systems that retained the sound of the guitar.

Development has continued and some of the systems now on the market are very good indeed. During the early 1980s several people started working on systems that could be used with a solid instrument to give an acoustic-like sound. It was as if the whole instrument had come full circle. During the mid-1980s, Roger Giffin at Giffin Guitars in London produced a fretless bass with piezo transducers in the saddles of an adapted Schaller bass bridge and the instrument certainly had a good sound.

Several companies now produce transducer saddles, or complete bridges with transducers built in, for a variety of guitar types and some manufacturers fit them as standard. The only problem with these systems is the fact that they need a different sort of amplification to the main guitar pick-up. There is no point trying to get a good acoustic sound from a piezo transducer bridge plugged into a distorting valve guitar amp! Should you choose to use this system it is advisable to give the transducer a separate output so that it can be amplified through the PA or another, more suitable, amplifier. This is easily achieved by routing the output via a stereo jack and running the lead into a splitter box, feeding the overdriven main guitar sound and the acoustic sound to their respective amplifiers.

WIRING THE WHOLE LOT TOGETHER

Once you have chosen your pick-ups you will need to connect them in such a way that the variety of tones they offer can be used to best advantage.

The earliest guitars were relatively simple, offering a choice of either pick-up or both, as on the Les Paul, while the Telecaster/Broadcaster had a choice of back pick-up, front pick-up or front pick-up through a large capacitor to make it very bassy (although this was later changed to be the same as the Les Paul), or a choice of one of three pick-ups on the Stratocaster. Each of these guitars had either one volume for everything or one for each pick-up and a

selection of tone controls that worked differently on each model.

As guitars developed other choices became available. The Fender Duo Sonic had a slider switch for each pick-up with three positions: rhythm/off/lead. The 'rhythm' position simply fed the signal through a small resistance to lower the output.

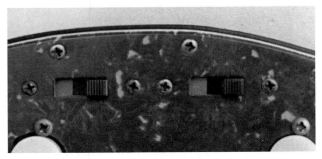

The slider switches on a Fender Duo Sonic.

The Fender Jaguar was covered in knobs and switches. As well as having standard tone and volume controls these were duplicated on the upper half of the instrument with knurled knobs set into the guitar. There were three switches; two were on/off controls for the pick-ups and the third was a rhythm and lead switch similar in function to that on the Duo Sonic.

At Gibson various modifications were made to the tone circuits of their guitars. In 1958 they introduced a three pick-up version of the Les Paul. This had a switch that offered back pick-up, middle and front together, and front alone. It was not possible to choose the middle pick-up alone, as on a Stratocaster, and the tone variation was not that different from a standard two pick-up guitar. They even kept two volumes and tones, one set working on two pick-ups.

At roughly the same time Gibson also introduced a semi-acoustic known as the Switchmaster. This was a development of the earlier ES5 which had three pick-ups with a separate volume for each and a master tone control. The outputs of the pick-ups were infinitely variable and many good tones could be found but it was fiddly. The Switchmaster also had three pick-ups but had a switch similar to a Stratocaster with four positions. This allowed each pick-up to be chosen individually or all three together. There was a tone and volume control for each pick-up. The same system was fitted to a few Les Pauls and these are very rare.

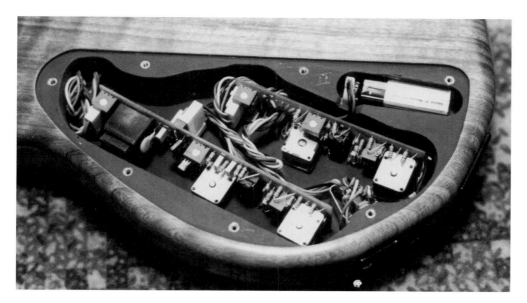

Some of the first guitars with active, or battery-powered, electrics were released in the 1960s. Many of these suffered from noisy pre-amps. Companies such as Alembic tackled the problem but it was not until the mid-1970s that truly effective circuits were in use on mainstream instruments. Typical of these is the Wal bass with its well-made and very effective pre-amp.

The Fender Jazz Bass had no switches. The earliest had two dual concentric knobs, effectively two controls on the same shaft, that gave a volume and tone for each pick-up. These could be mixed to varying degrees. Later versions had two volumes and a master tone. On some guitars with a volume for each pick-up, turning one volume all the way down when both pick-ups are selected cuts the guitar completely. The ES5 and the Jazz Bass both had a system that gave the option of turning just one pick-up off completely.

Gibson were also among the early users of tone filter systems. Their ES345 and ES355 had a feature called Varitone that altered the characteristics of the tone circuit. They also had an interesting system in their ES340 which had a two-way selector that gave both pick-ups on together, mixable via the volume controls, or both pick-ups on together out of phase.

Having pick-ups in and out of phase is something that offers a guitarist or bassist even more tonal options. When pick-ups are out of phase some of the signal, that which is identical in each coil, is cancelled and the result is a thinner, treblier tone with less volume. Reversing the polarity of one pick-up of a pair will not alter its sound when it is on alone but it will noticeably affect things when both pick-ups are on together.

The term 'out of phase' is sometimes used to describe the sound that is achieved when two pick-ups on a Stratocaster are on together, a feature that is much easier since the advent of five-position switches, although this is not actually what is happening since the pick-ups are in phase but wired in parallel. If you reverse the polarity of one pick-up of the pair they do become out of phase and the sound virtually disappears. It is not a pleasant sound.

Series or parallel wiring between two pick-ups or even between the coils of a humbucker can give a similar out-of-phase-like tone. Early Di Marzio pick-ups came with a switch and a wiring diagram that offered series/parallel wiring. This made the pick-ups sound as if they were single coil, as they were brighter in tone and slightly quieter but still humbucking. Another way of making a humbucker sound like a single coil pick-up is to turn one coil off, making it exactly like a single coil. This is known as 'coil-tapping'.

With the choice of switching active or passive pick-ups on and off, in phase and out of phase, series or parallel, coil-tapping or not, mixer controls and tone-altering devices, the possibilities on even a relatively simple guitar could get very confusing. As previously mentioned, the Brian May guitar has a single volume and tone and an on/off and phase reversal switch for each of its three pick-ups. When first made it also had an electronic fuzz unit built in. Hereby starts another area of possible sound variation (and potential confusion).

Many companies offer a variety of pre-amps that can vary from simple power boosters that pummel the input of your amplifier into submission, or fairly sophisticated active tone controls as seen on some of today's better amplifiers. Remember if you are going to choose something like this it needs to be incorporated in your design at the start.

For all of the above, there is a selection of components suited to guitars available from guitar shops and parts suppliers. These range from potentiometers for tone and volume controls through to switches of varying complexity and pre-amps. These will be described as we use each type.

Now it gets difficult. To make things simpler I will now describe in easy stages the more common components of the tone circuit and build up to some of the more complicated ones.

Volume and tone controls

The volume control on a guitar is simple. A potentiometer will be wired so that, as it turns, more and more of the signal is fed to earth (ground) until it finally cuts out. The input is on one side of the track, the output in the middle and the other end of the track is earthed. Which end of the track is earthed determines the direction in which the potentiometer (or pot) will work.

There are two types of pot that can be used. These are known as linear or logarithmic. The logarithmic pot is also referred to as the audio-taper. The linear pot gives a gradual and progressive change while the log pot has more of the resistance at one end of the track. The reason for this is that the human ear does not hear changes in volume but changes in loudness, and so if using a linear pot on a guitar,

although the current flowing through it will alter gradually, it will sound as if all the change is bunched at one end. The log pot is called the audio-taper as it is adjusted for the way we hear the change. Although the current change is not gradual, we hear it as if it is.

Since one end of the pot is different to the other it cannot be used in the other direction as it would sound even worse than a linear pot. This is the reason that many left-handed guitars have the controls wired in the same way as right-handed guitars. It might feel a little strange, as they appear to work in the wrong fashion, but the pots are working as efficiently as they can. It is possible to get reverse-taper pots that can be used for left-handed guitars, but if you desperately need to change the pots on your left-handed guitar so that they work in the normal sense, then it is wise to fit linear pots and suffer the slight change in how they work.

Most guitar pots are sold in 250K and 500K ohm values. Many manufacturers use 500K for everything. Fender used to use 1Meg (1000K) pots in the Telecaster. Gibson now use 300K pots on volume controls and 100K pots on tone. A good 'rule of thumb' is to use 500K log pots on the volume controls of guitars with humbucking pick-ups, 250K on guitars with single coils, and 250K for all tone controls. Some guitars with 500K pots on the tone control sound as if they have linear pots as the tonal change is bunched at one end of the rotation. This is due to it being the wrong value rather than the

Potentiometers come in a variety of styles, sizes and values. The enclosed pot on the right has a solid shaft that will only accept knobs with a grub screw fixing. The pot on the left has a smaller diameter screw fixing and a splined shaft to accept ordinary guitar knobs.

pot being log or linear. Changing the pot to one of a smaller value will often even this out.

Most pots for guitars have splined shafts to accept standard guitar knobs. Pots from other sources tend to have solid shafts and will not accept the same knobs. The Telecaster used solid shaft pots and had knobs that fixed with the help of a grub screw. Knobs like this are available but it is worth making sure that you can fit your chosen knobs onto your guitar.

Passive (i.e. not battery-powered) tone controls generally work in a similar way. Instead of earthing all the guitar's signal, it is filtered through a capacitor. Differing value capacitors will alter different frequencies.

The most commonly used capacitors used in guitar-making are between 0.001 mfd and 0.01 mfd. A higher value capacitor will cut more treble than a smaller value. For example, a capacitor of 0.05 mfd will cut more treble than a 0.02 mfd capacitor. Fender mainly use a 0.01 to 0.05 mfd capacitor and Gibson use a lot of 0.02 mfd capacitors.

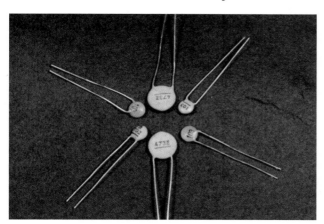

A selection of different value capacitors.

There are several different types of capacitor which all do the same job but are made of slightly differing materials. The most commonly used for guitars are ceramic disc capacitors. These cost just a few pence each and so it is worth buying several different values and experimenting to find the tone change that suits you best. Unfortunately I rarely use tone controls. I am one of those people that leave them full up and might as well not have them, but then I also wish that guitar knobs were marked up to 11!

Switches

Selector switches may vary but are generally either toggle or slider. Gibson always used to use Switchcraft leaf switches. These are very high quality toggle switches and have been copied by other manufacturers. They work on a simple 'make and break' principle and since the internals are plain to see, they are easy to wire up. One pick-up is wired to one set of contacts and the other pick-up is wired to the second set. With the switch in the central position both pick-ups are connected. By moving the toggle to one side, one set of contacts is broken, disconnecting the pick-up. These switches are quite big and need a certain amount of room inside the guitar. They are also available in vertical or horizontal form.

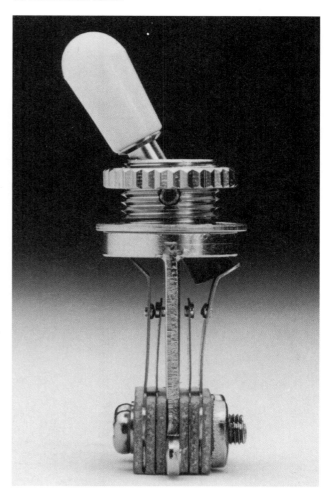

A leaf-type switch clearly showing how the contacts work.

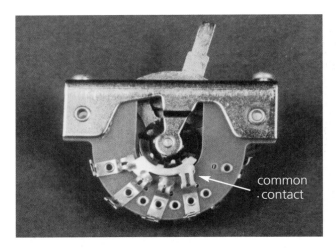

One side of a Stratocaster-type switch. One contact is connected in turn to the other three. The other side is identical and offers a wide variety of options.

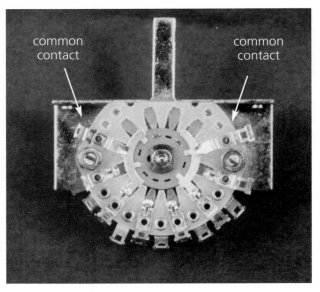

Switches with four times as many contacts as a standard Strat/Tele switch are now available. These offer a very wide variety of possible combinations and can be used with two pick-ups to provide phasing options and coil-tapping as well as pick-up selection. Visible on this view are the two sets of contacts on each face of the switch.

The Stratocaster and Telecaster use very similar switches, the only difference being that there are now two extra positions on the Strat switch between those on the Telecaster which allow two pick-ups to be on together. These are actually two switches in one. Each side of the switch operates independently. When joined together they can work to choose the pick-ups and feed the signal to the tone controls, as on a Stratocaster, or work as an on/off switch for either of two pick-ups with a combined output, as on a Telecaster. These switches are really like a rotary switch placed on its side.

Manufacturers are now producing even more complicated switches which operate in the same way as the more traditional switches but have more contacts, allowing switching options that were previously only available on rotary switches.

Smaller switches, both toggle and slider, can be used for a variety or purposes. The most basic are SPST, this acronym describing the switch as single-pole and single-throw, and are used just for turning on an item. A single-pole double-throw (SPDT) switch will have three contacts and will join either centre and left or centre and right. These can be used as an either/or switch to choose between functions. Some may also have an unconnected centre position. SPDT switches with a centre position that connects all three contacts – as would be used on a

The switch on the left is a double-pole quadruple-throw, or two DPST, on a common toggle. On the right is a standard DPDT mini toggle which has the same function as the switch on the base of the push–pull pot.

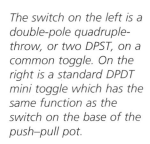

Different types of jack connector.

selector switch giving one, two or both pick-ups – are rare.

Double-pole double-throw (DPDT) switches are simply two SPDT switches sharing the same toggle. They can be used for a number of jobs including phase reversal and series/parallel wiring.

Even more complicated switches can be bought including three- and four-pole double-throw. They can be used for anything and are only limited by your imagination.

The last link in the chain is the socket. Most guitars are connected to their amplifier via a cord that has two ¼ in jack plugs. The jack plug has been around since just after the dinosaurs but they are common and they are reliable. They are available in several forms: stereo and mono, switched and skeletal or enclosed.

Stereo and switched sockets can be used to turn batteries inside the guitar (for pre-amps, etc.) on and off as well as for connecting the guitar to the amp. This is why guitars with active electrics inside should not be left plugged in.

It is possible to fit the guitar with a Canon-type audio-connector as found on most microphone cables. These are more robust than phone jacks, but are more expensive and will not, of course, accept a standard guitar lead. These can also be used to turn on or off the battery on an active tone circuit and I have used one on the eight-string bass.

WIRING

As with everything there is a minimum amount of tools that are needed to wire the guitar successfully. Most important is the soldering iron. If the iron is too powerful it can damage or even melt some small components, and if it is not powerful enough

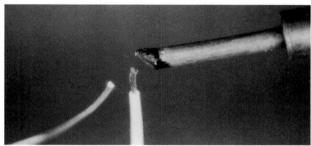

Tinning the end of a wire.

it will be unable to give a good joint on the back of potentiometers. An iron of about 25 watts is ideal. Alternatively you could use an instant heat soldering gun, although these are sometimes a little large to use in a confined space. A good pair of wire-cutters will be needed as will a good wire-stripper.

The ends of each wire should be stripped back for about ¼ in (6.3 mm) and the bare wire gently twisted to keep the strands together before tinning the wire with solder. After the wire has cooled it can be cut back to about ⅛ in (3 mm) from the sleeving before being soldered into place.

Long-nosed pliers will be essential for holding wires in place while the solder cools. Fingers could be used but they tend to be a little less heat-resistant.

Some guitar pots come with the back of the pot plated which can make soldering difficult if not impossible. This should be filed off to reveal the base metal before the solder joint is made.

Only just enough solder should be used for each joint, and when cool this should still look a little shiny. If the joint is a very dull grey colour the joint may well be dry and will need resoldering.

Stage by stage, how it works

The wiring options in this chapter have been kept deliberately simple since there are plenty of sources of information if a more complicated wiring design is needed. What I am intending to do here is provide the basis that can lead to further experimentation and to cover some of the more popular basic designs. I have also attempted to make the diagrams as user-friendly as possible by drawing them as they would appear when viewed from below, as would be the case if looking into the control cavity on a guitar with rear mounted pick-ups or on the underside of a scratchplate, rather than using schematics as in the first edition of this book. Inevitably some compromises need to be made and some aspects of the diagrams need to be simplified.

For the purposes of these diagrams, a single-coil pick-up will be represented like this (right):

The wires are shown as leaving either end of the coil. For the single-coil diagrams, the wire at the top or right, depending on the orientation of the pick-up in the diagram, represents the beginning of the winding of the coil. These are also drawn as if for a six-stringed instrument but is a diagrammatic representation only.

The live connection would normally be to the start of the coil and this would connect with the tip of the jack plug, or the centre core of the input wire. The other end of the coil would be connected to the earth in many cases and this would be to the screen of the input wire, which itself is connected to the shaft of the jack plug.

A Fender Stratocaster pick-up showing the start (right) and finish (left) points of the coil.

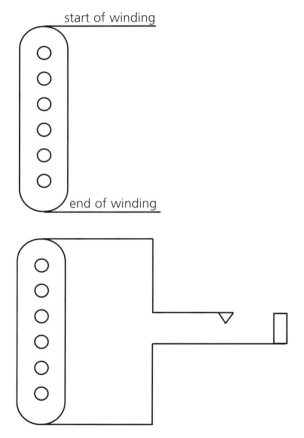

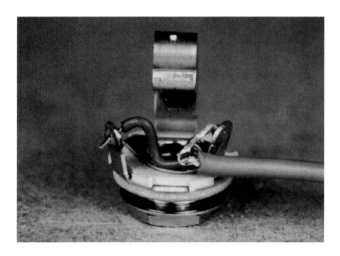

(left) A skeletal jack socket showing how the earth, in this case the screen on the cable, is attached to the sleeve of the jack and the hot wire is attached to the tip.

Since all earth wires are connected together there is no point including them in the diagrams as all they will do is confuse the issue. Therefore a single pickup is shown like this:

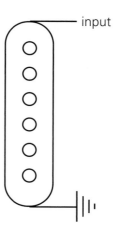

Very few people are ever likely to want their pickups connected directly to the amplifier and so tone and volume controls are wired in. The pot looks like this when viewed from below:

The outer tags are at either end of the resistance track. The centre connection is to the contact that sweeps across the track as the pot is turned, varying the resistance difference to each end of the track.

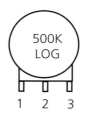

The schematic of the pot would be like this:

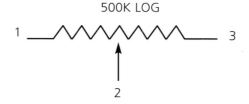

A volume control gradually earths the signal as it is rotated so one end needs to be connected to earth and the input and output wired to the others as here:

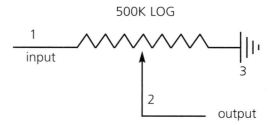

From underneath the pot, the volume control would look like this:

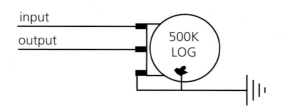

The earth wire from the pick-up would be connected to the back of the pot along with the earth wire from the output. A simple volume control will look like this:

Note the wires used are screened which helps prevent hum. The additional 0.001 mfd capacitor across the input and output of the pot helps prevent treble loss when the control is turned.

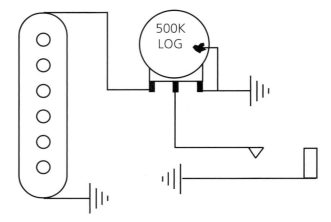

The full schematic of the pick-up and volume control of this would look like this:

All of the earth connections would be made to the back of the pot, as in the photograph, and an earth wire should also go to the bridge.

A tone control works by filtering some of the signal through a capacitor. This is the schematic:

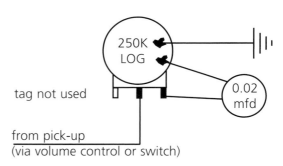

And this is the photograph:

Note how the connections are reversed from the diagram, with the capacitor on the centre tag (tag 2) and the input on the outer (tag 3). Either way will work as long as tag 1 is not used.

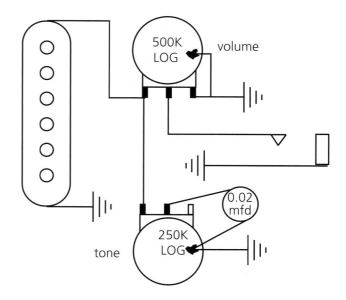

The tone control, added to our previous circuit, would look like this

As on the previous circuit the earths would be connected to the backs of the pot and the casings of the pots would be joined too.

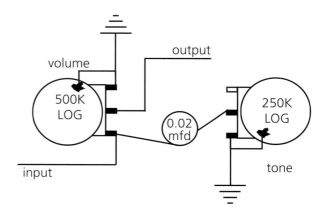

An alternative tone and volume circuit is sometimes used by Gibson. The effect is the same but the wiring slightly different:

Compare this with the photograph:

The input and output cables are very similar to those found on many Gibsons, with a braided screen that can be soldered directly to the back of a pot to make a good earth connection. The wire linking the two pots can also be seen.

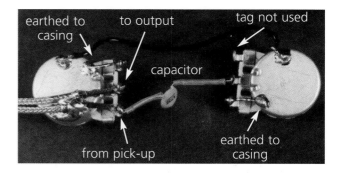

So far, the circuits have had just one pick-up. Adding another means adding a way of choosing or mixing them. A simple circuit, as used on the Fender Jazz Bass, sends each pick-up to its own volume control and to the output via the tone control which works on both pick-ups. It is important that the input from the pick-ups goes to the centre tag on the pot as if it goes to the end tag, as it could do on a single volume control, it will cut out the entire guitar when one volume is turned all the way down:

As in previous circuits, the backs of the pots are joined and the connections marked with the earth symbol are also soldered to the back of one of the pots.

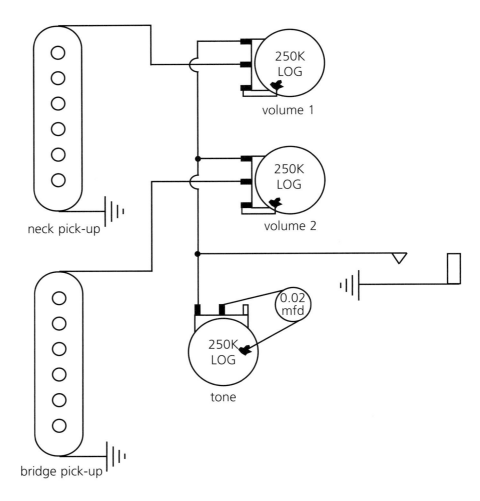

If more than one pick-up is to be used and a mixer circuit is not required then some form of switching is needed. The most common forms of switch used are the toggle and the Stratocaster-style 'cheesecutter'. The toggle will look like this (compare this with the photograph on page 161):

The casing or frame will be earthed (and for clarity is not shown in the diagrams) so if choosing between two pick-ups, it will look like this:

The two tags in the centre are joined for the output. The switch could be used in the Jazz Bass-style circuit for added flexibility. The switch would be wired into the circuit after the volume pots.

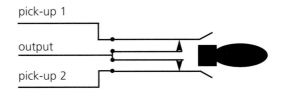

In the Les Paul and many other guitars, Gibson used a two pick-up arrangement with a volume and a tone for each pick-up. The pick-ups are wired to the volume and tone pots and the outputs are taken to the switch. There is no mixing facility on this circuit, so turning one pick-up down when both are selected will turn the guitar off.

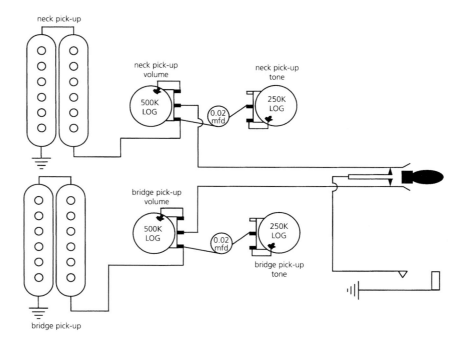

The 'cheesecutter' is, as we have seen, two switches, one either side. From beneath the switch looks like this:

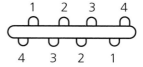

Not all manufacturers of these switches use the same order for the contacts; the common contact, terminal 4 in these diagrams, may be at the other end than in these drawings so it is wise to check. Also, some Japanese versions of this switch are encased in plastic and have the contacts in one long line. Finding which of these is connected to which others will require some investigation with a meter.

Contact 4 is connected to the others on that side in turn as the switch is moved. To choose between each of the three pick-ups it is a simple case of connecting like this:

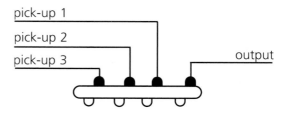

Five-way versions of this switch generally do not have five separate positions but in-between positions that bridge two of the contacts so connecting the common contact to 1, 1 and 2, 2, 2 and 3 and 3 alone.

If being used on a two pick-up guitar both sides of the switch need to be used so that, in the centre position, both pick-ups are on. In this case a three-position switch should be used as the additional two positions found on a Strat switch would have no effect.

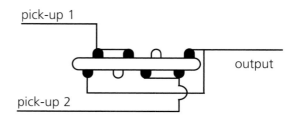

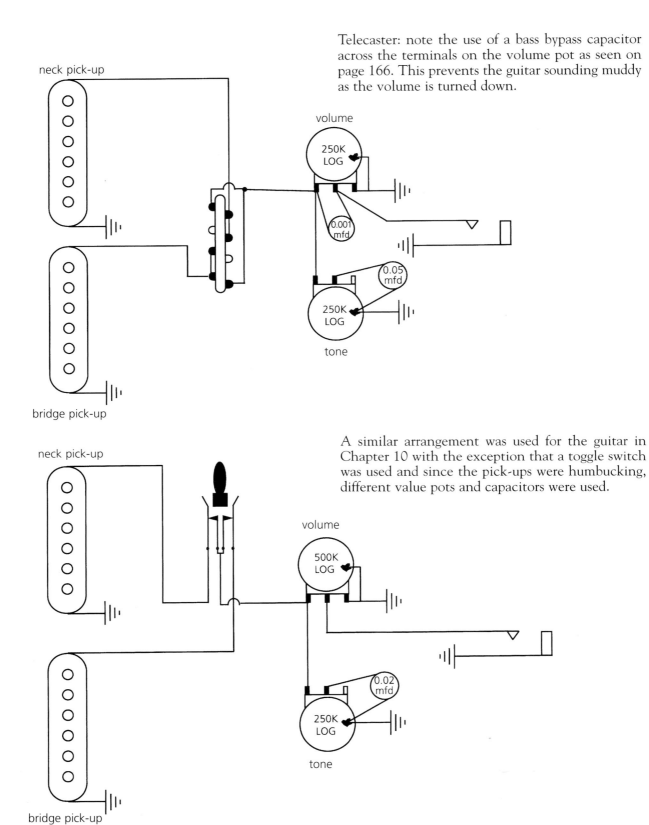

Telecaster: note the use of a bass bypass capacitor across the terminals on the volume pot as seen on page 166. This prevents the guitar sounding muddy as the volume is turned down.

neck pick-up

volume

250K LOG

0.001 mfd

0.05 mfd

250K LOG

tone

bridge pick-up

A similar arrangement was used for the guitar in Chapter 10 with the exception that a toggle switch was used and since the pick-ups were humbucking, different value pots and capacitors were used.

neck pick-up

volume

500K LOG

0.02 mfd

250K LOG

tone

bridge pick-up

The wiring on the Chapter 10 guitar.

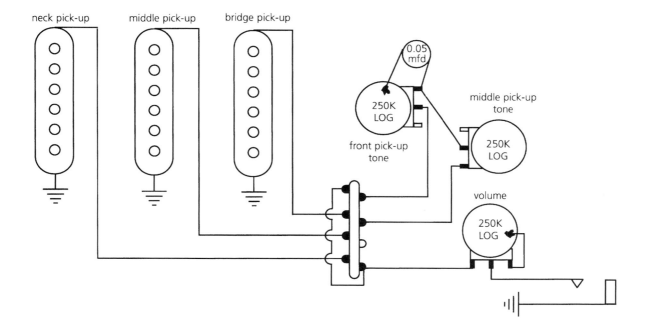

The standard Stratocaster wiring diagram that has been in use since 1954. Note how the second side of the switch is used to feed the tone controls. The normal system has no tone control for the bridge pick-up. This can be altered by simply adding a wire that bridges the remaining tag to its neighbour which will then give the middle and bridge pick-up a shared tone control.

The tone control for the front pick-up would normally be positioned next to the volume control but has been moved in the drawing for clarity. Also not drawn here are the earth connections to the backs of the pots. Many Stratocasters are shielded with foil under the scratchplate and this often provides the connection between the pots which make contact as they are fitted through the scratchplate. If there is no shielding on your guitar the backs of the pots should be connected together as in previous diagrams and all earth connections from the pick-ups and jack socket also connected to the back of the pots. An additional wire goes from the common earth to the bridge to earth the whole system.

An alternative to either of these switches is to use SPST or SPDT toggle or slider switches to turn the pick-ups on or off. The SPST will have just two contacts showing underneath which would connect with the switch in one position and remain disconnected in the other. The SPDT has three contacts, the centre contact being connected to each of the others depending on which way the toggle is pointed.

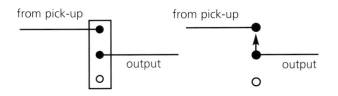

These can be used to select any number of pick-ups with the outputs linked and the casings earthed:

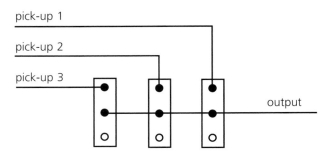

Humbucking pick-ups can add considerably to the complexity of the circuit. It makes little difference if it is to be used fully humbucking but if it is to be used more flexibly then both coils need to be shown.

Standard wiring on a humbucker is for the beginning of the first coil to be the live, the end of that coil and the beginning of the other to be connected and the end of the second coil to be the earth. This is series winding, with one coil feeding into the second. The magnets on the humbucker are arranged so that the coils are opposite polarity.

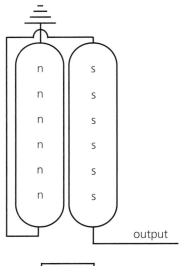

For ease of illustration I will draw them like this:

This is similar to how many older-style humbuckers with single core and screened wire actually look. They have the end of one coil and the beginning of the next joined and covered by a piece of tape. Before helpful pick-up-making companies provided wiring options, the only way of achieving some of the wiring tricks was to uncover this join so that each end of the pick-up could be accessed.

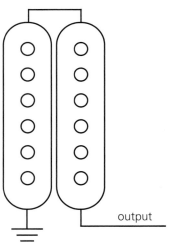

The simplest change is to cut off one coil, known as coil-tapping. A link is taken from the join between the two coils and earthed via an SPDT switch.

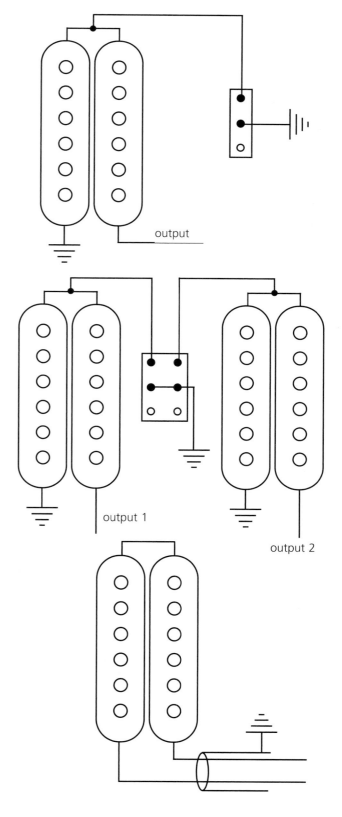

output

Since a DPDT switch is essentially two single-pole switches side by side, one can be used to coil-tap two pick-ups without causing any cross-connection. This is very useful when adding additional features to the circuit, as will be seen later in this chapter.

Push/pull pots have a DPDT switch that is activated when pulling the knob. This one is wired to coil-tap two pick-ups, the earth wire is extended to the middle contacts and when the switch is operated it shorts the two wires on the other two contacts to ground, as on the diagram right.

Phase switching can be done on any pick-up providing that the casing is not earthed. For this you will need two conductor wires and a separate screen. This does not just apply to humbuckers as any pick-up can be put out of phase with any other.

output 1

output 2

A phase switch requires a DPDT switch with no 'off' position in the centre. This simply reverses the direction that the current takes around the coil. When this pick-up is on with another, the phase reversal cancels out some of the signal giving a thinner, treblier sound with less volume. It has no effect when the pick-up is on alone.

It is not advisable to phase switch the two coils of a humbucker as this would cancel out virtually all its signal.

Phase switches can be used in conjunction with on/off switches as on Brian May's Red Special.

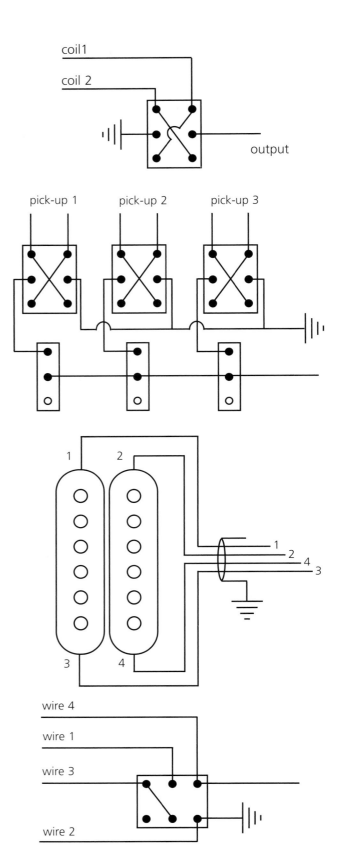

Most aftermarket humbuckers now come with four-conductor wiring which gives many more options. Each end of each coil is given its own wire and it is up to you to decide how to connect these. The wires are colour-coded and no two manufacturers use the same colours in the same way. It is essential therefore to refer to the literature that comes with each pick-up to ensure that it is wired correctly. Some pick-ups, for example those by Kent Armstrong, come without attached wiring so understanding the connections on the pick-up is advisable. Clearly, joining wires 3 and 4 together, using 1 as the ground and 2 as the live will give a standard humbucking sound. Routing 3 and 4 to a switch and earthing them with the switch thrown will give a coil-tap, cutting off the left-hand coil in this diagram.

Humbuckers are normally wired with their coils in series, the output of one going into the input of the other. Wiring them in parallel gives a sound similar to coil-tapping but the coils remain humbucking. Unlike coil-tapping, only one pick-up can be dealt with on a DPDT switch.

The guitar built in Chapter 9 has a coiltap that operates on both pick-ups, a single volume and tone, a three-way toggle selector and a push/pull switch on the tone control that gives a choice of frequency ranges. With the switch in the normal position the tone control works through a normal capacitor to give a normal treble cut. With the switch pulled, the signal is fed through another capacitor and a small tone choke. This is a resistance coil manufactured by Kent Armstrong which smooths out the signal and acts as a mid filter. It is very good for giving a thinner sound which is very usable in chord work.

Kent Armstrong's tone choke.

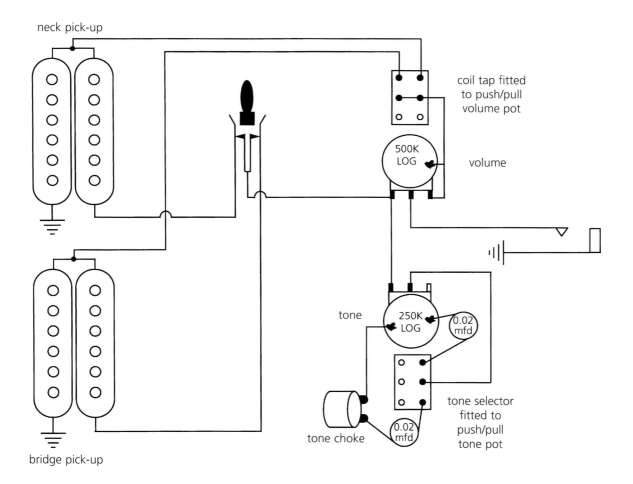

With this circuit it would have been just as easy to dispense with the tone choke and use the switch as a phase switch.

Three-pick-up guitars often do not use a switch that allows all three pick-ups to be on together or to be individually selected. The three-pick-up Gibson Les Paul and SG Customs are examples. They can select bridge, bridge and middle pick-up, or neck pick-up.

Changing the system to be more flexible is easy by using a volume for each pick-up and a master tone. A very similar circuit to this one was used on the Gibson ES5, the predecessor to the Switchmaster mentioned elsewhere.

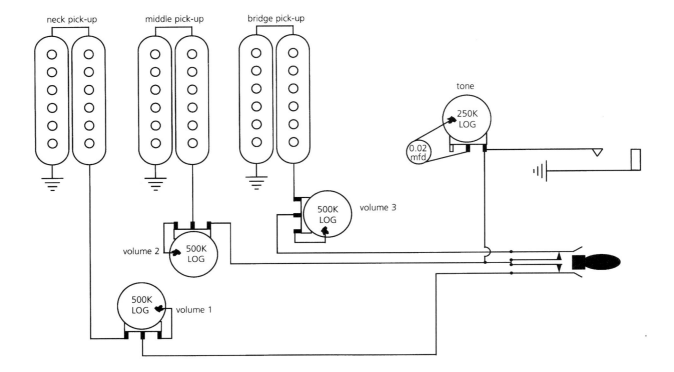

It would be a relatively simple job to fit coil-tap switches onto push/pull pots for each of the pick-ups. Alternatively, a coil tap could be used for two pickups and another for one leaving two other controls that could have phase switches for the bridge and neck pick-ups. The possibilities are almost endless.

It is possible to coil tap three humbucking Stratocaster-style pick-ups using just one DPDT switch. This works because the cheesecutter switch is two switches in one and can be used to feed the coil-tap wires to the tapping switch. The tone controls cannot also cover the bridge pick-up as they are fitted before the switch (facing page, top).

The Stratocaster-style guitar in Chapter 17 was fitted with two humbucking pick-ups and one single-coil. They are selected with a standard cheesecutter switch and a standard Stratocaster-style wiring circuit with the addition of a coil tap for the humbuckers and a switch that will turn on the bridge and neck pick-up together regardless of where the selector is positioned. This means that if the bridge pick-up is selected the neck pick-up can be added or vice versa, and if the centre pick-up is selected all three will be active – options not available on a standard Stratocaster (facing page, bottom).

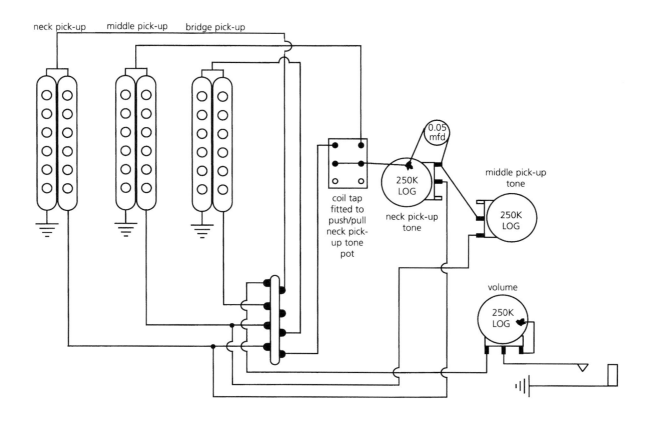

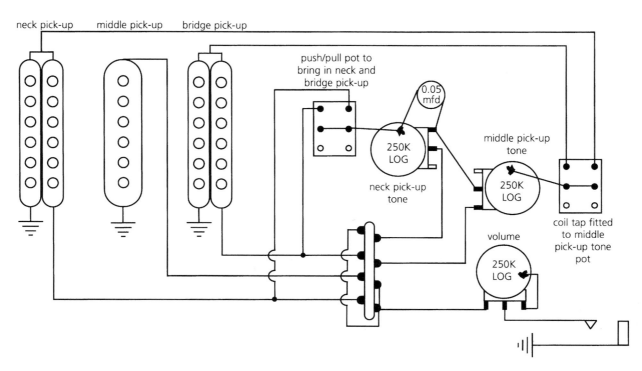

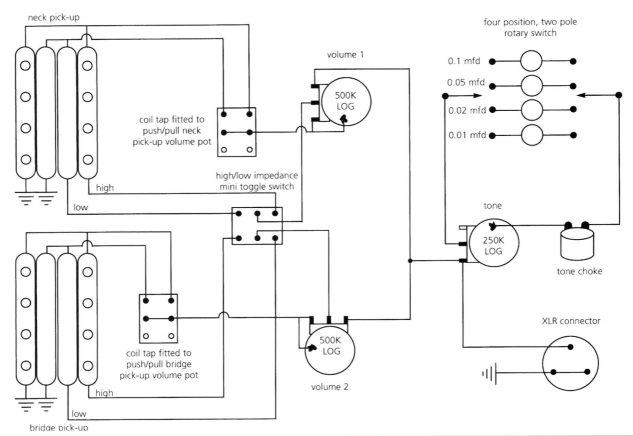

A Bartolini pre-amp.

The eight-string made in Chapter 11 has a circuit that is quite complicated. The pick-ups have four coils and are, in effect, two pick-ups in one. There is a normal high-impedance pair and a seperate low-impedance pair and a mini toggle switch chooses between these. Both sets are coil-tapped on push/pull pots on the volume controls which act as a mixer circuit. The tone control goes several stages further than the Chapter 9 guitar by having a choice of four capacitors of varying values fed through the tone choke. This is very similar to the system used on the Gibson ES345, known as Varitone. The final link in the chain is the XLR connector.

For even more variation in tone it is possible to fit active controls into any guitar. These do require a battery, so it either has to fit in the control cavity or have a battery cavity provided, but all manner of tonal variation can be provided. It is perhaps more suitable for bass guitars, but there is the added advantage that the system gives a slightly higher output due to there being no loss of signal along the guitar lead.

Screening

All electrical circuits pick up interference from other sources. Guitar circuits are no exception. For this reason guitars should be screened against this. Mounting the controls on a metal plate, as on the Telecaster, or adding a foil sheet underneath the scratchplate, as on a Stratocaster, will help but this is very directional.

The best way to ensure the guitar is protected as much as possible is to screen the control cavity with either copper tape or screening paint which is available from some specialist outlets. It is very important that all parts of the screen are earthed. It is not enough to use a lot of aluminium foil and hope. If using copper tape a common earth should be soldered across all pieces, or tape with a conductive adhesive should be used. If using screening paint it is best to choose one of the oil-based varieties. Water-based paints are available but will often be messy and rub off on hands and anything else that comes into contact with them. If using a paint it is a good idea to attach an earth wire into the cavity with a screw. The free end can be soldered on to the back of a pot and the screening paint, well and truly slapped over the screw, will provide a good contact. Using screened cable as much as possible inside the guitar will also help.

Pick-ups too can be screened. Some will come already screened and this is the reason many humbuckers have a metal cover – remove it at your peril! Others will benefit from being screened but beware: a pick-up is a fragile piece of equipment and the windings are easily broken. Do not attempt this without having taken advice and without being totally sure of what you are doing. It is better to have a slightly noisy guitar than a totally dead pick-up.

All of the above only touches the surface of what is available and what is possible. There are other publications that give far more detail than I can in this book and a lot of information can be found via the Internet. Part of the fun of guitar-making is experimenting.

A simple faults checklist

No signal	— Amplifier not turned on — Jack socket or another part of the circuit not connected — Check the wiring to make sure no live contact is touching the earth — Rock and roll has finally sent you deaf
Weak signal	— Check the output of each pick-up. If the signal dies when the tone control is turned down it is possible the pick-up has gone open circuit and the windings are broken — Check the screening wires inside the guitar for any loose strands that could be touching any other part of the circuit
Tone or volume controls work in reverse	— The two outside contacts on the pot have been wired the wrong way round. Desolder and rewire correctly
Pick-up selector works on wrong pick-up	— The pick-ups have been wired either to the wrong part of the selector switch or to the wrong part of the circuit. Check carefully against the wiring diagram
Loud buzz when strings are touched	— The live and earth wires on the jack may have been reversed causing the live to be connected to the strings via the bridge
Tone control does nothing	— Either it is wired incorrectly or the capacitor is not working. Check for dry solder joins
Guitar works intermittently	— Check for dry solder joins. Good connections should appear bright
Tone and volume controls crackle when turned	— Dirty potentiometers. Clean with good switch cleaner

15 Setting up the Guitar

Of course, by now your new masterpiece is almost finished and looking very much like the guitar you have always dreamed of owning, and the hordes of screaming fans you always knew would be there for you are waiting with bated breath for you to string up your guitar and amaze them with your natural virtuosity. However, it is no good just stringing your new guitar up and hoping it will play perfectly as soon as it is plugged in, as it will need some setting up so that it will give its optimum performance. We have already dealt with stoning the frets but there are now several more jobs to do.

FITTING THE STRINGS

After having invested a small fortune in your guitar, you will have a set of strings all ready and waiting to go onto it. It is at this stage that life can get very annoying if all is not well with your design or workmanship. Putting the strings on will show if your neck was not quite fitted straight or if the neck angle, or many other things, are substantially wrong. Of course, if you have planned carefully and executed the work correctly all should be well and life will be much easier.

CUTTING THE STRING SLOTS IN THE NUT

The first job to be attended to is the cutting of the string slots in the nut. It is only a small part of the guitar but it is very important. Its job is to hold the strings the correct distance above the fingerboard so that they do not foul the frets, the correct distance apart so that the guitar is easier to play, and to stop the strings' vibration carrying over towards the head. This last job is most important as if the nut is badly cut and the strings' vibration is not stopped it may rattle and buzz in its slot and the tuning will be affected.

The string must start vibrating at the fingerboard edge of the nut and not halfway across it, and the easiest way of achieving this is to angle the slots back gently. The four bottom string slots on a six-string, and all on a bass, are cut using some carefully chosen needle files that are a very shallow V in section or very small and round. The top two strings have their slots cut with a razor saw.

The positions of the strings are marked onto the nut in pencil and then they are lightly grooved so

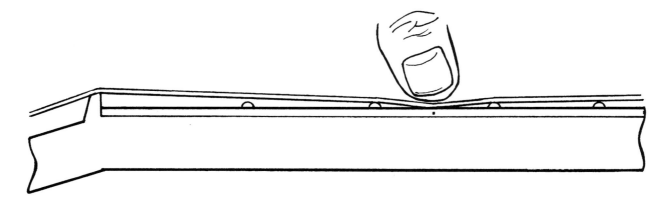

When cutting the string slots in the nut the strings should just clear the first fret when fretted at the third.

Using a small needle file to cut the nut slots in the carved top guitar. These should be cut carefully so that they do not curve over the nut as this could upset the intonation of the guitar; the string must start its vibration from the fingerboard side of the nut. The thicker slots can be cut with needle files but a small saw or specialised nut files can be used for the thinner slots. One good source for nut files is to serrate the edges of a set of feeler gauges. They even come marked with their thickness!

that the spacing of the string can be checked. There are now gauges available from some parts suppliers that make the marking out a doddle.

The slots are then cut a little at a time checking constantly that they are not going too deep. If the slot is too deep the string will rattle against the first fret or will even be damped completely. If, on the other hand, the slot is not deep enough the string will be difficult to fret at the first position and the force needed to fret it may cause the note to go out of tune. This is worth remembering as something to check for on any guitar. If the note at the first few frets is a little sharp the slots in the nut may be too shallow. To check that the slot is the correct depth the string should be fretted at the third fret. The string should then just clear the first fret.

When all of the slots have been successfully cut the nut can be cleaned up with a little wet-and-dry paper and the guitar can be tuned. The nut slots can be lubricated, but not with oil. One substance that is suitable and easily found is graphite dust. This is sold in convenient lengths which are encased in a small piece of wood, often with the letters HB on one end and the other end sharpened to a point. The graphite can be rubbed into the nut slots and will help to prevent the strings sticking. An extra use for the graphite is that, in emergencies, it can be used for writing shopping lists and notes to that wonderful person who caught your eye in the front

row of the gig . An alternative lubricant for the nut is petroleum jelly.

Cutting the nut slots on a fretless bass can be interesting. The notes played on the fingerboard will have a certain amount of buzz since the string has no fret to vibrate against and keep it slightly above the board. The nut, if cut as high as on a fretted bass, will make the bass sound different at the open positions.

The answer is to cut the nut so that the string is very slightly higher than the board, allowing the string to rattle a little against the board as it vibrates. Having a nut cut this low can produce problems if there is not enough angle over the nut to stop the string vibrating before it reaches the head. This is more common on Fender-style necks where there is no head angle. The answer is to fit more string retainers or to wind more of the string onto the machine-head post so that the string is pulled down into the slot.

TRUSS-ROD ADJUSTMENT

Before setting the action of the guitar the truss rod should be adjusted. It is a fallacy to assume that the neck of the guitar needs to be totally straight. There has to be an element of forward bow, known as neck relief, so that the string will not rattle against frets further along the neck. This does not have to be very great and the amount needed will

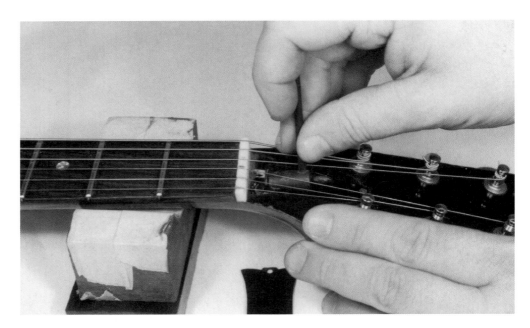

Adjusting the truss rod. It is important not to over-tighten the rod and to use the correct adjuster.

vary with guitars of different types and even with guitars of the same model and with different gauges of string.

The strings should be tuned and the top string fretted at the first and last fret. If the strings touch the frets all the way along the neck the neck is either bent backwards or is a little too straight. Either way the truss rod needs to be slackened off a little. If there is a space of more than about ¹⁄₆₄ in (0.4 mm) the neck is being pulled forward and the truss rod needs to be tightened.

With the string fretted at the first and last fret, the distance between the string and the top surface of the fret in the middle of the neck should be between ¹⁄₆₄ in (0.4 mm) and ¹⁄₃₂ (0.8 mm). Truss rods vary greatly in their sensitivity and a quarter of a turn on one neck may have little effect whereas a quarter of a turn on another may 'banana' the neck significantly. Fender's Precision Basses are prime examples; one apparently only has to breathe near the rod and the neck will move. As with so many things, the art of adjusting the neck rod on the guitar is to take it carefully and a little at a time.

Depending on the type of truss rod fitted to the guitar, too much or heavy-handed adjustment can damage either the rod or the guitar and so it is essential to proceed slowly. It is also important to use the correct tool to adjust the rod. Adjustment nuts come in many different styles and sizes and can be adjusted by spanner, allen key or even screwdriver but using the wrong tool can damage the adjustment

nut and make future adjustments difficult or even impossible. Basic adjustment of the rod should not, however, cause too many problems.

For all adjustments the guitar should be, if at all possible, strung and tuned to pitch. This is easy enough on guitars which have the truss-rod adjustment at the head but some guitars, for example many old-style Fenders and the Telecaster built in Chapter 10, have their adjustment at the end of the fingerboard and this can only be reached by removing the neck.

In these cases the rod needs to be adjusted a little at a time and the neck replaced onto the guitar and strung up so that the effect of each adjustment can be measured. It can be a time-consuming and frustrating business. The relief can be seen if one sights along the neck as one would do with a rifle. The string nearest the edge of the fingerboard will be a straight line and the amount that the fingerboard curves away can be estimated.

Sighting along the neck in this way is also helpful when trying to fathom out why a guitar will not play properly. In theory, the relief along the neck will be a gentle, even curve, the same one side as it is the other.

It is entirely possible that, if using very light strings, a neck will need no adjustment and may even be too straight. If this is the case the only alternative is to raise the action a little unless the truss rod is one of the two-way types that allow forward movement of the neck.

Setting the action on the Telecaster.

SETTING THE ACTION

The action is next to be set. For the lowest possible action the strings should be set so that they are almost touching the frets all the way along the neck and the action should then be raised to the point where the strings stop rattling on the frets and do not choke when they are bent across the neck.

Guitars with a more pronounced camber will need to have a slightly higher action than guitars with flatter fingerboards. The best way of setting the action on any guitar is by trial and error. If the fret stoning has been done properly there is no reason why a good low action is not possible, but equally if the action is too low the guitar can still be difficult to play as it may be difficult to get under a string to bend it.

Some players prefer a higher action. Gary Moore uses an action that would slice many people's fingers into small chunks and strings that are very thick compared to some people's choice. However, he gets a great tone and can play perfectly well.

INTONATION

Having now got the action of the guitar adjusted correctly and the nut adjusted properly the next step is to ensure that the guitar plays in tune all the way along the neck.

Most acoustic guitars have a saddle that slants so that the bass strings are a little longer than the treble and electric guitar bridges. Individual saddles are also adjusted in this way. The bridge is adjusted like this so that when any string is fretted, the stretching that takes place to get it to the fret does not put the whole guitar out of tune. This is known as compensation. Since the bass strings are usually a little higher off of the board than the treble strings and are more susceptible to changes in tension, these need more compensation than the treble strings, hence the angled saddle.

To set the string lengths properly the note at the 12th fret is compared with the harmonic at the same point. If the note is sharper than the harmonic the bridge piece needs to be moved back, and if the note is flatter than the harmonic the opposite applies as the string length is too long. It is possible to do this by ear if you have good natural pitch, but for those of us who do not, one of the electronic tuners on the market will help by visually showing the differences.

When fretting the string to check the intonation, care must be taken not to press the string too hard as if the fret is a little high the note can be changed. In the normal course of playing this may not be noticeable but if it is not recognised when the guitar is being set up, false readings on the tuner may confuse the issue. This problem is aggravated if extra-light strings are used. Each string can be adjusted in

Early Telecasters had just three saddles that made accurate intonation difficult. The trick was to even out the differences!

turn and the result should be a guitar that plays perfectly in tune all the way along the neck.

This, in most cases, will suffice but there are tuners on the market which give all the notes in the scale and so one can also test the guitar at the 19th or 24th fret positions. The notes at the 24th fret position, if your guitar goes up that far, should be the

same as the open strings but two octaves higher and, again, the fretted note should be the same as the harmonic. The notes at the 19th fret are different but the harmonic and the fretted note should match.

It is wise to remember that most musical instruments have tempered tuning, that is to say that there are slight imperfections built in to compensate for the fact that the pure mathematics of music does not always add up for every key that you may play in. These imperfections are very slight but may show up on a tuner and so the very slight differences in tuning on the higher frets can be averaged out or ignored if you do not tend to play that high. After all, having a guitar that is in tune where you play is more important than one that is almost in tune in areas you seldom use.

If the guitar still sounds out of tune as different notes are played on one string then the most probable cause is that the string is dud. If all of the strings are out of tune in some positions when in tune at other positions it is possible that the fingerboard on the guitar may have been made inaccurately. This, of course, can be tested with a chromatic tuner, and if it is severe it might be time to replace the board.

PICK-UP ADJUSTMENT

The last job in setting up the guitar is to adjust the pick-ups so that they are at the correct height under the strings. The nearer the pick-up is to the string the higher the output will be, but this does have

Adjusting the intonation. The differences between the fretted note and harmonic are best seen on an electronic tuner.

Adjusting the height on a humbucker. Some pick-ups, for example the Gibson P90, are not adjustable but their pole pieces are. Putting the pick-up right next to the string will give more output but will also give less dynamics and can cause tuning problems.

complications. Inside the pick-up is a magnet that, if it is too close to the string, may pull the string and cause tuning problems and can dampen the vibration. This is especially noticeable in the case of the Fender Stratocaster where the three pick-ups, if set too close to the strings, can make setting the intonation on the bass strings almost impossible. The answer to this is to set the pick-ups so that the bass side is lower than the treble. This is one of the reasons why Stratocasters sound the way they do.

If the string is too close to the pick-up it can cause nasty rattles when the top notes on the guitar are played, as the string can foul the pick-up. On some guitars this can damage the pick-up. The answer is to lower the pick-up and turn the amplifier up.

AT LAST

The guitar should now be ready for playing. This will give either a sense of achievement or one of relief. You may well have made one or two mistakes and it is probable that you have learned a lot more about how guitars work than you would have done if you had been boring and just spent your money buying a guitar. You may also have learned a lot about what is and is not possible with a little careful thought and planning.

All that there is now left to do is plan the next guitar . . .

16 Tremolo Systems

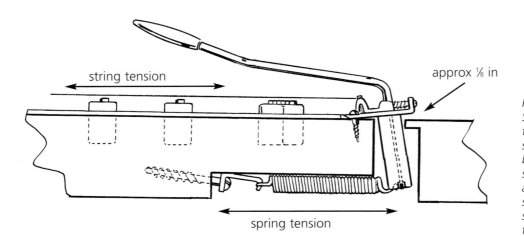

string tension

approx ⅛ in

spring tension

In order for the Stratocaster-style tremolo to work, the string tension needs to be balanced by the spring tension. This is adjusted using the two screws that hold the spring claw in place in the rear cavity.

Many guitars now feature a tremolo system. Both the slime green guitar made in Chapter 9 and the black Stratocaster-style guitar put together in Chapter 17 feature aftermarket tremolos. Both of these, and the majority of available systems, are based on the tried-and-tested system first seen on the Fender Stratocaster in 1954. There are exceptions, such as the Kahler systems that were very popular in the mid-1980s, but it is the Fender-derived systems that have remained popular because the original design was so well thought-out, and which are now by far the most numerous.

The standard Fender Stratocaster tremolo will give quite a wide range of temporary detunability while overall tuning stays largely stable. The replacement systems were designed to overcome any shortcomings in the original units although in practice these units can be just as unreliable as a badly adjusted Fender type.

The workings of the system are simplicity itself. The bridge plate pivots on six screws along its front edge. The strings are fed through a steel block which is attached to a number of springs. These counter the pull of the strings and pull the unit back into its original position after the tremolo arm has been

used. An added bonus to the system is that as tuning is lowered, with the bridgeplate pivoting forwards, the action is raised preventing string buzz. As long as the tension in the springs is adjusted carefully, the screws at the front of the plate not overtightened and the top nut kept lubricated, the system can be made to work quite well with all but the most energetic use. The most common cause for tuning problems that do arise is the amount of stretch in guitar strings. Strings need to be stretched when fitted so that tuning does not wander.

Enthusiastic use of the arm can lead to problems and the replacement systems were designed to get rid of some of the friction in the system. The new units were designed to pivot on hardened steel posts, as on both the Schaller and Wilkinson units seen in this book. The Floyd Rose design, licence-built by Schaller, also features a locking nut. The theory behind this is that if the strings are locked at the nut they cannot stick in the slots and get out of tune. Minor retuning is possible with the knurled tuning knobs built behind the saddles. However, if these units are not set up correctly or the strings not properly stretched, they will still go out of tune.

The rear view of the standard Fender system. Three springs are used in this guitar which is set up with strings from .009 to .046. The earth wire from the spring claw connects to the back of one of the control pots. Also visible in this view are the holes drilled through the tremolo block that take the strings. This causes the strings to pass over the saddles at a sharp angle giving better sustain.

Because the systems are designed to be in balance, setting one up can be frustrating as each adjustment will alter the tuning which has to be restored before any further adjustment.

The first stage in adjusting the tremolo is to decide how many springs you will attach. They will work with just two when using light gauge strings, but using three is most common. Using the full complement of five will give a firmer action and, in all cases, if the system is set up properly it will remain in tune.

The springs are adjusted by two screws in the rear cavity that move the spring claw. If using relatively light strings and three screws, setting the claw about

½ in (12.7 mm) away from the front edge of the rear cavity should be a good starting point. The screws on the front of the standard Fender type should be adjusted so they are loose enough for the plate to move but not so slack that the plate can ride up and down on the screws.

The guitar can then be strung and tuned, which itself takes time as each string will cause the tuning on the others to wander. Once the strings are on they should be stretched until there is no more tuning variance left in them.

The bridge plate should not sit flat on the front of the guitar as rearward motion of the arm will not be possible and the rear of the bridge plate should sit about ⅛ in (3 mm) above the face of the guitar. Again, each adjustment will cause the tuning to change and the guitar will need constant attention.

Setting the action on the guitar will also cause tuning problems. Raising or lowering the bridge saddles

The action on the Floyd Rose-type of tremolo system is set by the two screws which the bridge plate pivots upon. Individual string height is not easily adjustable. Intonation can also be difficult to set. It is not adjustable like a Fender-style bridge but is clamped in place. To adjust this it needs to be unclamped which is impossible if the string is under tension. The string first has to be slackened off, the locking screws undone and the saddle moved to the position required. It then needs to be retuned and checked. This can be very time-consuming but once set it stays in tune very well.

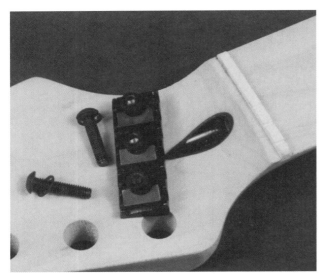

The locking nut supplied with the Floyd-Rose and Schaller units requires the head of the guitar to be altered as the unit replaces the nut. A flat area is routed and the screw holes need to be drilled through the neck. Once this has been machined, the only adjustment for string height at the nut is to deepen the rout or pack it with shims. Once fitted there is no going back! Other manufacturers use slightly different systems but for many people a locking nut may not be necessary.

Fine adjustment of the action on the Wilkinson. The screws holding the saddles in place need to be loosened and this can cause the saddle to move due to string tension. This, of course, will affect the intonation. The two hardened pillars that replace the six screws of a standard Fender unit can be seen. These are adjustable for overall height and the saddle adjustment can be used to match the camber of the fingerboard, a feature that is not available on a Floyd Rose-type tremolo. The mounting posts also position the bridge plate above the face of the guitar so less additional space is required beneath the rear edge.

will tighten or loosen the string tension and so alter the tuning. Raising or lowering the action on the Wilkinson or Schaller is easier as the whole unit moves up and down and tuning does not change. However, the Wilkinson does have individual adjustment to allow for matching the camber of the fretboard

The three things that all of these systems have in common is the need to ensure that friction is kept to a minimum, that the strings are stretched and that the adjustment is done carefully and methodically. If you want to 'dive bomb' with a tremolo you may

wish to use a replacement system but, with careful adjustment, you might be surprised just how good the original Fender system can be.

They can also be adapted to work more efficiently. Roger Giffin produced several guitars with standard Fender-style trems which were mounted onto a small metal plate set into the top of the guitar. This was curved on its upper surface so that the bridge plate was in minimal contact. The plate was held down by just the two outermost mounting screws and the system was very efficient. Even fairly 'industrial' use of the arm produced few tuning problems if the nut was lubricated with graphite (from a pencil) and the strings stretched properly.

17 Assembling Component Parts

One aspect of guitar-making that was left out of the first edition of this book was the construction of guitars from replacement parts. Basically, making a guitar in this way takes away the hard work of cutting, carving and sanding and means you just have to assemble your dream instrument. At least, that is the theory. In actual fact you are immediately limited to having what is on offer from whatever parts supplier you choose to use. For example, there is no point in dreaming about having a scaled-down Stratocaster-style instrument built with a shorter scale length and twin humbuckers if no one sells the parts for such a guitar. However, if you want something that is fairly traditional and will enable you to choose your preferred bridge, machine-heads, pick-ups and finish, then this might be a way to go.

There are pitfalls. Even though most of the spare parts are based on Leo Fender's designs and many are licensed by Fender it does not mean they will all fit together perfectly. Even parts from the same manufacturer might not always go together effortlessly. If you are going to make any guitar, even from component parts, you have to be ready to do a little work. You are also going to have to deal with the frets as shown in Chapter 7, finish it in some way as in Chapter 13, wire it as in Chapter 14 and set the guitar up as detailed in Chapter 15.

COMMON SENSE

Some aspects of the process of choosing your component parts is pure common sense. You may want a Telecaster-style body with a Stratocaster-style neck. If you look at the ends of the necks you will notice that a Strat neck is curved while a Tele neck is straight. This will also mean that the cut-out on the scratchplate that usually fits around the end of the neck will look a little untidy. There are two choices: put up with the untidiness, or either reshape the end of the neck (the hard way) or the scratchplate (the easy way) so that all is tidy.

One advantage of making a guitar in this way is that you have a certain amount of leeway in how you can adapt the guitar but, again, think it through first. For example, if you have always hankered after a '50s Fender Esquire, the single-pick up Telecaster, but prefer the contoured body of a Strat, you can do this quite easily without having to buy a vintage guitar and cut it about. Besides, vintage guitars should always be left as built. Likewise you can buy ready-cut bodies for Telecasters, Stratocasters with humbuckers, Precision Basses with added Jazz Bass pick-ups and even bodies that have no routings for pick-ups and controls so that you can choose your own.

The parts should be bought just as if you were buying a complete guitar. Do not be content to buy them mail order; whilst most companies are very fair not all components will be in A1 condition. This is inevitable when dealing with wood. Necks especially should be inspected for straightness. Some companies offer figured wood necks and bodies; the same comments as before apply. Often these will not be as stable as their plain-grained counterparts. Inspect them carefully. Necks can twist or bend and bodies can warp across their width and warranties may be void if work has already started on the parts before the defects were noted.

In order to show the amount of work that is needed on parts such as these I have included a photo section dealing with the assembly of guitars from component parts.

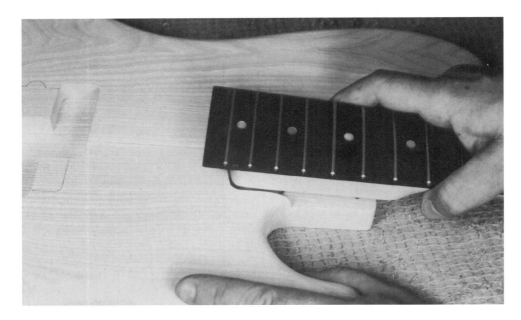

Having bought your parts they should be checked to see if they will fit together. This is a body from one company and a neck from another. The neck is over-size by about 3/64 in (1 mm) and so the cavity needs to be widened. This can be done with chisels but it can also be done carefully with a router. Remember that material needs to be taken from both sides of the cavity.

Of course, if the neck is too loose then some packing may be required and if the slot is too deep then you have real problems. Check the fit of the major parts before you buy if at all possible.

This bass is due to become a fretless with a Bartolini Musicman-style pick-up. This pick-up is both larger and a different shape to the standard Precision Bass-style pick-ups so the rout needs to be enlarged. The complete rout could be plugged before routing for the new pick-up if a neater job was required but this is to be covered with a scratch-plate. The first stage is to find the centre line of the guitar, which in this case was the join between the two pieces of ash that make up the body. The new shape can then be marked and checked to make sure that it will fit.

The Bartolini pick-up has been positioned so that the maximum amount of the old rout is covered. The remaining area can be seen in front of the pick-up. This was routed to 5/8 in (15.8 mm) which is standard for Fender pick-up routs and suits this pick-up too. This method would apply if fitting, for example, a humbucker to a Stratocaster-style body or an additional Jazz Bass-style pick-up to a Precision-style instrument.

Not all components necessarily fit. This apparently standard Strat-style jack cavity needs slight adjustment to accept this apparently standard Strat-style jackplate.

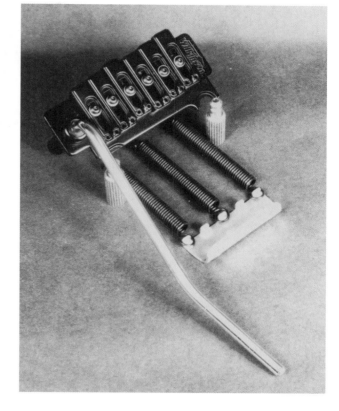

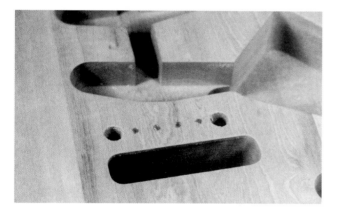

The studs for the Wilkinson are positioned on the outer two screw holes of the standard unit. Since this body was bought predrilled, the new wider diameter holes are drilled, centred on the existing holes, and the inner four holes are filled with small dowels which are then sanded flush with the body.

One advantage of assembling a guitar from aftermarket accessories is the choice of available hardware. I have chosen to assemble a Stratocaster-style guitar using an alder body, maple neck and with the Wilkinson tremolo. This is just one of a number of aftermarket tremolos that have been around for some years, although as this book went to press it was announced that these will no longer be available. A very similar version will be available, however, from the Japanese manufacturer Gotoh. This differs from a standard Fender unit in a number of ways, not least of which is its two-point mounting which is adjustable for height in addition to the adjustment available from the saddles. This unit is also very similar in height to a standard Fender Stratocaster tremolo so no neck angle adjustment is needed as might be the case with a Floyd Rose or one of the similar systems.

Machine-heads come in a variety of styles and sizes. I have chosen to fit Schaller lockable tuners to the Stratocaster-style guitar. These require a hole of 10 mm (a little more than ⅜ in). The Mighty Mite neck shown here is predrilled to accept these but the neck I eventually used had been drilled to accept vintage-style tuners and the original holes had to be reamed to fit. Reamers are by far the best way of increasing the diameter of a hole as trying to do this with a drill can be inaccurate and, in extreme cases, can split the head. For headstocks that have been predrilled to accept wide mounting machine-heads, fitting

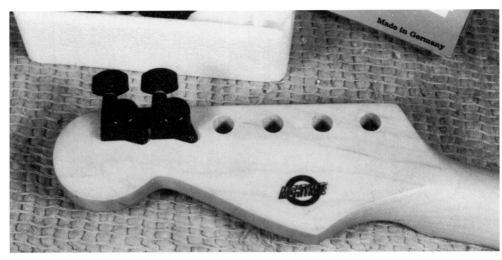

vintage types may require the holes to be plugged and redrilled. It is far easier to buy machine-heads to match your neck or vice versa.

The chosen bridge on the bass guitar is a Gotoh design. This is a very sturdy bridge that is similar to the Fender unit. The holes for the bridge mounting were not predrilled on the body and so, after careful measurement and checking of the bridge position, it was placed on the body and the mounting hole positions marked. Since this body has a join between the two pieces of wood right along the centre it is simple to use this line to position the bridge accurately. It is also important to drill the screw holes to the correct diameter. Too large and they will not tighten correctly and the bridge may pull off; too narrow and the screws could break as they are inserted.

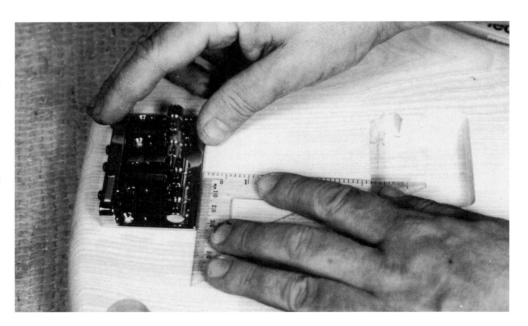

Removing the remains of a broken screw is one of the most annoying jobs that can ever be done on a guitar and is difficult to do without damaging the guitar further.

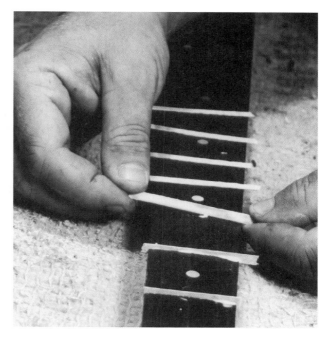

The fret slots are filled with strips of maple veneer glued into place with white PVA. This gives a visible line across the fingerboard in the fret position, making it easier for non-bass players, such as myself, to play. The strips are left to dry out thoroughly so they do not pull out at the next stage. Do not be tempted to simply file the frets level with the board. This will leave the tang in place and although this will also give a visible line, the tang will wear differently to the surrounding wood and the bass will start buzzing and rattling. Also, removing the fret tang at a later date to refret the guitar will not be easy as there will be nothing to grip.

The bass is to be a fretless. The chosen WD Products neck came fretted so these frets had to be removed. The endcutters seen on page 47 are used to gently prise the fret out of its slot. The fret is easier to remove if it is heated a little with a soldering iron. This releases oils in the wood around the fret tang making it easier to pull out without the tang studs tearing the board.

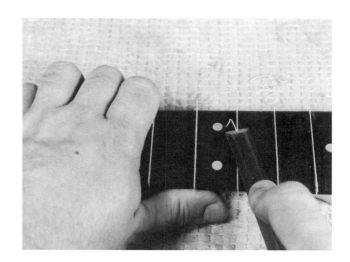

Once glued in, the worst of the excess can be pared off using a sharp chisel, taking care not to tip the chisel and mark the face of the board.

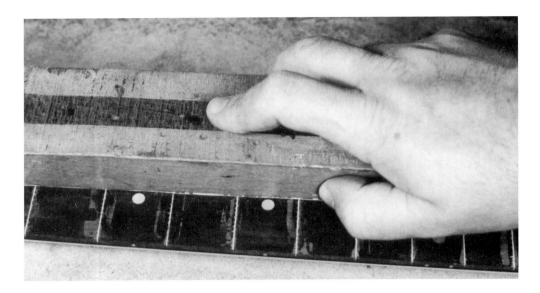

Preparing a fretless board is no different than preparing a fretted one. The sanding stick is used to flatten the maple lines. Since most of the work on the board has already been done at the factory, no reshaping of the contour should be necessary.

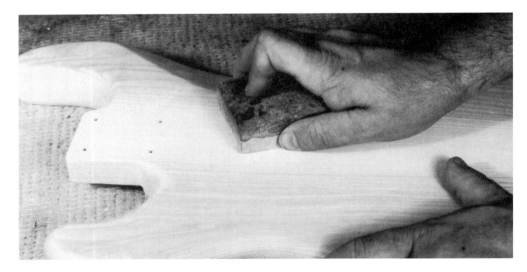

Although most bodies are sold ready for finishing and are often sanding sealed, some preparation is almost inevitable to deal with the wear and tear of transit and the minor knocks and abrasions that occur when the body is on display prior to sale. The P-bass body here was sanded along the grain with 220 grit paper over a cork block.

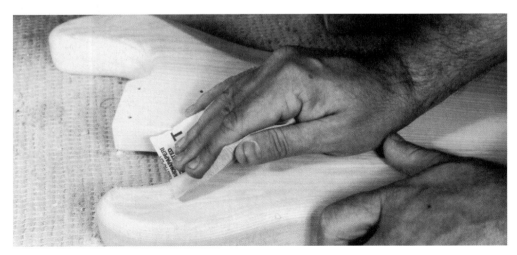

The edges of aftermarket guitar bodies frequently show signs of machining and the curves of the rounding-over are sometimes not blended with the front and sides too well. The best way of dealing with these areas is to wrap some paper over the fingers which provide the perfect flexible base.

The alder Stratocaster-style body was grainfilled before painting. This is not always necessary on an alder body but helped highlight some of the minor dings that it had collected in storage and while clumsy old me worked on it. This also helped blend the dowels at the front of the tremolo block into the surrounding surface. Here, the brass inserts for the mounting studs have been installed, as fitting after the body is painted could damage the finish. The threads are protected from paint by masking tape plugs. In this picture the hole that links the control cavity to the jack cavity and the hole that takes the earth wire into the back cavity where it is soldered to the spring claw can be clearly seen. This guitar was sprayed black with standard automotive paint (see page 149).

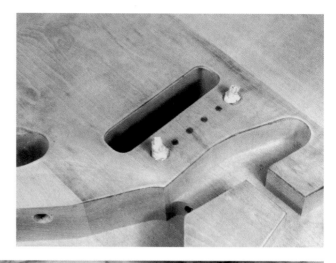

With the Tru-Oil finish applied and semi-glossed (see page 150), the bass can be assembled. The bridge is screwed into place with the earth wire that connects the common earth inside the bass to the bridge trapped beneath it.

Since there is no readily available scratchplate for a Precision bass-style guitar with a Musicman pick-up, one has to be made. The main shape was taken from an existing model and adapted, or a whole new design can be made. For this bass a template of thin card was made and attached to the bass with masking tape while the pick-up position was marked using the routing jig as a guide.

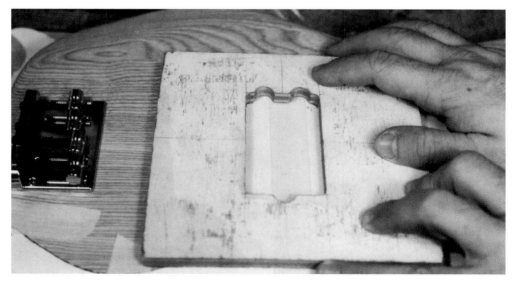

To make life a little easier (always a good option) the black single-layer scratchplate plastic is covered in masking tape while being worked on to protect the finish and to make sure any lines drawn on can be clearly seen. The pick-up position is routed, using the jig, and the card template is then positioned on the plastic so that it lines up correctly and is drawn around. The pickguard is cut out using a small electric jigsaw similar to that seen on page 88 before the edges are tidied using progressively finer grades of sandpaper, starting with 220 grit and going on to 1200 grit and finally metal polish to restore some of the shine. The face of the plastic is left masked as, while it is possible to remove some scratches, it is impossible to totally restore the original sheen. Keeping it covered for as long as possible is the best option. The scratchplate on this guitar could be made with a laminated black/white/black or

white/black/white plastic but the edges would need to be bevelled accurately to show the laminations. These bevels are machined on factory-produced plates but would have to be filed, sanded and scraped onto this one. Note also the screw holes have been drilled and countersunk and their position will be marked onto the body so they can be predrilled.

No such problem exists for the Stratocaster-style guitar which is fitted with a black/white/black laminate scratchplate from Mighty Mite. This has the standard routs for three pick-ups, a cheesecutter switch, master volume and two tones. This guitar is fitted with a standard Stratocaster-style pick-up in the centre (one of the Kent Armstrong designed Sky pick-ups), a Seymour Duncan Hot Rails at the bridge and a JB Junior at the neck. The two humbucking pick-ups should fit into the scratchplate without alteration but in fact a small amount of opening-up was necessary.

Unlike the guitar heads on the Stratocaster-style guitar which use a screwed-in bushing, the bass heads – and vintage styles of guitar head – have a bushing that is a press-fit. On the bass a very slight adjustment of the hole was needed with a small file before the fit was correct, These should need only light 'persuasion' to fit into the hole. The hammer is being used here to press the bushing into place rather than hammer it in and the wood block helps prevent damage. Over-zealous use of the hammer to fit a tight bushing can split a headstock. It is far better to slightly enlarge the hole.

Mounting holes for bass machine-heads vary far less than for guitars. Most aftermarket necks come predrilled to accept the large Kluson-style tuners, although the mounting holes for the backplates will often need drilling. The heads used on this bass are the Schaller equivalent of the old Kluson heads. They are used to mark the positions of the mounting holes, making sure they are kept correctly aligned. The holes are then drilled to $\frac{1}{16}$ in (1.5 mm). Note the piece of masking tape on the drill bit acting as a rudimentary depth guide which helps prevent over-enthusiastic drilling ruining the face of the head.

As mentioned elsewhere, setting up the fretless bass nut is a matter of taking the slots low enough so the strings can be played easily in the lower positions but not so low that they rattle against the board. The slots are cut using small round files. The nut shown here is a Graph Tech graphite nut.

If your chosen neck is not predrilled then aligning the neck and drilling the screw holes is one of the most important jobs and it is essential that this is done correctly. The bridge and scratchplate are fitted and the neck is clamped to the body using cauls to protect the wood. An old guitar string is used to check the alignment and if the clamp is fitted carefully both sides of the neck can be checked. Any adjustment can be made and the clamp retightened before marking the final position of the screw holes.

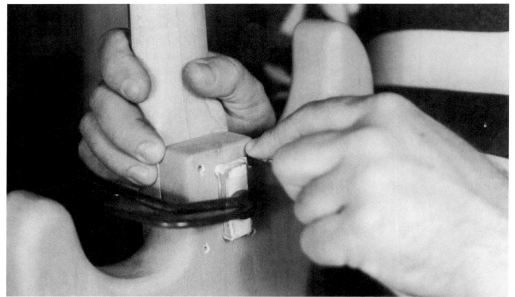

The neck holes can be marked while the neck is still clamped to the body but it is better to drill the holes with the neck removed. The fixing screws will go quite deep into the neck and drilling them with the aid of some some sort of depth gauge – even if it is only a piece of tape around the drill bit – will help prevent them from emerging from the front of the fingerboard by mistake.

It is a frustrating fact of guitar-making that no matter how much you learn or, for that matter, how much you include in a book, there is always something that will disprove a long-held belief and which will make you have to stop and think deeply about a problem before carrying on. This is no bad thing as it would probably not be fun if it were too easy. Problems are there to be solved. If you choose to build your own guitar, assemble one from aftermarket spare parts, or do a combination of both, you may come up against a problem I have not covered in this book.

Appendix 1 Fretting Tables

The following fretting charts cover the main scale lengths used in guitar-making. These have all been worked out using the system discussed in Chapter 7 on a Microsoft Excel spreadsheet. Both imperial and metric measurements are given and in each case the scale length has been converted as exactly as possible. For example, none have been rounded up or down.

As described in Chapter 7, the three columns show the distance between each fret (or in the case of the first, the position from the nut); the distance from the nut to each fret and the remainder of the scale length from that position to the bridge. No compensation has been made to allow for any string stretching raising the pitch of the note.

The remainder columns are useful for measuring the distance to the bridge at any position although this does not allow for any compensation either and the actual saddle positions may vary.

The amount of compensation needed depends upon a number of factors including action, string thickness and string tension. For a low action and light strings very little compensation might be required on the treble side of a bridge although up to ⅛ in (3 mm) might be needed depending on the set up of the guitar. The bass side will need approximately ⅛ – ³⁄₁₆ in (3–4 mm) more. Basses, due to their generally lower string tension, may only need about the same amount of compensation. This small amount of adjustment is usually well within the limits of the bridge.

The first of the charts is for the short 23 ½ in scale used on the Gibson Byrdland. This converts to 596.90 mm.

fret	Imperial			Metric		
	fret	nut	remainder	fret	nut	remainder
1	1.319	1.319	22.181	33.502	33.502	563.398
2	1.245	2.564	20.936	31.621	65.123	531.777
3	1.175	3.739	19.761	29.847	94.970	501.930
4	1.109	4.848	18.652	28.171	123.141	473.759
5	1.047	5.895	17.605	26.590	149.731	447.169
6	0.988	6.883	16.617	25.098	174.829	422.071
7	0.933	7.816	15.684	23.689	198.518	398.382
8	0.880	8.696	14.804	22.360	220.878	376.022
9	0.831	9.527	13.973	21.105	241.983	354.917
10	0.784	10.311	13.189	19.920	261.903	334.997
11	0.740	11.051	12.449	18.802	280.705	316.195
12	0.699	11.750	11.750	17.747	298.452	298.448
13	0.659	12.410	11.090	16.751	315.203	281.697
14	0.622	13.032	10.468	15.811	331.013	265.887
15	0.588	13.620	9.880	14.923	345.936	250.964
16	0.555	14.174	9.326	14.086	360.022	236.878
17	0.523	14.698	8.802	13.295	373.317	223.583
18	0.494	15.192	8.308	12.549	385.866	211.034
19	0.466	15.658	7.842	11.845	397.710	199.190
20	0.440	16.098	7.402	11.180	408.890	188.010
21	0.415	16.513	6.987	10.552	419.442	177.458
22	0.392	16.906	6.594	9.960	429.402	167.498
23	0.370	17.276	6.224	9.401	438.803	158.097
24	0.349	17.625	5.875	8.873	447.677	149.223

Make Your Own Electric Guitar

The second is for the 24 in (609.60 mm) scale as used on a Fender Jaguar.

fret	Imperial nut	Imperial remainder	fret	Metric nut	Metric remainder
1	1.347	22.653	34.215	34.215	575.385
2	2.618	21.382	32.294	66.509	543.091
3	3.819	20.181	30.482	96.990	512.610
4	4.951	19.049	28.771	125.761	483.839
5	6.020	17.980	27.156	152.917	456.683
6	7.029	16.971	25.632	178.549	431.051
7	7.982	16.018	24.193	202.742	406.858
8	8.881	15.119	22.835	225.578	384.022
9	9.730	14.270	21.554	247.131	362.469
10	10.531	13.469	20.344	267.475	342.125
11	11.287	12.713	19.202	286.677	322.923
12	12.000	12.000	18.124	304.802	304.798
13	12.674	11.326	17.107	321.909	287.691
14	13.309	10.691	16.147	338.056	271.544
15	13.909	10.091	15.241	353.297	256.303
16	14.476	9.524	14.385	367.682	241.918
17	15.010	8.990	13.578	381.260	228.340
18	15.515	8.485	12.816	394.076	215.524
19	15.991	8.009	12.097	406.172	203.428
20	16.441	7.559	11.418	417.590	192.010
21	16.865	7.135	10.777	428.367	181.233
22	17.265	6.735	10.172	438.539	171.061
23	17.643	6.357	9.601	448.140	161.460
24	18.000	6.000	9.062	457.202	152.398

Chart number three is for the 24⅝ in scale used by Gibson. This converts to 623.888 mm.

fret	Imperial nut	Imperial remainder	fret	Metric nut	Metric remainder
1	1.379	23.184	35.016	35.016	588.871
2	2.680	21.883	33.051	68.067	555.820
3	3.908	20.654	31.196	99.264	524.624
4	5.067	19.495	29.445	128.709	495.179
5	6.161	18.401	27.792	156.501	467.386
6	7.194	17.368	26.233	182.734	441.154
7	8.169	16.393	24.760	207.494	416.393
8	9.089	15.473	23.371	230.865	393.023
9	9.958	14.605	22.059	252.923	370.964
10	10.777	13.785	20.821	273.744	350.143
11	11.551	13.011	19.652	293.396	330.491
12	12.281	12.281	18.549	311.946	311.942
13	12.971	11.592	17.508	329.454	294.434
14	13.621	10.941	16.525	345.979	277.908
15	14.235	10.327	15.598	361.577	262.310
16	14.815	9.748	14.722	376.300	247.588
17	15.362	9.200	13.896	390.196	233.692
18	15.878	8.684	13.116	403.312	220.576
19	16.366	8.197	12.380	415.692	208.195
20	16.826	7.737	11.685	427.377	196.510
21	17.260	7.302	11.029	438.407	185.481
22	17.670	6.893	10.410	448.817	175.071
23	18.057	6.506	9.826	458.643	165.244
24	18.422	6.141	9.275	467.918	155.970

The full 24¾ in scale as used on many Gibson-style instruments converts to 628.650 mm.

fret	Imperial fret	Imperial nut	Imperial remainder	Metric fret	Metric nut	Metric remainder
1	1.389	1.389	23.361	35.284	35.284	593.366
2	1.311	2.700	22.050	33.303	68.587	560.063
3	1.238	3.938	20.812	31.434	100.021	528.629
4	1.168	5.106	19.644	29.670	129.691	498.959
5	1.103	6.208	18.542	28.005	157.696	470.954
6	1.041	7.249	17.501	26.433	184.129	444.521
7	0.982	8.231	16.519	24.949	209.078	419.572
8	0.927	9.159	15.591	23.549	232.627	396.023
9	0.875	10.034	14.716	22.227	254.854	373.796
10	0.826	10.860	13.890	20.980	275.834	352.816
11	0.780	11.639	13.111	19.802	295.636	333.014
12	0.736	12.375	12.375	18.691	314.327	314.323
13	0.695	13.070	11.680	17.642	331.969	296.681
14	0.656	13.725	11.025	16.652	348.620	280.030
15	0.619	14.344	10.406	15.717	364.337	264.313
16	0.584	14.928	9.822	14.835	379.172	249.478
17	0.551	15.479	9.271	14.002	393.174	235.476
18	0.520	16.000	8.750	13.216	406.391	222.259
19	0.491	16.491	8.259	12.475	418.865	209.785
20	0.464	16.954	7.796	11.774	430.640	198.010
21	0.438	17.392	7.358	11.114	441.753	186.897
22	0.413	17.805	6.945	10.490	452.243	176.407
23	0.390	18.195	6.555	9.901	462.144	166.506
24	0.368	18.563	6.187	9.345	471.489	157.161

Paul Reed Smiths use a 25 in, or 635.0 mm, scale length.

fret	Imperial fret	Imperial nut	Imperial remainder	Metric fret	Metric nut	Metric remainder
1	1.403	1.403	23.597	35.640	35.640	599.360
2	1.324	2.728	22.272	33.640	69.280	565.720
3	1.250	3.978	21.022	31.752	101.032	533.968
4	1.180	5.158	19.842	29.970	131.001	503.999
5	1.114	6.271	18.729	28.288	159.289	475.711
6	1.051	7.322	17.678	26.700	185.989	449.011
7	0.992	8.315	16.685	25.201	211.190	423.810
8	0.936	9.251	15.749	23.787	234.977	400.023
9	0.884	10.135	14.865	22.452	257.428	377.572
10	0.834	10.969	14.031	21.192	278.620	356.380
11	0.787	11.757	13.243	20.002	298.622	336.378
12	0.743	12.500	12.500	18.880	317.502	317.498
13	0.702	13.202	11.798	17.820	335.322	299.678
14	0.662	13.864	11.136	16.820	352.142	282.858
15	0.625	14.489	10.511	15.876	368.017	266.983
16	0.590	15.079	9.921	14.985	383.002	251.998
17	0.557	15.636	9.364	14.144	397.146	237.854
18	0.526	16.161	8.839	13.350	410.496	224.504
19	0.496	16.657	8.343	12.601	423.096	211.904
20	0.468	17.126	7.874	11.893	434.990	200.010
21	0.442	17.568	7.432	11.226	446.215	188.785
22	0.417	17.985	7.015	10.596	456.811	178.189
23	0.394	18.378	6.622	10.001	466.812	168.188
24	0.372	18.750	6.250	9.440	476.252	158.748

Fender's most popular scale length has also been used on Gibsons and many other makes. 25½ in converts to 647.70 mm.

fret	Imperial			Metric		
	fret	nut	remainder	fret	nut	remainder
1	1.431	1.431	24.069	36.353	36.353	611.347
2	1.351	2.782	22.718	34.313	70.665	577.035
3	1.275	4.057	21.443	32.387	103.052	544.648
4	1.204	5.261	20.239	30.569	133.621	514.079
5	1.136	6.397	19.103	28.853	162.474	485.226
6	1.072	7.469	18.031	27.234	189.708	457.992
7	1.012	8.481	17.019	25.705	215.414	432.286
8	0.955	9.436	16.064	24.263	239.676	408.024
9	0.902	10.338	15.162	22.901	262.577	385.123
10	0.851	11.189	14.311	21.615	284.193	363.507
11	0.803	11.992	13.508	20.402	304.595	343.105
12	0.758	12.750	12.750	19.257	323.852	323.848
13	0.716	13.466	12.034	18.176	342.028	305.672
14	0.675	14.141	11.359	17.156	359.185	288.515
15	0.638	14.779	10.721	16.193	375.378	272.322
16	0.602	15.380	10.120	15.284	390.662	257.038
17	0.568	15.948	9.552	14.427	405.089	242.611
18	0.536	16.484	9.016	13.617	418.706	228.994
19	0.506	16.990	8.510	12.853	431.558	216.142
20	0.478	17.468	8.032	12.131	443.689	204.011
21	0.451	17.919	7.581	11.450	455.140	192.560
22	0.425	18.344	7.156	10.808	465.947	181.753
23	0.402	18.746	6.754	10.201	476.148	171.552
24	0.379	19.125	6.375	9.629	485.777	161.923

Many classical guitars will have a scale length as long as 26 in, or 660.40 mm.

fret	Imperial			Metric		
	fret	nut	remainder	fret	nut	remainder
1	1.459	1.459	24.541	37.066	37.066	623.334
2	1.377	2.837	23.163	34.985	72.051	588.349
3	1.300	4.137	21.863	33.022	105.073	555.327
4	1.227	5.364	20.636	31.168	136.241	524.159
5	1.158	6.522	19.478	29.419	165.660	494.740
6	1.093	7.615	18.385	27.768	193.428	466.972
7	1.032	8.647	17.353	26.209	219.637	440.763
8	0.974	9.621	16.379	24.738	244.376	416.024
9	0.919	10.540	15.460	23.350	267.726	392.674
10	0.868	11.408	14.592	22.039	289.765	370.635
11	0.819	12.227	13.773	20.802	310.567	349.833
12	0.773	13.000	13.000	19.635	330.202	330.198
13	0.730	13.730	12.270	18.533	348.735	311.665
14	0.689	14.418	11.582	17.493	366.227	294.173
15	0.650	15.068	10.932	16.511	382.738	277.662
16	0.614	15.682	10.318	15.584	398.322	262.078
17	0.579	16.261	9.739	14.709	413.032	247.368
18	0.547	16.808	9.192	13.884	426.915	233.485
19	0.516	17.324	8.676	13.105	440.020	220.380
20	0.487	17.811	8.189	12.369	452.389	208.011
21	0.460	18.270	7.730	11.675	464.064	196.336
22	0.434	18.704	7.296	11.020	475.084	185.316
23	0.409	19.114	6.886	10.401	485.485	174.915
24	0.387	19.500	6.500	9.817	495.302	165.098

Some budget basses use a 30 in, or 762.0 mm, scale.

	Imperial			Metric		
	fret	nut	remainder	fret	nut	remainder
1	1.684	1.684	28.316	42.768	42.768	719.232
2	1.589	3.273	26.727	40.368	83.136	678.864
3	1.500	4.773	25.227	38.102	121.238	640.762
4	1.416	6.189	23.811	35.964	157.201	604.799
5	1.336	7.525	22.475	33.945	191.146	570.854
6	1.261	8.787	21.213	32.040	223.186	538.814
7	1.191	9.977	20.023	30.242	253.428	508.572
8	1.124	11.101	18.899	28.544	281.972	480.028
9	1.061	12.162	17.838	26.942	308.914	453.086
10	1.001	13.163	16.837	25.430	334.344	427.656
11	0.945	14.108	15.892	24.003	358.347	403.653
12	0.892	15.000	15.000	22.656	381.002	380.998
13	0.842	15.842	14.158	21.384	402.386	359.614
14	0.795	16.637	13.363	20.184	422.570	339.430
15	0.750	17.387	12.613	19.051	441.621	320.379
16	0.708	18.095	11.905	17.982	459.603	302.397
17	0.668	18.763	11.237	16.972	476.575	285.425
18	0.631	19.393	10.607	16.020	492.595	269.405
19	0.595	19.989	10.011	15.121	507.715	254.285
20	0.562	20.551	9.449	14.272	521.988	240.012
21	0.530	21.081	8.919	13.471	535.458	226.542
22	0.501	21.582	8.418	12.715	548.173	213.827
23	0.472	22.054	7.946	12.001	560.175	201.825
24	0.446	22.500	7.500	11.328	571.502	190.498

A 32 in bass scale converts to 812.80 mm.

	Imperial			Metric		
	fret	nut	remainder	fret	nut	remainder
1	1.796	1.796	30.204	45.619	45.619	767.181
2	1.695	3.491	28.509	43.059	88.678	724.122
3	1.600	5.091	26.909	40.642	129.320	683.480
4	1.510	6.602	25.398	38.361	167.682	645.118
5	1.426	8.027	23.973	36.208	203.890	608.910
6	1.346	9.373	22.627	34.176	238.065	574.735
7	1.270	10.643	21.357	32.258	270.323	542.477
8	1.199	11.841	20.159	30.447	300.770	512.030
9	1.131	12.973	19.027	28.738	329.508	483.292
10	1.068	14.041	17.959	27.125	356.634	456.166
11	1.008	15.049	16.951	25.603	382.237	430.563
12	0.951	16.000	16.000	24.166	406.403	406.397
13	0.898	16.898	15.102	22.810	429.212	383.588
14	0.848	17.746	14.254	21.529	450.741	362.059
15	0.800	18.546	13.454	20.321	471.062	341.738
16	0.755	19.301	12.699	19.180	490.243	322.557
17	0.713	20.014	11.986	18.104	508.347	304.453
18	0.673	20.686	11.314	17.088	525.434	287.366
19	0.635	21.321	10.679	16.129	541.563	271.237
20	0.599	21.921	10.079	15.223	556.787	256.013
21	0.566	22.486	9.514	14.369	571.156	241.644
22	0.534	23.020	8.980	13.563	584.718	228.082
23	0.504	23.524	8.476	12.801	597.520	215.280
24	0.476	24.000	8.000	12.083	609.603	203.197

Rickenbacker's basses and the eight-string in Chapter 11 use a 32½ in or 825.50 scale.

fret	Imperial fret	Imperial nut	Imperial remainder	Metric nut	Metric remainder
1	1.824	1.824	30.676	46.332	779.168
2	1.722	3.546	28.954	90.064	735.436
3	1.625	5.171	27.329	131.341	694.159
4	1.534	6.705	25.795	170.302	655.198
5	1.448	8.153	24.347	207.075	618.425
6	1.367	9.519	22.981	241.785	583.715
7	1.290	10.809	21.691	274.547	550.953
8	1.217	12.026	20.474	305.470	520.030
9	1.149	13.175	19.325	334.657	490.843
10	1.085	14.260	18.240	362.206	463.294
11	1.024	15.284	17.216	388.209	437.291
12	0.966	16.250	16.250	412.753	412.747
13	0.912	17.162	15.338	435.918	389.582
14	0.861	18.023	14.477	457.784	367.716
15	0.813	18.836	13.664	478.423	347.077
16	0.767	19.602	12.898	497.903	327.597
17	0.724	20.326	12.174	516.290	309.210
18	0.683	21.010	11.490	533.644	291.856
19	0.645	21.655	10.845	550.025	275.475
20	0.609	22.263	10.237	565.486	260.014
21	0.575	22.838	9.662	580.080	245.420
22	0.542	23.380	9.120	593.855	231.645
23	0.512	23.892	8.608	606.856	218.644
24	0.483	24.375	8.125	619.128	206.372

The Fender bass popularised the 34 in, or 863.60 mm, scale.

fret	Imperial fret	Imperial nut	Imperial remainder	Metric nut	Metric remainder
1	1.908	1.908	32.092	48.471	815.129
2	1.801	3.709	30.291	94.221	769.379
3	1.700	5.410	28.590	137.403	726.197
4	1.605	7.014	26.986	178.162	685.438
5	1.515	8.529	25.471	216.633	646.967
6	1.430	9.958	24.042	252.944	610.656
7	1.349	11.308	22.692	287.218	576.382
8	1.274	12.581	21.419	319.568	544.032
9	1.202	13.784	20.216	350.103	513.497
10	1.135	14.918	19.082	378.923	484.677
11	1.071	15.989	18.011	406.126	457.474
12	1.011	17.000	17.000	431.803	431.797
13	0.954	17.954	16.046	456.038	407.562
14	0.901	18.855	15.145	478.913	384.687
15	0.850	19.705	14.295	500.504	363.096
16	0.802	20.507	13.493	520.883	342.717
17	0.757	21.265	12.735	540.118	323.482
18	0.715	21.979	12.021	558.274	305.326
19	0.675	22.654	11.346	575.411	288.189
20	0.637	23.291	10.709	591.586	272.014
21	0.601	23.892	10.108	606.853	256.747
22	0.567	24.459	9.541	621.263	242.337
23	0.535	24.995	9.005	634.865	228.735
24	0.505	25.500	8.500	647.703	215.897

A 35 in scale converts to 889.0 mm.

	Imperial			Metric		
	fret	nut	remainder	fret	nut	remainder
1	1.964	1.964	33.036	49.896	49.896	839.104
2	1.854	3.819	31.181	47.096	96.992	792.008
3	1.750	5.569	29.431	44.452	141.444	747.556
4	1.652	7.221	27.779	41.957	183.402	705.598
5	1.559	8.780	26.220	39.603	223.004	665.996
6	1.472	10.251	24.749	37.380	260.384	628.616
7	1.389	11.640	23.360	35.282	295.666	593.334
8	1.311	12.951	22.049	33.302	328.967	560.033
9	1.237	14.189	20.811	31.432	360.400	528.600
10	1.168	15.357	19.643	29.668	390.068	498.932
11	1.102	16.460	18.540	28.003	418.071	470.929
12	1.041	17.500	17.500	26.431	444.503	444.497
13	0.982	18.482	16.518	24.948	469.451	419.549
14	0.927	19.409	15.591	23.548	492.998	396.002
15	0.875	20.284	14.716	22.226	515.224	373.776
16	0.826	21.110	13.890	20.979	536.203	352.797
17	0.780	21.890	13.110	19.801	556.004	332.996
18	0.736	22.626	12.374	18.690	574.694	314.306
19	0.695	23.320	11.680	17.641	592.335	296.665
20	0.656	23.976	11.024	16.651	608.985	280.015
21	0.619	24.595	10.405	15.716	624.702	264.298
22	0.584	25.179	9.821	14.834	639.536	249.464
23	0.551	25.730	9.270	14.001	653.537	235.463
24	0.520	26.250	8.750	13.216	666.753	222.247

36 in, or 914.40 mm, scales are used by some manufacturers of five- and six-string basses.

	Imperial			Metric		
	fret	nut	remainder	fret	nut	remainder
1	2.021	2.021	33.979	51.322	51.322	863.078
2	1.907	3.928	32.072	48.441	99.763	814.637
3	1.800	5.728	30.272	45.722	145.486	768.914
4	1.699	7.427	28.573	43.156	188.642	725.758
5	1.604	9.031	26.969	40.734	229.376	685.024
6	1.514	10.544	25.456	38.448	267.824	646.576
7	1.429	11.973	24.027	36.290	304.113	610.287
8	1.349	13.322	22.678	34.253	338.366	576.034
9	1.273	14.594	21.406	32.331	370.697	543.703
10	1.201	15.796	20.204	30.516	401.213	513.187
11	1.134	16.930	19.070	28.803	430.016	484.384
12	1.070	18.000	18.000	27.187	457.203	457.197
13	1.010	19.010	16.990	25.661	482.864	431.536
14	0.954	19.964	16.036	24.220	507.084	407.316
15	0.900	20.864	15.136	22.861	529.945	384.455
16	0.850	21.714	14.286	21.578	551.523	362.877
17	0.802	22.515	13.485	20.367	571.890	342.510
18	0.757	23.272	12.728	19.224	591.114	323.286
19	0.714	23.987	12.013	18.145	609.259	305.141
20	0.674	24.661	11.339	17.126	626.385	288.015
21	0.636	25.297	10.703	16.165	642.550	271.850
22	0.601	25.898	10.102	15.258	657.808	256.592
23	0.567	26.465	9.535	14.402	672.210	242.190
24	0.535	27.000	9.000	13.593	685.803	228.597

Appendix 2   Useful Addresses

The following is a selection of the companies and individuals that will supply parts and services for guitar-makers.

SPECIFIC GUITAR-MAKING SUPPLIERS

Luthiers Supplies
The Hall
Horebeech Lane
Horam
East Sussex, TN21 0HR
UK

Touchstone Tonewoods
44 Albert Road North
Reigate
Surrey, RH2 9EZ
UK

Craft Supplies
The Mill
Millers Dale
Derbyshire, SK17 8SN
UK

Luthiers Mercantile International
PO Box 774
412 Moore Lane
Healdsburg
CA 95448 USA
http://www.wco.com/~lmi/catalog.htm

Stewart MacDonald's Guitar Shop
Supply
21 N Shafer Street
PO Box 900
Athens
OH 45701 USA
http://www.stewmac.com

Timeless Instruments
PO Box 51
Tugaske
Saskatchewan
SOH 4BO, Canada
Website
www3.sk.sympatico.ca/timeless

Gerard Gilet
5/6 Booralee St
Botany
NSW 2019
Australia

Euphonon Company
PO Box 100-J
Orford
NH 03777 USA

Guitarmaker's Connection
(part of the Martin Company)
PO Box 329
Nazareth
PA 18064 USA

International Violin Company, Ltd.
1421 Clark View Road
Suite 118
Baltimore
MD 21209 USA

Guilds and associations

Guild of American Luthiers
8222 South Park Avenue
Tacoma
WA 98408 USA

Other companies mentioned in the text

Kent Armstong
9 North Orchard Road
Grafton
Vermont
05146 USA

Custom pick-ups

Aria (UK) Ltd
Unit 12
Heston Industrial Mall
Heston
Middlesex, TW5 0LD
UK

Selectron UK
Selectron House
Unit A
Jenkins Dale Industrial Estate
Chatham
Kent, ME4 5RT
UK

Seymour Duncan
5427 Hollister Avenue
Santa Barbara
CA 93111-2345 USA
http://www.seymourduncan.com

The following companies can supply various guitar-making woods

Allen Guitars
PO Box 1883
Colfax
CA 95713 USA

Luthiers supplies and specialist fret slotting service in a variety of scales.

Timberline
Unit 7
58–66 Morley Road
Tonbridge
Kent
TN9 1RP
UK

Wood and tool suppliers.

North Hiegham Sawmills
Paddock Street
Norwich
NR2 4TW
UK

Allied Lutherie
PO Box 217,
498 A Moore Lane,
Healdsburg, CA. 95448 USA
http://www.alliedlutherie.com

Associated Traders International
31949 36th Ave SW
Federal Way
WA 98023 USA

Craftsman Wood Service Co.
1735 W. Cortland Ct.
Addison
IL 60101 USA

Exotic Wood Company
444 Erial-Williams Road
PO Box 532
Sicklerville
NJ 08081 USA

Gilmer Wood Company
2211 N.W. St. Helens Road
Portland
OR 97210 USA
http://www.gilmerwood.com

Pacific Rim Tonewoods, Inc
420 16th Street
Bellingham, WA 98225

Tropical Exotic Hardwoods of Latin
America
P.O. Box 1806,
Carlsbad, CA. 92018
http://www.anexotichardwood.com

Kuau Technology Ltd.
PO Box 1031
Puunene
HI 96784 USA

M.C.R. Tonewoods
PO Box 31
Upperco
MD 21155 USA

Bruce L. Ross, Wood Broker
1148 Western Drive
Santa Cruz
CA 95060 USA

Sandy Pond Hardwoods, Inc.
921-A Lancaster Pike
Quarryville
PA 17566 USA

Sundance Tonewoods
2963 Gopher Canyon Rd
Vista
CA 92084 USA

Universal Hardwood Imports
PO Box 620595
Orangeville
CA 95662 USA

Vitali Import Co., Inc.
PO Box 249
5944-48 Atlantic Blvd.
Maywood
CA 90270 USA

International Luthiers Supply, Inc.
PO Box 580397
Tulsa
OK 74158 USA

Wood 'N' Guitars
PO Box 328
Honesdale
PA 18431 USA

Woodworkers Store, The
21801 Industrial Blvd.
Rogers
MN 55374 USA

A&M Wood Speciality
358 Eagle Street North
PO Box 32040
Cambridge
Ontario
N3H 5M2
Canada

Soveriegn
The Music Wood People
2612 St. Georges Avenue
North Vancouver
British Columbia
V7N 1T7
Canada

Lazarides Timber Agencies
3/1089 Kingsford Smith Drive
Eagle Farm
QLD 4009
Australia

Mathews Timber Pty Ltd
Rooks Rd
Vermont VIC 3133
Australia

Trend Timbers Pty Ltd
Cunneen St
Mulgrave
NSW 2756
Australia

Firma Andreas Gleissner
Mozartstrasse 12
D-91088 Bubenreuth
Germany
Website www.gleissner.franken.com

Fritz Kollitz
Fine Tonewood and Accessoirs
Kairlindacher Strasse 2
D-91085 Weisendorf
Germany

Woodland GmbH
Ton und Werthoelzer
Saalburgstrasse 3
D-61138 Niederdorfelden
Germany.

Maderas Barber S. A.
C. Sagunto 7
P. Industrial Fuente
Jarro
Valencia
46988 - Paterna
Spain

S.V.S. Tonewoods
Grosslingova 40
811 09 Bratislava
Slovakia

SPECIALIST GUITAR PARTS SUPPLIERS

Allparts
P. O. Box 1318
Katy
TX 77492 USA

Brandoni Music
Unit 3.6
Wembley Commercial Centre
East Lane
Wembley
Middlesex, HA9 7XT
UK

Rokas
5 Denmark Street
London
WC2H 8LP
UK

Central London guitar spares stockist

Pincotts
35 Jackson Court
Hazelmere
High Wycombe
Bucks, HP15 7TZ
UK

Fralin Pickups
2015 West Laburnum Ave.
Richmond, VA 23227
http://www.fralinpickups.com

Chandler Industries
370 Lang Road
Burlingame
CA 94010 USA

Jim Dunlop
PO Box 821
Benicia
CA 94510 USA

Fret wire and fretting supplies.

Goldo Music
Krausenstr.35
30171
Hanover
Germany

Warmoth Guitar Products
6424 112th St. E.
Puyallup
WA 98373 USA

Quality unfinished necks and bodies.

WD Music Products
4070 Mayflower road
Ft. Myers
FL 33916 USA

Pickguards, bodies, necks, hardware

WD Music Products UK.
Unit 31
Old Surrenden Manor
Bethersden
Kent, TN26 3DL
UK

Lollar Guitars
PO Box 2450
Vashon Island
WA 98070 USA

Pick-up making supplies

Subway Guitars
1800 Cedar Street
Berkeley,
CA94703 USA

Curtis Instrument Parts
PO Box 124
Lara
Victoria 3212
Australia

Guitar Factory (Gladesville)
Victoria Rd
Gladesville
NSW 2111
Australia

Kinman Guitar Craft
Baldock St
Moorooka
QLD 4105
Australia

Pick-ups and parts.

F Payton & Son
39 Whiting St
Artarmon
NSW 2064
Australia

Parts wholesalers.

Turramurra Music Pty Ltd
1267 Pacific Highway
Turramurra
NSW 2074
Australia
http://www.turramusic.com.au

Retail shop with a good selection of hardware.

ABM Hardware
Mueller & Sohn KG
Schlossgasse 5
D-91058 Erlangen
Germany

Rockinger Guitars
Krausenstr. 34-36
30171 Hannover
Germany
http://www.rockinger.com

Music Systeme
24 rue Victor Massé
75009 Paris
France

Retail shop with good selection of hardware.

Inlay suppliers, bone and ivory substitutes

Art Specialties International, Inc.
PO Box 215
Depew
NY 14043 USA

Supplier of Corion (used for nuts).

Duke of Pearl
18072 Greenhorn Road
Grass Valley
CA 95945 USA

Small Wonder Music Company
2 Summerhill Cottage
Chapmans Town Road
Rushlake Green
East Sussex, TN21 9PS
UK

Shell and inlay supplies, fretboards.

Fa. Shellex
Mortiz Strasse 12
6080 Gross Gerau
Germany

Mother-of-pearl, bone, fretwire, inlays.

Finishing and finishing supplies

Guitar Reranch
605 Pebble Creek
Garland
TX 75040 USA

Custom refinshing service. Supplier of custom colours in aerosol cans.

The Finishing Touch Ltd.
171-A Milbar Blvd.
Farmingdale,
NY 11735 USA

Veneers, lacquer, woods.

Durobond Northern
65 Old Pittwater Rd
Brookvale
NSW 2100
Australia

Suppliers of nitrocellulose lacquer for guitar finishing.

Specialist tools

Garrett Wade
161 Avenue Of The Americas
New York
NY 10013

Tools and finishing supplies.
Grizzly Imports, Inc.
PO Box 2969
Bellingham
WA 98227 USA

Imported woodworking machinery and tools.

Metropolitan Music Co.
PO Box 1415
Mountain Rd.
Stowe
VT 05672-9598 USA

High quality reemers, peg shavers, specialty tools and tonewoods.

Tool Shop
PO Box 25429
Greenville
SC 29616

Woodcraft Supply Corp.
41 Atlantic Ave.
PO Box 4000
Woburn
MA 01888USA

Woodworker's Supply of New Mexico
5604 Alameda, NE
Albuquerque
NM 87113 USA

Other important addresses and contacts

The photograph of Jimi Hendrix was kindly supplied by Caesar Glebbeek who runs a magazine devoted to Jimi and has a fine website which can be found at www.univibes.com. The magazine is published three times a year and further details can be had from:

UniVibes
Coppeen
Enniskeane
County Cork
Republic of Ireland

The elephant photograph on page 105 was supplied by Peter and Angie Smart who have asked that I publicise the conservation work done by:

Friends of Conservation
Sloane Square House
Holbein Place
London
SW1W 8NS

They are more than happy to receive your donations.

Every effort is made to keep this list as up-to-date as possible. Please report any mistakes, omissions or bad links or send your Les Paul Juniors to:

NBS Publications
PO Box 6292
Basingstoke
Hampshire, RG21 5YX
UK

melvynh@globalnet.co.uk

Appendix 3 Some Useful Templates

Throughout this book reference has been made to some standard guitar parts. What follows is a series of drawings that can be used to make jigs for these pieces. In all cases a centre line is shown for both length and width where necessary.

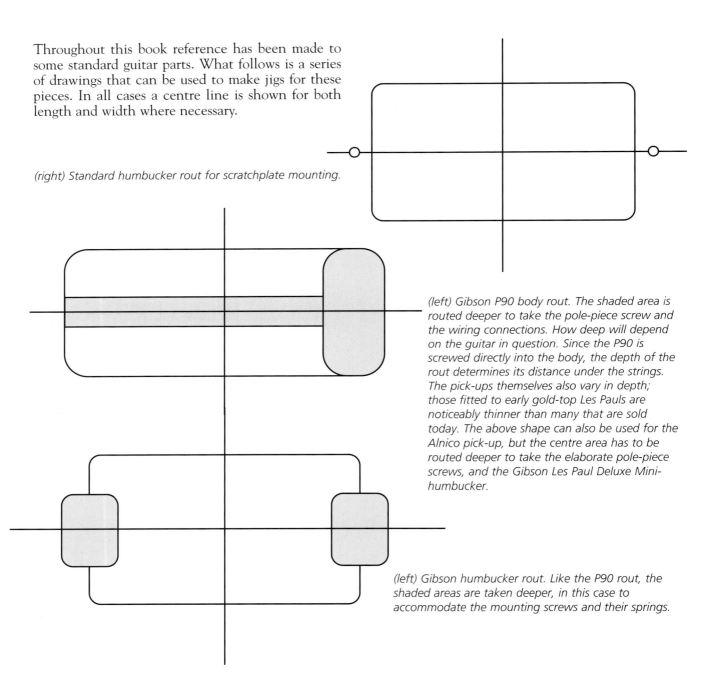

(right) Standard humbucker rout for scratchplate mounting.

(left) Gibson P90 body rout. The shaded area is routed deeper to take the pole-piece screw and the wiring connections. How deep will depend on the guitar in question. Since the P90 is screwed directly into the body, the depth of the rout determines its distance under the strings. The pick-ups themselves also vary in depth; those fitted to early gold-top Les Pauls are noticeably thinner than many that are sold today. The above shape can also be used for the Alnico pick-up, but the centre area has to be routed deeper to take the elaborate pole-piece screws, and the Gibson Les Paul Deluxe Mini-humbucker.

(left) Gibson humbucker rout. Like the P90 rout, the shaded areas are taken deeper, in this case to accommodate the mounting screws and their springs.

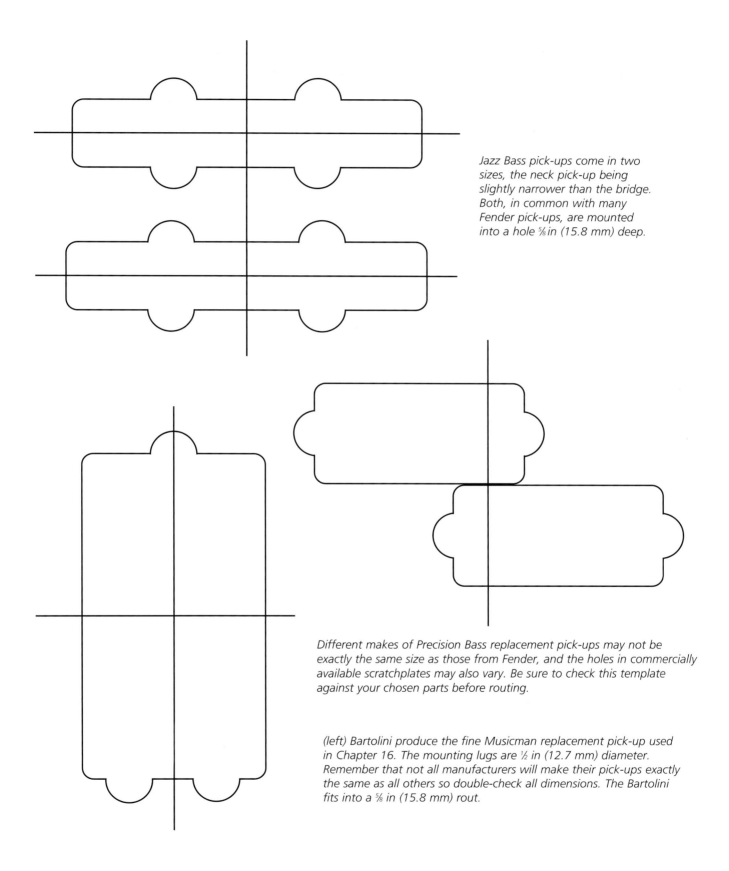

Jazz Bass pick-ups come in two sizes, the neck pick-up being slightly narrower than the bridge. Both, in common with many Fender pick-ups, are mounted into a hole ⅝ in (15.8 mm) deep.

Different makes of Precision Bass replacement pick-ups may not be exactly the same size as those from Fender, and the holes in commercially available scratchplates may also vary. Be sure to check this template against your chosen parts before routing.

(left) Bartolini produce the fine Musicman replacement pick-up used in Chapter 16. The mounting lugs are ½ in (12.7 mm) diameter. Remember that not all manufacturers will make their pick-ups exactly the same as all others so double-check all dimensions. The Bartolini fits into a ⅝ in (15.8 mm) rout.

The Stratocaster-style tremolo needs a cavity on the rear of the guitar to take the springs and their adjustment claw and a hole right through the guitar to take the tremolo block. Both of these drawings are for a right-handed instrument and are viewed as if looking at them in situ. The cavity for the front of the body should be routed all the way through and then the back cavity can be lined up with the forward edge of the deeper part, lined up with the forward edge of the hole through the body. The back cavity is routed to ⅝ in (15.8 mm) deep in common with many other Fender-designed body cavities and the shaded area on the drawing is routed through the body to within ⅛ in (3 mm) of the front surface.

If using a high-tech tremolo system such as the Floyd Rose or Wilkinson, the outer two mounting screw holes will be used and the others will not be required. Remember also that not all so-called standard systems are built exactly as the Fender so always double-check the dimensions of the unit you intend to use. The most common area for change is the distance between the six mounting screw holes.

Line these two
faces up

(left) A Stratocaster-style pick-up template for cutting a hole in a scratchplate.

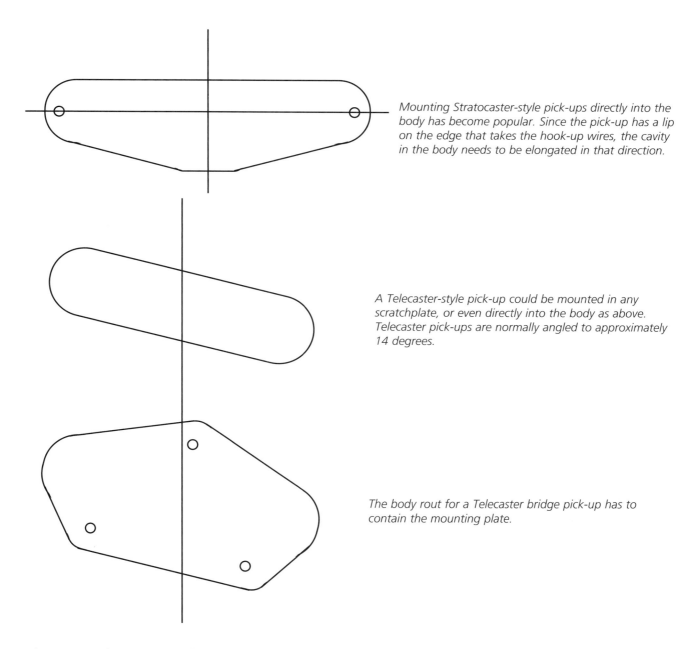

Mounting Stratocaster-style pick-ups directly into the body has become popular. Since the pick-up has a lip on the edge that takes the hook-up wires, the cavity in the body needs to be elongated in that direction.

A Telecaster-style pick-up could be mounted in any scratchplate, or even directly into the body as above. Telecaster pick-ups are normally angled to approximately 14 degrees.

The body rout for a Telecaster bridge pick-up has to contain the mounting plate.

These are only a few standard routs that may be required in guitar-making. I have not attempted to include standard control routs, or plans of body shapes, as it is up to you to design and build your own guitar. These, however, are the most common aftermarket accessories you are likely to find and are therefore more likely to build into your own instrument.

Appendix 4 Guitar-making and the Internet

The advent of the Internet as both a business and a communication tool has had a great effect on guitar-making. Just over 20 years ago when I started making guitars I had to pull things apart to find out how they worked. Now it is possible to not only buy books but to access a large amount of information and expertise on the Internet. This can range from lists of useful addresses and links to guitar spares companies, wood suppliers, specialist luthiers suppliers and sources of finishing materials to extremely useful discussion groups where anyone can post a message requesting help or advice and often find the answer in great detail, freely given by one or more of the many experienced luthiers who regularly log on to these groups. Since the Internet is growing at a rate that is only surpassed by the expansion of the universe in the moments after the Big Bang, it is certain that resources such as these will grow and expand. It is also likely that any suggestions of links given here in the book could well go out of date quite quickly.

The easiest way of finding a suitable newsgroup is to go via one of the established newsgroup operators such as Google (www.groups.google.com) who now look after the twenty year old Usenet archive which contains a wealth of information from past messages. These are split into categories and then split again into subjects. A little time spent searching through these to find those that relate to the guitar and to guitar-making is time well spent.

Searching through the many pages of links that are to be found on any site that relates to the electric guitar is often worth the time as some discussion groups are not part of a larger newsgroup set-up. These sites often feature a Frequently-Asked Questions (FAQ) database that will often solve a specific problem.

Another source of good information is the web-sites of some manufacturers and supply companies. Both Luthiers Mercantile International and Stewart MacDonald's Guitar Shop Supply have informative sites and a lot of information can be found on sites such as Seymour Duncan's (www.seymourduncan.com). This includes a lot of information about the pickups in the range, an FAQ section and a selection of useful wiring diagrams for standard guitars. There are also some hints and tips which are very useful. EMG also have a useful site (www.emginc.com) describing their products and featuring a lot of useful information.

General searches for information using the keywords of guitar-making or luthiers may only come up with a few relevant sites but will invariably have some very useful links to follow. Use search engines such as Google, Yahoo or Alta Vista.

Certainly, using the Internet as a means of contacting people and finding information is very effective. Just a quick look at one of the newsgroups (for example news:rec.music.makers.builders) will show postings from first-time builders and from experienced, and sometimes quite well known, luthiers. Answers are usually forthcoming to all questions and a regular check on the pages will reveal good sources for materials, advice on tools and where to get them at the best prices, as well as opinions on all aspects of the subject. There is also a Musical Instrument Makers Forum (www.mimf.com) where you can not only find answers to a host of questions and informative discussions, but also on-line training, plans for instruments, books and a lot of good advice.

Sites such as these are bound to grow and others to appear as more people discover how useful the internet can be. After all, some of the research for this book was done on the 'net!

Recommended Reading

Anderton, Craig, *Do-It-Yourself Projects for Guitarists*, Miller Freeman Books (1995).

Bacon, Tony & Day, Paul, *The Ultimate Guitar Book*, Balaphon (1991).

Benedetto, Bob, *Making an Archtop*, Limelite Press (1994).

Brosnac, Donald, *Guitar Electronics for Musicians*, Amsco Publications (1983).
        Scientific Guitar Design, The Bold Strummer (1996).

Cumpiano, William and Natelson, Jonathan, *Guitar Making Tradition and Technology*, Chronicle Books (1993).

Duchossoir, A, *The Fender Telecaster*, Hal Leonard Corporation (1991).
        Gibson Electrics: The Classic Years, Hal Leonard Corporation (1994).
        The Fender Stratocaster, Hal Leonard Corporation (1994).

Erlewine, Dan, *Guitar Player Repair Guide*, Miller Freeman Books (1994).

Foley, Bill, *Build Your Own Electric Guitar*, GVM Publishing (1986).

Flexner, Bob, *Understanding Wood Finishing*, Rodale Press (1994).

Fliegler, Ritchie, *The Complete Guide to Guitar and Amp Maintenance*, Hal Leonard Corporation (1994).

Guild of American Luthiers, *Lutherie Tools*, GAL Resource Book One (1990).

Kamimoto, Hideo, *Complete Guitar Repair*, Oak Publications (1978).
        Electric Guitar Set-ups, Amsco Publications (1994).

Legg, Adrian, *Customizing Your Electric Guitar*, Amsco Publications (1981)

Lollar, Jason, *Basic Pickup Winding and Complete Guide to Making Your Own Pickup Winder*.
                                        Lollar Publications (1999).

Patterson, James E., *Pearl Inlay*, Stewart-MacDonald's Guitar Shop Supply (1991).

Robinson, Larry, *The Art of Inlay*, Miller Freeman Books (1994).

Schatten, Les, *Standard Wiring Diagrams*, Schatten Designs (1993).

Siminoff, Roger, *Constructing a Solid Body Guitar*, Hal Leonard Corporation (1986).

Sloane, Irving, *Guitar Repair*, The Bold Strummer (1989).
        Steel String Guitar Construction, The Bold Strummer (1990)

Fret Work Step by Step, Stewart-MacDonald's Guitar Shop Supply

Trade Secrets; Book One, Stewart-MacDonald's Guitar Shop Supply

Wheeler, Tom, *American Guitars*, HarperPerennial (1992)

Young, David Russell, *Steel String Guitar Construction*, The Bold Strummer

Acknowledgements

At the beginning of this book is a dedication to Leo Fender. I would now like to add George Harrison who played *that* chord that got me started. RIP George.

I will also include, in no fixed order, Brian May, Orville Gibson, Les Paul, Seth Lover, Ted McHugh, Seymour Duncan, Roger Giffin, Kent Armstrong, Paul Chapman, Ian Waller and Pete Stevens, Dave King, Martin Bird, Micky Moody, Sid Bishop, Irving Sloane, Chris Moores, Phil Hargreaves, Vince Hastwell and Chris Bryant, who have all influenced my guitar-making to a greater or lesser degree. I should also thank the many players who have made my spine tingle playing as diverse a range of styles as is possible over the years, from that opening chord in the Beatles' *Hard Day's Night* through Chuck Berry, Jimi Hendrix, Chet Atkins, Danny Gatton Pete Townshend, Amos Garrett, Albert Lee, Mark Garvin, Bonnie Raitt, Jimmy Page and many others, and to those that will, no doubt make my spine tingle in the future, especially Jeff Beck.

I would like to thank the many people that have helped or influenced the production of this book or just kept me sane: Kent Armstrong and his dad, Dan, of Rainbow Products, David and Gilly Dyke of Luthiers Supplies, David Carroll of Touchstone Tonewoods, Clive Norris of Selectron UK and Martin Hartwell of Aria UK who were all generous to a fault with little or no prompting in supplying parts, Pete Stevens and Paul Herman of Wal, Marty from MMG Guitars, Chris Trigg of Vintage and Rare in London, Jack Waterson of Vintage Guitars in Los Angeles, Todd Taggart then of Luthiers Mercantile International, Mike Lindskold and everyone else at Stewart MacDonald's Guitar Shop Supply, Ron Muriel at Roka's, Andrea Corr, Mattia Valente, Reginald Mitchell, Garth Bloor, Ken Warmoth of Warmoth Guitars, George Waldman, Joan Osbourne, Bill Lester of Guitar ReRanch, Bruce Brand for the original push, Jackie Davidson, Vince Hastwell, Cyndi Lauper, Jeffrey Quill, Guinness the Cat, David Kinghorn, Barry Cox for boundless enthusiasm, Roger Giffin (again) for teaching me a hell of a lot and for lending me his workshop for those all-night sessions so long ago, Don Martin, my mum and dad, Jacques Latessa, Ward Meeker at *Vintage Guitar Magazine*, Shawn Colvin, Jasmin Dunlop Powell of Jim Dunlop Products, Ken Rearwin, Andrew McWhirter for the Australian input, Michael Palin, Ron Long for a long list of addresses, Dave Cammish, Peter and Angie Smart for the flump picture, Mel Blanc, Nick Magnus for the cartoons, Alex Henshaw, Jerry Lunn for printing the photographs and Peter Haskell for still having the negatives, Paul Hart for all the new diagrams, Pete Davies and all at Marlborough Photographic Services, Eddie Fret of Fret Music Southampton, Pete and Maureen Walker of P. J. Walker in Portsmouth, Karen Brazier for great copy-editing, Jill Lake and Alan Bathe for good publishing advice and everyone I have forgotten who answered requests for information, addresses and sources of parts.

Last and not least thanks to Carol for putting up with all this.

Index

Life's been good to me so far . . .

You can do it Duffy Moon . . .

COMPREHENSIVE

RADIOGRAPHIC
PATHOLOGY

COMPREHENSIVE
RADIOGRAPHIC
PATHOLOGY

RONALD L. EISENBERG, M.D., F.A.C.R.
Chairman of Imaging, Department of Radiology,
Highland General Hospital,
Oakland, California;
Clinical Professor of Radiology,
University of California at San Francisco and Davis

CYNTHIA A. DENNIS, R.T.
Director, School of Radiologic Technology,
Louisiana State University School of Medicine,
Shreveport, Louisiana

Second Edition

with 619 *illustrations*

St. Louis Baltimore Berlin Boston Carlsbad Chicago London Madrid
Naples New York Philadelphia Sydney Tokyo Toronto

Mosby
Dedicated to Publishing Excellence

Editor: Jeanne Rowland
Associate Developmental Editor: Lisa Potts
Project Manager: Mark Spann
Production Editors: Carl Masthay, Stephen C. Hetager
Designer: David Zielinski
Manufacturing Supervisor: Theresa Fuchs

SECOND EDITION
Copyright © 1995 by Mosby–Year Book, Inc.

Previous editions copyrighted 1990

Composition by Carlisle Communications, Inc.
Printed by Maple Vail Press
Printed in the United States of America

Mosby–Year Book, Inc.
11830 Westline Industrial Drive
St. Louis, Missouri 63146

ISBN 0-8151-3144-5

95 96 97 98 99 / 9 8 7 6 5 4 3 2

*To all students and radiographers
wishing to better understand
the value of the profession
of radiologic technology*

······ Preface

An understanding of basic principles of pathology and an awareness of the radiographic appearances of specific diseases are essential parts of the training of a radiologic technologist. This knowledge enables the radiologic technologist to become a more competent professional and a contributing member of the diagnostic team. An understanding of disease processes can aid the technologist in selecting proper modalities and in determining the need for retaking a radiograph that might be acceptable under different circumstances.

Unfortunately, many teaching programs currently use textbooks designed only for high school or college students or for medical students, or they use a set of teaching slides that require the active participation of a radiologist. Our solution has been to develop a well-illustrated, comprehensive textbook of pathology designed specifically for students of radiologic technology and as a reference guide for graduate radiographers.

In this new edition, readers will find updated discussions of ultrasound, CT, and MRI, and coverage of additional pathologies, such as rotator cuff tears, tears of the menisci of the knee, achalasia, esophageal diverticula, hippocampal sclerosis, and lead poisoning. We have also added practical explanations of endotracheal tubes, central venous catheters, Swan-Ganz catheters, and transvenous cardiac pacemakers.

Due to positive feedback, we have kept the organization consistent with the first edition. An introductory chapter discusses basic pathology (including the immune reaction and AIDS) and introduces the pathologic terms that are used throughout the book. It also describes the advantages and limitations of three widely used modalities: ultrasound, computed tomography, and magnetic resonance imaging. Each of the remaining chapters is a systematic approach to the diseases involving a specific organ system, organized in a manner that is conducive to progressive lesson planning. For each of the most common pathologic conditions there is a brief description of the disease itself and its clinical manifestations, followed by the imaging findings. Specific information relative to radiologic technology is included, such as the changes in technique needed for patients with specific conditions and any special handling of the patient that may be required. If multiple imaging modalities can be used, the most appropriate initial procedure is indicated, as well as the sequence in which various imaging studies should be performed.

Each chapter opens with a listing of goals and objectives designed to show the student what information should be thoroughly understood. This is followed by radiographer notes, which offer helpful suggestions for producing optimal radiographs of the specific organ system. Each chapter ends with a series of review questions to help readers assess their degree of comprehension of the material. An answer key is found at the back of the text.

Several appendices include material that is valuable to the radiologic technologist but applies to multiple chapters. An extensive glossary and a list of major prefixes, roots, and suffixes enable the reader to determine the meaning of unfamiliar words. In addition, there is a table detailing the diagnostic implications of abnormal values for important laboratory examinations.

RONALD L. EISENBERG
CYNTHIA A. DENNIS

Acknowledgments

Figures 4-1 to 4-29, 4-31 to 4-41, 4-43 to 4-53, and 4-55 to 4-100 were borrowed with permission from Eisenberg RL: Gastrointestinal radiology: a pattern approach, ed 2, Philadelphia, 1990, JB Lippincott Co.

The unnumbered figures in Chapters 2 through 10 were borrowed from Thibodeau GA, Patton KT: Anatomy and physiology, ed 2, St Louis, 1993, Mosby–Year Book, Inc.

Contents

4 Gastrointestinal System, 119

5 Urinary System, 174

6 Cardiovascular System, 205

COMPREHENSIVE

RADIOGRAPHIC
PATHOLOGY

CHAPTER 1

Introduction to Pathology

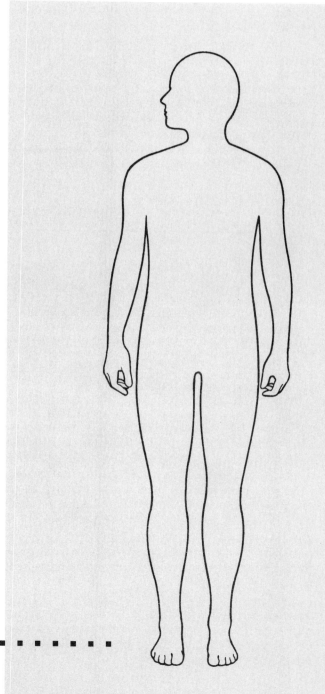

■ **Prerequisite Knowledge**

The student should have a basic knowledge of the normal anatomy and physiology of the human body. A good foundation in medical terminology, including word roots, prefixes, and suffixes (see Appendix A) will be most helpful in assimilating the somewhat difficult information presented in this and future chapters. In addition, proper learning and understanding of the material will be facilitated if the student has some clinical experience in all areas of radiography of the human body and film evaluation, including a concept of the changes in technique required to compensate for density differences produced by underlying pathologic conditions.

■ **Goals**

To acquaint the student radiographer with basic medical terminology used to describe various pathologic conditions occurring in the human body (including hereditary diseases, immune reactions, and AIDS) and to introduce the student to some specialized imaging techniques

■ **Objectives**

1. Be able to classify the more common diseases in terms of their penetrability to x rays
2. Be familiar with the changes in technical factors required for obtaining optimal quality radiographs in patients with various underlying pathologic conditions
3. Understand and be able to define or describe all bold-faced terms in this chapter
4. Describe inflammation, edema, infarction, hemorrhage, and neoplasia
5. Describe the various alterations of cell growth
6. Be able to describe the various immune reactions of the body

■ Radiographer Notes

Radiography of patients with underlying pathologic conditions can present problems for even the most experienced radiographers. Adjustments in patient position may be necessary to prevent excessive pain caused by the body's response to trauma or certain disease processes. A change in routine projections may be indicated to visualize subtle alterations in the normal radiographic appearance. Many disease processes also alter the density of the structures being radiographed and therefore require changes in technique. For example, extensive edema may require an increased technique, whereas severe atrophy may require a decreased technique. Unless the radiographer has access to previous films with recorded techniques, a standard technique chart should be used to determine the initial exposures. Any necessary adjustments can then be made on subsequent films. The box lists the changes in penetrability expected in advanced stages of various disease processes.

Certain diseases suppress the normal immune response. Immunocompromised patients (such as individuals with advanced leukemia) may require special care to prevent them from acquiring a disease from the radiographer. They may have to be placed in protective isolation (sometimes referred to as "reverse" isolation), and the radiographer may be required to mask, gown, and glove before approaching the patient. On the other hand, diseases such as AIDS and hepatitis require blood and body fluid protection for the radiographer. It is essential that the radiographer wear rubber gloves when touching any area of the patient that may have been contaminated with blood or body fluids. When examining a patient with AIDS who has a productive cough, the radiographer must wear a mask and possibly protective eye goggles if there is a need to be extremely close to a patient's face. It is important to remember that many patients being radiographed have not been diagnosed and thus all patients should be treated as though they may have a communicable disease. Therefore proper precautions should be taken whenever you are exposed to any type of body secretion or blood.

7. Be able to describe AIDS and the precautions necessary when radiographing patients with AIDS or any patient where contact with any body fluid is possible (Universal Precautions)
8. Be able to describe briefly the theory of image production with ultrasound, CT, and MRI

Disease

Pathology is the study of diseases that can cause abnormalities in the structure or function of various organ systems. In essence, a disease is the pattern of response of the body to some form of injury. Diseases may be hereditary or may result from a broad spectrum of traumatic, infectious, vascular, or metabolic processes. They may reflect alterations of cell growth, as in tumors, or even be caused by physicians and their treatment (iatrogenic). In some cases the underlying cause is unknown, and the disease is termed "idiopathic."

This chapter is a discussion of several basic reactions of the body that are the underlying mechanisms for the radiographic manifestations of most pathologic conditions. These processes include inflammation, edema, ischemia and infarction, hemorrhage, and alterations of cell growth leading to the development of neoplasms (tumors). In addition, this chapter deals with hereditary diseases and their radiographic appearances, as well as immune reactions and the acquired immunodeficiency syndrome (AIDS).

■ Inflammation

Acute inflammation is the initial response of body tissues to local injury. Among the various types of injury are blunt or penetrating trauma, infectious organisms, and irritating chemical substances. Regardless of the underlying cause, the inflammatory response consists of four overlapping events that occur sequentially:

1. Alterations in blood flow and vascular permeability
2. Migration of circulating white blood cells to the interstitium of the injured tissue
3. Phagocytosis and enzymatic digestion of dead cells and tissue elements
4. Repair of injury by regeneration of normal parenchymal cells or proliferation of granulation tissue and eventual scar formation

Penetrability by x rays of pathology of body systems for far-advanced disease states

SKELETAL SYSTEM
Additive (hard to penetrate)
  Acromegaly
  Acute kyphosis
  Callus
  Charcot joint
  Chronic osteomyelitis (healed)
  Exostosis
  Hydrocephalus
  Marble bone
  Metastasis (osteosclerotic)
  Osteochondroma
  Osteoma
  Paget's disease
  Proliferative arthritis
  Sclerosis
Destructive (easy to penetrate)
  Active osteomyelitis
  Active tuberculosis
  Aseptic necrosis
  Atrophy—disease or disuse
  Blastomycosis
  Carcinoma
  Coccidioidomycosis
  Degenerative arthritis
  Ewing's tumor (children)
  Fibrosarcoma
  Giant cell tumor
  Gout
  Hemangioma
  Hodgkin's disease
  Hyperparathyroidism
  Leprosy
  Metastasis (osteolytic)
  Multiple myeloma
  Neuroblastoma
  New bone (fibrosis)
  Osteitis fibrosa cystica
  Osteoporosis/osteomalacia
  Radiation necrosis
  Solitary myeloma

RESPIRATORY SYSTEM
Additive (hard to penetrate)
  Actinomycosis
  Arrested tuberculosis (calcification)
  Atelectasis
  Bronchiectasis
  Edema
  Empyema
  Encapsulated abscess
  Hydropneumothorax
  Malignancy
  Miliary tuberculosis
  Pleural effusion
  Pneumoconiosis
    Anthracosis
    Asbestosis
    Calcinosis
    Siderosis
    Silicosis
  Pneumonia
  Syphilis
  Thoracoplasty
Destructive (easy to penetrate)
  Early lung abscess
  Emphysema
  Pneumothorax

CIRCULATORY SYSTEM
Additive (hard to penetrate)
  Aortic aneurysm
  Ascites
  Cirrhosis of liver
  Enlarged heart

SOFT TISSUE
Additive (hard to penetrate)
  Edema
Destructive (easy to penetrate)
  Emaciation

From Thompson TT: *Cahoon's formulating x-ray techniques,* ed 9, Durham, NC, 1979, Duke University Press.

The earliest bodily response to local injury is dilation of arterioles, capillaries, and venules leading to a dramatic increase in blood flow in and around the injury site. This **hyperemia** produces the heat and redness associated with inflammation. As hyperemia develops, the venules and capillaries become abnor-mally **permeable,** allowing passage of a protein-rich plasma across vessel walls into the interstitium. This inflammatory **exudate** in the tissues produces the swelling associated with inflammation and puts pressure on sensitive nerve endings, which causes pain. The protein-rich exudate of inflammation must be differentiated from a **transduate,** a low-protein fluid such as the pulmonary edema that develops in congestive heart failure.

Very early in the inflammatory response, leukocytes (white blood cells, especially neutrophils and macrophages) of the circulating blood migrate to the area of injury. These white blood cells cross the capillary walls into the injured tissues, where they engulf and enzymatically digest infecting organisms and cellular debris, a process called **phagocytosis.**

The removal of necrotic debris and any injurious agents such as bacteria makes possible the repair of the injury that triggered the inflammatory response. In many tissues, such as the lung after pneumococcal pneumonia, regeneration of parenchymal cells permits reconstitution of entirely normal anatomy and function. However, some tissues, such as the heart after myocardial infarction, cannot heal by regeneration. The area of destroyed tissue is replaced by **granulation tissue** and eventually by a fibrous **scar.** Granulation tissue refers to a combination of young, budding capillaries and actively proliferating fibroblasts, which produce connective tissue fibers (collagen) that replace the dead tissue. Eventually, the strong connective tissue contracts to produce a fibrous scar. In the abdomen, such **fibrous adhesions** can narrow loops of intestine and result in an obstruction. The accumulation of excessive amounts of collagen (more common in blacks) may produce a protruding, tumorlike scar known as a **keloid.** Unfortunately, surgery to remove a keloid is usually ineffective because the subsequent incision tends to heal in the same way.

Many injuries heal by a combination of regeneration and scar tissue formation. An example is the response of the liver to repeated and persistent alcoholic injury that results in cirrhosis, in which irregular lobules of regenerated liver cells are crisscrossed and surrounded by bands of scar tissue.

The five clinical signs of acute inflammation are rubor (redness), calor (heat), tumor (swelling), dolor (pain), and loss of function. The local heat and redness result from increased blood flow in the microcirculation at the site of injury. The swelling and pain are the result of exudate causing an increase in interstitial fluid and pressure on nerve endings.

Acute inflammation can also lead to systemic manifestations. Fever is especially common in inflammatory states associated with the spread of organisms into the bloodstream. There is also an increase in the number of circulating white blood cells (leukocytosis).

Some bacterial organisms (such as staphylococci and streptococci) produce **toxins** that damage the tissues and incite an inflammatory response. **Pyogenic** bacteria lead to the production of a thick, yellow fluid called **pus,** which contains dead white blood cells, inflammatory exudate, and bacteria. An inflammation associated with pus formation is termed **suppurative.** When implanted beneath the skin or in a solid organ, a pyogenic infection produces an **abscess,** a localized collection of pus. All pyogens, wherever they become implanted, are capable of invading blood vessels to produce **bacteremia,** with the potential involvement of other organs and tissues in the body.

A **granulomatous** inflammation is a distinct pattern seen in relatively few diseases, including tuberculosis, syphilis, and sarcoidosis. A **granuloma** is a localized area of chronic inflammation, often with central necrosis. It is characterized by the accumulation of macrophages, some of which fuse to form multinucleated giant cells.

▪ Edema

Edema is the accumulation of abnormal amounts of fluid in the intercellular tissue spaces or body cavities. It can be localized, as in an inflammatory reaction, or generalized, with pronounced swelling of subcutaneous tissues throughout the body (**anasarca**). Localized edema may result from inflammation with the escape of protein-rich intravascular fluid into the extravascular tissue or a local obstruction to lymphatic drainage as in **filariasis,** in which a parasitic worm causes lymphatic obstruction and localized edema termed **elephantiasis.** Generalized edema occurs most frequently in patients with congestive heart failure, cirrhosis of the liver, and certain forms of renal disease. Generalized edema is usually most prominent in dependent portions of the body because of the effects of gravity. Thus ambulatory patients tend to accumulate fluid in tissues around the ankles and lower legs, whereas in patients who are lying down, the edema fluid is most prominent in the back and sacral areas and the lung.

Extravascular fluid can also accumulate in serous cavities to produce pleural and pericardial effusions and peritoneal ascites.

Edema may produce minimal clinical symptoms or be potentially fatal. If localized to the subcutaneous tissues, large amounts of edema may cause minimal functional impairment. In contrast, pulmonary edema, pericardial effusion, or edematous swelling of the brain may have dire consequences.

■ Ischemia and Infarction

Ischemia refers to interference with the blood supply to an organ or part of an organ that deprives its cells and tissues of oxygen and nutrients. Ischemia may be caused by narrowing of arterial structures, as in atherosclerosis, or by thrombotic or embolic occlusion. Depending on several factors, occlusion of an artery or vein may have little or no effect on the involved tissue, or it may cause death of the tissue and even the individual. A major determinant is the availability of an alternative or newly acquired route of blood supply (collateral vessels). Other factors include the rate of development of the occlusion, the vulnerability of the tissue to hypoxia, and the oxygen-carrying capacity of the blood. Slowly developing occlusions are less likely to cause death of tissue because they provide an opportunity for the development of alternative pathways of flow. Ganglion cells of the nervous system and myocardial muscle cells undergo irreversible damage if deprived of their blood supply for 3 to 5 minutes. Anemic or cyanotic patients tolerate arterial insufficiency less well than normal individuals do, and thus occlusion of even a small vessel in such an individual may lead to death of tissue.

An **infarct** is a localized area of ischemic necrosis (death) within a tissue or organ produced by occlusion of either its arterial supply or its venous drainage. The two most common clinical forms of infarction are myocardial and pulmonary. Almost all infarcts result from thrombotic or embolic occlusion. Infrequent causes include twisting of an organ (volvulus), compression of the blood supply of a loop of bowel in a hernia sac, or trapping of a viscus under a peritoneal adhesion.

Severe arterial disease of the lower extremities may result in necrosis of several toes or a large segment of the foot, a condition called **gangrene.**

Infarctions tend to be especially severe because they are more common in patients least able to withstand them. Thus infarcts tend to occur in elderly individuals with advanced atherosclerosis or impaired cardiac function. The postoperative and postdelivery periods are also times in which infarctions often occur.

■ Hemorrhage

The term **hemorrhage** implies rupture of a blood vessel. Rupture of a large artery or vein is almost always caused by some form of injury, such as trauma, atherosclerosis, or inflammatory or neoplastic erosion of the vessel wall. Hemorrhage may be external, or blood may be trapped within body tissues, resulting in an accumulation termed a **hematoma.** The accumulation of blood in a body cavity results in hemothorax, hemopericardium, hemoperitoneum, or hemarthrosis (blood in a joint). Minimal hemorrhages into the skin, mucous membranes, or serosal surfaces are called **petechiae;** slightly larger hemorrhages are termed **purpura.** A large (greater than 1 to 2 cm) subcutaneous hematoma, or "bruise," is called an **ecchymosis.**

The significance of hemorrhage depends on the volume of blood loss, the rate of loss, and the site of hemorrhage. Sudden losses of up to 20% of the blood volume or slow losses of even larger amounts may have little clinical significance. The site of the hemorrhage is critical. For example, an amount of bleeding that would have little clinical significance in the subcutaneous tissues may cause death when located in a vital portion of the brain. Large amounts of external bleeding lead to the chronic loss of iron from the body and anemia. In contrast, internal hemorrhages into body cavities, joints, or tissues permit the iron to be recaptured for the synthesis of hemoglobin and the development of normal red blood cells.

■ Alterations of Cell Growth

Changes in the number and size of cells, their differentiation, and their arrangement may develop in response to physiologic stimuli. **Atrophy** refers to a reduction in the size or number of cells in an organ or tissue, with a corresponding decrease in function. It must be distinguished from **hypoplasia** and **aplasia,** in which failure of normal development accounts for small size. An example is the **disuse atrophy** after immobilization of a limb by a plaster cast. There is a dramatic reduction in muscle mass of the encased limb. Because the cast also removes the stress and strain from the enclosed bone that normally stimulates new bone formation, normal bone resorption continues unchecked and loss of calcified bone can be seen on radiographs. In this situation, there is rapid recovery from the atrophic appearance when the cast is removed and normal function is resumed. Pathologic, irreversible atrophy may be caused by loss of innervation or hormonal stimulation or by decreased blood supply. For example, stenosis of a renal artery may cause atrophy of the kidney with shrinkage of individual nephrons and loss of interstitial tissue.

Hypertrophy refers to an increase in the size of cells of a tissue or organ in response to a demand for increased function. This must be distinguished from

hyperplasia, an increase in the number of cells in a tissue or organ. Hypertrophy occurs most often in cells that cannot multiply, especially those in myocardial and peripheral striated muscle. Myocardial hypertrophy is necessary to maintain cardiac output despite increased peripheral resistance in patients with arterial hypertension or aortic valve disease. Loss of a normal kidney is followed by hypertrophy of the kidney on the opposite side in an attempt to continue adequate renal function. Examples of hyperplasia include proliferation of granulation tissue in the repair of injury and the increased cellularity of bone marrow in patients with hemolytic anemia or after hemorrhage. Hyperplasia of the adrenal cortex is a response to increased ACTH secretion; hyperplasia of the thyroid gland occurs with increased thyrotropic hormone secretion by the pituitary gland.

Dysplasia is a loss in the uniformity of individual cells and their architectural orientation. It is typically associated with prolonged chronic irritation or inflammation. Removal of the irritant may result in a return to normal, but often the tissue change persists and may evolve into a totally abnormal growth pattern. Thus dysplasia is generally considered at least potentially premalignant—a borderline lesion that may heal or progress to cancer.

▪ Neoplasia

Neoplasia literally means "new growth" and refers to an abnormal proliferation of cells that are no longer controlled by factors that govern the growth of normal cells. Neoplastic cells act as parasites, competing with normal cells and tissues for their metabolic needs. Thus tumor cells may flourish while the patient becomes weak and emaciated, a condition termed **cachexia.**

Neoplasms are commonly referred to as "tumors"; indeed, the study of neoplasms is called **oncology,** which derives from the Greek word *oncos* meaning 'tumor'. Although the word **tumor** originally referred to any swelling that could also be produced by edema or hemorrhage into a tissue, the word is now used almost exclusively to refer to a neoplasm.

Neoplasms are divided into benign and malignant categories based on a judgment of their potential clinical behavior. **Benign** tumors closely resemble their cells of origin in structure and function. They remain localized, do not spread to other sites, and thus can usually be surgically removed with survival of the patient. Nevertheless, some benign tumors can have severe consequences because of their position or hormonal secretion. For example, a benign pituitary tumor can cause pressure atrophy and destruction of the surrounding gland, and a benign tumor of the islets of Langerhans in the pancreas can produce excessive amounts of insulin resulting in possibly fatal low levels of blood glucose. Other potentially dangerous benign tumors include those arising in the brain or spinal cord and tumors of the trachea or esophagus that may occlude the air supply or make it impossible to swallow.

Malignant neoplasms invade and destroy adjacent structures and spread to distant sites (metastasize) to cause death. They tend to be poorly differentiated so that it may be impossible to determine the organ from which they arise. Malignant tumors are collectively referred to as **cancers.** This term is derived from the Latin word for 'crab', possibly because the fingerlike projections they extend into underlying tissue resemble crablike claws.

All tumors, both benign and malignant, have two basic components: (1) the parenchyma, made up of proliferating neoplastic cells, and (2) the supporting stroma, made up of connective tissue, blood vessels, and possibly lymphatic vessels. The parenchyma of the neoplasm largely determines its biologic behavior and is the component from which the tumor derives its name.

Most benign tumors are composed of parenchymal cells that closely resemble the tissue of origin. They are named by adding the suffix *-oma* to the cell type from which the tumor arose. For example, benign tumors of fibrous tissue are termed "fibromas," whereas benign cartilaginous tumors are "chondromas." The term **adenoma** is the term for benign epithelial neoplasms that grow in glandlike patterns. Benign tumors that form large cystic masses are called **cystadenomas. Lipomas** are soft fatty tumors, **myomas** are tumors of muscle, and **angiomas** are tumors composed of blood vessels. An epithelial tumor that grows as a projecting mass on the skin or from an inner mucous membrane (like the gastrointestinal tract) is termed a **papilloma,** or **polyp.**

Malignant neoplasms of epithelial cell origin are called **carcinomas,** from the Greek word *karkinos* meaning 'crab'. Carcinomas affect epithelial tissues, skin, and mucous membranes lining body cavities. Malignancies of glandular tissues such as the breast, liver, and pancreas, as well as the cells lining the gastrointestinal tract, are called **adenocarcinomas. Squamous cell carcinoma** denotes a cancer in which the tumor cells resemble stratified squamous epithelium, as in the lung and head and neck regions. At times, the tumor grows in such a bizarre pattern that it is termed "undifferentiated" or "anaplastic" (without form).

Sarcomas are malignant tumors arising from connective tissues such as bone, muscle, and cartilage. Although less common than carcinomas, sarcomas tend to spread more rapidly and are highly malignant.

There is substantial evidence that most tumors arise from a single cell (monoclonal origin). The rate of growth generally correlates inversely with the level of parenchymal differentiation. Thus, well-differentiated tumors tend to grow slowly, whereas bizarre, undifferentiated neoplasms have a rapid growth rate.

Although the cause of cancer is still unknown, many possible causative factors (carcinogens) have been implicated. Chemical carcinogens may cause structural alteration of the DNA molecule (mutation), which may lead to the development of a neoplasm. Examples of chemical carcinogens include air or water pollution, cigarette smoke, asbestos, and a variety of other substances used in industry, food, cosmetics, and plastics. The development of specific types of cancer in certain families is suggestive of some genetic predisposition. Excessive exposure to ultraviolet radiation (sunshine) may lead to the development of skin cancer. Survivors of the atom bomb who received huge doses of radiation have demonstrated a high incidence of leukemia. A greater-than-expected rate of leukemia was also seen in persons working with x radiation before the need for proper protection was appreciated.

The study of experimental animal tumors has offered convincing evidence that neoplastic transformation can be induced by DNA and RNA viruses. Viruses that invade normal cells may alter their genetic material, leading to the abnormal cell divisions and rapid growth observed in malignant tumors.

The clinical symptoms of cancer vary with the site of malignancy. Bleeding in the stools, a change in bowel activity (intermittent constipation and diarrhea), or intestinal obstruction is suggestive of gastrointestinal malignancy. Difficulty in swallowing (dysphagia) or loss of appetite (anorexia), especially if accompanied by rapid weight loss, is suggestive of a neoplasm in the esophagus or stomach. Hematuria may be a sign of kidney or bladder cancer, whereas difficulties in urination (urgency, burning sensations, inability to start the stream of urine) in an older man may be a sign of prostate tumor. Hemoptysis (coughing up blood) or a persistent cough or hoarseness is suggestive of a neoplasm in the respiratory tract. Severe anemia may develop from internal bleeding or from malfunction of the bone marrow caused by growth of a malignant lesion in the skeleton. It should be stressed that these clinical symptoms may also be caused by benign disease. Nevertheless, since they may signal an underlying malignancy, these symptoms should be carefully investigated to exclude the presence of cancer.

Pain frequently is not an early sign of cancer. Unfortunately, pain often is appreciated only when the malignancy has spread too extensively to be curable. Secondary infections are common and an increasing cause of death. Most cancer patients are immunologically compromised, either because of their original disease or as a result of radiation or chemotherapy. In addition to typical bacterial and viral infections, immunocompromised patients with malignancy are especially susceptible to unusual **opportunistic** infections such as *Pneumocystis carinii* pneumonia and **cytomegalovirus.**

Some cancers that are still at a curable stage can be detected by screening procedures. Routine mammography may identify nonpalpable breast cancer; a Pap smear may show otherwise unsuspected cancer of the cervix. Surgical removal of these small tumors without metastatic spread offers an excellent prognosis.

Malignant neoplasms disseminate to distant sites by one of three pathways: (1) seeding within body cavities, (2) lymphatic spread, and (3) hematogenous spread.

Seeding (diffuse spread) of cancers occurs when neoplasms invade a natural body cavity. For example, a tumor of the gastrointestinal tract may penetrate the wall of the gut, permitting its metastases to enter the peritoneal cavity and implant at distant sites. A similar sequence may occur with lung cancers in the pleural cavity and neoplasms of the central nervous system (medulloblastoma, ependymoma) that spread from the cerebral ventricles by means of the cerebrospinal fluid to reimplant on the meningeal surfaces within the brain or in the spinal cord.

Lymphatic spread is the major metastatic route of carcinomas, especially those of the lung and breast. The pattern of lymph node involvement depends on the site of the primary neoplasm and the natural lymphatic pathways of drainage of that region. Carcinomas of the lung metastasize first to the regional bronchial lymph nodes and then to the tracheobronchial and hilar nodes. Carcinoma of the breast usually arises in the upper outer quadrant and first spreads to the axillary nodes. Medial breast lesions may drain through the chest wall to nodes along the internal mammary artery.

Hematogenous spread of cancer is a complex process involving several steps. Tumor cells invade and penetrate blood vessels and are released as neoplastic emboli into the circulation. These emboli of tumor cells are trapped in small vascular channels of distant organs, where they invade the wall of the arresting vessel and infiltrate and multiply in the adjacent tissue. The localization of hematogenous metastases tends to be determined by the vascular connections and anatomic relations between the primary neoplasm and the metastatic sites. For example, carcinomas arising in abdominal organs such as the gastrointestinal tract tend to metastasize to the liver because of the flow of portal vein blood to that organ. Cancers arising in midline organs close to the vertebral column (e.g., prostate, thyroid) tend to embolize through the paravertebral venous plexus to seed the vertebral column. Neoplasms in organs drained by the inferior and superior vena cava, such as the kidney, tend to metastasize to the lung. However, there are several well-defined patterns of metastatic spread that are not easily explained by vascular-anatomic relationships. Some examples include the tendency for carcinoma of the lung to involve the adrenal glands, simultaneous metastatic deposits in the brain and adrenal glands, and pituitary metastases occurring from breast carcinomas.

The **grading** of a malignant tumor assesses its aggressiveness, or degree of malignancy. The grade of a tumor usually indicates its biologic behavior and may allow prediction of its responsiveness to certain therapeutic agents. **Staging** refers to the extensiveness of a tumor at its primary site and the presence or absence of metastases to lymph nodes and distant organs such as the liver, lungs, and skeleton. The staging of a tumor is often critical to the choice of appropriate therapy. Well-localized tumors without evidence of metastases may be surgically removed. Fast-growing, undifferentiated tumors such as Hodgkin's disease may respond best to **radiation therapy**. **Hormonal therapy** is used to treat cancer of the prostate, either by the removal of the sources of male gonadal hormones that stimulate tumor growth or by the administration of the female gonadal hormone estrogen that inhibits it. **Chemotherapy** is the use of one or a combination of cytotoxic substances that kill neoplastic cells but also may injure many normal cells and result in significant complications.

▪ Hereditary Diseases

Hereditary diseases are passed from one generation to the next through the genetic information contained in the nucleus of each cell. They reflect an abnormality in the DNA (deoxyribonucleic acid), which is the blueprint for protein synthesis within the cell. In many hereditary diseases, there is an error in a single protein molecule that can lead to enzyme defects; defects in membrane receptors and transport systems; alterations in the structure, function, or quantity of nonenzyme proteins; and unusual reactions to drugs.

The most common hereditary abnormality is an enzyme deficiency. This leads to a metabolic block that results in a decreased amount of a substance needed for normal function or an accumulation of a metabolic intermediate that may cause injury. An example of the first mechanism is albinism, the absence of pigmentation resulting from an enzymatic deficiency that prevents the synthesis of the pigment melanin. An example of the second mechanism is phenylketonuria, in which absence of an enzyme leads to the accumulation of toxic levels of the amino acid phenylalanine.

A defect in the structure of the globin molecule leads to the development of the hemoglobinopathies such as sickle cell disease and thalassemia. An example of a genetically determined adverse reaction to drugs is glucose 6-phosphate dehydrogenase deficiency, in which an insufficient amount of the enzyme results in a severe hemolytic anemia in patients receiving a common antimalarial drug.

Despite our extensive knowledge of the biochemical basis of many genetic disorders, there are a large number of conditions for which the underlying mechanism is unknown. This list includes cystic fibrosis, neurofibromatosis, retinoblastoma, familial colonic polyposis, and Huntington's disease.

Each human cell contains 46 chromosomes divided into 23 pairs. The chromosomes, in turn, contain thousands of genes, each of which is responsible for the synthesis of a single protein. Forty-four of the chromosomes are called **autosomes;** the other two are the X and Y chromosomes, which determine the sex of the person. A combination of XY chromosomes results in a male, whereas an XX configuration results in a female.

Half of each person's chromosomes are inherited from each parent. If the genes inherited from each parent are the same for a particular trait, the person is called **homozygous.** If the genes are different (e.g., one for brown eyes and one for blue eyes), the person is **heterozygous.** Genes that always produce an effect regardless of whether the person is homozygous or heterozygous are called **dominant;** genes that manifest themselves only when the person is homozygous for the trait are termed **recessive.** In determining eye color, brown is dominant, whereas blue is recessive. It must be remembered that although a recessive trait must have been contributed by both parents it is possible that neither parent demonstrated that trait. For example, two parents each with one gene for brown eyes and one gene for blue eyes would show the dominant brown coloration, though they could each contribute a blue-eye gene to their offspring, who would manifest the recessive blue-eye trait.

In some traits, genes are **codominant** so that both are expressed. An example is the AB blood type, in which the gene for factor A is inherited from one parent and that for factor B is inherited from the other.

Mutations are alterations in the DNA structure that may become permanent hereditary changes if they affect the gonadal cells. Mutations may result from radiation, chemicals, or viruses. They may have minimal effect and be virtually undetectable or be so serious that they are incompatible with life and cause the death of a fetus and spontaneous abortion.

Autosomal dominant disorders are transmitted from one generation to the next. Both males and females are affected, and both can transmit the condition. When an affected person marries an unaffected person, half the children (on the average) will have the disease. The clinical manifestations of autosomal dominant disorders can be modified by reduced penetrance and variable expressivity. Reduced penetrance means that not everyone who has the gene will demonstrate the trait; variable expressivity refers to the fact that a dominant gene may be manifest somewhat differently among several individuals (e.g., polydactyly may be expressed in the toes or in the fingers as one or more extra digits). Examples of autosomal dominant disorders include achondroplasia, neurofibromatosis, Marfan's syndrome, and familial hypercholesterolemia.

Autosomal recessive disorders result only when a person is homozygous for the defective gene. The trait does not usually affect the parents, though siblings may show the disease. On average, siblings have a one-in-four chance of being affected; two out of four will be carriers, and one will be normal. Recessive genes appear more frequently in a family, and close intermarriage (as between first cousins) increases the risk of the particular disease. Unlike autosomal dominant diseases, the expression of the defect tends to be uniform in autosomal recessive diseases and the age of onset is frequently early in life. Examples of autosomal recessive disorders include phenylketonuria, cystic fibrosis, galactosemia, glycogen and lipid storage diseases, Tay-Sachs disease, and sickle cell anemia.

Sex-linked disorders generally result from defective genes on the X chromosome, since the Y chromosome is small and carries very few genes. Most of these conditions are transmitted by heterozygous carrier females virtually only to sons, who have only the single, affected X chromosome. Sons of a heterozygous woman have a one-in-two chance of receiving the mutant gene. An affected male does not transmit the disorder to sons, but all his daughters are carriers. In rare cases a female may have the sex-linked disease if she is homozygous for the recessive gene. Virtually all sex-linked disorders are recessive. The most common example of a sex-linked disorder is color blindness. Other conditions include glucose 6-phosphate dehydrogenase deficiency and some types of hemophilia and muscular dystrophy.

▪ Radiographic Manifestations of Hereditary Diseases

Down's syndrome (mongolism)

Down's syndrome is the most common of the trisomy disorders that are caused by the presence of an extra autosomal chromosome that results in an individual having three strands of a certain chromosome (number 21) instead of the normal two. It is usually diagnosed from birth because of the characteristic clinical appearance—mental deficiency, short stature, poor muscle tone, short neck, and a straight skin crease that extends across the palm of the hand. The typical facial appearance includes widely set eyes, short and flat nose, and a coarse tongue, which often protrudes through a partially open mouth.

The major skeletal abnormality in infancy is in the pelvis, where there is a decrease in the acetabular and iliac angles with hypoplasia and noticeable lateral flaring of the iliac wings (Figure 1-1). Other common skeletal abnormalities include shortening of the middle phalanx of the fifth finger, squaring of the vertebral bodies (superoinferior length becoming equal to or greater than the anteroposterior measurement), hypoplasia of the nasal sinuses, and delayed closure of the cranial sutures.

Congenital heart disease, especially septal defects, occurs in about 40% of patients with Down's syndrome. There is also a greater-than-normal incidence of duodenal obstruction (duodenal atresia or annular pancreas) and Hirschsprung's disease, as well as a substantially increased likelihood of developing leukemia.

Turner's syndrome

Turner's syndrome (gonadal dysgenesis) is characterized by primary amenorrhea (no ovulation or menstruation), sexual infantilism, short stature, and bilateral tiny gonads. Although the patient appears to be female, she has only one X chromosome.

A characteristic, but nonspecific, skeletal abnormality is shortening of the fourth metacarpal and

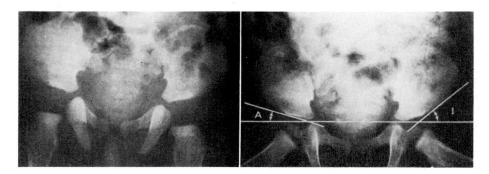

Figure 1-1 Down's syndrome. Two examples of typical pelvis in Down's syndrome showing flared iliac wings and diminished acetabular, *A*, and iliac, *I*, angles. (From James AE, Merz P, Janower ML, et al: *Clin Radiol* 22:417-433, 1971.

sometimes also the fifth metacarpal (Figure 1-2). This produces a positive metacarpal sign, in which a line drawn tangentially to the distal ends of the heads of the fifth and fourth metacarpals passes through the head of the third metacarpal (indicating the disproportionate shortening of the fourth and fifth metacarpals), rather than extending distally to the head of the third metacarpal as in a normal person.

Various urinary tract anomalies, especially horseshoe kidney and other types of malrotation, are often seen in patients with gonadal dysgenesis. Coarctation of the aorta is the most common cardiovascular anomaly. Because coarctation of the aorta most often affects men, its appearance in a woman should indicate the possibility of underlying gonadal dysgenesis.

Klinefelter's syndrome

Klinefelter's syndrome is a disorder characterized by small testes that fail to mature or produce sperm. The fundamental defect is the presence in a male of two or more X chromosomes. At puberty, the breasts enlarge, and a female distribution of hair develops. The affected individual is tall, mentally deficient, and sterile.

Radiographically, the skeletal changes are both less common and less pronounced than in patients with Turner's syndrome, its female counterpart. A positive metacarpal sign is seen in fewer than 25% of the patients. Hypogonadism may lead to delayed epiphyseal fusion and retarded bone maturation.

Phenylketonuria

Phenylketonuria is an inborn error of metabolism in which an enzyme deficiency results in the impaired conversion of phenylalanine to tyrosine. If the condition is not diagnosed and treated early, the patient usually suffers profound retardation, hyperactivity,

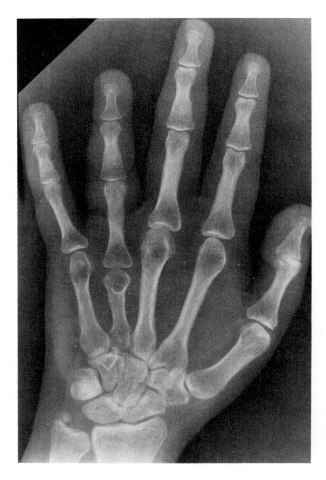

Figure 1-2 Turner's syndrome. Frontal projection of hand shows short fourth metacarpal.

and seizures, all related to brain atrophy that can be demonstrated as dilatation of the ventricles and sulci on computed tomography (CT) or magnetic resonance imaging (MRI). Because of an inadequate amount of tyrosine, there is impaired production of the pigment melanin, and the patient is very light in color.

Homocystinuria

Homocystinuria is an inborn error of the metabolismof the amino acid methionine that causes a defect in the structure of collagen or elastin. The most frequent and striking radiographic feature of homocystinuria is osteoporosis of the spine, which is often associated with biconcave deformities of the vertebral bodies (Figure 1-3). Osteoporosis with cortical thinning is also common in the long bones. Patients with homocystinuria have a tendency to develop arterial and venous thrombosis, and premature occlusive vascular disease is the major cause of death.

Alkaptonuria and ochronosis

Alkaptonuria is a rare inborn error of metabolism in which an enzyme deficiency leads to an abnormal accumulation of homogentisic acid in the blood and urine. The urine is either very dark on voiding or becomes black after standing or being alkalinized. The disorder often goes unrecognized until middle

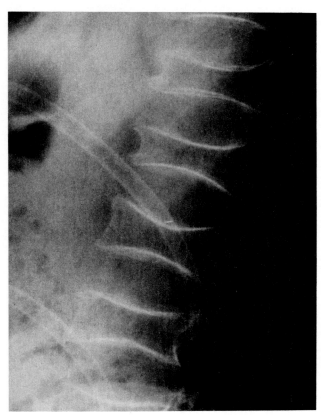

Figure 1-3 Homocystinuria. Striking osteoporosis of spine is associated with biconcave deformities of vertebral bodies. (From Thomas PS, Carson NAJ: *Ann Radiol* 21:95, 1978.

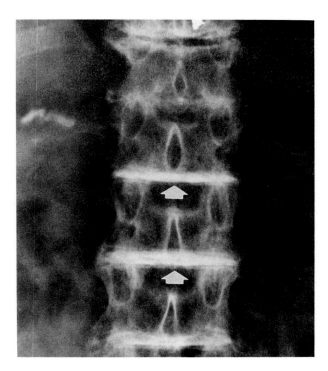

Figure 1-4 Ochronosis. Frontal projection of lumbar spine shows dense laminated calcification of multiple intervertebral disks (*arrows*).

life, when deposition of the black pigment of oxidized homogentisic acid in cartilage and other connective tissue produces a distinctive form of degenerative arthritis (ochronosis). The pathognomonic radiographic finding is dense laminated calcification of multiple intervertebral disks (Figure 1-4) that begins in the lumbar spine and may extend to involve the dorsal and cervical regions.

Cystinuria

Cystinuria is an inborn error of amino acid transport characterized by impaired tubular absorption and excessive urinary excretion of several amino acids. Large amounts of cystine in the urine predispose to the formation of renal, ureteral, and bladder stones. Pure cystine stones are not radiopaque and can be demonstrated only on excretory urography, where they appear as filling defects in the urinary tract. Stones containing the calcium salts of cystine are radiopaque and can be detected on plain abdominal radiographs.

Glycogen storage diseases

The glycogen storage diseases are a group of genetic disorders involving the pathways for the storage of carbohydrates as glycogen (in the liver) and for its

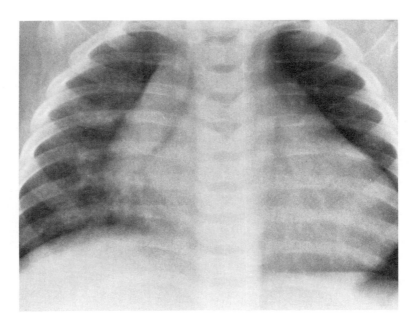

Figure 1-5   Glycogen storage disease. Generalized globular cardiac enlargement with left ventricular prominence.

use in maintaining blood glucose and providing energy. An excess amount of normal or abnormal glycogen infiltrates and enlarges multiple organs, especially the heart and liver (Figure 1-5).

Gaucher's disease

Gaucher's disease is an inborn error of metabolism characterized by the accumulation of abnormal quantities of complex lipids in the reticuloendothelial cells of the spleen, liver, and bone marrow. The most striking changes occur in the skeletal system. Infiltration of the bone marrow with abnormal lipid-containing cells causes a loss of bone density with expansion and cortical thickening of the long bones, especially the femur. Marrow infiltration of the distal femur causes abnormal modeling and flaring and the characteristic (but nonspecific) Erlenmeyer flask deformity (Figure 1-6).

Aseptic necrosis (especially involving the femoral heads) is a common complication. The spleen is usually greatly enlarged, and hepatomegaly is common.

Marfan's syndrome

Marfan's syndrome is an inherited generalized disorder of connective tissue with ocular, skeletal, and cardiovascular manifestations. Most patients are tall and slender and appear emaciated because of the decrease in subcutaneous fat. A typical feature of Marfan's syndrome is bilateral dislocation of the lens of the eye caused by weakness of its supporting

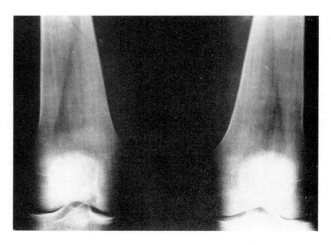

Figure 1-6   Gaucher's disease. The distal ends of the femurs show typical underconstriction and cortical thinning. (From Levin B: *AJR* 85:685-696, 1961.)

tissues. A laxity of ligaments about the joints leads to loose-jointedness or double-jointedness, recurrent dislocations, and flat feet. The major radiographic abnormality is elongation and thinning of the tubular bones (Figure 1-7), most pronounced in the hands and feet and seen clinically as arachnodactyly (spiderlike digits). Almost all patients with Marfan's syndrome have abnormalities of the cardiovascular system. Necrosis of the medial portion of the aortic wall causes progressive dilatation of the ascending aorta that produces a bulging of the upper right

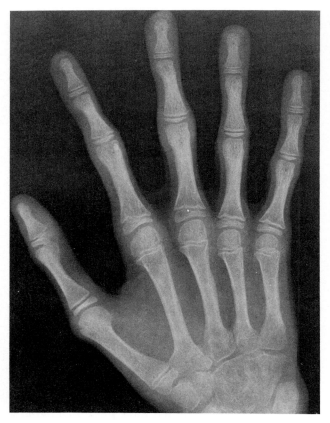

Figure 1-7 Arachnodactyly in Marfan's syndrome. Metacarpals and phalanges are unusually long and slender.

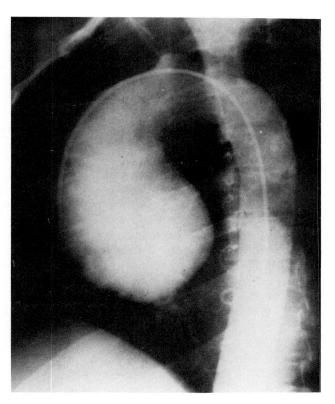

Figure 1-8 Marfan's syndrome. Arteriogram shows enormous dilatation of aneurysmal ascending aorta. (From Ovenfors CO, Godwin JD: In Eisenberg RL, Amberg JR, editors: *Critical diagnostic pathways in radiology: an algorithmic approach,* Philadelphia, 1981, Lippincott.

portion of the cardiac silhouette (Figure 1-8) and an unusual prominence of the pulmonary outflow tract as it is displaced by the dilated aorta. Dissecting aneurysm is a serious complication that may kill the patient in early life.

Osteogenesis imperfecta

See page 69.

Achondroplasia

See page 69.

▪ Disorders of Immunity

The immune reaction of the body provides a powerful defense against invading organisms by allowing it to recognize foreign substances (antigens), such as bacteria, viruses, fungi, and toxins, and to produce antibodies to counteract them. The antibody binds together with the antigen to make the antigen harmless. Once antibodies have been produced, a person becomes **immune** to the antigen.

Antibodies, or **immunoglobulins,** are formed in lymphoid tissue, primarily in the lymph nodes, thymus gland, and spleen. Although an infant is born with some immunity, most immunity is acquired either naturally by exposure to a disease or artificially by immunization. There are two types of artificial immunity, active and passive. In **active immunity,** a person forms antibodies to counteract an antigen in the form of a vaccine or toxoid. A **vaccine** consists of a low dose of dead or deactivated bacteria or viruses. Although these organisms cannot cause disease, they are foreign proteins containing antigens that stimulate the body to produce antibodies against them. A **toxoid** is a chemically altered **toxin,** the poisonous material produced by a pathogenic organism. As with a vaccine, the toxin cannot cause disease but does trigger the development of antibodies to it. Examples of active immunity are the vaccines given to prevent smallpox, polio, measles, tetanus, and diphtheria. Active immunity persists for a long time, though a relatively long time is required to build up immunity, and a booster shot is frequently given for a stronger effect.

Passive immunity refers to the administration of a dose of preformed antibodies from immune serum of an animal, usually a horse. This type of immunity acts immediately but lasts for a relatively short time. It is used in situations when a person is exposed to a serious disease (hepatitis, rabies, tetanus) but has no immunity against it and thus requires an immediate supply of antibodies to prevent a possibly fatal infection.

There are several fundamental mechanisms of immunologic responses to antigens. The first type is a rapidly occurring reaction in which antigens are attacked by antibodies previously bound to the surface of mast cells. The mast cells release **histamine,** which causes a local increase in vascular permeability and smooth muscle contraction. Disorders resulting from localized reactions of this type (which probably have a genetically determined predisposition) include hay fever, asthma, and gastrointestinal allergies. Generalized, or systemic, **anaphylactic** reactions are characterized by hypotension and vascular collapse (shock) with urticaria (hives), bronchiolar spasm, and laryngeal edema. This reaction is the cause of acute death in patients who are hypersensitive ("allergic") to the sting of bees, wasps, and other insects and to medications such as penicillin and the iodinated contrast materials used in radiology.

In the second (cytotoxic) type of immune reaction, the antigen is either a component of a cell or is attached to the wall of red blood cells, white blood cells, platelets, or vascular endothelial cells. The reaction with an antibody leads to cell destruction by lysis or phagocytosis. Examples of this type of immune reaction include the transfusion reaction occurring after the administration of ABO-incompatible blood and erythroblastosis fetalis, the hemolytic anemia of the Rh-positive newborn whose Rh-negative mother has produced anti-Rh antibodies.

The third type of immune reaction is a delayed reaction that occurs in an individual previously sensitized to an antigen. As an example, the first time a person touches poison ivy there is no reaction. However, on the next exposure to poison ivy, antibodies are present to attack the antigen, and the patient develops the typical rash and irritation. A similar process is involved in the reaction to tuberculosis, leprosy, many fungal diseases, and other infections. It is also the principal component of rejection in organ transplants.

▪ Acquired Immunodeficiency Syndrome (AIDS)

The acquired immunodeficiency syndrome (AIDS), which most commonly affects young homosexual males and intravenous drug abusers, is character-

ized by a profound and sustained impairment of cellular immunity that results in recurrent or sequential opportunistic infections and a particularly aggressive form of Kaposi's sarcoma. AIDS has also been reported in a substantial number of hemophiliacs, recipients of transfusions, and increasingly in heterosexual partners of affected individuals.

AIDS is attributable to infection with retroviruses known as human immunodeficiency viruses (HIV). It predominantly involves the lungs, gastrointestinal tract, and central nervous system. Pulmonary infections are extremely common in patients with AIDS and are frequently caused by organisms that only rarely produce disease in individuals with normal immune systems. About 60% of AIDS victims develop one or more attacks of *Pneumocystis carinii* pneumonia, which is characterized by a sudden onset, a rapid progression to diffuse lung involvement, and a considerable delay in resolution. The typical early radiographic finding of this protozoan infection is a hazy, perihilar granular infiltrate that spreads to the periphery and appears predominantly interstitial. In later stages the pattern progresses to patchy areas of air space consolidation with air bronchograms, indicating the alveolar nature of the process (Figure 1-9). The radiographic appearance may closely resemble pulmonary edema or bacterial pneumonia. Because *Pneumocystis carinii* cannot be cultured and the disease it causes is usually fatal if untreated, an open-lung biopsy is often necessary if a sputum examination reveals no organisms in a patient suspected of having this disease.

Gastrointestinal manifestations of AIDS include a variety of sexually transmitted diseases involving

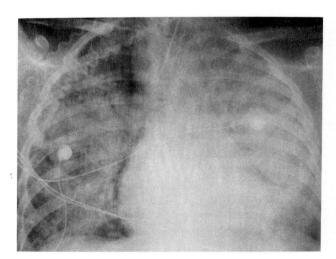

Figure 1-9   *Pneumocystis carinii* pneumonia. Diffuse bilateral air-space consolidation suggestive of severe bacterial pneumonia or pulmonary edema.

the rectum and colon, infectious processes (such as shigellosis, amebiasis, candidiasis, and giardiasis), and alimentary tract dissemination (spread) of Kaposi's sarcoma. Kaposi's sarcoma is a systemic disease that characteristically affects the skin and causes an ulcerated hemorrhagic dermatitis. Metastases to the small bowel are relatively common and consist of multiple reddish or bluish red nodules that intrude into the lumen of the bowel (Figure 1-10). Similar lesions can develop throughout the gastrointestinal tract. Central ulceration of the metastases causes gastrointestinal bleeding and a characteristic radiographic appearance of multiple "bull's-eye" lesions simulating metastatic melanoma.

About 40% of all AIDS victims have neurologic symptoms, most commonly progressive dementia. Focal neurologic symptoms and signs are common in patients who develop mass lesions of the brain. The multiple manifestations of AIDS in the central nervous system are best demonstrated on MRI, where they appear as areas of increased signal intensity on T_2-weighted images. Atypical brain abscesses and meningeal infection often occur, most commonly as a result of toxoplasmosis, cryptococcosis, cytomegalovirus, and herpesvirus (Figure 1-11). Increasing evidence indicates that there also may be cerebral infections by the human immunodeficiency virus (HIV) itself. Patients with AIDS also have a high incidence of lymphoma involving the central nervous system.

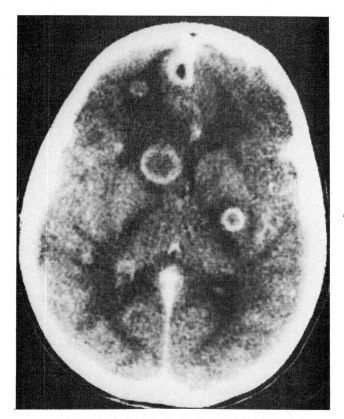

A

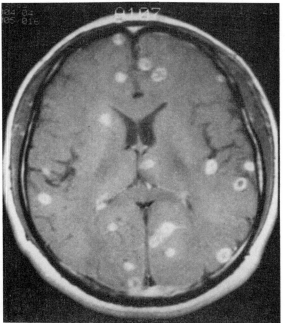

B

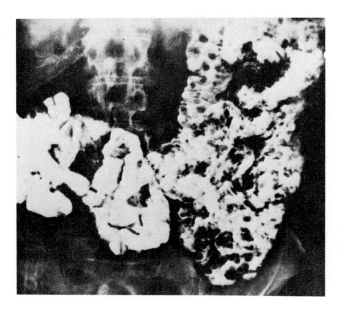

Figure 1-10 Kaposi's sarcoma. Small bowel study shows multiple intramural nodules (predominantly involving the jejunum) that distort the mucosal pattern and produce contour defects and intraluminal lucencies. (From Bryk D, et al: *Gastrointest Radiol* 3:425, 1978.)

Figure 1-11 Neurologic manifestations of acquired immunodeficiency syndrome (AIDS). **A,** CT scan shows multiple ring-enhancing lesions caused by cryptococcal brain abscesses. **B,** magnetic resonance image after intravenous administration of contrast medium, demonstrating multiple enhancing abscesses caused by toxoplasmosis.

Specialized Imaging Techniques

▪ Ultrasound

Ultrasound (Figure 1-12) is a noninvasive imaging modality in which high-frequency sound waves that are produced by electrical stimulation of a specialized crystal are passed through the body (reduced in intensity) in relation to the acoustic properties of the tissues through which they travel. The crystal is mounted in a transducer, which also acts as a receiver to record echoes that are reflected back from the body whenever the sound wave strikes an interface between two tissues that have different acoustic impedances. A water-tissue interface produces strong reflections (echoes), whereas a solid tissue mass that contains only small differences in composition causes weak reflections. The display of the ultrasound image on a television monitor shows both the intensity level of the echoes and the position in the body from which they arose. Ultrasound images may be displayed as static gray-scale scans or as multiple images that permit movement to be viewed in real time.

In general, fluid-filled structures have intense echoes at their borders, no internal echoes, and good transmission of the sound waves. Solid structures produce internal echoes of variable intensity. Since the solid structure tends to attenuate the sound waves, the posterior margin is less sharply defined than the anterior margin, and only a portion of the beam is transmitted.

The major advantage of ultrasound is its safety. Up to now there has been no evidence of any adverse effect on human tissues at the intensity level currently used for diagnostic procedures. Therefore ultrasound is the modality of choice for examination of children and pregnant women, in whom there is potential danger from the radiation exposure of other imaging studies. It is by far the best technique for evaluating fetal age, congenital anomalies, and complications of pregnancy (Figure 1-13). Ultrasound is used extensively to evaluate the intraperitoneal and retroperitoneal structures (except for internal lesions of the gastrointestinal tract), to detect abdominal and pelvic abscesses, to diagnose obstruction of the biliary and urinary tracts, and to assess the patency of major blood vessels. Ultrasound may be used as a quick, inexpensive procedure to evaluate postoperative complications, though it may be difficult to perform in these patients because of overlying dressings, retention sutures, drains, and open wounds, which may prevent the transducer from being in direct contact with the skin. In children with open fontanelles, ultrasound can be used to examine intracranial structures. Other uses of ultrasound include breast imaging (to differentiate solid from cystic masses) (Figure 1-14), prostate imaging (to detect and accurately stage neoplasms), and Doppler studies (to evaluate narrowing or obstruction of blood vessels). High-resolution, real-time ultrasound systems can assist surgeons during operative procedures. This technique has been applied to the neurosurgical localization of brain and spine neoplasms, evaluation of intraven-

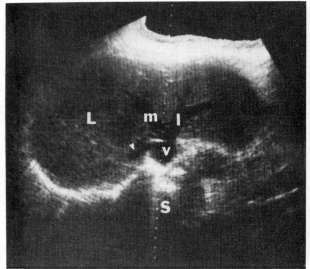
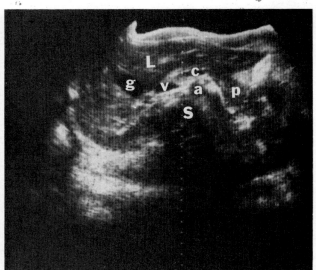

A   **B**

Figure 1-12   Normal abdominal ultrasound images. **A,** Upper portion of liver. **B,** Lower portion of liver. *a,* Aorta; *g,* gallbladder; *L,* liver; *l,* left hepatic vein; *m,* middle hepatic vein; *p,* tail of pancreas; *S,* spine; *v,* inferior vena cava; *arrowhead,* right hepatic vein.

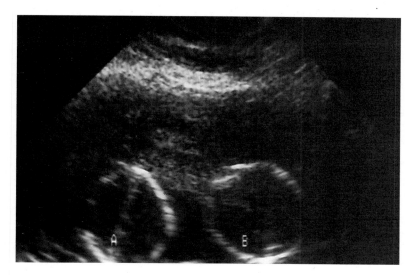

Figure 1-13 Ultrasonogram of twin pregnancy shows the two fetal skulls, *A* and *B*. (From Krebs CA, Giyanani VL, Eisenberg RL: *Ultrasound Atlas of disease processes,* Norwalk, CT, 1993, Appleton & Lange.)

A

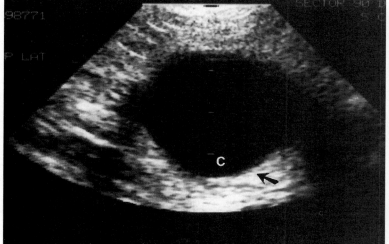

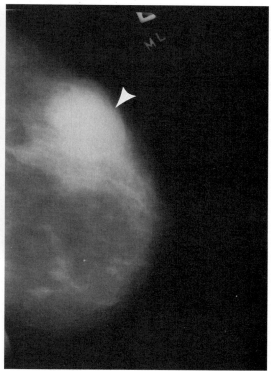

B

Figure 1-14 Ultrasound in breast imaging. **A,** Sonogram shows an anechoic mass *(C)* with well-defined back wall and distal enhancement *(arrow).* **B,** Mammography also shows this simple breast cyst *(arrowhead).* (From Krebs CA, Giyanani VL, Eisenberg RL: *Ultrasound atlas of disease processes,* Norwalk, CT, 1993, Appleton & Lange.)

tricular shunt tube placement, localization of renal calculi, and surgical procedures involving the hepatobiliary system and pancreas.

The latest technology in ultrasound is the color flow duplex system, in which conventional real-time imaging is combined with Doppler imaging (to produce quantitative data) as well as color to depict motion and the direction and velocity of blood flow.

The color and intensity represent the direction of flow and the magnitude of velocity, respectively.

The major limitation of ultrasound is the presence of acoustic barriers, such as air, bone, and barium. For example, air reflects essentially all the ultrasound beam, and so structures beneath it cannot be imaged. This is a special problem when one is attempting to image the solid abdominal organs in a patient with adynamic ileus and is the major factor precluding the ultrasound examination of the thorax. For an ultrasound examination of the pelvis, the patient is usually given large amounts of fluid to fill the bladder, thus displacing the air-filled bowel from the region of interest.

▪ Computed Tomography

Computed tomography (CT) (Figure 1-15) is a radiographic technique for producing cross-sectional tomographic images by first scanning a "slice" of tissue from multiple angles with a narrow x-ray beam, then calculating a relative linear attenuation coefficient (amount of radiation absorbed in tissue for the various tissue elements in the section), and finally displaying the computed reconstruction as a gray-scale image on a television monitor. Unlike other imaging modalities (except for the more recent magnetic resonance imaging), CT permits the radiographic differentiation among a variety of soft tissues. It is extremely sensitive to slight differences (1%) in tissue densities; for comparison, differences in tissue density of at least 5% are required for detection by conventional screen-film radiography. Thus, in the head, CT can differentiate between blood clots, white matter and gray matter, cerebrospinal fluid, cerebral edema, and neoplastic processes. The CT number reflects the attenuation of a specific tissue relative to that of water, which is arbitrarily given a CT number of 0. The highest CT number is that of bone; the lowest is that of air. Fat has a CT number less than 0, whereas soft tissues have CT numbers higher than 0.

Technical improvements in CT instrumentation have greatly reduced the time required to produce a single slice (1 to 2 seconds), and this permits the CT evaluation of virtually any portion of the body. In most instances, some type of preliminary film is obtained (either a radiograph or a CT-generated image) for localization, the detection of potentially interfering high-density material (metallic clips, barium, electrodes), and correlation with the CT images. An overlying grid with numeric markers permits close correlation between the subsequent CT scans and the initial scout film.

The intravenous injection of iodinated contrast material is an integral part of many CT examinations. Scanning during or immediately after the administration of contrast material permits the differentiation of vascular from nonvascular solid structures. Differences in the degree and the time course of contrast enhancement may permit the detection of neoplastic or infectious processes within

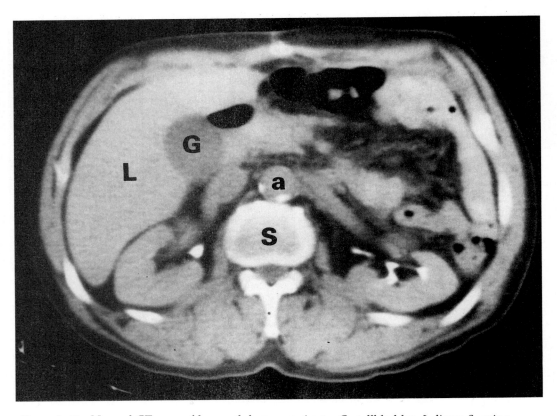

Figure 1-15   Normal CT scan of lower abdomen. *a*, Aorta; *G*, gallbladder; *L*, liver; *S*, spine.

normal parenchymal structures. Because of its relatively low CT number, fat can serve as a natural contrast material and can outline parenchymal organs. In patients with malignant lesions, the loss of adjacent fat planes is highly suspicious for tumor extension. For abdominal studies, especially those of the pancreas and retroperitoneum, dilute oral contrast material is frequently given to demonstrate the lumen of the gastrointestinal tract and permit the distinction between loops of bowel and solid abdominal structures.

High-resolution CT uses thin sections to produce a very detailed display of lung anatomy. It is far more sensitive and specific than plain chest radiographs (or conventional CT) for the diagnosis of parenchymal lung disease (Figure 1-16).

The newest technology in CT is spiral scanning. In this technique, continual CT scanning is performed as the patient is moved through the gantry (unlike the multiple single scans in conventional CT). This permits much faster scanning without respiratory motion and provides data that can be reformatted in coronal and sagittal planes as well as the standard axial plane. Spiral CT can permit reconstruction of images in three dimensions and offers the potential of demonstrating vascular lesions without the need for arteriography (Figure 1-17).

▪ Magnetic Resonance Imaging

Magnetic resonance imaging (MRI) (Figure 1-18), once called nuclear magnetic resonance (NMR), has in a few short years become an important clinical

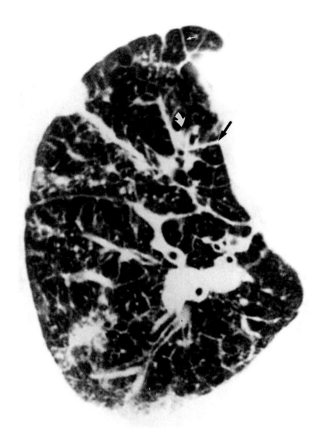

Figure 1-16 High-resolution CT of the lung. Lymphangitic carcinomatosis produces extensive abnormalities with thickening of interlobular septa *(straight arrows),* major fissure, and bronchovascular bundles *(curved arrows).* (From Muller NM: *Semin Roentgenol* 26:132-142, 1991.)

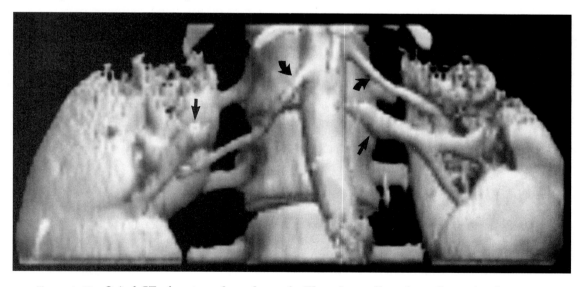

Figure 1-17 Spiral CT of aorta and renal vessels. There is excellent three-dimensional visualization of the normal renal arteries *(curved arrows)* and the dependent, partially filled renal veins *(straight arrows).* (From Rubin GD, Dake MD, Napel SA, et al: *Radiology* 186:147-152, 1993.)

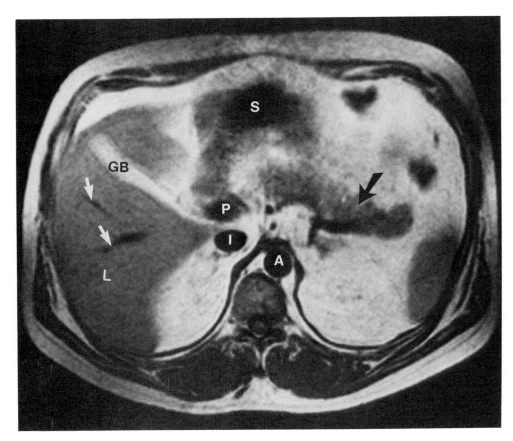

Figure 1-18   Normal MR image of upper abdomen. Transverse scan shows liver *(L)* and
branches of portal veins *(white arrows)*. Gallbladder *(GB)* has high intensity in this fasting
person. Pancreas *(black arrow)* and stomach *(S)* are easily seen. Inferior vena cava *(I)*, aorta *(A)*,
and main portal vein *(P)* are seen with signal void because they contain flowing blood.

tool for a variety of conditions. Although the physics of MRI is beyond the scope of this book, the
technique basically consists in inducing transitions
between energy states by causing certain atoms to
absorb and transfer energy. This is accomplished by
directing a radiofrequency pulse at a substance
placed within a large magnetic field. Various measures of the time required for the material to return
to a baseline energy state (relaxation time) can be
translated by a complex computer program to a
visual image on a television monitor. The two time
constants associated with relaxation are T_1 and T_2
(explained below). To generate an MR image, the
radiographer selects a pulse sequence, which represents a set of radiofrequency magnetic pulses and
the time spacing between these pulses. The most
commonly used pulse sequence is the spin echo.
Other terminology used to describe the pulse sequences includes repetition time (TR) and echo delay
time (TE). The TR is the time between the initiation
of a pulse sequence and the beginning of the suc-
ceeding pulse sequence. The TE is the time between

the generation of the radiofrequency pulse and the
time at which the image is obtained.

MRI has many of the advantages offered by other
imaging modalities without the associated disadvantages. Like ultrasound, MRI is nonionizing and
capable of imaging in multiple planes. Unlike ultrasound, MRI depends less on the operator's skill or
the habitus of the patient and can penetrate bone
without significant decrease in intensity (attenuation) so that the underlying tissue can be clearly
imaged. MRI provides excellent spatial resolution,
equal to that of CT, and far better contrast resolution
of soft tissue. The intravenous injection of contrast
material is unnecessary with MRI because flowing
blood produces a signal void that contrasts sharply
with adjacent structures.

Unlike other imaging modalities that depend on
information from one parameter (such as CT, which
depends on electron density), MRI has the advantage that it derives information from multiple parameters such as hydrogen density and T_1 and T_2
relaxation times. Different imaging sequences dem-

onstrate the effect of one or a combination of these parameters, allowing for a superb display of the differences between normal and abnormal tissues. In general, a pulse sequence using a short TR (500 to 700 msec) and short TE (20 to 30 msec) provides a T_1-weighted image. A pulse sequence using a long TR (2000 to 2500 msec) and a long TE (60 to 80 msec) provides a T_2-weighted image.

Although the degree of signal intensity of various substances on MR scans is complex and depends on multiple factors, some generalizations can be made. On T_1-weighted images, substances causing high signal intensity (bright) include fat, subacute hemorrhage, highly proteinaceous material (e.g., mucus), and slow flowing blood. Water, as in cerebrospinal fluid or simple cysts, has a relatively low signal intensity and appears dark. Soft tissue has an intermediate level of signal.

On T_2-weighted images, water has a high signal intensity (bright), whereas muscle and other soft tissues (including fat) tend to have low signal intensity and appear dark. Bone, calcium, and air appear very dark on all imaging sequences.

Although MRI has improved the sensitivity of detecting abnormal tissue, up to now it has not had a significant effect on specificity. In the head, for example, infarction, edema, tumor, infection, and demyelinating disease all produce identical high signal intensity on T_2-weighted images. Other disadvantages of MRI include a slower scanning time, leading to image degradation resulting from patient motion; the possibility of patient claustrophobia; and the contraindication to imaging patients with pacemakers (may prevent proper operation) or ferromagnetic intracranial aneurysm clips (may slip and result in hemorrhage).

An exciting new technique is MR angiography. This permits high-quality images of the arterial and venous systems without the need for contrast material (Figure 1-19). Further technical refinements and

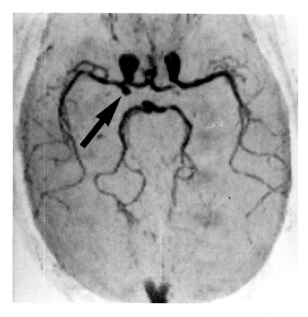

Figure 1-19   MR angiography. Lateral reconstruction shows a posterior communicating artery aneurysm *(arrow)*. (From Stark DD, Bradley WG: *Magnetic resonance imaging,* St Louis, 1993, Mosby.)

clinical experience will expand the role of this modality and may allow MR angiography to eventually supplant contrast angiography in the diagnosis of vascular disease.

In the future, spectroscopic examinations using high magnetic fields and assessing various chemical elements may permit the sophisticated biochemical analysis of tissues in vivo. Improved hardware and software and the development of specific magnetic contrast agents should improve the specificity of this modality and make MRI the imaging procedure of choice for a broad spectrum of clinical findings.

QUESTIONS

1. The accumulation of abnormal amounts of fluid in the spaces between cells or in body cavities is termed _____ .

2. _____ is the process by which white blood cells surround and digest infectious organisms.

3. A tumorlike scar is referred to as a _____ .

4. Inflammation with pus formation is termed _____ .

5. An interruption in the blood supply to an organ or body part is referred to as _____ .

6. A localized area of ischemic necrosis in an organ or tissue is termed an _____ .

7. A swelling caused by bleeding into an enclosed area is termed _____ .

8. A decrease in function of an organ or tissue, because of a reduction in the size or number of cells, is termed _____ .

9. The term _____ means new growth.

10. The term for benign epithelial neoplasms that have a glandlike pattern is _____ .

11. _____ Soft fatty tumors

12. _____ Tumors composed of blood vessels

13. _____ Malignant neoplasms of epithelial cell origin

14. _____ Tumors of muscle

15. _____ Large cystic, benign tumor masses

16. _____ Malignant tumors from connective tissues such as bone, muscle, and cartilage

17. _____ Term meaning without form

18. _____ Loss of appetite

19. _____ Difficulty in swallowing

20. _____ Coughing up blood

21. _____ Major metastatic route of carcinomas

A. Cachexia
B. Myomas
C. Dysphagia
D. Lymphatic
E. Staging
F. Lipomas
G. Hemoptysis
H. Cystadenomas
I. Angiomas
J. Grading
K. Vaccine
L. Antigen
M. Polyp
N. Chemotherapy
O. Sarcomas
P. Anorexia
Q. Carcinomas
R. *Pneumocystis* pneumonia
S. Anaphylactic
T. Anaplastic

22. _____ Assessing the aggressiveness of a malignant tumor

23. _____ Refers to extensiveness of a tumor and whether or not it has metastasized

24. _____ Use of cytotoxic substances that kill neoplastic cells and may cause injury to normal cells

25. _____ Foreign substances produced by invading organisms

26. _____ Consists of a low dose of dead or deactivated bacteria or viruses

27. _____ Critical reaction that can cause death

28. _____ Tumor cells grow well, patient becomes weak and emaciated

29. _____ Opportunistic infection

30. _____ Epithelial tumor that grows as a projecting mass arising on the skin or a mucous membrane

BIBLIOGRAPHY

General radiology

Eisenberg RL: *Diagnostic imaging in internal medicine*, New York, 1985, McGraw-Hill.

Eisenberg RL: *Diagnostic imaging in surgery*, New York, 1986, McGraw-Hill.

Juhl JH, Crummy AB: *Essentials of radiologic imaging*, Philadelphia, 1987, Lippincott.

Putman CE, Ravin CE: *Textbook of diagnostic imaging*, Philadelphia, 1988, Saunders.

Ultrasound

Mittelstaedt CA: *Abdominal ultrasound*, New York, 1987, Churchill Livingstone.

Sarti DA: *Diagnostic ultrasound: text and cases*, St Louis, 1987, Mosby.

Computed tomography

Greenberg M, Greenberg BM: *Essentials of body computed tomography*, Philadelphia, 1983, Saunders.

Lee JKT, Sagel SS, Stanley RJ: *Computed body tomography with MRI correlation*, New York, 1989, Raven Press.

Moss AA, Gamsu G, Genant HK: *Computed tomography of the body*, Philadelphia, 1992, Saunders.

Magnetic resonance imaging

Edelman RR, Hesselink JR: *Clinical magnetic resonance imaging*, Philadelphia, 1990, Saunders.

Stark DD, Bradley WG: *Magnetic resonance imaging*, St Louis, 1993, Mosby.

CHAPTER 2

Respiratory System

■ **Prerequisite Knowledge**

The student should have a basic knowledge of the anatomy and physiology of the respiratory system. In addition, proper learning and understanding of the material will be facilitated if the student has some clinical experience in chest radiography and film evaluation, including a concept of the changes in technique required to compensate for density differences produced by the underlying pathologic conditions.

■ **Goals**

To acquaint the student radiographer with the pathophysiology and radiographic manifestations of all of the common and some of the unusual disorders of the respiratory system

■ **Objectives**

1. Be able to classify the more common diseases in terms of their penetrability to x rays
2. Be familiar with the changes in technical factors required for obtaining optimal quality radiographs in patients with various underlying pathologic conditions
3. Understand and be able to define or describe all bold-faced terms in this chapter
4. Describe the physiology of the respiratory system
5. Identify anatomic structures on both diagrams and radiographs of the respiratory system
6. Be able to describe the more common pathologic conditions affecting the respiratory system, as well as their radiographic manifestations

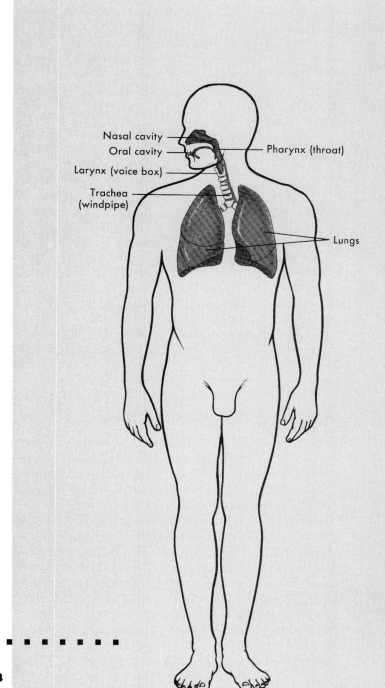

■ Radiographer Notes

Proper positioning and the use of correct exposure factors are especially important in radiography of the respiratory system, so that the radiologist can detect the subtle changes in pulmonary and vascular structures necessary to make a precise diagnosis. Ideally, follow-up studies should be performed with the same exposure factors used in making the initial radiographs. In this way, any density changes can be attributed to true pathologic findings rather than to mere technical differences.

Except for those few pathologic conditions requiring expiration films, all chest radiography should be performed with the patient in full inspiration (inhalation). In an ideal film the upper 10 posterior ribs should be visualized above the diaphragm. Poor expansion of the lungs may cause a normal-sized heart to appear enlarged and makes it difficult to evaluate the lung bases. To obtain a full-inspiration radiograph, the patient should be instructed to take a deep breath, exhale, and inhale again (maximal inspiration), at which time the exposure should be made. This technique avoids the *Valsalva effect*, which is forced expiration against the closed glottis that increases the intrapulmonary pressure. The Valsalva effect results in compression and a large decrease in size of the heart and adjacent blood vessels and thus an inability to evaluate heart size and pulmonary vascularity accurately.

The patient must be precisely positioned for chest radiography to ensure symmetry of the lung fields and a true appearance of the heart and pulmonary vasculature. Whenever possible, all chest radiographs should be taken with the patient in the erect position. The only exception is the patient with a suspected pathologic condition that requires a lateral decubitus position. Although recumbent radiographs may be necessary in immobile or seriously ill patients, they are less than satisfactory because in this position the abdominal contents tend to prevent the diaphragm from descending low enough to permit visualization of well-expanded lung bases or fluid levels. A 72-inch focal-film distance should be used when possible to minimize magnification of the heart and mediastinal structures. Correct positioning with absence of rotation in the frontal projection can be demonstrated by symmetry of the sternoclavicular joints. The shoulders must be rolled forward (anteriorly) to remove the scapulas from overlying the lungs. In large-breasted women, it is often necessary to elevate and separate the breasts to allow good visualization of the lung bases. Nipple shadows of both men and women occasionally appear as soft-tissue masses. If the nature of these soft-tissue masses is unclear, it may be necessary to repeat the examination using small lead markers placed on the nipples. Collimation of the radiograph is required to reduce scattered radiation, though it is essential that both costophrenic angles be visualized.

Radiographs exhibiting a long scale of contrast are necessary to visualize the entire spectrum of

■ Physiology of the Respiratory System

The major role of the respiratory system is the oxygenation of blood and the removal of waste products of the body in the form of carbon dioxide. The trachea, bronchi, and bronchioles are tubular structures responsible for conducting air from the outside of the body into the lungs. The single trachea branches out into two bronchi (one to each lung) and then on to progressively smaller bronchioles to produce a structure termed the "bronchial tree" because its appearance resembles an inverted tree. The tracheobronchial tree is lined with a mucous membrane (respiratory epithelium) containing numerous hairlike projections called "cilia." During inspiration, the air is moistened and warmed as it passes to the lungs. The cilia act as miniature sweepers to prevent dust and foreign particles from reaching the lungs. Any damage to the respiratory epithelium and its cilia permits bacteria and viruses (entering with the inspired or inhaled air) to proliferate and produce an infection.

The vital gas exchange within the lung takes place within the alveoli, extremely thin-walled sacs surrounded by blood capillaries, which represent the true parenchyma of the lung. Oxygen in the inhaled air diffuses from the alveoli into the blood capillaries, where it attaches to hemoglobin molecules in red blood cells and is carried to the various tissues of the body. Carbon dioxide, a waste product of cellular metabolism, diffuses in the opposite direction from the blood capillaries into the alveoli and is thus removed from the body during expiration (exhalation). Because individual alveoli are extremely small, densities within the thoracic cavity (mediastinum, heart, lung markings, pulmonary vasculature) and the surrounding bony thorax. Most authorities agree that a minimum of 120 kVp should be used with an appropriate ratio grid for all adult chest radiography. If it is necessary to decrease the overall density, this should be accomplished by reduction of the milliampere-seconds (mAs) rather than the kVp. Decreasing the kVp tends to enhance the bony thorax, which may obscure vascular details and cause underpenetration of the mediastinal structures. In general the density and contrast should be such that the thoracic vertebrae and intervertebral disk spaces are faintly visible through the shadow of the mediastinum without obscuring the lung markings and pulmonary vascularity.

Short exposure times (10 msec or less) must be used in chest radiography because longer times may not eliminate the involuntary motion of the heart. Automatic exposure devices are generally recommended, and they help to ensure that follow-up studies will have a similar film density. An exception is the expiration (exhalation) chest radiograph, which should be exposed with a manual technique because the preset density of an automatic exposure device may cause excessive blackening of the lungs and thus obscure a small pneumothorax.

Compensatory filters are sometimes needed to overcome the broad range of different tissue densities within the chest. They are especially important to allow good visualization of the mediastinum without overexposing the lungs. The use of compensatory filters generally requires that the radiographic exposure be twice that used in the absence of additional filtration.

To demonstrate fluid levels, the patient should be in an erect position, and a horizontal x-ray beam must be used. Any angulation of the beam prevents a parallel entrance to the air-fluid interface. In some clinical situations (small pneumothorax, pleural thickening versus free pleural fluid) it is necessary to use a horizontal beam with the patient placed in the lateral decubitus position.

Certain pathologic conditions of the respiratory system require that the radiographer alter the routine technical factors. Some disorders produce increased density that is harder to penetrate, whereas others decrease the density of the lungs so that they are easier to penetrate than normal. It is important to remember that these changes may vary for a single disease, since the chest structures may be easier or harder to penetrate, depending on the stage of the disease process. Unless the radiographer has access to previous films with recorded techniques, the initial exposures should be made using a standard technique chart. Adjustments and technical factors can then be made if necessary on subsequent films. Table 1-1 lists the changes in penetrability expected in advanced stages of various disesase processes.

chest radiographs can demonstrate only a cluster of alveoli and their tiny terminal bronchioles, which is the basic anatomic unit of the lung, which is termed the "acinus."

Respiration is controlled by a center in the medulla at the base of the brain. The respiratory center is regulated by the level of carbon dioxide in the blood. Even a slight increase in the amount of carbon dioxide in the blood increases the rate and depth of breathing, as when an individual exercises. The accumulation of waste gases that must be removed from the body (as well as the body's need for additional oxygen) causes the respiratory center to stimulate the muscles of respiration—the diaphragm and the intercostal muscles between the ribs. Contraction of the muscles of respiration causes the volume of the chest cavity to increase. This decreases the pressure within the lungs and forces air to move into the lungs through the tracheobronchial tree. As the respiratory muscles relax, the volume of the chest cavity decreases, and air is forced out of the lungs. Special muscles of expiration (abdominal and internal intercostal muscles) may be needed for difficult breathing or in patients with narrowed airways as in emphysema.

Unlike most other organs, the lung has two different blood supplies. The pulmonary circulation is a low-pressure, low-resistance system through which oxygen enters and carbon dioxide is removed. The bronchial circulation, which is a part of the high-pressure systemic circulation, supplies oxygenated blood to nourish (support) the lung tissue itself.

The lungs are encased by a double membrane consisting of two layers of pleura. The visceral pleura covers the lung, and the parietal pleura lines the inner chest wall (thoracic cavity). Although a potential space, the pleural cavity normally contains only a small amount of fluid to lubricate the surfaces to prevent friction as the lungs expand and contract. The airtight space between the lungs and the chest wall has a pressure a bit less than that in the lungs. This difference in pressure acts like a vacuum to prevent the lungs from collapsing. An inflammatory or neoplastic process that involves the pleura may produce fluid within the potential space (pleural effusion).

▪ Inflammatory Disorders

Pneumonia

Acute pneumonia is an inflammation of the lung that can be caused by a variety of organisms, most commonly bacteria and viruses. Regardless of the cause, pneumonias tend to produce one of three basic radiographic patterns.

Alveolar, or air-space, pneumonia, exemplified by pneumococcal pneumonia, is produced by an organism that causes an inflammatory exudate that replaces air in the alveoli so that the affected part of the lung is no longer air containing but rather appears solid (Figure 2-1). The inflammation spreads from one alveolus to the next by way of communicating channels and may involve a whole lobe or even the entire lung. Consolidation of the lung parenchyma with little or no involvement of the airways produces the characteristic air-bronchogram sign (Figure 2-2). The sharp contrast between air within the bronchial tree and the sur-

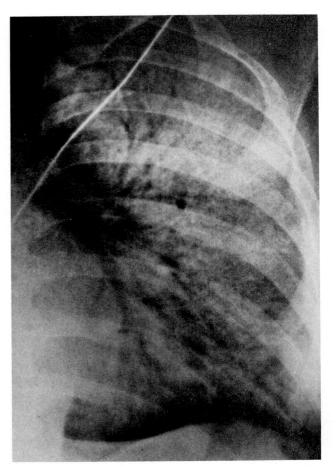

Figure 2-2 Air-bronchogram sign in pneumonia. Frontal chest radiograph demonstrates air within intrapulmonary bronchi in patient with diffuse alveolar pneumonia of left lung.

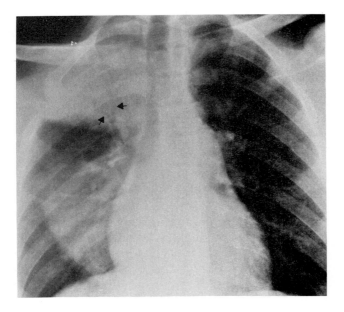

Figure 2-1 Alveolar pneumonia (pneumococcal). Homogeneous consolidation of right upper lobe and medial and posterior segments of right lower lobe. Notice associated air bronchograms *(arrows)*.

rounding airless lung parenchyma permits the normally invisible bronchial air column to become seen radiographically. The appearance of an air bronchogram requires the presence of air within the bronchial tree, an implication that the bronchus is not completely occluded at its origin. An air bronchogram excludes a pleural or mediastinal lesion, since there are no bronchi in these regions. Because air in the alveoli is replaced by an equal or almost equal quantity of inflammatory exudate, and since the airways leading to the affected portions of the lung remain open, there is no evidence of volume loss in alveolar pneumonia.

Bronchopneumonia, typified by staphylococcal infection, is primarily an inflammation that originates in the airways and spreads to adjacent aveoli. Because alveolar spread in the peripheral air spaces is minimal, the inflammation tends to produce small patches of consolidation that may be seen throughout the lungs but are separated by an abundance of air-containing lung tissue (Figure 2-3). Bronchial inflammation causing airway obstruction leads to atelectasis with loss of lung volume; air bronchograms are absent.

Interstitial pneumonia is most commonly produced by viral and mycoplasmal infections. In this type of pneumonia the inflammatory process predominantly involves the walls of the alveoli and the interstitial supporting structures of the lung, producing a linear or reticular pattern (Figure 2-4). When seen on end, the thickened interstitium may appear as multiple small nodular densities.

Extensive inflammation of the lung can cause a mixed pattern of alveolar, bronchial, and interstitial pneumonia.

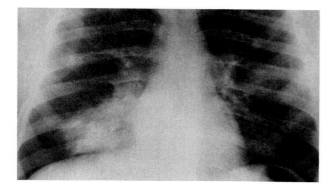

Figure 2-3 Bronchopneumonia (staphylococcal). Ill-defined consolidation at right base.

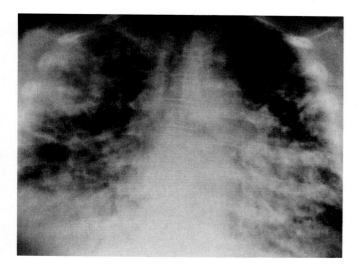

Figure 2-4 Interstitial pneumonia (viral). Diffuse peribronchial infiltrate with associated air-space consolidation obscures heart border (shaggy heart sign). Patchy alveolar infiltrate is present in right upper lung. (From Eisenberg R: *Atlas of signs in radiology,* Philadelphia, 1984, Lippincott.)

Aspiration pneumonia

The aspiration of esophageal or gastric contents into the lung can lead to the development of pneumonia. Aspiration of esophageal material can occur in patients with esophageal obstruction (tumor, stricture, achalasia), diverticula (Zenker's), or neuromuscular disturbances in swallowing. Aspiration of liquid gastric contents is most often related to general anesthesia, tracheostomy, coma, or trauma. Both types of aspiration cause multiple alveolar densities, which may be distributed widely and diffusely throughout both lungs (Figure 2-5). Because the anatomic distribution of pulmonary changes is affected by gravity, the posterior segments of the upper and lower lobes are most commonly affected, especially in debilitated or bedridden patients. Early diagnosis of aspiration pneumonia and the prompt institution of corticosteroid and antibiotic therapy are essential to improve the otherwise grave prognosis in this condition.

Lung abscess

Lung abscess is a necrotic area of pulmonary parenchyma containing purulent (puslike) material. A lung abscess may be a complication of bacterial pneumonia, bronchial obstruction, aspiration, a foreign body, or the hematogenous spread of organisms to the lungs either in a patient with diffuse bacteremia or as a result of septic emboli.

The earliest radiographic finding of lung abscess is a spherical density that characteristically has a dense center with a hazy, poorly defined periphery. If there is communication with the bronchial tree, the fluid contents of the cavity are partly replaced

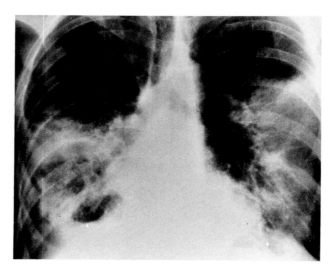

Figure 2-5 Aspiration pneumonia. Bilateral, nonsegmental air-space consolidation.

by air, producing a typical air-fluid level within the abscess (Figure 2-6). A cavitary lung abscess usually has a thickened wall with a shaggy, irregular inner margin.

Clinically, a patient with lung abscess has a fever and cough and produces copious amounts of foul-smelling sputum. An important complication of lung abscess is the development of a brain abscess, which is produced by infected material carried by the blood from the lung to the left side of the heart and then on to the brain.

Tuberculosis

Tuberculosis is caused by *Mycobacterium tuberculosis*, a rod-shaped bacterium with a protective waxy coat that permits it to live outside the body for a long time. Tuberculosis spreads mainly by droplets in the air, which are produced in huge numbers by the coughing of an infected patient. Therefore it is essential that respiratory precautions be followed when radiographing patients with active disease. The organisms may be inhaled from sputum that has dried and been changed into dust. They are rapidly killed by direct sunlight but may survive a long time in the dark. Tuberculosis also may be acquired by drinking the milk of infected cows. However, routine pasteurization of milk has virtually eliminated this route of infection.

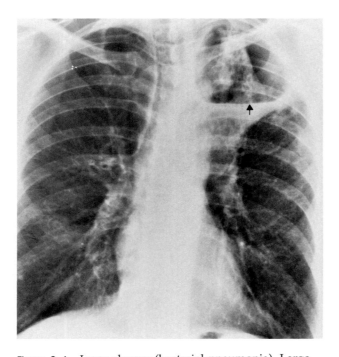

Figure 2-6 Lung abscess (bacterial pneumonia). Large, thick-walled left upper lobe abscess with air-fluid level *(arrow)* and associated infiltrate.

Unlike most bacteria, mycobacteria do not stain reliably by Gram's method. However, once the stain is taken up, the mycobacteria are difficult to decolorize by either acid or alcohol, and thus the organisms are often called "acid-fast bacilli."

Tuberculosis is primarily a disease of the lungs, though it can spread to involve the gastrointestinal, genitourinary, and skeletal systems. In the initial tuberculous infection (primary lesion), a collection of inflammatory cells collects around a clump of tuberculosis bacilli to form a small mass (tubercle) that is visible to the naked eye. The outcome of this initial infection depends on the number of bacilli and the resistance of the infected tissue. If the resistance is good and the dose is small, the proliferation of fibrous tissue around the tumor limits the spread of infection and produces a mass of scar tissue. In the lung, tuberculous scars are commonly found in the apices. They often contain calcium, which is deposited as healing occurs. If the dose of bacilli is larger or if the resistance of the patient is lowered, the disease tends to progress slowly. Within the center of the tubercle, inflammatory cells are killed by the bacilli so that the core becomes a necrotic, cheeselike mass (caseation). The caseous material may eventually become liquified so that a cavity is formed. Coalescence of several small cavities can result in the formation of a large cavity, which may contain an air-fluid level. Rupture of blood vessels crossing a cavity causes bleeding and the coughing up of blood (hemoptysis). If the infection is overwhelming and resistance is minimal, there is diffuse destruction throughout the lung with the formation of huge cavities and often a fatal outcome.

Previous tuberculous infection can be detected by the tuberculin test, in which a purified protein derivative (PPD) of the tuberculosis bacillus is injected into the skin and the injection site examined 2 to 3 days later. A visible and palpable swelling 10 mm or larger indicates that the individual has developed antibodies to a previous exposure to tuberculosis. If there is no such reaction, the individual has either not been exposed to the tuberculosis bacilli or is anergic (immunologically nonreacting). It is important to remember that the tuberculin test is not positive during an acute infection and for several weeks thereafter.

Primary tuberculosis

Primary pulmonary tuberculosis has traditionally been considered a disease of children and young adults. However, with the dramatic decrease in the prevalence of tuberculosis (especially in children and young adults), primary pulmonary disease can develop at any age.

There are four basic radiographic patterns of primary pulmonary tuberculosis. The infiltrate may be seen as a lobar or segmental air-space consolidation that is usually homogeneous, dense, and well defined (Figure 2-7). Associated enlargement of hilar or mediastinal lymph nodes is very common (Figure 2-8). Indeed, the combination of a focal parenchymal lesion and enlarged hilar or mediastinal nodes produces the classic primary complex (Ghon lesion), an appearance strongly suggestive of primary tuberculosis. Pleural effusion is common,

especially in adults (Figure 2-9). Most primary tuberculous pleural effusions are unilateral and clear rapidly with treatment. Miliary tuberculosis refers to dissemination of the disease by way of the blood-stream. Radiographically, this produces innumerable fine discrete nodules distributed uniformly throughout both lungs (Figure 2-10).

Tuberculous pneumonia may resolve completely and leave a normal lung. However, if necrosis and caseation develop, some fibrous scarring occurs. Calcification may develop within both the parenchymal

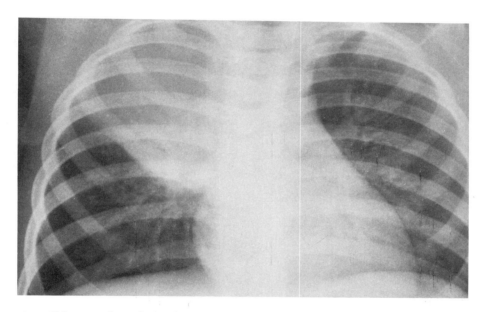

Figure 2-7 Primary tuberculosis. Consolidation of right upper lobe.

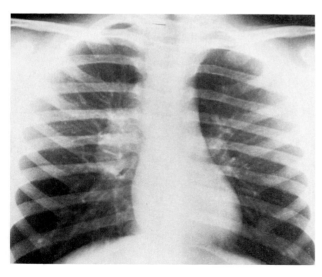

Figure 2-8 Primary tuberculosis. Enlargement of right hilar lymph nodes without discrete parenchymal infiltrate.

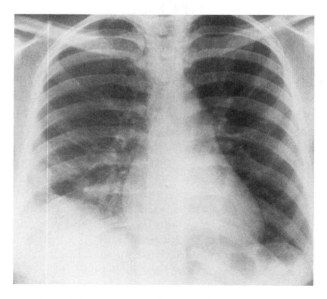

Figure 2-9 Primary tuberculosis. Unilateral right tuberculous pleural effusion without parenchymal or lymph node involvement.

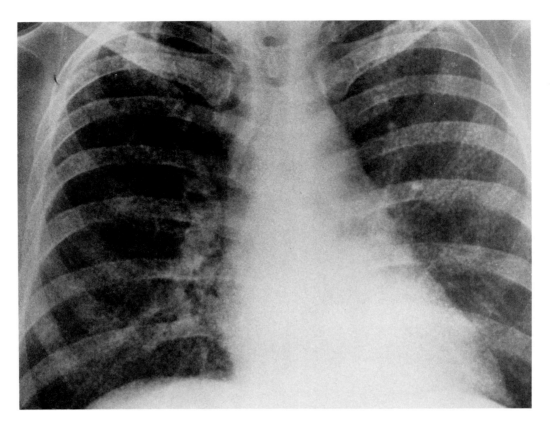

Figure 2-10   Miliary tuberculosis.

and the nodal lesions, and this may be the only residue of primary tuberculous infection on subsequent films. If the disease responds poorly to therapy and continues to progress (especially in patients with immunodeficiency or diabetes and in those receiving steroid therapy), the pneumonia may break down into multiple necrotic cavities or a single large abscess filled with caseous material (Figure 2-11).

Secondary (reactivation) tuberculosis

Reactivation of organisms from previously dormant tubercles is termed a "secondary lesion." At times, the tuberculosis bacillus may remain inactive for may years before a secondary lesion develops, often because of a decrease in the body's immune defense.

Secondary tuberculosis most commonly affects the upper lobes, especially the apical and posterior segments (Figure 2-12). It initially is seen as a nonspecific hazy, poorly marginated alveolar infiltrate that often radiates outward from the hilum. Necrosis and liquefaction commonly lead to the development of tuberculous cavities, which typically have thick walls with ill-defined inner margins. Secondary pulmonary tuberculosis heals slowly

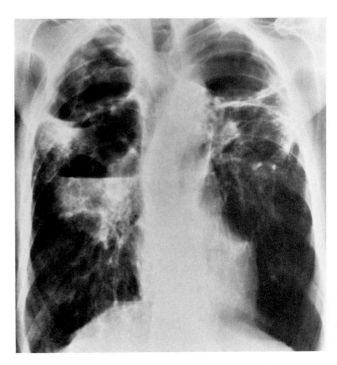

Figure 2-11   Tuberculosis. Multiple large cavities with air-fluid levels in both upper lobes. Notice chronic fibrotic changes and upward retraction of hila.

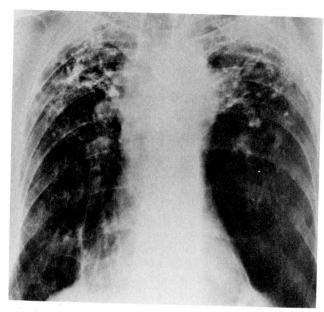

Figure 2-12   Secondary tuberculosis. Bilateral fibrocalcific changes at apices. Notice upward retraction of hila.

with extensive fibrosis. Contraction of the fibrous scars causes loss of volume of the involved segment or lobe and a decrease in the size of the hemithorax. The trachea and other mediastinal structures are retracted to the involved side; in upper lobe disease the hilum is elevated.

Because it is difficult to radiographically determine the activity of secondary tuberculosis, comparison with previous films is essential. An unchanged appearance of fibrosis and calcification on serial films is usually considered evidence of "healing" of the tuberculous process. Nevertheless, even densely calcified lesions can contain central areas of necrosis in which viable organisms can still be found even after long periods of apparent inactivity. Of course, new cavitation or an increasing amount of pulmonary infiltrate indicates active disease.

Tuberculoma

A tuberculoma is a sharply circumscribed parenchymal nodule, often containing viable tuberculosis bacilli, that can develop in either primary or secondary disease. Although the residual localized caseation may remain unchanged for a long period or permanently, a tuberculoma is potentially dangerous because it may break down at any time and lead to dissemination of the disease. Radiographically, tuberculomas appear as single or multiple pulmonary nodules, usually 1 to 3 cm in diameter. They can occur in any part of the lung but are most common in the periphery and in the upper lobes. A

central nidus of calcification (which may only be detectable on tomograms) is strongly suggestive of the lesion representing a tuberculoma (Figure 2-13). However, the lack of calcification is of no diagnostic value.

Histoplasmosis

Histoplasmosis, caused by the fungus *Histoplasma capsulatum,* is a common disease that often produces a radiographic appearance simulating that of tuberculosis.

The primary form of histoplasmosis is usually relatively benign and often passes unnoticed. Chest radiographs may demonstrate single or multiple areas of pulmonary infiltration that are most often in the lower lung and are frequently associated with hilar lymph node enlargement. Although this pattern simulates the primary complex of tuberculosis, pleural effusion rarely occurs with histoplasmosis. In children, striking hilar adenopathy, which may cause bronchial compression, may develop without radiographic evidence of parenchymal disease. Hilar lymph node calcification is common in adults. A frequent manifestation of pulmonary histoplasmosis is a solitary, sharply circumscribed, granulomatous nodule (histoplasmoma), which is usually less than 3 cm in diameter and is most often in a lower lobe. Central, rounded calcification within the mass (target lesion) is virtually pathognomonic of this disease (Figure 2-14). Multiple soft-tissue nodules scattered throughout both lungs may simulate miliary tuberculosis. These shadows may clear completely or may fibrose and persist, often appearing on subsequent chest radiographs as widespread punctate calcifications (Figure 2-15).

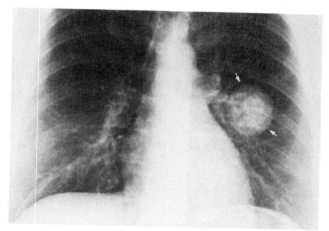

Figure 2-13   Calcified tuberculoma. Large soft-tissue mass in left lung *(arrows)* that contains dense central calcification.

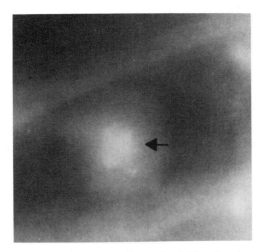

Figure 2-14 Histoplasmoma. Central calcification *(arrow)* in solitary pulmonary nodule.

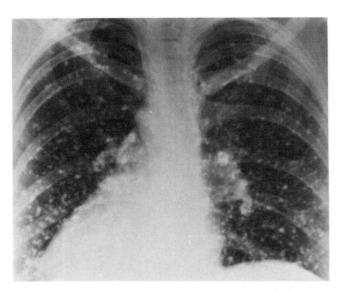

Figure 2-15 Histoplasmosis. Diffuse calcifications in lungs produce snowball pattern.

The more chronic form of histoplasmosis is characterized by zones of parenchymal consolidation, often large and with a loss of lung volume, that usually develop in an upper lobe. Cavitation is common, and the radiographic appearance closely simulates reinfection tuberculosis.

Histoplasmosis can incite progressive fibrosis in the mediastinum. This can cause obstruction of the superior vena cava, pulmonary arteries, and pulmonary veins, as well as severe narrowing of the esophagus.

Diffuse calcification in the liver, spleen, and lymph nodes is virtually diagnostic of histoplasmo-sis, especially in areas in which the disease is endemic (e.g., the Mississippi and Ohio valleys of the United States). These calcifications tend to be small, multiple, dense, and discrete, though occasionally they may appear as moderately large, solidly calcified granulomas.

Bronchiectasis

Bronchiectasis refers to permanent abnormal dilatation of one or more large bronchi as a result of destruction of the elastic and muscular components of the bronchial wall. The origin of the destructive process is nearly always a bacterial infection, which may either be a severe necrotizing pneumonia or a result of a local or systemic abnormality that impairs the body's defense mechanisms and promotes bacterial growth. Since the advent of antibiotic therapy, the incidence of bronchiectasis has substantially decreased.

The patient with bronchiectasis typically has a chronic productive cough, often associated with recurrent episodes of acute pneumonia and hemoptysis. The disease usually involves the basal segments of the lower lobes and is bilateral in about half of the cases. Plain chest radiographs may show a coarseness and loss of definition of interstitial markings caused by peribronchial fibrosis and retained secretions (Figure 2-16). In more advanced disease, oval or circular cystic spaces can develop. These cystic dilatations can be up to 2 cm in diameter and often

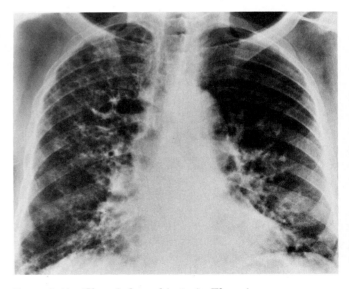

Figure 2-16 Chronic bronchiectasis. There is severe coarsening of interstitial markings involving bases and right upper lobe. Oval and circular cystic spaces, producing somewhat of a honeycomb pattern, are best seen in right upper lobe.

contain air-fluid levels. In very severe disease, coarse interstitial fibrosis surrounding local areas of dilatation can produce a honeycomb pattern.

Although plain radiographs may strongly indicate bronchiectasis, bronchography is necessary to fill the dilated cystic spaces with contrast material and to establish the diagnosis unequivocally. (Figure 2-17).

Croup

Croup is primarily a viral infection of young children that produces inflammatory obstructive swelling localized to the subglottic portion of the trachea. On frontal radiographs of the lower neck, there is a characteristic smooth, fusiform, tapered narrowing of the subglottic airway (Figure 2-18, *A*), unlike the broad shouldering seen normally (Figure 2-18, *B*).

Epiglottitis

Acute infections of the epiglottis, most commonly caused by *Haemophilus influenzae* in children, causes thickening of epiglottic tissue and surrounding pharyngeal structures. On lateral projections of the neck using soft, tissue techniques, a rounded thickening of the epiglottic shadow gives it the configuration and approximate size of an adult's thumb (Figure 2-19), in contrast to the normal, narrow epiglottic

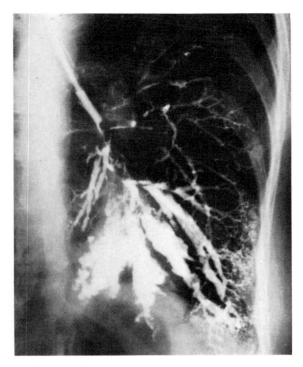

Figure 2-17 Chronic bronchiectasis. Bronchogram shows severe dilatation of basal bronchi of left lower lobe. (From Fraser RG, Paré JAP: *Diagnosis of diseases of the chest*, Philadelphia, 1979, Saunders.)

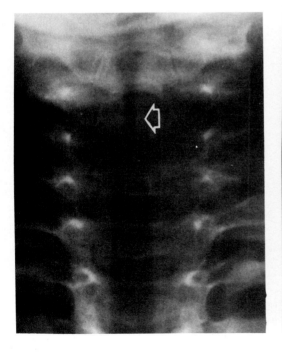

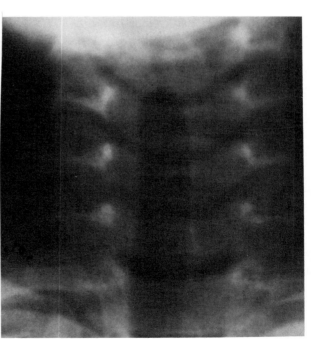

A **B**

Figure 2-18 Croup. **A,** Arrow indicates smooth, tapered narrowing of subglottic portion of trachea (Gothic arch sign). **B,** Normal trachea with broad shouldering in subglottic region.

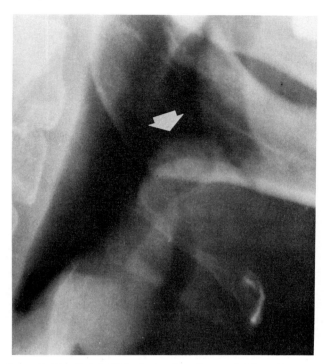

Figure 2-19 Epiglottitis. Lateral radiograph of neck demonstrates wide, rounded configuration of inflamed epiglottis *(arrow)*. (From Podgore JK, Bass JW: *J Pediatr* 88:154-155, 1976.)

shadow resembling an adult's little finger. The prompt recognition of acute epiglottitis is imperative because the condition may result in sudden complete airway obstruction.

■ Diffuse Lung Disease

Chronic obstructive pulmonary disease

Chronic obstructive pulmonary disease (COPD) includes several conditions in which chronic obstruction of the airways leads to an ineffective exchange of respiratory gases and difficulty breathing. Chronic bronchitis is characterized by excessive tracheobronchial mucus production leading to the obstruction of small airways. Emphysema refers to the distention of distal air spaces as a result of the destruction of alveolar walls and the obstruction of small airways. Predisposing factors to chronic obstructive lung disease include cigarette smoking, infection, air pollution, and occupational exposure to harmful substances such as asbestos.

Chronic bronchitis

Chronic inflammation of the bronchi leads to severe coughing with the production of sputum. Bronchitis may be a complication of respiratory infection or be

the result of long-term exposure to air pollution or cigarette smoking.

About half the patients with chronic bronchial disease demonstrate no changes on chest radiographs. The most common radiographic abnormality in chronic bronchitis is a generalized increase in bronchovascular markings (Figure 2-20), especially in the lower lungs ("dirty chest"). Thickening of bronchial walls and peribronchial inflammation can cause parallel or slightly tapered tubular line shadows ("tramlines") or appear as thickening of bronchial shadows when viewed end on. Eventually, excessive production of mucus and swelling of the bronchial mucosa may lead to narrowing of the airways and overinflation of the lungs (emphysema).

Emphysema

Emphysema is a crippling and debilitating condition in which obstructive and destructive changes in small airways lead to a dramatic increase in the volume of air in the lungs. In many patients, the development of emphysema is closely associated with heavy cigarette smoking. Other predisposing factors are chronic bronchitis, air pollution, and

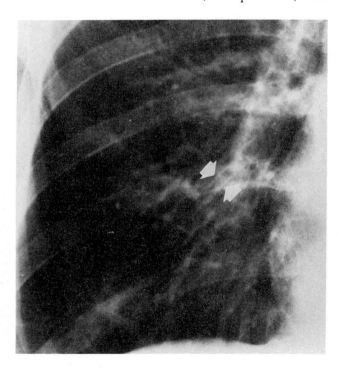

Figure 2-20 Chronic bronchitis. Coned view of right lower lung demonstrates coarse increase in interstitial markings. Arrows point to characteristic parallel line shadows ("tramlines") outside boundary of pulmonary hilum. (From Eisenberg R: *Atlas of signs in radiology,* Philadelphia, 1984, Lippincott.)

long-term exposure to irritants of the respiratory tract.

Irritating smoke, fumes, and pollutants injure the fine hairs (cilia) of the respiratory mucosa, which can no longer sweep away foreign particles. This causes mucosal inflammation and the secretion of excess mucus that plugs up the air passages and leads to an increase in airway resistance. Collateral air drift permits the ventilation of lung parenchyma served by the obstructed airways. However, bronchial narrowing and loss of elasticity make it very difficult for the patient to exhale the stale air. The resulting air trapping and overinflation of the lung lead to alveolar distention and eventually to the rupture of alveolar septa. As the walls between alveoli are destroyed, these tiny air sacs become transformed into large air-filled spaces called bullae, which do not permit efficient transfer of oxygen into the bloodstream. As the lungs become less able to move air in and out, the heart is strained and eventually enlarges. The large air sacs (bullae) may rupture, leading to the entry of air into the pleural space (pneumothorax) and collapse of the lung (atelectasis).

The major radiographic signs of emphysema are related to pulmonary overinflation, alterations in the pulmonary vasculature, and bullae formation.

The hallmark of pulmonary overinflation is flattening of the domes of the diaphragm (Figure 2-21). Another important sign on lateral chest radiographs is increased size and lucency of the retrosternal air space, the distance between the posterior side of the sternum and the anterior wall of the ascending aorta. There is also an increase in the anteroposterior (AP) diameter of the chest (barrel chest). Air trapping may be detected fluoroscopically as a decrease in the normal movement of the diaphragm during respiration.

The major vascular change in patients with emphysema is a reduction in the number and size of the peripheral arteries. As the pressure in the pulmonary arteries increases, the main and central pulmonary arteries become more prominent, which further accentuates the appearance of rapid tapering of peripheral vessels.

Bullae appear as air-containing cystic spaces whose walls are usually of hairline thickness. They range in size from 1 to 2 cm in diameter up to an entire hemithorax (Figure 2-22). These large, radiolucent, air-filled sacs are found predominantly at the apices or at the bases and may become so large that they cause respiratory insufficiency by compressing the remaining relatively normal lung.

A less common radiographic appearance of emphysema is the increased-markings pattern. Instead of being narrowed, the vascular markings in this condition are more prominent than normal and tend to be irregular and indistinct, producing a "dirty chest" appearance.

Emphysema can occasionally occur in young patients who have hereditary disorders of connective

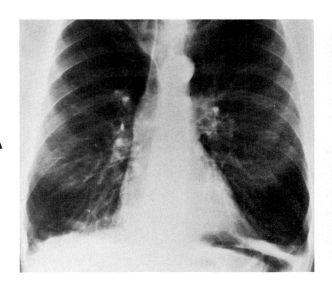
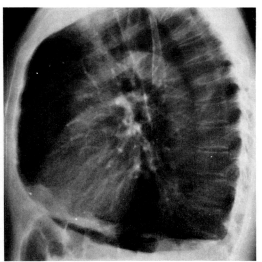

A

B

Figure 2-21 Emphysema. **A,** Frontal and, **B,** lateral projections of chest demonstrate severe overinflation of lungs along with flattening and even a superiorly concave configuration of hemidiaphragms. There is also increased size and lucency of retrosternal air space, increase in anteroposterior diameter of chest, and reduction in number and caliber of peripheral pulmonary arteries.

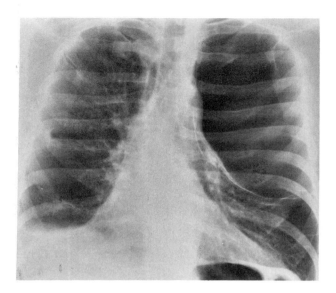

Figure 2-22   Giant emphysematous bulla. Air-containing mass fills most of left hemithorax.

tissue (osteogenesis imperfecta). Striking lower lobe predominance develops in young patients who have a deficiency of the enzyme α-antitrypsin, which leads to destruction of elastic and connective tissue in the lungs.

In patients with advanced stages of pulmonary emphysema who have large amounts of air trapped in their lungs, it is necessary to reduce exposure factors for chest radiography.

Asthma

Asthma is a very common disease in which widespread narrowing of the airways develops because of an increased responsiveness of the tracheobronchial tree to various substances (allergens). Common allergens include house dust, pollen, molds, animal dander, certain fabrics, and various foods. The hypersensitivity reaction to one or more of these allergens leads to swelling of the mucous membranes of the bronchi, excess secretion of mucus, and spasm of the smooth muscle in the bronchial walls, all of which lead to severe narrowing of the airways. This makes breathing (especially expiration) difficult and results in the characteristic wheezing sound that is produced by air passing through the narrowed bronchial tubes.

Early in the course of the disease, chest radiographs obtained between acute episodes demonstrate no abnormalities. During an acute asthmatic attack, bronchial narrowing and difficulty in expiration lead to an increased volume of the hyperlucent lungs with flattening of the hemidiaphragms and an increase in the retrosternal air space. In contrast to

emphysema, the pulmonary vascular markings in asthma are of normal size. In patients with chronic asthma, especially those with a history of repeated episodes of superinfection, thickening of bronchial walls can produce prominence of interstitial markings and the "dirty chest" appearance (Figure 2-23).

Pneumoconiosis

Prolonged occupational exposure to certain irritating dusts can cause severe pulmonary disease and a spectrum of radiographic findings. These inhaled dusts cause a chronic interstitial inflammation that leads to pulmonary fibrosis and a diffuse nonspecific radiographic pattern of linear streaks and nodules throughout the lungs. The most common of the pneumoconioses are silicosis, asbestosis, and coal worker's disease. Other causes include exposure to such dusts as tin, iron oxide, barium, and beryllium.

Silicosis

The inhalation of high concentrations of silicon dioxide primarily affects workers engaged in mining, foundry work, and sandblasting. Although acute silicosis can develop within 10 months of exposure in workers exposed to sandblasting in confined spaces, 15 to 20 years of long-term, relatively less intense exposure is required to produce radiographic changes.

The classic radiographic pattern in silicosis consists of multiple nodular shadows scattered throughout the lungs. These nodules are usually fairly well circumscribed and of uniform density and may

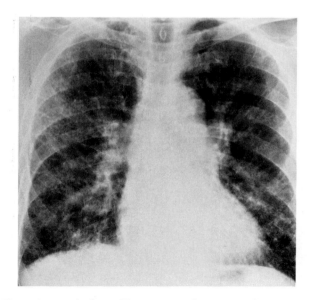

Figure 2-23   Asthma. Recurrent pulmonary infections have led to development of diffuse pulmonary fibrosis and prominence of interstitial markings in lungs.

become calcified (Figure 2-24). As the pulmonary nodules increase in size, they tend to coalesce and form conglomerates of irregular masses in excess of 1 cm in diameter (progressive massive fibrosis) (Figure 2-25). These masses are usually bilateral and relatively symmetric and are almost always restricted to the upper half of the lungs. Occasionally, a single large homogeneous mass in the perihilar area of one lung may closely simulate bronchogenic carcinoma. Hilar lymph node enlargement is common. The deposition of calcium salts in the periphery of enlarged lymph nodes produces the charac-teristic eggshell appearance (Figure 2-26), which is virtually pathognomonic of silicosis.

Asbestosis

Asbestosis may develop in improperly protected workers engaged in the manufacture of asbestos or in those handling building materials or insulation that is composed of asbestos. The radiographic hall-mark of asbestosis is involvement of the pleura. Initially, pleural thickening appears as linear plaques of opacification, which are most often along the lower chest wall and diaphragm. A virtually pathog-nomonic appearance of asbestosis is calcification of pleural plaques, especially in the form of thin, cur-vilinear densities conforming to the upper surfaces of the diaphragm bilaterally (Figure 2-27). This pleural calcification generally does not develop until at least 20 years after the first exposure to asbestos (Figure 2-28).

In the lungs, round or irregular opacities produce a combined linear and nodular pattern that may obscure the heart border to produce the so-called shaggy heart. The major complication of asbestosis is the development of malignant neoplasms in the chest. Pleural mesothelioma is a highly malignant tumor that appears as an irregular scalloped or nodular density within the pleural space. It is frequently associated with a large pleural effusion that may obscure the underlying tumor. In addition to mesothelioma, bronchogenic carcinoma is also unusually common in patients with asbestosis, especially those who are cigarette smokers.

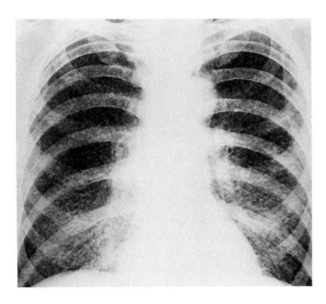

Figure 2-24 Silicosis. Calcification in miliary nodules scattered throughout both lungs.

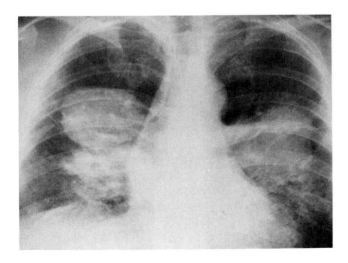

Figure 2-25 Progressive massive fibrosis in silicosis. Large, irregular nodules in both perihilar regions.

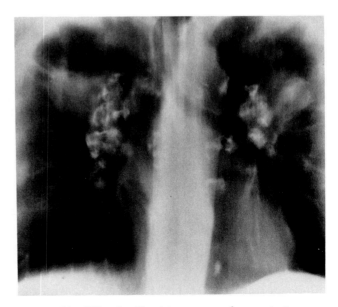

Figure 2-26 Silicosis. Chest tomogram demonstrates characteristic eggshell lymph-node calcification associated with bilateral perihilar masses.

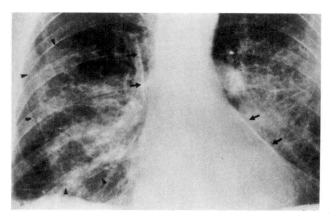

Figure 2-27 Asbestosis. Frontal film shows en face pleural calcifications on right *(arrowheads)*, linear calcifications in profile in mediastinal reflection of pleura on right and in pericardium on left *(horizontal arrows)*, and linear calcification in left diaphragmatic pleura *(vertical arrow)*. From Sargent EN, Jacobson G, Gordonson JS: *Semin Roentgenol* 12:287-297, 1977.)

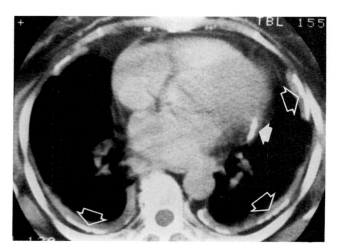

Figure 2-28 Asbestosis. CT scan shows calcified pleural plaques along lateral and posterior chest wall *(open arrows)* and adjacent to heart *(solid arrow)*.

Coal worker's pneumoconiosis

Coal miners, especially those working with anthracite (hard coal), are susceptible to developing pneumoconiosis by inhaling high concentrations of coal dust. Initially, multiple small, irregular opacities produce a reticular pattern similar to that of silicosis (Figure 2-29). However, the nodules tend to be somewhat less well defined than those of silicosis and are of a granular density, unlike the homogeneous density of silicosis nodules. With advanced disease, the pattern of progressive massive fibrosis can develop. This appears as one or more masses of

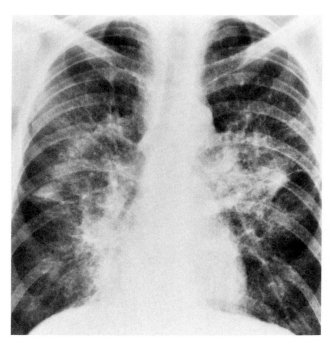

Figure 2-29 Coal worker's pneumoconiosis. Diffuse reticular pattern throughout both lungs associated with ill-defined masses of fibrous tissue in perihilar region that extend to right base.

fibrous tissue with smooth, well-defined lateral borders that gradually migrate toward the hilum, leaving a zone of overinflated emphysematous lung between them and the chest wall. A single large homogeneous mass in the perihilar area of one lung may simulate bronchogenic carcinoma; the detection of the underlying background of pneumoconiosis is essential for the proper diagnosis.

▪ Vascular Diseases

Pulmonary embolism

Pulmonary embolism is a potentially fatal condition that is by far the most common pathologic process involving the lungs of hospitalized patients. In about 80% of patients with this disorder, the condition does not cause symptoms and is thus unrecognized because the emboli are too small or too few to occlude blood flow to a substantial portion of the lung. Even when symptomatic, pulmonary embolism may be difficult to diagnose. More than 95% of pulmonary emboli arise from thrombi that develop in the deep venous system of the lower extremities because of venous stasis. The remainder come from thrombi that occur in the right side of the heart or in brachial or cervical veins and are trapped by capillaries in the pulmonary artery circulation. Thrombi originating in the left side of the heart can embolize

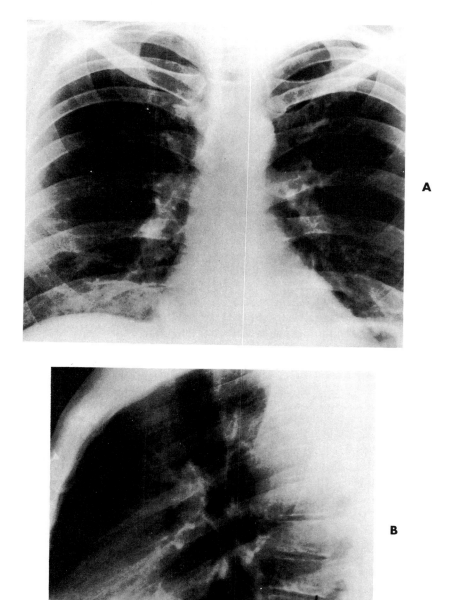

Figure 2-30   Pulmonary embolism. **A,** Frontal and, **B,** lateral projections of chest demonstrate fairly well circumscribed shadow of homogeneous density occupying posterior-based segment of right, lower lobe. On lateral projection pleural-based density has shape of truncated cone and is convex toward hilum (Hampton's hump; *arrows*). (From Fraser RG, Paré JAP: *Diagnosis of diseases of the chest,* Philadelphia, 1978, Saunders.)

to the peripheral arterial circulation, where they are trapped in arterioles or capillaries before they can return in the venous blood to the heart and the pulmonary circulation. Most embolic occlusions occur in the lower lobes because of the preferential blood flow to these regions.

The physiologic consequences of embolic occlusion of the pulmonary arteries depend on the size of the embolic mass and the general state of the pulmonary circulation. In young persons with good cardiovascular function and adequate collateral circulation, the occlusion of a large central vessel may be associated with minimal, if any, functional impairment. In contrast, in patients with cardiovascular disease or severe debilitating illnesses, pulmonary vascular occlusion often leads to infarction.

Most patients with thromboembolism without infarction have a normal chest radiograph. Nevertheless, some subtle, yet distinctive, abnormalities on plain radiographs can be strongly suggestive of the diagnosis. A large-vessel pulmonary embolism causes a focal reduction in blood volume without a substantial change in air or tissue volume. This leads to focal pulmonary oligemia and relative lucency of the involved portion of lung. Another sign of pul-

monary embolism is enlargement of the ipsilateral main pulmonary artery caused by distention of the vessel by the bulk of the thrombus. This sign is of most value when serial radiographs demonstrate progressive enlargement of the affected vessel.

Pulmonary embolism with infarction appears radiographically as an area of lung consolidation. A highly characteristic, though somewhat uncommon, appearance of pulmonary infarction is the so-called Hampton's hump (Figure 2-30). This is a pleura-based, wedge-shaped density that has a rounded apex and is most commonly seen at the base of the lung, often in the costophrenic sulcus. In many instances an infarction merely produces a nonspecific parenchymal density that simulates acute pneumonia. A pleural effusion often develops (Figure 2-31).

Because the chest radiograph is usually either normal or nonspecific, the radionuclide lung scan is generally considered the most effective screening test for significant pulmonary embolism. On a perfusion scan that measures blood flow to the lungs, the area of lung distal to an embolus appears as a defect on the radionuclide scan. (Figure 2-32). Unfortunately, false-positive scans may be recorded in portions of the lung that are poorly perfused be-

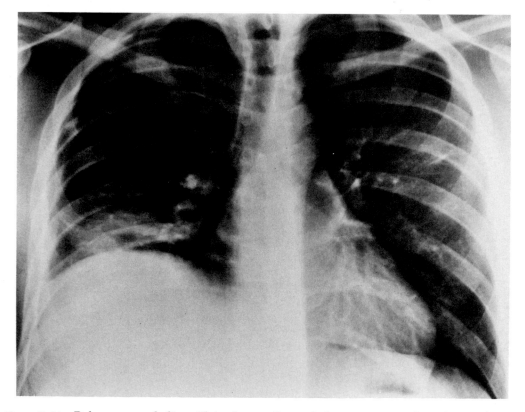

Figure 2-31 Pulmonary embolism. Plain chest radiograph demonstrates atelectasis at right base, which is associated with elevation of right hemidiaphragm that represents a large subpulmonic effusion.

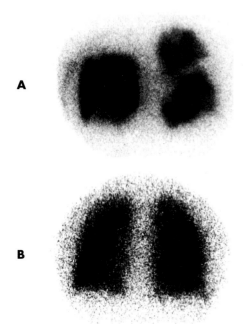

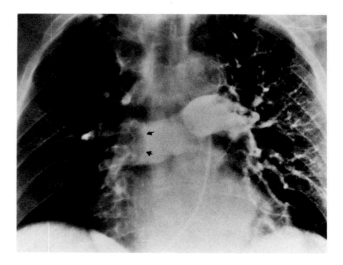

Figure 2-33   A pulmonary arteriogram shows virtually complete obstruction *(arrows)* of the right pulmonary artery.

Figure 2-32   Pulmonary embolism. **A,** Radionuclide perfusion lung scan shows multiple areas of absent isotope uptake in both lungs, consistent with a shower of pulmonary emboli. **B,** Normal lung scan in another patient for comparison. (Courtesy Shelby Miller, M.D., Oakland, Calif.)

cause of impaired ventilation, even if no obstructing vascular lesion is present. Therefore ventilation lung scans are also performed to increase the diagnostic accuracy. The ventilation scan is usually relatively normal in patients with pulmonary embolism, whereas it generally demonstrates defects corresponding to areas of decreased perfusion in patients with chronic pulmonary disease.

Pulmonary arteriography is the definitive technique for evaluating the patient with suspected pulmonary embolism (Figure 2-33). However, it is associated with a small, though definite, risk of morbidity and mortality. The unequivocal arteriographic diagnosis of pulmonary embolism requires the demonstration of an abrupt occlusion (cutoff) of a pulmonary artery or a persistent intraluminal filling defect within it. More recently, MRI has been used to show a pulmonary embolus either as a moderate- to high-intensity signal within the black flow void of the normal pulmonary artery or as a generalized increased signal intensity caused by slow blood flow in an obstructed pulmonary vessel.

Septic embolism

Septic embolism refers to a shower of bacteria that enter the pulmonary circulation and are trapped within the lung. Septic emboli primarily arise from

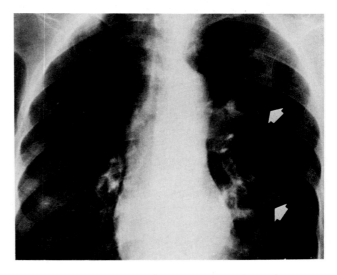

Figure 2-34   Septic pulmonary emboli. Large cavitary lesions *(arrows)* in left lung of intravenous drug abuser with septic thrombophlebitis.

either the heart (bacterial endocarditis) or the peripheral veins (septic thrombophlebitis). Many patients have a history of intravenous drug abuse. Septic emboli are almost always multiple and appear radiographically as ill-defined, round or wedge-shaped opacities in the periphery of the lung. They often present a migratory pattern, first appearing in one area and then in another as the older lesions resolve. Cavitation frequently develops (Figure 2-34).

Pulmonary arteriovenous fistula

Pulmonary arteriovenous fistula is an abnormal vascular communication from a pulmonary artery to a

A

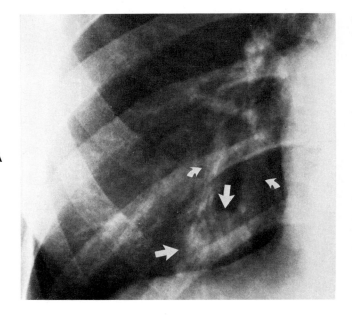

B

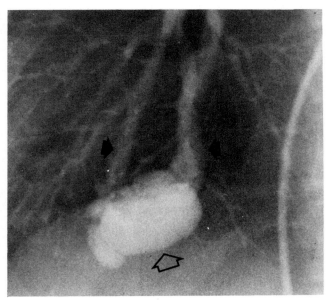

Figure 2-35　Pulmonary arteriovenous fistula. **A,** Film of right lung shows round soft-tissue mass *(straight arrows)* at base. Feeding and draining vessels *(curved arrows)* extend to lesion. **B,** Arteriogram clearly shows feeding artery and draining veins *(solid arrows)* associated with arteriovenous malformation *(open arrow)*.

pulmonary vein. Pulmonary arteriovenous fistulas are multiple in about one third of patients; up to two thirds of patients with these pulmonary malformations have similar arteriovenous communications elsewhere (hereditary hemorrhagic telangiectasia). Very large or multiple fistulas can cause so much shunting of blood from the pulmonary arteries to the pulmonary veins that the blood cannot be adequately oxygenated and cyanosis results.

A pulmonary arteriovenous fistula typically appears as a round or oval, lobulated soft-tissue mass that is most commonly situated in the lower lobes. A pathognomonic finding is the identification of a feeding artery and a draining vein (Figure 2-35, *A*). This may be difficult to demonstrate on plain radiographs and often requires tomography or arteriography (Figure 2-35, *B*). Pulmonary arteriography is required before surgical removal, not only to confirm the diagnosis, but also to detect smaller, unsuspected vascular malformations that cannot be identified on routine radiographs.

▪ Neoplasms

Bronchial adenoma

Bronchial adenomas are neoplasms of low-grade malignancy that constitute about 1% of all bronchial

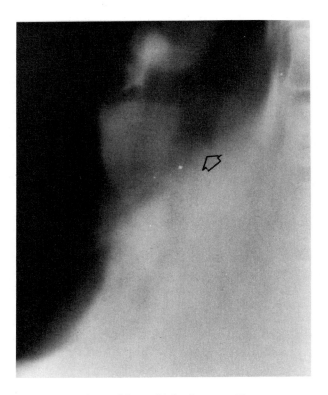

Figure 2-36　Central bronchial adenoma. Tomogram shows ill-defined mass causing high-grade obstruction of right lower lobe bronchus *(arrow)*.

neoplasms. They are at least as common in women as in men and are found in a younger age group than bronchogenic carcinoma. Hemoptysis and recurring pneumonia are the most common symptoms.

Because about 80% of bronchial adenomas are located centrally in major or segmental bronchi, bronchial obstruction with peripheral atelectasis and postobstructive pneumonitis is the most common radiographic finding. This characteristically produces a homogeneous increase in density corresponding exactly to a lobe or one or more segments, usually with a substantial loss of volume. If large enough, a central bronchial adenoma that has caused peripheral atelectasis and pneumonia may be identifiable as a discrete, lobulated, soft-tissue mass. If the tumor is too small to obstruct the lumen, the chest radiograph appears normal. Tomography may demonstrate the rounded tumor mass within an air-filled bronchus (Figure 2-36). Peripheral bronchial adenomas do not cause bronchial obstruction and appear as nonspecific solitary pulmonary nodules (Figure 2-37).

Bronchogenic carcinoma

Primary carcinoma of the lung arises from the mucosa of the bronchial tree. Although the precise cause is unknown, bronchogenic carcinoma is closely linked to smoking and to the inhalation of cancer-causing agents (carcinogens) such as air pollution, exhaust gases, and industrial fumes.

Bronchogenic carcinoma produces a broad spectrum of radiographic abnormalities that depend on the site of the tumor and its relation to the bronchial tree. The tumor may appear as a discrete mass or be undetectable and identified only by virtue of secondary postobstructive changes caused by tumor within or compressing the bronchus.

The most common type of lung cancer is squamous carcinoma, which typically arises in the major central bronchi and causes gradual narrowing of the bronchial lumen. Adènocarcinomas usually arise in the periphery of the lung rather than in the larger central bronchi. Small cell (oat cell) carcinomas characteristically cause bulky enlargement of hilar lymph nodes that is often bilateral. The least common type of lung tumor is bronchiolar (alveolar cell) carcinoma, which has a spectrum of appearances varying from a well-circumscribed, peripheral solitary nodule to a poorly defined mass simulating pneumonia or multiple nodules scattered throughout both lungs.

A major form of bronchogenic carcinoma is the solitary pulmonary nodule within the lung parenchyma. This presents a diagnostic dilemma between malignancy and a benign process (tumor or granuloma). Although malignant tumors generally have ill-defined, irregular, or fuzzy borders (Figure 2-38) in contrast to the sharp margins of benign lesions

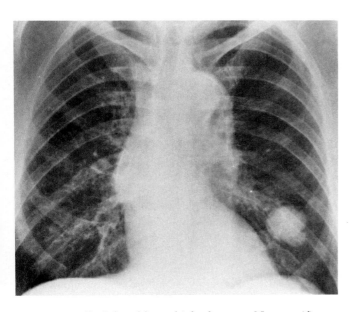

Figure 2-37 Peripheral bronchial adenoma. Nonspecific solitary pulmonary nodule at left base.

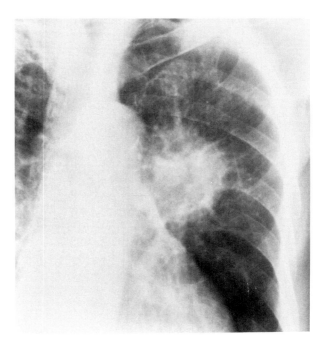

Figure 2-38 Malignant solitary pulmonary nodule (bronchogenic carcinoma). Notice fuzzy, ill-defined margins.

(Figure 2-39), there are many exceptions to this rule. The presence of central target or popcorn calcification is almost certain proof of an inflammatory cause (Figure 2-40). A comparison with previous films is essential because a nodule that is unchanged in size on radiographs made 2 or more years previously can be assumed to be benign. The growth rate of a solitary pulmonary nodule (doubling time) has been used to determine the likelihood of its being malignant. A pulmonary nodule that doubles in volume in less than 1 month or more than 18 months is usually benign. However, the overlapping of growth rates of benign and malignant lesions, particularly among rapidly growing nodules, makes the use of doubling time unreliable as an absolute indicator of malignancy. In the patient older than 35 to 40 years of age, a solitary pulmonary nodule should be resected unless it can be unequivocally demonstrated to be benign.

Airway obstruction by bronchogenic carcinoma may cause atelectasis of a segment of lung and often leads to postobstructive pneumonia that develops in the lung distal to the obstructed bronchus. An important sign differentiating postobstructive pneumo-

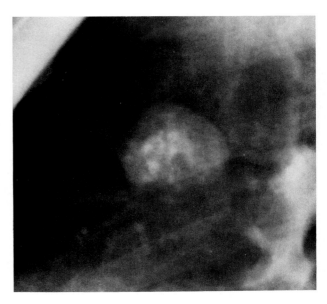

Figure 2-40   Benign solitary pulmonary nodule (tuberculoma). Notice central calcification characteristic of benign lesion.

nia from simple inflammatory disease is the absence of an air bronchogram in the former, since this sign can be detected only if there is an open airway leading to the area of consolidation.

Unilateral enlargement of the hilum, best appreciated on serial chest radiographs, may be the earliest sign of bronchogenic carcinoma. The enlarged hilum represents either a primary carcinoma arising in the major hilar bronchus or metastases to enlarged pulmonary lymph nodes from a small primary lesion elsewhere in the lung (Figure 2-41).

Cavitation is common in bronchogenic carcinoma. It most often involves upper lung lesions and represents central necrosis of the neoplasm. The cavities usually resemble acute lung abscesses and have thick walls with irregular, often nodular, inner surfaces (Figure 2-42).

Although the diagnosis of bronchogenic carcinoma may be made by detection of cancer cells in the sputum, a precise diagnosis usually requires biopsy of the tumor during bronchoscopy (direct visualization of the tracheobronchial tree using a tube inserted through the nose) or a needle biopsy in the radiology department under CT or fluoroscopic guidance.

The prognosis of bronchogenic carcinoma is poor, except when the tumor is in the form of a solitary pulmonary nodule that can be surgically removed. Direct lymphatic spread of a tumor can cause enlargement of hilar or mediastinal lymph nodes (Figure 2-43). Distant metastases most frequently involve the bones, where they cause osteolytic

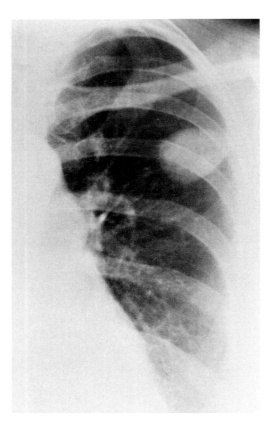

Figure 2-39   Benign solitary pulmonary nodule (tuberculoma). Notice sharp, well-defined borders of this left upper lobe mass.

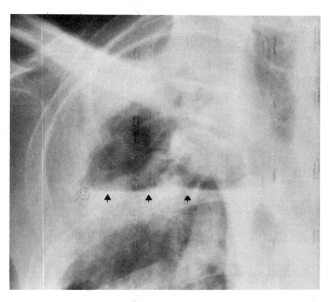

Figure 2-41 Bronchogenic carcinoma. Tomography demonstrates bilateral bulky hilar adenopathy typical of oat cell carcinoma.

Figure 2-42 Bronchogenic carcinoma. Large cavitary right upper lobe mass with air-fluid level *(arrows)* and associated rib destruction.

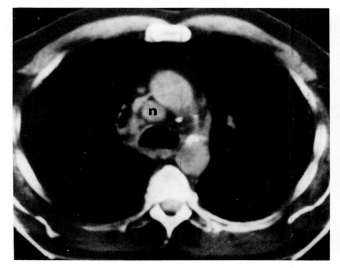

A

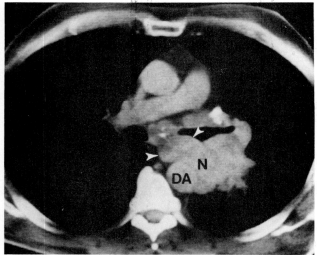

B

Figure 2-43 Spread of bronchogenic carcinoma to mediastinum. **A,** CT scan shows enlarged lymph node *(n)* in pretracheal region, consistent with unresectable mediastinal spread. **B,** In another patient, CT scan shows obliteration of fat plane around descending aorta *(DA)* by adjacent neoplasm *(N)*. In addition, tumor extends deep into mediastinum *(arrowheads)* behind left main-stem bronchus and in front of descending aorta. (From Lee JKT, Sagel SS, Stanley RJ, editors: *Computed body tomography,* New York, 1989, Raven.)

destruction. Metastases to the liver, brain, and adrenal glands commonly develop.

Pulmonary metastases

Up to one third of patients with cancer develop pulmonary metastases; in about half of these patients, the only demonstrable metastases are confined to the lungs. Pulmonary metastases may develop from hematogenous or lymphatic spread, most commonly from musculoskeletal sarcomas, myeloma, and carcinomas of the breast, urogenital tract, thyroid, and colon. Carcinomas of the breast, esophagus, or stomach may directly extend to involve the lungs. Primary lung lesions may metastasize by spread through the bronchial tree.

Hematogenous metastases typically appear radiographically as multiple, relatively well-circumscribed, round or oval nodules throughout the lungs (Figure 2-44). The pattern may vary from fine miliary nod-

ules (Figure 2-45) produced by highly vascular tumors (kidney or thyroid gland carcinomas, sarcoma of bone, trophoblastic disease) to huge, well-defined masses (cannonball lesions) caused by metastatic sarcomas. Carcinoma of the thyroid gland typically

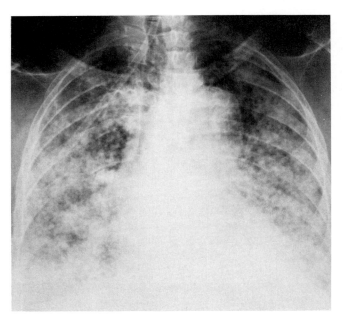

Figure 2-45 Metastatic thyroid carcinoma. Multiple fine miliary nodules throughout both lungs.

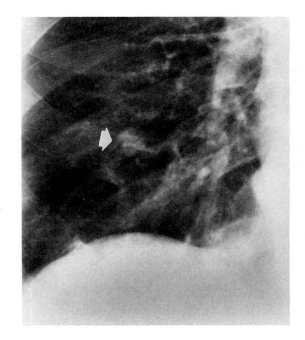

Figure 2-44 Hematogenous metastases. Multiple, well-circumscribed nodules scattered diffusely throughout both lungs.

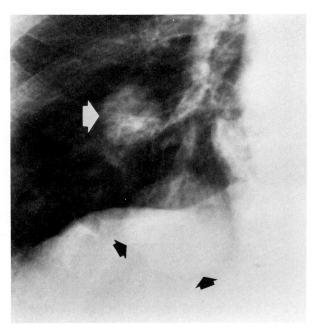

Figure 2-46 Pulmonary metastases. **A,** Solitary metastasis *(arrow).* **B,** Repeat examination 5 months later shows rapid growth of previous solitary nodule *(white arrow).* Second huge nodule *(black arrows)* was not appreciated on previous examination because it projected below right hemidiaphragm.

causes a snowstorm of metastatic deposits yet remains unchanged for a prolonged period because of a very low grade of malignancy.

Solitary metastases, which occur in about 25% of cases, may be indistinguishable from primary bronchogenic carcinoma may permit the detection of 2-46). In such cavity masses that cannot be seen on additional pulmonographs.

standard commonly is a complication of carci-
Lymphatic metastatic spread throughout the
lu the breast, stomach, thyroid, pancreas, lung cervix, or prostate. The radiographic appearance consists of coarsened interstitial markings that are of irregular contour and poorly defined (Figure 2-47). They are most prominent in the lower lobes and may simulate interstitial pulmonary edema.

■ Miscellaneous Lung Disorders

Atelectasis

Atelectasis refers to a condition in which there is diminished air within the lung associated with reduced lung volume. It is most commonly the result of bronchial obstruction, which may be attributable to a neoplasm, foreign body (peanut, coin, or tooth), or mucus plug. Mucoid obstruction may be attributable to an excessive secretion in patients with

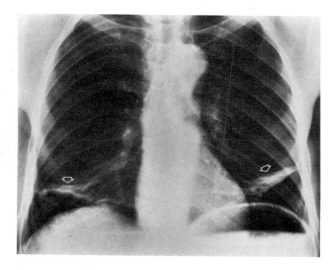

Figure 2-48   Platelike atelectasis. There are horizontal linear streaks of opacity *(arrows)* in lower portions of both lungs.

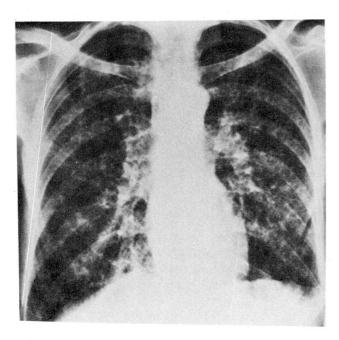

Figure 2-47   Lymphangitic metastases. Coarsened bronchovascular markings of irregular contour and poor definition in this patient with metastatic carcinoma of stomach.

chronic bronchitis or be a complication of abdominal surgery, in which mucus collects in the bronchi as a result of the irritative effect of anesthesia and coughing is decreased because of the pain of the abdominal wound. Atelectasis may also be attributable to compression of the lung by pneumothorax, pleural fluid, a tumor, a lung abscess, or a large emphysematous bulla. Regardless of the precise cause, air is unable to enter that part of the lung supplied by the obstructed bronchus. As the air already in the lung is absorbed into the bloodstream, the lung collapses.

The most common radiographic sign of atelectasis is a local increase in density caused by airless lung that may vary from thin platelike streaks (Figure 2-48) to lobar collapse (Figure 2-49). Indirect signs of atelectasis reflect an attempt by the remaining lung to compensate for the loss of the collapsed portion. These signs include elevation of the ipsilateral hemidiaphragm; displacement of the heart, mediastinum, and hilum toward the atelectatic segment; and compensatory overinflation of the remainder of the ipsilateral lung. An important direct sign of atelectasis is displacement of interlobar fissures, which shift and become bowed, conforming to the contour of the collapsed segment.

An important iatrogenic cause of atelectasis is the improper placement of an endotracheal tube below the level of the tracheal bifurcation. Because of geometric factors, the endotracheal tube tends to enter the right main-stem bronchus, effectively blocking the left bronchial tree and causing collapse of part or all of the left lung (Figure 2-50).

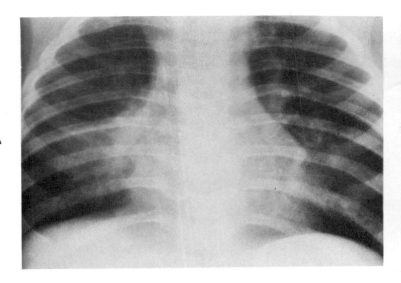
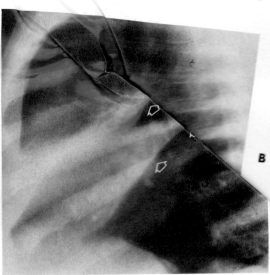

Figure 2-49 Right middle lobe and lingular collapse. **A,** Frontal chest radiograph demonstrates obliteration of right and left borders of heart. **B,** Lateral projection demonstrates collapse of right middle lobe and lingula *(arrows)*.

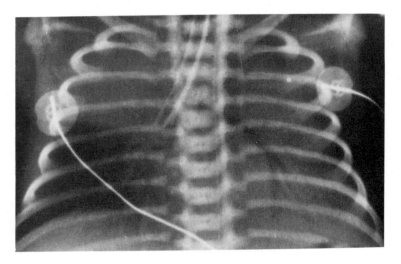

Figure 2-50 Malpositioned endotracheal tube. Excessively low position of endotracheal tube in bronchus intermedius causes collapse of right upper lobe and entire left lung.

Cystic fibrosis

Cystic fibrosis (mucoviscidosis) is a hereditary disease characterized by the secretion of excessively viscous mucus by all the exocrine glands.

In the lungs, thick mucus secreted by the trachea and bronchi blocks the air passages and leads to focal areas of lung collapse. Recurrent pulmonary infections are common, since bacteria that are normally carried away by mucosal secretions adhere to the sticky mucus produced in this condition. Radiographically, cystic fibrosis causes generalized irregu-

lar thickening of linear markings throughout the lungs that, when combined with the almost invariable hyperinflation, produces an appearance similar to severe chronic lung disease in adults (Figure 2-51).

In the pancreas, blockage of the ducts by mucus plugs prevents pancreatic enzymes from entering the duodenum. This impairs the digestion of fat, resulting in failure of the child to gain weight and the production of large, bulky, foul-smelling stools. In about 10% of newborns with cystic fibrosis, the

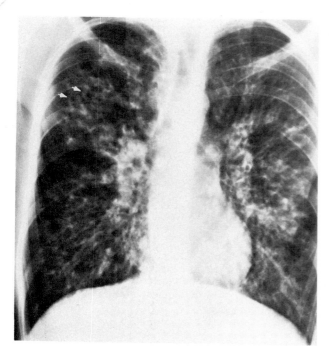

Figure 2-51 Cystic fibrosis. Multiple small cysts superimposed on diffuse, coarse, reticular pattern.

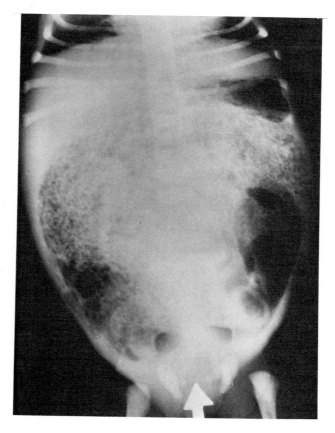

Figure 2-52 Meconium ileus in cystic fibrosis. Massive small bowel distention with profound soap-bubble effect of gas mixed with meconium. (From Swischuk LE: *Radiology of the newborn and young infant,* Baltimore, 1980, Williams & Wilkins.)

thick mucus causes obstruction of the small bowel (meconium ileus) (Figure 2-52). Bowel perforation with subsequent fatal peritonitis may occur.

Involvement of the sweat glands in cystic fibrosis causes the child to perspire excessively. This leads to a loss of large amounts of salt (sodium, potassium, and chloride), so that the patients are extremely susceptible to heat exhaustion in hot weather. The presence of excessive chloride on the skin is the basis for the "sweat test," a simple and reliable test for cystic fibrosis.

Hyaline membrane disease

Hyaline membrane disease is one of the most common causes of respiratory distress in the newborn. It primarily occurs in premature infants, especially those who have diabetic mothers or who have been delivered by cesarean section. Hypoxia and increasing respiratory distress may not be immediately evident at birth but almost always appear within 6 hours of delivery.

The progressive underaeration of the lungs in hyaline membrane disease results from a lack of **surfactant.** This lipoprotein is normally produced by cells in the walls of the alveoli and is responsible for maintaining the surface tension within the alveoli that permits them to remain inflated.

In addition to pronounced underaeration, the radiographic hallmark of hyaline membrane disease is a finely granular appearance of the pulmonary parenchyma (Figure 2-53). A peripherally extending air bronchogram develops because the small airways dilate and stand out clearly against the atelectatic surrounding lung.

The treatment of hyaline membrane disease includes the use of positive pressure ventilators that pump air (often with high concentrations of oxygen) into the lungs through an endotracheal tube. The high ventilator pressure may cause leakage of air from overinflated alveoli or small terminal bronchioles, leading to interstitial emphysema, pneumothorax, and pneumopericardium, all of which further decrease the expansion of the lungs.

Adult respiratory distress syndrome

The term **adult respiratory distress syndrome (ARDS)** is used to describe a clinical picture of severe, unexpected, and life-threatening acute respiratory distress that develops in patients who have a variety of medical and surgical disorders but no major underlying lung disease. It occurs most commonly

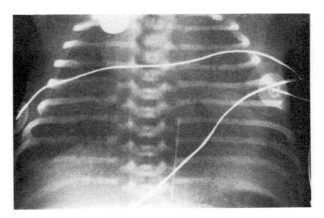

Figure 2-53 Hyaline membrane disease. Diffuse granular pattern of pulmonary parenchyma associated with air bronchograms *(arrows)*.

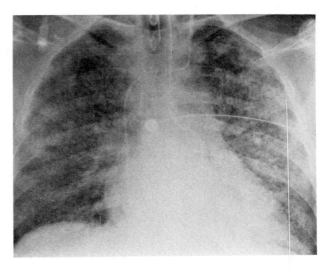

Figure 2-54 Adult respiratory distress syndrome. Ill-defined areas of alveolar consolidation scattered throughout both lungs.

in patients with nonthoracic trauma who develop hypotension and shock and thus is often called "shock lung." Other conditions that may lead to the adult respiratory distress syndrome include severe pulmonary infection, aspiration or inhalation of toxins and irritants, and drug overdose. Regardless of the cause, there is a complete breakdown in the structure of the lung, leading to massive leakage of cells and fluid into the interstitial and alveolar spaces and severe hypoxemia caused by a pronounced respiratory impairment in the ability to oxygenate blood. Radiographically, there are patchy, ill-defined areas of alveolar consolidation scattered throughout both lungs (Figure 2-54). Unlike pulmonary edema caused by heart failure, in the adult respiratory distress syndrome the heart is usually of normal size, and there is no evidence of redistribution of blood flow to the upper zones.

The hypoxemia in adult respiratory distress syndrome may be fatal, even with intensive medical therapy. Continuous positive-pressure ventilation may cause air to enter the interstitium of the lung and lead to pneumothorax and pneumomediastinum. Diffuse interstitial and patchy air-space fibrosis may produce a coarse reticular pattern. If the patient recovers completely, the radiographic abnormalities may clear completely, and there may be only a mild decrease in pulmonary function.

Intrabronchial foreign bodies

The aspiration of solid foreign bodies into the tracheobronchial tree occurs almost exclusively in young children. Although some foreign bodies are radiopaque and easily detected on plain chest radiographs, most aspirated foreign bodies are nonopaque and can be diagnosed only by observation of secondary signs in the lungs caused by partial or complete bronchial obstruction. The lower lobes are almost always involved, the right more often than the left.

The complete obstruction of a major bronchus leads to resorption of trapped air, alveolar collapse, and atelectasis of the involved segment or lobe. Extensive volume loss causes a shift of the heart and mediastinal structures toward the affected side along with elevation of the ipsilateral hemidiaphragm and narrowing of the intercostal spaces.

Partial bronchial obstruction may produce air trapping as a result of a check-valve phenomenon. Air freely passes the partial obstruction during inspiration but remains trapped distally as the bronchus contracts normally during expiration (Figure 2-55). Hyperaeration of the affected lobes causes a shift of the heart and mediastinum toward the normal, contralateral side. This finding is accentuated during forced expiration because the hyperaerated segment does not contract. This classic appearance of partial bronchial obstruction is dramatically demonstrated at fluoroscopy as the mediastinum shifts away from the affected side during deep expiration and returns toward the midline on full inspiration.

A malpositioned endotracheal tube can act as an intrabronchial foreign body. The tube tends to extend down the right main-stem bronchus, causing hyperlucency of the right lung and obstructive atelectasis of the left lung.

Mediastinal emphysema (pneumomediastinum)

Air within the mediastinal space may appear spontaneously or be the result of chest trauma; perfora-

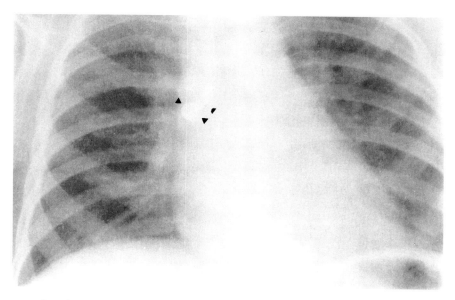

Figure 2-55 Intrabronchial foreign body. Nail *(arrows)* lies in right main-stem bronchus. (From Cappitanio MA et al: *Radiology* 103:460-461, 1972.)

tion of the esophagus or tracheobronchial tree; or the spread of air along fascial planes from the neck, peritoneal cavity, or retroperitoneal space. Spontaneous pneumomediastinum usually results from a sudden rise in intra-alveolar pressure (e.g., severe coughing, vomiting, or straining) that causes alveolar rupture and the dissection of air along blood vessels in the interstitial space to the hilum and mediastinum. Air may also extend peripherally and rupture into the pleural space, causing an associated pneumothorax.

On frontal chest radiographs, air causes lateral displacement of the mediastinal pleura, which appears as a long linear opacity that is parallel to the heart border but separated from it by the air (Figure 2-56). On lateral projections, air typically collects behind the sternum, extending in streaks downward and anterior to the heart. Chest radiographs may also demonstrate air outlining the pulmonary arterial trunk and aorta, as well as dissecting into the soft tissues of the neck.

In infants, mediastinal air causes elevation of the thymus. Loculated air confined to one side produces an appearance similar to that of a windblown sail. Bilateral mediastinal air elevates both thymic lobes to produce an angel-wings configuration (Figure 2-57).

Subcutaneous emphysema

Subcutaneous emphysema is caused by penetrating or blunt injuries that disrupt the lung and parietal pleura so that air is forced into the tissues of the chest wall. The resulting radiographic appearance is

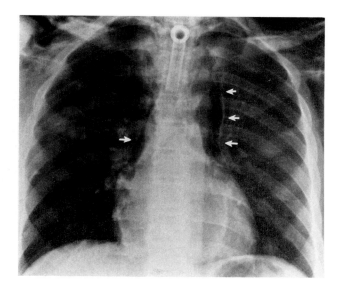

Figure 2-56 Mediastinal emphysema. Mediastinal pleura is displaced laterally and appears as long linear opacity *(arrows)* parallel to heart border but separated from it by gas.

bizarre, with streaks of lucency outlining muscle bundles (Figure 2-58).

▪ Disorders of the Pleura

Pneumothorax

Pneumothorax refers to the presence of air in the pleural cavity that results in a partial or complete collapse of the lung (Figure 2-59). It most commonly results from rupture of a subpleural bulla, either as a

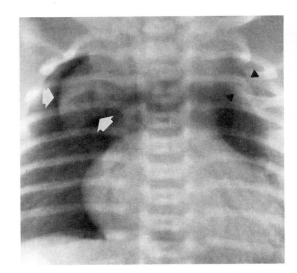
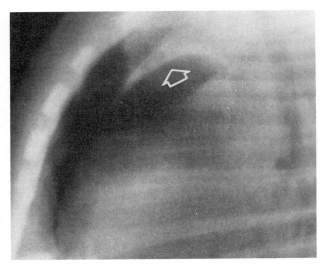

Figure 2-57   Mediastinal emphysema in infant. **A,** Elevation of both lobes of thymus by mediastinal air *(arrows)* produces angel-wings sign. **B,** Lateral projection shows mediastinal air lifting thymus off pericardium and great vessels *(arrows* and *arrowheads).* (From Eisenberg R: *Atlas of signs in radiology,* Philadelphia, 1984, Lippincott.)

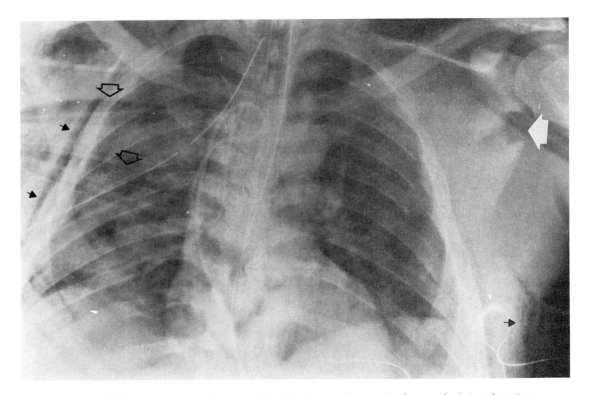

Figure 2-58   Subcutaneous emphysema. Frontal chest radiograph of severely injured patient shows streaks and bubbles of subcutaneous air *(black arrows)* in soft tissues along lateral borders of thorax, as well as broad lucencies outlining muscle bundles *(open arrows)* overlying anterior chest wall. Notice fracture of left scapula *(white arrows)* and multiple rib fractures.

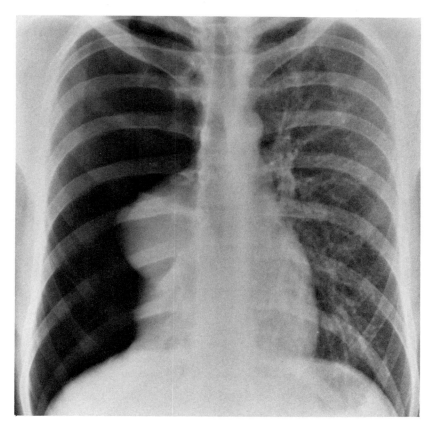

Figure 2-59 Spontaneous pneumothorax. Complete collapse of right lung.

complication of emphysema or as a spontaneous event in an otherwise healthy young adult. Other causes of pneumothorax include trauma (stabbing, gunshot, or fractured rib), iatrogenic causes (after lung biopsy or the introduction of a chest tube for thoracentesis), and as a complication of neonatal hyaline membrane disease requiring prolonged assisted ventilation. Regardless of the cause, the increased air in the pleural cavity compresses the lung and causes it to collapse, resulting in the patient experiencing sudden, severe chest pain and difficulty breathing. A pneumothorax appears radiographically as a hyperlucent area in which all pulmonary markings are absent. The radiographic hallmark of pneumothorax is the demonstration of the visceral pleural line, which is outlined centrally by air within the lung and peripherally by air within the pleural space. A large pneumothorax can cause collapse of an entire lung. Chest radiographs for pneumothorax should be taken with the patient in the upright position, since it may be very difficult to identify this condition if the patient is supine. In addition to routine full-inspiration films, a PA (or AP) radiograph should be obtained with the lung in full expiration to allow identification of small pneumothoraces (Figure

2-60). This maneuver causes the lung to decrease in volume and become relatively denser, while the volume of air in the pleural space remains constant and is easier to detect. Another technique for demonstrating small pneumothoraces is a film obtained with a horizontal x-ray beam while the patient is in the lateral decubitus position. In this position, air rising to the highest point in the hemithorax is more clearly visible over the lateral chest wall than on erect views, in which a small amount of air in the apical region may be obscured by overlying bony densities. In obtaining any expiration radiograph an automatic exposure device (AED) is *not* recommended, since the preset density may produce a film blackness capable of concealing a small pneumothorax. Using a manual technique, the exposure factor for an expiration radiograph should be about one third greater than that for an inspiration film.

Small pneumothoraces usually reabsorb spontaneously. Larger pneumothoraces may require chest tube drainage.

Tension pneumothorax is a medical emergency in which air continues to enter the pleural space but cannot leave it. The accumulation of air within the pleural space causes complete collapse of the lung

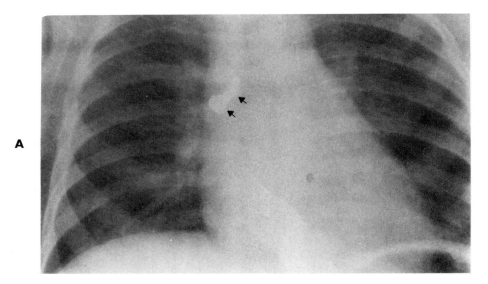

A

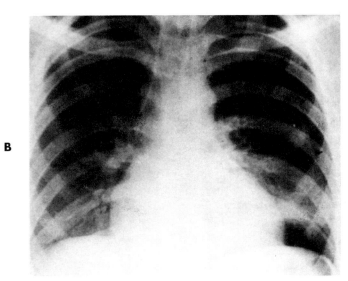

B

Figure 2-60   Pneumothorax. **A,** On routine frontal chest film, there is a faint rim of pleura *(arrows)* at left apex separated from thoracic wall by area containing air but no pulmonary vasculature. **B,** On expiratory film, left pneumothorax *(arrows)* is clearly seen. (From Eisenberg RL: *Diagnostic imaging in surgery,* New York, 1987, McGraw-Hill.)

on that side and depression of the hemidiaphragm (Figure 2-61). The heart and mediastinal structures are shifted toward the unaffected side, severely compromising cardiac output because the elevated intrathoracic pressure decreases venous return to the heart. If a tension pneumothorax is not treated promptly, the resulting circulatory collapse may be fatal.

Pleural effusion

The accumulation of fluid in the pleural space is a nonspecific finding that may be caused by a wide variety of pathologic processes. The most common causes include congestive heart failure, pulmonary embolism, infection (especially tuberculosis), pleurisy, neoplastic disease, and connective tissue disorders. Pleural effusion also can be the result of abdominal disease, such as recent surgery, ascites, subphrenic abscess, and pancreatitis.

The earliest radiographic finding in pleural effusion is blunting of the normally sharp angle between the diaphragm and the rib cage along with an upward concave border of the fluid level (meniscus) (Figure 2-62). Because the costophrenic angles are deeper posteriorly than laterally, small pleural effusions are best seen posteriorly on the routine lateral

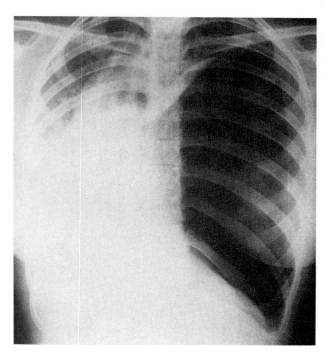

Figure 2-61 Tension pneumothorax. Left hemithorax is completely radiolucent and lacks vascular markings. There is dramatic shift of mediastinum to right. Left hemidiaphragm is greatly depressed, and there is spreading of left ribs.

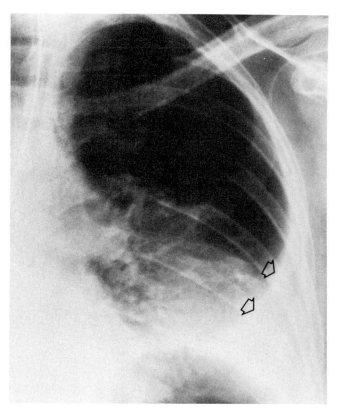

Figure 2-62 Pleural effusion. Blunting of normally sharp angle between diaphragm and rib cage *(arrows)* along with characteristic upward concave (meniscus) of fluid level.

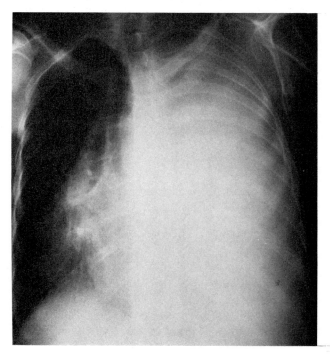

Figure 2-63 Pleural effusion causing shift of mediastinum. Left hemithorax is virtually opaque, and there is a shift of mediastinal structures to right.

projection. As much as 400 ml of pleural fluid may be present and still not produce blunting of the lateral costophrenic angles on erect frontal views of the chest. Larger amounts of pleural fluid produce a homogeneous whiteness that may obscure the diaphragm and adjacent borders of the heart. Massive effusions may compress the adjacent lung and even displace the heart and mediastinum to the opposite side (Figure 2-63).

Small pleural effusions may be difficult to distinguish from pleural thickening and fibrosis, which results from previous pleural inflammation and appears radiographically as a soft-tissue density along the lateral chest wall. The diagnosis of a small pleural effusion is best made by use of a horizontal x-ray beam with the patient in a lateral decubitus position with the affected side down. As little as 5 ml of pleural fluid can be seen layering out at a linear opacification along the dependent chest wall. At times, however, a collection of pleural fluid may be loculated (fixed in place by fibrous adhesions) and therefore will not layer out on decubitus views.

Pleural effusions may produce less common appearances on chest radiographs. A pleural fluid collection that has become fixed by inflammatory fibrosis may mimic a solid mass. At times, pleural fluid may collect below the inferior surface of the lung

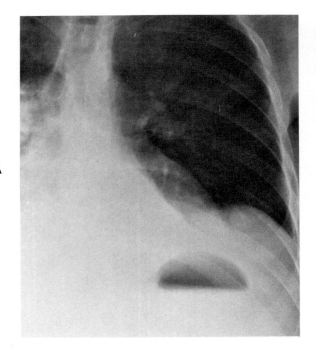
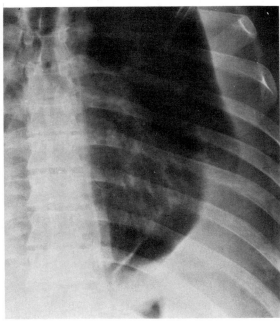

Figure 2-64 Pleural effusion. **A,** Frontal projection of chest demonstrates large distance between gastric air bubble and top of false left hemidiaphragm in this patient with large subpulmonic effusion. Notice retrocardiac paraspinal density *(arrows)* that simulates left lower lobe infiltrate or atelectasis. **B,** Left lateral decubitus projection shows that retrocardiac density represents large amount of free pleural fluid. (From Vix VA: *Semin Roentgenol* 12:277-286, 1977.)

(subpulmonic effusion) and give the radiographic appearance of an elevated hemidiaphragm (Figure 2-64). In patients with congestive heart failure, an effusion may develop in an interlobar fissure to produce a round or oval density resembling a solitary pulmonary nodule. As the patient's heart condition improves, repeat examinations demonstrate decreased size or complete resolution of these "phantom tumors" (see Figure 6-10).

Empyema

Empyema refers to the presence of infected liquid or frank pus in the pleural space. Usually the result of the spread of an adjacent infection (bacterial pneumonia, subdiaphragmatic abscess, lung abscess, esophageal perforation), empyemas may also occur after thoracic surgery, trauma, or instrumentation of the pleural space. Since the development of antibiotics, empyemas are rare.

Radiographically, an empyema is initially indistinguishable from pleural effusion. As the empyema develops, it becomes loculated and appears as a discrete mass that may vary in size from a large lesion filling much of the hemithorax (Figure 2-65) to a small mass along the chest wall or in an

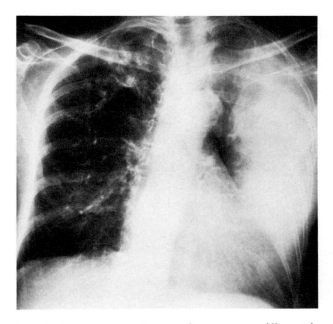

Figure 2-65 Empyema. Large soft-tissue mass fills much of left hemothorax. (From Eisenberg RL: *Diagnostic imaging in surgery,* New York, 1987, McGraw-Hill.)

interlobar fissure. Air within a free or loculated empyema causes an air-fluid level and indicates communication with a bronchus or the skin surface. Needle aspiration of an empyema may be performed by fluoroscopic guidance; if there is a loculated mass adjacent to the chest wall, ultrasound may be used to guide the aspiration needle.

▪ Mediastinal Masses

Because various types of mediastinal masses tend to occur predominantly in specific locations, the medi-astinum is often divided into anterior, middle, and posterior compartments. The anterior compartment extends from the sternum back to the trachea and the anterior border of the heart. The middle medi-astinum contains the heart and great vessels, the central tracheobronchial tree and lymph nodes, and the phrenic nerves. The posterior compartment is composed of the space behind the pericardium.

Major lesions of the anterior mediastinum include thymomas (Figure 2-66), teratomas, thyroid masses, lipomas, and lymphoma. The middle mediastinum is involved with lymph node disorders (lymphoma,

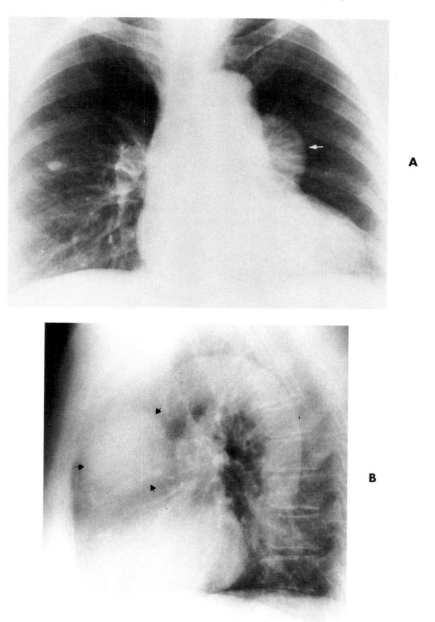

A

B

Figure 2-66   Anterior mediastinal mass. **A,** Frontal and, **B,** lateral projections of chest demonstrate large mass (thymoma) in anterior mediastinum *(arrows)*.

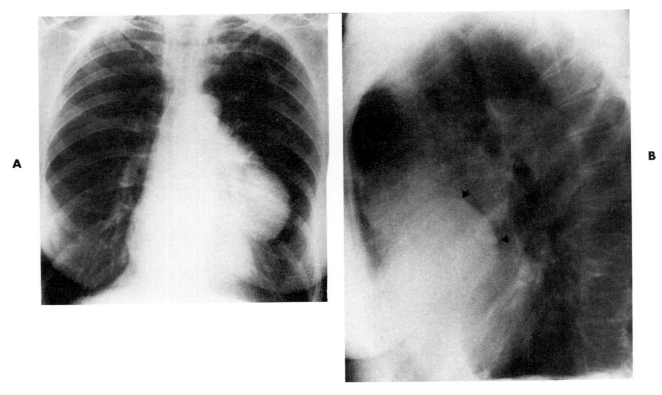

Figure 2-67   Middle mediastinal mass. **A,** Frontal and, **B,** lateral projections of chest demonstrate smooth-walled, spherical mediastinal mass *(arrows)* projecting into left lung and left hilum (bronchogenic cyst).

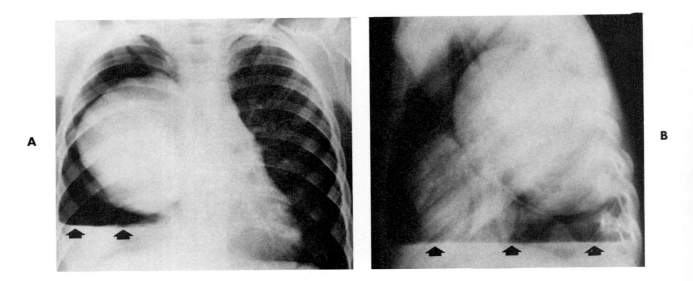

Figure 2-68   Posterior mediastinal mass. **A,** Frontal and, **B,** lateral projections of chest demonstrate large, oval, homogeneous mass in posterior mediastinum (neurenteric cyst). Notice right hydropneumothorax *(arrows)* with long air-fluid level that developed as complication of diagnostic needle biopsy.

metastatic carcinoma, granulomatous processes), bronchogenic cysts (Figure 2-67), vascular anomalies, and various masses situated in the anterior costophrenic angle (pericardial cysts, foramen of Morgagni hernia). The posterior mediastinum is the site of neurogenic tumors, neurogenic cysts (Figure 2-68), aneurysms of the descending aorta, and extramedullary hematopoiesis.

The configuration of a mediastinal mass depends to a large degree on its consistency. Cystic masses are often compressed between blood vessels and the tracheobronchial tree, producing a multiloculated appearance. In contrast, solid masses tend to compress and displace adjacent structures.

About one third of patients with mediastinal masses are asymptomatic, and the lesion is detected on a routine chest radiograph. Chest pain, cough, dyspsnea, and symptoms caused by compression or invasion of structures in the mediastinum (dysphagia, hoarseness as a result of recurrent laryngeal nerve involvement, superior vena cava obstruction) are highly suggestive of malignancy. In addition to plain chest radiographs, conventional tomography and contrast studies of the esophagus may be of value in defining the anatomic location and borders of the mass. CT of the chest after the intravenous injection of contrast material may help in distinguishing between vascular and nonvascular lesions, as well as in determining whether a lesion is cystic and thus most probably benign (Figures 2-69 and 2-70).

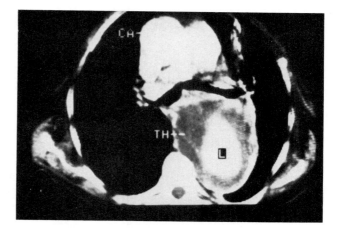

Figure 2-70 CT of posterior mediastinal mass. Contrast-enhanced scan at level just below carina shows large aneurysm of descending aorta. Large mural thrombus *(TH)* surrounds greatly dilated lumen of descending aorta *(L)*. Notice also prominently dilated ascending aorta *(OA)*.

▪ Disorders of the Diaphragm

The diaphragm is the major muscle of respiration that separates the thoracic and abdominal cavities. Radiographically, the height of the diaphragm varies considerably with the phase of respiration. On full inspiration, the diaphragm is usually about the level of the tenth posterior intercostal space. On expiration, it may appear two or three intercostal spaces higher. The average range of diaphragmatic motion with respiration is 3 to 6 cm, but in patients with emphysema this may be substantially reduced. The level of the diaphragm falls as the patient moves from a supine to an upright position. In an erect patient, the dome of the diaphragm tends to be about half an interspace higher on the right than on the left. However, in about 10% of normal individuals the hemidiaphragms are at the same height, or the left is higher than the right.

Diaphragmatic paralysis

Elevation of one or both leaves of the diaphragm can be caused by paralysis resulting from any process that interferes with the normal function of the phrenic nerve. This paralysis may be attributable to accidental surgical transection of the phrenic nerve, involvement of the nerve by primary bronchogenic carcinoma or metastatic malignancy in the mediastinum, or a variety of intrinsic neurologic diseases (Figure 2-71). The radiographic hallmark of diaphragmatic paralysis is paradoxical movement of the diaphragm that is best demonstrated at fluoroscopy by having the patient sniff. This rapid but shallow inspiration causes a quick downward thrust

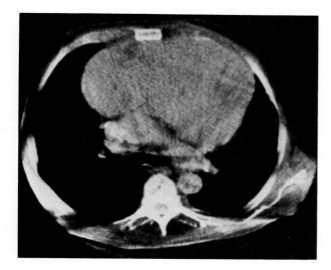

Figure 2-69 CT of anterior mediastinal mass. Enormous soft-tissue mass (thymoma) causes posterior displacement of other mediastinal structures. No difference in density can be seen between mass and heart behind it.

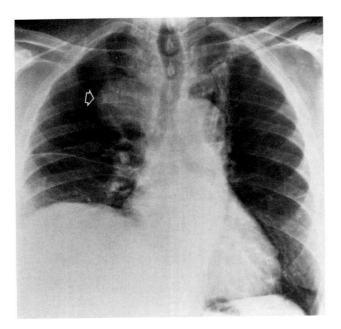

Figure 2-71   Paralysis of right hemidiaphragm because of involvement of phrenic nerve by primary carcinoma of lung *(arrow)*.

of a normal leaf of the diaphragm, whereas a paralyzed hemidiaphragm tends to rise with inspiration because of the increased intra-abdominal pressure. During expiration, the normal hemidiaphragm rises and the paralyzed one descends. The demonstration of a pronounced degree of paradoxical motion is a valuable aid in differentiating paralysis of the diaphragm from limited diaphragmatic motion resulting from intrathoracic or intra-abdominal disease.

Eventration of the diaphragm

Eventration of the diaphragm is a rare congenital abnormality in which one hemidiaphragm (very rarely both) is poorly developed and is too weak to permit the upward movement of abdominal contents into the thoracic cage. This leads to the radiographic appearance of a localized bulging or generalized elevation of the diaphragm (Figure 2-72). The condition is usually asymptomatic and is most common on the left. An eventration must be distinguished from a diaphragmatic hernia, through which abdominal contents are displaced into the chest. Oral administration of barium should permit the differentiation between the normal contours of the bowel below a diaphragmatic eventration and the crowding of these structures and narrowing of their afferent and efferent limbs when trapped in a hernia sac.

Other causes of elevation of the diaphragm

Diffuse elevation of one or both leaves of the diaphragm can be caused by ascites, obesity, pregnancy, or any other process in which the intra-abdominal volume is increased (Figure 2-73). Intra-abdominal inflammatory diseases, such as subphrenic abscess,

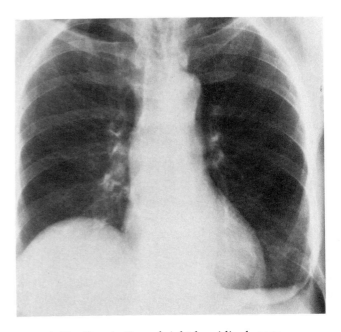

Figure 2-72   Eventration of right hemidiaphragm.

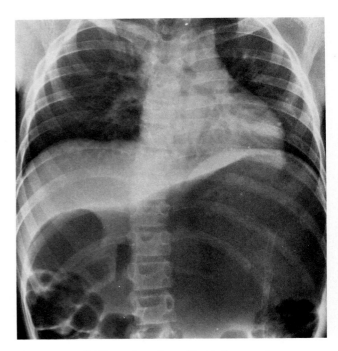

Figure 2-73   Diffuse elevation of both leaves of diaphragm caused by severe, acute gastric dilatation.

can lead to elevation of a hemidiaphragm with severe limitations of diaphragmatic motion. Cystic or tumor masses arising in the upper quadrants can cause localized or generalized bulging of the diaphragm. Acute intrathoracic processes (chest-wall injury, atelectasis, pulmonary embolism) can produce diaphragmatic elevation caused by splinting of the diaphragm. An apparent elevation of a hemidiaphragm may be caused by a subpulmonic pleural effusion, which can be correctly diagnosed on a chest radiograph performed with a horizontal x-ray beam and the patient in a lateral decubitus position.

QUESTIONS

1. Describe the proper breathing instructions to be given to a patient for chest radiography.

2. In what portion of the respiratory system does the vital gas exchange take place?

3. The covering of the lungs is termed the _____ .

4. A necrotic area of pulmonary parenchyma containing purulent or puslike material is called a _____ .

5. What radiographic procedure is often required to confirm the diagnosis of bronchiectasis when routine chest radiographs are inconclusive?

6. Flattening of the domes of the diaphragm, increased AP diameter of the chest, and increased lucency of the retrosternal air space are suggestive of a diagnosis of _____ .

7. The three most common pneumoconioses are _____ , _____ , and _____ .

8. An abnormal vascular communication between a pulmonary artery and pulmonary vein is termed a _____ .

9. _____ is a disease of newborns characterized by progressive underaeration of the lungs and a granular appearance.

10. What medical emergency has occurred when air continues to enter the pleural space and cannot escape, leading to complete collapse of a lung and shift of the heart and mediastinal structures?

11. Pus in the pleural space is called _____ .

12. The major muscle of respiration is the _____ .

13. Describe why a true horizontal beam is desirable when one is performing any chest radiograph.

14. The Valsalva maneuver can cause the heart and major blood vessels to:
    A. Appear enlarged
    B. Appear smaller
    C. Appear elevated
    D. Show no change

15. Place an "H" by those pathologic conditions that are harder to penetrate and an "E" by those that are easier to penetrate:
    _____ Pleural effusion   _____ Empyema
    _____ Miliary tuberculosis _____ Asbestosis
    _____ Emphysema   _____ Pneumonia
    _____ Lung abscess   _____ Atelectasis
    _____ Pulmonary edema   _____ Brochiectasis

16. Describe the pulmonary circulation of the lungs.

17. Describe the bronchial circulation of the lungs.

18. The lining of the thoracic cavity is called the _____ .

19. A lung inflammation caused by bacteria or viruses is called a _____ .

20. For technologist safety, it is important to remember that tuberculosis is spread mainly by _____ , which produces infectious _____ .

21. What medical term is used to describe the entry of air into the pleural space?

22. An increased volume of air in the lungs is seen in _____ .

23. Inhalation of irritating dusts leading to chronic inflammation and pulmonary fibrosis is called _____ .

24. Trapping of bacteria in the pulmonary circulation that occurs in patients with a history of intravenous drug abuse is called _____ .

25. _____ is a hereditary disease in which thick mucus is secreted by all the exocrine glands.

26. Reduced air volume within a lung leading to collapse is termed _____ .

27. Blunt or penetrating trauma to the chest can produce _____ , which appears as streaks of air that outline muscles of the thorax and sometimes the neck.

28. Name the two positions that are sometimes used to demonstrate a pneumothorax that are different from the routine chest radiograph positions.

29. An abnormal connection between the esophagus and trachea is termed _____ .

30. At what costal interspace does the diaphragm lie when the lungs are fully inflated?
    A. Eighth   C. Tenth
    B. Ninth   D. Eleventh

31. What radiographic position is sometimes helpful in the diagnosis of very small pleural effusions?

32. Air collecting behind the sternum and dissecting up into the soft tissues of the neck is called _____ .

33. An accumulation of fluid in the pleural space, sometimes caused by heart failure or pulmonary embolus, is called:
    A. Empyema   C. Effusion
    B. Edema   D. Abscess

BIBLIOGRAPHY
Chest
Felson B: *Chest roentgenology*, Philadelphia, 1971, Saunders.
Heitzman ER: *The lung; radiologic-pathologic correlations*, St Louis, 1984, Mosby.

Paré JAP, Fraser RG: *Synopsis of diseases of the chest*, Philadelphia, 1983, Saunders.
Reed JC: *Chest radiology: patterns and differential diagnoses*, St Louis, 1981, Mosby.

CHAPTER 3

Skeletal System

■ **Prerequisite Knowledge**

The student should have a basic knowledge of the anatomy and physiology of the skeletal system. In addition, proper learning and understanding of the material will be facilitated if the student has some clinical experience in skeletal radiography and film evaluation, including a concept of the changes in technique required to compensate for density differences produced by the underlying pathologic conditions.

■ **Goals**

To acquaint the student radiographer with the patho-physiology and radiographic manifestations of all of the common and some of the unusual disorders of the skeletal system.

■ **Objectives**

1. Be able to classify the more common diseases in terms of their penetrability to x rays
2. Be familiar with the changes in technical factors required for obtaining optimal-quality radiographs in patients with various underlying pathologic conditions
3. Understand and be able to define or describe all bold-faced terms in this chapter
4. Describe the physiology of the skeletal system
5. Identify anatomic structures on both diagrams and radiographs of the skeletal system
6. Be able to describe the various pathologic conditions affecting the skeletal system as well as their radiographic manifestations

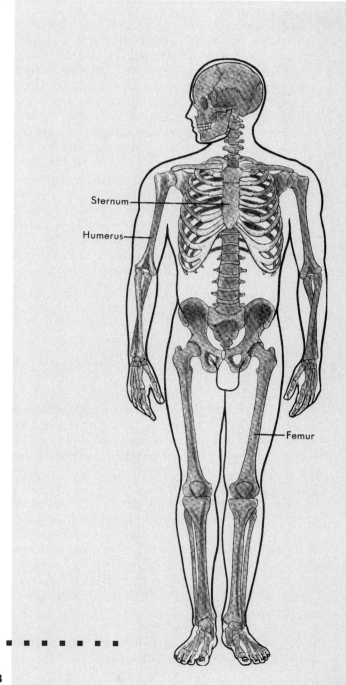

■ ■ ■ ■ ■ ■ ■ ■ ■ ■ ■ **Radiographer Notes**

Proper positioning, correct tube-part-film alignment, and the use of exposure factors designed to produce an optimal contrast level and visibility of detail are critical factors in radiography of the skeletal system. In patients with suspected fractures, two projections as close as possible to 90 degrees to each other must always be obtained. A variety of projections (oblique, tangential, coned-down) may be required to identify obscure fractures. At times, the poor condition of a patient may require ingenuity on the part of the radiographer to obtain diagnostic radiographs when routine positioning methods cannot be used.

Patients with bone tumors, arthritis, or recent trauma are frequently in severe pain and extremely frightened of being injured further or suffering more discomfort. It is essential that the patient be reassured of the radiographer's awareness of his or her pain or discomfort and that the radiographer will be as careful as possible. Remember that a radiographer can easily cause further injury to the patient if proper moving techniques are not used. At times, it may be necessary to perform cross-table or tube-angulation projections to obtain the required films without having to move the patient. In such cases, the tube-part-film alignment is critical because variations of these relationships can obscure pathologic bone conditions or lead to errors in interpretation of the alignment of fracture fragments. The radiographic tube must be perpendicular to the image receptor and the body part to prevent image distortion.

Bone radiographs require a short scale of contrast to provide maximal visibility of detail. The periosteum, cortex, and internal bone structure (trabeculae) must be well demonstrated to detect the often subtle changes of fractures, demineralization, and bone destruction. For example, periosteal new bone formation may indicate underlying tumor, infection, or prior trauma, whereas minute juxta-articular erosions are often seen in arthritis. The scale of contrast must be such that the soft tissues and muscles also are well visualized. Soft-tissue swelling, calcifications, opaque foreign bodies, muscle wasting, and the presence of gas are all important radiographic findings.

It is recommended that lower- to mid-kVp ranges be used in all skeletal radiography. To achieve the necessary scale of contrast, the extremities should be examined by use of an exposure in the 40 to 69 kVp range, whereas a range of 70 to 80 kVp is recommended for studies of the spine, pelvis, thoracic cage, and shoulder. Appropriate ratio grids, or Bucky devices, should be used for all body parts 10 cm or greater.

■ Physiology of the Skeletal System

The skeletal system is primarily composed of two highly specialized connective tissues: bone and cartilage. Bone consists of an organic matrix in which inorganic salts (primarily calcium and phosphate) are deposited. The outer surfaces of bone are covered by a fibrous membrane termed the **periosteum,** except at joint surfaces where the bone is covered with articular cartilage that acts as a protective cushion. The periosteum contains a network of blood vessels from which nutrient arteries penetrate into the underlying bone. The main shaftlike portion is termed the **diaphysis,** and the ends of the bone are called **epiphyses.** The hollow, tubelike structure within the diaphysis is the **medullary,** or **marrow,** cavity, which is lined by an inner membrane termed the **endosteum.**

There are two major types of bone. The outer layer is composed of **compact bone,** which to the naked eye is dense and structureless. Under the microscope, the matrix of compact bone consists of complex structural units called "haversian systems." **Cancellous (spongy) bone** is composed of a weblike arrangement of marrow-filled spaces separated by thin processes of bone, called **trabeculae,** that are visible to the naked eye. The relative amount of each type of bone depends on the degree of strength required and thus varies from bone to bone and in different portions of the same bone. For example, the shafts of long bones such as the femur and tibia have a thick outer layer of compact bone, whereas the layer of compact bone is relatively thin in irregular bones, such as vertebral bodies and facial bones, or short bones, such as the carpal and tarsal bones.

Most bones form from models composed of hyaline cartilage (enchondral ossification). In a typical long bone, a primary ossification center appears in the center of the cartilage precursor about the eighth week of intrauterine life, and bone formation extends so that the entire shaft is usually ossified before birth. Just before or after birth, secondary

Special techniques such as magnification or tomography may be necessary to detect subtle fractures or other pathologic bone conditions. For example, the navicular bone of the wrist typically requires the use of the magnification technique. For 2× linear or 4× area magnification, the part in question must be an equal distance from the radiographic tube and the image receptor. For 3× linear or 9× area magnification, the part must be twice as far from the image receptor as from the x-ray tube. Close collimation is extremely important to prevent undercutting the image. A radiographic tube with a fractional focal spot of 0.3 mm or less is mandatory, since larger focal spot sizes cause excessive distortion and an image that appears to have motion and lack detail as a result of excessive penumbra (blurring). Tomography may be required to make a definite diagnosis if the plain radiographs are equivocal or to delineate precisely the extent of bone involvement. For example, tomography is frequently needed in the evaluation of fractures of the tibial plateau and spine.

As a general rule, it is essential to prevent motion of the part of the body being radiographed. To accomplish this, the patient should be made as comfortable as possible, immobilization devices should be used when necessary, and the shortest possible exposure time should be used. However, a few portions of the skeletal system are better visualized using a motion technique. These include the sternum, lateral thoracic spine, transthoracic lateral projection of the upper humerus, and "wagging jaw," or Ottonello method, for obtaining an AP projection of the cervical spine. For the first three, a breathing technique is used while the patient remains immobilized. A minimum exposure time of about 5 seconds and a very low milliamperage should be used. The patient is instructed to breathe rhythmically during the entire exposure to blur out overlying ribs and lung markings. In the Ottonello method, movement of the jaw blurs out the image of the mandible, which otherwise would be superimposed on the upper portion of the cervical spine.

Certain pathologic conditions of the skeletal system require that the radiographer alter the routine technical factors. Some disorders produce increased density (sclerosis, increased bone growth), which is harder to penetrate; others decrease the density of the bony structures (lytic bone destruction, loss of calcium from bone), and so they are easier to penetrate (see box on p. 3). It is important to remember that the necessary technical changes may vary depending on the stage of the underlying condition.

ossification centers appear in the epiphyses, the ends of developing long bones. Until the linear growth of bone is complete, the epiphysis remains separated from the diaphysis by a cartilaginous plate called the **epiphyseal cartilage.** The epiphyseal cartilage persists until the growth of the bone is complete. At that time, the epiphyseal plate ossifies, and the epiphysis and diaphysis fuse (various ages for specific bones).

The increase in length of a developing long bone occurs by growth of the epiphyseal cartilage followed by ossification. Bones grow in diameter by the combined action of two special types of cells called **osteoblasts** and **osteoclasts.** Osteoclasts enlarge the diameter of the medullary cavity by removing the bone of its walls. At the same time, osteoblasts from the periosteum produce new bone around its outer circumference. Osteoblasts and osteoclasts are continuously active in resorbing old bone and producing new bone. This constant process of remodeling occurs until the bone assumes its adult size and shape.

The radiographic determination of bone age is useful in the evaluation of physiologic age, growth potential, and prediction of adult stature. The most well-known and widely accepted method of determining skeletal bone age (skeletal maturation) is that of Greulich and Pyle in their radiographic atlas compiled from thousands of examinations of American children at different ages. This atlas contains standard radiographs for age and sex that permit an assessment of bone age based on the presence or absence of ossification centers and their configuration and the fusion of epiphyses in various portions of the hand and wrist.

Throughout life, bone formation **(ossification)** and bone destruction **(resorption)** continue to occur. They are in balance during the early and middle years of adulthood. After about 40 years of age, however, bone loss at the inner or endosteal surface exceeds bone gain at the outer margins. Thus in long bones the thickness of compact bone in the diaphyses decreases, and the diameter of the medullary cavity increases. The bone eventually resembles a hollow shell and is less able to resist compressive and bending forces. This process may lead to collapse and loss of height of vertebral bodies and fractures of long bones after relatively mild injury.

Bones can also develop within a connective tissue membrane **(intramembranous ossification).** The clavicles and flat bones of the skull have no cartilaginous stage and begin to take shape when groups of primitive cells differentiate into osteoblasts, which secrete matrix material and collagenous fibrils. Deposition of complex calcium salts in the organic bone matrix produces rodlike trabeculae that join in a network of interconnecting spicules to form spongy or cancellous bone. Eventually, plates of compact or dense bone cover the core layer of spongy bone. Flat bones grow in size by the addition of osseous tissue to their outer surfaces **(appositional growth).** They cannot grow by expansion as is the case with enchondral bone growth.

Bones perform five basic functions. They serve as the supporting framework of the body and protect the vital organs (skull protecting the brain, rib cage protecting the heart and lungs). Bones serve as levers on which muscles can contract and shorten and thus produce movement at a joint. Red bone marrow within certain bones (spinal column, upper humerus, and upper femur in the adult) is the major site of production of blood cells. Finally, bone serves as the major storehouse for calcium salts. The maintenance of a normal level of calcium, which is essential for survival, depends on a balance in the rates of calcium movement between the blood and bones.

■ Congenital/Hereditary Diseases of Bone

Vertebral anomalies

A **transitional vertebra** is one that has characteristics of vertebrae on both sides of a major division of the spine. Transitional vertebrae most frequently occur at the lumbosacral junction and contain expanded transverse processes, which may form actual unilateral or bilateral joints with the sacrum. When unilateral, this process often leads to degenerative change involving the opposite hip and the intervertebral disk space above it. At the thoracolumbar junction, the first lumbar vertebra may have rudimentary ribs articulating with the transverse processes. The seventh cervical vertebra may also have a rudimentary rib (Figure 3-1). This **cervical rib** may compress the brachial nerve plexus (causing pain or numbness in the upper extremity) or the subclavian artery (decreasing blood flow to the arm) and therefore require surgical removal.

Spina bifida

Spina bifida refers to a posterior defect of the spinal canal resulting from failure of the posterior elements to fuse properly. A mild, insignificant form is **spina bifida occulta,** in which there is a splitting of the bony neural canal at the L5 or S1 level (Figure 3-2). Large defects are associated with spinal cord abnor-

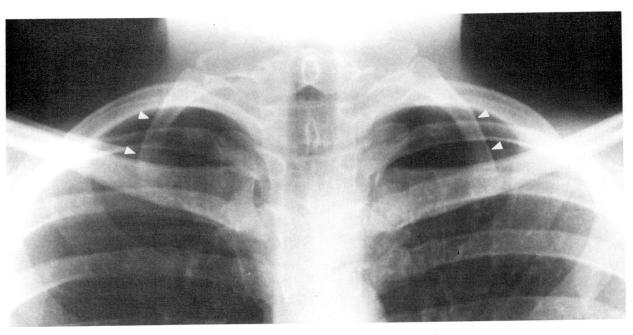

Figure 3-1   Bilateral cervical ribs *(arrowheads).*

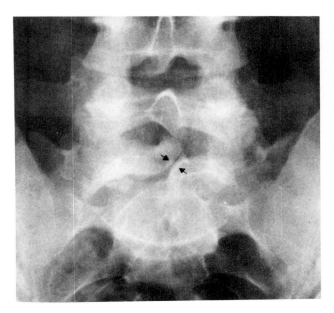

Figure 3-2 Spina bifida occulta *(arrows)*.

malities and may lead to a variety of muscular abnormalities and lack of bladder or bowel control. In many cases a slight dimpling of the skin or tuft of hair over the vertebral defect indicates the site of the lesion.

Large defects in the lumbar or cervical spine may be accompanied by herniation of the meninges **(meningocele)** or of the meninges and a portion of the spinal cord or nerve roots **(myelomeningocele).** Almost all patients with myelomeningocele have the Chiari II malformation, with caudal displacement of posterior fossa structures into the cervical canal. Hydrocephalus is a frequent complication. These lesions are associated with large bony defects, absence of the laminae, and increased interpedicular distance (Figure 3-3). The herniated spinal contents are seen as a soft-tissue mass posterior to the spine. Myelography, CT, or MRI can demonstrate the presence of the spinal cord or nerve roots within the herniated sac. Prenatal real-time ultrasound can now demonstrate this serious malformation in utero.

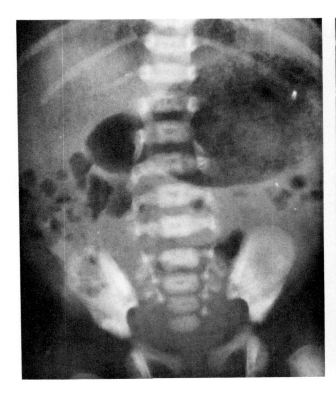
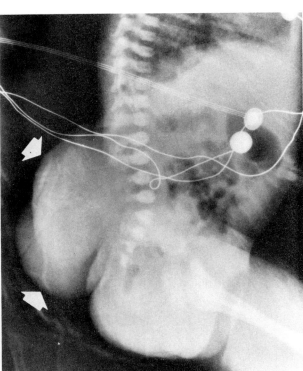

Figure 3-3 Meningomyelocele. **A,** Frontal projection of abdomen shows greatly increased interpedicular distance of lumbar vertebrae. **B,** In another patient, lateral projection demonstrates large soft-tissue mass *(arrows)* situated posterior to spine. Notice absence of posterior elements in lower lumbar and sacral regions.

A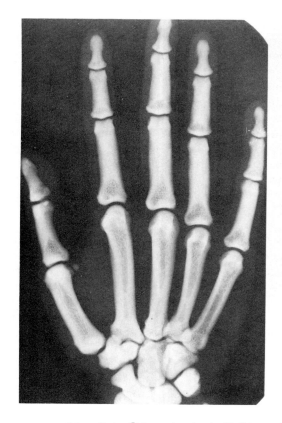

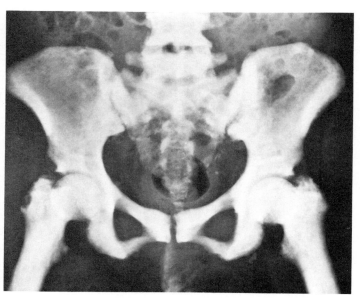 B

Figure 3-4   Osteopetrosis. **A,** Striking sclerosis of bones of hand and wrist. **B,** Generalized increased density of lower spine, pelvis, and hips.

A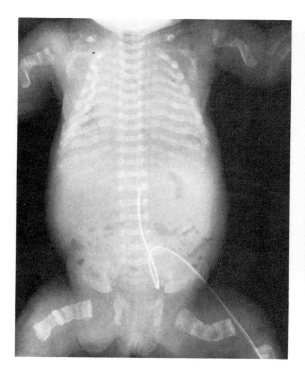

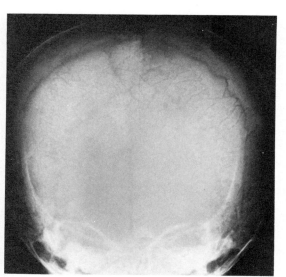 B

Figure 3-5   Osteogenesis imperfecta. **A,** Generalized flattening of verebral bodies associated with fractures of multiple ribs and long bones in infant. **B,** Multiple wormian bones.

Osteopetrosis

Osteopetrosis (marble bones) is a rare hereditary bone dysplasia in which failure of the resorptive mechanism of calcified cartilage interferes with its normal replacement by mature bone. This results in a symmetric, generalized increase in bone density (Figure 3-4). Osteopetrosis varies in severity and age of clinical presentation from a fulminant, often fatal condition involving the entire skeleton at birth or in utero to an essentially asymptomatic form that is an incidental radiographic finding.

Osteogenesis imperfecta

Osteogenesis imperfecta is an inherited generalized disorder of connective tissue characterized by multiple fractures and an unusual blue color of the normally white sclera of the eye. Patients with this condition suffer repeated fractures caused by the severe osteoporosis and the thin, defective cortices (Figure 3-5, *A*). The fractures often heal with exuberant callus formation (often so extensive as to simulate a malignant tumor) and may cause bizarre deformities. Ossification of the skull progresses slowly, leaving wide sutures and multiple juxtasutural accessory bones within a suture (wormian bones), which produce a mosaic appearance (Figure 3-5, *B*).

Achondroplasia

Achondroplasia is the most common form of dwarfism that results from diminished proliferation of cartilage in the growth plate (decreased enchondral bone formation). Because membranous bone formation is not affected, the individual has short limbs, which contrast with the nearly normal length of the trunk. Other characteristic physical features include a large head with frontal bulging, saddle nose, a prognathous (jutting) jaw, and prominent buttocks that give the false impression of lumbar lordosis. Typical radiographic findings include progressive narrowing of the interpedicular distances from above downward, the opposite of normal, and scalloping of the posterior margins of the lumbar vertebral bodies (Figure 3-6).

▪ Metabolic Bone Disease

Osteoporosis

Osteoporosis is a generalized or localized deficiency of bone matrix in which the mass of bone per unit volume is decreased in amount but normal in composition. Bone is a living, constantly changing tissue, and normally there is a balance between the amount of old bone being removed and the amount of new

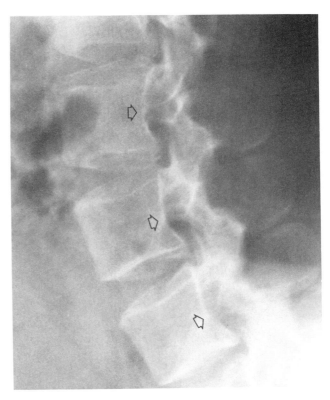

Figure 3-6   Achondroplasia. Posterior scalloping of multiple vertebral bodies *(arrows).*

bone replacing it. Osteoporosis is usually caused by accelerated resorption of bone, though decreased bone formation may lead to osteoporosis in such entities as Cushing's syndrome, prolonged steroid administration, and disuse or immobilization osteoporosis as in a casted extremity (Figure 3-7). Loss of mineral salts causes osteoporotic bone to become more lucent than normal. This may be difficult to detect, since about 30% of the bone density must be lost before it can be demonstrated as a lucent area on routine radiographs. In patients with osteoporosis it is essential to use the lowest practical kVp. This technique provides the extremely short scale of contrast necessary to visualize the demineralized osteoporotic bones.

The major causes of generalized osteoporosis are aging and postmenopausal hormonal changes. As a person ages, the bones lose density and become more brittle, fracturing more easily and healing more slowly. Many elderly persons also are less active and have poor diets that are deficient in protein. In postmenopausal osteoporosis there is a deficiency in the gonadal hormonal levels and decreased bone formation.

Regardless of the cause, the radiographic appearance is somewhat similar in all conditions producing

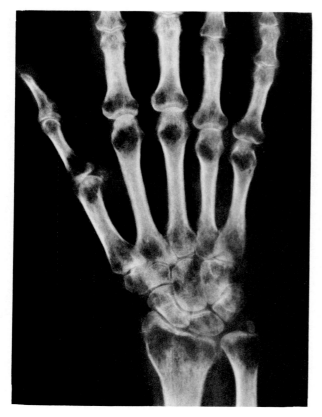

Figure 3-7   Disuse osteoporosis. Severe periarticular demineralization after prolonged immobilizaton of extremity.

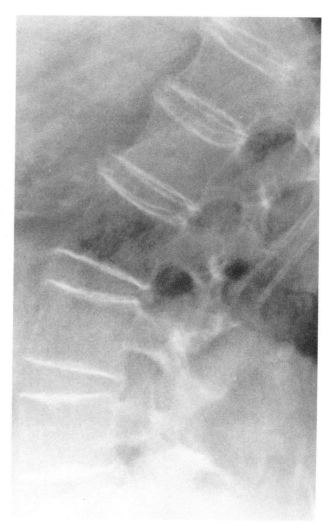

Figure 3-8   Osteoporosis of aging. Generalized demineralization of spine in postmenopausal woman. Cortex appears as thin line that is relatively dense and prominent (picture-frame pattern).

osteoporosis. The most striking change is cortical thinning with irregularity and resorption of the endosteal (inner) surfaces (Figure 3-8). These findings are most evident in the spine and pelvis. As the bone density of a vertebral body decreases, the cortex appears as a thin line that is relatively dense and prominent, producing the typical picture-frame pattern. Because of the severe loss of bone density, anterior wedging or compression fractures of one or more vertebral bodies may result, most commonly in the middle and lower thoracic and upper lumbar areas. The intervertebral disk may expand into the weakened vertebral bodies and produce characteristic concave contours of the superior and inferior disk surfaces. In the skull, the calvarium may show a spotty loss of density, and there is commonly deossification (bone loss) of the floor of the sella turcica and dorsum sellae.

Osteomalacia

Osteomalacia refers to insufficient mineralization of the adult skeleton. There is normally a balance between osteoid formation and mineralization. Os-

teomalacia is the result of either excessive osteoid formation or, more frequently, insufficient mineralization. Proper calcification of osteoid requires that adequate amounts of calcium and phosphorus be available at the mineralization sites. Failure of calcium and phosphorus deposition in bone matrix in osteomalacia may be attributable to an inadequate intake or failure of absorption of calcium, phosphorus, or vitamin D, which is necessary for intestinal absorption of calcium and phosphorus and may have a direct effect on bone. At times, the level of vitamin D is sufficient but the material is not used because of resistance to the action of the vitamin at end organs, such as the kidneys. Other nonnutritional causes of osteomalacia include chronic kidney failure and certain renal diseases in which calcium is lost in the urine and bone is broken down in an attempt to maintain a normal calcium level in the blood.

Regardless of the cause, osteomalacia appears radiographically as a loss of bone density because of the presence of nonmineralized osteoid. Although the cortex is thinned, it may stand out more prominently than normal because of the uniform deossification of medullary bone (Figure 3-9). In contrast to osteoporosis, the cortical borders in osteomalacia are often indistinct. Fine-detail radiographs of the hands in patients with osteomalacia often demonstrate intracortical lines caused by local resorption or lack of mineralization, a finding not seen in osteoporosis.

Bones that are softened by osteomalacia may bend or give way as a result of weight-bearing. Bowing deformities primarily involve the pelvis, vertebral column, thorax, and proximal extremities. In the pelvis, there may be characteristic inward bending of the sidewalls with deepening of the acetabular cavities (protrusio acetabuli) (Figure 3-10).

Rickets

Rickets is a systemic disease of infancy and childhood that is the equivalent of osteomalacia in the

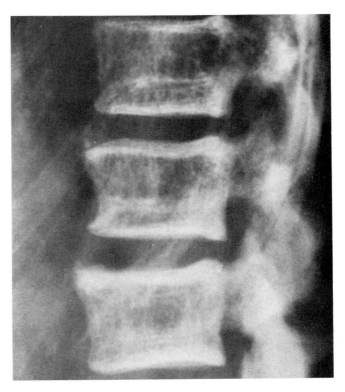

Figure 3-9 Osteomalacia. Striking prominence of cortices of vertebral bodies with increased trabeculation of spongy bone.

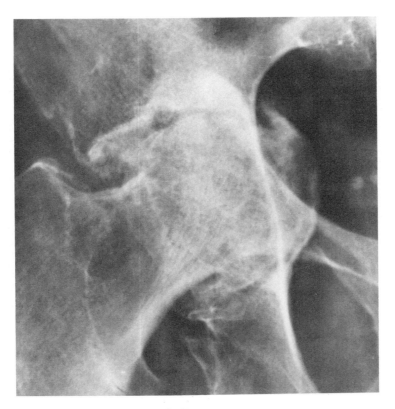

Figure 3-10 Protrusio acetabuli.

mature skeleton. In this condition, calcification of growing skeletal elements is defective because of a deficiency of vitamin D in the diet or a lack of exposure to ultraviolet radiation (sunshine), which converts the sterols in the skin into vitamin D. Rickets is most common in premature infants and usually develops between the ages of 6 months and 1 year.

The early radiographic changes in rickets are best seen in the fastest growing portions of bone, such as the sternal ends of the ribs, proximal ends of the tibia and humerus, and distal ends of the radius and ulna. An overgrowth of noncalcified osteoid tissue appears radiographically as a characteristic increased distance between the ossified portion of the epiphysis and the end of the shaft. In response to the pull of muscular and ligamentous attachments, the metaphyseal ends of the bone become cupped and frayed, and the normally sharp metaphyseal lines disappear (Figure 3-11). Lack of calcification leads to a delayed appearance of the epiphyseal ossification centers. Because of poor mineralization, bowing of weight-bearing bones (especially the tibia) develops once the infant begins to stand or walk. Extensive osteoid tissue in the sternal ends of the ribs produces a characteristic beading (rachitic rosary).

Softening of the vertebral bodies leads to the development of kyphosis. In females, narrowing of the pelvic inlet may make normal delivery impossible in later life.

Gout

Gout is a disorder of purine metabolism (a component of nucleic acids) in which an increase in the blood levels of uric acid leads to the deposition of uric acid crystals in the joints, cartilage, and kidney. Several inherited enzyme defects can cause overproduction of uric acid (primary gout). In secondary gout, hyperuricemia can be caused by an overproduction of uric acid because of increased turnover of nucleic acids (metastatic carcinoma, myeloma, hemolytic anemia), drugs (chemotherapy, thiazides used to treat hypertension), or a decrease in the excretion of uric acid because of kidney failure.

The primary manifestation of acute gout is an exquisitely painful arthritis that initially attacks a single joint, primarily the first metatarsophalangeal joint. Radiographic changes develop late in the disease and only after repeated attacks. Therefore negative radiographs do not exclude gout and thus are of no help in early diagnostic evaluation.

A 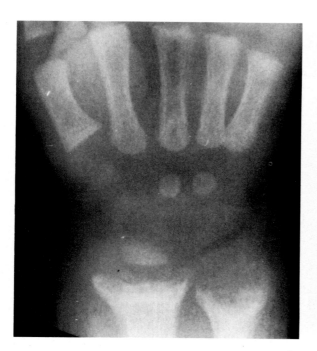 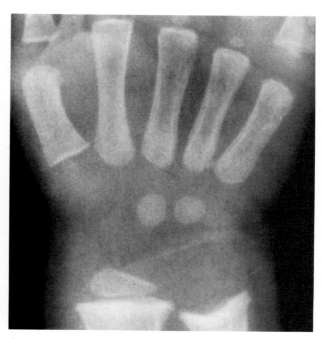 B

Figure 3-11 Rickets. **A,** Initial film of wrist shows characteristic cupping and fraying of metaphyseal ends of radius and ulna, with disappearance of normally sharp metaphyseal lines. **B,** After therapy with vitamin D, there is remineralization of metaphyseal ends of radius and ulna, increased sharpness of metaphyseal lines, and return of epiphyseal centers to normal density and sharpness of outline.

Deposition of nonopaque urate crystals in the joint synovial membrane and on the surface of articular cartilage incites an inflammatory reaction that produces the earliest radiographic signs of joint effusion and periarticular swelling (Figure 3-12). Clumps of urate crystals (tophi) form along the margins of the articular cortex and erode the underlying bone, producing small, sharply marginated, punched-out defects at the joint margins of the small bones of the hand and foot. These erosions often have the appearance of cystlike lesions with thin sclerotic margins and characteristic overhanging edges ("rat bite") (Figure 3-13). In advanced disease, severe destructive lesions are associated with joint space narrowing and even fibrous ankylosis. Because patients are relatively free of symptoms between acute exacerbations of the disease, the bone density remains relatively normal, and diffuse osteoporosis is not part of the radiographic appearance.

Continued deposition of urate crystals in the periarticular tissues causes the development of characteristic large, lumpy soft-tissue swellings representing gouty tophi. In addition to the first metatarsophalangeal joints, other common sites of tophi

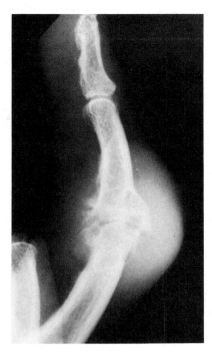

Figure 3-12 Gout. Severe joint effusion and periarticular swelling of proximal interphalangeal joint of finger. Notice associated erosion of articular cartilage.

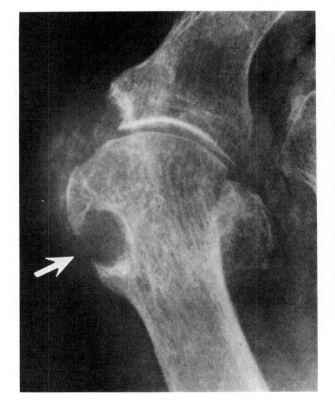

A

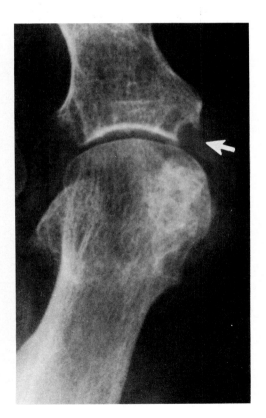

B

Figure 3-13 Two examples of typical rat-bite erosions about first metatarsophalangeal joint *(arrows)*. Cystlike lesions have thin sclerotic margins and characteristic overhanging edges.

include the ear, the olecranon bursa, and the insertion of the Achilles tendon. Tophi consisting only of sodium urate are of soft-tissue density. Deposition of calcium in these urate collections causes the tophaceous periarticular masses to become radiopaque (Figure 3-14).

Although some renal dysfunction occurs in almost all patients with gouty arthritis, no radiographic abnormalities in the urinary tract can be demonstrated unless uric acid stones are formed. Pure uric acid stones are not radiopaque and can only be demonstrated on excretory urograms, where they appear as filling defects in the pelvocalyceal system or ureter. Stones containing the calcium salts of uric acid are radiopaque and can be detected on plain abdominal radiographs.

Paget's disease

Paget's disease (osteitis deformans) is one of the most common chronic diseases of the skeleton. Destruction of bone followed by a reparative process results in weakened, deformed, and thickened bony structures that tend to fracture easily. The disease is seen most commonly during middle life, affects men twice as often as women, and has been reported to occur in about 3% of all persons older than 40 years of age. Although the destructive phase often predominates initially, there is most frequently a combination of destruction and repair; in the pelvis and weight-bearing bones of the lower extremities, the reparative process may begin early and be the prominent feature. Often involving multiple bones, Paget's disease particularly affects the pelvis, femurs, skull, tibias, vertebrae, clavicles, and ribs.

In the skull, Paget's disease begins as an area of sharply demarcated radiolucency (osteoporosis circumscripta) that represents the destructive phase of the disease (Figure 3-15, *A*). During the reparative

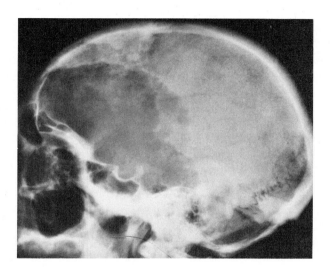

A

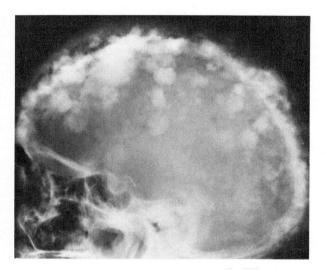

B

Figure 3-15 Paget's disease of skull. **A,** Radiograph obtained during destructive phase of disease demonstrates area of sharply demarcated radiolucency (osteoporosis circumscripta) that primarily involves frontal portion of calvarium. **B,** During reparative phase in another patient, irregular areas of sclerosis produce characteristic cotton-wool appearance of skull.

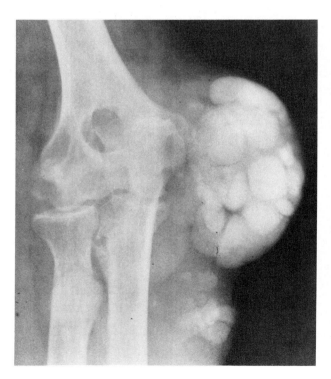

Figure 3-14 Gout. Massive deposition of calcium in long-standing tophaceous lesion about elbow.

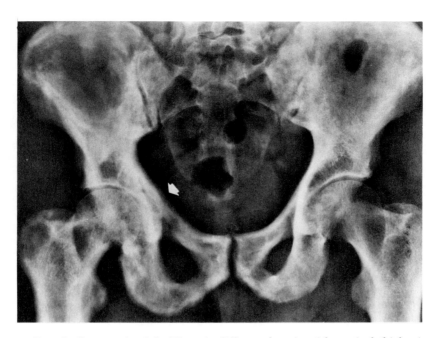

Figure 3-16   Paget's disease of pelvis. There is diffuse sclerosis with cortical thickening involving right femur and both iliac bones. Notice characteristic thickening and coarsening of iliopectineal line *(arrow)* on involved right side.

process, the development of irregular islands of sclerosis and cortical thickening results in a mottled, cotton wool appearance (Figure 3-15, *B*). In the spine, Paget's disease characteristically causes enlargement of the vertebral body. Increased trabeculation, which is most prominent at the periphery of the bone, produces a rim of thickened cortex and a picture-frame appearance. Uniform dense sclerosis of one or more vertebral bodies (ivory vertebrae) may occur.

The pelvis is the most common and often the initial site of Paget's disease. A distinctive early sign is coarsening of the trabeculae along the iliac margins, which produces thickening of the pelvic brim (Figure 3-16).

In the long bones, the destructive phase almost invariably begins at one end of the bone and extends along the shaft for a variable distance before ending in a typical sharply demarcated, V-shaped configuration (blade of grass appearance). In the reparative stage the bone is enlarged, with an irregularly widened cortex and coarse, thickened trabeculae (Figure 3-17). Although dense, the bones are soft, and deformities are common.

Paget's disease may lead to severe clinical complications. The downward thrust of the heavy head on the softened bone of the spine may compress the brainstem and cause numerous cranial nerve deficits. Expansion and distortion of softened vertebral bodies, sometimes with pathologic fractures, may

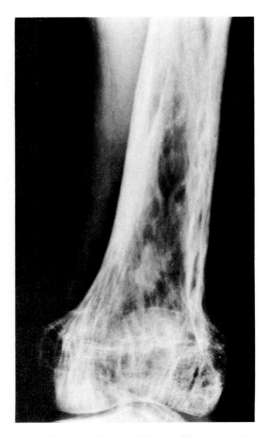

Figure 3-17   Paget's disease of knee. Characteristic cortical thickening, destruction of fine trabeculae, and accentuation of secondary trabeculae.

compress the spinal cord and produce nerve root deficits. Multiple microscopic arteriovenous malformations in pagetoid bone may result in high-output cardiac failure. The most serious complication of Paget's disease is the development of osteosarcoma, which fortunately occurs in less than 1% of patients with this condition.

■ Benign Bone Tumors

Osteochondroma (exostosis) is a benign projection of bone with a cartilaginous cap that arises in childhood or the teens, especially about the knee. The cortex of an osteochondroma blends with that of normal bone, and the long axis of the tumor characteristically is parallel to the parent bone and points away from the nearest joint (Figure 3-18).

Enchondromas are slow-growing benign cartilaginous tumors arising in the medullary canal. They are most frequently found in children and young adults and primarily involve the small bones of the hands and feet. Enchondromas are slow growing and often multiple. As the well-demarcated tumor grows, it expands bone locally, causing thinning and endosteal scalloping of the cortex that

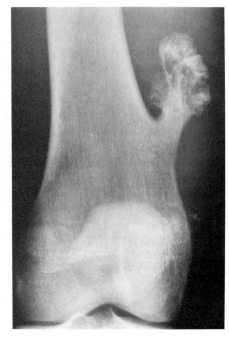

Figure 3-18   Osteochondroma. Long axis of tumor is parallel to that of femur and points away from knee joint.

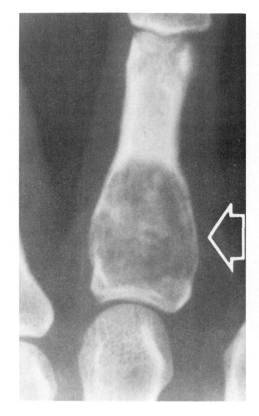

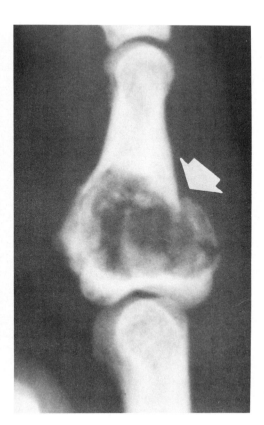

Figure 3-19   Enchondroma. **A,** Well-demarcated tumor *(arrow)* expands bone and thins cortex. **B,** Pathologic fracture *(arrow)*.

often leads to a pathologic fracture with minimal trauma (Figure 3-19). A characteristic finding of enchondroma is calcifications within the lucent matrix.

Giant cell tumor typically arises at the end of the distal femur or proximal tibia of a young adult after epiphyseal closure. It begins as an eccentric lucent lesion in the metaphysis and characteristically extends to the immediate subarticular cortex of the bone but does not involve the joint (Figure 3-20). As the tumor expands toward the shaft, it produces the characteristic radiographic appearance of multiple large bubbles separated by thin strips of bone.

Osteomas most often arise in the outer table of the skull, the paranasal sinuses (especially frontal and ethmoid), and the mandible. They appear radiograhically as well-circumscribed, extremely dense round lesions that are rarely larger than 2 cm in diameter (Figure 3-21).

Osteoid osteoma usually develops in teenagers or young adults and produces the classic clinical symptom of local pain that is worse at night and is dramatically relieved by aspirin. Most osteoid osteomas occur in the femur and tibia. The tumor typically is seen as a small, round or oval, lucent center

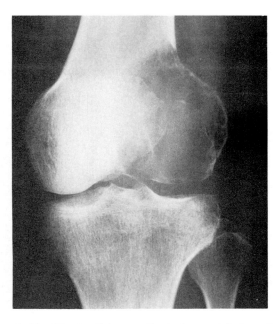

Figure 3-20 Giant cell tumor. Typical eccentric lucent lesion in distal femoral metaphysis extends to immediate subarticular cortex. Surrounding cortex, though thinned, remains intact.

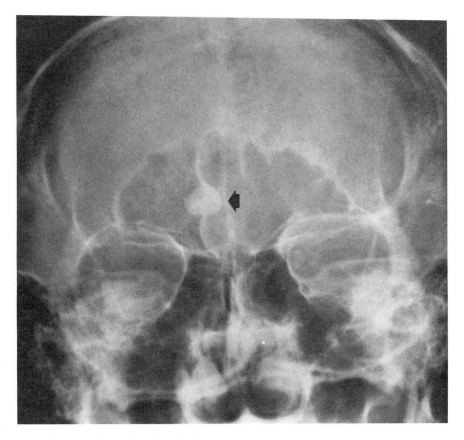

Figure 3-21 Osteoma *(arrow)* in frontal sinus.

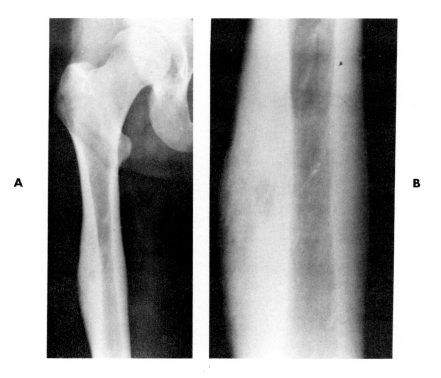

Figure 3-22 Osteoid osteoma. **A,** Full and, **B,** coned projections of midshaft of femur demonstrate dense sclerotic zone of cortical thickening laterally, which contains small oval lucent nidus *(arrowhead).*

(nidus), less than 1 cm in diameter, that is surrounded by a large, dense sclerotic zone of cortical thickening (Figure 3-22). Because this dense reaction may obscure the nidus on conventional radiographs, overpenetrated films or tomography (conventional or computed) may be necessary for its demonstration. Surgical excision of the nidus is essential for cure; it is not necessary to remove the reactive calcification, even though it may form the major part of the lesion.

A **simple bone cyst** is a true fluid-filled cyst with a wall of fibrous tissue. Although not a true neoplasm, a simple bone cyst may resemble one radiographically and clinically. Solitary bone cysts are asymptomatic and are discovered either incidentally or after pathologic fracture. It appears as an expansile lucent lesion that is sharply demarcated from adjacent normal bone and may have a thin rim of sclerosis around it. A simple bone cyst has an oval configuration, with its long axis parallel to that of the host bone (Figure 3-23).

An **aneurysmal bone cyst,** rather than being a true neoplasm or cyst, consists of numerous blood-filled arteriovenous communications. In long bones, an aneurysmal bone cyst is an expansile, eccentric, cystlike lesion that causes pronounced ballooning of the thinned cortex (Figure 3-24). At times, the cortex

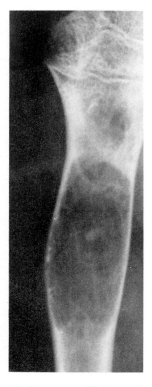

Figure 3-23 Simple bone cyst. This cyst in proximal humerus has oval configuration, with its long axis parallel to that of host bone.

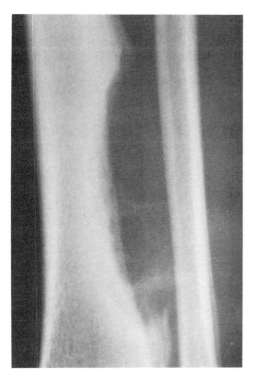

Figure 3-24 Aneurysmal bone cyst. Expansile, eccentric, cystic lesion of tibia with multiple fine internal septa. Because severely thinned cortex is difficult to detect, tumor resembles malignant process.

may be so thin that it is invisible on plain radiographs, and thus this benign lesion may be mistaken for a malignant bone tumor.

Bone islands are solitary, sharply demarcated areas of dense compact bone that occur most commonly in the pelvis and upper femurs but may be seen in every bone except the skull (Figure 3-25). Although almost half the bone islands enlarge over a period of years and many show activity on radionuclide scans, bone islands are asymptomatic and completely benign and must be distinguished from osteoblastic metastases.

▪ Malignant Bone Tumors

Osteogenic sarcoma generally occurs in the end of a long bone (especially about the knee). Most osteogenic sarcomas arise in persons between 10 and 25 years of age, though a smaller peak incidence is seen in older age groups in whom the tumor is superimposed on a preexisting bone disorder, particularly Paget's disease. The usual initial complaints are local pain and swelling, sometimes followed by fever, weight loss, and secondary anemia. Pulmonary metastases develop early, and a plain chest radiograph should be obtained to exclude this unfavorable

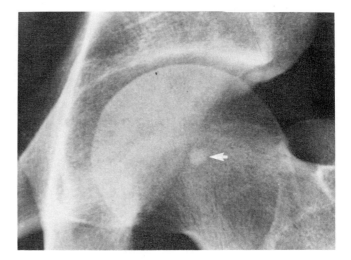

Figure 3-25 Bone island *(arrow)* in femoral head.

prognostic sign. If no metastases to the lung are detected by this modality, CT should be performed.

The typical radiographic appearance of osteogenic sarcoma is a mixed destructive and sclerotic lesion associated with a soft-tissue mass, irregular periosteal reaction, and reactive new bone formation (Figure 3-26, *A*). In the classic sunburst pattern, horizontal bony spicules extend in radiating fashion into the soft-tissue mass (Figure 3-26, *B*). A characteristic finding is elevation of the periosteum at the periphery of a lesion with subsequent new bone formation (Codman's triangle) (Figure 3-27).

Chondrosarcoma is a malignant tumor of cartilaginous origin that may originate anew or within a preexisting cartilaginous lesion (osteochondroma, enchondroma). The tumor is about half as common as osteogenic sarcoma, develops at a later age (half the patients are older than 40 years of age), grows more slowly, and metastasizes later. In addition to the bone destruction seen with all malignant tumors, chondrosarcoma often contains punctate or amorphous calcification within its cartilaginous matrix (Figure 3-28).

Ewing's sarcoma is a primary malignant tumor arising in the bone marrow. A tumor of children and young adults, Ewing's sarcoma has a peak incidence in the midteens and is rare over 30 years of age. The major clinical complaint is local pain, often of several months' duration, that persistently increases in severity and may be associated with a tender soft-tissue mass. Patients with this tumor characteristically have malaise and appear sick, often with fever and leukocytosis, suggestive of osteomyelitis. The classic radiographic appearance of Ewing's sarcoma is an ill-defined permeative area of bone destruction that involves a large central portion of the shaft of a

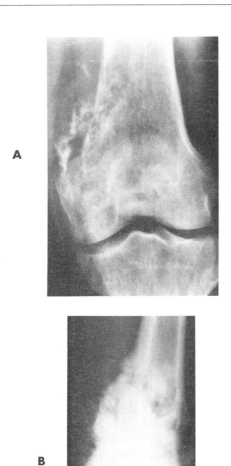

A

B

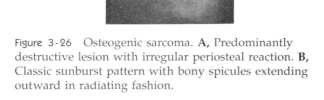

Figure 3-26   Osteogenic sarcoma. **A,** Predominantly destructive lesion with irregular periosteal reaction. **B,** Classic sunburst pattern with bony spicules extending outward in radiating fashion.

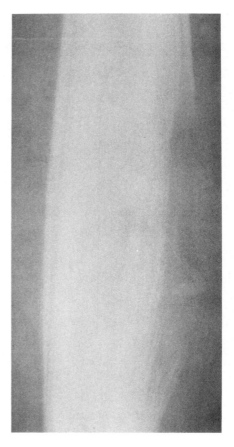

Figure 3-27   Codman's triangle. Thin periosteal elevation and subsequent new bone formation at periphery of this neoplastic lesion.

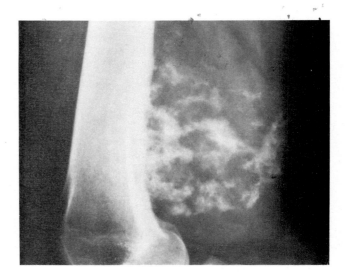

Figure 3-28   Chondrosarcoma. Prominent dense calcification in large neoplastic mass.

long bone and is associated with a fusiform layered periosteal reaction parallel to the shaft (Figure 3-29).

Multiple myeloma is a disseminated (widespread) malignancy of plasma cells that may be associated with bone destruction, bone marrow failure, hypercalcemia, renal failure, and recurrent infections. The disease primarily affects persons between 40 and 70 years of age. Typical laboratory findings include an abnormal spike of monoclonal immunoglobulin and the presence of Bence Jones protein in the urine. The classic radiographic appearance of multiple myeloma is multiple punched-out osteolytic lesions scattered throughout the skeletal system and best seen on lateral views of the skull (Figures 3-30 and 3-31). Because the bone destruction is attributable to the proliferation of plasma cells distributed throughout the bone marrow, the flat bones containing red marrow (vertebrae, skull, ribs, pelvis) are primarily affected. The appearance may be indistinguishable from that of a metastatic carcinoma, though the lytic defects in multiple myeloma tend to be more discrete and uniform in size. Extensive plasma cell proliferation in the bone marrow with no tendency to form discrete tumor masses may produce generalized skeletal deossifications simulating postmenopausal osteoporosis. In the spine, decreased bone density and destructive changes in multiple myeloma are usually limited to the vertebral bodies, sparing the pedicles (lacking red marrow) that are frequently destroyed by metastatic disease. The severe loss of bone substance in the spine often results in multiple vertebral compression fractures (Figure 3-32). Because multiple myeloma causes little or no stimulation of new bone formation, radionuclide bone scans may be normal even with extensive skeletal infiltration.

CT and MRI can precisely define the location of a malignant bone tumor, as well as its extension into the medullary cavity and spread to surrounding structures (Figures 3-33 and 3-34).

■ Bone Metastases

Metastases are the most common malignant bone tumors, spreading by means of the bloodstream or

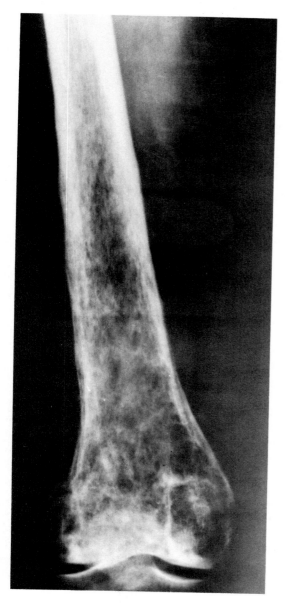

Figure 3-29 Ewing's sarcoma. Diffuse permeative destruction with mild periosteal response involving distal half of femur.

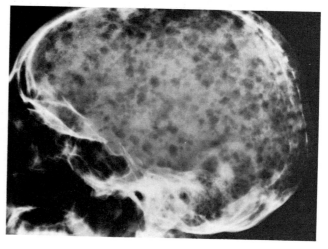

Figure 3-30 Multiple myeloma. Diffuse punched-out osteolytic lesions scattered throughout skull.

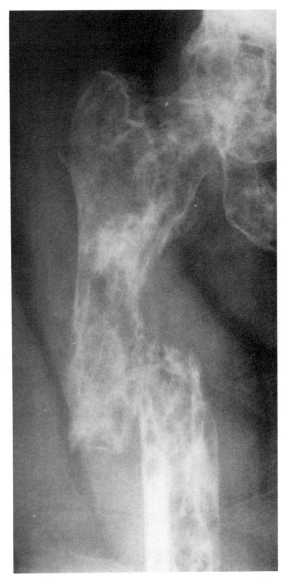

Figure 3-31 Diffuse destructive bone lesion that has led to pathologic fracture of femur.

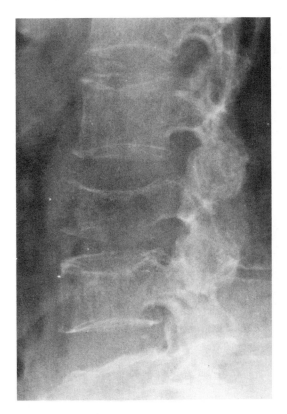

Figure 3-32 Multiple myeloma. Diffuse myelomatous infiltration causes generalized demineralization of vertebral bodies and compression fracture of L2.

lymphatic vessels or by direct extension. The most common primary tumors are carcinomas of the breast, lung, prostate, kidney, and thyroid. Favorite sites of metastatic spread are bones containing red marrow, such as the spine, pelvis, ribs, skull, and the upper ends of the humerus and femur. Metastases distal to the knees and elbows are infrequent but do occur, especially with bronchogenic (lung) tumors.

The detection of skeletal metastases is critical in the management of patients with known or suspected neoplastic disease, both at the time of initial staging and during the period of continuing followup care. The presence of metastases may exclude

some patients from the radical "curative" therapy that is offered to those without disseminated (widespread) disease, thus sparing them from fruitless, high-morbidity procedures for a nonremediable condition. The best screening examination for the detection of asymptomatic skeletal metastases is the radionuclide bone scan (Figure 3-35), which is unquestionably more sensitive than the radiographic "skeletal survey." Because almost half the mineral content of a bone must be lost before the loss is detectable on plain radiographs, the skeletal survey should be abandoned as a general screening examination for the detection of asymptomatic skeletal metastases. The only false-negative bone scans occur with aggressively osteolytic lesions, especially in patients with multiple myeloma. The role of plain radiographs in screening for metastases is to further evaluate focal abnormalities detected on radionuclide scanning, since a variety of lesions (e.g., infections, benign tumors, fibrous dysplasia, bone islands) can also give positive bone scans. Because the presence of multiple focal abnormalities is typical of metastatic disease, it is only necessary to radiographically examine a single lesion or area to con-

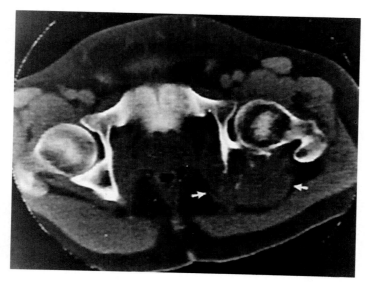

Figure 3-33 CT of osteogenic sarcoma. Scan through level of femoral heads shows destruction of left ischium that was seen on plain radiographs. In addition, CT scan demonstrates large soft-tissue mass *(arrows)* in area covered by gluteus maximus muscle and separated from rectum. Mass was not clinically palpable. (From deSantos LA, Bernardino ME, and Murray JA: *AJR* 132:535-540, 1979.)

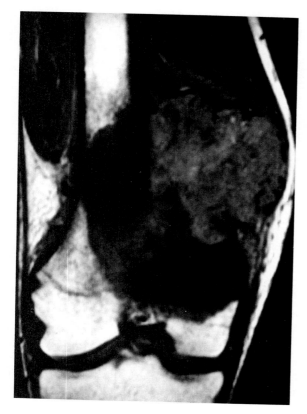

Figure 3-34 Magnetic resonance image of osteogenic sarcoma. Coronal image shows the intramedullary and soft-tissue extent of the mass. (From Stark DD, Bradley WG Jr: *Magnetic resonance imaging,* ed 2, St Louis, 1991, Mosby.)

firm the diagnosis. In addition, because of the occasional false-negative bone scan, it is imperative that all *symptomatic* sites in patients with neoplastic disease be examined by plain radiographs unless the radionuclide bone scan unequivocally demonstrates diffuse metastatic disease.

Metastatic disease may produce a broad spectrum of radiographic appearances. Osteolytic metastases cause destruction without accompanying bone proliferation. They develop from tumor embolic deposits in the medullary canal and eventually extend to destroy cortical bone. The margins of the lucent lesions are irregular and poorly defined, rarely sharp and smooth. The most common primary lesions causing osteolytic metastases are carcinomas of the breast, kidney, and thyroid. Metastases from carcinomas of the kidney and thyroid typically produce a single large metastatic focus that may appear as an expansile trabeculated lesion ("blow-out") (Figure 3-36). Metastases from breast carcinoma are most often multiple when first detected.

In the spine, osteolytic metastases tend to involve not only the vertebral bodies but also the pedicles and posterior arches. Destruction of one or more pedicles may be the earliest sign of metastatic disease and may help in differentiating this process from multiple myeloma, in which the pedicles are much less often involved. Because cartilage is resistant to invasion by metastases, preservation of the intervertebral disk space may help to distinguish metastases from an inflammatory process. Pathologic

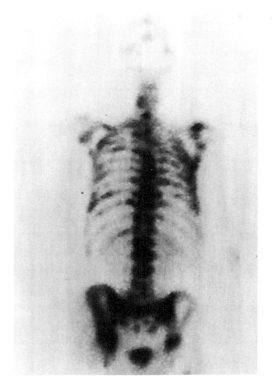

Figure 3-35   Screening radionuclide bone scan. Multiple focal areas of radionuclide uptake in axial skeleton, representing metastases from prostate carcinoma.

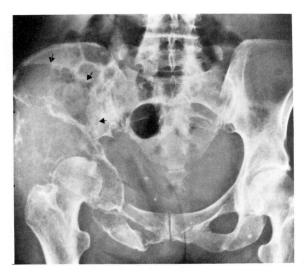

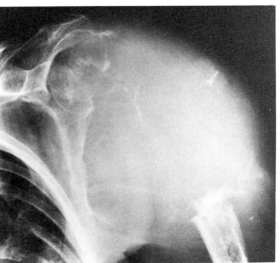

Figure 3-36   Blow-out metastases. **A,** Lytic expansile destruction of left ilium *(arrows)* in metastatic thyroid carcinoma. **B,** Osteolytic metastasis to humerus from carcinoma of kidney.

collapse of vertebral bodies frequently occurs in advanced disease.

Osteoblastic metastases are generally considered evidence of slow growth in a neoplasm that has allowed time for a proliferation of reactive bone. In men, osteoblastic metastases are usually a result of carcinoma of the prostate gland; carcinoma of the breast is the most common primary site of osteoblastic metastases in women. These lesions initially appear as ill-defined areas of increased density that may progress to complete loss of normal bony architecture. They may vary from small, isolated round foci of sclerotic density to a diffuse sclerosis involving most or all of a bone (Figure 3-37). In the spine, this may produce the characteristic uniform density of an "ivory" vertebral body (Figure 3-38).

The combination of destruction and sclerosis in the mixed type of metastasis causes the affected bone to have a mottled appearance, with intermixed areas of lucency and increased density.

Bone destruction by metastases and associated extension of tumor in the adjacent soft tissues can be well demonstrated by CT and MRI (Figure 3-39).

▪ Arthritis

Rheumatoid arthritis

Rheumatoid arthritis is a chronic systemic disease of unknown cause that primarily is seen as a nonsuppurative (noninfectious) inflammatory arthritis of the small joints of the hands and feet. Women are affected about three times more frequently than men, and the average age of onset in adults is 40 years. Rheumatoid arthritis usually has an insidious origin and may either run a protracted and progressive course, leading to a crippling deformity of affected joints, or undergo spontaneous remissions

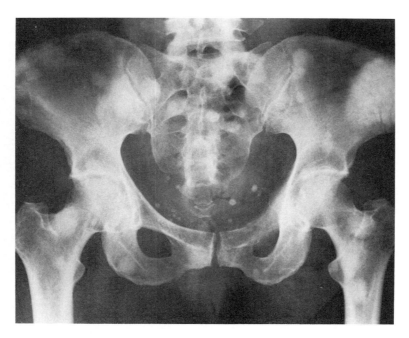

Figure 3-37   Osteoblastic metastases. Multiple areas of increased density involving pelvis and proximal femurs representing metastases from carcinoma of urinary bladder.

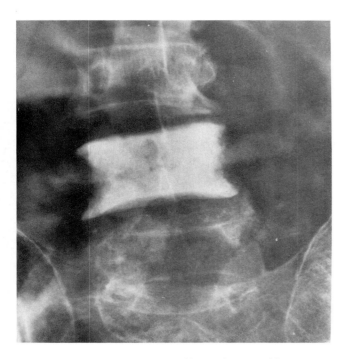

Figure 3-38   Ivory vertebra. Diffuse sclerosis of L4 vertebral body from metastatic carcinoma of prostate.

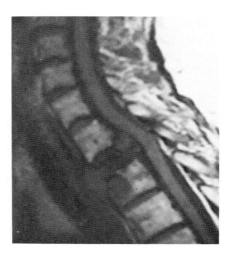

Figure 3-39   Magnetic resonance image of metastases. Sagittal scan shows gross metastatic destruction and replacement of the body of T2, which has collapsed. The metastasis has a lower signal than that of vertebral marrow or the spinal cord. The spinal cord is focally indented and displaced posteriorly by the tumor. There is also a low-signal-intensity lytic metastasis involving the anterior portion of T3. (From Stark DD, Bradley, WG Jr: *Magnetic resonance imaging*, ed 2, St Lous, 1991, Mosby.)

of variable length. There is usually symmetric involvement of multiple joints, and the disease often progresses proximally toward the trunk until practically every joint in the body is involved.

Rheumatoid arthritis begins as an inflammation of the synovial membrane that lines the joints. The resulting mass of thickened granulation tissue (pannus) causes erosion of the articular cartilage and underlying bony cortex, fibrous scarring, and even the development of ankylosis (bony fusion across a joint). A combination of fusion of joint surfaces combined with inflammatory laxity of ligaments leads to the development of crippling deformities in the end stage of the disease (Figure 3-40).

The earliest radiographic evidence of rheumatoid arthritis is fusiform periarticular soft-tissue swelling caused by joint effusion and hyperplastic synovial inflammation. Disuse and local hyperemia (increased blood flow) lead to periarticular osteoporosis that initially is confined to the portion of bone adjacent to the joint but may extend to involve the entire bone (Figure 3-41). Extension of the pannus from the synovial reflections onto the bone causes characteristic small foci of destruction at the edges of the joint, where articular cartilage is absent. These typical marginal erosions have poorly defined edges without a sclerotic rim and sometimes may be seen only on oblique or magnification views. Destruction of articular cartilage causes narrowing of the joint space. The laying down of bony trabeculae across a narrow joint space may completely obliterate the joint cavity and produce solid bony ankylosis, which most frequently involves the bones of the wrist.

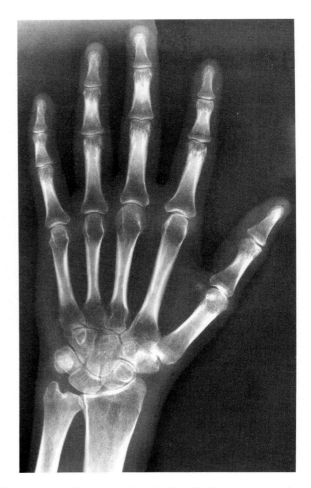

Figure 3-41 Rheumatoid arthritis. Striking periarticular osteoporosis. (From Brown JC, Forrester DM: Arthritis. In Eisenberg RL, Amberg JR, editors: *Critical diagnostic pathways in radiology*, Philadelphia, JB Lippincott, 1981.)

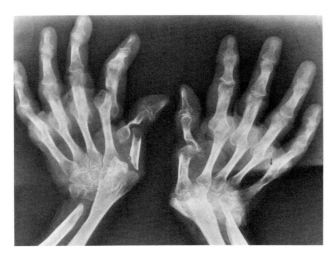

Figure 3-40 Multilating rheumatoid arthritis. Severe, bilaterally symmetric destructive changes of hands and wrists with striking subluxations.

Ligamentous involvement produces a variety of contractures and subluxations and the common ulnar deviation of the hands. In the cervical spine, rheumatoid arthritis characteristically produces atlantoaxial subluxation (Figure 3-42), an increased distance between the anterior border of the odontoid and the superior border of the anterior arch of the atlas (normally less than 2.5 mm), which is caused by weakening of the transverse ligaments from synovial inflammation.

Rheumatoid nodules are soft-tissue masses that usually appear over the extensor surfaces on the ulnar aspect of the wrist or the olecranon but occasionally are seen over other body prominences, tendons, or pressure points. These characteristic nodules are seen in no other disease and develop in about 20% of patients with rheumatoid arthritis.

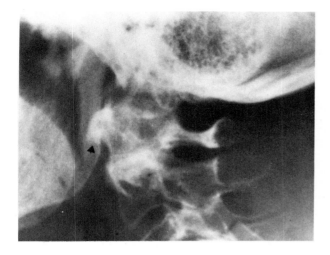

A

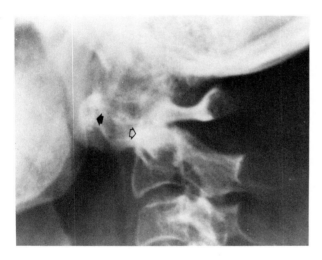

B

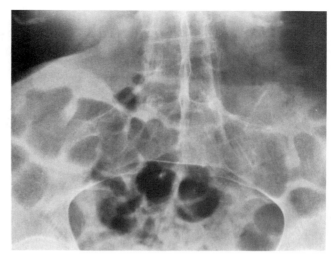

Figure 3-43   Ankylosing spondylitis. Bilateral, symmetric obliteration of sacroiliac joints and "bamboo spine."

Figure 3-42   Subluxation of atlantoaxial joint in rheumatoid arthritis. **A,** Routine lateral film of cervical spine shows normal relation between anterior border of odontoid process and superior portion of anterior arch of atlas *(arrow).* **B,** With flexion, there is wide separation between anterior arch of atlas *(solid arrow)* and odontoid *(open arrow).*

Rheumatoid variants

Ankylosing spondylitis, Reiter's syndrome, and psoriatic arthritis are variants of rheumatoid arthritis. **Ankylosing spondylitis** almost always begins in the sacroiliac joints, causing bilateral and usually symmetric involvement. Blurring of the articular margins and patchy sclerosis generally progress to narrowing of the joint space and may lead to complete fibrous and bony ankylosis (Figure 3-43). The disease typically progresses from the lumbar spine upward. Ossification in the paravertebral tissues

and longitudinal spinal ligaments combines with extensive lateral bony bridges (syndesmophytes) between vertebral bodies to produce the characteristic "bamboo spine" of advanced disease. Limitation of activity leads to generalized skeletal osteoporosis and a tendency to fracture in response to the stress of minor trauma (Figure 3-44).

Reiter's syndrome is characterized by arthritis, urethritis, and conjunctivitis. It primarily affects young adult men and appears to be a postinfectious syndrome after certain types of venereal or gastrointestinal infections. Reiter's syndrome most frequently involves the sacroiliac joints, heel, and toes (Figure 3-45). Unlike ankylosing spondylitis, sacroiliac involvement is usually bilateral but asymmetric, and Reiter's syndrome tends to cause only minimal changes in the spine. Although the radiographic changes in peripheral joints often mimic rheumatoid arthritis, Reiter's syndrome tends to be asymmetric and primarily involves the feet rather than the hands (Figure 3-46).

Psoriatic arthritis refers to a rheumatoid-like destructive process involving peripheral joints that develops in patients with typical skin changes of psoriasis (Figure 3-47). Unlike rheumatoid arthritis, psoriatic arthritis predominantly involves the distal rather than the proximal interphalangeal joints of the hands and feet, produces asymmetric rather than symmetric destruction, and causes little or no periarticular osteoporosis. Characteristic findings include bony ankylosis of the interphalangeal joints of the hands and feet and resorption of the terminal tufts of the distal phalanges (Figure 3-48).

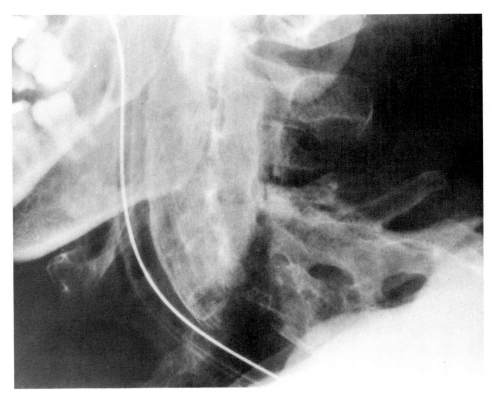

Figure 3-44 Ankylosing spondylitis. Oblique fracture of midcervical spine with anterior dislocation of superior segment is seen in patient who fell dancing and struck his head. Fracture extends through lateral mass and lamina.

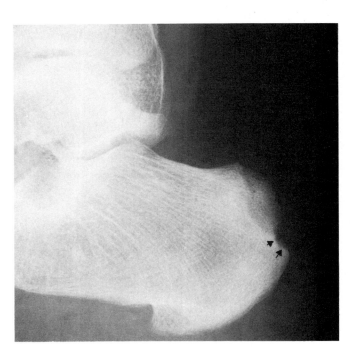

Figure 3-45 Reiter's syndrome. Striking bony erosion *(arrows)* at insertion of Achilles tendon on posterosuperior margin of calcaneus.

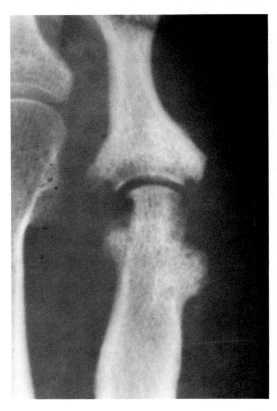

Figure 3-46 Reiter's syndrome. Erosive changes about metatarsophalangeal joint of fifth digit. Erosions involve juxta-articular region, leaving articular cortex intact.

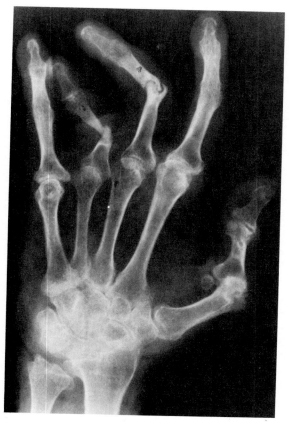

Figure 3-47   Psoriatic arthritis. Bizarre pattern of asymmetric bone destruction, subluxation, and ankylosis. Notice particularly pencil-in-cup deformity of third proximal interphalangeal joint and bony ankylosis involving wrist and phalanges of second and fifth digits.

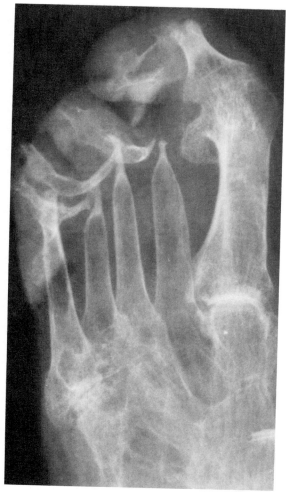

Figure 3-48   Psoriatic arthritis. Severe mutilating arthritis of foot and ankle. There is extreme pencil-like destruction of metatarsals and phalanges with ankylosis of almost all tarsal joints.

Osteoarthritis (degenerative joint disease)

Osteoarthritis is an extremely common generalized disorder that is characterized pathologically by loss of joint cartilage and reactive new bone formation. Part of the wear and tear of the aging process, degenerative joint disease tends to predominantly affect the weight-bearing joints (spine, hip, knee, ankle) and the interphalangeal joints of the fingers. A secondary form of degenerative joint disease may develop in a joint that has been repeatedly traumatized or subjected to abnormal stresses because of orthopedic deformities, or may be a result of a septic or inflammatory arthritis that destroys cartilage.

The earliest radiographic findings in degenerative joint disease are narrowing of the joint space, caused by thinning of the articular cartilage, and development of small bony spurs (osteophytes) along the margins of the articular edges of the bones. In contrast to the smooth, even narrowing of the joint space in rheumatoid arthritis, the joint space narrowing in degenerative joint disease is irregular and more pronounced in that part of the joint in which weight-bearing stress is greatest and degeneration of the articular cartilage is most noticeable. The articular ends of the bones become increasingly dense (periarticular sclerosis). Erosion of the articular cortex may produce typical irregular, cystlike lesions with sclerotic margins in the subchondral bone near the joint. Calcific or ossified loose bodies may develop, especially at the knee. With advanced disease, relaxation of the joint capsule and other ligamentous structures may lead to subluxation. Local osteoporosis does not occur unless pain causes prolonged disuse of the joint.

In the fingers, degenerative joint disease primarily involves the distal interphalangeal joints (Figure 3-49). Marginal spurs produce well-defined bony protuberances that appear clinically as the palpable

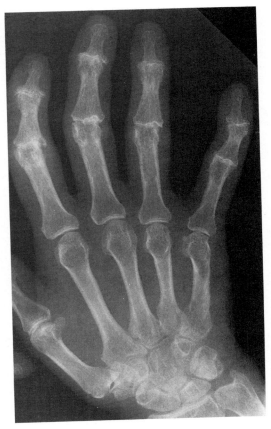

Figure 3-49 Osteoarthritis of fingers. Narrowing of interphalangeal joints with spurring and erosions.

and visible knobby thickening of Heberden's nodes. In the hip, the most prominent finding is asymmetric narrowing of the joint space that predominantly involves the superior and lateral aspects of the joint, where the stress of weight bearing is greatest (Figure 3-50). Joint-space narrowing is also asymmetric in the knee, where it predominantly involves the medial femorotibial compartment (Figure 3-51).

Infectious arthritis

Pyogenic (pus-forming) organisms may gain entry into a joint by the hematogenous route, by direct extension from an adjacent focus of osteomyelitis, or from trauma to the joint (surgery, needling). The onset of bacterial arthritis is usually abrupt, with high fever, shaking chills, and one or a few severely tender and swollen joints.

Soft-tissue swelling is the first radiographic sign of acute bacterial arthritis. In children, fluid distention of the joint capsule may cause widening of the joint space and actual subluxation, especially about the hip and shoulder. Periarticular edema displaces or obliterates adjacent tissue fat planes (Figure 3-52, A). Rapid destruction of articular cartilage causes joint space narrowing early in the course of the disease. The earliest bone changes, which tend to appear 8 to 10 days after the onset of symptoms, are small focal erosions in the articular cortex. Because of the delay in bone changes, detection of the char-

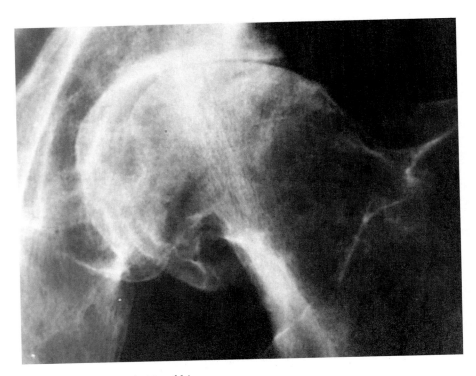

Figure 3-50 Osteoarthritis of hip.

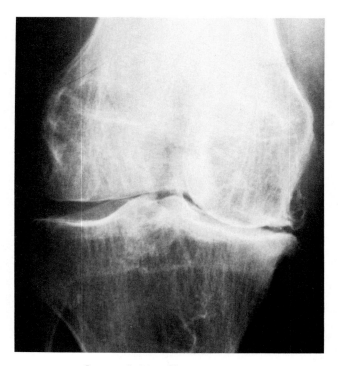

Figure 3-51   Osteoarthritis of knee.

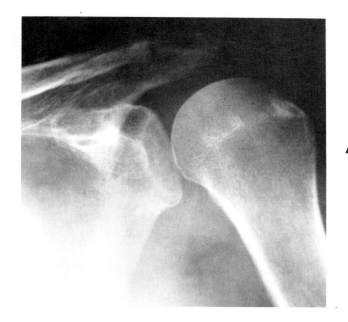

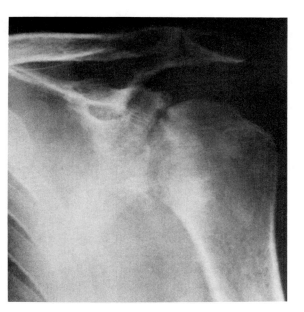

acteristic soft-tissue abnormalities is essential for early diagnosis. Severe, untreated infections cause extensive destruction and a loss of the entire cortical outline (Figure 3-52). With healing, sclerotic bone reaction results in an irregular articular surface. If the articular cartilage has been completely destroyed, bony ankylosis usually follows.

Tuberculous arthritis is a chronic, indolent infection that has an insidious onset and a slowly progressive course (Figure 3-53). Usually involving only one joint, tuberculous arthritis primarily affects the spine, hips, and knees. Most patients have a focus of tuberculosis elsewhere in the body, most commonly the lungs.

A distinctive early radiographic feature of tuberculous arthritis is extensive juxta-articular osteoporosis that precedes bone destruction in contrast to bacterial arthritis, in which osteoporosis is a relatively late finding. Joint effusion leads to a nonspecific periarticular soft-tissue swelling. Cartilage and bone destruction occur relatively late in the course of tuberculous arthritis and tend to initially involve the periphery of the joint, sparing the maximal weight-bearing surfaces that are destroyed in pyogenic arthritis. Therefore joint-space narrowing occurs late in tuberculous arthritis in contrast to the early narrowing with bacterial infections. As in pyogenic arthritis, the earliest evidence of bone destruction is usually erosion at the margins of the articular

Figure 3-52   Acute staphylococcal arthritis. **A,** Several days after instrumentation of shoulder for joint pain, there is separation of humeral head from glenoid fossa caused by fluid in joint space. **B,** Six weeks later, there is pronounced cartilage and bone destruction, with sclerosis on both sides of glenohumeral joint.

ends of bone. With progressive disease there is ragged destruction of the articular cartilage and subchondral cortex and disorganization of the joint, often with preservation of necrotic fragments of bone (sequestra) that may involve apposing surfaces ("kissing sequestra").

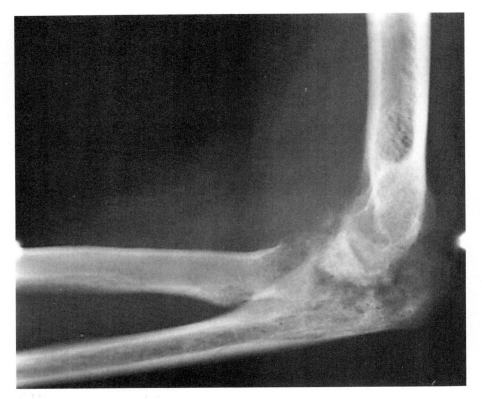

Figure 3-53   Tuberculous arthritis of elbow. Complete destruction of joint space. Notice large chronic granulomatous mass in antecubital region. (From Forrester DM, Brown JC, Nesson JW: *The radiology of joint disease,* Philadelphia, 1978, Saunders.)

Bursitis

Bursitis refers to an inflammation of the bursae, small fluid-filled sacs located near the joints that reduce friction on movement. The major radiographic manifestation of this condition is the deposition of calcification in adjacent tendons, which is a common cause of pain, limitation of motion, and disability about a joint. Calcific tendinitis most commonly involves the shoulder, and calcification may be demonstrated radiographically in about half the patients with persistent pain and disability in the shoulder region (Figure 3-54). However, calcification may also be detected in asymptomatic persons; on the other hand, severe clinical symptoms may occur without evidence of calcification. Calcific tendinitis appears as amorphous calcium deposits that most frequently occur about the shoulder in the supraspinatous tendon, where they are seen directly above the greater tuberosity of the humerus. The deposits vary greatly in size and shape, from thin curvilinear densities to large calcific masses.

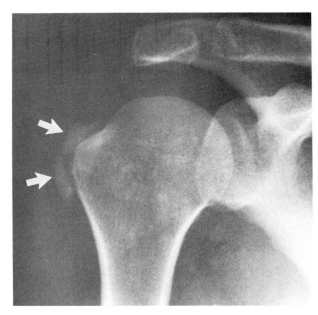

Figure 3-54   Calcific tendinitis. Frontal view of shoulder demonstrates amorphous calcium deposits *(arrows)* in supraspinatus tendon.

Rotator cuff tears

The rotator cuff of the shoulder is a musculotendinous structure composed of the teres minor, infraspinatus, supraspinatus, and subscapularis muscles. Rupture of the rotator cuff produces a communication between the shoulder joint and the subacromial bursa that can be demonstrated by arthrography (the injection of contrast material directly into the shoulder joint) (Figure 3-55). Currently, MRI is considered the modality of choice for demonstrating a rotator cuff disorder. The normal rotator cuff is well shown as a black structure, but tears cause it to have high signal intensity (Figure 3-56).

Tears of the menisci of the knee

Meniscal tears are a common cause of knee pain. Although occasionally the result of acute trauma, meniscal tears more frequently reflect a degenerative process caused by the chronic trauma inherent in human knee function. In the past, meniscal tears were best demonstrated by arthrography; now, MRI is clearly the imaging modality of choice.

MRI demonstrates a tear as a sharply marginated line of high signal intensity that crosses the normally dark, triangular meniscus (Figure 3-57). In addition, this modality can show the often-associated tears of the anterior and posterior cruciate ligaments as well as changes in the underlying bone.

▪ Osteomyelitis

Bacterial osteomyelitis

Osteomyelitis is an inflammation of the bone (osteitis) and bone marrow (myelitis) that is caused by a broad spectrum of infectious organisms that reach bone by hematogenous spread, by extension from an adjacent site of infection, or by direct introduction of organisms (trauma or surgery). Acute hematogenous osteomyelitis tends to involve bones with rich red

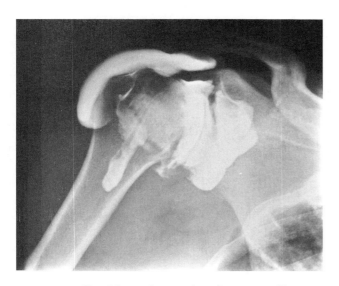

Figure 3-55 Shoulder arthrography of rotator cuff tear. Opacification of subacromial and subdeltoid bursae indicates abnormal communication between them and glenohumeral joint cavity, thus confirming the diagnosis. (From Greenspan A: *Orthopedic radiology*, Philadelphia, 1988, Lippincott.)

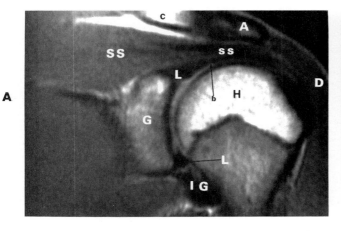
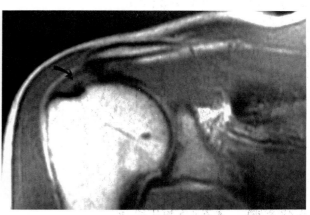

Figure 3-56 Magnetic resonance image of rotator cuff tear. **A,** Normal patient. Notice the low signal of the suspraspinatus tendon *(ss)*. A, Acromion; C, clavicle; D, deltoid muscle; G, glenoid fossa; H, humeral head; IG, inferior glenohumeral ligament; L, glenoid labrum. **B,** Degenerative tear. There is a high signal *(arrow)* within the rotator cuff. (From Stark DD, Bradley WG Jr: *Magnetic resonance imaging*, ed 2, St Louis, 1991, Mosby.)

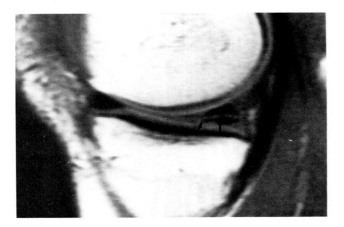

Figure 3-57 Meniscal tear. Sagittal magnetic resonance scan of knee shows horizontal line of high signal intensity *(arrow)* crossing dark posterior horn of medial meniscus. (From Stark DD, Bradley WG Jr: *Magnetic resonance imaging,* ed 2, St. Louis, 1991, Mosby.)

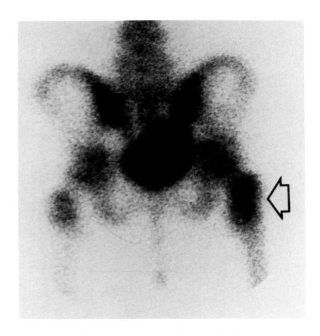

Figure 3-58 Osteomyelitis. Radionuclide bone scan (posterior projection) demonstrates increased uptake of radionuclide in trochanteric portion of right femur *(arrow)*. Plain film of pelvis and hips obtained at same time showed no detectable abnormality.

marrow. In infants and children, the metaphyses of long bones, especially the femur and tibia, are most often affected; staphylococci and streptococci are the most common organisms. In adults, acute hematogenous osteomyelitis primarily occurs in the vertebrae and rarely involves the long bones. Although the incidence and severity of osteomyelitis have decreased since the advent of antibiotics, this disease has recently become more prevalent as a complication of intravenous drug abuse. In diabetic patients and those with other types of vascular insufficiency, a soft-tissue infection may spread from a skin abscess or a decubitus ulcer, usually in the foot, to cause cellulitis and eventually osteomyelitis in adjacent bones.

Osteomyelitis begins as an abscess of the bone. Pus produced by the acute inflammation spreads down the medullary cavity and outward to the surface. Once the infectious process has reached the outer margin of the bone, it raises the periosteum from the bone and may spread along the surface for a considerable distance.

Because the earliest changes of osteomyelitis are usually not evident on plain radiographs until about 10 days after the onset of symptoms, radionuclide bone scanning is the most valuable imaging modality for the early diagnosis of osteomyelitis. Increased nuclide uptake, reflecting the inflammatory process and increased blood flow, is evident within hours of the onset of symptoms (Figure 3-58).

On plain radiographs the earliest evidence of osteomyelitis in a long bone is a localized, deep soft-tissue swelling adjacent to the metaphysis. The inflammation causes displacement or obliteration of

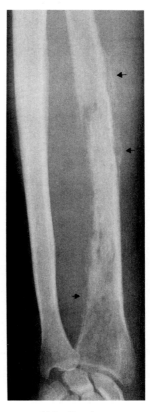

Figure 3-59 Osteomyelitis. Patchy pattern of bone destruction involves much of shaft of radius. Notice early periosteal new bone formation *(arrows)*.

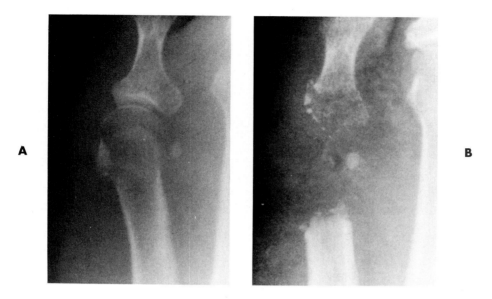

Figure 3-60 Staphylococcal osteomyelitis. **A,** Initial film of first metatarsophalangeal joint shows soft-tissue swelling and periarticular demineralization because of increased blood flow to region. **B,** Several weeks later, there is severe bony destruction about metatarsophalangeal joint.

the normal fat planes adjacent to and between the deep muscle bundles, unlike skin infections, in which the initial swelling is superficial. The initial bony change is subtle areas of metaphyseal lucency reflecting resorption of necrotic bone. Soon, bone destruction becomes more prominent, producing a ragged, moth-eaten appearance (Figures 3-59 and 3-60). The more virulent the organism, the larger is the area of destruction. Subperiosteal spread of inflammation elevates the periosteum and stimulates the deposition of layers of new bone parallel to the shaft. This results in a layered periosteal reaction that is characteristic of benign diseases, especially infection. Eventually, a large amount of new bone surrounds the cortex in a thick, irregular bony sleeve (involucrum). Disruption of cortical blood supply leads to bone necrosis. Segments of avascular dead bone (sequestra) remain as dense as normal bone and are clearly differentiated from the demineralized bone, infected granulation tissue, and pus about them (Figure 3-61).

After the acute infection has subsided, a pattern of chronic osteomyelitis develops. The bone appears thickened and sclerotic with an irregular outer margin. The cortex may become so dense that the medullary cavity is difficult to demonstrate. Reactivation of infection may appear as the recurrence of deep soft-tissue swelling, periosteal calcification, or the development of lytic abscess cavities within the bone. However, plain radiographs are often inadequate to determine whether an active infection is

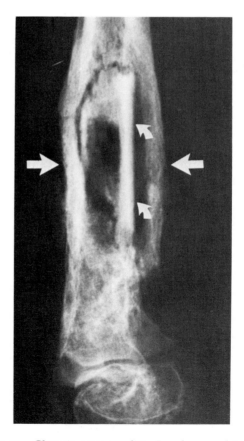

Figure 3-61 Chronic osteomyelitis. Involucrum (*straight arrows*) surrounds sequestrum (*curved arrows*).

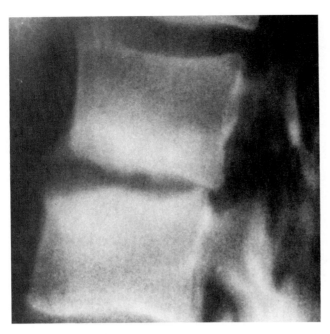

Figure 3-62   Bacterial vertebral osteomyelitis. Narrowing of intervertebral disk space with irregularity of end plates and reactive sclerosis.

present. Radionuclide scanning is much more sensitive and accurate in establishing a recurrence.

The earliest sign of vertebral osteomyelitis is subtle erosion of the subchondral bony plate with loss of the sharp cortical outline. This may progress to total destruction of the vertebral body associated with a paravertebral soft-tissue abcess (Figure 3-62). Unlike neoplastic processes, osteomyelitis usually affects the intervertebral disk space and often involves adjacent vertebrae. Depending on the site of disease, anterior extension of osteomyelitis may cause retropharyngeal abscess, mediastinitis, empyema, pericarditis, subdiaphragmatic abscess, psoas muscle abscess, or peritonitis; posterior extension of inflammatory tissue can compress the spinal cord or produce meningitis if the infection penetrates the dura to enter the subarachnoid space.

CT can be of value in the diagnosis of osteomyelitis, especially that involving the spine. This modality can precisely define the size of the surrounding soft-tissue mass, its relation to nearby vital structures (aorta, spinal cord), and the presence of abscess cavities requiring surgical drainage.

Tuberculous osteomyelitis

Tuberculous osteomyelitis most commonly involves the thoracic and lumbar spine. The infection tends to begin in the anterior part of the vertebral body adjacent to the intervertebral disk (Figure 3-63, *A*). Irregular, poorly marginated bone destruction within the vertebral body is often associated with a characteristic paravertebral abscess, an accumulation of purulent material that produces a fusiform soft-tissue mass about the vertebra. The spread of tuberculous osteomyelitis causes narrowing of the adjacent intervertebral disk and the extension of infection and bone destruction across the disk to involve the adjacent vertebral body. Unlike bacterial infection, tuberculous osteomyelitis is rarely associated with periosteal reaction or bone sclerosis. In the untreated patient, progressive vertebral collapse and anterior wedging lead to a characteristic sharp kyphotic angulation (gibbous deformity) (Figure 3-63, *B*).

Tuberculosis can produce a low-grade chronic infection of the long bones that appears radiographically as a generally destructive lytic process with minimal or no periosteal reaction. The spectrum of radiographic appearances is wide, varying from localized, well-circumscribed, expansile lesions to diffuse uniform, honeycomb-like areas of destruction that are often associated with pathologic fractures. Chronic draining sinuses may develop, especially in children.

▪ Fractures

Fractures are the most common skeletal abnormality seen in a general radiology practice. A fracture is defined as a disruption of bone caused by mechanical forces applied either directly to the bone or transmitted along the shaft of a bone. Although often obvious, some fractures are subtle and difficult to detect. A fracture typically appears as a radiolucent line crossing the bone and disrupting the cortical margins. However, the fracture line may be thin and easily overlooked, whereas overlap of fragments may produce a radiopaque line. Secondary signs of underlying fracture include joint effusion, soft-tissue swelling, and interruption of the normal pattern of bony trabeculae.

Fractures are described and classified by the extent, direction, position, and number of fracture lines and the integrity of the overlying skin (Figure 3-64). A fracture that results in discontinuity between two or more fragments is **complete;** an **incomplete** fracture causes only partial discontinuity, with a portion of the cortex remaining intact. In **closed** fractures, the overlying skin is intact; if the overlying skin is disrupted, the fracture is **open,** or **compound.** Although this is a clinical distinction, the radiographic demonstration of bone clearly protruding through the skin and the presence of air and soft tissues about the fracture site on immediate postinjury radiographs are findings that are highly suggestive of an open fracture.

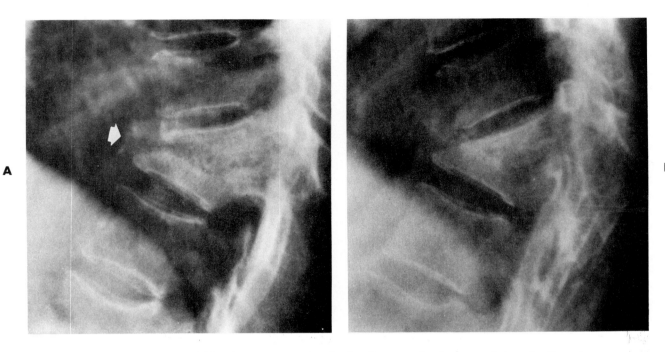

Figure 3-63 **A,** Initial film demonstrates vertebral collapse and anterior wedging of adjacent midthoracic vertebrae *(arrow).* Residual intervertebral disk space can barely be seen. **B,** Several months later there is virtual fusion of collapsed vertebral bodies, producing characteristic sharp kyphotic angulation (gibbous deformity).

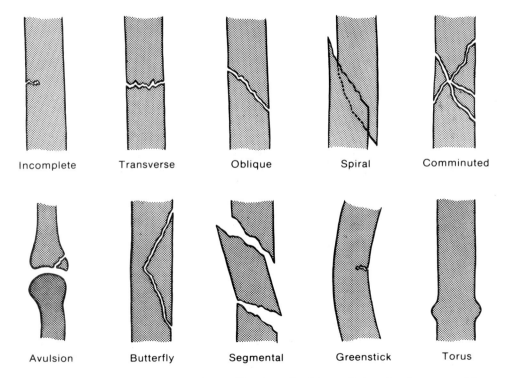

Figure 3-64 Classification of fractures. (From Eisenberg R: *Diagnostic imaging in surgery,* New York, 1987, McGraw-Hill.)

The direction of a fracture is determined by its relation to the long axis of long and short bones and to the longest axis of irregular bones (e.g., the talus or carpal navicular). A **transverse** fracture runs at a right angle to the long axis of a bone and is most commonly the result of a direct blow or a fracture within pathologic bone. An **oblique** fracture runs a course of approximately 45 degrees to the long axis of the bone and is the result of angulation or both angulation and compression forces. A **spiral** fracture encircles the shaft, is generally longer than an oblique fracture, and is caused by torsional forces. **Avulsion** fractures are generally small fragments torn off from bony prominences; they are usually the result of indirectly applied tension forces within attached ligaments and tendons rather than direct blows.

A **comminuted** fracture is composed of more than two fragments. A **butterfly** fragment is an elongated triangular fragment of cortical bone generally detached from two other larger fragments of bone; a **segmental** fracture consists of a segment of the shaft isolated by proximal and distal lines of fracture.

A **compression** fracture results from a compression force that causes compaction of bone trabeculae and results in decreased length or width of a portion of a bone. Compression fractures most commonly occur in the vertebral body as a result of flexion of the spine; they may also be seen as impacted fractures of the humeral or femoral heads. A **depressed** fracture occurs in the skull or tibial plateau. In the skull, a small object with great force can produce a comminuted fracture with portions of the fracture fragments driven inward. In the knee, the relatively hard lateral femoral condyle may impact on the relatively soft lateral tibial plateau with sufficient force to push the cortical surface of the tibia into the underlying cancellous bone.

A **stress,** or **fatigue,** fracture is the response of bone to repeated stresses, no one of which is sufficient to cause a fracture. The earliest pathologic process in a stress fracture is osteoclastic resorption, followed by the development of periosteal callus in an attempt to repair and strengthen the bone. A **pathologic** fracture occurs in bone at an area of weakness, caused by such processes as tumor, infection, or metabolic bone disease.

A **greenstick** fracture is an incomplete fracture with the opposite cortex intact. Greenstick fractures are found almost exclusively in infants and children because of the softness of their cancellous bone. A **torus (buckle)** fracture is one in which one cortex is intact with buckling or compaction of the opposite cortex. A **bowing** fracture is a plastic deformation caused by a stress that is too great to permit a complete recovery of normal shape but is less than the stress required to produce a fracture.

A fracture is **undisplaced** when a plane of cleavage exists in the bone without angulation or separation. **Displacement** refers to separation of bone fragments; the direction of displacement is described by the relation of the distal fragment with respect to the proximal fragment and is usually measured in terms of the thickness of the shaft. **Angulation** indicates an angular deformity between the axes of the major fragments and is also described by the position of the distal fragment with respect to the proximal one. **Dislocation** refers to displacement of a bone so that it is not in contact with its normal articulation. If there is only partial loss of continuity of the joint surfaces, the displacement is called a **subluxation.**

Radiographs are essential in the diagnosis and management of fractures. Initially, a radiograph documents the clinically suspected fracture and determines whether the underlying bone is normal or whether the fracture is pathologic and has occurred in abnormal bone. After the orthopedic reduction of a fracture, repeat radiographs are required to determine whether the fracture fragments are in good position. Over the next several weeks or months, additional radiographs are obtained to assess fracture healing and to exclude possible complications.

In all cases of trauma, it is essential to have at least two projections of the injured part, preferably taken at 90 degrees to each other. It is also important to demonstrate the joint above and below the fracture to search for a dislocation or second fracture that may have resulted from transmission of the mechanical force. An example of this mechanism is the fracture or dislocation of the head of the fibula that frequently occurs with a fracture of the distal part of the tibia at the ankle.

Fracture treatment

The overall goal of fracture treatment is to restore function and stability with an acceptable cosmetic result and a minimum of residual deformity. In **external,** or **closed,** reduction the fracture is treated by manipulation of the affected body part without surgical incision. **Open reduction** is a surgical procedure in which there is direct or indirect manipulation of the fracture fragments and usually the application or insertion of some type of appliance or device to achieve and maintain the reduction (Figure 3-65). **External fixation** is accomplished by the use of splints or casts; **internal fixation** uses metal plates and screws, wires, rods, or nails, either alone or in combination, to maintain the reduction.

Most reduced fractures are immobilized or protected by an overlying cast. The radiopaque cast

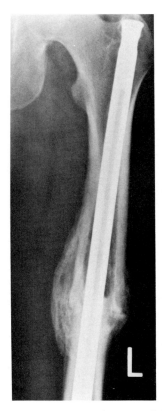

Figure 3-65 Open reduction with internal fixation. Intramedullary rod has been placed across fracture of femoral shaft. Notice extensive callus formation about fracture site.

Figure 3-66 Normal union of fracture. There is dense callus formation bridging previous fracture of midshaft of femur. Original fracture line is completely obliterated.

causes some obscuration of fine bony detail and, in severely osteoporotic bone, may make it difficult to visualize the fracture site. Therefore, if there is a question of healing that requires the demonstration of early callus formation or if there is a possibility of osteomyelitis, it is essential that the cast be removed by the physician before obtaining radiographs so that there is sufficient visibility of bone detail to resolve these questions.

Fracture healing

The radiographic evidence of fracture healing is a continuous external bridge of callus (calcium deposition) that extends across the line of fracture and unites the fracture fragments (Figure 3-66). The callus is uniformly ossified and approaches the density of normal bone. It is essential that at least two views be taken (preferably 90 degrees to each other) to be certain that there is callus about the fracture line in all directions. Proper exposure of the radiograph is required because underexposed films may produce the illusion of obliteration of the fracture line by bony trabeculae, whereas a properly exposed film would demonstrate the continued presence of

the fracture line and the lack of healing. If the findings are equivocal, conventional tomography or computed tomography (CT) may be required to determine the degree of union. "Stress" films, a series of radiographs obtained with the injured part in the neutral position and during the application of stress by a physician or designated assistant on the distal fragment or part in the plane of suspected motion, may demonstrate a change in the alignment of the fragment that indicates a lack of union.

Malunion is the healing of fragments of a fracture in a faulty position. This leads to impairment of normal function or cosmetic appearance that may require surgical correction (Figure 3-67).

Delayed union is an ill-defined term that is arbitrarily applied to any fracture that takes longer to heal than the average fracture at that anatomic location. Delayed union may result from infection or inadequate immobilization or from limited blood supply or loss of bone at the fracture site.

Nonunion refers to a condition in which the fracture healing process has completely stopped and the fragments will remain ununited even with pro-

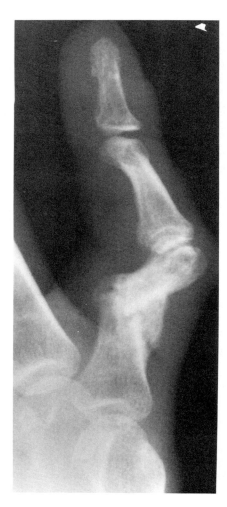

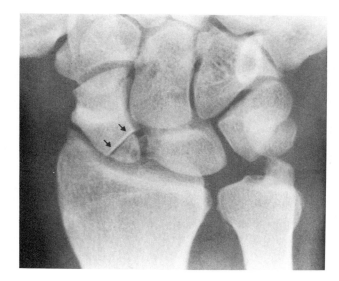

Figure 3-68 Nonunion of fracture of carpal navicular. Twenty years after initial injury, there is smooth, well-defined line of sclerosis *(arrows)* about fracture margin.

Figure 3-67 Malunion. Healing of proximal phalangeal fracture in poor position led to impairment of normal function.

longed immobilization. Radiographically, nonunion characteristically appears as smooth, well-defined sclerosis about the fracture margins with occlusion of the medullary canal by sclerotic bone (Figure 3-68). There is a persistent defect between the fragments, consisting of fibrous tissue and cartilage. Nonunion predominantly occurs in adults, is rare in children, and requires operative intervention to reinitiate the healing process.

Pathologic fractures

Pathologic fractures are those occurring in bone that has been weakened by a preexisting condition. The most common underlying process is metastatic malignancy or multiple myeloma. In children, developmental diseases such as osteogenesis imperfecta, osteopetrosis, or nutritional deficiencies (rickets, scurvy) may result in pathologic fractures. Pathologic fractures also may occur in benign causes of

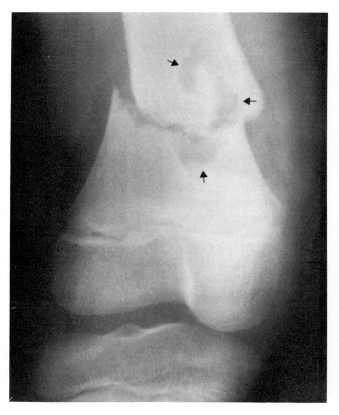

Figure 3-69 Pathologic fracture. There is transverse fracture crossing large benign tumor *(arrows)* of distal femur.

weakened bone, such as simple bone cyst, enchondroma, aneurysmal bone cysts, and fibrous dysplasia. Metabolic disorders causing a diffuse loss of bone substance (osteoporosis, osteomalacia, hyperparathyroidism) also make the skeleton more susceptible to injury.

Clinically, pathologic fractures arise from minor trauma that would not affect normal bone. Radiographically, the fracture crosses an area of abnormal thinning, expansion, or bone destruction (Figure 3-69). The most frequent sites of pathologic fractures are the spine, femur, and humerus, areas in which metastatic disease is most common. In the spine, a pathologic fracture results in collapse of the vertebral body; indeed, a compressed vertebra in a patient older than 40 years of age should indicate underlying myeloma or metastatic disease.

Remember that patients with suspected pathologic fractures must be handled with extreme care lest the radiographer cause either further injury to the bone in question or an additional pathologic fracture in another area.

Stress fractures

Stress (fatigue) fractures are the result of repeated stresses to a bone that would not be injured by isolated forces of the same magnitude. The type of stress fracture and the site where it occurs vary with the activity. Regardless of location, the activities resulting in stress fractures are usually strenuous, often new or different, and repeated with frequency before producing pain. Stress fractures frequently occur in soldiers during basic training ("march" fracture). The most common sites are the shafts of the second and third metatarsals, the calcaneus, the proximal and distal shafts of the tibia and fibula, the shaft and neck of the femur, and the ischial and pubic rami.

Initially, plain radiographs of the symptomatic area are within normal limits (Figure 3-70, *A*). The stress fracture is first visualized 10 to 20 days after the onset of symptoms as either a thin line of transverse or occasionally oblique radiolucency or as fluffy periosteal callus formation without evidence of a fracture line. When this radiographic appearance is detected at a site where stress fractures are common, it is important to elicit a history of athletic or other unusual activity as the underlying cause.

Radionuclide bone scans can demonstrate a stress fracture before it can be detected on plain radiographs (Figure 3-71).

Battered-child syndrome

The battered-child syndrome refers to multiple, repeated physically induced injuries in young children

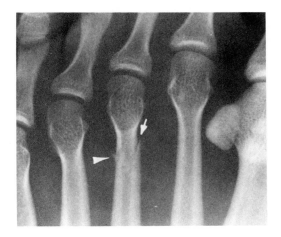

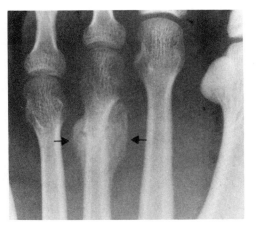

Figure 3-70 Stress fracture of third metacarpal. Initial radiograph was within normal limits. **A,** Radiograph obtained 14 days after onset of symptoms demonstrates thin oblique lucency *(arrow)* interrupting one cortex and small amount of fluffy periosteal callus formation *(arrowhead)* along opposite cortex. There is no evidence of complete fracture line. **B,** Three weeks later, repeat radiograph shows dense callus formation *(arrows)* about fracture site.

caused by parents or guardians. The radiographic findings in this syndrome include multiple fractures of varying age in various stages of healing, fractures of the corners of metaphyses with or without associated epiphyseal displacement, and exuberant subperiosteal new bone formation along the shafts of long bones (Figure 3-72). Skull fractures or widening of the cranial sutures are commonly associated. Another highly suggestive finding is one or more fractures at otherwise unusual sites (fractured only by direct blows), such as the ribs, scapula, sternum, spine, or lateral ends of the clavicles. Prompt and accurate diagnosis of the battered-child syndrome is essential to minimize the extent of physical and

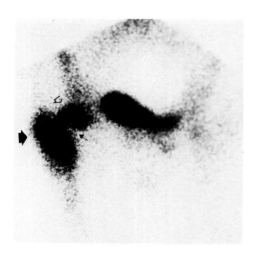

Figure 3-71   Radionuclide bone scan of stress fracture. Greatly increased radionuclide uptake in femoral neck *(open arrow)* and intertrochanteric region *(solid arrow),* with lack of uptake at actual fracture site *(thin arrow).* Plain radiograph and tomograms showed only minimal trabecular disruption and slight callus formation. (From Dorn HL, Lander PH: *AJR* 144:343-347, 1985.)

psychologic damage and, in some areas, to prevent a fatal injury.

Common fractures and dislocations

Colles' fracture is a transverse fracture through the distal radius with dorsal (posterior) angulation and often overriding of the distal fracture fragment (Figure 3-73). In more than half the cases there is an associated avulsion fracture of the ulnar styloid process. Colles' fracture is usually caused by a fall on the outstretched hand and is the most common fracture about the wrist.

Navicular fractures are the most common fractures involving the carpal bones. They are usually transverse and occur through the central part (waist) of the bone. Although most navicular fractures can be identified on routine frontal projections of the wrist, subtle fractures may be identified only on specific oblique and angulated projections or on films made using magnification techniques. In some cases, a navicular fracture cannot be detected on the initial examination despite strong clinical suspicion

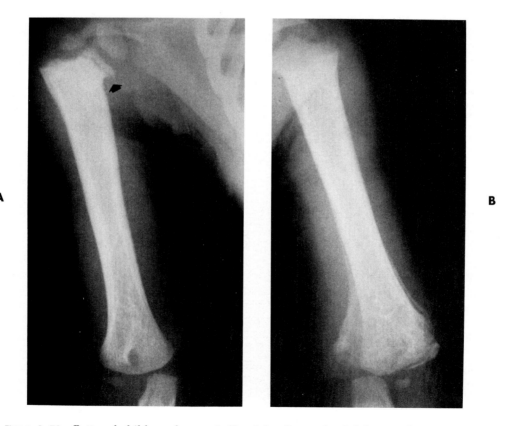

Figure 3-72   Battered-child syndrome. **A,** Frontal radiograph of right arm demonstrates corner fracture *(arrow)* of proximal humerus. **B,** Frontal radiograph of left arm shows healing displaced fracture of distal humerus. (From Sty JR, Starshak RJ: *Radiology* 146:369-375, 1983.)

(Figure 3-74, *A*). In this situation, the wrist should be placed in a cast or plaster splint and reexamined (out of plaster) in 7 to 10 days. At this time, resorption of bone at the margins of the fracture widens the fracture line and makes it more apparent radiographically (Figure 3-74, *B*).

Nonunion is a serious complication of navicular fractures (see Figure 3-68). Its incidence is increased by motion or displacement of the fracture fragments caused either by poor immobilization or by neglected, untreated fractures. Because the blood supply to the navicular is derived primarily from the

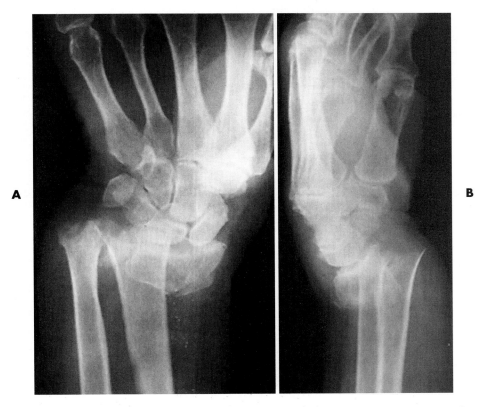

Figure 3-73   Colles' fracture. **A,** Frontal and, **B,** lateral projections of wrist show overriding and dorsal displacement of distal fragment. There is also displaced fracture of distal ulna.

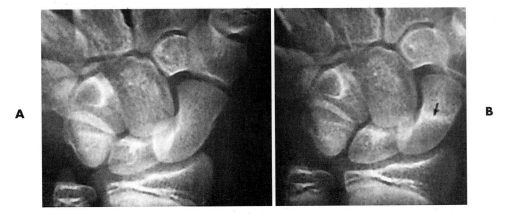

Figure 3-74   Fracture of navicular. **A,** On radiograph obtained immediately after injury, fracture cannot be detected. **B,** On repeat radiograph obtained 3 weeks later, fracture is clearly identified by sclerotic band *(arrow)* of opaque internal callus. (From Silverman FN: *Caffey's pediatric x-ray imaging,* St Louis, 1985, Mosby.)

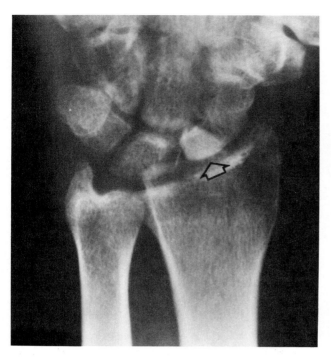

Figure 3-75 Avascular necrosis of navicular fracture. There is increased bone density in avascular proximal fragment *(arrow)*.

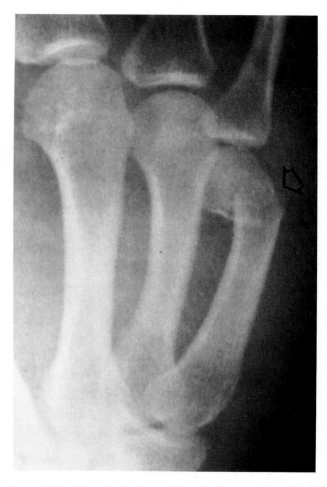

Figure 3-76 Boxer's fracture. There is fracture at neck of fifth metacarpal *(arrow)* with volar angulation of distal fragment.

distal portion, the proximal fragment may become avascular and undergo ischemic necrosis. This appears as an increase in bone density associated with collapse of bone or loss of volume in the affected fragment (Figure 3-75).

A boxer's fracture refers to a transverse fracture of the neck of the fifth metacarpal with volar (palmar) angulation of the distal fragment (Figure 3-76). This injury typically is the result of a blow struck with the fist.

In the detection of fractures about the elbow, a valuable clue is displacement of the normal elbow fat pads (fat pad sign). On lateral projections of the elbow, the anterior fat pad normally appears as a radiolucency closely applied to the anterior surface of the distal end of the humerus. The posterior fat pad is normally hidden in the depths of the olecranon fossa and should not be visible on standard lateral projections of the elbow. Any process producing synovial or hemorrhagic effusion within the elbow joint displaces the fat pads. The normally hidden posterior fat pad is posteriorly displaced and becomes visible as a crescentic lucency behind the lower end of the humerus (Figure 3-77). The anterior fat pad becomes more rounded and further separated from the underlying bone. The posterior fat pad is by far the more sensitive indicator of an

elbow joint effusion. Its presence on the lateral projection of the patient with elbow trauma is strongly suggestive of an underlying fracture, especially of the radial head, and indicates the need for oblique projections if no fracture is seen on standard projections. If no fracture is identified, a repeat radiograph obtained 2 weeks or more after appropriate immobilization will often show a fracture by demonstrating a fracture line or callus formation indicating healing.

Most fractures of the forearm involve both the radius and ulna. If only one bone is fractured, it is essential to examine both the elbow and the wrist to exclude the possibility of proximal or distal joint dislocation. A Monteggia fracture (Figure 3-78) refers to an isolated fracture of the shaft of the ulna associated with anterior dislocation of the radius at the elbow. A Galeazzi fracture refers to the combina-

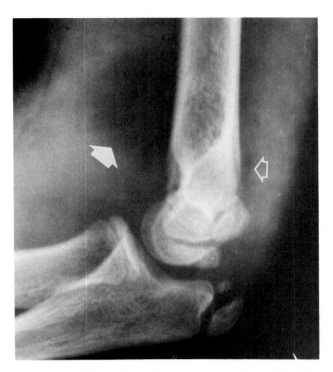

Figure 3-77 Elbow fat pad sign. Anterior fat pad *(solid arrow)* is clearly lifted from its fossa as result of large joint effusion in this child with supracondylar fracture of distal humerus. Normally hidden posterior fat pad is posteriorly displaced by effusion *(open arrow)*.

tion of a fracture of the shaft of the radius and dorsal (posterior) dislocation of the ulna at the wrist.

Pott's fracture involves both malleoli (of tibia and fibula) with dislocation of the ankle joint. A bimalleolar fracture refers to one involving both the medial and the lateral malleoli (Figure 3-79). Because of the mechanism of injury, the fracture on one side is transverse, whereas the opposite fracture is oblique or spiral. Trimalleolar fractures involve the posterior lip of the tibia in addition to the medial and lateral malleoli and usually represent fracture dislocations.

One of the most frequent injuries of the foot is a transverse fracture at the base of the fifth metatarsal (Jones' fracture) (Figure 3-80). This fracture represents an avulsion injury that results from plantar flexion and inversion of the foot as in stepping off a curb or falling while walking on stairs. It is important to distinguish this fracture from the longitudinally oriented apophysis that is normally found in children at the lateral margin of the base of the fifth metatarsal.

The shoulder is by far the most commonly dislocated joint in the body (Figure 3-81). About 95% of shoulder dislocations are anterior and the result of external rotation and abduction of the arm. As the anterior displacement occurs, the posterolateral surface of the humeral head impacts against the anterior or anteroinferior surface of the glenoid fossa and

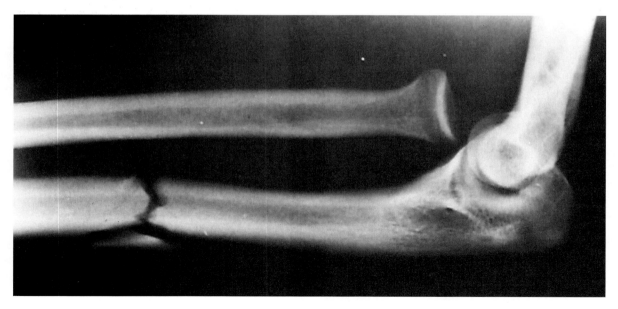

Figure 3-78 Monteggia fracture. Displaced fracture of ulnar shaft is associated with anterior dislocation of radial head.

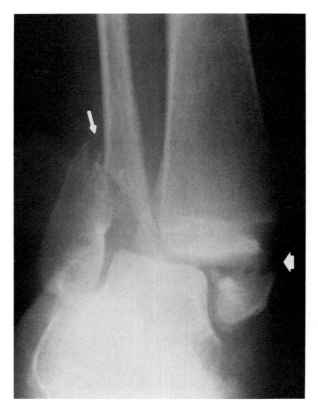

Figure 3-79 Bimalleolar fracture of ankle. There is transverse fracture of medial malleolus *(broad arrow)* associated with low oblique fracture of distal fibula *(thin arrow)*.

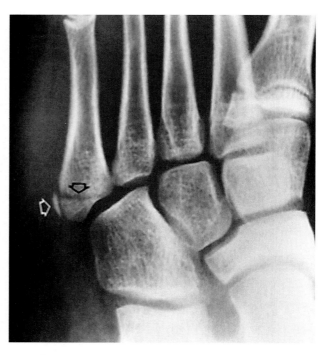

Figure 3-80 Fracture of base of fifth metatarsal. Notice that fracture line is transverse *(black arrow)*, whereas normal apophysis in this child has vertical orientation *(white arrow)*.

A

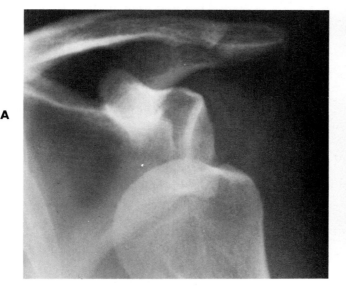

B

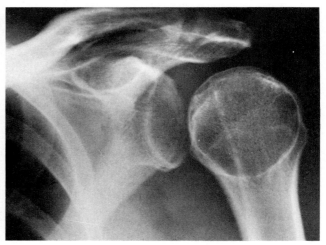

Figure 3-81 Dislocation of shoulder. **A,** Anterior. **B,** Posterior.

may result in a compression fracture of the humeral head, a fracture of the glenoid rim, or both. In most cases, the humeral head is displaced medially and anteriorly and comes to rest beneath the coracoid process.

Dislocations of the hip, with or without associated fracture of the acetabulum, are caused by severe injuries such as automobile collisions, pedestrian accidents, or falls from a great height. Unlike the shoulder, posterior dislocations of the hip are far more common than anterior dislocations and account for 85% to 90% of the cases (Figure 3-82).

■ **Fractures and Dislocations of the Spine**

Fractures and dislocations of the spine may be the result of direct trauma, hyperextension-flexion injuries (whiplash), or normal stresses in abnormal bone (osteoporosis, metastatic destruction). In the patient with spinal injury, the major goal of the radiographic evaluation is to determine whether a fracture or dislocation is present and whether the injury is

stable or unstable. The spine can be considered as consisting of two major columns. The anterior column is composed of the vertebral bodies, intervertebral disks, and anterior and posterior longitudinal ligaments. The posterior column is formed by the facets, apophyseal joints, pedicles, laminae, spinous processes, and all the intervening ligaments. If one of the two columns remains intact, the injury is considered **stable.** If both columns are disrupted, the injury is considered **unstable.**

If there is a strong suspicion of injury to the cervical spine, the initial radiograph should be a horizontal-beam lateral projection with the patient supine. This cross-table lateral radiograph *must* be checked by the physician before any other projections are obtained. It is essential to include all seven cervical vertebrae on the film lest the relatively common injuries of C6 and C7 be overlooked (Figure 3-83). This may require supine oblique projections or films made in the swimmer's projection, in which one arm of the patient is extended over the head while the other arm remains by the side so as to

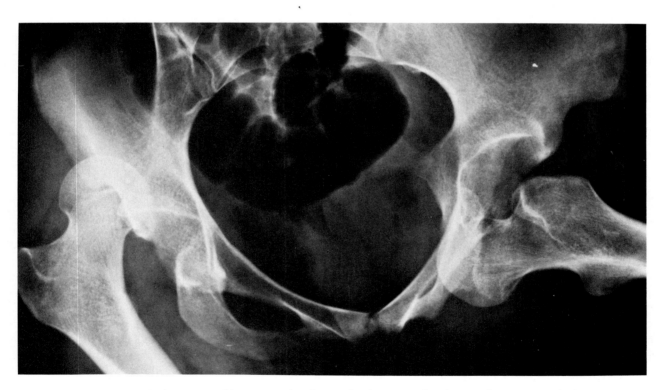

Figure 3-82 Dislocations of hip. Frontal radiograph of teen-aged girl injured in motor vehicle collision demonstrates right posterior dislocation and left anterior dislocation of hip. Right posterior dislocation is characterized by typical superolateral displacement of femoral head, fixed adduction, and internal rotation (lesser trochanter superimposed on femoral shaft). Left anterior dislocation is manifested by characteristic inferomedial displacement of femoral head, which has come to overlie obturator foramen; fixed abduction; and external rotation (lesser trochanter depicted in profile). (From Bassett, LW, Gold, RH, Epstein HC: *AJR* 141:385-386, 1983.)

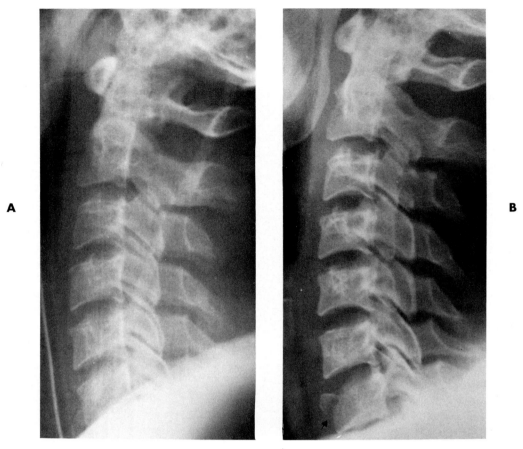

Figure 3-83 Fracture of C7 vertebral body. **A,** On initial lateral radiograph, only upper six cervical vertebrae can be seen. Patient's shoulders overlie seventh cervical vertebra. **B,** With shoulders pulled down to expose seventh cervical vertebra, anterosuperior fracture *(arrow)* is clearly identified.

slightly oblique the upper torso and permit visualization of the cervicothoracic junction. A frontal projection of the spine and an open-mouth projection of the atlas and axis (C1 and C2) should be obtained next. In an acutely injured patient, oblique or flexion and extension projections should be performed *only* under the direct supervision of the attending physician. Computed or even conventional tomography may be used to confirm the presence or absence of a fracture (especially of the posterior elements) and to visualize otherwise obscured areas of the spine such as the craniovertebral and cervicothoracic junctions. CT can precisely localize fracture fragments in relation to the spinal canal and detect otherwise obscure fractures of the posterior elements. Myelography may be performed in patients with a spinal cord injury in the absence of an obvious fracture or dislocation to identify a condition amenable to surgical removal or repair (herniated disk fragment; epidural hematoma of the spinal cord).

There are several types of fractures peculiar to the cervical spine. A **Jefferson fracture** is a comminuted fracture of the ring of the atlas that involves both the anterior and posterior arches and causes displacement of the fragments. The characteristic appearance on frontal radiographs or tomograms is a bilateral offset or spreading of the lateral articular masses of C1 in relation to the apposing articular surfaces of C2 (Figure 3-84).

Fractures of the odontoid process are usually transverse and located at the base of the dens at its junction with the body (Figure 3-85). On an open-mouth view, a lucency between the upper central incisor teeth often overlaps the dens; this must be differentiated from a rare vertical fracture of the dens.

The **hangman's fracture** is the result of acute hyperextension of the head on the neck. This appears as a fracture of the arch of C2 anterior to the inferior facet and is usually associated with anterior subluxation of C2 on C3 (Figure 3-86). Although

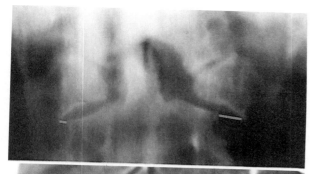

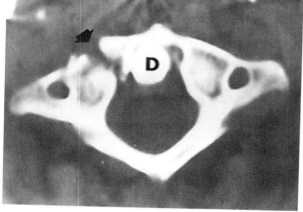

Figure 3-84 Jefferson fracture. **A,** On frontal projection, there is lateral displacement of lateral masses of C1 bilaterally *(white lines).* **B,** CT scan in another patient shows unilateral break in arch of C1 *(arrow). D,* Dens.

originally described in patients who had been hanged, this injury is now far more commonly the result of motor vehicle accidents.

Clay shoveler's fracture refers to an avulsion fracture of a spinous process in the lower cervical or upper thoracic spine. The fracture is difficult to demonstrate on emergency cross-table lateral radiographs because the shoulders frequently obscure the lower cervical region. One can make the diagnosis on the frontal view by noting the double shadow of the spinous processes caused by the caudad displacement of the avulsed fragment (Figure 3-87). This double–spinous-process sign must be differentiated from a bifid spinous process, which usually lies at a higher level and on a more horizontal plane.

Most fractures of the thoracolumbar spine are attributable to compressive forces that cause anterior wedging or depression of the superior end plate of a vertebral body (Figure 3-88). The **"seat belt fracture"** refers to a transverse fracture of a lumbar vertebra that is often associated with significant visceral injuries (Figure 3-89). In this condition, a horizontal fracture of the vertebral body extends to involve some or all of the posterior elements.

▪ Herniation of Intervertebral Disks

The intervertebral disks act as shock absorbers between the vertebrae, cushioning the movements of the spine. They consist of a fibrous outer cartilage (annulus) surrounding a central nucleus pulposus,

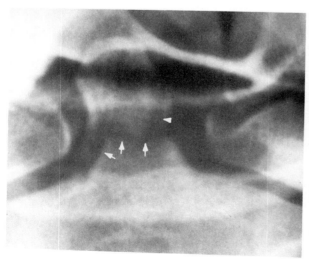

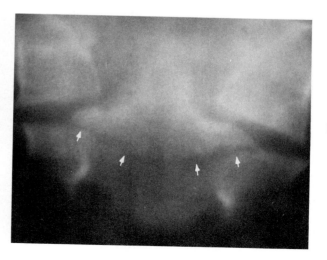

Figure 3-85 Fracture of odontoid process. **A,** Open-mouth frontal projection shows combined oblique and transverse fracture at base of dens *(arrows).* There is also separate cortical fragment on left *(arrowhead),* which most likely remains attached to alar ligament. **B,** In another patient, frontal tomogram shows low fracture *(arrows)* through body of C2.

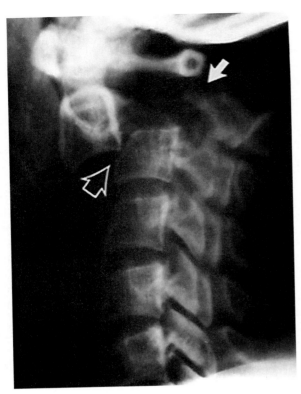

Figure 3-86 Hangman's fracture. Neural arch fracture *(solid arrow)* associated with complete C2-3 subluxation *(open arrow)*. (From Osborn, AG: Head trauma. In Eisenberg RL, Amberg JR, editors: *Critical diagnostic pathways in radiology*, Philadelphia, 1981, Lippincott.)

which is the essential part of the disk. The nucleus pulposus is a highly elastic, semifluid mass compressed like a spring between the vertebral surfaces. In youth, it contains a large amount of fluid to cushion the motion of the spine. With increasing age, the fluid and elasticity gradually diminish, leading to degenerative changes and back pain. Protrusion, or herniation, of a lumbar intervertebral disk is the major cause of severe acute, chronic, or recurring low back and leg pain. It most frequently involves the L4-5 and L5-S1 levels in the lumbar region where it often causes sciatica, pain that radiates down the sciatic nerve to the back of the thigh and lower leg. Other major sites are the C5-6 and C6-7 levels in the neck and the T9 through T12 levels in the thoracic region.

Patients with symptoms suggestive of disk herniation are initially treated conservatively with bed rest, muscle relaxants, and analgesics before being subjected to radiographic studies. Although plain radiographs show characteristic narrowing of the intervertebral disk spaces with hypertrophic spur formation, bony sclerosis, spurs impinging on the neural foramina, and the vacuum phenomenon (lucent collections overlying the intervertebral disks), these findings are nonspecific and frequently occur in patients with minimal symptoms (Figure 3-90). The diagnosis of herniation of an intervertebral disk requires CT, MRI, or myelography to demonstrate impression of the disk on the spinal cord or individual nerve roots (Figures 3-91 to 3-95).

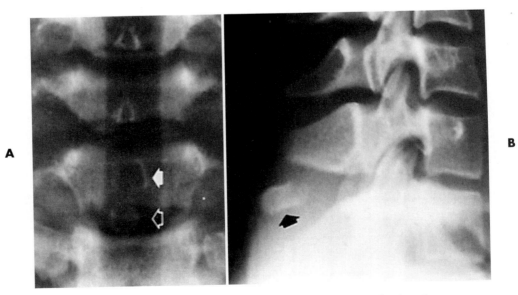

Figure 3-87 Clay shoveler's fracture. **A,** Frontal projection of cervical spine shows characteristic double-spinous-process sign resulting from caudad displacement of avulsed fragment *(open arrow)* with respect to normal position of major portion of spinous process *(solid arrow).* **B,** Lateral projection clearly shows avulsed fragment *(arrow).*

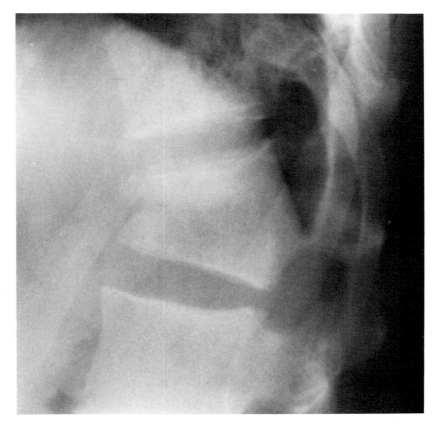

Figure 3-88 Vertebral body fracture. Characteristic anterior wedging of superior end plate of L1 vertebral body.

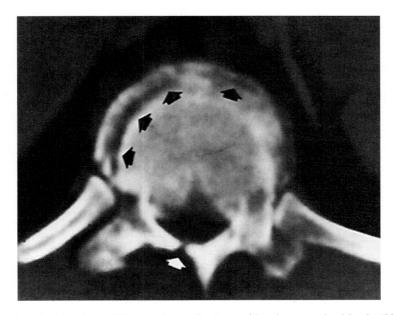

Figure 3-89 Seat belt fracture. CT scan shows fracture of lumbar vertebral body *(black arrows)* associated with lamina fracture at same level *(white arrow).*

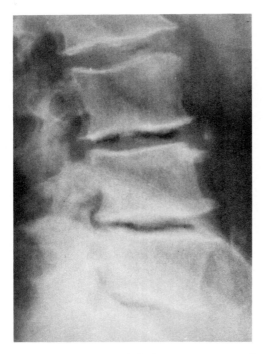

Figure 3-90   Degenerative disk disease. Hypertrophic spurring, intervertebral disk space narrowing, and reactive sclerosis. Notice linear lucent collections *(vacuum phenomenon)* overlying several of intervertebral disks.

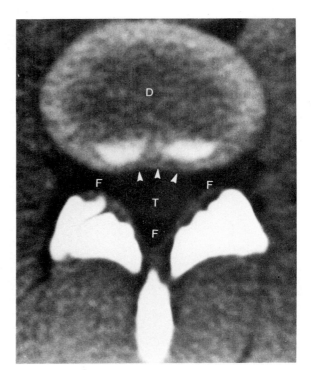

Figure 3-92   CT of normal lumbar disk *(D) (arrow).* Normal lumbar intervertebral disk has concave posterior border *(arrowheads).* Notice normal epidural fat *(F)* surrounding thecal sac *(T).*

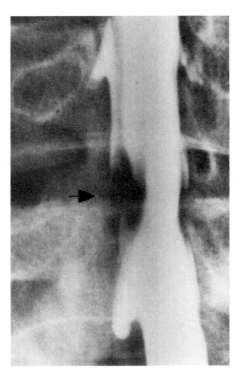

Figure 3-91   Lumbar disk herniation. Myelogram shows extradural lesion *(arrow)* at level of intervertebral disk space. Notice amputation of nerve root by disk compression.

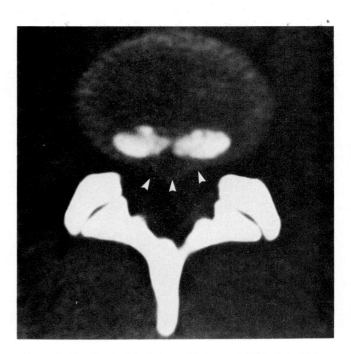

Figure 3-93   Central bulging of intervertebral disk. CT scan shows convex posterior border of disk *(arrowheads).* Notice preservation of epidural fat.

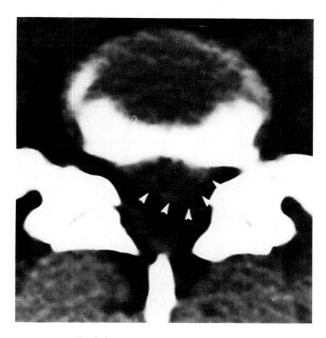

Figure 3-94 Disk herniation at L5-S1 level. CT shows herniation of disk *(arrowheads)* to left with obliteration of epidural fat. (From Eisenberg RL: *Diagnostic imaging in surgery,* New York, 1987, McGraw-Hill.)

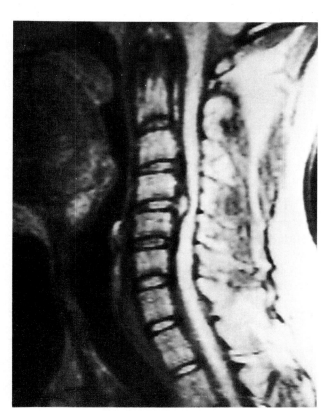

Figure 3-95 Magnetic resonance image of intervertebral disk herniation in cervical region. Notice extradural impression on spinal cord *(arrowhead).*

■ Fibrous Dysplasia

Fibrous dysplasia is a disorder that usually begins during childhood and is characterized by the proliferation of fibrous tissue within the medullary cavity. The disease may be confined to a single bone (monostotic) or the bones of one extremity, or it may be widely distributed throughout the skeleton (polyostotic).

Fibrous dysplasia primarily involves the long bones (especially the femur and tibia), ribs, and facial bones. Fibrous replacement of the medullary cavity typically produces a well-defined radiolucent area, which may vary from completely radiolucent to a homogeneous ground-glass density, depending on the amount of fibrous or osseous tissue deposited in the medullary cavity (Figure 3-96). Irregular bands of sclerosis may cross the cystlike lesion, giving it a multilocular appearance (Figure 3-97). The bone is often locally expanded, and the cortex may be eroded from within, predisposing to pathologic fractures. In severe and long-standing disease, affected bones may be bowed or deformed.

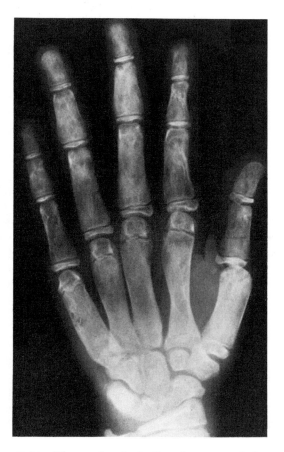

Figure 3-96 Fibrous dysplasia. Smudgy, ground-glass appearance of medullary cavities with failure of normal modeling.

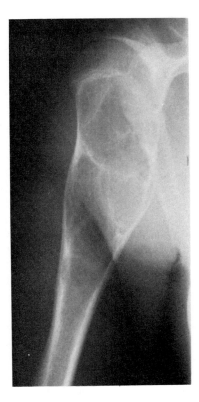

Figure 3-97   Fibrous dysplasia. Expansile lesion of humerus containing irregular bands of sclerosis giving it multilocular appearance.

Fibrous dysplasia is the most common cause of an expansile focal rib lesion, which usually has a ground-glass or soap-bubble appearance.

■ Spondylolysis and Spondylolisthesis

Spondylolysis refers to a cleft in the pars interarticularis that is situated between the superior and inferior articular processes of a vertebra. Occurring in about 5% of the population, these clefts are usually bilateral, most commonly involve the fifth lumbar vertebra, and predispose to the forward displacement of one vertebra on the other. Spondylolysis is the term for a defect in the pars interarticularis without displacement; if displacement occurs, the condition is called **spondylolisthesis.**

A plain lateral radiograph of the lower lumbar spine clearly shows any spondylolisthesis and may demonstrate the lucent cleft in the pars interarticularis even if no displacement has occurred (Figure 3-98). In grading spondylolisthesis of the lumbosacral junction on the lateral projection, the superior surface of the sacrum is divided into four equal parts. A forward displacement of the fifth lumbar vertebra up to one fourth the thickness of the sacrum is called a first-degree spondylolisthesis; half

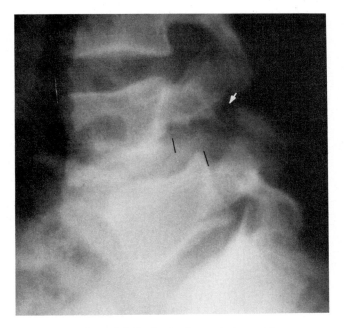

Figure 3-98   Spondylolisthesis. Lateral view of lower lumbar spine shows break in pars interarticularis *(arrow),* with resultant anterior slippage of L4 with respect to L5. Vertical black lines indicate posterior margins of vertebral bodies.

the thickness, a second-degree spondylolisthesis, and so on.

The diagnosis of spondylolysis without displacement may require an oblique projection of the lumbar spine, on which the appearance of the posterior elements has been likened to that of a Scotty dog (Figure 3-99). The pedicle and transverse process form the eye and nose; the superior and inferior articular processes form the ear and leg; and the pars interarticularis forms the neck, which is "fractured" in a patient with spondylolysis.

■ Ischemic Necrosis of Bone

Ischemic necrosis of bone results from the loss of blood supply, which in turn can result from such varied conditions as thrombosis, vasculitis, disease of surrounding bone, or single or repeated episodes of trauma disrupting the blood supply. Among the many conditions associated with ischemic necrosis are acute trauma (fracture or dislocation), steroid therapy or Cushing's disease, hemolytic anemia (especially sickle cell disease), chronic alcoholism and chronic pancreatitis, Gaucher's disease, radiation therapy, and caisson disease (a complication of underwater diving, the so-called "bends").

The femoral head is the most frequent site of ischemic necrosis. Initially, the ischemic bone may appear denser than adjacent viable bone. The first

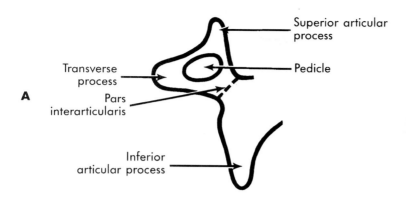

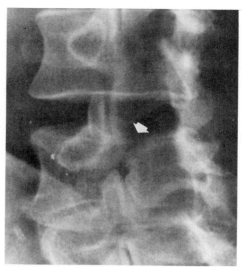

Figure 3-99 Spondylolysis. **A,** Diagram of Scotty dog sign. **B,** Oblique projection of lumbar spine demonstrates defect in pars interarticularis, which appears as fracture through neck of Scotty dog *(arrow).*

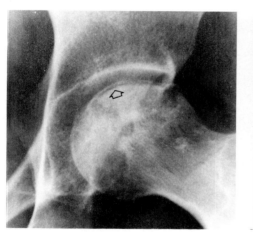

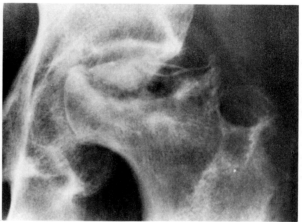

Figure 3-100 Ischemic necrosis of femoral head. **A,** Arclike radiolucent cortical band (crescent sign) *(arrow)* in femoral head represents fracture line. Notice lucent cortical band *(arrow).* **B,** Eventually, there is combination of lytic and sclerotic areas with severe flattening of femoral head.

sign of structural failure is the development of a radiolucent subcortical band (crescent sign) representing a fracture line (Figure 3-100, *A*). As the disorder progresses, fragmentation, compression, and resorption of dead bone, along with proliferation of granulation tissue, revascularization, and production of new bone, produce a pattern of lytic and sclerotic areas with flattening of the femoral head and periosteal new bone formation (Figure 3-100, *B*). Mechanical distortion about the hip leads to uneven weight bearing and accelerated secondary osteoarthritis.

It is often necessary to obtain two radiographs in patients with ischemic necrosis. The first is taken with normal density, whereas the second is made with increased kVp to allow for adequate penetration of the more opaque ischemic bone.

Radionuclide bone scanning is more sensitive than plain radiography for detecting changes of ischemic necrosis. In the initial stages of infarction, nuclide activity is absent in the area of involvement. As the disease progresses, this area of decreased activity may become rimmed by a zone of increased activity as a result of the reparative process.

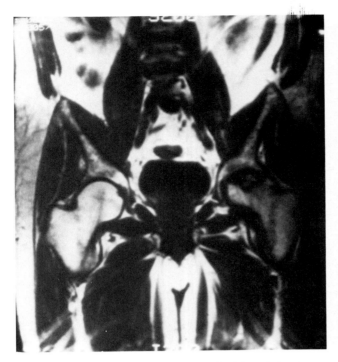

Figure 3-101   Ischemic necrosis. On this T_1-weighted image, ischemic left femoral head has lost normal bright signal intensity and appears dark.

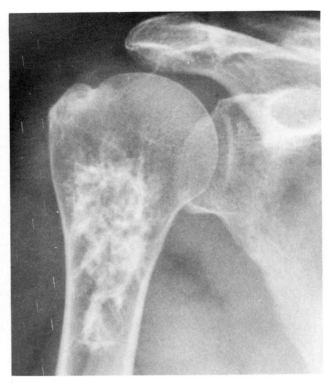

Figure 3-102   Bone infarct. Densely calcified area in medullary cavity of humerus with dense streaks extending from central region.

MRI may be even more sensitive than radionuclide bone scanning for detecting ischemic necrosis. Infarction at the end of a bone causes changes in the fatty marrow, sharply reducing the normal intense T_1-weighted signal from the marrow so that the infarcted area becomes gray or black (Figure 3-101).

In addition to ischemic changes in the subchondral areas of bone, infarction may involve the shaft of a long bone. In many cases this type of bone infarction is asymptomatic and is detected only on radiographs obtained for another purpose. A mature infarct in the shaft of a bone appears as a densely calcified area in the medullary cavity (Figure 3-102). It may be sharply limited by a dense sclerotic zone or associated with dense streaks extending from the central region. Bone infarction must be differentiated from a calcified enchondroma, which contains amorphous, spotty calcific densities, is not surrounded by a sclerotic rim, and may expand the bone.

QUESTIONS

1. The shaft of any long bone is termed the
   A. Epiphysis
   B. Diaphysis
   C. Metaphysis
   D. Periosteum

2. The end of a long bone is referred to as the
   A. Epiphysis
   B. Diaphysis
   C. Metaphysis
   D. Periosteum

3. The special types of cells responsible for the diameter growth of bones are
   A. Osteoblasts
   B. Osteoclasts
   C. Chondroblasts
   D. Both A and B

4. The common area(s) of the body radiographed for bone age determination is/are
   A. Skull
   B. Wrist
   C. Hand
   D. Both B and C

5. What pathologic condition is present if the posterior elements of one or more vertebrae fail to unite?
   A. Meningocele
   B. Spina bifida
   C. Myelomeningocele
   D. Spondylolisthesis

6. In patients with advanced osteoporosis, what type of radiographic technique is preferred?
   A. Low kVp; short scale contrast
   B. High kVp; short scale contrast
   C. Low kVp; long scale contrast
   D. High kVp; long scale contrast

7. The major causes of generalized _____ are aging and postmeno-pausal hormonal changes.
   A. Osteogenesis imperfecta
   B. Osteoporosis
   C. Osteopetrosis
   D. Osteomalacia

8. An inherited generalized disorder of connective tissue characterized by multiple fractures and a bluish color of the sclera of the eye is
   A. Osteogenesis imperfecta
   B. Osteoporosis
   C. Osteopetrosis
   D. Osteomalacia

9. Lack of vitamin D in the diet of infants and children can cause a systemic disease called
   A. Achondroplasia
   B. Rickets
   C. Osteomalacia
   D. Osteopetrosis

10. A disorder of metabolism causing an increased blood level of uric acid is called
   A. Achondroplasia
   B. Rickets
   C. Gout
   D. Urasia

11. A benign projection of bone with cartilage-like cap occurring around the knee in children or adolescents is
   A. Osteochondroma
   B. Enchondroma
   C. Achondroplasia
   D. Osteoma

12. An example of a malignant bone tumor is
   A. Osteogenic sarcoma
   B. Chondrosarcoma
   C. Ewing's sarcoma
   D. All of the above

13. The form of noninfectious arthritis characterized by osteoporosis, soft-tissue swelling, and erosions of the metacarpophalangeal joints and ulnar styloid processes is
   A. Reiter's
   B. Rheumatoid
   C. Psoriatic
   D. Osteoarthritis

14. The extremely common form of arthritis that is characterized by loss of joint cartilage and reactive new bone growth and is part of the normal wear of aging is
   A. Reiter's
   B. Rheumatoid
   C. Psoriatic
   D. Osteoarthritis

15. Inflammation of the small fluid-filled sacs located around joints that reduce friction is termed
   A. Tendinitis
   B. Arthritis
   C. Bursitis
   D. Both A and C

16. In what type of fracture is the skin broken?
   A. Open
   B. Compound
   C. Comminuted
   D. Both A and C

17. What type of fracture consists of more than two fragments?
   A. Open
   B. Compound
   C. Comminuted
   D. Both A and C

18. What term applies to the new calcium deposits that unite fracture sites?
   A. Bone
   B. Callus
   C. Periosteum
   D. Both A and C

19. What type of fracture occurs in bone weakened by some preexisting condition such as a metastatic lesion or multiple myeloma?
   A. Stress
   B. Colles'
   C. Pott's
   D. Pathologic

20. What is the name for the type of fracture that can occur from falling on the outstretched hand and involves the distal portion of the radius?
   A. Stress
   B. Colles'
   C. Pott's
   D. Pathologic

21. What name is applied to a fracture involving both malleoli?
   A. Stress
   B. Colles'
   C. Pott's
   D. Pathologic

22. What is the name applied to the fracture resulting from acute hyperextension of the head on the neck that usually effects C2 and C3?
   A. Hangman's
   B. Jefferson
   C. Boxer's
   D. Monteggia

23. What area of the spine does a clay shoveler's fracture involve?
   A. Lower thoracic and upper lumbar
   B. Lumbar only
   C. Lower cervical and upper thoracic
   D. Cervical only

24. Diagnosis of an intervertebral disk herniation requires which radiographic procedure(s)?
   A. Myelography
   B. CT
   C. MRI
   D. A or B or C

25. What medical term refers to a cleft in the pars interarticularis commonly involving the fifth lumbar vertebra?
   A. Spondylolisthesis
   B. Spondylolysis
   C. Spondylitis
   D. A or B or D

26. What pathologic condition sometimes occurs after trauma, causing an interrupted blood supply to a bone?
   A. Vasculitis
   B. Ischemic necrosis
   C. Cushing's
   D. Stress fracture

27. Place an "H" by those pathologic conditions that are harder to penetrate and an "E" by those that are easier to penetrate:
   _____ Callus
   _____ Ischemic necrosis
   _____ Atrophy
   _____ Osteolytic lesions
   _____ Acromegaly
   _____ Multiple myeloma
   _____ Osteoporosis
   _____ Osteosclerotic lesions

BIBLIOGRAPHY

Brower AC: *Arthritis in black and white,* Philadelphia, 1988, Saunders.

Greenfield GB: *Radiology of bone diseases,* ed 4, Philadelphia, 1990, Lippincott.

Greenspan A: *Orthopedic radiology: a practical approach,* Philadelphia, 1992, Lippincott.

Helms CA: *Fundamentals of skeletal radiology,* Philadelphia, 1989, Saunders.

Resnick D, Niwayama G: *Diagnosis of bone and joint disorders,* Philadelphia, 1988, Saunders.

Rogers LF: *Radiology of skeletal trauma,* New York, 1992, Churchhill Livingstone.

CHAPTER 4

Gastrointestinal System

■ **Prerequisite Knowledge**

The student should have a basic knowledge of the anatomy and physiology of the gastrointestinal system. In addition, proper learning and understanding of the material will be facilitated if the student has some clinical experience in gastrointestinal radiography and film evaluation, including a concept of the changes in technique required to compensate for density differences produced by a few of the underlying pathologic conditions.

■ **Goals**

To acquaint the student radiographer with the pathophysiology and radiographic manifestations of all of the common and some of the unusual disorders of the gastrointestinal system.

■ **Objectives**

1. Be able to classify the more common diseases in terms of their penetrability to x rays
2. Be familiar with the changes in technical factors required for obtaining optimal quality radiographs in patients with various underlying pathologic conditions
3. Understand and be able to define or describe all bold-faced terms in this chapter
4. Describe the physiology of the gastrointestinal system
5. Identify anatomic structures on both diagrams and radiographs of the gastrointestinal system
6. Be able to describe the various pathologic conditions affecting the gastrointestinal system as well as their radiographic manifestations

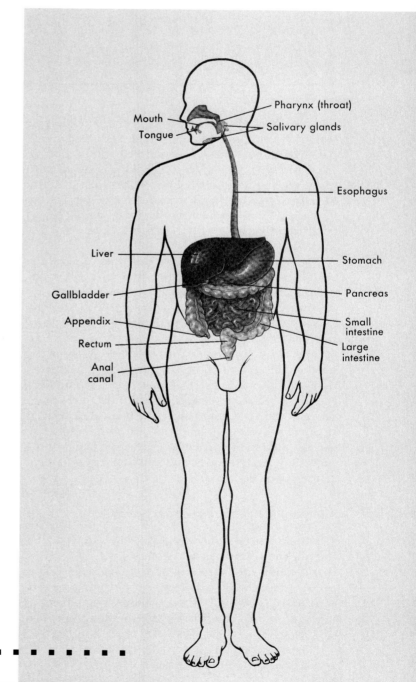

Mouth
Tongue
Pharynx (throat)
Salivary glands
Esophagus
Liver
Stomach
Gallbladder
Pancreas
Appendix
Small intestine
Rectum
Large intestine
Anal canal

∎ **Radiographer Notes**

Plain abdominal radiographs and contrast studies of the digestive tract remain the most common imaging examinations of the gastrointestinal system. Ultrasound and CT are the major imaging modalities for the pancreas and biliary tract, and MRI is now being used in some institutions to screen for hepatic metastases.

Plain abdominal radiographs must show an appropriately wide scale of contrast to demonstrate the many different densities in the abdominal cavity. Depending on the screen-film combination, this requires the use of a kVp in the middle to high range. Bony structures, such as the lumbar spine and its transverse processes, must be well demonstrated, as well as soft-tissue shadows of the liver, kidney, and psoas muscle. For barium studies of the gastrointestinal tract, adequate penetration of the dense barium solution requires a high kVp (about 120 kVp). For double-contrast (air-barium) studies, a kVp in the range of 90 kVp is needed to allow for penetration of the barium combined with excellent visualization of mucosal detail. Gallbladder studies require a shorter scale of contrast than other abdominal examinations and therefore are usually performed using a low to middle range of kVp (about 70 kVp).

As with other body systems, certain pathologic conditions require alterations in technical factors. In patients with ascites, a common complication of advanced cirrhosis, an increased kVp is required to penetrate the additional fluid content of the abdomen. On the other hand, a decreased kVp is needed in patients with suspected large or small bowel obstruction because of the excessive amount of gas in the abdominal cavity.

The radiographer usually is called on to assist the radiologist during fluoroscopic examinations of the gastrointestinal tract. Indeed, it is generally the radiograher's task to coerce the patient into drinking and not vomiting the rather unpleasant-tasting contrast material and to urge the patient to turn around several times to provide adequate mucosal coating for the double-contrast upper gastrointestinal series. Similarly, the radiographer may have to convince the patient to retain barium and air during the often uncomfortable barium enema examinations. It is frequently time well spent for the radiographer to explain fully to the patient both the mechanics of the procedure and the extreme importance of patient cooperation.

■ **Physiology of the Digestive System**

The basic function of the digestive system is to alter the chemical and physical composition of food so that it can be absorbed and used by body cells. This process depends on secretions of the endocrine and exocrine glands and the controlled movement of ingested food through the tract so that absorption can occur.

Digestion begins in the mouth with chewing **(mastication),** the mechanical breakdown of food. The secretion of saliva moistens the food in preparation for swallowing. Swallowing **(deglutition)** is a complex process that requires coordination of many muscles in the head and neck and the precise opening and closing of esophageal sphincters. Digestion continues in the stomach with the churning movement of gastric contents that have been mixed with hydrochloric acid and the proteolytic enzyme pepsin. The resulting milky white **chyme** is propelled through the pyloric sphincter into the duodenum by rhythmic smooth muscle contractions called **peristalsis.** The greatest amount of digestion occurs in the duodenum, the first part of the small bowel. In addition to intestinal secretions containing mucus and enzymes, digestion in this region is enhanced by secretions of the pancreas and liver. The pancreas secretes enzymes for the digestion of protein (trypsin and chymotrypsin), fat (lipase), and carbohydrate (amylase). It also secretes an alkaline solution to neutralize the acid carried into the small intestine from the stomach. Bile is secreted by the liver, stored in the gallbladder, and enters the duodenum through the common bile duct. Bile is an **emulsifer,** a substance that acts like soap by dispersing the fat into very small droplets that permit it to mix with water.

When digestion is complete, the nutrients are absorbed through the intestinal mucosa into blood capillaries and lymph vessels of the wall of the small bowel. The inner surface area of the small bowel is increased by the formation of numerous fingerlike projections **(villi),** which provide the largest amount of surface area possible for digestion and absorption.

Material that has not been digested passes into the colon, where water and minerals are absorbed and the remaining matter is excreted as feces. If the contents of the lower colon and rectum move at a rate that is slower than normal, extra water is absorbed from the fecal mass to produce a hardened stool and **constipation. Diarrhea** results from increased motility of the small bowel, which floods the colon with an excessive amount of water that cannot be completely absorbed.

The vermiform (worm-shaped) appendix arises from the inferomedial aspect of the cecum about 3 cm below the ileocecal valve. Although the appendix has no functional importance in digestion, it is often classified as an accessory digestive organ merely because of its location.

The liver is the largest gland in the body and is responsible for several vital functions. Liver cells detoxify (make harmless) a variety of poisonous substances that enter the blood from the intestines. Toxic chemicals that are changed to nontoxic compounds in the liver include ammonia (converted to urea and excreted by the kidneys), alcohol, and barbiturates. Liver cells secrete about 1 pint of bile each day. As mentioned, bile is an emulsifier that is essential for the digestion and absorption of dietary fat and the fat-soluble vitamins A, D, E, and K. Bile is a greenish liquid consisting of water, bile salts, cholesterol, and bilirubin (breakdown product of hemoglobin).

Liver cells play a vital role in the metabolism of proteins, fats, and carbohydrates. The liver is the major site of synthesis of the enzymes necessary for various cellular activities throughout the body. Liver cells also synthesize blood proteins, such as albumin, which maintains the correct amount of fluid within blood vessels, and the essential proteins required for blood clotting (fibrinogen and prothrombin). Therefore liver damage may result in edema (excess water in the soft tissues) and a serious bleeding tendency. The liver plays an important role in maintaining the proper level of glucose in the blood by taking up excess glucose absorbed by the small intestine and storing it as **glycogen.** When the level of circulating glucose falls below normal, the liver breaks down glycogen and releases glucose into the bloodstream. Liver cells also store iron and vitamins A, B_{12}, and D.

The gallbladder is a pear-shaped sac that lies on the undersurface of the liver. Its function is to store bile that enters it by way of the hepatic and cystic ducts and to concentrate the bile by absorbing water. In response to the presence of dietary fat in the small bowel, the gallbladder contracts and ejects the concentrated bile into the duodenum.

The pancreas controls the level of circulating blood glucose by secreting insulin and glucagon in the islands of Langerhans. An increased concentra-

tion of glucose in the blood stimulates the beta cells to increase insulin secretion, which decreases the blood glucose level probably by accelerating the transport of glucose into cells. A blood glucose concentration less than normal triggers the alpha cells to secrete glucagon, which accelerates the breakdown of glycogen into glucose by the liver.

As discussed, pancreatic secretions are vital for digestion. Pancreatic enzymes that pass through the pancreatic duct into the duodenum are necessary for the breakdown of protein, carbohydrate, and fat.

▪ Esophagus
Esophagitis
Reflux

Although the reflux of gastric acid contents is the most common cause of acute esophagitis, infectious and granulomatous disorders, physical injury (caustic agents, radiation injury), and medication may produce a similar inflammatory response. Regardless of the cause, acute esophagitis produces burning chest pain that may simulate the pain of heart disease. The esophagus is often dilated with a loss of effective peristalsis. Nonpropulsive peristaltic waves, ranging from mild tertiary contractions to severe segmental spasms, are an early finding.

Reflux esophagitis develops when the lower esophageal sphincter fails to act as an effective barrier to the entry of gastric acid contents into the distal esophagus. Although there is a higher-than-normal likelihood of gastroesophageal reflux in patients with sliding hiatal hernias, reflux esophagitis can be endoscopically demonstrated in only about one fourth of patients with them. On the other hand, esophagitis is often encountered in patients in whom no hiatal hernia can be demonstrated.

Several radiographic approaches have been suggested for the demonstration of gastroesophageal reflux. One procedure is to increase intraabdominal pressure by straight-leg raising or manual pressure on the abdomen, often with Valsalva's maneuver (forced expiration with the glottis closed). Turning the patient from prone to supine or vice versa may demonstrate reflux of barium from the stomach into the esophagus. A new technique for demonstrating and measuring gastroesophageal reflux is to scan the lower esophagus and stomach after the oral administration of a radioactive substance (Figure 4-1). It must be remembered, however, that the failure to demonstrate reflux radiographically does not exclude the possibility that a patient's esophagitis is related to reflux. As long as typical radiographic findings of reflux esophagitis are noted, there is little reason to persist in strenuous efforts to actually

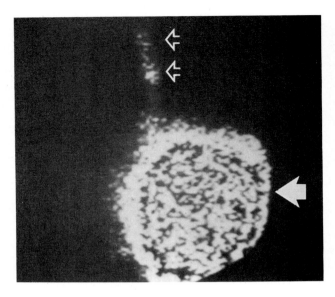

Figure 4-1   Gastroesophageal reflux. Notice reflux of orally administered radionuclide into esophagus *(open arrows)* from stomach *(solid arrow)*.

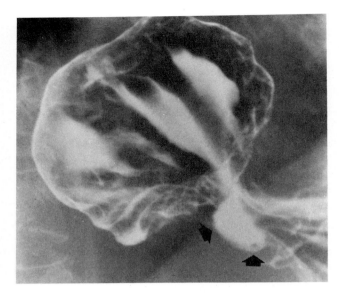

Figure 4-3   Ulcer *(arrows)* in large hiatal hernia sac.

Figure 4-2   Large, penetrating ulcer *(arrow)* in reflux esophagitis.

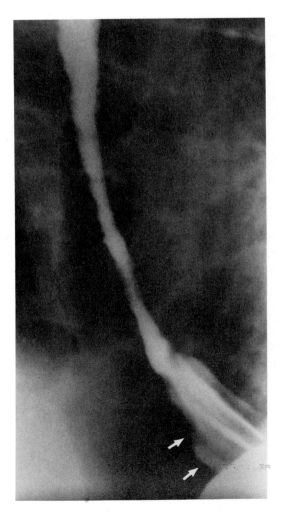

Figure 4-4   Long esophageal stricture caused by reflux esophagitis. Notice the associated hiatal hernia *(arrows)*.

demonstrate retrograde flow of barium from the stomach into the esophagus.

The earliest radiographic findings in reflux esophagitis are detectable on double-contrast studies. They consist of superficial ulcerations or erosions that appear as streaks or dots of barium superimposed on the flat mucosa of the distal esophagus. In single-contrast studies of patients with esophagitis the outer borders of the barium-filled esophagus are not sharply seen, but rather have a hazy, serrated appearance with shallow, irregular protrusions that are indicative of erosions of varying length and depth. Widening and coarsening of edematous longitudinal folds can simulate filling defects. In addition to diffuse erosion, reflux esophagitis can result in large, discrete penetrating ulcers in the distal esophagus (Figure 4-2) or in a hiatal hernia sac (Figure 4-3). Fibrotic healing of diffuse reflux esophagitis or a localized penetrating ulcer may cause

narrowing of the distal esophagus. Strictures resulting from reflux esophagitis tend to be smooth and tapering with no demonstrable mucosal pattern (Figure 4-4).

Barrett's esophagus

Barrett's esophagus is a condition related to severe reflux esophagitis in which the normal squamous lining of the lower esophagus is destroyed and replaced by columnar epithelium similar to that of the stomach. Ulceration in Barrett's esophagus typically occurs at the squamocolumnar junction. Although a hiatal hernia with gastroesophageal reflux is commonly demonstrated, the Barrett's ulcer is usually separated from the hiatal hernia by a variable length of normal-appearing esophagus (Figure 4-5), in contrast to reflux esophagitis, in which the distal esophagus is abnormal down to the level of the hernia. As with reflux esophagitis, fibrotic heal-

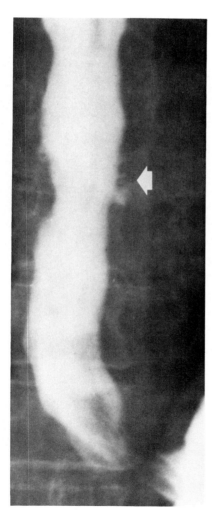

Figure 4-5 Barrett's esophagus. Ulcerations *(arrow)* have developed at a distance from esophagogastric junction.

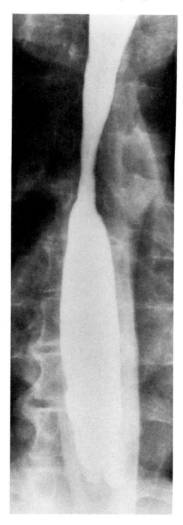

Figure 4-6 Barrett's esophagus. Notice smooth, tapered stricture in upper thoracic esophagus.

ing of the ulceration in a Barrett's esophagus often leads to a smooth, tapered stricture (Figure 4-6). In addition to postinflammatory stricture, Barrett's esophagus has an unusually high propensity for developing malignancy in the columnar cell–lined portion. These tumors are almost always adenocarcinoma, which is otherwise very rare in the esophagus.

Because the distal esophagus consists of a gastric type of mucosa in Barrett's esophagus, it actively takes up the intravenously injected radionuclide pertechnetate. The demonstration of a continuous concentration of the isotope from the stomach into the distal esophagus to a level that corresponds approximately to that of the ulcer or stricture is indicative of Barrett's esophagus.

Candida and *Herpesvirus*

Candida and *Herpesvirus* are the organisms most often responsible for infectious esophagitis, which usually occurs in patients with widespread malig-

nancy who are receiving radiation therapy, chemotherapy, corticosteroids, or other immunosuppressive agents. It also can develop in patients with AIDS and even in otherwise healthy adults who have received antibiotics (especially tetracycline) for upper respiratory infection. The classic radiographic appearance is an irregular cobblestone pattern with a shaggy marginal contour of the esophagus caused by deep ulcerations and sloughing of the mucosa (Figure 4-7).

Ingestion of corrosive agents

The ingestion of alkaline corrosive agents produces acute inflammatory changes in the esophagus. Superficial penetration of the toxic agent results in only minimal ulceration. Deeper penetration of the submucosa and muscular layers causes sloughing of destroyed tissue and deep ulceration. Drug-induced esophagitis may occur in patients who have delayed esophageal transit time, which permits prolonged mucosal contact with the ingested substance. The most common drug causing esophageal ulceration is

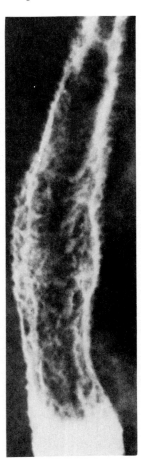

Figure 4-7 *Candida* esophagitis. Multiple ulcers and nodular plaques produce grossly irregular contour of shaggy esophagus. This manifestation of far-advanced candidiasis has become infrequent because of earlier and better treatment of the disease.

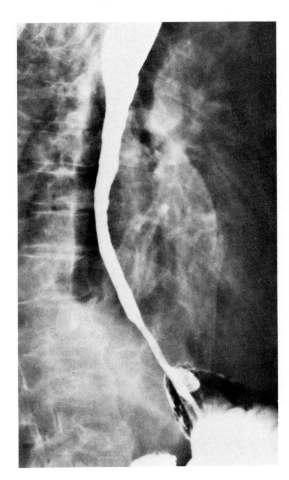

Figure 4-8 Corrosive stricture resulting from ingestion of lye.

potassium chloride in tablet form. Other medications that can cause esophagitis are weak caustic agents that are harmless when they pass rapidly through the esophagus.

Healing of the intense mucosal and intramural inflammation of acute esophagitis may lead to pronounced fibrosis and stricture formation. These benign strictures tend to be long lesions with tapered margins and relatively smooth mucosal surfaces (Figure 4-8), in contrast to the irregular narrowing, mucosal destruction and overhanging margins that are generally associated with malignant processes.

Hiatal hernia

Hiatal hernia is the most frequent abnormality detected on upper gastrointestinal examination. Its broad radiographic spectrum ranges from large esophagogastric hernias, in which much of the stomach lies within the thoracic cavity and there is a predisposition to volvulus (twisting), to small hernias that emerge above the diaphragm only under certain circumstances (related to changes in intraabdominal or intrathoracic pressure) and easily slide back into the abdomen through the hiatus. The

symptoms associated with hiatal hernia, as well as its complications (esophagitis, esophageal ulcer, esophageal stenosis), are related to the presence of esophageal reflux rather than the hiatal hernia itself. Most hiatal hernias do not produce symptoms and are clinically of no importance.

Although the diagnosis of hiatal hernia generally requires a barium study (Figure 4-9), at times a large hiatal hernia may appear on plain chest radiographs as a soft-tissue mass in the posterior mediastinum, often containing a prominent air-fluid level (Figure 4-10).

Cancer of the esophagus

Progressive difficulty in swallowing (dysphagia) in a person older than 40 years of age must be assumed to be caused by cancer until proved otherwise. Because the symptoms of esophageal carcinoma tend to appear late in the course of the disease and since the lack of a limiting outer layer (serosa) commonly permits direct extension of the tumor by the time of initial diagnosis, carcinoma of the esophagus has a dismal prognosis. Most carcinomas of the esophagus are of the squamous cell type. The incidence of carcinoma of the esophagus is far higher in men than in women. There is a strong correlation between excessive alcohol intake, smoking, and esophageal carcinoma.

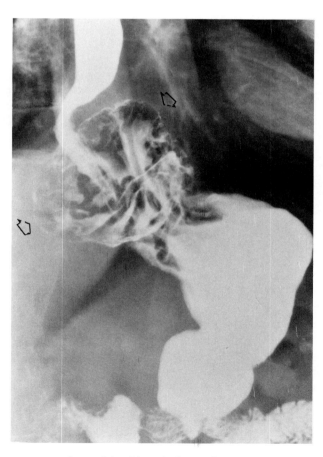

Figure 4-9   Large hiatal hernia *(arrows)*.

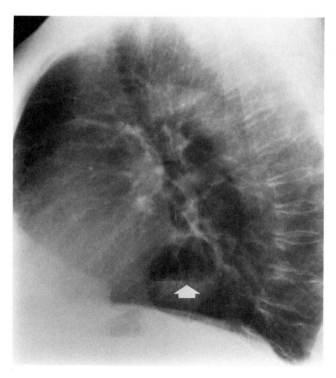

Figure 4-10   Air-fluid level *(arrow)* in hiatal hernia seen on lateral chest radiograph.

The earliest radiographic appearance of infiltrating carcinoma of the esophagus is a flat, plaquelike lesion, occasionally with central ulceration, that involves one wall of the esophagus (Figure 4-11). At this stage there may be minimal reduction in the caliber of the lumen. Unless the patient is carefully examined in various positions, this earliest form of esophageal carcinoma can be missed. As the infiltrating cancer progresses, irregularity of the wall is seen, indicating mucosal destruction. Advanced lesions encircle the lumen completely, causing annular constrictions with overhanging margins and often some degree of obstruction. The lumen through the stenotic area is irregular, and mucosal folds are absent or severely ulcerated (Figure 4-12). Less commonly, carcinoma of the esophagus can appear as a localized polypoid mass, often with deep ulceration and a fungating appearance.

Luminal obstruction as a result of carcinoma causes proximal dilatation of the esophagus and may result in aspiration pneumonia. Extension of the tumor to adjacent mediastinal structures may lead to fistula formation, especially between the esophagus and the respiratory tract (see Figure 4-19).

CT has become a major method for staging patients with esophageal carcinoma. It can provide information on tumor size, extension, and resectability that was previously available only at thorac-

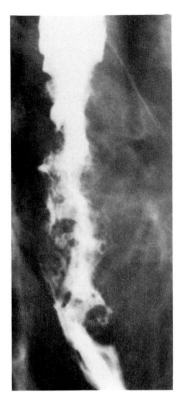

Figure 4-12 Carcinoma of esophagus. Irregular narrowing with ulceration involves extensive segment of thoracic portion of esophagus.

otomy (Figure 4-13). Evidence of spread of tumor includes the obliteration of fat planes between the esophagus and adjacent structures (left atrium, aorta), the formation of a fistula to the tracheobronchial tree, and evidence of metastatic disease (low-density masses in the liver; enlargement of draining lymph nodes).

Esophageal varices

Esophageal varices are dilated veins in the wall of the esophagus that are most commonly the result of increased pressure in the portal venous system (portal hypertension), which is usually a result of cirrhosis of the liver. In patients with portal hypertension, much of the portal blood cannot flow along its normal pathway through the liver to the inferior vena cava and then on to the heart. Instead, it must go by a circuitous collateral route, and increased blood flow through these dilated veins causes the development of esophageal (and gastric) varices. Esophageal varices are infrequently demonstrated in the absence of portal hypertension. "Downhill" varices are produced when venous blood from the head and neck cannot reach the heart because of an

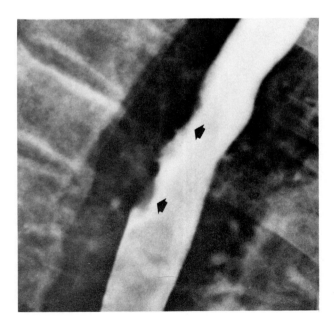

Figure 4-11 Early carcinoma of esophagus. Flat, plaquelike lesion (arrows) involves posterior wall of esophagus.

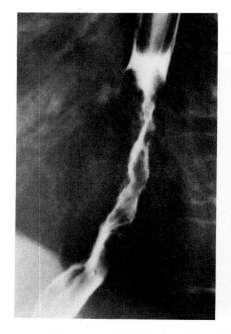

A

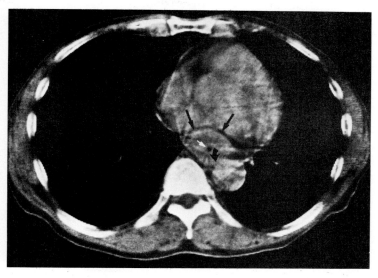

B

Figure 4-13 CT staging of esophageal carcinoma. **A,** Esophagram demonstrates infiltrating lesion causing irregular narrowing of distal part of esophagus. **B,** CT scan shows mass of bulky carcinoma *(black arrows)* filling most of lumen *(white arrow)*. Obliteration of fat plane adjacent to aorta *(curved arrow)* indicates mediastinal invasion.

obstruction of the superior vena cava caused by tumors or inflammatory disease in the mediastinum. In this situation blood flows "downhill" through the esophageal veins before eventually entering the portal vein, through which it flows to the inferior vena cava and the right atrium.

The characteristic radiographic appearance of esophageal varices is serpiginous thickening of folds, which appear as round or oval filling defects resembling the beads of a rosary (Figure 4-14). Precise technique is required to demonstrate esophageal varices. Complete filling of the esophagus with barium may obscure varices, whereas powerful contractions of the esophagus may squeeze blood out of the varices and make them impossible to detect.

The major complication of esophageal varices is bleeding. Their appearance in patients with cirrhotic liver disease implies significant portal venous hypertension and is an ominous sign, since up to 90% of the deaths from liver disease in patients with cirrhosis occur within 2 years of the diagnosis of varices.

Achalasia

Achalasia is a functional obstruction of the distal section of the esophagus with proximal dilation

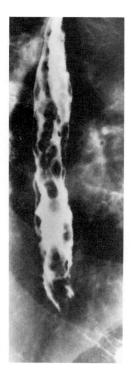

Figure 4-14 Esophageal varices. Notice diffuse round and oval filling defects, which resemble rosary beads.

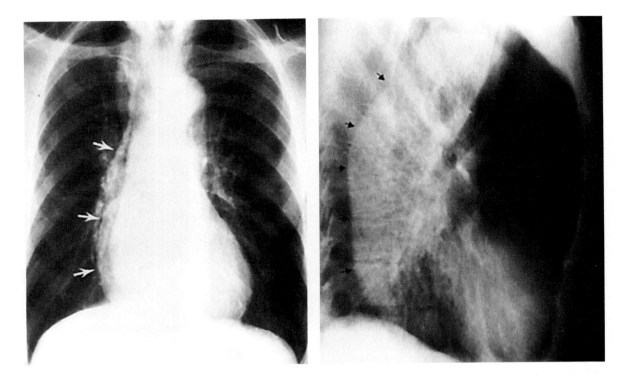

Figure 4-15   Achalasia. Frontal chest radiograph demonstrates margin of dilated tortuous aorta *(arrows)* parallel with right border of heart. (From Eisenberg RL: *Gastrointestinal radiology: a pattern approach*, Philadelphia, 1990, Lippincott.)

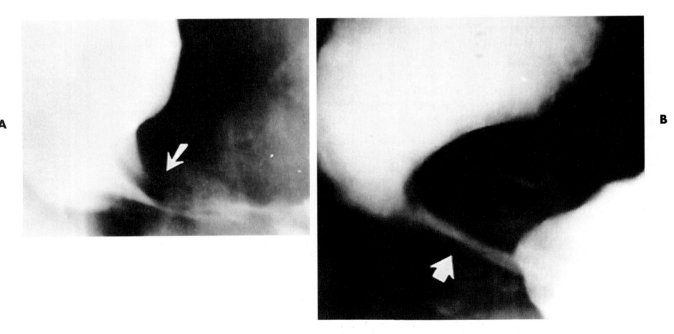

Figure 4-16   Achalasia. **A,** "Rat-tail" narrowing of distal part of the esophagus *(arrow).* **B,** Small spurt of barium *(arrow)* enters stomach through narrowed distal segment (jet effect). (From Eisenberg RL: *Gastrointestinal radiology: a pattern approach*, Philadelphia, 1990, Lippincott.)

caused by incomplete relaxation of the lower esophageal sphincter. It is related to a paucity or absence of ganglion cells in the myenteric neural plexuses of the distal esophageal wall. On plain chest radiographs, the dilated, tortuous esophagus may produce a widened mediastinum (often with an air-fluid level) on the right side adjacent to the cardiac shadow (Figure 4-15). The hallmark of achalasia, seen on barium studies, is a gradually tapered, smooth, conical 1 to 3 cm narrowing of the distal esophageal segment ("rat-tail" or "beak" appearance) (Figure 4-16). On sequential radiographs, especially with the patient upright, only small spurts of barium pass through the narrowed distal segment to enter the stomach.

Esophageal diverticula

Esophageal diverticula are common lesions that either contain all layers of the wall (traction) or are composed of only mucosa and submucosa herniating through the muscular layer (pulsion). Zencker's diverticula arise from the posterior wall of the upper (cervical) esophagus (Figure 4-17). Occasionally, they can become so large that they almost occlude the esophageal lumen. Diverticula of the thoracic

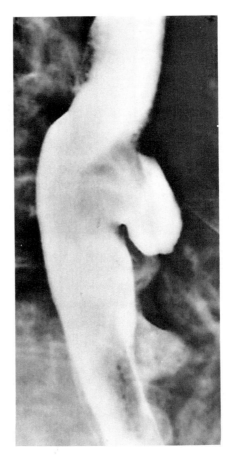

Figure 4-18 Traction diverticulum of midthoracic portion of esophagus. (From Eisenberg RL: *Gastrointestinal radiology: a pattern approach*, Philadelphia, 1990, Lippincott.)

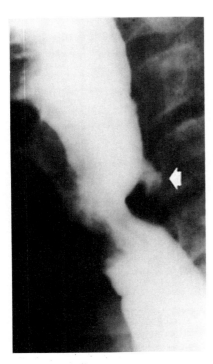

Figure 4-17 Small Zencker's diverticulum. Saccular outpouching *(arrow)* arising posteriorly just proximal to impression produced by cricopharyngeus muscle. (From Eisenberg RL: *Gastrointestinal radiology: a pattern approach*, Philadelphia, 1990, Lippincott.)

portion of the esophagus are primarily found opposite the bifurcation of the trachea in the region of the hilum of the lung (Figure 4-18). These traction diverticula develop in response to the pull of fibrous adhesions after infection of the mediastinal lymph nodes. Epiphrenic diverticula arise in the distal 10 cm of the esophagus (Figure 4-19). They are associated with incoordination of esophageal peristalsis and sphincter relaxation, which increases the intraluminal pressure in this segment.

Foreign bodies

A wide spectrum of foreign bodies can become impacted in the esophagus, usually in the cervical esophagus at or just above the level of the thoracic inlet (Figure 4-20). Most metallic objects, such as pins, coins, and small toys, are very radiopaque and are easily visualized on radiographs or during fluoroscopy. Objects made of aluminum and some light

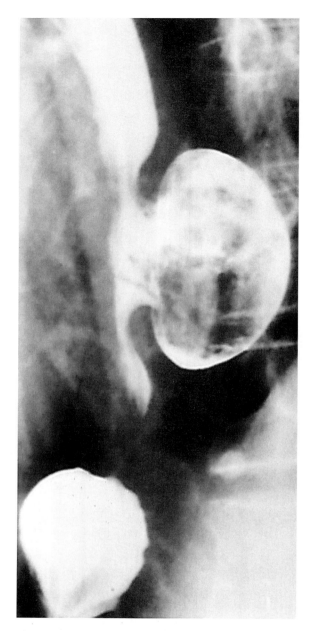

Figure 4-19 Epiphrenic diverticulum. (From Eisenberg RL: *Gastrointestinal radiology: a pattern approach,* Philadelphia, 1990, Lippincott.)

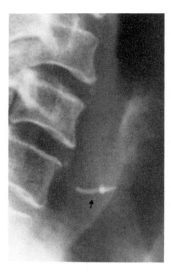

Figure 4-20 Fish bone *(arrow)* impacted in lower cervical portion of esophagus.

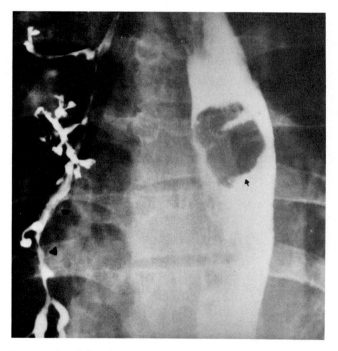

Figure 4-21 Meat impaction in esophagus. Large bolus of hot dog *(arrow)* is trapped in midesophagus of patient with quadriplegia. Notice barium in bronchial tree *(arrowheads)* caused by aspiration.

alloys may be impossible to detect radiographically because the density of these metals is almost equal to that of soft tissue. It is essential that any suspected foreign body be evaluated on two projections to be certain that the object projected over the esophagus truly lies within it.

Nonopaque foreign bodies in the esophagus, especially pieces of poorly chewed meat, can be demonstrated only after the ingestion of barium (Figure 4-21). Such foreign bodies usually become impacted in the distal esophagus just above the level of the diaphragm and are often associated with a distal stricture. These intraluminal filling defects usually have an irregular surface and may resemble a completely obstructing carcinoma.

Perforation of the esophagus

Perforation of the esophagus may be a complication of esophagitis, peptic ulcer, neoplasm, external trauma, or instrumentation. At times, perforation of a previously healthy esophagus can result from severe vomiting or coughing, often from dietary or alcoholic indiscretion. Complete rupture of the wall of the esophagus may cause the sudden development of severe upper gastric pain simulating myocardial infarction. In the Mallory-Weiss syndrome, an increase in intraluminal and intramural pressure associated with vomiting after an alcoholic bout causes superficial mucosal laceration or fissures near the esophagogastric junction that produce severe hemorrhage.

A perforation that extends throughout the entire esophageal wall can lead to free air in the mediastinum or periesophageal soft tissues. The administration of radiopaque contrast material may demonstrate extravasation through the perforation (Figure 4-22) or an intramural dissection channel separated by an intervening lucent line from the normal esophageal lumen.

Tracheoesophageal fistula

Congenital type

Congenital tracheoesophageal (TE) fistulas result from failure of a satisfactory esophageal lumen to develop completely separate from the trachea. Esophageal atresia and TE fistulas are often associated with other congenital malformations involving

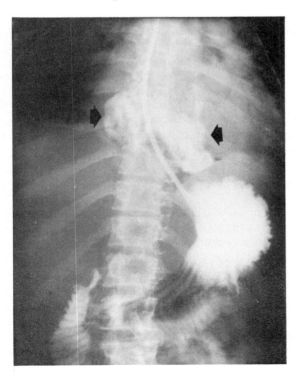

Figure 4-22 Esophageal perforation. Extravasation of contrast material *(arrows)* is seen in previously healthy patient who experienced severe vomiting after excessive ingestion of alcohol.

the skeleton, cardiovascular system, and gastrointestinal tract.

The most common type of TE fistula, type III (85% to 90%), consists of an upper segment ending in a blind pouch at the level of the bifurcation of the trachea or slightly above it and a lower segment attached to the trachea by a short fistulous tract. Radiographic demonstration of looping of a small esophageal feeding tube indicates that the proximal esophagus ends in a blind pouch (Figure 4-23, A). Plain radiographs of the abdomen demonstrate the presence of air in the bowel that has freely entered the stomach through the fistulous connection between the trachea and distal esophagus.

In the next most common type of esophageal anomaly, type I, both the upper and lower segments of the esophagus are blind pouches. This anomaly can be differentiated from the type III lesion only by plain abdominal radiographs, which demonstrate the absence of air below the diaphragm in the type I lesion and air below the stomach in the type III lesion.

In the type II form of TE fistula, the upper esophageal segment communicates with the trachea, whereas the lower segment ends in a blind pouch. Because there is no connection between the trachea and the stomach, there is no radiographic evidence of gas within the abdomen. The oral administration of contrast material in this condition immediately outlines the tracheobronchial tree.

There are two forms of type IV TE fistula. In one, the upper and lower esophageal segments end in blind pouches, both of which are connected to the tracheobronchial tree. In this case gas is seen in the stomach, and oral contrast material outlines both fistulas and the bronchial tree. In the other form of type IV fistula (H fistula), both the trachea and the esophagus are intact. These two structures are connected by a single fistulous tract that can be found at any level from the cricoid cartilage of the trachea to the tracheal bifurcation (Figure 4-23, B). Unlike the other forms of TE fistula, the H fistula may not be identified in infancy and, if it is small and only occasionally causes emptying of material into the lungs, can permit survival into adulthood.

Acquired type

About 50% of acquired fistulas between the trachea and esophagus are caused by malignancy in the mediastinum. Almost all the rest result from infectious processes or trauma.

Fistulization between the esophagus and the respiratory tract is a major late complication of esophageal carcinoma and is often a terminal event (Figure 4-24). A fistula can also be a complication of erosion

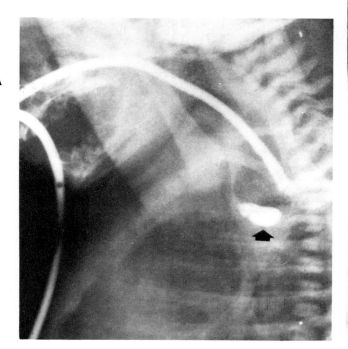

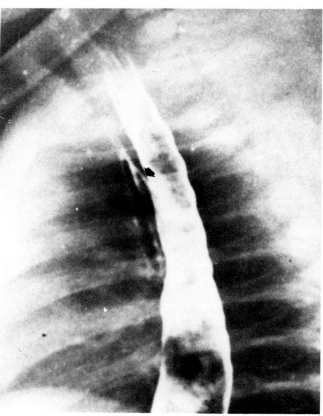

Figure 4-23 Congenital tracheoesophageal fistula. **A,** Type III fistula *(arrow),* in which contrast material injected through feeding tube demonstrates occlusion of proximal esophageal pouch. **B,** Type IV, or H, fistula *(arrow).*

into the esophagus by carcinoma of the lung arising near or metastasizing to the middle mediastinum or by mediastinal metastases from other primary sites. Regardless of therapy, the overall prognosis of malignant TE fistulas is dismal, and more than 80% of patients with this complication die within 3 months from uncontrollable hemorrhage or from pulmonary infection caused by repeated episodes of aspiration pneumonia.

Fistulous communications between the esophagus and the tracheobronchial tree can be the result of esophageal instrumentation and perforation. This is most common after esophagoscopy but may also occur after instrumental dilatation of strictures by bougienage, pneumatic dilatation of the esophagus for the treatment of achalasia, or even the insertion of a nasogastric tube. Blunt or penetrating trauma to the chest, especially after crush injury, can result in esophageal perforation and fistulization. After traumatic perforation of the thoracic esophagus, chest radiographs may demonstrate air dissecting within

the mediastinum and soft tissues, often with pleural effusion or hydropneumothorax. The introduction of an oral contrast agent may demonstrate the site of perforation and the extent of fistulization.

▪ Stomach

Gastritis

Inflammation of the stomach can be the result of a variety of irritants including alcohol, corrosive agents, and infection. Alcoholic gastritis may produce thickening of gastric folds (Figure 4-25), multiple superficial gastric erosions, or both. In corrosive gastritis, the acute inflammatory reaction heals by fibrosis and scarring, which results in severe narrowing of the antrum and may cause gastric outlet obstruction. In bacterial (phlegmonous) gastritis, inflammatory thickening of the gastric wall causes narrowing of the stomach that may mimic gastric cancer. The diagnosis of infectious gastritis can be made if there is evidence of bubbles of gas

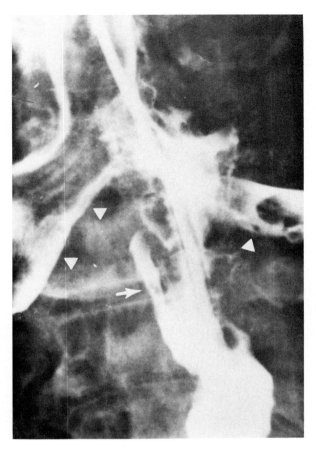

Figure 4-24   Esophagorespiratory fistula between esophagus *(arrow)* and bronchial tree *(arrowheads),* seen as complication of esophageal carcinoma.

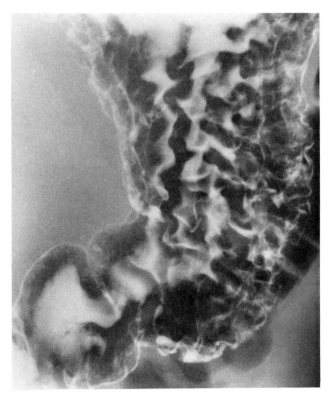

Figure 4-25   Gastritis. Notice pronounced thickening of rugal folds throughout stomach.

(produced by the bacteria) in the stomach wall (Figure 4-26).

Chronic atrophic gastritis refers to severe mucosal atrophy (wasting) that causes thinning and a relative absence of mucosal folds, with the fundus or entire stomach having a bald appearance. This is a nonspecific radiographic pattern that can be related to such factors as age, malnutrition, medication, and complications of alcoholism. Chronic atrophic gastritis also occurs in patients with pernicious anemia, who cannot absorb vitamin B$_{12}$ because of an inability of the stomach to secrete intrinsic factor (or hydrochloric acid).

Peptic ulcer disease

Peptic ulcer disease is an inflammatory process involving the stomach and duodenum caused by the action of acid and the enzyme pepsin secreted by the stomach. The spectrum of peptic ulcer disease varies from small and shallow superficial erosions to huge ulcers that may perforate through the bowel wall.

The major complications of peptic ulcer disease are hemorrhage, perforation, and gastric outlet obstruction. Peptic ulcer disease is the most common cause of acute upper gastrointestinal bleeding. Free perforation of a peptic ulcer is the most frequent cause of pneumoperitoneum with peritonitis (see page 169). Narrowing of the lumen of the distal stomach or duodenal bulb caused by peptic ulcer disease is by far the most common cause of gastric outlet obstruction.

Duodenal ulcer

Duodenal ulcer is the most common manifestation of peptic ulcer disease. More than 95% of duodenal ulcers occur in the first portion of the duodenum (duodenal bulb). An unequivocal diagnosis of active duodenal ulcer requires the demonstration of the ulcer crater, which appears in profile as a small collection of barium projecting from the lumen. When seen en face, the ulcer niche appears as a rounded or linear collection of contrast material surrounded by lucent folds that often radiate toward the crater (Figure 4-27). Secondary signs of duodenal ulcer disease are thickening of mucosal folds and deformity of the duodenal bulb. Acute ulcers incite

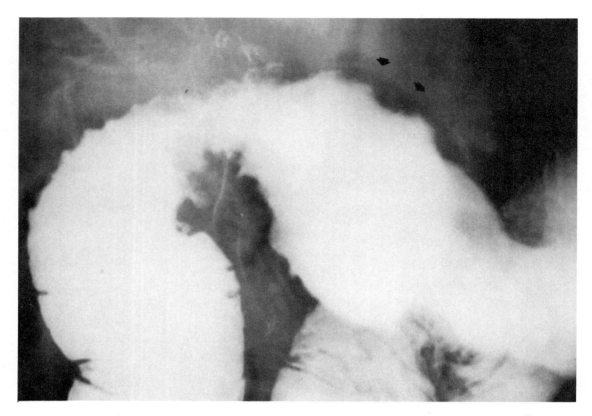

Figure 4-26   Phlegmonous emphysematous gastritis. Notice severe, irregular ulceration of distal stomach, with air in wall *(arrows)*.

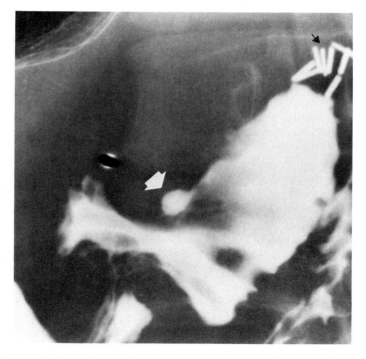

Figure 4-27   Duodenal ulcer. Ulcer niche appears as rounded collection of barium *(white arrow)* surrounded by lucent edema. Of incidental note are multiple surgical clips *(black arrow)*.

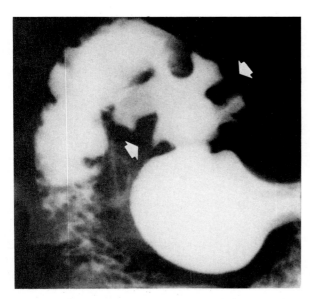

Figure 4-28 Chronic duodenal ulcer disease. Typical clover-leaf deformity is visible *(arrows.)*

muscular spasm leading to deformity of the margins of the duodenal bulb that may be inconstant and varied during the examination. With chronic ulceration, fibrosis and scarring cause a fixed deformity that persists even though the ulcer heals. Symmetric narrowing of the duodenal bulb in its midportion may produce the typical cloverleaf deformity of chronic duodenal ulcer disease (Figure 4-28).

Gastric ulcer

Unlike duodenal ulcers, which are virtually always benign, up to 5% of gastric ulcers are malignant. Radiographic signs that indicate whether a gastric ulcer is more likely to be benign or malignant have been described. The classic sign of a benign gastric ulcer on profile views is penetration, the clear projection of the ulcer outside the normal barium-filled gastric lumen because the ulcer represents an excavation in the wall of the stomach (Figure 4-29). A thin lucency at the base of the ulcer reflecting mucosal edema caused by inflammatory exudate is another sign of benignancy. When viewed en face, a gastric ulcer appears as a persistent collection of barium surrounded by a halo of edema (Figure 4-30). A hallmark of benign gastric ulcer is radiation of mucosal folds to the edge of the crater. However, since radiating folds can be identified in both malignant and benign ulcers, the character of the folds must be carefully assessed. If the folds are smooth and slender and appear to extend into the edge of the crater, the ulcer is most likely benign (Figure 4-31, A). In contrast, irregular folds that merge into a mound of polypoid tissue around the crater are

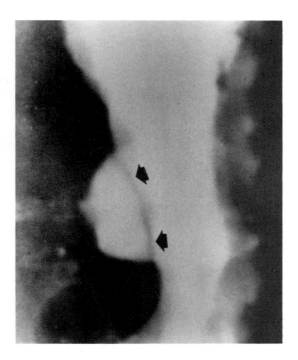

Figure 4-29 Benign gastric ulcer. Penetration of contrast material outside normal barium-filled gastric lumen associated with thin, sharply demarcated, lucent line with parallel straight margins *(arrows)* representing edema at base of ulcer crater.

Figure 4-30 Benign gastric ulcer. On *en face* projection, prominent radiating folds extend directly to ulcer. Lucency around ulcer *(arrows)* represents inflammatory mass effect. (From Margulis AR, Burhenne JH, editors: *Alimentary tract radiology,* ed 4, St. Louis, 1989, Mosby.)

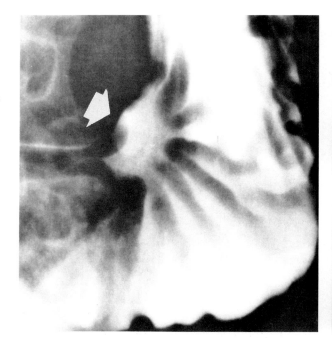

Figure 4-31   Radiating folds in gastric ulcers. **A,** Small, slender folds extending to edge of crater *(arrow)* indicate benign nature of ulcer. **B,** In this malignant gastric ulcer, thick folds radiate to irregular mound of tissue around ulcer *(arrow).*

suggestive of malignancy (Figure 4-31, B). Although the size, shape, number, and location of gastric ulcers were formerly suggested as criteria for distinguishing between benign and malignant lesions, these findings are of little practical value. One exception is ulcers in the gastric fundus above the level of the esophagogastric junction, essentially all of which are malignant.

An abrupt transition between the normal mucosa and the abnormal tissues surrounding a gastric ulcer is characteristic of a malignant lesion (Figure 4-32), in contrast to the diffuse and almost imperceptible transition between the normal gastric mucosa and the mound of edema surrounding a benign ulcer. Neoplastic tissue surrounding a malignant ulcer is usually nodular, unlike the smooth contour of the edematous mound around a benign ulcer. A malignant ulcer does not penetrate beyond the normal gastric lumen but remains within it because the ulcer merely represents a necrotic area within an intramural or intraluminal mass.

Most benign gastric ulcers heal completely with medical therapy (Figure 4-33). Complete healing does not necessarily mean that the stomach returns to an absolutely normal radiographic appearance; bizarre deformities can result because of fibrotic retraction and stiffening of the wall of the stomach. Although many malignant ulcers show significant

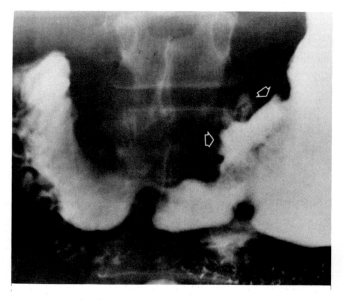

Figure 4-32   Malignant gastric ulcer. There is abrupt transition between normal mucosa and abnormal tissue surrounding irregular gastric ulcer *(arrows).*

healing, there is almost never complete disappearance of the ulcer crater.

The role of endoscopy in evaluating patients with gastric ulcers is controversial. At present, endoscopy is indicated whenever the radiographic findings are not typical of a benign ulcer, if healing of the ulcer

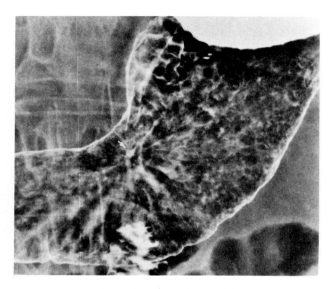

Figure 4-33 Healing of gastric ulcer. Folds converge to residual central depression *(arrow)*.

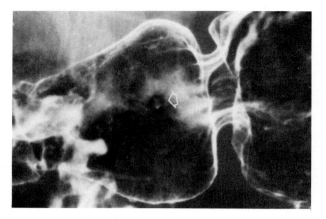

Figure 4-34 Superficial gastric erosions in patient with gastritis. Collection of barium represents shallow erosion surrounded by radiolucent halo *(arrow)*.

does not progress at the expected rate, or if the mucosa surrounding a healed ulcer crater has a nodular surface or any other feature suggestive of an underlying early gastric cancer.

Superficial gastric erosions

Superficial gastric erosions are ulcerations that are so small and shallow that they are rarely demonstrated on conventional single-contrast upper gastrointestinal examinations. With the increasing use of double-contrast techniques, a superficial gastric erosion typically appears radiographically as a tiny fleck of barium, which represents the erosion, surrounded by a radiolucent halo, which represents a mound of edematous mucosa (Figure 4-34). Possible factors implicated in the production of superficial gastric erosions include alcohol, anti-inflammatory drugs (aspirin, steroids), Crohn's disease (see page 151), and candidiasis (see page 124).

Cancer of the stomach

Because pain is infrequently an early symptom, carcinoma of the stomach is rarely noted until the disease is far advanced and thus has a dismal prognosis. The incidence of gastric cancer varies widely throughout the world. It is very high in Japan, Chile, and parts of Eastern Europe. It is low in the United States, where for an unknown reason the incidence of the disease has been decreasing. Several conditions appear to predispose persons to the development of carcinoma of the stomach. There is an increased risk of gastric cancer in patients with atrophic gastric mucosa, as a pernicious anemia, and

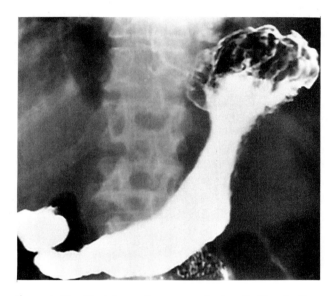

Figure 4-35 Gastric carcinoma producing linitis plastica pattern.

in persons 10 to 20 years after a partial gastrectomy for peptic ulcer disease. A suggestive laboratory sign is achlorhydria, the absence of hydrochloric acid in gastric secretions obtained by means of a stomach tube.

Gastric carcinoma can present a broad spectrum of radiographic appearances. Tumor infiltration of the gastric wall may stimulate intense fibrosis, which produces diffuse thickening, narrowing, and fixation of the stomach wall (linitis plastica pattern) (Figure 4-35). The stomach is contracted into a tubular structure without normal pliability. This fibrotic process usually begins near the pylorus and progresses slowly upward with the fundus being

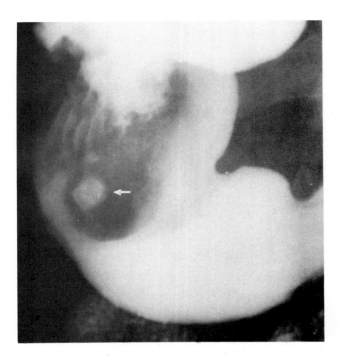

Figure 4-36 Gastric carcinoma producing large polypoid mass with associated ulceration *(arrow)*.

the area least involved. Another major form of gastric carcinoma is a large polypoid mass. Irregularity and ulceration within the mass are suggestive of malignancy, whereas the presence of a stalk or normal-appearing gastric folds extending to the tumor are signs of benignancy. Ulceration can develop in any gastric carcinoma. This varies from shallow erosions in relatively superficial mucosal lesions to huge excavations within fungating polypoid masses (Figure 4-36).

CT is of major value in the staging and treatment planning of gastric carcinoma, in assessing the response to therapy, and in detecting tumor recurrence (Figure 4-37). Carcinoma of the stomach may appear as thickening of the gastric wall or as an intraluminal mass. Obliteration of the fat planes (covering layers of fat) around the stomach is a reliable indicator of the extragastric spread of tumor. CT can demonstrate direct tumor extension to intraabdominal organs and distant metastases, especially to the liver.

Lymphoma of the stomach

See page 287.

▪ Small Bowel

Small bowel obstruction

Fibrous adhesions caused by previous surgery or peritonitis account for almost 75% of all small bowel

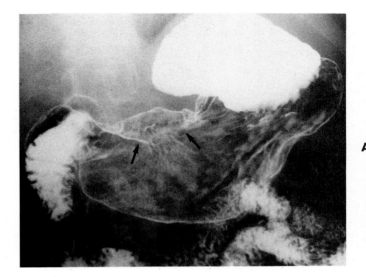

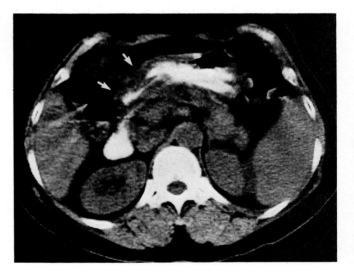

Figure 4-37 CT staging of gastric carcinoma. **A,** Double-contrast study demonstrates large lesser-curvature mass *(arrows).***B,** CT scan shows narrowing of antrum by gastric carcinoma *(white arrows),* and adjacent lymph node metastases *(curved arrow).*

obstructions. External hernias (inguinal, femoral, umbilical, incisional) are the second most frequent cause. Other general causes of mechanical small bowel obstruction include luminal occlusion (gallstone, intussusception) and intrinsic lesions of the bowel wall (neoplastic or inflammatory strictures, vascular insufficiency).

Distended loops of small bowel containing gas and fluid can usually be recognized within 3 to 5 hours of the onset of complete obstruction. Almost all gas proximal to a small bowel obstruction represents swallowed air. On upright or lateral decubitus

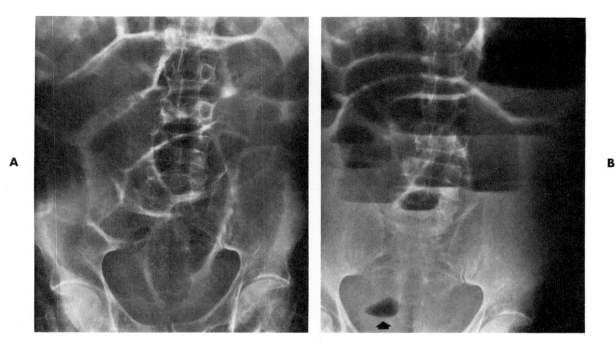

Figure 4-38 Small bowel obstruction. **A,** Supine and, **B,** upright projections demonstrate large amounts of gas in dilated loops of small bowel with multiple prominent air-fluid levels. Single, small collection of gas *(arrow)* remains in colon.

projections, the interface between gas and fluid forms a straight horizontal margin. Gas-fluid levels are occasionally present normally, but more than two gas-fluid levels in small bowel distal to the duodenum are generally considered to be abnormal (Figure 4-38). Although the presence of gas-fluid levels at different heights in the same loop has traditionally been considered evidence for mechanical obstruction, an identical pattern can also be demonstrated in some patients with adynamic ileus.

As time passes, the small bowel may become so distended as to be almost indistinguishable from the colon. To make the critical differentiation between small and large bowel obstruction, it is essential to determine which loops of bowel contain abnormally large amounts of air. Small bowel loops generally occupy the more central portion of the abdomen, whereas colonic loops are positioned laterally around the periphery of the abdomen or inferiorly in the pelvis (Figure 4-39). Gas within the lumen of the small bowel outlines the thin valvulae conniventes, which completely encircle the bowel. In contrast, colonic haustral markings are thicker and farther apart and occupy only a portion of the transverse diameter of the bowel.

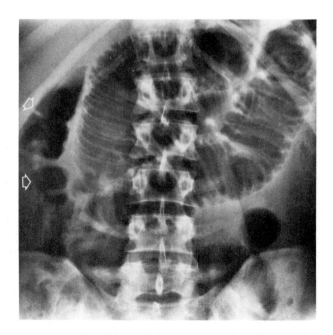

Figure 4-39 Small bowel obstruction. Dilated loops of small bowel occupy central portion of abdomen, with nondilated cecum and ascending colon positioned laterally around periphery of abdomen *(arrows).*

The site of obstruction can usually be predicted with considerable accuracy if the number and position of dilated bowel loops are analyzed. The presence of a few dilated loops of small bowel located high in the abdomen (in the center or slightly to the left) indicates an obstruction in the distal duodenum or jejunum. The involvement of more small bowel loops is suggestive of a lower obstruction. As additional loops are affected, they appear to be placed one above the other upward and to the left, producing a characteristic stepladder appearance (Figure 4-40). The point of obstruction is always distal to the lowest loop of dilated bowel.

In patients with complete mechanical small bowel obstruction, little or no gas is found in the colon. This is a valuable point in the differentiation between mechanical obstruction and adynamic ileus, in which gas is seen within distended loops throughout the bowel. Although a small amount of gas or fecal accumulations may be present at an early stage of a small bowel obstruction (Figure 4-39), the detection of a large amount of gas in the colon effectively eliminates this diagnosis.

The bowel proximal to an obstruction can contain no gas but be completely filled with fluid. This may produce a confusing picture of a normal-appearing abdomen or a large soft-tissue abdominal mass.

Plain abdominal radiographs are occasionally not sufficient for a distinction to be made between small and large bowel obstruction. In these instances a carefully performed barium enema examination will document or eliminate the possibility of large bowel obstruction. If it is necessary to determine the precise site of small bowel obstruction, barium can be administered in either a retrograde (by means of an enema) or an antegrade (by way of the mouth) manner. Orally administered barium (*not* water-soluble agents) is the most effective contrast material for demonstrating the site of small bowel obstruction (Figure 4-41). The large amount of fluid proximal to a small bowel obstruction prevents any trapped barium from hardening or increasing the degree of obstruction. The density of barium permits excellent visualization far into the intestine, unlike water-soluble agents, which are lost to sight because of dilution and absorption. It must be em-

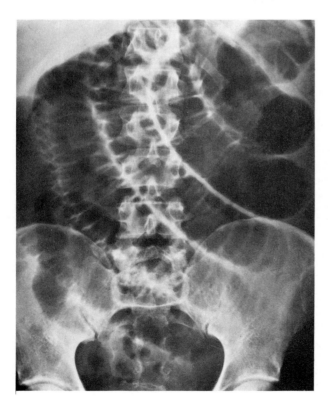

Figure 4-40 Low small bowel obstruction. Dilated loops of gas-filled bowel appear to be placed one above other, upward and to left, producing characteristic stepladder appearance.

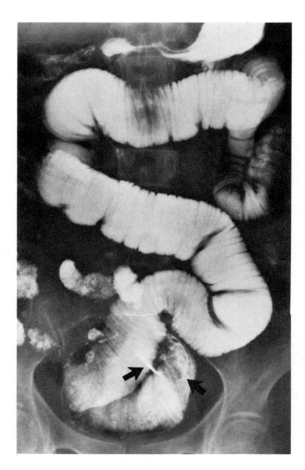

Figure 4-41 Barium upper gastrointestinal series demonstrates impacted bezoar *(arrows)* to be cause of small bowel obstruction.

phasized that if plain radiographs clearly demonstrate a mechanical small bowel obstruction, *any* contrast examination is unnecessary.

Strangulation of bowel caused by interference with the blood supply is a serious complication of small bowel obstruction. In a closed-loop obstruction (volvulus, incarcerated hernia), both the loops going toward (afferent) and away from (efferent) the area of narrowing become obstructed. The involved segments are usually filled with fluid and appear radiographically as a tumorlike soft-tissue mass. A closed loop is a clinically dangerous form of obstruction, since the continuing outpouring of fluid into the enclosed space can raise intraluminal pressure and rapidly lead to occlusion of the blood supply to that segment of bowel. Because venous pressure is normally lower than arterial pressure, blockage of venous outflow from the strangulated segment occurs before obstruction of the mesenteric arterial supply. Ischemia can rapidly cause necrosis of the bowel with sepsis, peritonitis, and a potentially fatal outcome.

CT may aid in demonstrating small bowel obstruction when the plain abdominal radiographs are normal or nonspecific. In addition to showing the site, level, and cause of the obstruction, this modality may indicate whether there is strangulation of the involved loops of bowel. CT appears to be most valuable in patients with a history of abdominal malignancy and in those who have signs of infection, bowel infarction, or a palpable abdominal mass (Figure 4-42).

Adynamic ileus

Adynamic ileus is a common disorder of intestinal motor activity in which fluid and gas do not progress normally through a nonobstructed small and large bowel. A variety of neural, hormonal, and metabolic factors can precipitate reflexes that inhibit intestinal motility. Adynamic ileus occurs to some extent in almost every patient who undergoes abdominal surgery. Other causes of adynamic ileus include peritonitis, medication that decreases intestinal peristalsis (atropine-like effect), electrolyte and metabolic disorders, and trauma. The clinical appearance of patients with adynamic ileus varies from minimal symptoms to generalized abdominal distention with a sharp decrease in the frequency and intensity of bowel sounds.

The radiographic hallmark of adynamic ileus is the retention of large amounts of gas and fluid in dilated small and large bowel. Unlike the appearance

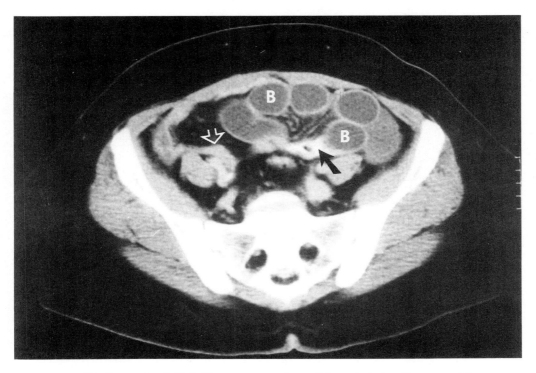

Figure 4-42 CT diagnosis of clinically unsuspected small bowel obstruction caused by adhesions. Notice transition point between dilated loops of small bowel *(B)* and collapsed ileum *(black arrow)*. Notice collapsed terminal ileum *(open arrow)*. (From Jeffrey RB: *CT and sonography of the acute abdomen,* New York, 1989, Raven.)

in mechanical small bowel obstruction, the entire small and large bowel in adynamic ileus appears almost uniformly dilated with no demonstrable point of obstruction (Figure 4-43).

There are two major variants of adynamic ileus. **Localized ileus** refers to an isolated distended loop of small or large bowel (sentinel loop) that is often associated with an adjacent acute inflammatory process. The portion of the bowel involved can offer a clue to the underlying disease. Localized segments of the jejunum or transverse colon are frequently dilated in patients with acute pancreatitis. Similarly, the hepatic flexure of the colon can be distended in acute cholecystitis, the terminal ileum can be dilated in acute appendicitis, the descending colon can be distended in acute diverticulitis, and dilated loops can be seen along the course of the ureter in acute ureteral colic (Figure 4-44). Unfortunately, isolated segments of distended small bowel are commonly seen in patients with abdominal pain and thus the "sentinel loop" may be found guarding the wrong area.

Colonic ileus refers to selective or disproportionate gaseous distention of the large bowel without an obstruction (Figure 4-45). Massive distention of the cecum, which is often horizontally oriented, characteristically dominates the radiographic appearance. Colonic ileus usually accompanies or follows an acute abdominal inflammatory process or abdominal surgery. The clinical presentation and the findings on plain abdominal radiographs simulate those of mechanical obstruction of the colon. A barium

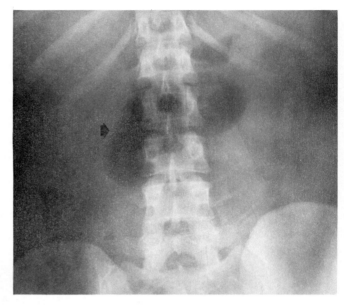

Figure 4-44   Localized ileus in patient with acute ureteral colic. Arrow points to impacted ureteral stone.

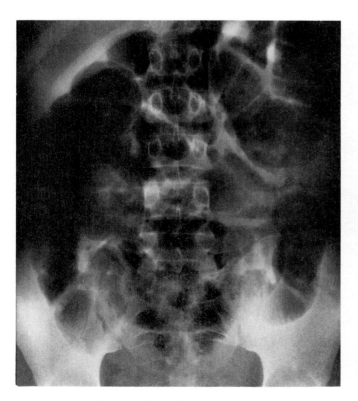

Figure 4-43   Adynamic ileus. Large amounts of gas and fluid are retained in loops of dilated small and large bowel. Entire small and large bowel appear almost uniformly dilated with no demonstrable point of obstruction.

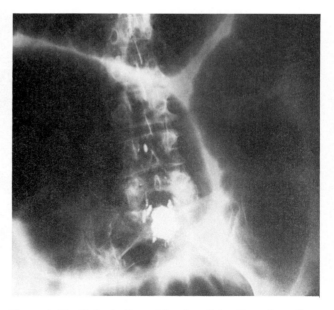

Figure 4-45   Colonic ileus. Massive distention of small bowel without obstruction in patient with severe diabetes and electrolyte abnormalities.

enema examination is usually necessary to exclude an obstructing lesion.

Crohn's disease (regional enteritis)

Crohn's disease is a chronic inflammatory disorder of unknown cause that most often involves the terminal area of the ileum but can affect any part of the gastrointestinal tract. Although it can occur at any age, Crohn's disease is most common in young adults. The underlying cause is unknown, though there appears to be some psychogenic element; stress or emotional upsets are frequently related to the onset or relapse of the disease.

The granulomatous inflammatory process in Crohn's disease is frequently discontinuous, with diseased segments of bowel separated by apparently healthy portions ("skip areas"). Diffuse inflammation with edema involves all layers of the intestinal wall. Ulceration is common, and fistulas running in the bowel wall or extending to other organs are not infrequent.

The clinical spectrum of Crohn's disease is broad, ranging from a relatively benign course with unpredictable acute attacks and remissions to severe diarrhea and an acute abdomen. Although acute Crohn's disease may produce right lower quadrant pain simulating appendicitis, there is often blood in the stools in Crohn's disease as a result of bleeding from the intensely congested mucous membranes. Small bowel obstruction and fistula formation occur in up to half of patients. Rectal fissures and perirectal abscesses occur in about one third.

In the small bowel, the earliest radiographic changes of Crohn's disease include irregular thickening and distortion of mucosal folds caused by submucosal inflammation and edema. Transverse and longitudinal ulcerations can separate islands of thickened mucosa and submucosa, leading to a characteristic rough cobblestone appearance (Figure 4-46). Rigid thickening of the entire bowel wall produces pipelike narrowing. Continued inflammation and fibrosis can result in a severely narrowed, rigid segment of small bowel in which the mucosal pattern is lost (string sign) (Figure 4-47). When several areas of small bowel are diseased, involved segments of varying length are often sharply separated from radiographically normal segments (skip lesions).

Fistula formation is a hallmark of chronic Crohn's disease found in at least half of all patients with this condition (Figure 4-48). The diffuse inflammation of the serosa and mesentery in Crohn's disease causes involved loops of bowel to be firmly matted together by fibrous peritoneal and mesenteric bands. Fistulas apparently begin as ulcerations that burrow through

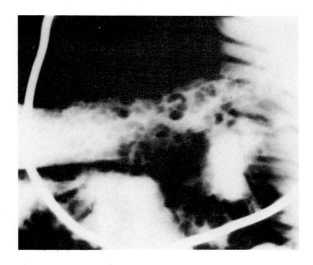

Figure 4-46 Crohn's disease. Cobblestone appearance is produced by transverse and longitudinal ulcerations separating islands of thickened mucosa and submucosa.

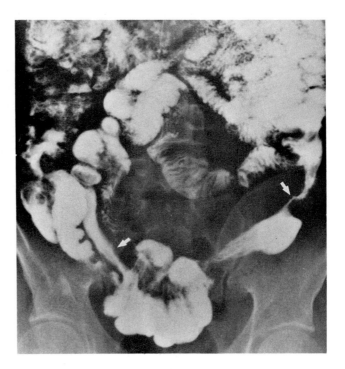

Figure 4-47 Crohn's disease. Arrows point to widely separated areas of disease (skip lesions), which appear as greatly narrowed segments of small bowel (string sign).

the bowel wall into adjacent loops of small bowel and colon. In addition to fistulas between loops of bowel, a characteristic finding in Crohn's disease is the appearance of fistulous tracts ending blindly in abscess cavities surrounded by dense inflammatory tissue. These abscess cavities can produce palpable

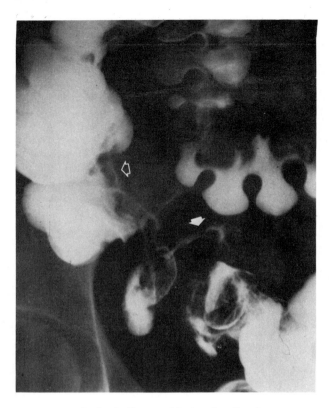

Figure 4-48 Crohn's disease. Notice fistulization between terminal ileum and sigmoid colon *(solid arrow)* as well as along cecum *(open arrow)*.

able small bowel changes. The two major radiographic appearances are (1) small bowel dilatation with normal folds (Figure 4-49) and (2) a pattern of generalized, irregular, distorted small bowel folds (Figure 4-50).

Intussusception

Intussusception is a major cause of bowel obstruction in children; it is much less common in adults. Intussusception is the telescoping of one part of the intestinal tract into another because of peristalsis, which forces the proximal segment of bowel to move distally within the ensheathing outer portion. Once such a lead point has been established, it gradually progresses forward and causes increased obstruction. This can compromise the vascular supply and produce ischemic necrosis of the intussuscepted bowel.

In children, intussusception is most common in the region of the ileocecal valve. The clinical onset tends to be abrupt, with severe abdominal pain, blood in the stool ("currant jelly"), and often a palpable right-sided mass. If the diagnosis is made

masses, persistent fever, or pain. Although less common than bowel-bowel fistulas, internal fistulas extending from the bowel to the bladder or vagina can occur. A common complication is the development of external gastrointestinal fistulas, which usually extend to the perianal area and may be associated with fissures and perirectal abscesses.

Whenever possible, Crohn's disease is treated with medications, and surgery is performed only if complications require it. Surgical resection of an involved segment of small bowel is associated with a high incidence of Crohn's disease recurring adjacent to the anastomosis.

Malabsorption disorders

The term **malabsorption disorders** refers to a multitude of conditions in which there is defective absorption of carbohydrates, proteins, and fats from the small bowel. Regardless of the cause, malabsorption results in steatorrhea—the passage of bulky, foul-smelling, high-fat-content stools that float.

Many of the diseases causing malabsorption produce radiographic abnormalities in the small bowel, though malabsorption can exist without any detect-

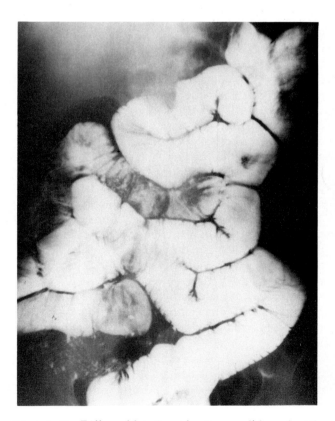

Figure 4-49 Diffuse dilatation of entire small bowel with excessive intraluminal fluid in patient with malabsorption caused by sprue.

Figure 4-50 Diffuse, irregular thickening of small bowel folds in patient with malabsorption secondary to Whipple's disease.

early and therapy instituted promptly, the mortality of intussusception in children is less than 1%. However, it treatment is delayed more than 48 hours after the onset of symptoms, the mortality increases dramatically. In adults, intussusception is often chronic or subacute and is characterized by irregular recurrent episodes of colicky pain, nausea, and vomiting. A specific cause of intussusception often cannot be detected in children. In adults, however, the leading edge is frequently a polypoid tumor with a stalk (pedunculated) or an inflammatory mass.

Radiographically, an intussusception produces the classic coiled-spring appearance of barium trapped between the intussusceptum and the surrounding portions of bowel (Figure 4-51, A). Reduction of a colonic intussusception can sometimes be accomplished by a barium enema examination (Figure 4-51, B, and C), though great care must be exercised to prevent excessive intraluminal pressure, which may lead to perforation of the colon. Reduction of intussusceptions by rectal insufflation of air (instead of barium) has been reported to be an effective technique in children. In older children and adults, a repeat barium enema after reduction is

necessary to determine whether there is an underlying polyp or tumor causing the intussusception.

▪ Appendicitis

Acute appendicitis develops when the neck of the appendix is blocked by a fecalith or by postinflammatory scarring that creates a closed-loop obstruction within the organ. Because of inadequate drainage, fluid accumulates in the obstructed portion and serves as a breeding ground for bacteria. High intraluminal pressure causes distention and thinning of the appendix distal to the obstruction that interferes with the circulation and may lead to gangrene and perforation. If the process evolves slowly, adjacent organs (terminal ileum, cecum, omentum) may wall off the appendiceal area so that a localized abscess develops; rapid vascular compromise may permit free perforation with the spilling of fecal material into the peritoneal cavity and the development of generalized peritonitis.

The clinical symptoms of acute appendicitis are usually so characteristic that there is no need for routine radiographs to make the correct diagnosis. The presence of severe right lower quadrant pain, low-grade fever, and slight leukocytosis, especially in younger adults, is presumed to be evidence of appendicitis. However, in some patients, especially the elderly, the clinical findings may be obscure or minimal. In addition, because the appendix is mobile and may be in unusual locations, the pain of acute appendicitis may mimic cholecystitis, diverticulitis, or pelvic inflammatory disease. When the symptoms are confusing, radiographic examination may be necessary for prompt diagnosis and surgical intervention before perforation occurs.

Plain abdominal radiographs may demonstrate a round or oval, laminated calcified fecalith in the appendix (appendicolith) (Figure 4-52). Surgical experience indicates that the presence of an appendicolith in combination with symptoms of acute appendicitis usually implies that the appendix is gangrenous (necrotic) and likely to perforate. Most appendicoliths are located in the right lower quadrant overlying the iliac fossa. Depending on the length and position of the appendix, however, an appendicolith can also be seen in the pelvis or in the right upper quadrant (retrocecal appendix), where it can simulate a gallstone.

Because of the danger of perforation, barium enema examination is usually avoided in acute appendicitis. If it is performed, an irregular impression of the base of the cecum (caused by inflammatory edema), in association with failure of barium to enter the appendix, is a characteristic finding.

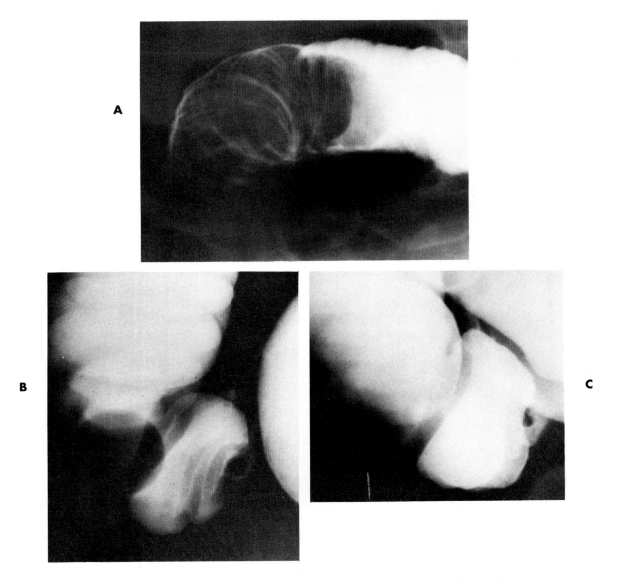

Figure 4-51 Intussusception. **A,** Obstruction of colon at hepatic flexure produces characteristic coiled-spring appearance of intussuscepted bowel. **B,** Partial and, **C,** complete reduction of intussusception by careful barium enema examination.

Nevertheless, failure of barium to fill the appendix is not a reliable sign of appendicitis, since the appendix does not fill in about 20% of normal patients. Partial filling of the appendix with distortion in its shape or caliber is strongly suggestive of acute appendicitis (Figure 4-53), especially if there is a cecal impression. In contrast, a patent (open) appendiceal lumen effectively excludes the diagnosis of acute appendicitis, especially when barium extends to fill the rounded appendiceal tip.

When the clinical presentation is unclear, high-resolution ultrasound with graded compression has become the imaging modality of choice for diagnosing acute appendicitis. A noncompressible appendix measuring 7 mm or more in maximal outer diameter is considered virtually pathognomonic of acute appendicitis (Figure 4-54).

CT shows an appendiceal abscess as a round or oval mass of soft-tissue density that may contain gas. This modality provides a more precise evaluation of the nature, extent, and location of the pathologic process and can detect intra-abdominal disease unrelated to appendicitis, which may explain the patient's clinical presentation.

▪ Colon

Diverticulosis

Colonic diverticula are outpouchings that represent acquired herniations of mucosa and submucosa through the muscular layers at points of weakness in the bowel wall. The incidence of colonic diverticulosis increases with age. Rare in persons less than 30 years of age, diverticula can be demonstrated in up to half of persons over 60 years of age. Diverticula occur most commonly in the sigmoid colon and decrease in frequency in the proximal colon. Although most patients with diverticulosis have no symptoms, a substantial number have chronic or intermittent lower abdominal pain, frequently related to meals or emotional stress, and alternating bouts of diarrhea and constipation. Bleeding may be caused by inflammatory erosion of penetrating blood vessels at the base of the diverticulum.

Colonic diverticula appear radiographically as round or oval outpouchings of barium projecting

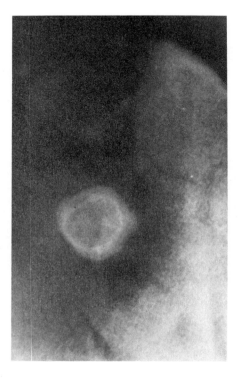

Figure 4-52   Laminated calcification in appendicolith.

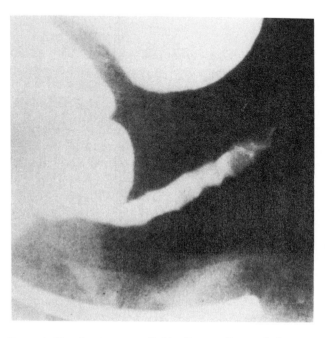

Figure 4-53   Acute appendicitis. Spot radiograph from barium enema examination shows incomplete filling of appendix. (From Rice RP et al: *Radiographics* 4:393-409, 1984).

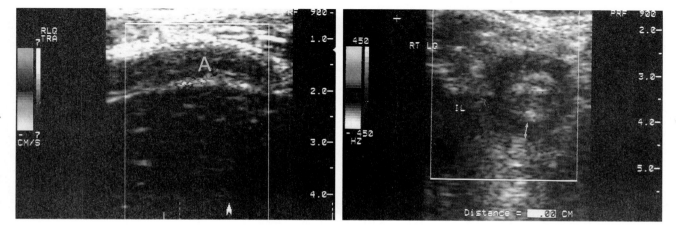

Figure 4-54   Ultrasound of appendicitis. **A,** Sagittal sonogram shows inflamed appendix *(A),* which is elongated and hypoechoic. **B,** Transverse scan shows appendiceal lumen surrounded by hypoechoic inflamed tissue *(arrows).* (Courtesy Carol Krebs, R.T., Shreveport, Louisiana.)

beyond the confines of the lumen. They vary in size from barely visible dimples to saclike structures 2 cm or more in diameter. Giant sigmoid diverticula of up to 25 cm in diameter, which probably represent slowly progressing chronic diverticular abscesses, may appear as large, well-circumscribed, lucent cystic structures in the lower abdomen.

Diverticula are usually multiple and tend to occur in clusters, though a solitary diverticulum is occasionally found. With multiple diverticula, deep crisscrossing ridges of thickened circular muscle can produce a characteristic series of sacculations (sawtoothed configuration) (Figure 4-55).

Diverticula also commonly occur in the esophagus and duodenum and infrequently may develop in the jejunum and ileum.

Diverticulitis

Diverticulitis is a complication of diverticular disease of the colon, especially in the sigmoid region, in which perforation of a diverticulum leads to the development of a peridiverticular abscess. It is estimated that up to 20% of patients with diverticulosis eventually develop acute diverticulitis. Retained fecal material trapped in a diverticulum by the narrow opening of the diverticular neck causes inflammation of the mucosal lining, which then leads to perforation of the diverticulum. This usually results in a localized peridiverticular abscess that is walled off by fibrous adhesions. The inflammatory process may localize within the wall of the colon and produce an intramural mass, or it may dissect around the colon, causing segmental narrowing of the lumen. Extension of the inflammatory process along the colon wall can involve adjacent diverticula, resulting in a longitudinal sinus tract along the bowel wall. A common complication of diverticulitis is the development of fistulas to adjacent organs (bladder, vagina, ureter, small bowel).

The radiographic diagnosis of diverticulitis requires direct or indirect evidence of diverticular perforation. The most specific sign is extravasation, which can appear either as a tiny projection of contrast material from the tip of a diverticulum (Figure 4-56, *A*) or as obvious filling of a pericolic abscess (Figure 4-56, *B*). A more common, though somewhat less specific, sign of diverticulitis is the demonstration of a pericolic soft-tissue mass that is attributable to a localized abscess and represents a walled-off perforation. This extraluminal mass appears as a filling defect causing eccentric narrowing

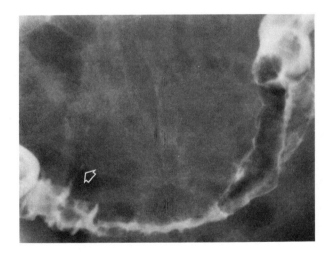

A

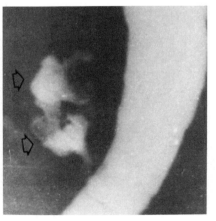

B

Figure 4-56 Diverticulitis. **A,** Thin projection of contrast *(arrow)* implies extravasation from colonic lumen. Notice severe spasm of sigmoid colon caused by intense adjacent inflammation. **B,** Obvious contrast filling of pericolic abscess *(arrows)*.

Figure 4-55 Diverticulosis. Typical saw-toothed configuration produced by thickened circular muscle associated with multiple diverticula.

of the bowel lumen. The adjacent diverticula are spastic, irritable, and attenuated and frequently seem to drape over the mass. It is important to remember, however, that a peridiverticular abscess caused by diverticulitis can occur without radiographically detectable diverticula (Figure 4-57).

Severe spasm or fibrotic healing of diverticulitis can cause rigidity and progressive narrowing of the colon that simulates annular carcinoma. Although radiographic distinction from carcinoma may be impossible, findings favoring the diagnosis of diverticulitis include the involvement of a relatively long segment, a gradual transition from diseased to normal colon, a relative preservation of mucosal detail, and fistulous tracts and intramural abscesses. At times, colonoscopy or surgery may be required to make a definitive diagnosis.

Ulcerative colitis

Ulcerative colitis is primarily a disease of young adults that is highly variable in severity, clinical course, and ultimate prognosis. The cause is unknown, though an autoimmune cause has been suggested and a psychogenic factor may be involved because the condition is often aggravated by stress. The onset of the disease, as well as subsequent exacerbations, can be insidious or abrupt. The main symptoms include bloody diarrhea, abdominal pain, fever, and weight loss. A characteristic feature of ulcerative colitis is alternating periods of remission and relapse. Most patients have intermittent episodes of symptoms with complete remission between attacks. In fewer than 15% of patients, ulcerative colitis is an acute severe process with a far higher incidence of serious complications such as toxic megacolon (extreme dilatation of a segment of colon with systemic toxicity) and free perforation into the peritoneal cavity.

In the radiographic evaluation of a patient with known or suspected ulcerative colitis, plain abdominal radiographs are essential. Large nodular protrusions of hyperplastic mucosa, deep ulcers outlined by intraluminal gas, or polypoid changes along with a loss of haustral markings (normal indentations in the wall of the colon) may indicate the diagnosis. Plain abdominal radiographs can also demonstrate evidence of toxic megacolon, a dramatic and ominous complication of ulcerative colitis that is characterized by extreme dilatation of a segment of colon (Figure 4-58), or of an entire diseased colon, combined with systemic toxicity (abdominal pain and tenderness, tachycardia, fever, and leukocytosis). Toxic megacolon can lead to spontaneous perforation of the colon, which can be dramatic and sudden and can cause irreversible shock. Because there is such a high danger of spontaneous perforation, barium enema examination is absolutely contraindicated during a recognized attack of toxic megacolon.

Ulcerative colitis has a strong tendency to begin in the rectosigmoid area. Although by radiographic criteria alone the rectum appears normal in about 20% of patients with ulcerative colitis, true rectal

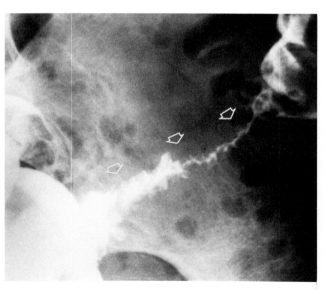

Figure 4-57 Sigmoid diverticulitis. Severe narrowing of long, involved portion of sigmoid colon (arrows) in patient with no radiographically detectable diverticula.

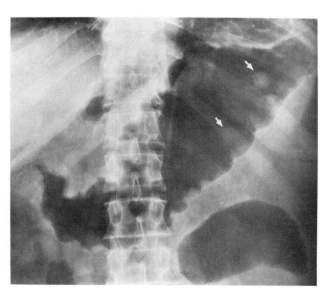

Figure 4-58 Toxic megacolon in ulcerative colitis. Notice dilatation of transverse colon with multiple pseudopolypoid projections extending into lumen (arrows).

sparing is infrequent, and there is usually evidence of disease on sigmoidoscopy or rectal biopsy. Although ulcerative colitis may spread to involve the entire colon (pancolitis), isolated right colon disease with a normal left colon does not occur. The disease is almost always continuous, without evidence of the skip areas seen in Crohn's disease. Except for "backwash ileitis" (minimal inflammatory changes involving a short segment of terminal ileum), ulcerative colitis does not involve the small bowel, a feature distinguishing it from Crohn's disease, which may involve both the large and the small intestines.

On double-contrast studies, the earliest detectable radiographic abnormality in ulcerative colitis is fine granularity of the mucosa corresponding to the hyperemia and edema seen endoscopically (Figure 4-59). Once superficial ulcers develop, small flecks of adherent barium produce a stippled mucosal pattern. As the disease progresses, the ulcerations become deeper. Extension into the submucosa may produce broad-based ulcers with a collar-button appearance (Figure 4-60). Perirectal inflammation can cause widening of the soft-tissue space between the anterior sacrum and the posterior rectum (retrorectal space).

With chronic disease, fibrosis and muscular spasm cause progressive shortening and rigidity of the colon (Figure 4-61). The haustral pattern is absent, and the bowel contour is relatively smooth because of ulcer healing and subsequent reepithelialization. Eventually, the colon may appear as a symmetric, rigid tubular structure (lead-pipe colon).

Carcinoma of the colon is about 10 times more frequent in patients with ulcerative colitis than in the general population. During the first 10 years of disease, there is only a small risk of malignancy. Thereafter, it is estimated that there is a 20% chance per decade that a patient with ulcerative colitis will develop carcinoma. Malignant lesions in ulcerative colitis generally occur at a much younger age than those in the general population and tend to be extremely virulent. Carcinoma of the colon in patients with chronic ulcerative colitis often appears as a bizarre stricture rather than with the more characteristic polypoid or apple-core appearance of a primary colonic malignancy (Figure 4-62). The tumor typically produces a narrowed segment with an eccentric lumen, irregular contours, and margins that are rigid and tapered. Because it is frequently difficult to distinguish carcinoma from benign stricture in patients with ulcerative colitis, colonoscopy or surgery is often required for an unequivocal diagnosis.

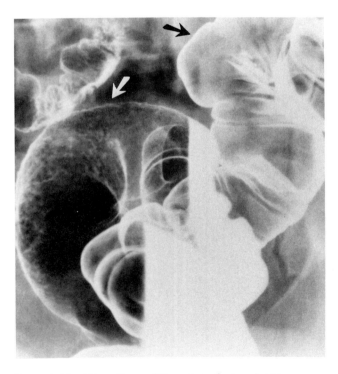

Figure 4-59 Ulcerative colitis primarily involving rectosigmoid. Distal rectosigmoid mucosa *(white arrow)* is finely granular, compared with normal-appearing mucosa *(black arrow)* in the more proximal colon.

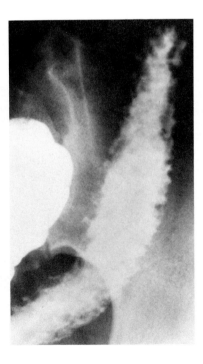

Figure 4-60 Ulcerative colitis. Progression of disease results in deep ulcerations (collar-button ulcers) extending into submucosal layer.

Crohn's colitis

Crohn's disease of the colon is identical to the same pathologic process involving the small bowel and must be distinguished from ulcerative colitis. The

proximal portion of the colon is most frequently involved in Crohn's disease; associated disease of the terminal ileum is seen in up to 80% of the patients. Unlike ulcerative colitis, in Crohn's colitis the rectum is often spared, and isolated rectal disease very rarely occurs. Crohn's disease usually has a patchy distribution, with involvement of multiple noncontiguous segments of colon (skip lesions), unlike the continuous colonic involvement in ulcerative colitis. Perirectal abnormalities (fissures, abscesses, fistulas) occur at some point during the course of disease in half of patients with Crohn's colitis but are rare in ulcerative colitis.

The earliest radiographic findings of Crohn's disease of the colon are seen on double-contrast examinations. Isolated tiny, discrete erosions (aphthous ulcers) appear as punctate collections of barium with a thin halo of edema around them (Figure 4-63). Aphthous ulcers in Crohn's disease have a patchy distribution against a background of normal mucosa, unlike the blanket of abnormal granular mucosa seen in ulcerative colitis.

As Crohn's colitis progresses, the ulcers become deeper and more irregular, with a great variation in size, shape, and overall appearance. Deep linear, transverse, and longitudinal ulcers often separate intervening mounds of edematous but nonulcerating mucosa, producing a characteristic cobblestone appearance (Figure 4-46). If the penetrating ulcers extend beyond the contour of the bowel, they can coalesce to form long tracts running parallel to the

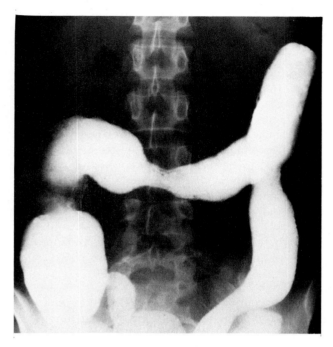

Figure 4-61 Chronic ulcerative colitis (lead-pipe colon). Muscular hypertrophy and spasm cause shortening and rigidity of colon with loss of haustral markings.

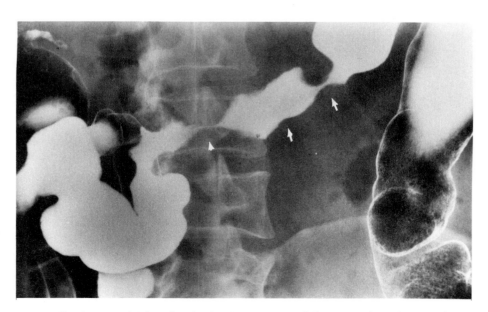

Figure 4-62 Carcinoma of colon developing in patient with long-standing chronic ulcerative colitis. Long, irregular lesion with bizarre pattern is visible in transverse colon *(arrows)*.

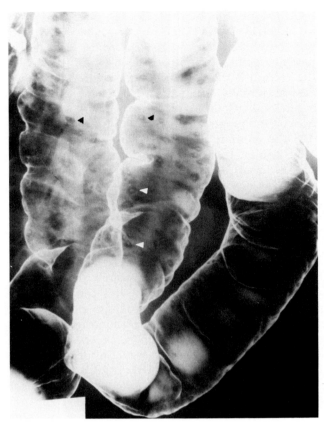

Figure 4-63 Diffuse aphthous ulcers *(arrowheads)* in early Crohn's colitis. (From Caroline DF, Evers K: *Radio Clin North Am* 25:47-66, 1987.)

long axis of the colon (Figure 4-64). The penetration of ulcers into adjacent loops of bowel or into the bladder, vagina, or abdominal wall causes fistulas, which can often be demonstrated radiographically.

Inflammatory and fibrotic thickening of the bowel wall leads to narrowing of the lumen and stricture formation. Occasionally, an eccentric stricture with a suggestion of overhanging edges can be difficult to distinguish from annular carcinoma (Figure 4-65). In most instances, however, characteristic features of Crohn's disease elsewhere in the colon (deep ulcerations, pseudopolyps, skip lesions, sinus tracts, fistulas) clearly indicate the correct diagnosis.

Patients with Crohn's colitis appear to have a higher incidence of developing colon cancer than the general population, though this association is less striking than between colon cancer and ulcerative colitis. Carcinoma complicating Crohn's colitis is most common in the proximal portion of the colon and usually appears radiographically as a fungating mass with typical malignant features, unlike the mildly irregular stricture characteristic of colon cancer in patients with ulcerative colitis.

Ischemic colitis

Ischemic colitis is characterized by the abrupt onset of lower abdominal pain and rectal bleeding. Diarrhea is common, as is abdominal tenderness on physical examination. Most patients are older than 50 years of age, and many have a history of prior cardiovascular disease.

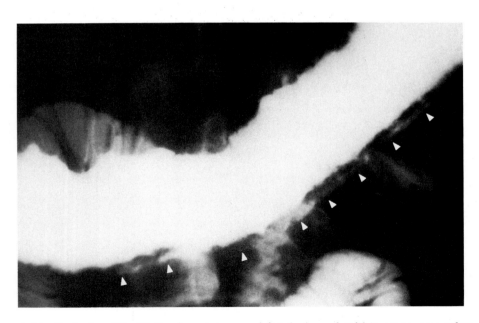

Figure 4-64 Crohn's colitis. Notice long intramural fistula *(arrowheads)* in transverse colon. (From Lichtenstein JE: *Radiol Clin North Am* 25:3-23, 1987.)

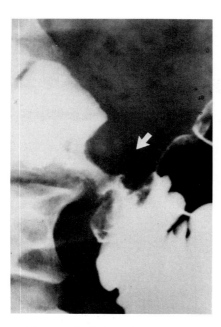

Figure 4-65 Chronic Crohn's colitis. Benign stricture with overhanging edges in transverse colon simulates carcinoma *(arrow)*.

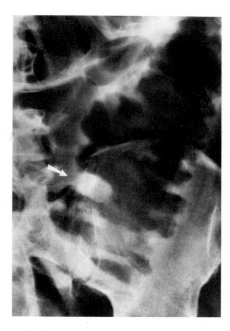

Figure 4-66 Ischemic colitis. Soft-tissue polypoid densities *(arrow)* protrude into lumen of descending colon in patient with acute abdominal pain and rectal bleeding.

The initial radiographic appearance of ischemic colitis is fine superficial ulceration caused by inflammatory edema of the mucosa. As the disease progresses, deep penetrating ulcers, pseudopolyps, and characteristic "thumbprinting" can be demonstrated. Thumbprinting refers to sharply defined, fingerlike indentations along the margins of the colon wall (Figure 4-66). In most cases the radiographic appearance of the colon returns to normal within 1 month if good collateral circulation is established. Extensive fibrosis during the healing phase can cause tubular narrowing and a smooth stricture. If blood flow is insufficient, acute bowel necrosis and perforation may result.

Irritable bowel syndrome

The term **irritable bowel syndrome** refers to several conditions that have an alteration in intestinal motility as the underlying pathophysiologic abnormality. Patients with this condition may complain primarily of chronic abdominal pain and constipation (spastic colitis), chronic intermittent watery diarrhea, often without pain, or alternating bouts of constipation and diarrhea. Although there are no specific radiographic findings in the irritable bowel syndrome, patients with this condition usually undergo a barium enema examination to exclude another chronic disorder as the cause of the symptoms. When the patient is symptomatic, the barium enema may demonstrate areas of irritability and spasticity and accentuated haustration, though similar radiographic findings may be observed in normal asymptomatic persons, especially those who have received laxatives and enemas.

Cancer of the colon

Carcinoma of the colon and rectum is the leading cause of death from cancer in the United States, though it can be more easily diagnosed than most other malignant neoplasms. About half of colon carcinomas occur in the rectum and sigmoid, where they can be felt by rectal examination or seen with a sigmoidoscope. Carcinoma of the colon and rectum is primarily a disease of older persons, with a peak incidence in the 50- to 70-year range. Two diseases predispose to development of cancer of the colon: long-standing ulcerative colitis and familial polyposis, a hereditary disease in which innumerable polyps develop in the colon and elsewhere in the intestinal tract.

Because cancer of the colon is curable if discovered early in the course, delay in diagnosis is the most significant factor in the poor prognosis. There is considerable evidence to indicate that many, if not most, carcinomas of the colon arise in preexisting polyps. Therefore the early diagnosis of colonic cancer is basically an exercise in polyp detection. Malignant polyps (Figure 4-67) tend to be sessile

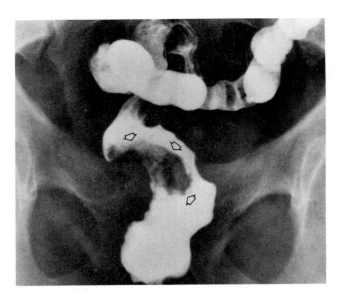

Figure 4-67   Carcinoma of rectum. Bulky lesion *(arrows)* could be felt on rectal examination.

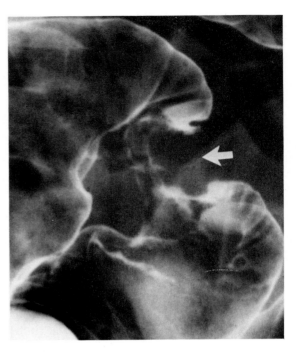

Figure 4-68   Annular carcinoma of sigmoid colon. Notice sharply defined proximal and distal margins of this relatively short, apple-core lesion *(arrow).*

lesions (without stalks) with an irregular or lobulated surface, unlike benign polyps that are usually smooth and often have a stalk (pedunculated). Other radiographic criteria suggestive that a polyp is malignant include large size (especially if greater than 2 cm in diameter), retraction or indentation (puckering) of the colon wall seen on profile view at the site of origin of a sessile polyp, and evidence of interval growth of a polyp on sequential examinations.

Annular carcinoma (apple-core, napkin-ring) is one of the most typical forms of primary colonic malignancy (Figure 4-68). Annular carcinomas appear to arise from flat plaques of tumor (saddle lesions) that involve only a portion of the circumference of the colon wall. Unless there is meticulous care in searching for an area of minimal straightening or slight contour defects, the small and subtle, but lethal, saddle carcinomas can easily be overlooked. As the tumor grows, it characteristically infiltrates the bowel wall rather than forming a bulky intraluminal mass. This produces a classic bilateral contour defect with ulcerated mucosa, eccentric and irregular lumen, and overhanging margins. Progressive constriction of the bowel can cause complete colonic obstruction, most commonly in the sigmoid region.

Ulceration is common in carcinoma of the colon. It can vary from an excavation within a large fungating mass to mucosal destruction within an annular apple-core tumor.

A patient with carcinoma of the colon has a 1% risk of having multiple synchronous (same time) colon cancers. Therefore it is essential to examine

carefully the rest of the colon once an obviously malignant lesion has been detected. In addition, such a patient has a 3% risk of developing additional metachronous cancers at a later date.

CT is a major modality for staging carcinoma of the colon and in allowing assessment of tumor recurrence (Figure 4-69). Carcinoma causes asymmetric or circumferential thickening of the bowel wall with narrowing and deformity of the lumen. CT can demonstrate local extension of tumor to the pelvic organs as well as lymphadenopathy and metastases to the adrenal glands or liver.

Large bowel obstruction

About 70% of large bowel obstructions are a result of primary colonic carcinoma. Diverticulitis and volvulus account for most other cases. Colonic obstructions tend to be less acute than small bowel obstructions; the symptoms develop more slowly, and fewer fluid and electrolyte disturbances are produced.

The radiographic appearance of colonic obstruction depends on the competency of the ileocecal valve. If the ileocecal valve is competent, obstruction causes a large, dilated colon with a greatly distended, thin-walled cecum and little small bowel gas (Figure 4-70). The colon distal to the obstruction is usually collapsed and free of gas. If the ileocecal valve is incompetent, there is distention of gas-filled

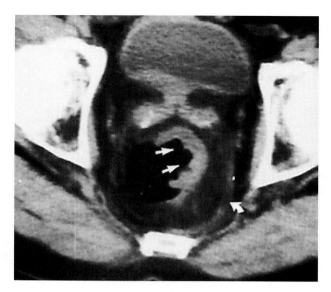

Figure 4-69   CT of rectal carcinoma, showing a soft-tissue mass on lateral wall of rectum containing central ulceration *(straight arrows)*. Thickening of perirectal fascia *(curved arrow)*, presence of multiple lymph nodes (on more cephalad images), and increased soft-tissue density of perirectal fat was suggestive of tumor extension beyond bowel wall, which was confirmed at surgery. (From Butch RJ: In Taveras JM, Ferruci JT, editors: *Radiology: diagnosis-imaging-intervention,* Philadelphia, 1987, Lippincott.)

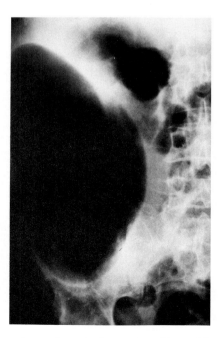

Figure 4-70   Large bowel obstruction. Huge dilatation of cecum (to 13 cm in diameter) without perforation.

loops of both colon and small bowel, and it may simulate an adynamic ileus.

The major danger in colonic obstruction is perforation. If the ileocecal valve is competent, the colon behaves like a closed loop, and the increased pressure caused by the obstruction cannot be relieved. Because the cecum is spherical and has a large diameter, it is the most likely site for perforation. In acute colonic obstruction, perforation is very likely if the cecum distends to more than 10 cm; in intermittent or chronic obstruction, however, the cecal wall can become hypertrophied, and the diameter of the cecum can greatly exceed 10 cm without perforation (Figure 4-70). In the patient with suspected large bowel obstruction, a low-pressure barium enema can be safely performed and will demonstrate the site and often the cause of the obstruction (Figure 4-71).

Volvulus of the colon

Volvulus refers to a twisting of the bowel on itself that may lead to intestinal obstruction. Because twisting of the bowel usually requires a long, movable mesentery, volvulus of the large bowel most frequently involves the cecum and sigmoid colon. The transverse colon, which has a short mesentery, is rarely affected by volvulus.

Cecal volvulus

The ascending colon and the cecum may have a long mesentery as a fault of rotation and fixation during the embryonic development of the gut. This situation predisposes to volvulus, with the cecum twisting on its long axis. It should be stressed, however, that only a few patients with an extremely mobile cecum ever develop cecal volvulus.

In cecal volvulus, the distended cecum tends to be displaced upward and to the left, though it can be found anywhere within the abdomen. A pathognomonic sign of cecal volvulus is a kidney-shaped mass (representing the twisted cecum) with the twisted and thickening mesentery mimicking the renal pelvis (Figure 4-72, A). A barium enema examination is usually required for definite confirmation of the diagnosis. This study demonstrates obstruction of the contrast column at the level of the stenosis, with the tapered edge of the column pointing toward the site of the twist (Figure 4-72, B).

Sigmoid volvulus

A long, redundant loop of sigmoid colon can undergo a twist on its mesenteric axis and form a closed-loop obstruction. In sigmoid volvulus, the greatly inflated sigmoid loop appears as an inverted U-shaped shadow that rises out of the pelvis in a vertical or oblique direction and can even reach the

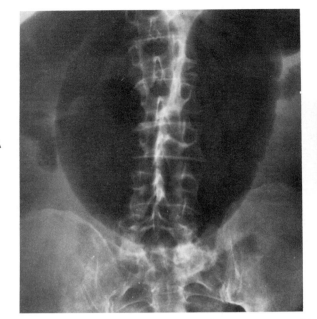
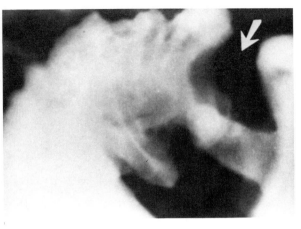

Figure 4-71   Large bowel obstruction caused by annular carcinoma of sigmoid. **A,** Plain abdominal radiograph demonstrates pronounced dilatation of gas-filled transverse and ascending colon. **B,** Barium enema demonstrates typical apple-core lesion *(arrow)* producing the colonic obstruction.

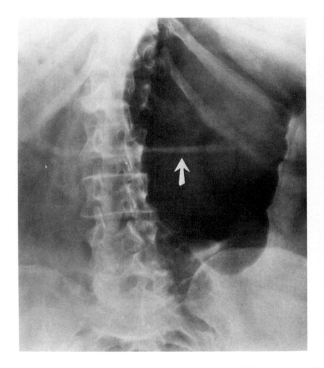
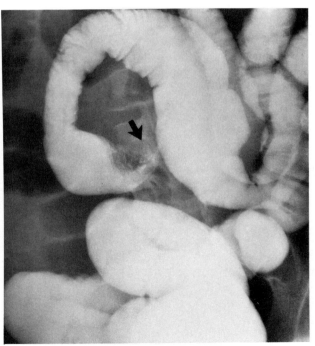

Figure 4-72   Cecal volvulus. **A,** Dilated, gas-filled cecum appears as kidney-shaped mass with twisted and thickening mesentery *(arrow)* mimicking renal pelvis. **B,** Barium enema examination demonstrates obstruction of contrast column at level of stenosis *(arrow)* with tapered edge of column pointing toward torsion site.

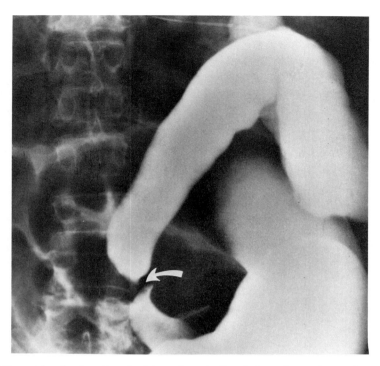

Figure 4-73 Sigmoid volvulus. Luminal tapering at site of stenosis produces characteristic bird's-beak configuration.

level of the diaphragm. The affected loop appears devoid of haustral markings and has a sausage or balloon shape. A barium enema examination demonstrates an obstruction to the flow of contrast material at the site of volvulus and considerable distention of the rectum. The lumen of the sigmoid tapers toward the site of stenosis, and a pathognomonic bird's beak appearance is produced (Figure 4-73).

Hemorrhoids

Hemorrhoids are varicose veins of the lower end of the rectum that cause pain, itching, and bleeding. As with varicose veins in the leg, hemorrhoids are caused by increased venous pressure. The most common cause of increased pressure is chronic constipation with resulting excessive muscular straining needed to empty the bowel. Increased venous pressure can also be produced by a pelvic tumor or a pregnant uterus.

On barium enema examinations, hemorrhoids occasionally can produce single or multiple rectal filling defects that simulate polyps (Figure 4-74). The proper diagnosis can easily be made by inspection, digital examination, or direct vision through the anoscope.

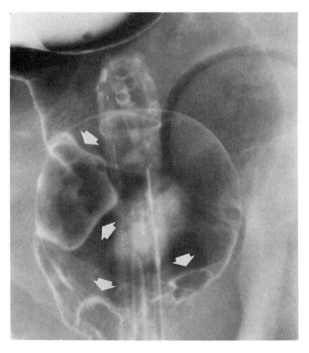

Figure 4-74 Hemorrhoids. Multiple rectal filling defects *(arrows)* simulate polyps.

▪ Gallbladder

Gallstones (cholelithiasis)

Gallstones can develop whenever bile contains insufficient bile salts and lecithin in proportion to cholesterol to maintain the cholesterol in solution. This situation can result from a decrease in the amount of bile salts present (because of decreased reabsorption in the terminal ileum as a result of inflammatory disease or surgical resection) or can be caused by increased hepatic synthesis of cholesterol. Because cholesterol is not radiopaque, most gallstones are radiolucent and visible only on contrast examinations or ultrasound. In up to 20% of patients, however, gallstones contain sufficient calcium to be detectable on plain abdominal radiographs (Figure 4-75). Gallstones can have a central nidus (focus) of calcification, be laminated (alternating opaque and lucent rings), or have calcification around the periphery. Occasionally, a nonopaque

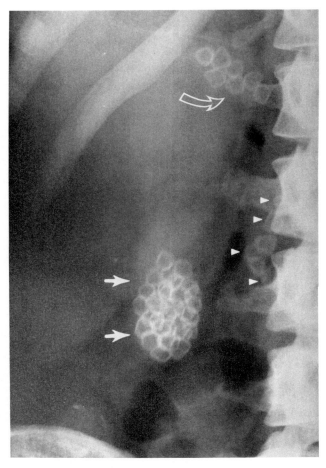

Figure 4-75 Calculi in gallbladder *(solid arrows)* and bile ducts *(open arrow)*. Calculi *(arrowheads)* lie in common bile duct, some of which overlie spine and are difficult to detect. (Courtesy Stephen R. Baker, New York, N.Y.)

stone may contain gas-filled fissures that produce the "Mercedes-Benz" sign, a characteristic triradiate pattern similar to the German automobile trademark (Figure 4-76).

Oral cholecystography (OCG) has been the traditional technique for the diagnosis of gallstones, though it has been replaced in most institutions by ultrasound (see below). Gallstones appear as freely movable filling defects in the opacified gallbladder. They fall by gravity to the dependent portion of the gallbladder and frequently layer out at a level that depends on the relation of the specific gravity of the stone to that of the surrounding bile (Figure 4-77). Solitary gallstones are usually rounded; multiple stones are generally faceted. Large numbers of stones can have a sandlike or gravel-like consistency and be visible only when they layer out on radiographs obtained with the patient in an erect or lateral decubitus position using a horizontal beam. Infrequently, a gallstone is coated with tenacious mucus and adheres to the gallbladder wall.

Malabsorption of the radiopaque contrast, hepatocellular dysfunction (serum bilirubin ≥ 2 mg/dl), and intrinsic disease of the gallbladder (cystic duct obstruction, chronic cholecystitis) can lead to nonvisualization of the gallbladder on OCG. If these causes can be excluded, failure of the gallbladder to opacify after the administration of two doses of orally administered cholecystographic contrast material is highly reliable evidence of gallbladder disease.

Ultrasound is now the major imaging modality for demonstrating gallstones. This noninvasive tech-

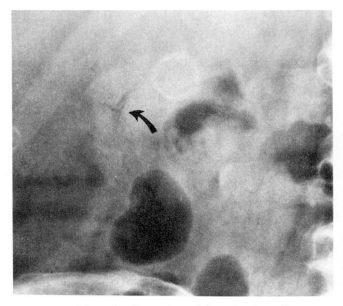

Figure 4-76 Mercedes-Benz sign of fissuring in gallstone *(arrow)*. Notice adjacent gallstone with radiopaque rim.

A　**B**

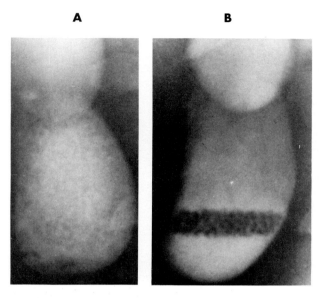

Figure 4-77　Oral cholecystogram showing multiple gallstones. **A,** With the patient supine, the stones are poorly defined and have a gravel-like consistency. **B,** On an erect film taken with a horizontal beam, the innumerable gallstones layer out and are easily seen.

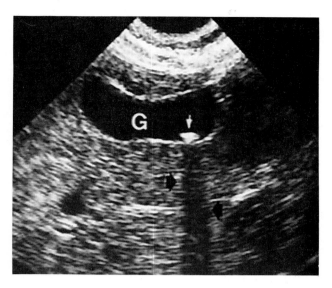

Figure 4-78　Ultrasound of gallstones. Echogenic focus *(white arrow)* in otherwise sonolucent gallbladder *(G)* represents large gallstone. Notice acoustic shadowing immediately inferior to stone *(black arrows).*

nique is equal in accuracy to OCG, is independent of hepatic function, and does not rely on patient compliance in taking oral contrast agents. In addition to imaging the gallbladder, ultrasound can provide important additional information by effectively demonstrating the biliary tree and hepatic parenchyma. Gallstones appear on ultrasound as foci of high-amplitude echoes associated with posterior acoustic shadowing (Figure 4-78). The mobility of free-floating gallstones may be demonstrated by performing the examination with the patient in various positions.

Acute cholecystitis

Acute cholecystitis usually occurs after obstruction of the cystic duct by an impacted gallstone. Either ultrasound or radionuclide scanning can be used. The sonographic diagnosis of acute cholecystitis requires the demonstration of a distended gallbladder containing gallstones. Important additional findings include edema of the gallbladder wall and focal tenderness elicited directly over the gallbladder. A normal gallbladder ultrasound virtually excludes the diagnosis of acute cholecystitis. Because many disorders may mimic acute cholecystitis, ultrasound can also be used to evaluate the remainder of the right upper quadrant to detect any other acute abnormality.

The normal radionuclide cholescintigram demonstrates the bile ducts, the gallbladder, and early excretion of radionuclide into the duodenum and proximal jejunum within 30 minutes of the intravenous injection of isotope (Figure 4-79, A). Failure to accumulate radioactivity in the gallbladder is highly sensitive and specific for cystic duct obstruction (Figure 4-79, B). If associated with appropriate symptoms, this finding is virtually diagnostic of acute cholecystitis.

Emphysematous cholecystitis

Emphysematous cholecystitis is a rare condition in which the growth of gas-forming organisms in the gallbladder is facilitated by stasis and ischemia caused by cystic duct obstruction (most often by stones). Emphysematous cholecystitis occurs most frequently in elderly men and in patients with poorly controlled diabetes mellitus. Plain abdominal radiographs demonstrate gas in the gallbladder lumen that dissects into the wall or pericholecystic tissues to produce the pathognomonic appearance of a rim of lucent bubbles or streaks of gas outside of and roughly parallel to the gallbladder lumen (Figure 4-80).

Porcelain gallbladder

Porcelain gallbladder refers to extensive calcification in the wall of the gallbladder, which forms an oval density that corresponds to the size and shape of the organ (Figure 4-81). The term reflects the blue discoloration and brittle consistency of the gallbladder wall. The calcification in a porcelain gallbladder can

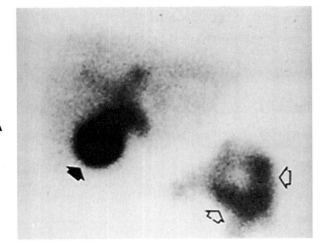
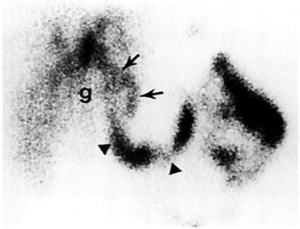

Figure 4-79   Acute cholecystitis. **A,** Normal radionuclide cholescintigram demonstrates bile ducts, gallbladder *(solid arrow),* and early excretion of radionuclide into douodenum and proximal jejunum *(open arrows).* **B,** In patient with acute cholecystitis, cholescintigram shows no visualization of gallbladder *(g)* but good visualization of common bile duct *(arrows)* and duodenum *(arrowheads),* indicating obstruction of cystic duct. (From Harned RE: In Eisenberg RL, Amberg JR, editors: *Critical diagnostic pathways in radiology,* Philadelphia, 1981, Lippincott.)

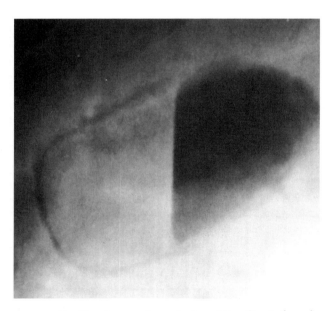

Figure 4-80   Emphysematous cholecystitis. Gas is found in both lumen and wall of gallbladder. (From Eisenberg RL: *Gastrointestinal radiology: a pattern approach,* Philadelphia, 1990, Lippincott.)

appear as a broad continuous band in the muscular layers or be multiple and punctate and occur in the glandular spaces of the mucosa. The detection of extensive calcification in the wall of the gallbladder should indicate the possibility of carcinoma. Although a porcelain gallbladder is uncommon in cases of carcinoma of the gallbladder, there is a striking incidence of carcinoma in porcelain gallbladders (up to 60% of the cases). Therefore, even if they are asymptomatic, patients with porcelain gallbladders are usually subjected to prophylactic cholecystectomy.

▪ Liver

Cirrhosis of the liver

Cirrhosis refers to chronic destruction of liver cells and structure with nodular regeneration of liver parenchyma and fibrosis. The major cause of cirrhosis is chronic alcoholism, in which damage to the liver is related either to the toxic effect of alcohol or the malnutrition that frequently accompanies chronic alcoholism. Other causes of liver destruction leading to cirrhosis include postnecrotic viral hepatitis, hepatotoxic drugs and chemicals that destroy liver cells, disease of the bile ducts (primary and secondary biliary cirrhosis), and excessive deposition of iron pigment within the liver (hemochromatosis). Regardless of the cause, the destroyed liver cells are replaced by fibrous connective tissue that has no liver cell function. Initially the liver is enlarged because of regeneration, but it eventually becomes smaller as the fibrous connective tissue contracts and the surface becomes bumpy and nodular.

Cirrhosis causes many physiologic changes that can be detected clinically or radiographically. In alcoholic cirrhosis a large amount of fat accumulates

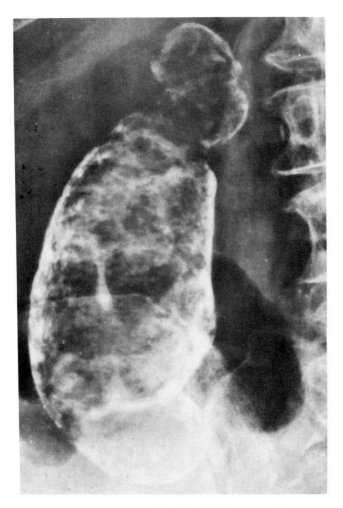

Figure 4-81 Porcelain gallbladder. Notice extensive mural calcification around perimeter of gallbladder.

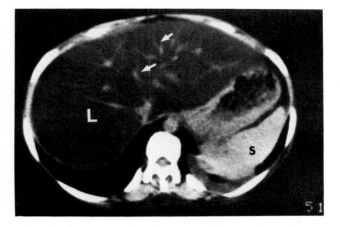

Figure 4-82 Fatty infiltration of liver in cirrhosis. CT scan shows generalized decrease in attenuation value of liver *(L)*, which is far less than that of spleen *(S)*. Portal veins appear as high-density structures *(arrows)* surrounded by background of low-denisity hepatic fat.

within the liver. This fatty infiltration is beautifully demonstrated on CT. In normal individuals the liver always appears brighter than the spleen, whereas in cirrhosis the liver is much darker because of the large amount of fat (Figure 4-82). The portal veins appear as high-density structures surrounded by a background of low density caused by hepatic fat, the opposite of the normal pattern of portal veins as low-density channels on noncontrast scans.

Nodular regeneration of the liver combined with fibrosis causes obstruction of the portal vein, which drains blood from the gastrointestinal tract through the liver before emptying into the inferior vena cava near the heart. Increased pressure within this vessel causes pronounced enlargement of the spleen (splenomegaly). Because blood cannot flow through the obstructed portal vein, it must find an alternative route to bypass the liver. This leads to the development of collateral circulation, with large dilated veins becoming prominent on the abdominal wall in the area of the umbilicus. Another alternative route for blood to return to the heart is the periesophageal veins, which dilate to become esophageal varices, which can rupture and lead to fatal hemorrhage (Figure 4-14).

Destruction of liver cells substantially decreases the ability of the organ to synthesize proteins, such as albumin and several of the multiple factors required for blood clotting. A deficiency of albumin (hypoalbuminemia) results in fluid leaking out of the circulation and the development of generalized edema. Edema can be seen as swelling of the lower extremity; when it involves the wall of the intestinal tract, edema can produce regular, uniform thickening of small bowel folds.

One of the most characteristic symptoms of cirrhosis is the accumulation of fluid in the peritoneal cavity (ascites), which causes characteristic abdominal distention. Ascites develops because of a combination of albumin deficiency and increased pressure within obstructed veins, which permits fluid to leak into the abdominal cavity. Large amounts of ascitic fluid are easily detectable on plain abdominal radiographs as a general abdominal haziness (ground-glass appearance) (Figure 4-83, A). With the patient in a supine position, the peritoneal fluid tends to gravitate to dependent portions of the pelvis and accumulate within the pelvic peritoneal reflections, thus filling the recesses on both sides of the bladder and producing a symmetric density resembling dog's ears. Smaller amounts of fluid (300 to 1000 ml) may widen the flank stripe and obliterate the right lateral inferior margin of the liver (hepatic angle).

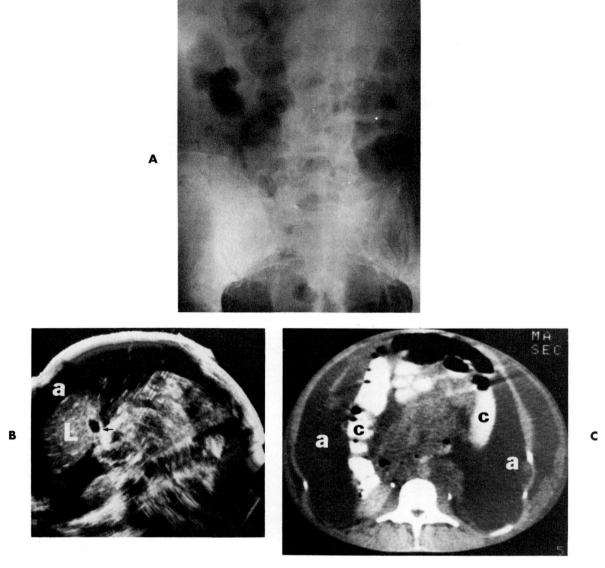

Figure 4-83 Ascites. **A,** Plain radiograph shows general abdominal haziness (ground-glass appearance). **B,** On ultrasound, large amount of sonolucent ascitic fluid *(a)* separates liver *(L)* and other soft-tissue structures from anterior abdominal wall. Notice relative thickness of gallbladder wall *(arrow)*. **C,** CT scan through lower abdomen shows huge amount of low-density ascitic fluid *(a)* with medial displacement of ascending and descending colon *(c)*.

Ascites is exquisitely shown on ultrasound as a mobile, echofree fluid region shaped by adjacent structures (Figure 4-83, B) or on CT as an extravisceral collection of fluid with a low attenuation value (Figure 4-83, C).

Cirrhosis may lead to the development of jaundice, either from destruction of liver cells or obstruction of bile ducts. Because the liver cannot perform its usual task of inactivating the small amounts of female sex hormones secreted by the adrenal glands in both men and women, men with cirrhosis often develop breast enlargement (gynecomastia). The inability of necrotic liver cells to detoxify harmful substances leads to an accumulation of ammonia and other poisonous material in the circulation. The patient becomes confused and disoriented, develops a typical flapping tremor or shaking, becomes abnormally sleepy (somnolence), and may lapse into potentially fatal hepatic coma.

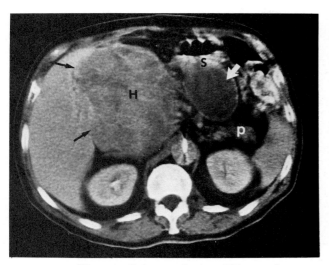

Figure 4-84 Hepatocellular carcinoma. CT scan shows huge mass *(H)* with attenuation value slightly less than that of normal liver. Black arrows point to interface between tumor and normal liver. Of incidental note is pancreatic pseudocyst *(white arrow)* in lesser sac between stomach *(S)* and pancreas *(p)*.

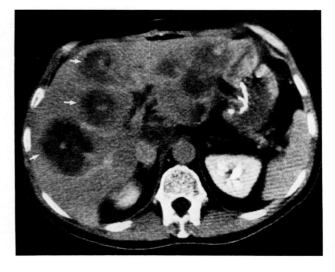

Figure 4-85 Hepatic metastases. CT scan shows multiple low-density metastases with high-density centers *(arrows)*.

Hepatocellular carcinoma

In the United States, primary liver cell carcinoma most commonly occurs in patients with underlying diffuse hepatocellular disease, especially alcoholic or postnecrotic cirrhosis. The clinical presentation varies from mild right upper quadrant discomfort and weight loss to hemorrhagic shock from massive intraperitoneal bleeding, which reflects rupture of the tumor into the peritoneal cavity. Invasion of the biliary tree may produce obstructive jaundice.

CT is the modality of choice in the diagnosis of hepatocellular carcinoma. The tumor appears as a large mass, with an attenuation value close to normal parenchyma, that tends to alter the contour of the liver by projecting beyond its outer margin (Figure 4-84). After the rapid administration of intravenous contrast material, there usually is dense, diffuse, and nonuniform enhancement of the tumor. Unlike metastases, hepatocellular carcinoma tends to be solitary or produce a small number of lesions. Hepatocellular carcinoma tends to invade the hepatic and portal venous systems, and tumor thrombi within these veins are well demonstrated on CT.

Although the overall prognosis of hepatocellular carcinoma remains bleak, radiographic studies can determine whether the patient can successfully undergo surgical removal of the tumor. If the tumor is confined to one lobe of the liver and there is no evidence of metastases, arteriography is usually indicated to demonstrate the precise surgical anatomy and to detect small, staining tumor nodules that cannot be identified with noninvasive imaging techniques.

Hepatic metastases

Metastases are by far the most common malignant tumors involving the liver. Although some types of metastases (especially mucinous carcinoma of the colon or rectum) may produce diffuse, finely granular calcifications seen on plain radiographs, the diagnosis of hepatic metastases usually requires CT, ultrasound, MRI, or radionuclide studies. CT and MRI are probably the most sensitive techniques for detecting hepatic metastases. On CT, most metastases are relatively well marginated and appear less dense than normal liver parenchyma (Figure 4-85). Although frequently detectable on noncontrast scans, most metastatic lesions are best seen as areas of increased density adjacent to normally enhancing hepatic parenchyma after the administration of intravenous contrast material. MRI demonstrates liver metastases as areas of low signal intensity on T_1-weighted sequences and bright lesions on T_2-weighted sequences.

Ultrasound and radionuclide scans can demonstrate hepatic metastases, but these modalities are slightly less sensitive than CT. CT has the additional advantage of being able to detect extrahepatic metastases, such as those to abdominal lymph nodes.

▪ Pancreas

Acute pancreatitis

Acute pancreatitis is an inflammatory process in which protein- and lipid-digesting enzymes become activated within the pancreas and begin to digest the organ itself. Occasionally, this necrotic process extends into blood vessels, causing bleeding (acute hemorrhagic pancreatitis), which may be life-threatening.

The most common cause of acute pancreatitis is excessive alcohol consumption. Less frequently, acute pancreatitis is related to gallstones, which may enter the common bile duct and obstruct the ampulla of Vater and force bile to reflux into the pancreas and cause an inflammatory reaction.

Acute pancreatitis usually presents with the sudden onset of severe, steady abdominal pain that radiates to the back and may indicate a perforated ulcer. Nausea and vomiting are common, and jaundice may develop if inflammatory edema of the head of the pancreas is sufficient to obstruct the common bile duct. If a large area of the pancreas is affected, the absence of lipid enzymes from the pancreas is affected, the absence of lipid enzymes from the pancreas prevents the proper absorption of fat, leading to the malabsorption syndrome. On blood tests and urinalysis, there is typically a high level of the pancreatic enzyme amylase, which confirms the diagnosis of acute pancreatitis.

Plain abdominal radiographs are often normal in the patient with acute pancreatitis; even when abnormal, the findings are usually nonspecific and consistent with any intra-abdominal inflammatory disease. The most frequent abnormalities include a localized adynamic ileus, usually involving the jejunum ("sentinel loop"); generalized ileus with diffuse gas-fluid levels; isolated distention of the duodenal sweep; and localized distention of the transverse colon to the level of the splenic flexure (colon cutoff sign). Pancreatic calcifications indicate that the patient has chronic pancreatitis, and moreover they may indicate an exacerbation of the inflammatory disease.

Ultrasound and CT are the imaging modalities that most precisely define the degree of pancreatic inflammation and the pathways of its spread throughout the abdomen. They also are of great clinical importance in the early diagnosis of complications of acute pancreatitis, such as abscess, hemorrhage, and pseudocyst formation.

CT in acute pancreatitis demonstrates diffuse or focal enlargement of the gland. In the normal patient the margins of the pancreas are sharply delineated by surrounding peripancreatic fat. Spread of inflammation and edema beyond the confines of the pancreas obscures the peripancreatic soft tissues and often thickens the surrounding fascial planes (Figure 4-86).

Acute pancreatitis may alter both the size and the parenchymal echogenicity of the gland on ultrasound examination. Although the pancreas usually enlarges symmetrically and retains its initial shape, nonspecific enlargement of the pancreatic head or tail can simulate focal pancreatic carcinoma. The accompanying interstitial inflammatory edema causes the pancreas to appear relatively sonolucent when compared with the adjacent liver (Figure 4-87). One limitation of ultrasound in patients with acute pancreatitis is the frequent occurrence of adynamic ileus with excessive intestinal gas, which may prevent adequate visualization of the gland.

Chronic pancreatitis

Pancreatic calcifications are an essentially pathognomonic finding in chronic pancreatitis, developing in about one third of patients with this disease (Figure 4-88). The small, irregular calcifications are seen most frequently in the head of the pancreas and can extend upward and to the left to involve the body and tail of the organ.

On ultrasound examination, the major feature of chronic pancreatitis is an alteration of the intrinsic echo pattern caused by calcification and fibrosis. The pancreas may be atrophic as a result of fibrous scarring or appear significantly enlarged during recurrences of acute inflammation. Dilatation of the pancreatic duct as a result of gland atrophy and obstruction can be seen, though a similar pattern can be produced by the ductal obstruction in pancreatic cancer. CT can also demonstrate ductal dilatation, calcification, and atrophy of the gland in patients with chronic pancreatitis. However, since similar information can be obtained less expensively and without ionizing radiation by ultrasound, CT is usually reserved for patients with chronic pancreatitis in whom technical factors make ultrasound suboptimal.

Enlargement of the pancreatic head can cause widening and pressure changes on the inner aspect of the duodenal sweep on barium studies. This produces narrowing of the lumen (double-contour effect) and spiny protrusions of mucosal folds (spiculation) that can be indistinguishable from pancreatic carcinoma.

Pancreatic pseudocyst

Pancreatic pseudocysts are loculated (walled-off) fluid collections arising from inflammation, necrosis, or hemorrhage associated with acute pancreatitis or

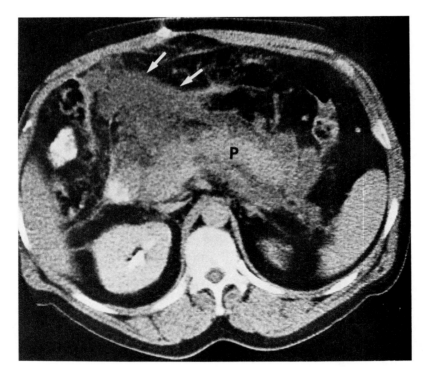

Figure 4-86   Acute pancreatitis. CT scan demonstrates diffuse enlargement of pancreas (P) with obliteration of peripancreatic fat planes by inflammatory process. There is extension of inflammatory reaction into tansverse mesocolon (arrows). (From Jeffrey RB, Federle MD, Laing FC: Radiology 147:185-192, 1983.)

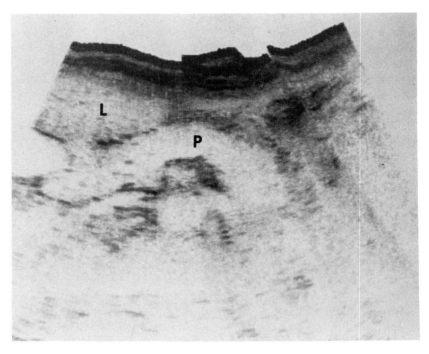

Figure 4-87   Acute pancreatitis. Transverse sonogram demonstrates diffuse enlargement of gland (P) with retention of its normal shape. Notice relative sonolucency of pancreas when compared with echogenicity of adjacent liver (L).

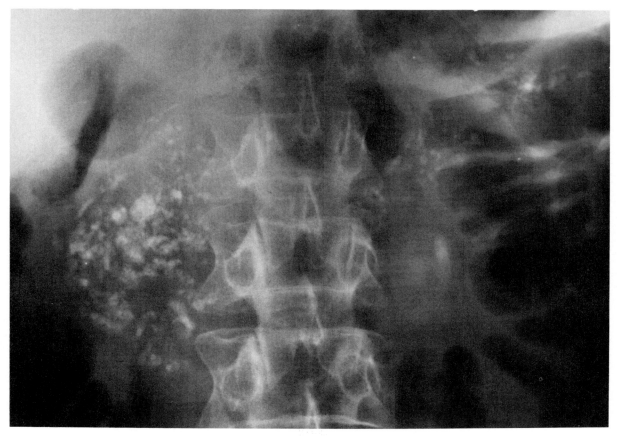

Figure 4-88　Chronic pancreatitis. Diffuse pancreatic calcifications.

trauma (Figure 4-89). On ultrasound examination, a pseudocyst typically appears as an echo-free cystic structure with a sharp posterior wall (Figure 4-90). Hemorrhage into the pseudocyst produces a complex fluid collection containing septations of echogenic areas. CT demonstrates pseudocysts as sharply marginated, fluid-filled collections that are often best delineated after the administration of intravenous contrast material (Figure 4-91).

Large pseudocysts are visible on plain radiographs of the abdomen when they displace the gas-filled stomach and bowel. Similarly, pseudocysts in the head of the pancreas can cause pressure defects and widening of the duodenal sweep, whereas those arising from the body or tail of the pancreas can displace and deform the stomach, proximal jejunum, or colon. However, since ultrasound is highly accurate in diagnosing pancreatic pseudocysts, it has completely replaced plain abdominal radiographs and barium studies, which display only indirect signs.

Pseudocysts may undergo spontaneous resolution or persist as chronic collections that may require surgical intervention. Because ultrasound is relatively inexpensive and without ionizing radiation, serial sonograms are usually used to monitor the progression of a pancreatic pseudocyst.

Cancer of the pancreas

The most common pancreatic malignancy is adenocarcinoma, which often is far advanced before it is detected and thus has an extremely poor survival rate. Several less common pancreatic tumors are hormone-secreting neoplasms of the islet cells of the islands of Langerhans. Production of insulin by an insulinoma can lower blood glucose, leading to attacks of weakness, unconsciousness, and insulin shock. Ulcerogenic islet cell tumors (gastrinomas) produce the Zollinger-Ellison syndrome, which is characterized by intractable ulcer symptoms, hypersecretion of gastric acid, and diarrhea. Diarrheagenic islet cell tumors produce the WDHA syndrome; this acronym stands for *w*atery *d*iarrhea, *h*ypokalemia (low serum potassium), and *a*chlorhydria (low serum chloride), which are major features of the clinical picture. ACTH production by pancreatic islet cell

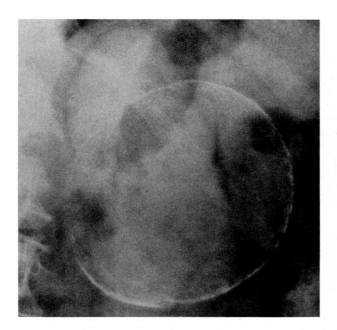

Figure 4-89 Calcified pancreatic pseudocyst.

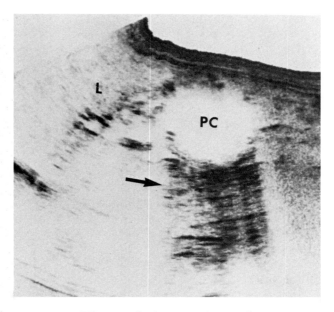

Figure 4-90 Ultrasound of pancreatic pseudocyst. Longitudinal sonogram of right upper quadrant demonstrates irregularily marginated pseudocyst *(PC)* with acoustic shadowing *(arrow). L,* Liver.

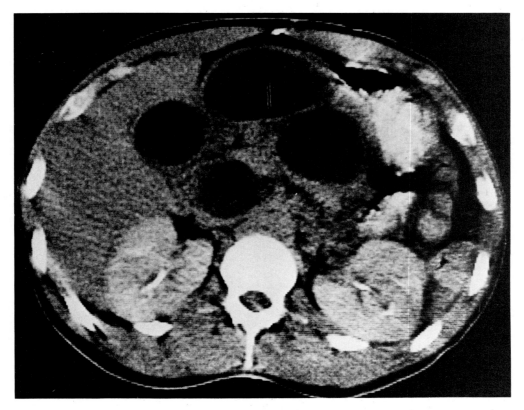

Figure 4-91 Multiple pancreatic pseudocysts. CT scan after intravenous administration of contrast material demonstrates four sharply marginated, fluid-filled collections.

tumors causes Cushing's syndrome; the release of serotonin by pancreatic tumors may cause the carcinoid syndrome. Because these functional islet cell tumors usually become apparent by their hormonal effects rather than by the consequences of tumor bulk, they are often small and difficult to detect.

Because it is noninvasive and relatively inexpensive, ultrasound is often the initial screening in a patient suspected of pancreatic carcinoma. Ultrasound can demonstrate most tumors greater than 2 cm in diameter that lie in the head of the pancreas; lesions in the body and tail of the pancreas are more difficult to detect by this modality. Pancreatic carcinoma typically causes the gland to have an irregular contour and a semisolid pattern of intrinsic echoes (Figure 4-92).

CT is the most effective modality for detecting pancreatic cancer in any portion of the gland and for defining its extent. CT can demonstrate the mass of the tumor and ductal dilatation and invasion of neighboring structures. After the administration of intravenous contrast material, the relatively avascular tumor appears as an area of decreased attenuation when compared with the normal pancreas (Figure 4-93). CT is the best procedure for staging pancreatic carcinoma and may prevent needless surgery in patients with nonresectable lesions. This technique may permit detection of hepatic metastases or involvement of regional vessels and adjacent retroperitoneal lymph nodes.

Cytologic examination of tissue obtained by percutaneous fine-needle aspiration under ultrasound or CT guidance can often provide the precise histologic diagnosis of a neoplastic mass, thus making surgical intervention unnecessary.

Carcinoma of the head of the pancreas often causes obstructive jaundice and the appearance of narrowing of the distal common bile duct on transhepatic cholangiography (Figure 4-94) or ERCP. Percutaneous biliary drainage may represent an alterna-

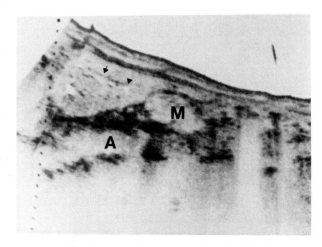

Figure 4-92 Carcinoma of pancreas. Longitudinal sonogram demonstrates irregular mass *(M)* with semisolid pattern of intrinsic echoes. Notice associated dilatation of intrahepatic bile ducts *(arrows)*. *A,* Aorta.

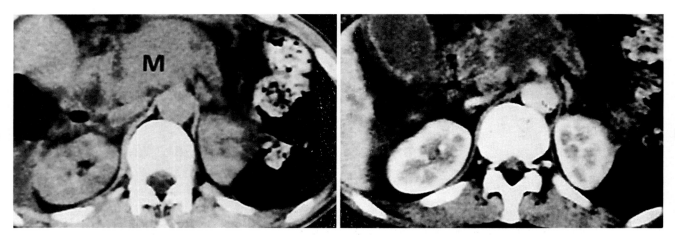

Figure 4-93 Carcinoma of pancreas. **A,** Noncontrast scan demonstrates homogeneous mass *(M)* in body of pancreas. **B,** After ingestion of intravenous bolus of contrast material, there is enhancement of normal pancreatic parenchyma and surrounding vascular structures. The pancreatic carcinoma remains unchanged and thus appears as a low-density mass. (From Federle MP, Goldberg HL: In Moss AA, Gamsu G, Genant HK, editors: *Computed tomography of the body,* Philadelphia, 1992, Saunders.)

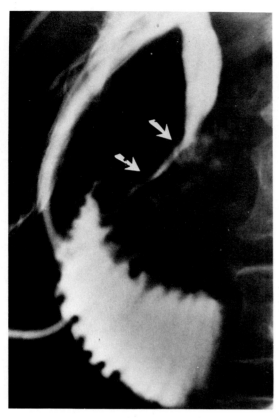

Figure 4-94 Carcinoma of head of pancreas. Transhepatic cholangiogram shows irregular narrowing of common bile duct *(arrows).* Calcifications reflect underlying chronic pancreatitis.

tive to surgical intervention for relieving biliary obstruction in patients with pancreatic carcinoma who cannot be cured. Although the transhepatic insertion of biliary drainage tubes does not alter the dismal prognosis, it can reduce patient morbidity and the need for hospitalization.

Barium upper gastrointestinal series demonstrate distortion of the mucosal pattern and configuration of the duodenal sweep in about half of patients with carcinoma of the head of the pancreas. Early or small lesions, however, rarely produce detectable radiographic abnormalities; tumors of the body or tail of the pancreas must be quite large to be visible on barium examinations.

▪ Pneumoperitoneum

Free air in the peritoneal cavity associated with significant abdominal pain and tenderness is often caused by perforation of a gas-containing viscus and indicates a surgical emergency. Less frequently, pneumoperitoneum results from abdominal, gyne-

cologic, intrathoracic, or iatrogenic causes and does not require operative intervention.

The radiographic demonstration of free air in the peritoneal cavity is a valuable sign in the diagnosis of perforation of the gastrointestinal tract. As little as 1 cc of free intraperitoneal gas can be identified. Free air is best demonstrated by examination of the patient in the upright position with a horizontal beam (Figure 4-95). Because the gas rises to the highest point in the peritoneal cavity, it accumulates beneath the domes of the diaphragm. Free intraperitoneal gas appears as a sickle-shaped lucency that is easiest to recognize on the right side between the diaphragm and the homogeneous density of the liver. On the left, the normal gas and fluid shadows present in the fundus of the stomach can be confusing. The free air is shown to best advantage if the patient remains in an upright (or lateral decubitus) position for 10 minutes before a radiograph is obtained.

If the patient is too ill to sit or stand, a lateral decubitus view (preferably with the patient on the left side) can be used. In this position, free air moves to the right and collects between the lateral margin of the liver and the abdominal wall (Figure 4-96). Some gas also collects in the right iliac fossa and, when large amounts are involved, can be seen along the flank down to the pelvis.

When the patient is in the supine position, free intraperitoneal gas accumulates between the intestinal

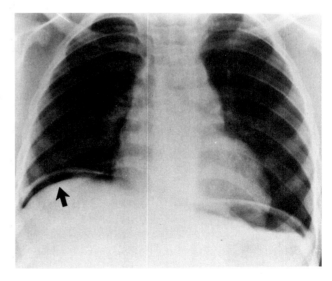

Figure 4-95 Pneumoperitoneum. Gas accumulating beneath dome of right hemidiaphragm *(arrow)* appears as sickle-shaped lucency on this erect chest film, obtained with horizontal beam.

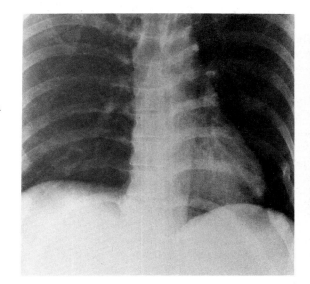

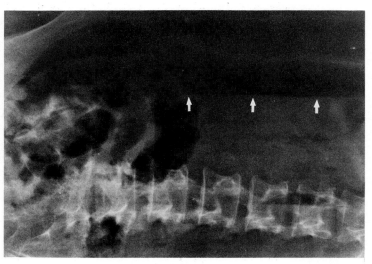

Figure 4-96 Pneumoperitoneum. **A,** Semierect projection obtained without a horizontal beam shows no evidence of free intraperitoneal gas beneath domes of diaphragm. **B,** On lateral decubitus projection obtained with horizontal beam on same patient, free intraperitoneal gas is clearly seen collecting under right side of abdominal wall *(arrows)*. Gas can even be seen extending down flank to region of pelvis.

loops and is much more difficult to demonstrate. However, a large quantity of gas can be diagnosed indirectly because it permits visualization of the outer margins of the intestinal wall (Figure 4-97). The distinct demonstration of the inner and outer contours of the bowel wall is often the only sign of pneumoperitoneum in patients in such poor condition that they cannot be turned on their side or be examined upright.

In children, pneumoperitoneum can be manifest as a generalized greater-than-normal lucency of the entire abdomen. An important sign of pneumoperitoneum on the supine radiograph is demonstration of the falciform ligament. This almost vertical, curvilinear, water-density shadow in the upper abdomen to the right of the spine is outlined only when there is gas on both sides of it, as in a pneumoperitoneum (Figure 4-98).

The most frequent cause of pneumoperitoneum with associated inflammation is perforation of a peptic ulcer, either gastric or duodenal. Colonic perforations, especially those involving the cecum, give the most abundant quantities of free intraperitoneal gas. Septic infection of the peritoneal cavity by gas-forming organisms can result in the production of a substantial amount of gas and the radiographic appearance of pneumoperitoneum. Pneumoperitoneum can also develop after penetrating injuries of the abdominal wall and after blunt trauma causing rupture of a hollow viscus.

Iatrogenic pneumoperitoneum is generally asymptomatic and usually follows abdominal surgery. Postoperative pneumoperitoneum can be radiographically detectable for up to 3 weeks after surgery, but usually can no longer be demonstrated after the first postoperative week. Rarely, free air in the peritoneal cavity may be the result of perforation during an endoscopic procedure.

▪ Spleen

Enlargement

Enlargement of the spleen (splenomegaly) is associated with numerous conditions, including infections (subacute bacterial endocarditis, tuberculosis, infectious mononucleosis, malaria), connective tissue disorders, neoplastic hematologic disorders (lymphoma, leukemia), hemolytic anemia and hemoglobinopathies, and portal hypertension (cirrhosis).

Plain abdominal radiographs can demonstrate the inferior border of the enlarged spleen well below the costal margin. An enlarged spleen can elevate the left hemidiaphragm, impress the greater curvature of the barium-filled stomach, and displace the entire stomach toward the midline. Splenomegaly can also cause downward displacement of the left kidney and the splenic flexure of the colon.

CT is of value when it is unclear whether a mass felt in the left upper quadrant represents an enlarged spleen or a separate abdominal mass. When sple-

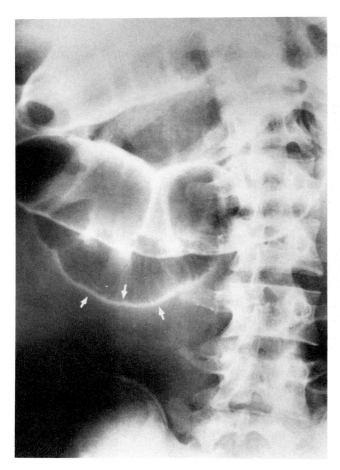

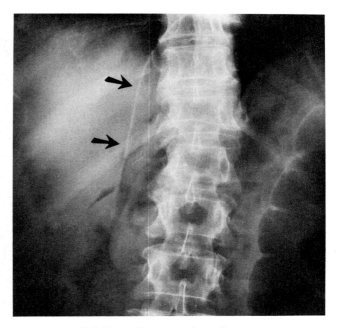

Figure 4-98 Falciform ligament sign of pneumoperitoneum. On supine projection, falciform ligament appears as curvilinear water-density shadow *(arrows)* in upper abdomen to right of spine. This finding implies that there is pneumoperitoneum with gas on both sides of ligament.

Figure 4-97 Double-wall sign of pneumoperitoneum demonstrated on supine projection. Large quantities of free intraperitoneal gas may be diagnosed indirectly because gas permits visualization of both inner and outer margins of intestinal wall *(arrows)*.

nomegaly is present, CT findings may indicate the cause of the splenic enlargement by demonstrating a tumor (Figure 4-99), abscess, or cyst. Associated abdominal lymph node enlargement is suggestive of lymphoma; characteristic alterations in the size and shape of the liver and prominence of collateral venous structures in the splenic hilum indicate that splenomegaly may be a result of cirrhosis and portal hypertension.

Rupture

Rupture of the spleen is usually caused by trauma. Infrequently, it may be a complication of palpation of a spleen enlarged by infection (especially infectious mononucleosis) or leukemia. In many patients suffering traumatic rupture of the spleen, the severity of clinical symptoms and the rapid loss of blood into the abdominal cavity require immediate surgery without radiographic investigation. However,

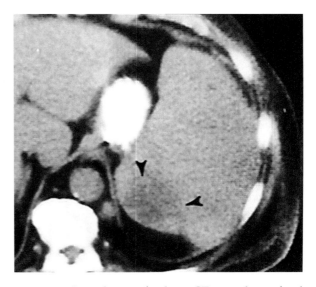

Figure 4-99 Lymphoma of spleen. CT scan shows focal low-attenuation lesion *(arrowheads)* posteriorly in greatly enlarged spleen. (From Koehler RE: Spleen. In Lee JKT, Sagel SS, Stanley RJ, editors: *Computed body tomography,* New York, 1983, Raven Press.)

in patients in whom bleeding stops temporarily or in whom there is slow bleeding over several days, radiographic studies may be of diagnostic value.

CT is the best imaging procedure for screening patients with blunt abdominal trauma for the presence of splenic injury. Indeed, its almost 100% sensitivity in detecting splenic injury has substantially decreased the need for abdominal arteriography and exploratory surgery. Subcapsular hematomas appear on CT as crescentic collections of fluid that flatten or indent the lateral margin of the spleen (Figure 4-100). Splenic lacerations, which may occur with or without an accompanying subcapsular hematoma, produce a CT appearance of splenic enlargement, an irregular cleft or defect in the splenic border, and free blood in the peritoneal cavity.

Before the advent of CT, splenic arteriography was the procedure of choice for demonstrating splenic rupture. Major positive findings include extravasation of contrast material into the splenic parenchyma; obstruction of a major splenic artery; and vascular defects in an enlarged spleen, indicating sites of rupture and hematoma.

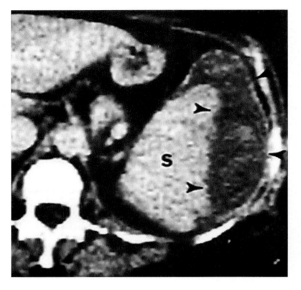

Figure 4-100 Traumatic subcapular splenic hematoma. Contrast enhanced CT scan shows hematoma as large zone of decreased attenuation *(arrowheads)* that surrounds and flattens lateral and anteromedial borders of adjacent spleen *(S)*. (From Koehler RE: Spleen. In Lee JKT, Sagel SS, Stanley RJ, editors: *Computed body tomography,* New York, 1983, Raven Press.)

QUESTIONS

1. Visualization of which of the following structures is an indication of the correct contrast scale of a plain abdominal radiograph?
   I. Liver, kidneys, and psoas muscle shadows
   II. Lumbar spine and transverse processes
   III. Kidneys and psoas muscle shadows
   IV. Lumbar spine and psoas shadows
   A. Both I and IV   C. I only
   B. Both I and II   D. IV only

2. The rhythmic smooth muscle contractions found in the upper gastrointestinal system are called
   A. Chyme   C. Peristalsis
   B. Digestion   D. Mastication

3. The greatest amount of digestion occurs in which portion of the intestines?
   A. Duodenum   C. Ileum
   B. Jejunum   D. Colon

4. Detoxification of poisonous substances takes place in which organ?
   A. Kidneys   C. Pancreas
   B. Liver   D. Spleen

5. Which organ controls the level of glucose in the circulating blood?
   A. Kidneys   C. Pancreas
   B. Liver   D. Spleen

6. The telescoping of one part of the intestinal tract into another is termed _____ .
   A. Intussusception   C. Crohn's disease
   B. Volvulus   D. Ileus

7. Twisting of the bowel upon itself is termed

   _____ .
   A. Intussusception   C. Crohn's disease
   B. Volvulus   D. Ileus

8. What is now considered to be the major imaging modality for the demonstration of gallstones?
   A. OCG   C. CT
   B. MRI   D. Ultrasound

9. What is the major cause of cirrhosis in the United States and Europe?
   A. Hepatitis   C. Alcoholism
   B. Elevated   D. Cholecystitis
      cholesterol

10. Rupture of the spleen as a result of blunt abdominal trauma can best be demonstrated by what imaging procedure?
    A. OCG   C. CT
    B. MRI   D. Ultrasound

11. If a patient is too ill to stand, what projection can be used to demonstrate pneumoperitoneum?
    A. Right lateral decubitus, patient on left side

B. Right lateral decubitus, patient on right side

C. Left lateral decubitus, patient on left side

D. Left lateral decubitus, patient on right side

12. Extensive calcification in the wall of the gall-bladder is termed _____ .
    A. Cholelithiasis
    B. Porcelain gallbladder
    C. Cholecystitis
    D. A or B

13. Varicose veins of the rectum are termed

    _____ .
    A. Polyps
    B. Hemorrhoids
    C. Ulcerations
    D. Carcinomas

14. *Apple-core* and *napkin-ring* are common descriptive terms for annular carcinoma of the

    _____ .
    A. Small intestine
    B. Stomach
    C. Jejunum
    D. Colon

15. Crohn's disease occurs in what organ(s)?
    A. Colon
    B. Small bowel
    C. Stomach
    D. All of the above

16. Large amounts of gas and fluid in uniformly dilated loops of small and large bowel, often seen after abdominal surgery, is termed

    _____ .
    A. Adynamic ileus
    B. Localized ileus
    C. Colonic ileus
    D. Ileus

17. What medical term is used to denote difficulty in swallowing?
    A. Mastication
    B. Dysphagia
    C. Deglutition
    D. B and C

18. Gastric contents that have mixed with hydrochloric acid and pepsin are called

    _____ .
    A. Chyme
    B. Digest
    C. Enzyme
    D. Emulsifier

19. To demonstrate esophageal reflux, the patient is often asked to perform the _____ .
    A. Trendelenburg's maneuver
    B. Sims' maneuver
    C. Fowler's maneuver
    D. Valsalva maneuver

20. An abnormal accumulation of fluid in the peritoneal cavity is termed _____ .
    A. Pneumoperitoneum
    B. Ascites
    C. Volvulus
    D. Hydroperitoneum

21. Herniations, or outpouchings, of the walls of a hollow organ are termed _____ .
    A. Ulcers
    B. Diverticula
    C. Hemorrhoids
    D. Polyps

22. A colon intussusception can sometimes be reduced by what radiographic procedure?
    A. Upper GI series
    B. Small bowel series
    C. Enteroclysis
    D. Barium enema

23. Patients over 40 years of age with a history of difficulty in swallowing are usually assumed, until proved otherwise, to have what pathologic condition?
    A. Esophageal varices
    B. Esophageal carcinoma
    C. Esophageal fistula
    D. Esophageal hernia

24. What is the most common manifestation of peptic ulcer disease?
    A. Gastric ulcer
    B. Esophageal ulcer
    C. Duodenal ulcer
    D. Peritoneal ulcer

25. If loops of bowel are distended by abnormally large amounts of air and are occupying the central portion of the abdomen, the patient most likely has a _____ .
    A. Small bowel obstruction
    B. Large bowel obstruction
    C. Gastric obstruction
    D. A and B

BIBLIOGRAPHY

Eisenberg RL: *Gastrointestinal radiology: a pattern approach*, Philadelphia, 1990, Lippincott.

Gore RM, Levine MS, Laufer I: *Textbook of Gastrointestinal radiology*, Philadelphia, 1993, Saunders.

Jones B, Braver JM: *Essentials of gastrointestinal radiology*, Philadelphia, 1982, Saunders.

Margulis AR, Burhenne HJ: *Alimentary tract radiology*, ed 4, St Louis, 1989, Mosby.

Meyers MA: *Dynamic radiology of the abdomen*, New York, 1994, Springer-Verlag.

CHAPTER 5

Urinary System

■ **Prerequisite Knowledge**

The student should have a basic knowledge of the anatomy and physiology of the urinary system. In addition, proper learning and understanding of the material will be facilitated if the student has some clinical experience in urinary radiography and film evaluation.

■ **Goals**

To acquaint the student radiographer with the pathophysiology and radiographic manifestations of all of the common and some of the unusual disorders of the urinary system

■ **Objectives**

1. Be able to classify the more common diseases in terms of their penetrability to x rays
2. Be familiar with the changes in technical factors required for obtaining optimal-quality radiographs in patients with various underlying pathologic conditions
3. Understand and be able to define or describe all bold-faced terms in this chapter
4. Describe the physiology of the urinary system
5. Identify anatomic stuctures on both diagrams and radiographs of the urinary system
6. Be able to describe the various pathologic conditions affecting the urinary system as well as their radiographic manifestations

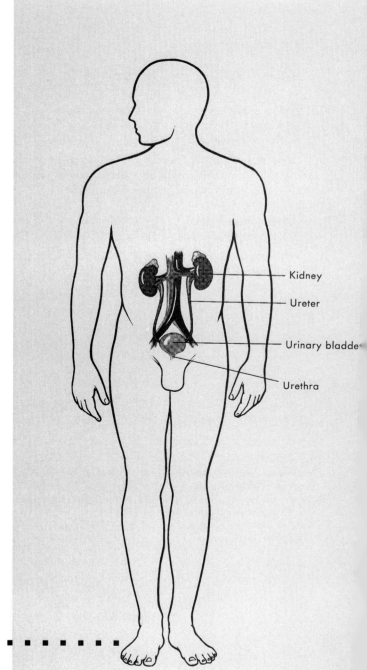

— Kidney

— Ureter

— Urinary bladde-

— Urethra

▪ Radiographer Notes

Although ultrasound and CT are being used with increasing frequency, plain radiography with contrast material introduced intravenously or by means of a catheter remains a major technique for imaging the urinary system. For excretory urography, the radiographer is responsible for preparing sterile injections of contrast material in addition to proper operation of equipment and positioning of the patient. In some instances the radiographer may have to perform these functions in an operating room using sterile technique.

All radiographic studies begin with a "scout" film that is obtained before the injection of any contrast material. The radiographer should evaluate this film for proper technique and positioning so that any required alterations can be made on subsequent radiographs during the procedure. A film with correct density and contrast should demonstrate the kidney and psoas muscle shadows and the lumbar vertebrae and their transverse processes. A correctly positioned film should show all of both kidneys down to the superior portion of the public bones (to ensure that all of the bladder is included). The radiograph must be in a true anteroposterior position with the pelvis appearing symmetric and the spinous processes of the lumbar vertebrae projected over the central portions of the vertebral bodies. The radiologist evaluates the scout radiograph to make certain that the technique and positioning are appropriate for the clinical problem and to evaluate proper patient preparation. The radiograph is also checked for any radiopaque calculi or other abnormality that might be obscured after the injection of contrast material.

The radiographer must be alert to the possibility of an allergic reaction whenever contrast agents are used. It is essential that the radiographer be aware of the proper procedures to follow in the event of an allergic reaction and be able to initiate and maintain basic life support until advanced life-support personnel have arrived. Depending on departmental policy, it is usually the radiographer's responsibility to assist during resuscitation procedures. Therefore it is essential that the radiographer be familiar with the contents of the emergency cart and be responsible for ensuring that the cart is completely stocked with appropriate medications.

All radiographs of the urinary system must be made with the patient in full exhalation so that the diaphragm assumes its highest position and does not compress the abdominal contents. Depending on the specific area being evaluated, the radiographer may have to perform oblique or erect projections, coned-down views of the kidneys or bladder, tomograms, or films made with abdominal compression. In certain pathologic conditions radiographs must be obtained at precisely timed intervals, and delayed films may be necessary.

▪ Physiology of the Urinary System

The urinary system consists of the kidneys, ureters, and bladder. The functional unit of the kidney is the nephron. Each kidney contains more than a million nephrons, which filter waste products from the blood, reabsorb water and nutrients (e.g., glucose, amino acids) from the tubular fluid, and secrete excess substances in the form of urine. In an average person, about 190 L of water is filtered out of glomerular blood each day. This enormous amount is many times the total volume of blood in the body. However, only a small proportion of this water (1 to 2 L) is excreted in the urine. Therefore more than 99% of water is reabsorbed into tubular blood.

The formation of urine begins in the **glomerulus,** a tuft of capillaries with very thin walls and a large surface area. The blood pressure within the glomerulus is higher than that in the surrounding **Bowman's capsule.** This causes the filtration of fluid into Bowman's capsule that is equivalent to plasma containing neither protein nor red blood cells (if the nephron is healthy). The initial urine proceeds into the **proximal convoluted tubule,** where a large amount of water and virtually all nutrients are reabsorbed by means of blood capillaries surrounding the tubules. The amount of sodium and chloride reabsorbed is determined by the concentration of these substances in the body and occurs at a variable rate designed to keep the osmotic pressure of the body constant. This process is greatly influenced by two hormones, antidiuretic hormone (ADH), secreted by the posterior pituitary gland, and aldosterone, secreted by the adrenal glands.

After passing through the proximal tubule, the fluid flows through the **loop of Henle,** a complex structure consisting of a descending limb, a loop, and an ascending limb. In addition to reabsorption of salt and water, the loop of Henle permits the excretion of a concentrated urine by actively secreting substances such as potassium (K^+) and hydrogen (H^+) ions, and some drugs. In this way the kidney plays an essential role in maintaining **electrolyte (salt) balance** and **acid-base balance** of blood and body fluids.

To maintain a healthy metabolism, the pH must be maintained in the very limited range of 7.35 to 7.45. If the pH of blood is lower than this (too acidic), the kidney excretes an acid urine to remove H^+; if the pH of blood is higher than 7.5 (too alkaline), the kidney preserves H^+ and secretes an alkaline urine.

Eventually, urine passes from the **collecting tubules,** whose openings are in the papillae, into the calyces, and on to the funnel-shaped renal pelvis and tubular ureters. Peristaltic waves (about 1 to 5/ min) force the urine down the ureters and into the bladder. The ureters enter the bladder through an oblique tunnel that functions as a valve to prevent backflow of urine into the ureters (vesicoureteral reflux) during bladder contraction.

The bladder acts as a reservoir for the urine before it leaves the body. The openings of the two ureters lie at the posterior corners of the triangular-shaped floor (**trigone**), and the urethral opening is situated at the anterior and lower corner. Filling of the bladder (about 250 ml in the average person) stimulates autonomic nerve endings in the wall that are perceived as a distended sensation and the desire to void (**micturate**). A complicated sequence of bladder contractions and relaxation of the sphincter muscles permits the bladder to expel urine from the body through the urethra. Voluntary contraction of the external sphincter to prevent or terminate micturition is learned and is possible only if the motor system is intact. Nervous system injury (cerebral hemorrhage, cord injury) results in involuntary emptying of the bladder at intervals (**incontinence**).

The kidney is also important in the production of red blood cells and the control of blood pressure. **Erythropoietin,** a substance produced by the kidney, stimulates the rate of production of red blood cells. Therefore renal failure is often associated with a severe anemia. The juxtaglomerular apparatus refers to specialized cells within renal arterioles that secrete **renin,** an enzyme that acts with one of the plasma proteins to produce **angiotensin.** Decreased blood flow through these arterioles increases the secretion of renin and thus the blood level of angiotensin, which constricts peripheral arterioles throughout the body and elevates the blood pressure.

■ Congenital/Hereditary Diseases of the Urinary Tract

Anomalies of number and size

Unilateral **renal agenesis** (solitary kidney) is a rare anomaly that may be associated with a variety of other congenital malformations (Figure 5-1). Before the diagnosis can be made, it is essential to exclude a nonfunctioning, diseased kidney or a prior nephrectomy. Ultrasound or CT can demonstrate the absence of renal tissue. A solitary kidney tends to be larger than expected, reflecting compensatory hypertrophy.

A **supernumerary kidney** is also a rare anomaly. The third kidney is usually small and rudimentary and possesses a separate pelvis, ureter, and blood supply.

A small, **hypoplastic** kidney often appears as a miniature replica of a normal kidney, with good function and normal relation between the amount of

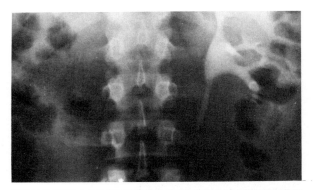

A

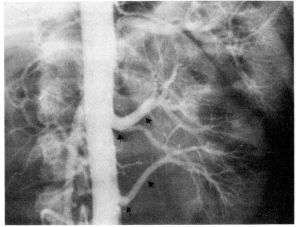

B

Figure 5-1   Solitary kidney. **A,** Excretory urogram demonstrates normal left kidney with no evidence of right renal tissue. **B,** Aortogram shows two renal arteries to left kidney (*arrows*) and no evidence of right renal artery, thus confirming diagnosis of unilateral renal agenesis.

parenchyma and the size of the collecting system (Figure 5-2.). Renal hypoplasia must be differentiated from an acquired atrophic kidney, which is small and contracted because of vascular or inflammatory disease that has reduced the volume of renal parenchyma.

Compensatory hypertrophy is an acquired condition that develops when one kidney is forced to perform the function normally carried out by two kidneys (Figure 5-2). This phenomenon may follow unilateral renal agenesis, atrophy, or nephrectomy. The ability of the kidney to undergo compensatory hypertrophy is greatest in children and diminishes in adulthood.

Anomalies of rotation, position, and fusion

Malrotation of one or both kidneys may produce a bizarre appearance of the renal parenchyma, calyces, and pelvis that is suggestive of a pathologic condition when in reality the kidney is otherwise entirely normal (Figure 5-3). Abnormally positioned kidneys **(ectopic kidney)** may be found in various locations, from the true pelvis **(pelvic kidney)** (Figure 5-4) to above the diaphragm **(intrathoracic kidney)** (Figure 5-5). Whenever only one kidney is seen on excretory urography, a full view of the abdomen is essential to search for an ectopic kidney. Although the ectopic kidney usually functions, the nephrogram and the pelvocalyceal system may be obscured by overlying bone and fecal contents.

Horseshoe kidney is the most common type of fusion anomaly. In this condition, both kidneys are

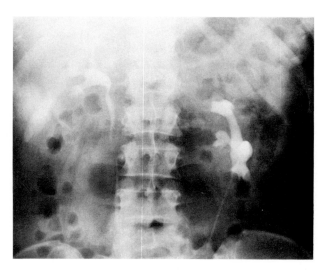

Figure 5-3   Malrotation of left kidney. Notice apparent lateral displacement of upper ureter and elongation of pelvis.

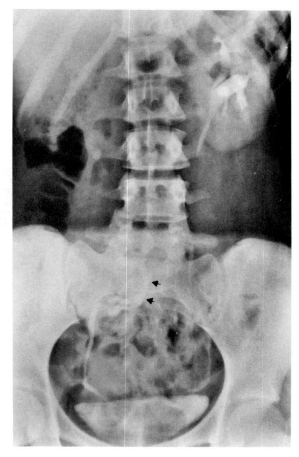

Figure 5-4   Pelvic kidney. Arrows point to collecting system.

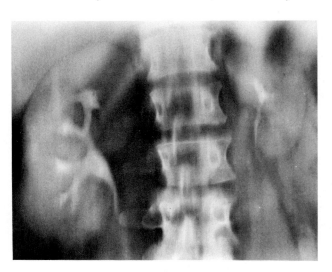

Figure 5-2   Hypoplastic kidney with compensatory hypertrophy. Small left kidney (miniature replica of a normal kidney) has good function and normal relation between amount of parenchyma and size of collecting system. Greatly enlarged right kidney represents compensatory hypertrophy.

malrotated and their lower poles are joined by a band of normal renal parenchyma (isthmus) or connective tissue (Figure 5-6). The ureters arise from the kidneys anteriorly instead of medially and the lower pole calyces point medially rather than later-

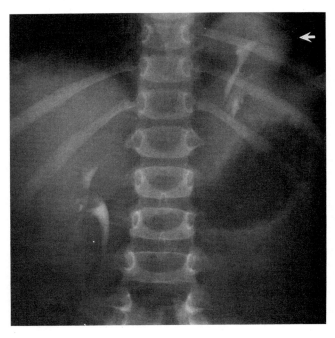

Figure 5-5   Intrathoracic kidney *(arrow)*.

ally. The pelves are often large and flabby and may simulate obstruction. **Crossed ectopia** refers to a situation in which an ectopic kidney lies on the same side as the normal kidney and is most commonly fused with it. **Complete fusion** of the kidneys is a rare anomaly that produces a single irregular mass that has no resemblance to a renal structure. The resulting bizarre appearance has been given such varied names as disk, cake, lump, and doughnut kidney.

Anomalies of renal pelvis and ureter

Duplication (duplex kidney) is a common anomaly that may vary from a simple bifid pelvis to a completely double pelvis, ureter, and ureterovesical orifice. The ureter draining the upper renal segment enters the bladder below the ureter draining the lower renal segment. Complete duplication can be complicated by obstruction or by vesicoureteral reflux with infection. Vesicoureteral reflux and infection more commonly involve the ureter draining the lower renal segment; obstruction more frequently affects the upper pole, where it can cause a hydronephrotic mass that displaces and compresses the lower calyces.

Ureterocele

A ureterocele is a cystic dilatation of the distal ureter near its insertion into the bladder. In the simple

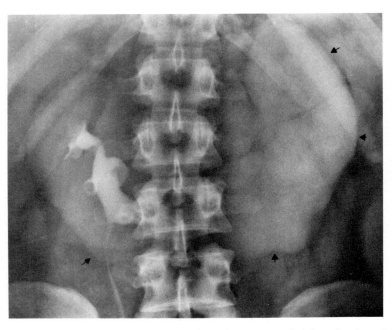

Figure 5-6   Horeshoe kidney *(arrows)*. Prolonged nephrogram and delayed calyceal filling on left are caused by obstructing stone at ureteropelvic junction on that side.

(adult) type, the opening in the ureter is situated at or near the normal position in the bladder, usually with stenosis of the ureteral orifice and with varying degrees of dilatation of the proximal ureter. The stenosis leads to prolapse of the distal ureter into the bladder and dilatation of the lumen of the prolapsed segment. The appearance on excretory urography depends on whether opaque medium fills the ureterocele. If it is filled, the lesion appears as a round or oval density surrounded by a thin radiolucent halo representing the wall of the prolapsed ureter and the mucosa of the bladder (cobra head sign) (Figure 5-7, *A*). When the ureterocele is not filled with contrast material, it appears as a radiolucent mass within the opacified bladder in the region of the ureteral orifice (Figure 5-7, *B*).

Ectopic ureteroceles are found almost exclusively in infants and children; most are associated with ureteral duplication. On excretory urography, an ectopic ureterocele typically appears as a large, eccentric filling defect impressing the floor of the bladder (Figure 5-8). The ureterocele arises from the ureter draining the upper segment of the duplicated collecting system. A mass effect, representing hydronephrosis, often involves the upper pole of the kidney and causes downward and lateral displacement of the lower portion of the collecting system.

Posterior urethral valves

Posterior urethral valves are thin transverse membranes, found almost exclusively in males, that cause bladder outlet obstruction and may lead to severe hydronephrosis and renal damage (Figure 5-9).

■ Inflammatory Disorders

Glomerulonephritis

Glomerulonephritis is a nonsuppurative inflammatory process involving the tufts of capillaries (glomeruli) that filter the blood within the kidney. It represents an antigen-antibody reaction that most commonly occurs several weeks after an acute upper respiratory or middle ear infection with certain strains of hemolytic streptococci. The inflammatory process causes the glomeruli to be extremely permeable, allowing albumin and red blood cells to leak into the urine (proteinuria, hematuria). Decreased glomerular filtration rate causes oliguria, a smaller-than-normal amount of urine.

Most cases of acute glomerulonephritis resolve completely, and the kidney returns to normal. In some patients, however, chronic inflammation with periods of remission and exacerbation lead to a fibrotic reaction that results in shrinkage of the kidneys with loss of renal function and the development of uremia.

The excretory urographic findings in glomerulonephritis depend on the duration and severity of the disease process and on the level of renal function. In patients with acute glomerulonephritis, the kidneys may be normal or diffusely increased in size with smooth contours and normal calyces. A loss of renal substance in chronic glomerulonephritis produces bilateral small kidneys (Figure 5-10). The renal outline remains smooth and the collecting system is normal, unlike the irregular contours and blunted calyces seen in chronic pyelonephritis.

A 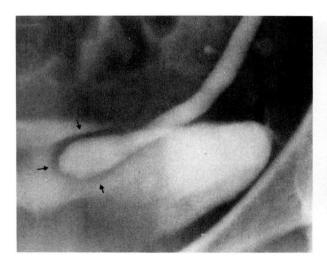 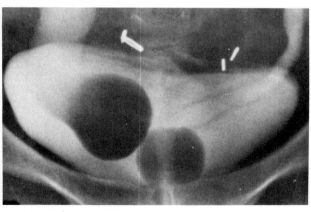 **B**

Figure 5-7 Simple ureteroceles. **A,** Unilateral ureterocele *(arrows)* filled with contrast material. **B,** Bilateral ureteroceles without contrast material appear as radiolucent masses in bladder.

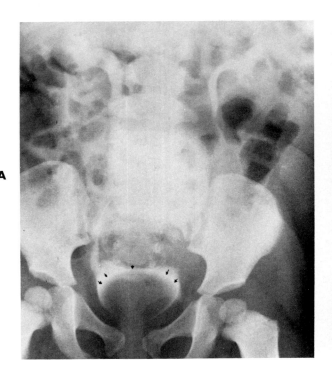
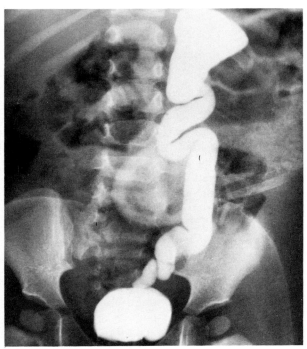

Figure 5-8　Ectopic ureteroceles. **A,** Excretory urogram demonstrates large lucency *(arrows)* filling much of bladder. There is slight downward and lateral displacement of visualized pelvocalyceal system on left. **B,** Cystogram shows contrast material undergoing reflux to fill greatly dilated collecting system draining upper pole of left kidney. Notice severe dilatation and tortuosity of ureter.

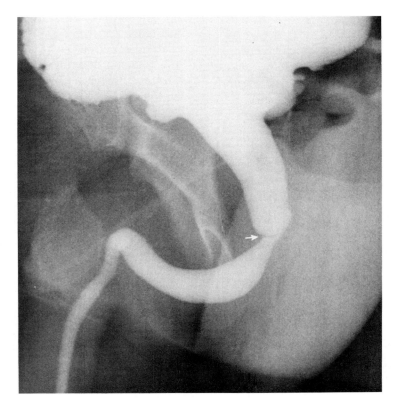

Figure 5-9　Posterior urethral valve. Voiding cystourethrogram shows characteristic thin transverse membrane of valve *(arrow)*. Distally, caliber of bulbous urethra is normal. (From Friedland GW et al: *Clin Radiol* 27:367-373, 1976.)

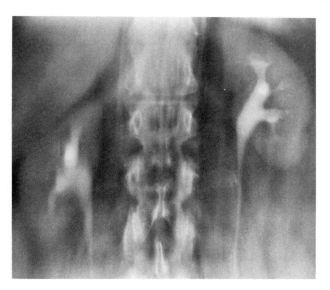

Figure 5-10 Chronic glomerulonephritis. Nephrotomogram shows bilateral small smooth kidneys. Uniform reduction in parenchymal thickness is particularly apparent in right kidney. Notice that pelvocalyceal system is well opacified and without irregular contours and blunted calyces seen in chronic pyelonephritis.

Pyelonephritis

Pyelonephritis is a suppurative inflammation of the kidney and renal pelvis caused by pyogenic (pus-forming) bacteria. Unlike glomerulonephritis, which primarily involves the parenchyma (glomeruli and tubules) of the kidney, the inflammatory process of pyelonephritis affects the interstitial tissue between the tubules. The infection is patchy in distribution, often involves only one kidney, and is asymmetric if both kidneys are involved. Although the infection may spread from the bloodstream or lymphatics, the infection usually originates in the bladder and ascends by means of the ureter to involve the kidneys. Pyelonephritis often occurs in women and children. The disease frequently develops in patients with obstruction of the urinary tract (enlarged prostate gland, kidney stone, congenital defect), which causes stagnation of the urine and provides a breeding ground for infection. Instrumentation or catheterization of the ureter is also an important contributing factor to the development of pyelonephritis.

Patients with pyelonephritis have high fever, chills, and sudden back pain that spreads over the

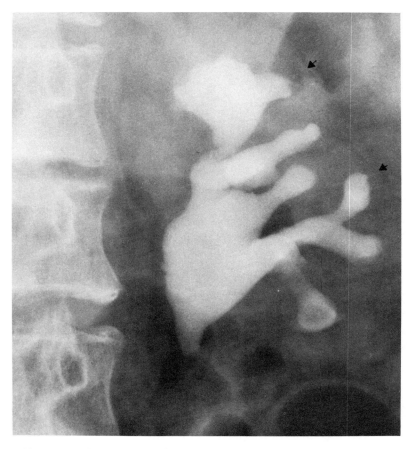

Figure 5-11 Chronic pyelonephritis. Diffuse rounded clubbing of multiple calyces with atrophy and thinning of overlying renal parenchyma. Arrows indicate outer margin of kidney.

abdomen. Painful urination (dysuria) usually occurs. Large amounts of pus may be detected in the urine (pyuria), and bacteria can be cultured from the urine or observed in the urinary sediment.

With the availability of antibiotic therapy, pyelonephritis generally heals without complication. However, fibrous scarring can cause irregular contraction of the kidney. Severe infection can destroy large amounts of renal tissue leading to uremia or septicemia as a result of diffuse spread of infection throughout the body.

In most patients with acute pyelonephritis, the excretory urogram is normal. Occasional abnormalities include generalized enlargement of the kidney on the symptomatic side, delayed calyceal opacification, and decreased density of the contrast material. A characteristic finding is linear striation in the renal pelvis, which probably represents mucosal edema. The urographic hallmark of chronic pyelonephritis is patchy calyceal clubbing with overlying parenchymal scarring (Figure 5-11). Initially, there is blunting of the calyces, which then become rounded or clubbed. Fibrotic scarring causes a cortical depression overlying the dilated calyx. Progressive cortical atrophy and thinning may be so extensive that the tip of the blunted calyx appears to lie directly beneath the renal capsule. The urographic findings may be unilateral or bilateral and are often most pronounced at the poles. If calyceal changes are minimal, the overlying cortical depressions may simulate lobar infarctions or normal kidney lobulations. However, in chronic pyelonephritis the cortical depression lies directly over a calyx, rather than between calyces as in lobar infarctions or congenital lobulation. Chronic pyelonephritis may progress to end-stage renal disease with small, usually irregular, poorly functioning kidneys.

Emphysematous pyelonephritis

Emphysematous pyelonephritis is a severe form of acute parenchymal and perirenal infection with gas-forming bacteria that occurs virtually only in diabetic patients and causes an acute necrosis of the entire kidney. The presence of radiolucent gas shadows within and around the kidney is pathognomonic of emphysematous pyelonephritis (Figure 5-12), a surgical emergency that is lethal if treated medically.

Tuberculosis

The hematogenous spread of tuberculosis may lead to the development of small granulomas scattered in the cortical portion of the kidneys. Spread of infection to the renal pyramid causes an ulcerative, de-

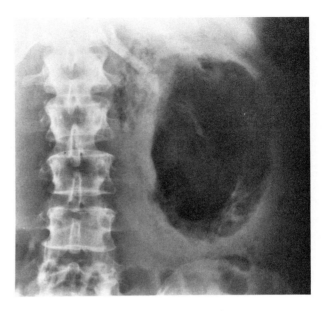

Figure 5-12   Emphysematous pyelonephritis.

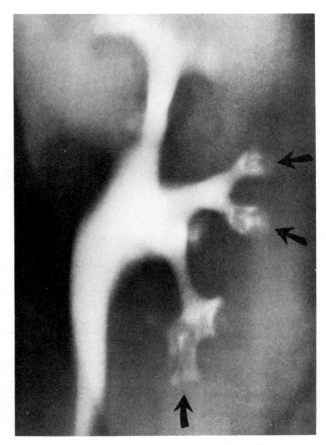

Figure 5-13   Tuberculosis. Early stage of papillary destruction (arrows). (From Tonkin AK, Witten DM: Semin Roentgenol 14:305-318, 1979.)

structive process in the tips of the papillae with irregularity and enlargement of the calyces (Figure 5-13). Fibrosis and stricture formation lead to cortical scarring and parenchymal atrophy, which may simulate the appearance of chronic bacterial pyelonephritis. Flecks of calcification may develop in multiple tuberculous granulomas. With progressive disease, gross amorphous and irregular calcifications can form. Eventually, the entire nonfunctioning renal parenchyma may be replaced by massive calcification (autonephrectomy) (Figure 5-14).

Tuberculosis can also involve the ureter and bladder. Initially, there are multiple ulcerations that result in a ragged, irregular appearance of the ureteral wall. As the disease heals, there are usually multiple areas in which the ureteral strictures alternate with dilated segments, producing a beaded, or corkscrew, appearance. In advanced cases, the wall of the ureter may become thickened and fixed with no peristalsis;

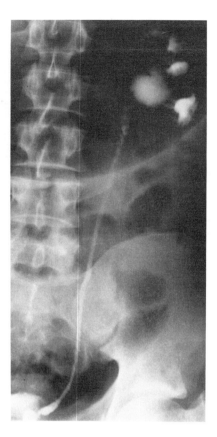

Figure 5-15   Ureteral tuberculosis.

this results in a pipestem ureter that runs a direct course toward the bladder (Figure 5-15). Tuberculous involvement of the urinary bladder may produce mural irregularities simulating carcinoma or, more commonly, a small, contracted bladder with a thickened wall.

Papillary necrosis

Papillary necrosis refers to a destructive process involving a varying amount of the medullary papillae and renal pyramids. It is most often seen in patients with diabetes, pyelonephritis, urinary tract infection or obstruction, sickle cell disease, or phenacetin abuse. The necrotic process causes cavitation of the central portion of the papillae or complete sloughing of the papillary tip (Figure 5-16). When a piece of medullary tissue has been completely separated from the rest of the renal parenchyma, an excretory urogram shows a characteristic ring of contrast material surrounding a triangular lucent filling defect representing the sloughed necrotic tissue. The remaining calyx has a round, saccular, or club-shaped configuration. The sloughed papilla may stay in place and become calcified, or it may

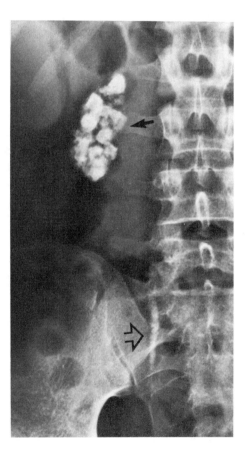

Figure 5-14   Tuberculous autonephrectomy. Plain film shows coarse irregular calcification that retains a kidney-like shape *(solid arrow)*. Notice also tuberculous calcification of right distal ureter *(open arrow)*. (From Tonkin AK, Witten DM: *Semin Roentgenol* 14:305-318, 1979.)

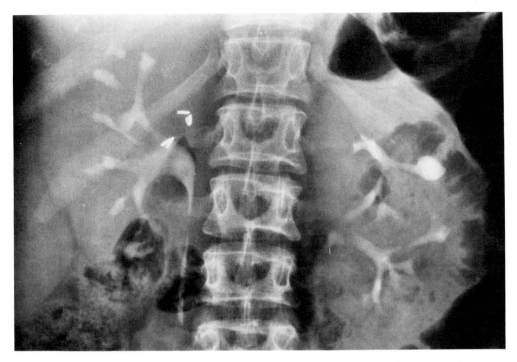

Figure 5-16 Papillary necrosis. Generalized saccular or club-shaped configuration of most calyces bilaterally in patient with sickle cell disease. Notice surgical clips.

pass down the ureter, where it may simulate a stone and even cause obstruction.

Cystitis

Inflammation of the urinary bladder is most common in women because of their shorter urethra. The major cause is the inadvertent spread of bacteria present in fecal material, which reaches the urinary opening and travels upward to the bladder. Instrumentation or catheterization of the bladder is another important cause of cystitis, which is the most common infection in hospitalized patients (nosocomial infection). Cystitis also can develop from sexual intercourse with the spread of infecting organisms from around the vaginal opening. Urinary frequency, urgency, and a burning sensation during urination are typical clinical findings.

Although acute inflammation of the bladder generally does not produce changes detectable on excretory urography, chronic cystitis causes a decrease in bladder size that is often associated with irregularity of the bladder wall (Figure 5-17). In candidal cystitis, fungus balls may produce lucent filling defects in the opacified bladder. Similar lucent filling defects in the bladder may reflect blood clots in patients with hemorrhagic cystitis and may complicate chemotherapy in the treatment of leukemia and lymphoma. A dramatic radiographic appearance is produced by emphysematous cystitis, an inflammatory disease of the bladder that most often occurs in diabetic patients and is caused by gas-forming bacteria. Characteristic plain film findings are a ring of lucent gas outlining all or a part of the bladder wall and the presence of gas within the bladder lumen (Figure 5-18).

■ Kidney Stones

Urinary calculi most commonly form in the kidney. They are asymptomatic until they lodge in the ureter and cause partial obstruction, resulting in extreme pain that radiates from the area of the kidney to the groin. The cause of kidney stones is varied and often reflects an underlying metabolic abnormality, such as hypercalcemia, resulting from hyperparathyroidism or any cause of increased calcium excretion in the urine. Urinary stasis and infection are also important factors in promoting stone formation.

More than 80% of symptomatic renal stones contain enough calcium to be radiopaque and detectable on plain abdominal radiographs (Figure 5-19). Completely radiolucent calculi contain no calcium and are composed of a variety of substances that are in excessive concentration in the urine. Excretory urography is used to detect these otherwise invisible nonopaque stones, which appear as filling defects in the contrast-filled collecting system. In patients with acute renal colic caused by an obstructing stone in

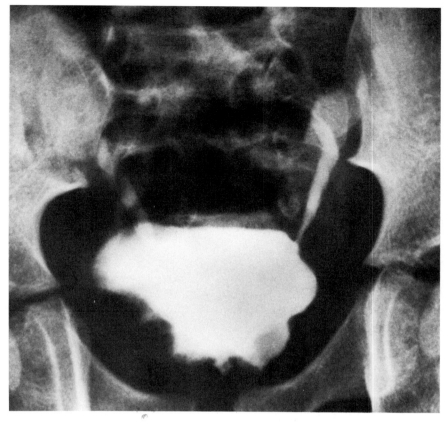

Figure 5-17 Cystitis. Excretory urogram shows irregular, lobulated filling defects (representing intense mucosal edema) at base of bladder.

A

B

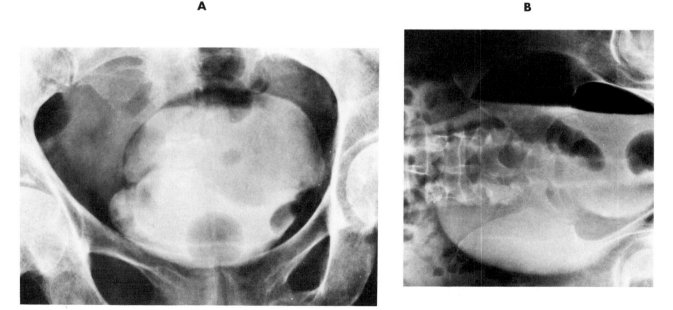

Figure 5-18 Emphysematous cystitis. **A,** Film from cystogram shows thin rim of lucency surrounding much of contrast-filled bladder. **B,** Right lateral decubitus view clearly shows long air-fluid level.

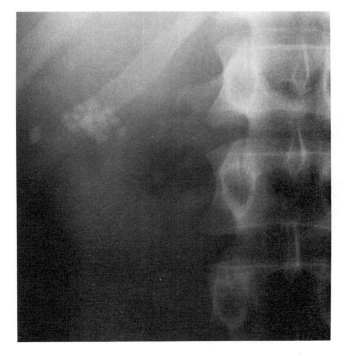
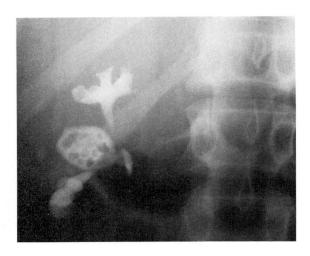

Figure 5-19 Cystine stones. **A,** Plain film shows multiple radiopaque calculi. **B,** Excretory urogram demonstrates stones as lucent filling defects in opacified renal pelvis. (From Eisenberg, R: *Gastrointestinal radiology: a pattern approach*, 1990, Philadelphia, Lippincott.)

the ureter, excretory urography may demonstrate the point of cutoff and dilatation of the proximal ureter and pelvocalyceal system. With acute obstruction, the intrapelvic pressure may increase to such an extent that there is little or no glomerular filtration, resulting in a delayed but prolonged nephrogram and a lack of calyceal filling on the affected side.

Small renal stones may pass spontaneously in the urine. At times, a stone may completely fill the renal pelvis (staghorn calculus) (Figure 5-20), blocking the flow of urine. In the past, surgery was frequently necessary to remove large kidney stones. More recently, medication introduced into the upper urinary tract by means of a percutaneous catheter has been used to dissolve large kidney stones into smaller pieces that pass easily. A new technique is lithotripsy, in which the patient is immersed in a tank of water into which acoustic shock waves are introduced. These shock waves shatter the hard stones into sand-sized particles that are then excreted in the urine.

Calcium can also deposit within the renal parenchyma (nephrocalcinosis) (Figure 5-21). This calcification varies from a few scattered punctate densities to very dense and extensive calcifications throughout both kidneys. The most common causes of nephrocalcinosis include hyperparathyroidism, increased intestinal absorption of calcium (sarcoidosis, hypervitaminosis D, milk-alkali syndrome), and renal tubular acidosis, a disorder in which the kidney is unable to excrete an acid urine (below pH 5.4).

Stones can also form in other portions of the genitourinary tract. Ureteral calculi almost invariably result from the downward movement of kidney stones (Figure 5-22). They are usually small, irregular, and poorly calcified and are therefore easily missed on abdominal radiographs that are not of good quality. Calculi most commonly lodge in the lower portion of the ureter, especially at the ureterovesical junction and at the pelvic brim (Figure 5-23). They are often oval, with their long axes paralleling the course of the ureter. Ureteral calculi must be differentiated from the far more common phleboliths, which are spherical and are located in the lateral portion of the pelvis below a line joining the ischial spines. In contrast, ureteral stones are situated medially above the interspinous line.

Stone formation in the bladder is primarily a disorder of elderly men with obstruction or infection of the lower urinary tract (Figure 5-24, *A*). Frequently associated lesions include bladder-outlet obstruction, urethral strictures, neurogenic bladder, and bladder diverticula (Figure 5-24, *B*). At times,

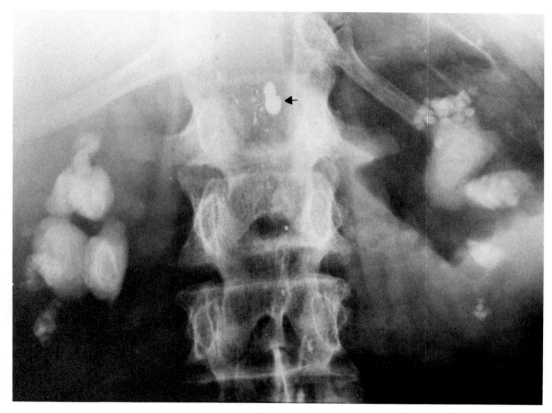

Figure 5-20 Staghorn calculi. Calculi fill renal pelves bilaterally. Of incidental note is residual contrast material *(arrow)* from prior myelogram.

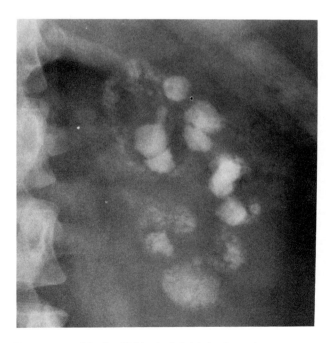

Figure 5-21 Nephrolithiasis. Multiple deposits are scattered throughout parenchyma of left kidney.

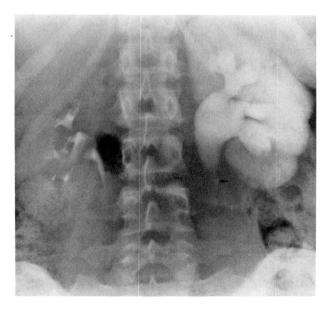

Figure 5-22 Obstructing ureteral calculus. Excretory urogram demonstrates prolonged nephrogram and pronounced dilatation of collecting system and pelvis proximal to obstructing stone *(arrow)*.

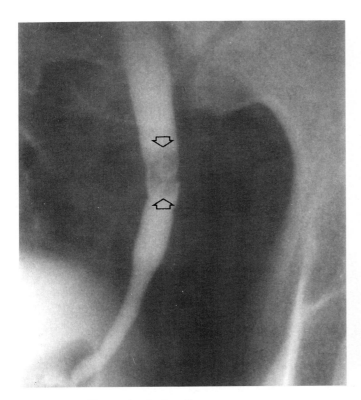

Figure 5-23   Ureteral calculus. Stone appears as nonopaque filling defect *(arrows)* in distal portion of ureter.

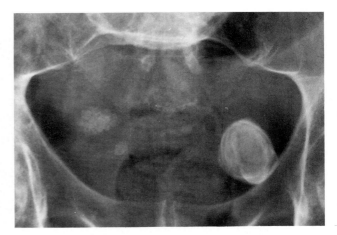

A

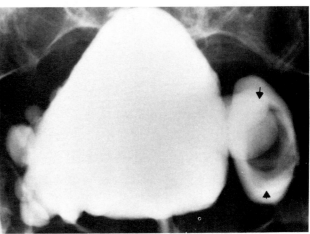

B

Figure 5-24   Bladder calculi. **A,** Plain radiograph of pelvis shows large laminated stone on left and multiple smaller calculi on right. **B,** Excretory urogram demonstrates large stone *(arrows)* in left-sided bladder diverticulum. Notice that multiple smaller calculi on right have been obscured by overlying constrast material.

upper urinary tract stones migrate down the ureter and are retained in the bladder. Bladder calculi can be single or multiple. They vary in size from tiny concretions, each the size of a grain of sand, to an enormous single calculus occupying the entire bladder lumen. Most bladder calculi are circular or oval; however, almost any shape can be encountered. They can be amorphous, laminated (layered), or even spiculated. One unusual type with a characteristic radiographic appearance is the hard burr, or jackstone, variety, which gets its name from the many irregular prongs that project from its surface and simulate the child's toy.

▪ Urinary Tract Obstruction

Urinary tract obstruction produces anatomic and functional changes that vary with the rapidity of onset, the degree of occlusion, and the distance between the kidney and the obstructing lesion. In adults, urinary calculi, pelvic tumors, urethral strictures, and enlargement of the prostate gland are the major causes. In children, congenital malformations (ureteropelvic junction narrowing, ureterocele, retrocaval ureter, posterior urethral valve) are usually

responsible for mechanical obstruction. Normal points of narrowing, such as the ureteropelvic and ureterovesical junctions, the bladder neck, and the urethral meatus, are common sites of obstruction. Blockage above the level of the bladder causes unilateral dilatation of the ureter (hydroureter) and renal pelvocalyceal system (hydronephrosis); if the lesion is at or below the level of the bladder, as in prostatic hypertrophy or tumor, bilateral involvement is the rule.

In acute urinary tract obstruction, diminished filtration of urographic contrast material results in delayed parenchymal opacification compared with the nonobstructed kidney. The nephrogram eventually becomes more dense than normal because of a decreased flow rate of fluid through the tubules, which results in enhanced water reabsorption by the nephrons and greater concentration of the contrast material (Figure 5-25). There is delayed and decreased pelvocalyceal filling because of dilatation and elevated pressure in the collecting system. The radiographic study may have to be prolonged up to 48 hours after the administration of contrast material to determine the precise site of obstruction.

In the patient with acute urinary tract obstruction, the kidney is generally enlarged, and the calyces are moderately dilated. An uncommon but pathognomonic urographic finding in acute unilateral obstruction (usually caused by ureteral stone) is pacification of the gallbladder 8 to 24 hours after the injection of contrast material. This "vicarious excretion" is related to increased liver excretion of contrast material that cannot be promptly excreted by the kidneys.

As an obstruction becomes more chronic, the predominant urographic finding is a greatly dilated pelvocalyceal system and ureter proximal to the obstruction (Figure 5-26). Prolonged increased pressure

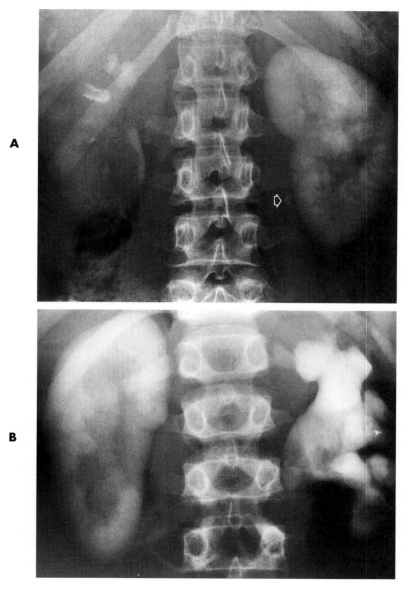

Figure 5-25 Urinary tract obstruction. **A,** Excretory urogram demonstrates prolonged nephrogram on left and no calyceal filling. Arrow points to obstructing stone in proximal left ureter. **B,** In another patient, there is prolonged and intensified obstructive nephrogram of right kidney. On left, there is pronounced dilatation of pelvocalyceal system but no persistent nephrogram, reflecting intermittent chronic obstruction on this side.

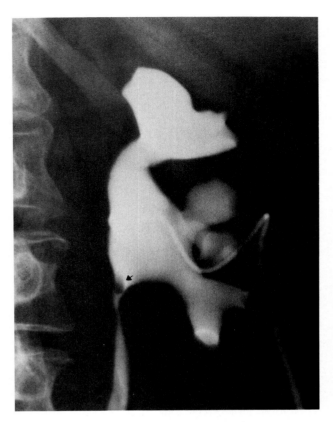

Figure 5-26 Hydronephrosis. Dilatation of entire pelvocalyceal system proximal to obstructing *Cryptococcus* fungus ball *(arrow)* at ureteropelvic junction.

causes progressive papillary atrophy, leading to calyceal clubbing. Gradual enlargement of the calyces and renal pelvis with progressive destruction of renal parenchyma may continue until the kidney becomes a nonfunctioning hydronephrotic sac in which normal anatomy is obliterated.

Whenever possible, the site of obstruction should be demonstrated. Although excretory urography with delayed films may accomplish this purpose, antegrade pyelography is often required. In this procedure, a catheter or needle is placed percutaneously into the dilated collecting system under ultrasound or fluoroscopic guidance, and contrast material is then introduced. This approach has the added advantage of providing immediate and certain decompression of a unilateral obstructing lesion.

Ultrasound is of particular value in detecting hydronephrosis in patients with such severe urinary tract obstruction and renal dysfunction that there is no opacification of the kidneys and collecting systems on excretory urograms. The dilated calyces and pelvis become large, hydronephrotic, echo-free sacs separated by septa of compressed tissue and vessels (Figure 5-27, *A*). With increased duration and severity of hydronephrosis, the intervening septa may disappear, leaving a large fluid-filled sac with no evidence of internal structure and no normal parenchyma apparent at its margins (Figure 5-27, *B*).

A physiologic form of hydronephrosis often develops during pregnancy. The enlarging uterine

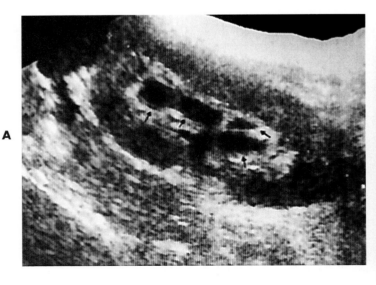
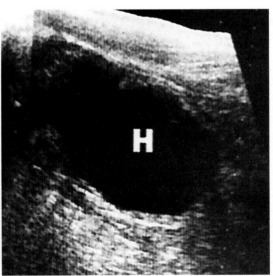

Figure 5-27 Hydronephrosis. **A,** In patient with moderately severe disease, dilated calyces and pelvis appear on ultrasound as echo-free sacs *(arrows)* separated by septa of compressed tissue and vessels. **B,** In patient with severe hydronephrosis, intervening septa have disappeared, leaving large fluid-filled sac *(H)* with no evidence of internal structure and no normal parenchyma apparent at its margins.

mass and physiologic hormonal changes cause extrinsic pressure on the ureter, leading to progressive dilatation of the proximal collecting systems (Figure 5-28). Often bilateral, the dilatation usually is more prominent and develops earlier on the right side. After delivery, the urinary tract returns to normal within several weeks. In some women, however, persistent dilatation of the ovarian vein can compress the ureter and result in prolonged postpartum hydronephrosis.

▪ Cysts and Tumors

Renal cyst

Simple renal cysts are the most common unifocal masses of the kidney. They are fluid-filled and usually unilocular though septa sometimes divide the cyst into chambers, which may or may not communicate with each other. Cysts vary in size, and they may occur at single or multiple sites in one or both kidneys. Thin curvilinear calcifications can be demonstrated in the wall of about 3% of simple cysts.

However, this peripheral type of calcification is not pathognomonic of a benign process, since malignant kidney lesions can produce a similar pattern.

As a simple renal cyst slowly increases in size, its protruding portion elevates the adjacent edges of the cortex. The cortical margin appears on nephrotomography as a very thin, smooth radiopaque rim about the bulging lucent cyst (beak sign) (Figure 5-29). Although the beak sign is generally considered to be characteristic of benign renal cysts, it is merely a reflection of slow expansion of a mass and thus may occasionally be seen in slow-growing solid lesions, including carcinoma. Thickening of the rim about a lucent mass is suggestive of bleeding into a cyst, cyst infection, or a malignant lesion. Renal cysts cause focal displacement of adjacent portions of the pelvocalyceal system. The displaced, attenuated collecting structures remain smooth, unlike the shagginess and obliteration that often occur when focal displacement is caused by a malignant neoplasm.

Ultrasound is the modality of choice for distinguishing fluid-filled simple cysts from solid mass lesions. Fluid-filled cysts classically appear as echo-free structures with strongly enhanced posterior walls (Figure 5-30), in contrast to solid or complex lesions, such as tumors, that appear as echo-filled

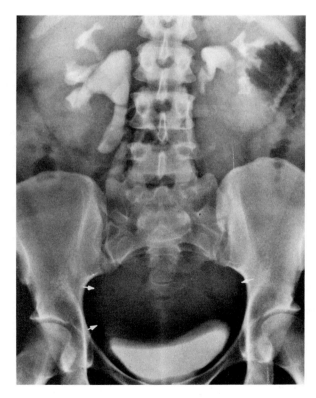

Figure 5-28 Hydronephrosis of pregnancy. Excretory urogram performed 3 days post partum demonstrates bilateral large kidneys with dilatation of ureters and pelvocalyceal systems, especially on right. Large pelvic mass (arrows) indenting superior surface of bladder represents uterus, which is still causing extrinsic pressure on ureters.

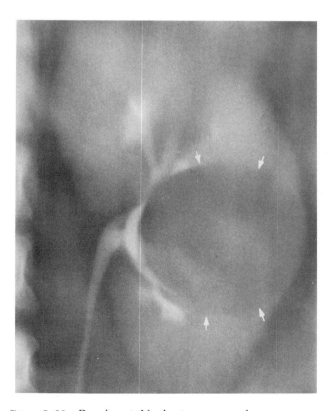

Figure 5-29 Renal cyst. Nephrotomogram shows smooth-walled, fluid-filled mass (arrows).

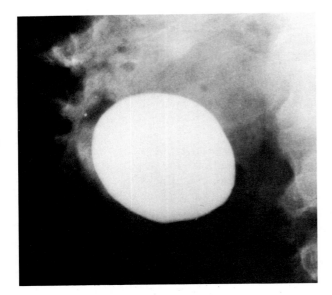

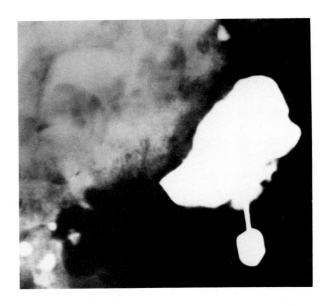

A

B

Figure 5-30 Renal cyst puncture. **A,** Instillation of contrast material shows smooth inner wall characteristic of benign cyst. **B,** In another patient, introduction of contrast material reveals greatly irregular inner border of necrotic renal cell carcinoma.

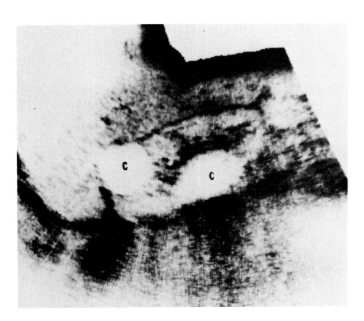

Figure 5-31 Renal cysts. Anechoic fluid-filled masses *(C)* with strongly enhancing posterior walls.

masses without posterior wall enhancement. CT is also highly accurate in detecting and characterizing simple renal cysts. On unenhanced scans, the cyst has a uniform attenuation value near that of water. After the injection of contrast material, a simple cyst becomes more apparent as the contrast material is concentrated by the normal surrounding parenchyma (Figure 5-31). The cyst itself shows no change in attenuation value, unlike a solid renal neoplasm, which always shows a small but definite increase in density. Because of the accuracy of CT and ultrasound, percutaneous cyst puncture is rarely necessary if these modalities provide unequivocal evidence of a simple cyst. However, because abscesses, cystic or necrotic tumors, and inflammatory or hemorrhagic cysts can mimic simple cysts, cyst puncture should be performed if there is an atypical appearance or a strong clinical suspicion of abscess, or if the patient has hematuria or hypertension. Fluid aspirated from a renal cyst can be clearly differentiated from that obtained from an abscess or renal tumor. The introduction of contrast material or air after the cyst fluid has been removed demonstrates the smooth inner wall of the cyst and further decreases the possibility of missing a malignant neoplasm (Figure 5-32).

Polycystic kidney disease

Polycystic kidney disease is an inherited disorder in which multiple cysts of varying size cause lobulated enlargement of the kidneys and progressive renal impairment, which is presumably a result of cystic compression of nephrons, which causes localized intrarenal obstruction. One third of patients with this condition have associated cysts of the liver, which do not interfere with hepatic function. About 10% have one or more saccular (berry) aneurysms of cerebral arteries, which may rupture and produce a fatal subarachnoid hemorrhage. Many patients with

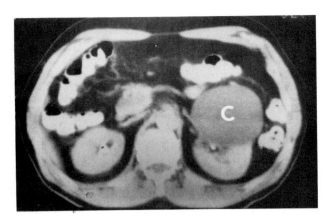

Figure 5-32 Renal cyst. Nonenhancing left renal mass (C with sharply marginated border and thin wall.

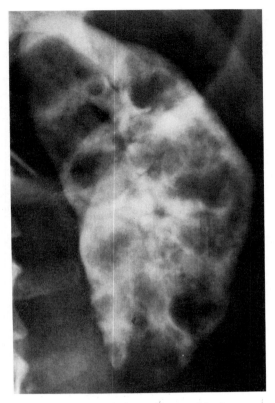

Figure 5-33 Polycystic kidney disease. Nephrogram phase from selective arteriography of left kidney demonstrates innumerable cysts ranging from pinhead size to 2 cm. Opposite kidney had identical appearance.(From Bosniak MA, Ambos MA: *Semin Roentgenol* 10:133-143, 1975.)

polycystic disease are hypertensive, a condition that may cause further deterioration of renal function and increase the likelihood that a cerebral aneurysm will rupture. Because patients tend to be asymptomatic during the first three decades of life, early diagnosis is made either by chance or as a result of a specific search prompted by the discovery of a positive family history.

Excretory urography demonstrates enlarged kidneys with a multilobulated contour. The pelvic and infundibular structures are elongated, effaced, and often displaced around larger cysts to produce a crescentic outline. The nephrogram typically has a distinctive mottled or Swiss cheese pattern caused by the presence of innumerable lucent cysts of varying size throughout the kidneys (Figure 5-33). Plaques of calcification occasionally occur in cyst walls.

Ultrasound demonstrates grossly enlarged kidneys containing multiple cysts that vary considerably in size and are randomly distributed throughout the kidney (Figure 5-34). The demonstration of similar hepatic cysts further strengthens the diagnosis. Ultrasound is also of value in screening family members of a patient known to have this hereditary disorder. In patients with bilateral kidney enlargement and poor renal function, ultrasound permits the differentiation of polycystic kidney disease from multiple solid masses.

The multiple cysts in polycystic kidney disease can also be detected on CT (Figure 5-35) and MRI. Although most individual cysts are histologically identical to simple cysts, intracystic hemorrhage is common. Unlike the low attenuation seen in simple renal cysts on CT, hemorrhagic cysts have high attenuation values. On MRI a hemorrhagic cyst has high signal intensity on both T_1- and T_2-weighted

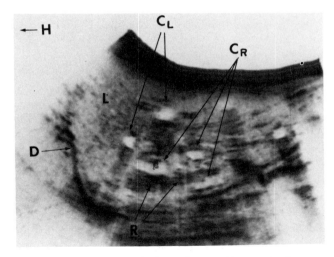

Figure 5-34 Polycystic kidney disease. Parasagittal sonogram shows multiple cysts (C_R, C_L) in right kidney (R) and liver (L). D, Diaphragm; H, head. (From Friedland GW et al., editors: *Uroradiology: an integrated approach*, New York, 1983, Churchill Livingstone.)

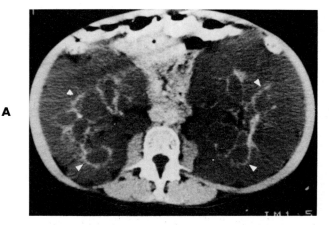

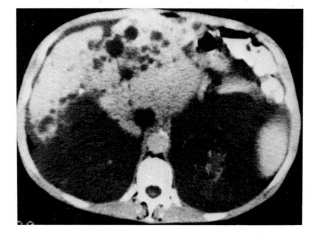

Figure 5-35   Polycystic kidney disease. **A,** CT scan shows contrast-enhancing rims *(arrowheads)* in severely thinned renal parenchyma about innumerable large renal cysts. **B,** CT scan at higher level also shows diffuse cystic involvement of liver.

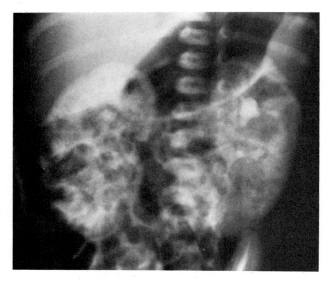

Figure 5-36   Infantile polycystic kidney disease. Excretory urogram in young boy with large, palpable abdominal masses demonstrates renal enlargement with characteristic streaky densities leading to calyceal tips. There is only minimal distortion of calyces.

Renal carcinoma

Renal cell carcinoma (hypernephroma) is the most common renal neoplasm, predominantly occurring in patients older than 40 years and often presenting with painless hematuria. About 10% of hypernephromas contain calcification that is usually located in reactive fibrous zones about areas of tumor necrosis. In the differentiation of solid tumor from fluid-filled benign cysts, the location of calcium within the mass is more important than the pattern of calcification. Of all masses containing calcium in a nonperipheral location, almost 90% are malignant. Although peripheral curvilinear calcification is much more suggestive of a benign cyst, hypernephromas can have a calcified fibrous pseudocapsule that results in an identical radiographic appearance.

Hypernephromas typically produce urographic evidence of localized bulging or generalized renal enlargement. The tumor initially causes elongation of adjacent calyces; progressive enlargement and infiltration lead to distortion, narrowing, or obliteration of part or all of the collecting system (Figure 5-37). Large tumors may partially obstruct the pelvis or upper ureter and cause proximal dilatation. Complete loss of function on excretory urography usually indicates tumor invasion of the renal vein.

On nephrotomography, a hypernephroma generally appears as a mass with indistinct outlines and a density similar to that of normal parenchyma, unlike the classic radiolucent mass with sharp margins

images, unlike the low signal intensity found on T_1-weighted images of simple renal cysts.

A rare, usually fatal form of polycystic disease can present at birth with diffusely enlarged kidneys, renal failure, and maldevelopment of intrahepatic bile ducts. The margins of the kidneys are smooth in infantile polycystic disease, unlike the irregular renal contours in the adult form of polycystic disease that are attributable to the protrusion of innumerable cysts from the kidney surface. When renal function is sufficient, excretory urography results in a striking nephrogram in which a streaky pattern of alternating dense and lucent bands reflects contrast material puddling in elongated cystic spaces that radiate perpendicularly to the cortical surface (Figure 5-36). Ultrasound shows distortion of the intraparenchymal architecture, though the individual cysts are too small to be visualized.

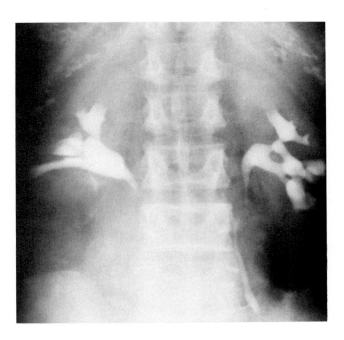

Figure 5-37 Renal cell carcinoma. Upward displacement of right kidney and distortion of collecting system by large lower pole mass.

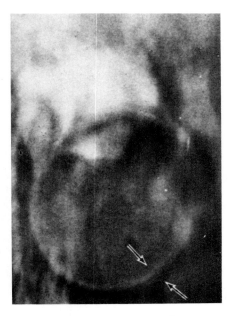

Figure 5-38 Renal cell carcinoma. Nephrotomogram demonstrates lucent, well-demarcated renal mass with thick wall *(arrows)*. (From Bosniak MA, Faegenburg D: *Radiology* 84:692-698, 1965.)

and a thin wall that represents a benign cyst. Necrotic neoplasms can also appear cystic, though they are usually surrounded by thick, irregular walls (Figure 5-38).

Ultrasound shows a renal carcinoma as a solid mass with numerous internal echoes and no evidence of the acoustic enhancement seen with renal cysts (Figure 5-39). On unenhanced CT scans, a hypernephroma appears as a solid neoplasm that is often not homogeneous and has an attenuation value near that of normal renal parenchyma, unlike a simple cyst, which has a uniform attenuation value near that of water. After the injection of contrast material, a simple cyst shows no change in attenuation value, whereas a solid renal neoplasm demonstrates a small but definite increase in density that is probably attributable primarily to vascular perfusion. However, this increased density is much less than that of surrounding normal parenchyma, which also tends to concentrate the contrast material, and thus renal neoplasms become more apparent on contrast-enhanced scans (Figure 5-40). CT is also an accurate method for detecting local and regional spread of hypernephroma. It can usually distinguish between neoplasms confined to the renal capsule and those that have extended beyond it. CT is also the most accurate method for detecting enlargement of para-aortic, paracaval, and retrocrural lymph nodes and spread to the ipsilateral renal vein and inferior vena cava (Figure 5-41).

MRI allows detailed demonstration of the renal anatomy and approaches the accuracy of CT in staging the abdominal extent of tumor in the patient with renal cell carcinoma (Figure 5-42, *A*) Advantages of MRI include its ability to determine the origin of the mass, to detect perihilar and perivascular lymph node metastases, and to demonstrate tumor invasion of adjacent organs. The superb delineation of blood vessels with MRI permits evaluation of tumor thrombus extension into the renal veins and inferior vena cava without the need for intravenous contrast material (Figure 5-42, *B*).

The most common sites of metastasis from renal cell carcinoma include the lungs, liver, bones, and brain.

Wilms' tumor (nephroblastoma)

Wilms' tumor is the most common abdominal neoplasm of infancy and childhood. The lesion arises from embryonic renal tissue, may be bilateral, and tends to become very large and appear as a palpable mass.

Wilms' tumor must be differentiated from neuroblastoma, a tumor of adrenal medullary origin that is the second most common malignancy in children. Peripheral cystic calcification occurs in about 10% of Wilms' tumors, in contrast to the fine, granular, or stippled calcification seen in about half of the cases of neuroblastoma. At excretory urography, the intrarenal Wilms' tumor causes pronounced distortion

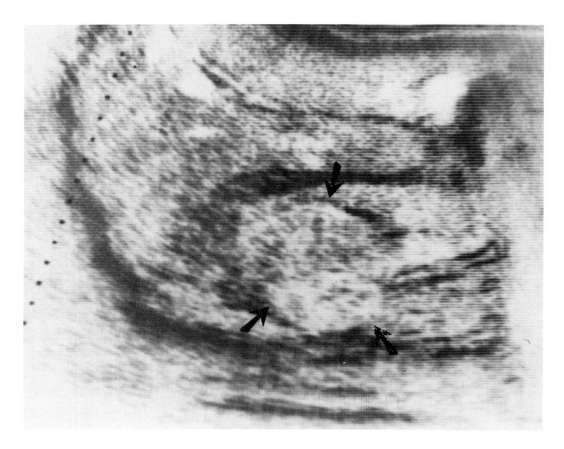

Figure 5-39   Renal cell carcinoma. Ultrasound shows echo-filled solid mass *(arrows)* with no posterior enhancement.

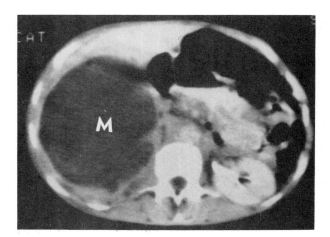

Figure 5-40   Necrotic renal cell carcinoma. CT shows huge nonenhancing, cystlike mass *(M)* that has irregular margins (especially on its medial and posterior aspects).

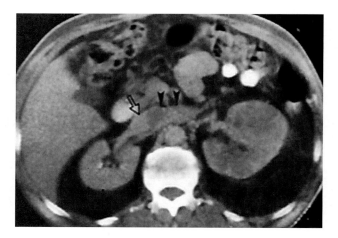

Figure 5-41   Renal cell carcinoma with left renal vein invasion. Postcontrast CT scan shows dilated left renal vein filled with tumor thrombus *(arrowheads)*. Thrombus extends to inferior vena cava *(arrow)*. (From McClennan BL, Lee JKT: Kidney. In Lee JKT, Sagel SS, Stanley RJ, editors: *Computed body tomography*, New York, 1983, Raven Press.)

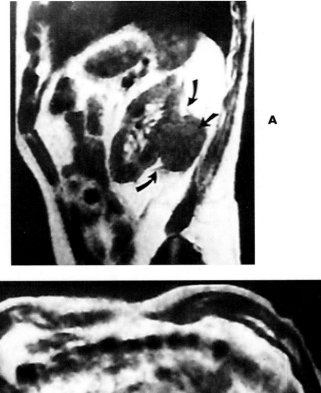

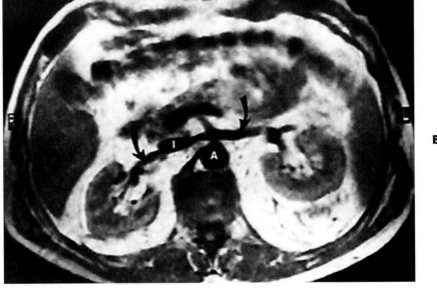

Figure 5-42   Renal cell carcinoma. **A,** Sagittal T_1-weighted magnetic resonance image through left kidney demonstrates large renal cell carcinoma *(straight arrow)* arising from posterior aspect of kidney and displacing Gerota's fascia outward *(curved arrows).* **B,** Transverse MR image at level of renal veins *(arrows)* and inferior vena cava *(I)* demonstrates normal signal from flowing blood without evidence of tumor thrombus. This modality is especially useful for staging renal cell carcinoma because of its multiplanar capability and its ability to allow assessment of vascular invasion. *A,* Aorta.

and displacement of the pelvocalyceal system (Figure 5-43). The major effect of the extrarenal neuroblastoma is to displace the entire kidney downward and laterally. Because the kidney itself is usually not invaded, there is not distortion of the pelvocalyceal system.

Ultrasound is of value in distinguishing Wilms' tumor from hydronephrosis, another major cause of a palpable renal mass in a child. Wilms' tumors typically have a solid appearance with gross distortion of the renal structure (Figure 5-44), unlike the precise organization of symmetrically positioned fluid-filled spaces in hydronephrosis. Ultrasound can also demonstrate the intrarenal location of Wilms' tumor, in contrast to the extrarenal origin of a neuroblastoma.

Although it entails the use of ionizing radiation, CT can show the full extent of the tumor (including invasion of the inferior vena cava) and can detect any recurrence of the neoplasm after surgical removal (Figure 5-45). Coronal T_1-weighted MR images can accurately differentiate Wilms' tumor from renal or hepatic lesions (Figure 5-46). This also is extremely useful in defining the extent of the lesion and showing possible tumor thrombus within the renal vein or inferior vena cava. Because MRI has no ionizing radiation, it is an ideal modality for follow-up evaluation after surgical removal of the tumor.

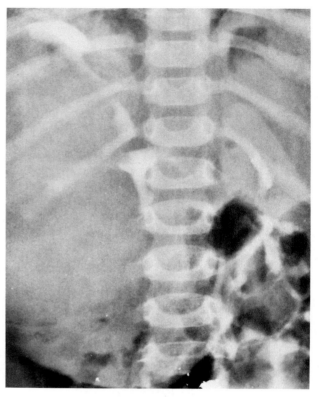

Figure 5-43 Wilms' tumor. Huge mass in right kidney distorts and displaces pelvocalyceal system. (From Friedland GW et al, editors: *Uroradiology: an integrated approach,* New York, 1983, Churchill Livingstone.)

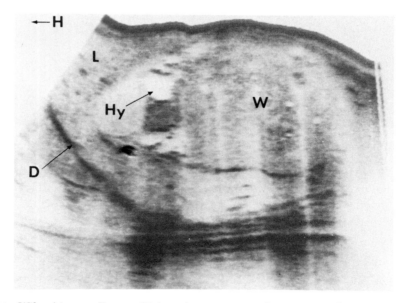

Figure 5-44 Wilms' tumor. Parasagittal supine sonogram demonstrates huge mass *(W)* involving lower pole of right kidney and resulting in hydronephrosis of upper collecting system *(Hy)*. Wilms' tumors tend to have moderately low internal echogenicity and, as in this patient, often contain multiple tiny cystic spaces. Large mass dramatically displaces liver *(L)*. D, Diaphragm; H, head. (From Friedland GW et al, editors: *Uroradiology: an integrated approach,* New York, 1983, Churchill Livingstone.)

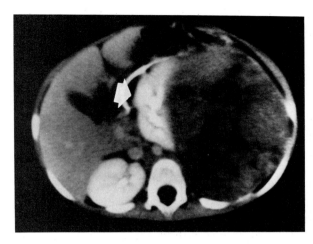

Figure 5-45 Wilms' tumor. Large low-density mass pushing functioning portion of left kidney *(arrow)* across midline.

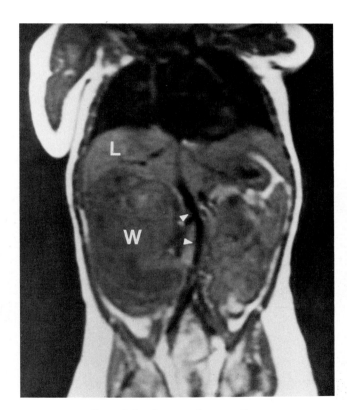

Figure 5-46 T_1-weighted coronal magnetic resonance scan shows sharply marginated infrahepatic mass *(W)* that is clearly distinct from liver. Inferior vena cava *(arrowheads)*, while displaced by mass, shows no evidence of tumor extension into it. *L,* Liver. (From Merten DE, Kirks DR: In Eisenberg RL, editor: *Diagnostic imaging: an algorithmic approach,* Philadelphia, 1988, Lippincott.

Carcinoma of the bladder

Bladder carcinoma is usually seen in men after 50 years of age. Many industrial chemicals have been-implicated as factors in the development of carcinoma of the bladder. Cigarette smoking has also been associated with bladder tumors, presumably because of carcinogenic metabolites being excreted in the urine. The incidence of bladder cancer is especially high in Egypt, most likely related to the widespread prevalence of the parasitic infection schistosomiasis in that country.

Carcinoma of the bladder may produce fingerlike projections into the lumen or infiltrate the bladder wall. Plain radiographs may demonstrate punctate, coarse, or linear calcifications that are usually encrusted on the surface of the tumor but occasionally lie within it. On excretory urograms, bladder cancer appears as one or more polypoid defects arising from the bladder wall or as focal bladder wall thickening (Figure 5-47). However, urography can detect only about 60% of bladder carcinomas because most are small when first symptomatic and are located on the trigone, where they can be difficult to visualize. Therefore all patients with lower urinary tract hematuria should undergo cystoscopy to exclude a bladder neoplasm.

CT with fill distention of the bladder demonstrates a neoplasm as a mass projecting into the bladder lumen or as focal thickening of the bladder wall (Figure 5-48, *A*). This modality is the method of choice for preoperative staging because it can

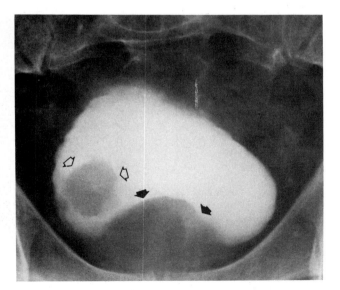

Figure 5-47 Carcinoma of bladder. Irregular tumor *(open arrows)* that is associated with large filling defect *(solid arrows)*, representing benign prostatic hypertrophy, at base of bladder.

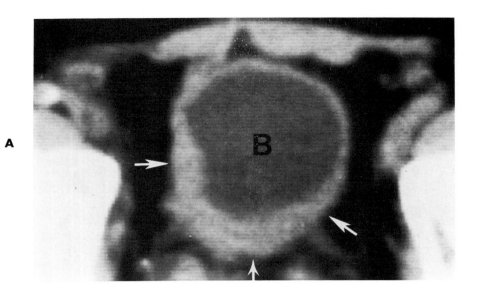

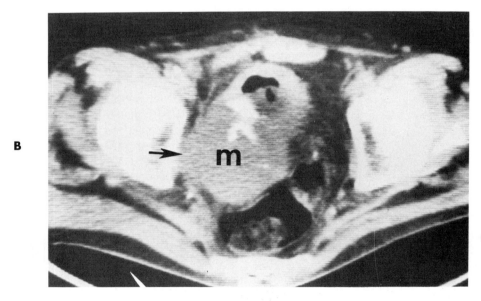

Figure 5-48   CT of bladder carcinoma *(B)*. **A,** Focal thickening of posterior wall *(arrows)*. **B,** In this patient, extensive bladder cancer *(m)* has extended to involve sidewall of pelvis *(arrow)*. (From Friedland GW et al, editors: *Uroradiology: an integrated approach,* New York, 1983, Churchill Livingstone.)

determine the presence and degree of extravesical extension, involvement of the pelvic sidewalls (Figure 5-48, *B*), and enlargement of pelvic or paraaortic lymph nodes.

Many carcinomas of the bladder have a low grade of malignancy, though they tend to recur repeatedly after surgical removal. More invasive tumors require removal of the entire bladder with transplantation of the ureters into a loop of ileum.

▪ Renal Vein Thrombosis

Renal vein thrombosis occurs most frequently in children who are severely dehydrated. In the adult, thrombosis is most often a complication of another renal disease (chronic glomerulonephritis, amyloidosis, pyelonephritis), trauma, the extension of a thrombus from the inferior vena cava, or direct invasion or extrinsic pressure resulting from renal tumors.

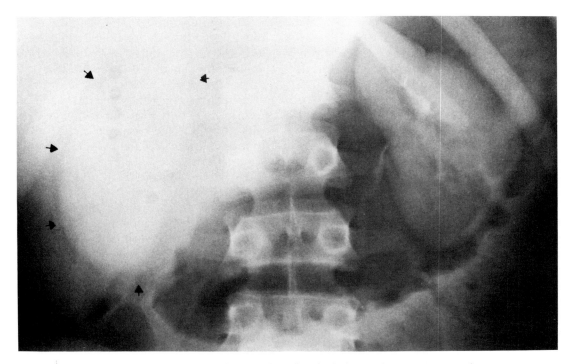

Figure 5-49 Acute renal vein thrombosis. Film of right kidney taken 5 minutes after injection of contrast material shows dense nephrogram *(arrows)* and absence of calyceal filling.

Renal vein thrombosis may be unilateral or bilateral. The clinical and radiographic findings are greatly influenced by the rapidity with which venous occlusion occurs. Sudden total occlusion causes striking kidney enlargement with minimal or no opacification on excretory urograms (Figure 5-49). If unresolved, this acute venous occlusion leads to the urographic appearance of a small, atrophic, nonfunctioning kidney.

When venous occlusion is partial or accompanied by adequate collateral formation, the kidney is large and smooth but with some degree of contrast excretion. There is stretching and thinning of the collecting system as a result of surrounding interstitial edema. Enlargement of collateral pathways for renal venous outflow (gonadal and ureteric veins) produces characteristic notching of the upper ureter.

The confirmation of renal vein thrombosis requires venographic demonstration of vessel occlusion or a localized filling defect (Figure 5-50). An examination of the inferior vena cava with a catheter placed well below the renal veins is often performed initially to exclude caval thrombosis with proximal extension before the renal veins are catheterized directly.

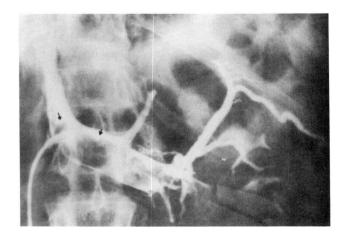

Figure 5-50 Renal vein thrombosis. Renal venogram demonstrates large filling defect in left renal vein *(arrows)* that extends into vena cava. (From Cohn LH et al: *Surgery* 64:387-396, 1968.)

■ **Acute Renal Failure**

Acute renal failure refers to a rapid deterioration in kidney function that is sufficient to result in the accumulation of nitrogen-containing wastes in the blood and a characteristic odor of ammonia on the breath. In prerenal failure, there is decreased blood flow to the kidneys cause by low blood volume (e.g., hemorrhage, dehydration, surgical shock), cardiac failure, or obstruction of both renal arteries. Postrenal failure is caused by obstruction of the urine outflow from both kidneys, most commonly a result of prostatic disease or functional obstruction of the bladder neck. Acute renal failure may also be the result of specific kidney diseases, such as glomerulonephritis, bilateral acute pyelonephritis, and malignant (severe) hypertension. Other causes of acute renal failure include nephrotoxic agents (antibiotics, radiographic contrast material, anesthetic agents, heavy metals, organic solvents), intravascular hemolysis, and large amounts of myoglobin (muscle protein) in the circulation resulting from muscle trauma or ischemia.

Because it is independent of renal function, ultrasound is especially useful in the evaluation of patients with acute renal failure. In addition to demonstrating dilatation of the ureters and pelves caused by postobstructive hypernephrosis, ultrasound can assess renal size and the presence of focal kidney lesions or diffuse renal cystic disease. In the patient with prerenal failure, ultrasound can aid in distinguishing low blood volume from right-sided heart failure. In the latter there is dilatation of the inferior vena cava and hepatic veins that does not occur in patients with low circulating blood volume.

Plain film tomography can often demonstrate renal size and contours. Bilaterally enlarged, smooth kidneys are suggestive of acute renal parenchymal dysfunction; small kidneys usually indicate chronic, preexisting renal disease. Plain film tomograms can also demonstrate bilateral renal calcification, which may indicate either secondary hyperparathyroidism caused by chronic renal disease or bilateral stones that have obstructed both ureters to produce postrenal failure.

Excretory urography in the patient with acute renal failure demonstrates bilateral renal enlargement with a delayed but prolonged nephrogram (Figure 5-51); vicarious excretion of contrast material by the liver occasionally results in opacification of the gallbladder. However, in most instances excretory urography is unnecessary in the patient with acute renal failure, especially since many authors believe that intravenous contrast material can cause further damage to the kidneys in this condition.

▪ Chronic Renal Failure

Like acute renal failure, chronic kidney dysfunction may reflect prerenal, postrenal, or intrinsic kidney disease. Therefore underlying causes of chronic renal failure include bilateral renal artery stenosis,

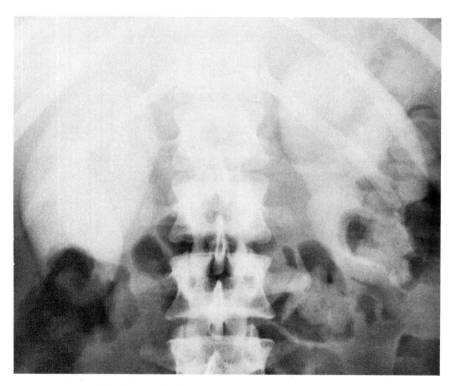

Figure 5-51   Acute renal failure. Film from excretory urogram 20 minutes after injection of contrast material shows bilateral persistent nephrograms with no calyceal filling.

bilateral ureteral obstruction, and intrinsic renal disorders such as chronic glomerulonephritis, pyelonephritis, and familial cystic diseases.

A failure to clear nitrogen-containing wastes adequately from the circulation leads to the accumulation of excessive blood levels of urea and creatinine (waste products of protein metabolism) in the blood. This condition is called **uremia** and produces toxic effects on many body systems. Irritation of the gastrointestinal tract produces nausea, vomiting, and diarrhea. In the nervous system, uremia causes drowsiness, dim vision, decreased mental ability, convulsions, and eventually coma. A decreased ability of the kidney to synthesize erythropoietin, which helps regulate the production of red blood cells, leads to the development of anemia. In the skin, uremia causes intense itching (pruritus) and a sallow, yellow coloring resulting from the combined effects of anemia and retention of a variety of pigmented metabolites (urochromes).

Because of the kidney's role in maintaining water balance and regulating acid-base balance and electrolyte levels, chronic renal failure causes abnormalities involving all these vital functions. Retention of sodium leads to increased water retention and the development of generalized edema and congestive heart failure. An elevated serum potassium level is potentially life threatening because of its direct effect on cardiac muscle contractility and the possibility of causing an arrhythmia or cardiac arrest. A reduction of serum calcium can produce the muscle twitching commonly seen in uremic patients. Low calcium levels also lead to increased activity of the parathyroid glands, which results in the removal of calcium from bones and a high incidence of renal stones.

Because it is independent of renal function, ultrasound is often the initial procedure in the evaluation of patients with chronic renal failure (Figure 5-52). It is of special value in diagnosing treatable diseases such as hydronephrosis and intrarenal or perirenal infections. This modality can also allow assessment of renal size and the presence of focal kidney lesions or diffuse renal cystic disease and can localize the kidneys for percutaneous renal biopsy.

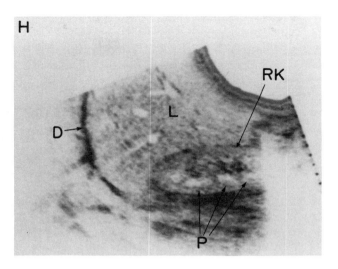

Figure 5-52 Chronic renal failure. Parasagittal sonogram of right kidney *(RK)* shows irregular echo pattern with echogenicity of renal cortical tissue increased to such an extent that it is greater than that of hepatic parenchyma *(L)*. Renal medullary pyramids *(P)* are clearly visible in right kidney. *H*, Head; *D*, diaphragm. (From Friedland GW et al, editors: *Uroradiology: an integrated approach,* New York, 1983, Churchill Livingstone.)

Even in patients with chronic renal failure and uremia, excretory urography with tomography may produce sufficient opacification of the kidneys to be of diagnostic value. However, excretory urography is infrequently required because similar information can be provided by ultrasound or retrograde pyelography. An initial plain abdominal radiograph may demonstrate bilateral renal calcifications (nephrocalcinosis) or obstructing ureteral stones (Fig. 5-25). Small kidneys with smooth contours are suggestive of chronic glomerulonephritis (Fig. 5-10), nephrosclerosis, or bilateral renal artery stenosis. Small kidneys with irregular contours, thin cortices, and typical clubbing of the calyces are consistent with chronic pyelonephritis (Fig. 5-11). Large kidneys are suggestive of obstructive disease, infiltrative processes (lymphoma, myeloma, amyloidosis) renal vein thrombosis (Fig. 5-49), or polycystic kidney disease (Fig. 5-38).

QUESTIONS

1. The imaging criteria for a pyelogram are the same as for an abdominal radiograph but must include all of the _____ to the

   _____ .

   A. Diaphragm:
      kidneys
   B. Kidneys; pelvis

   C. Kidneys; superior
      pubis
   D. A and B

2. What organ of the body plays an essential role in maintaining the acid-base balance of the blood and body fluids, as well as the electrolyte balance.

   A. Nephron
   B. Glomerulus

   C. Bladder
   D. Kidney

3. A bacterial inflammation of the kidney and renal pelvis is termed _____
   A. Renitis
   B. Pyelonephritis
   C. Glomerulitis
   D. None of the above

4. The medical term used to describe dilated calyces and renal pelvis is _____ .
   A. Hydronephrosis
   B. Pyelonephritis
   C. Nephrosis
   D. None of the above

5. What is the name for the most common abdominal neoplasm of infants and children?
   A. Polycystic disease
   B. Pyelonephritis
   C. Wilms' tumor
   D. Hypernephroma

6. What is the name of the most common fusion anomaly of the kidneys?
   A. Complete fusion
   B. Crossed ectopia
   C. Pelvic kidney
   D. Horseshoe kidney

7. What is the name for a cystic dilatation of the distal ureter near the bladder?
   A. Compensatory hypertrophy
   B. Renal agenesis
   C. Ureterocele
   D. Hypoplastic

8. Name the first portion of the kidney to visualize after injection of a contrast agent.
   A. Nephron
   B. Glomerulus
   C. Bowman's capsule
   D. Calyces

9. What term is used to describe a kidney not in the normal area of the abdomen?
   A. Horseshoe
   B. Duplex
   C. Ectopic
   D. Ectopic ureterocele

10. The medical term for painful urination is

    _____ .

    A. Dysuria
    B. Anuria
    C. Micturition
    D. Exacerbation

BIBLIOGRAPHY

Davidson AJ: *Radiology of the kidney*, Philadelphia, 1985, Saunders.

Pollack HM: *Clinical urography: an atlas and textbook of urological imaging*, Philadelphia, 1990, Saunders.

CHAPTER 6

Cardiovascular System

■ **Prerequisite Knowledge**

The student should have a basic knowledge of the anatomy and physiology of the cardiovascular system. In addition, proper learning and understanding of the material will be facilitated if the student has some clinical experience in chest radiography and film evaluation, including a concept of the changes in technique required to compensate for density differences produced by the underlying pathologic conditions. Previous experience in a cardiac catheterization laboratory would be beneficial.

■ **Goals**

To acquaint the student radiographer with the pathophysiology and radiographic manifestations of all of the common and some of the unusual disorders of the cardiovascular system

■ **Objectives**

1. Understand and be able to define or describe all bold-faced terms in this chapter
2. Describe the physiology of the cardiovascular system
3. Identify anatomic structures on both diagrams and radiographs of the cardiovascular system
4. Be able to describe the various pathologic conditions affecting the cardiovascular system as well as their radiographic manifestations
5. Be familiar with the special procedures that are indicated for imaging of particular pathologic conditions

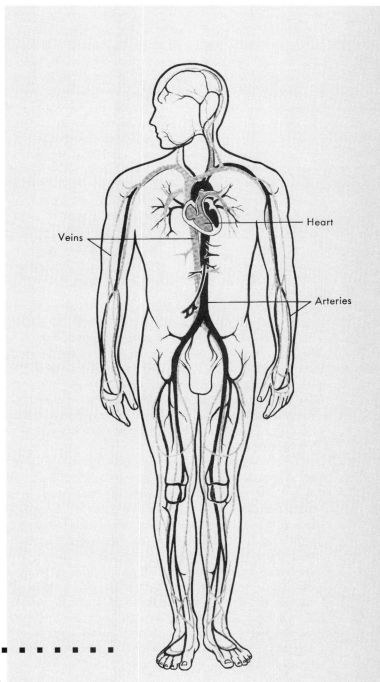

▪ Radiographer Notes

Plain chest radiography and fluoroscopy of the cardiovascular system are used to identify abnormalities in the size and shape of the heart and to detect calcification of heart valves, coronary arteries, or the pericardium. The presence and extent of functional disorders are better achieved using angiography, ultrasound, radionuclide imaging, and magnetic resonance.

As with all chest radiographs, it is essential that the radiographer perform cardiovascular studies with the patient positioned correctly and using proper technical factors. To this end, it would be helpful for the reader to review the radiographer notes at the beginning of the chapter on the respiratory system. An abnormality identified on a chest radiograph may be the first evidence of cardiovascular disease in an asymptomatic patient.

Radiographers now can specialize in invasive diagnostic and therapeutic cardiovascular procedures and be employed by heart catheterization laboratories. Angiocardiography is a diagnostic procedure performed to identify the exact anatomic location of an intracardiac disorder. Coronary angioplasty is a therapeutic procedure in which a narrowed coronary artery is dilated by inflation of a balloon that is attached to a catheter and manipulated fluoroscopically to the site of the stenosis. Because both angiocardiography and angioplasty involve the use of contrast material in patients who often have severe preexisting medical conditions, it is essential that the radiographer be continually alert to the possibility of cardiac or respiratory arrest and be prepared to immediately assist with basic and advanced life support.

The injection of contrast material into arteries (arteriograms) and veins (venograms) can be performed in almost any portion of the body. As in the heart, these invasive studies use potentially dangerous substances so that the radiographer must be alert for possible complications and be prepared to assist in cardiorespiratory emergencies. In addition, all these examinations require that the radiographer be trained in sterile technique and be familiar with the various types of catheters that are inserted into the vascular system for the delivery of contrast material.

▪ Physiology of the Cardiovascular System

The function of the cardiovascular system is to maintain an adequate supply of blood to all the tissues of the body. This is accomplished by the rhythmic contractions of the heart, the rate of which is controlled by the autonomic nervous system. The vagus nerve slows heart action by transmitting the chemical acetylcholine, whereas the sympathetic nervous system stimulates the release of epinephrine that accelerates the heart rate and increases the force of its contractions.

The heart consists of four chambers whose walls are composed of smooth muscle (myocardium), and it is lined with a smooth delicate membrane (endocardium) that is continuous with the inner surface of the blood vessels. The heart consists of two atria and two ventricles, with a partition (septum) separating the right and left sides of the heart. The ventricles are considerably larger and thicker walled than the atria because they have a substantially heavier pumping load. Between each atrium and its associated ventricle are the right and left atrioventricular valves that permit blood to flow in only one direction. These valves consist of flaps (cusps) of endocardium that are anchored to the papillary muscles of the ventricles by cordlike structures called "chordae tendineae." The **mitral,** or biscuspid, **valve** between the left atrium and left ventricle has two cusps, whereas the **tricuspid valve** between the right atrium and right ventricle has three cusps. The semilunar valves separate the ventricles from the great vessels leaving the heart. The **pulmonary valve** lies between the right ventricle and pulmonary artery, whereas the **aortic valve** separates the aorta from the left ventricle.

Deoxygenated venous blood is returned to the heart from the body through the superior and inferior venae cavae, which empty into the right atrium. Blood flows from the right atrium across the triscuspid valve into the right ventricle, which in turn pumps blood through the pulmonary valve into the pulmonary artery. Within the capillaries of the lungs, the red blood cells take up oxygen and release carbon dioxide. The freshly oxygenated blood then passes through the pulmonary veins into the left atrium, from which it flows across the mitral valve into the left ventricle. Contraction of the left ventricle forces oxygenated blood through the aortic valve into the aorta and the rest of the arterial tree to provide oxygen and nourishment to tissues throughout the body. The general circulation of the body is termed the **systemic circulation,** whereas the circulation of blood through the lungs is called the pulmonary circulation. Because greater pressure is needed to pump blood through the systemic circulation than through the pulmonary circulation, the wall of the left ventricle is considerably thicker than that of the right ventricle.

The atria and ventricles alternately contract and relax. The contracting phase is called **systole,** whereas the heart chambers relax and fill with blood during **diastole.** The normal cardiac impulse that stimulates mechanical contraction of the heart arises in the sinoatrial (SA) node, or pacemaker, which is situated in the right atrial wall near the opening of the superior vena cava. The impulse passes slowly through the atrioventricular (AV) node, which is located in the right atrium along the lower part of the interatrial septum, and then spreads quickly throughout the ventricles by way of the fibrous bundle of His, which terminates in Purkinje's fibers that can conduct impulses throughout the muscle of both ventricles and stimulate them to contract almost simultaneously. Specialized pacemaker cells in the SA node possess an **intrinsic rhythm,** so that even without any stimulation by the autonomic nervous system the node itself initiates impulses at regular intervals (about 70 to 75 beats per minute). If the SA node for some reason is unable to generate an impulse, pacemaker activity shifts to some other excitable component of the conduction system. These **ectopic pacemakers** also generate impulses rhythmically, though at a much slower rate. For example, if the AV node controls pacemaker activity, the heart would beat 40 to 60 times per minute. If the conduction system of the heart is unable to maintain an adequate rhythm, the patient may receive an artificial pacemaker that electrically stimulates the heart either at a set rhythm or only when the heart rate decreases below a preset minimum.

The heart muscle is supplied with oxygenated arterial blood by way of the right and left coronary arteries. These small vessels arise from the aorta just above the aortic valve. Unoxygenated blood from the myocardium drains into the coronary veins, which lead into the coronary sinus before opening into the right atrium.

The heart is surrounded by a double membranous sac termed the **pericardium.** The pericardium has a well-lubricated lining that protects against friction and permits the heart to move easily during contraction.

▪ Acquired Heart Disease

Coronary artery disease

Narrowing of the coronary arteries causes oxygen deprivation of the myocardium and ischemic heart disease. In most patients narrowing of the lumen of one or more of the coronary arteries is attributable to the deposition of fatty material on the inner arterial wall (atherosclerosis). Factors predisposing to the development of coronary artery disease include hypertension, obesity, smoking, a high-cholesterol diet, and lack of exercise.

The speed and degree of luminal narrowing determines whether an atherosclerotic lesion causes significant and clinically evident ischemia. Temporary oxygen insufficiency causes angina pectoris, a feeling of severe chest pain that may radiate to the neck, jaw, and left arm and is often associated with the sensation of chest tightness or suffocation. Attacks of angina pectoris are often related to a sudden increase in the demand of the myocardium for oxygen, as after strenuous exercise, a heavy meal, emotional stress, or exposure to severe cold. The placing of a nitroglycerin tablet under the tongue causes dilatation of the coronary arteries, which permits an adequate flow to the myocardium.

Occlusion of a coronary artery deprives an area of myocardium of its blood supply and leads to the death of muscle cells (myocardial infarction) in the area of vascular distribution. The size of the coronary artery that is occluded determines the extent of heart muscle damage. The greater the area affected, the poorer the prognosis. A favorable prognostic factor is the development of collateral circulation, through which blood from a surrounding area is channeled into the damaged tissue. If the patient survives, the infarcted region heals with fibrosis. Long-term complications include the development of thrombi on the surface of the damaged area and the production of a local bulge (ventricular aneurysm) at the site of the weakness of the myocardial wall.

Radionuclide thallium perfusion scanning is the major noninvasive study for assessment of regional blood flow to the myocardium (Figure 6-1). Focal decreases in thallium uptake that are observed immediately after exercise but are no longer identified on delayed scans usually indicate transient ischemia associated with significant coronary artery stenosis or spasm. After exercise, focal defects that are unchanged on delayed scans more frequently reflect scar formation. A normal thallium exercise scan makes the diagnosis of myocardial ischemia unlikely, though in about 10% of patients with significant obstructive disease the presence of sufficient collateral vessels can prevent the radionuclide demonstration of regional ischemia.

Radionuclide scanning using technetium pyrophosphate or other compounds that are taken up by acutely infarcted myocardium is a new noninvasive technique for detecting, localizing, and classifying

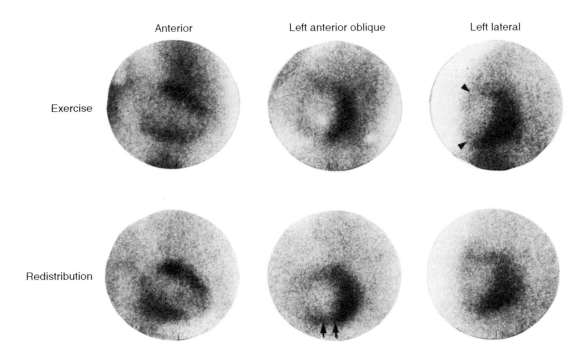

Anterior   Left anterior oblique   Left lateral

Exercise

Redistribution

Figure 6-1   Radionuclide thallium perfusion scan in myocardial infarction. On images obtained immediately after exercise, extensive regions of reduced isotope uptake can be seen on all three projections. This reduced uptake is most noticeable in anterior wall *(arrowheads)*, as seen on left lateral view. Virtually no redistribution into this region occurred at 4 hours *(bottom row)*, a finding suggestive of extensive scar formation. Notice small region at apex *(double arrows)* in which redistribution of thallium did occur. This is suggestive of presence of transiently ischemic yet viable myocardium in this area. (From Ashburn WL, Tubau J: *Radiol Clin North Am* 18:467-486, 1980.)

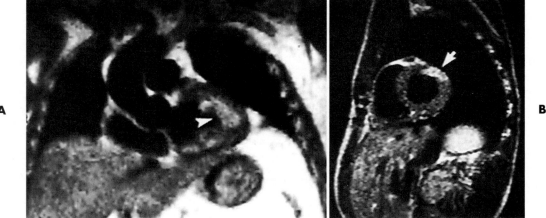

Figure 6-2   Magnetic resonance image of acute myocardial infarction. **A,** T_2-weighted coronal image obtained in patient 10 days after acute myocardial infarction demonstrates area of increased signal intensity (indicating edema associated with muscle necrosis) in subendocardial regions of lateral wall *(arrowhead)*. **B,** Short-axis view of another patient shows acute transmural infarction *(arrow)* of anterolateral wall. (From Stark DD, Bradley WG, editors: *Magnetic resonance imaging*, St. Louis, 1988, Mosby.)

myocardial necrosis. On CT, areas of myocardial ischemia appear as regions of decreased attenuation value because of the increased water content caused by intramyocardial cellular edema. Initial studies have indicated that MRI will also be of value in detecting early signs of muscular necrosis in myocardial infarction (Figure 6-2).

Plain chest radiographs are usually normal or nonspecific in most patients with ischemic heart disease. Calcification of a coronary artery, though infrequently visualized on routine chest radiographs and usually requiring cardiac fluoroscopy, is strongly suggestive of the presence of hemodynamically significant coronary artery disease (Figure 6-3). Plain chest radiographs are also entirely normal in many if not most patients after myocardial infarction. They are primarily of value in detecting evidence of pulmonary venous congestion in patients who develop congestive heart failure as a result of an inability of the remaining heart muscle to propel blood through the circulation adequately.

Coronary arteriography is generally considered the definitive test for determining the presence and assessing the severity of coronary artery disease. About 30% of significant stenoses involve a single vessel, most commonly the anterior descending artery. Two vessels are involved in 30%, and significant stenosis of the three main vessels can be demonstrated in the remaining 40%.

Aortocoronary bypass grafting, usually using sections of saphenous vein, is an increasingly popular procedure in patients with ischemic heart disease. Arteriography has been the procedure of choice in demonstrating the patency and functional efficiency of aortocoronary bypass grafts. Patent functioning grafts demonstrate prompt clearing of contrast material and good filling of the grafted artery. Stenotic or malfunctioning grafts demonstrate areas of narrowing, filling defects, and slow flow with delayed washout of contrast material.

Percutaneous transluminal angioplasty using a balloon catheter is now a recognized procedure for the treatment of patients with narrowing of one or more coronary arteries (Figure 6-4). As in other types of percutaneous transluminal angioplasty, a catheter is placed under fluoroscopic guidance into the affected coronary artery, and an arteriogram is performed for localization. The angioplasty balloon is then positioned at the level of the stenosis and inflated. After dilatation, coronary arteriography is repeated to show the subsequent appearance of the stenosis and to detect any complications of the procedure. Symptomatic improvement occurs in 50% to 70% of dilatations. About 3% to 8% of patients who undergo percutaneous angioplasty develop either persistent coronary insufficiency or sudden occlusion of a coronary artery at the site of dilatation at the time of the procedure. Therefore the procedure should be done at a time when an operating room, an anesthetist, and a cardiac surgeon are available so that immediate coronary bypass surgery can be performed if necessary. The mortality of coronary angioplasty is less than 1%.

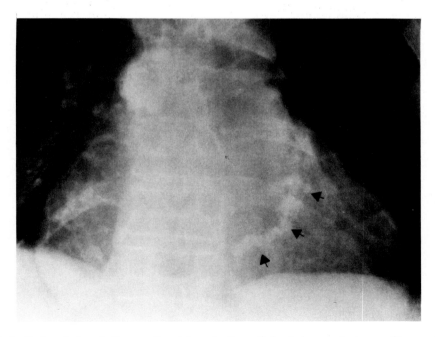

Figure 6-3 Ischemic heart disease. Frontal projection of chest demonstrates cardiomegaly with typical linear calcification in coronary artery *(arrows)*.

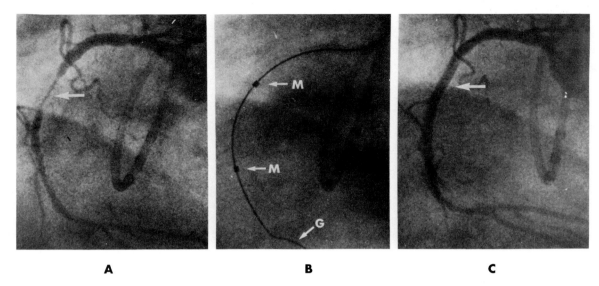

A   **B**   **C**

Figure 6-4   Percutaneous transluminal coronary angioplasty. **A,** Initial right coronary angiogram shows severe narrowing *(arrow)* of midportion of right coronary artery. **B,** During percutaneous transluminal coronary angioplasty, steerable wire guide *(G)* has been passed down coronary artery and through coronary stenosis. Tip lies within distal right coronary artery. Radiopaque markers *(M)* identify balloon portion of dilating catheter that has been advanced over wire guide through coronary stenosis. **C,** Immediately after angioplasty, previous site of stenosis *(arrow)* is now patent. (From Fischell TA, Block PC: *Cardiovasc Reviews Reports* 6:89-99, 1985.)

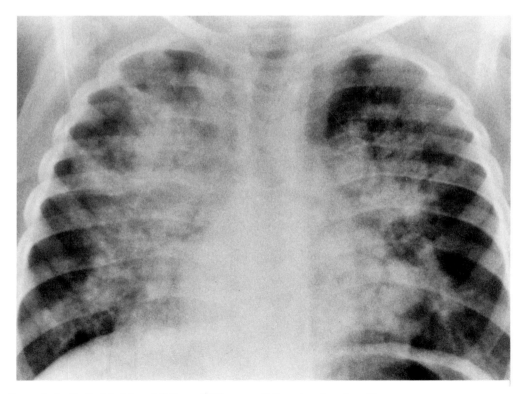

Figure 6-5   Left-sided heart failure. Diffuse perihilar alveolar densities.

Congestive heart failure

Congestive heart failure refers to the inability of the heart to propel blood at a sufficient rate and volume to provide an adequate supply to the tissues. It may be caused by an intrinsic cardiac abnormality or by hypertension or any obstructive process that abnormally increases the peripheral resistance to blood flow.

Left-sided heart failure produces a classic radiographic appearance of cardiac enlargement, redistribution of pulmonary venous blood flow (enlarged superior pulmonary veins and decreased caliber of the veins draining the lower lungs), interstitial edema, alveolar edema (irregular, poorly defined patchy densities), and pleural effusions (Figure 6-5). In acute left ventricular failure resulting from coronary thrombosis, however, there may be severe pulmonary congestion and edema with very little cardiac enlargement. The major causes of left-sided heart failure include coronary heart disease, valvular disease, and hypertension.

In right-sided heart failure, dilatation of the right ventricle and right atrium is present (Figure 6-6). The transmission of increased pressure may cause dilatation of the superior vena cava, widening of the right superior mediastinum, and edema of the lower extremities. The enlargement of a congested liver may elevate the right hemidiaphragm. Common causes of right-sided heart failure include pulmonary valvular stenosis, emphysema, and pulmonary hypertension resulting from pulmonary emboli.

Pulmonary edema

Pulmonary edema refers to an abnormal accumulation of fluid in the extravascular pulmonary tissues. The most common cause of pulmonary edema is an elevation of the pulmonary venous pressure. This is most often attributable to left-sided heart failure but may also be caused by pulmonary venous obstruction (mitral valve disease, left atrial tumor) or lymphatic blockade (fibrotic, inflammatory, or metastatic disease involving the mediastinal lymph nodes). Other causes of pulmonary edema include uremia, narcotic overdose, exposure to noxious fumes, excessive oxygen, high altitudes, fat embolism, adult respiratory distress syndrome, and various neurologic abnormalities.

Transudation of fluid into the interstitial spaces of the lungs is the earliest stage of pulmonary edema. However, in patients with congestive heart failure or pulmonary venous hypertension, increased pulmonary venous pressure first appears as a redistribution of blood flow from the lower to the upper lung zones. This phenomenon, probably caused by reflex venous spasm, causes prominent enlargement of the superior

A 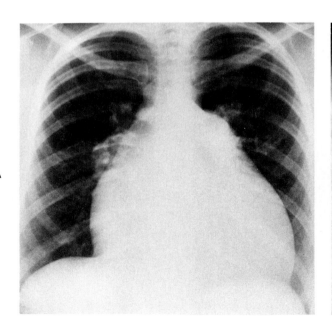 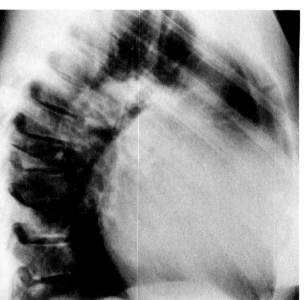 **B**

Figure 6-6 Right-sided heart failure. **A,** Frontal and, **B,** lateral projections of chest in patient with primary pulmonary hypertension show pronounced globular cardiomegaly with prominence of pulmonary trunk and central pulmonary arteries. Peripheral pulmonary vascularity is strikingly reduced. Right ventricular enlargement has obliterated retrosternal air space on lateral projection.

pulmonary veins and decreased caliber of the veins draining the inferior portions of the lung. Edema fluid in the interstitial space causes a loss of the normal sharp definition of pulmonary vascular markings (Figure 6-7). Accentuation of the vascular markings about the hila produces a perihilar haze. Fluid in the interlobular septa produces characteristic thin horizontal lines of increased density at the axillary margins of the lung inferiorly (Kerley-B lines).

A further increase in pulmonary venous pressures leads to the development of alveolar or pleural transudates. Alveolar edema appears as irregular, poorly defined patchy densities scattered throughout the lungs. The classic radiographic finding of alveolar pulmonary edema is the butterfly (or bat's-wing) pattern, a diffuse, bilaterally symmetric, fan-shaped infiltration that is most prominent in the central portion of the lungs and fades toward the periphery (Figure 6-8).

Pleural effusion associated with pulmonary edema usually occurs on the right side (Figure 6-9). When bilateral, the effusion tends to be more noticeable on the right. There is often an associated thickening of the interlobar fissures.

After adequate treatment of pulmonary edema, the interstitial, alveolar, and pleural abnormalities may disappear within several hours. Loculated pleural fluid within a fissure (especially the minor fissure) may resorb more slowly and appear as a sharply defined, elliptical or circular density that simulates a solid parenchymal mass (Figure 6-10).

Most patients with pulmonary edema caused by congestive failure or other heart disease have evidence of cardiomegaly. In noncardiogenic causes of pulmonary edema the heart often remains normal in size (Figure 6-11).

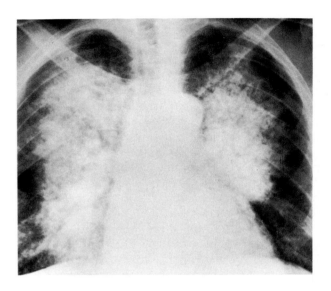

Figure 6-8 Butterfly pattern of severe pulmonary edema. Diffuse bilateral symmetric infiltration of central portion of lungs along with relative sparing of periphery produces butterfly pattern. (From Fraser RG, Paré JAP: *Diagnosis of diseases of the chest*, Philadelphia, 1979, Saunders.)

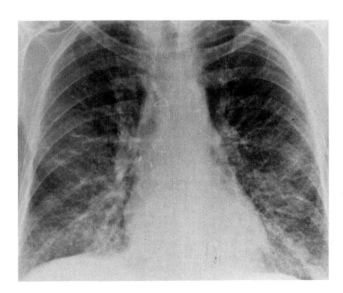

Figure 6-7 Interstitial pulmonary edema. Edema fluid in interstitial space causes loss of normal sharp definition of pulmonary vascular markings and perihilar haze. At bases, notice thin horizontal lines of increased density (Kerley-B lines), which represent fluid in interlobular septa.

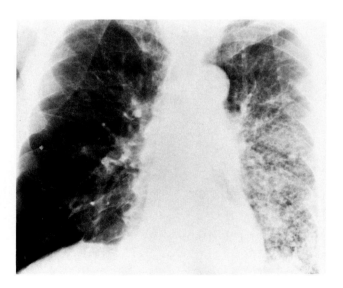

Figure 6-9 Unilateral pulmonary edema. Diffuse alveolar pattern limited to left lung because of effect of gravity on patient lying on left side.

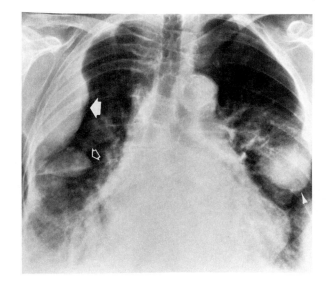

A

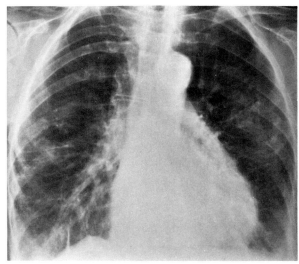

B

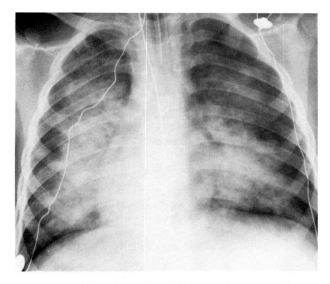

Figure 6-11   Near-drowning. Diffuse pulmonary edema pattern with normal-sized heart.

Figure 6-10   Loculated pleural fluid (phantom tumors). **A,** Frontal chest radiograph taken during episode of congestive heart failure demonstrates pronounced cardiomegaly with bilateral pleural effusions. Notice fluid collections along lateral chest wall *(solid arrow),* in minor fissure *(open arrow),* and in left major fissure *(arrowhead).* **B,** With improvement in patient's cardiac status, phantom tumors have disappeared. Bilateral small pleural effusions persist.

Hypertension

Hypertension, or high blood pressure, is the leading cause of strokes and congestive heart failure. The blood pressure is a function of cardiac output, the amount of blood pumped per minute by the heart, and the total peripheral resistance, which reflects the condition of the walls of the blood vessels throughout the body. Although the peripheral resistance and cardiac output may fluctuate rapidly, depending on

such factors as whether a person sits or stands and is quiet or excited, the systemic blood pressure remains remarkably constant in a normal person.

A blood pressure reading consists of two parts. The systolic pressure is the highest pressure in the peripheral arteries that occurs when the left ventricle contracts. The diastolic pressure is the pressure in the peripheral arteries when the left ventricle is relaxing and filling with blood from the left atrium. High blood pressure is defined as elevation of the systolic pressure above 140 millimeters of mercury (mm Hg) and of the diastolic pressure above 90 mm Hg. In patients older than 40 years of age, the systolic pressure may be somewhat higher and still be considered within normal limits. As a rough rule of thumb, a person is allowed an additional 10 mm Hg in the systolic pressure for each decade over 40 years of age.

Most patients with elevated blood pressure have essential, or idiopathic, hypertension. The benign form of essential hypertension is characterized by a gradual onset and a prolonged course, often of many years. In the much less common malignant form, the elevated blood pressure has an abrupt onset, runs a rapid course, and often leads to renal failure or cerebral hemorrhage.

About 6% of patients have secondary hypertension resulting from another disease. Although some patients in this group have adrenal abnormalities (Cushing's syndrome, primary aldosteronism, pheochromocytoma) in which there is an abnormality of the regulation of salt and water content (and thus the blood volume) or the secretion of a substance that increases vascular tone and peripheral arterial resistance, most have renal parenchymal or vascular disease as the underlying cause of hypertension.

The standard screening test for renovascular hypertension has been the rapid-sequence (hypertensive) excretory urogram, in which radiographs are obtained at each of the first 5 minutes after the rapid injection of contrast material. Features suggestive of renal ischemia include (1) unilateral delayed appearance and excretion of contrast material; (2) difference in kidney size greater than 1.5 cm (Figure 6-12, A); (3) irregular contour of the renal silhouette, suggestive of segmental infarction or atrophy; (4) indentations on the ureter or renal pelvis caused by dilated, tortuous ureteral arterial collaterals; and (5) hyperconcentration of contrast material in the collecting system of the smaller kidney on delayed films. Although up to 25% of patients with renovascular hypertension have a normal rapid-sequence excretory urogram, this modality is also of value in detecting other less frequent causes of hypertension such as tumor, polynephritis, polycystic kidneys, or renal infarction.

Arteriography is the most accurate screening examination for detecting renovascular lesions. The most common cause of renal artery obstruction is arteriosclerotic narrowing, which usually occurs in

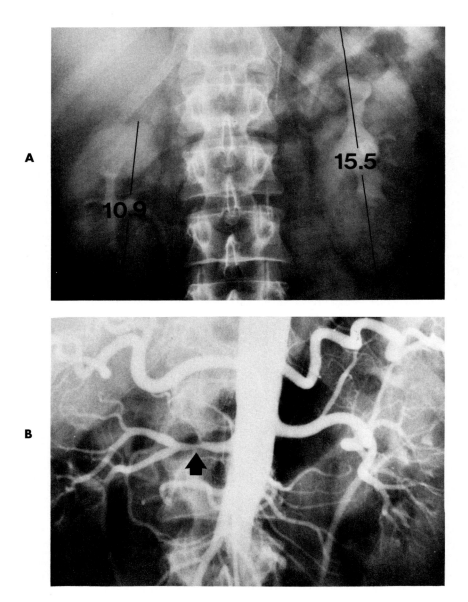

Figure 6-12   Renovascular hypertension. Diminished size of right kidney, **A,** caused by renal artery stenosis, **B.** *Arrow,* Stenosis. (From Burko H et al: In Eisenberg RL, Amberg JR, editors: *Critical diagnostic pathways in radiology: an algorithmic approach,* Philadelphia, 1981, Lippincott.)

the proximal portion of the vessel close to its origin from the aorta (Figure 6-12, *B*). Bilateral renal artery stenoses are noted in up to one third of the patients. Oblique projections, which demonstrate the vessel origins in profile, are often required to demonstrate renal artery stenosis.

The other major cause of renovascular hypertension is fibromuscular dysplasia. This disease is most frequent in young adult women and is often bilateral. The most common radiographic appearance of fibromuscular dysplasia is the string-of-beads pattern, in which there are alternating areas of narrowing and dilatation (Figure 6-13). Smooth, concentric stenoses occur less frequently.

The mere presence of a renovascular lesion does not mean that it is the cause of hypertension; indeed, many patients with normal blood pressure have severe renal artery disease. Therefore bilateral renal vein catheterization for the measurement of plasma renin activity is used to assess the functional significance of any stenotic lesion. A renal vein renin concentration on the abnormal side that is more than 50% greater than the renin level in the renal vein on the normal side indicates the functional significance of a lesion with an accuracy rate of about 85%.

Surgery has been the traditional treatment for a patient with arteriographically demonstrated renal artery studies and confirmatory renal vein renin studies. Recently, percutaneous transluminal angioplasty has been shown to be effective in dilating renal artery stenoses (Figure 6-14). Although insufficient time has elapsed to compare the long-term results of renal transluminal angioplasty with corrective surgical procedures, initial studies demonstrate the improvement or cure of hypertension in about 80% of patients treated with angioplasty.

Prolonged high blood pressure forces the heart to overwork, causing the left ventricle to enlarge and eventually fail. Since the high blood pressure affects all arteries of the body, including the coronary and carotid vessels, this condition increases the risk of coronary occlusion and myocardial infarction, as well as carotid narrowing leading to a stroke.

Decreased function of the kidneys leads to the retention of water and salt, which increases the blood volume and elevates the blood pressure. Long-standing hypertension causes atherosclerosis of the renal artery, which reduces blood flow to the kidneys and further damages them.

Hypertensive heart disease

Long-standing high blood pressure causes narrowing of systemic blood vessels and an increased resistance to blood flow. The left ventricle is forced to assume an increased work load, which initially causes hypertrophy and little if any change in the radiographic appearance of the cardiac silhouette.

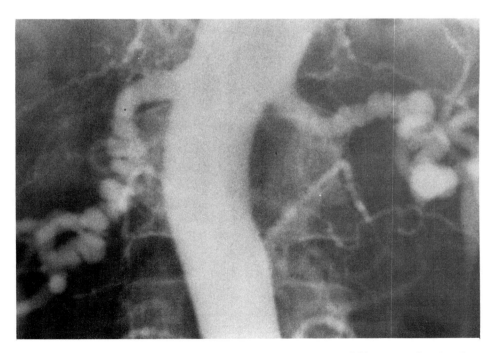

Figure 6-13 Renovascular hypertension. String-of-beads pattern of fibromuscular dysplasia bilaterally.

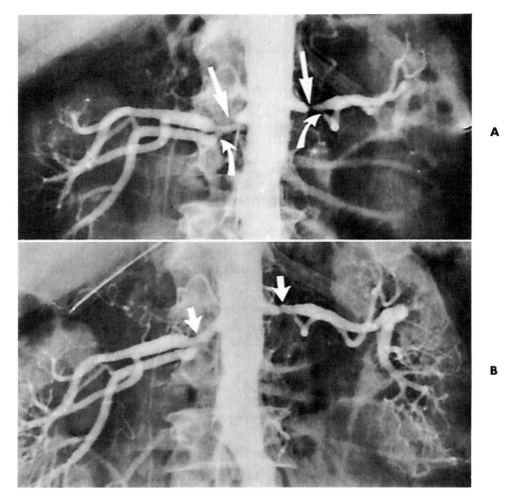

Figure 6-14 Percutaneous transluminal angioplasty for renovascular hypertension. **A,** Abdominal aortogram demonstrates severe bilateral stenoses of main renal arteries *(straight arrows)* and stenoses at origins of early bifurcations *(curved arrows)*. **B,** Aortogram after angioplasty of both renal arteries shows irregularities in areas of previous atherosclerotic narrowing *(arrows)* but improved residual lumen in both main renal arteries. After procedure, patient's previous severe hypertension was controllable to normal levels with only minimal dosages of diuretic medication. (From Waltman AC: In Athanasoulis CA et al, editors: *Interventional radiology,* Philadelphia, 1982, Saunders.)

Eventually, the continued strain on the heart leads to dilatation and enlargement of the left ventricle (Figure 6-15) along with downward displacement of the cardiac apex, which often projects below the left hemidiaphragm. Aortic tortuosity with prominence of the ascending portion commonly occurs (Figure 6-16). Failure of the left ventricle leads to increased pulmonary venous pressure and congestive failure.

Aneurysm

An aneurysm is a localized dilatation of an artery that most commonly involves the aorta, especially its abdominal portion. A **saccular** aneurysm involves only one side of the arterial wall, whereas bulging of the entire circumference of the vessel wall is termed **fusiform.** An aneurysm represents a weakness in the wall of a blood vessel caused by atherosclerosis, syphilis or other infection, trauma, or a congenital defect such as Marfan's syndrome. The presence of multiple small aneurysms is suggestive of a generalized arterial inflammation (arteritis). In the abdominal aorta, most aneurysms occur below the origin of the renal arteries, and thus the aneurysm can be surgically replaced by a prosthetic graft without injuring the kidneys. The danger of an aneurysm is its tendency to increase in size and rupture, leading

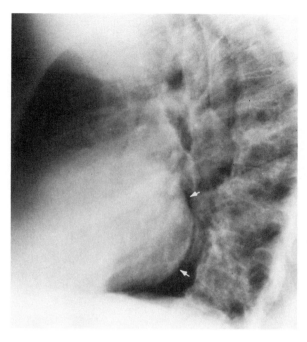

Figure 6-15 Hypertensive heart disease. Lateral projection of chest shows prominence of left ventricle *(arrows).*

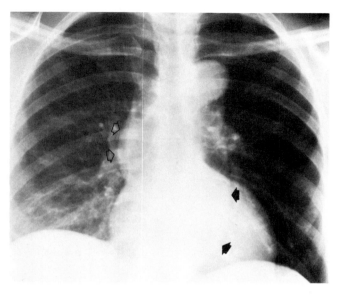

Figure 6-16 Hypertensive heart disease. Generalized tortuosity and elongation of ascending aorta *(open arrows)* and descending aorta *(solid arrows).*

to massive hemorrhage, which may be fatal if it involves a critical organ such as the brain.

Although plain abdominal radiographs can demonstrate curvilinear calcification in the wall of an aneurysm (Figure 6-17), ultrasound is the modality of choice for detection of an abdominal aortic aneurysm. The sonographic definition of aneurysmal dilatation of the abdominal aorta is an enlargement of the structure to a diameter greater than 3 cm. Ultrasound can demonstrate an intraluminal clot (Figure 6-18, *A*), and the noninvasive nature of ultrasound permits an evaluation of the enlargement of an aneurysm on serial studies. CT and MRI also can demonstrate the location and extent of an aneurysm. The major value of arteriography in patients with abdominal aortic aneurysm is as a presurgical road map to define the extent of the lesion and whether the renal arteries or other major branches are involved. Because the lumen of an aneurysm may be filled with clot, aortography often produces an underestimation of the extent of aneurysmal dilatation.

In the chest, CT after the intravenous injection of contrast material is the most efficient technique for demonstrating the size and extent of an aortic aneurysm and for differentiating this vascular lesion from a solid mediastinal mass. Unlike aortography, CT is relatively noninvasive and can directly identify an intraluminal thrombus (seen as a soft-tissue

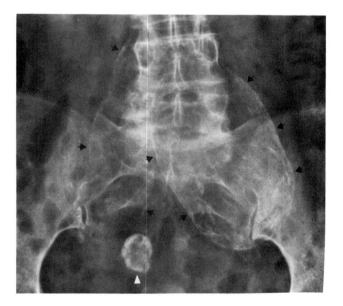

Figure 6-17 Calcification in walls of aneurysms of lower abdominal aorta and both common iliac arteries *(arrows).* Of incidental note is calcified uterine fibroid *(arrowhead)* in pelvis. (From Eisenberg, R: *Gastrointestinal radiology: a pattern approach,* Philadelphia, 1990, Lippincott.)

density separating the contrast-filled portion of the lumen from the aortic wall), which can only be inferred on contrast examination (Figure 6-18, *B*). CT can also demonstrate aortic mural calcification and effects of the aneurysm on adjacent structures,

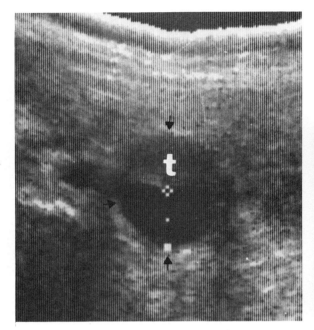

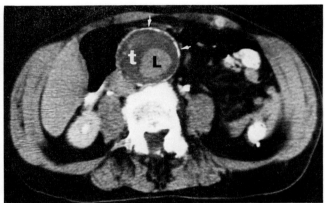

Figure 6-18   Abdominal aortic aneurysm. **A,** Ultrasound shows large aneurysm *(arrows)* with echogenic thrombus *(t)* filling anterior half of sac. **B,** CT scan of abdominal aortic aneurysm in another patient shows low-density thrombus *(t)* surrounding blood-filled lumen *(L).* Wall of aneurysm contains high-density calcification *(arrows).*

such as displacement of the mediastinum or bone erosion. Because of its ability to demonstrate flowing blood as a signal void and clot as a heterogeneous collection of signal intensities, MRI can provide information about an aneurysm that is comparable to that obtained from CT without the need for intravenous contrast material (Figure 6-19).

Traumatic rupture of the aorta

Traumatic rupture of the aorta is a potentially fatal complication of closed chest trauma (rapid deceleration, blast, compression). In almost all cases the aortic tear occurs just distal to the left subclavian artery at the site of the ductus arteriosus. On plain chest radiographs, hemorrhage into the mediastinum causes widening of the mediastinal silhouette and loss of a discrete aortic knob shadow. Associated rib or sternal fractures may be apparent. However, because nonspecific mediastinal widening is a frequent finding, especially on the supine, anteroposterior portable radiographs taken after trauma, other plain film signs are of diagnostic importance (Figure 6-20). These include displacement of an opaque nasogastric tube to the right (because of a hematoma that displaces the esophagus), widening of the right paratracheal stripe (Figure 6-21), and a collection of blood over the apex of the left lung (apical pleural

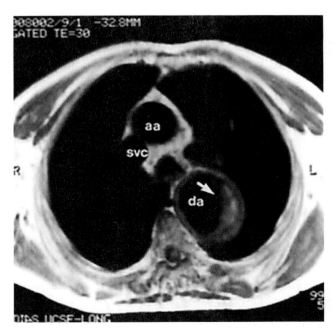

Figure 6-19   Magnetic resonance image of aortic aneurysm. Transverse scan with cardiac gating permits differentiation of large mural thrombus *(arrow)* from signal void of rapidly flowing intraluminal blood. *aa,* Ascending aorta; *da,* descending aorta; *svc,* superior vena cava. (From Thoeni RF, Margulis AR: In Eisenberg RL, editor: *Diagnostic imaging: an algorithmic approach,* Philadelphia, 1988, Lippincott.)

cap sign). Emergency aortography is the definitive examination for the evaluation of possible laceration or rupture of the aorta.

Dissection of the aorta

Dissection of the aorta is a potentially life-threatening condition in which disruption of the

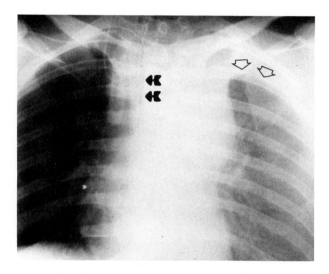

Figure 6-20 Traumatic aneurysm of aorta. There is widening of mediastinum and deviation of nasogastric tube to right *(solid arrows)*. Open arrows point to collection of fluid over left apex (apical pleural cap) in this patient after severe blunt chest trauma. (From Fisher RG, Hadlock FP, Ben-Menachem Y: *Radiol Clin North Am* 19:91-112, 1981.)

intima (inner layer) permits blood to enter the wall of the aorta and separate its layers. Most aortic dissections occur in patients with arterial hypertension. Some are a result of trauma, whereas others are attributable to a congenital defect such as Marfan's syndrome. An acute dissection typically causes sudden sharp or excruciating pain in the chest or abdomen. Although the pain passes, death frequently occurs some days later from rupture of the aneurysm into the chest or abdominal cavity.

Most aortic dissections begin as a tear in the intima immediately above the aortic valve. In two thirds of these (type I), the dissection continues into the descending aorta, often extending as far as the level of the iliac bifurcation. In the remainder (type II), the dissection is limited to the ascending aorta and stops at the origin of the innominate artery. In type III disease, the dissection begins in the thoracic aorta distal to the subclavian artery and extends for a variable distance proximally and distally to the original site.

On plain chest radiographs, aortic dissection causes progressive widening of the aortic shadow, which may have an irregular or wavy outer border (Figure 6-22). However, this is a nonspecific appearance and a definite diagnosis of dissection must be made on the basis of aortography or CT. In the patient with a suspected acute dissection of thoracic aorta, aortography is the procedure of choice. The diagnosis of aortic dissection depends on the demonstration of two channels separated by a thin radiolucent intimal flap (Figure 6-23). The false

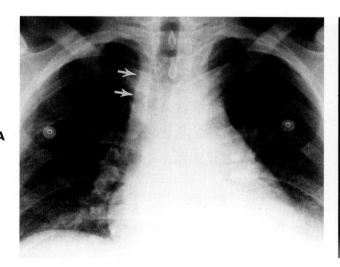

A

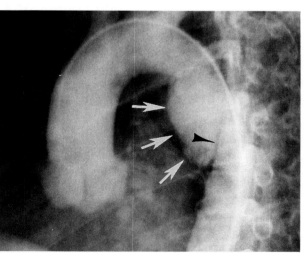

B

Figure 6-21 Traumatic aneurysm of aorta. **A,** Supine chest radiograph in patient with blunt chest trauma shows thickening of right paratracheal stripe *(arrows)*, which measures 1 cm in width. **B,** Aortogram demonstrates pseudoaneurysm at level of aortic isthmus *(arrows)*. Arrowhead indicates intimal flap. (From Woodring JH, Pulmano CM, Stevens RK: *Radiology* 143:605-608, 1982.)

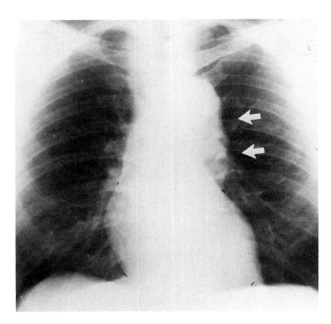

Figure 6-22 Aortic dissection. Plain chest radiograph shows diffuse widening of descending aorta with irregular, wavy outer border *(arrows)*. (From Ovenfors CO, Godwin JD: In Eisenberg RL, editor: *Diagnostic imaging: an algorithmic approach*, Philadelphia, 1988, Lippincott.)

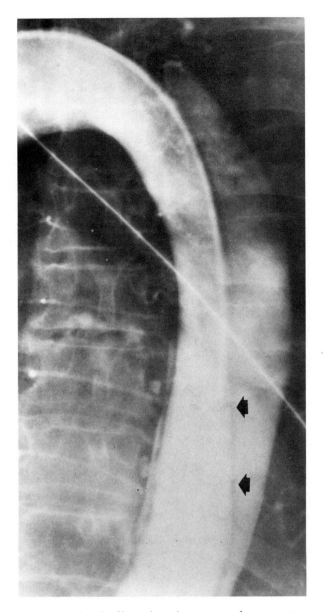

Figure 6-23 Aortic dissection. Aortogram demonstrates thin radiolucent intimal flap *(arrows)* separating true and false aortic channels.

channel may be filled with clot and be impossible to opacify with contrast material. In this case, the diagnosis can be made by demonstration of narrowing and compression of the true channel. When both the true and false lumens fill with contrast material, it is important to demonstrate the distal reentry point where the false lumen joins the true lumen. If the dissection extends below the diaphragm, arteriography can provide presurgical information about which major vessel branches from the aorta are blocked and which remain patent.

In the patient in whom nonacute aortic dissection is considered in the differential diagnosis of chest pain, CT and MRI offer low-risk alternative diagnostic methods to aortography. CT demonstrates an aortic dissection as a double channel with an intimal flap. With dynamic scanning and the rapid injection of a bolus of contrast material, differential filling of the true and false channels can be observed as with aortography. The major limitation of CT in the patient with suspected acute dissection is that only a single level can be evaluated on a given slice, as opposed to the rapid series of images covering a large portion of the aorta that can be obtained with aortography.

The high contrast between rapidly flowing blood, vessel wall, and adjacent soft-tissue structures per-

mit identification of vessels by MRI without the need for intravenous injection of contrast material. This technique can demonstrate aortic dissections and show their extent. The intimal flap is usually detected as a linear, medium-intensity structure separating the true and false lumens (Figure 6-24). Rapidly flowing blood in these lumens appears as a signal void. If the false lumen is thrombosed, or even if it is open but the flow is slow, the intimal flap may not be visualized. In this situation, aortic dissection is difficult to differentiate from an aortic aneurysm with mural thrombus, and aortography may be required to make this distinction.

Atherosclerosis

The major cause of vascular disease of the extremities is atherosclerosis, in which fatty deposits called plaques develop in the intima and produce progressive narrowing and often complete occlusion of large and medium-sized arteries. In the abdomen, the disease primarily involves the aorta and the common iliac arteries, often sparing the external iliac

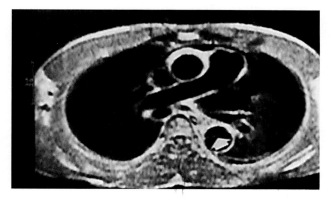

Figure 6-24 Magnetic resonance image of aortic dissection. Axial scan at level of main and right pulmonary arteries clearly shows intimal flap *(arrow)* in descending aorta. (From Ovenfors CO, Godwin JD: In Eisenberg RL, editor: *Diagnostic imaging: an algorithmic approach,* Philadelphia, 1988, Lippincott.)

vessels. In the lower extremities, arteriosclerotic narrowing most commonly affects the superficial femoral artery just above the knee. Plaque formation and luminal narrowing often involve the coronary and cerebral arteries, thus decreasing the blood flow to the heart muscle and the brain and leading to a myocardial infarction or stroke (cerebrovascular accident).

Arteriosclerotic plaques often calcify and appear on plain radiographs as irregularly distributed densities along the course of an artery (Figure 6-25). Small vessel calcification, especially in the hands and feet, is often seen in patients with accelerated arteriosclerosis, especially those with diabetes mellitus.

Doppler ultrasound is an effective noninvasive technique for screening patients with clinically suspected peripheral arteriosclerotic disease. Definitive diagnosis requires arteriographic demonstration of the peripheral vascular tree. Evidence of arteriosclerosis includes diffuse vascular narrowing, irregularity of the lumen, and filling defects. In patients with severe stenosis or obstruction, arteriography demonstrates the degree and source of collateral circulation and the status of the vessels distal to an area of narrowing (Figure 6-26).

Percutaneous transluminal angioplasty using a balloon catheter is now a recognized procedure for the alleviation of symptoms of peripheral ischemia in patients with arteriosclerosis (Figure 6-27). It is of special value in patients who are extremely ill and those who would not benefit from reconstructive arterial surgery.

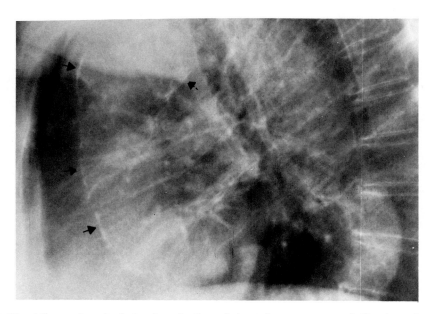

Figure 6-25 Atherosclerosis. Lateral projection of chest demonstrates calcification of anterior and posterior walls of ascending aorta *(arrows)*. Descending thoracic aorta is tortuous.

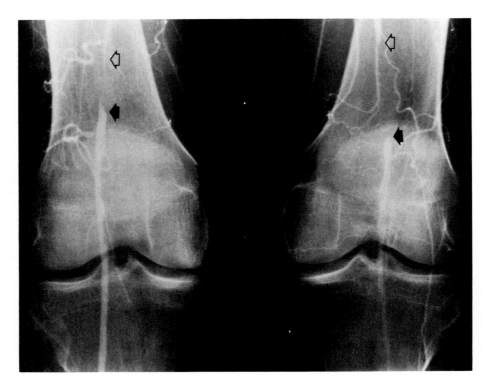

Figure 6-26   Bilateral atherosclerotic occlusion of superficial femoral arteries. Arteriogram demonstrates occlusion of both distal superficial femoral arteries *(open arrows)* with reconstitution by collateral vessels *(solid arrows).*

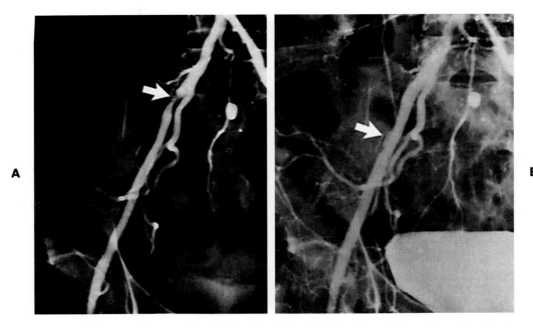

Figure 6-27   Percutaneous transluminal angioplasty of right external iliac artery stenosis. **A,** Initial film in patient with claudication demonstrates narrowing of proximal right external iliac artery *(arrow).* **B,** After angioplasty, there is relief of stenosis *(arrow)* and of symptoms. (From Waltman AC: In Athanasoulis CA et al, editors: *Interventional radiology,* Philadelphia, 1982, Saunders.)

Thrombosis and embolism

The blood-clotting mechanism is the major protective device of the body in response to the escape of blood from a vessel (hemorrhage). This same mechanism can occur in intact blood vessels, leading to the development of an intravascular clot called a thrombus. Three factors lead to the development of intravascular thrombosis. Clots tend to form where blood flow is slow and thus develop much more commonly in veins than in arteries. Thrombi especially occur in areas of stasis (slow circulation) in patients who are inactive or immobilized, as after abdominal surgery.

Changes in the wall of blood vessels can lead to thrombosis. Normally, the inner wall of a blood vessel has a very smooth lining (endothelium), and platelets cannot stick, or adhere, to it. However, when the endothelium is destroyed by injury or inflammation, platelets rapidly adhere to the rough spot, and a clot begins to form from the blood as it flows past. Arteriosclerosis is the major cause of endothelial irregularity and subsequent thrombosis. Nodules of vegetation on heart valves caused by rheumatic heart disease are also important predisposing factors for thrombus formation.

Changes in the blood itself can lead to thrombosis. A low level of oxygen within the blood, as in some forms of heart disease, forces the body to compensate by increasing the number of red blood cells (polycythemia). This causes the blood to become more viscous and increases the risk of thrombosis. Changes in the clotting and fibrinolytic mechanism also may increase the risk of thrombus formation.

Anticoagulants such as heparin and coumadin are often used to prevent intravascular clotting. Heparin prevents platelets from sticking together and to the vessel wall, so that a thrombus is not formed. Coumadin acts by antagonizing the action of vitamin K, which is necessary for blood clotting. However, these medications also interfere with the person's normal ability to stop bleeding and may lead to severe hemorrhage from relatively minor trauma or to potentially fatal bleeding in the brain and gastrointestinal tract. Recent reports have suggested the value of aspirin to prevent intravascular clotting because of its inhibition of platelet aggregation.

Once a thrombus is formed, it may follow one of three courses. The thrombus may contract or become canalized so that blood can once again flow through the lumen. The thrombus may continually enlarge or become converted into fibrous tissue, resulting in permanent occlusion of the vessel. A potentially catastrophic event is the production of an embolus, which refers to part or all of a thrombus that becomes detached from the vessel wall and enters the bloodstream. Embolization is especially likely to occur if there is infected tissue around the thrombus or if there is a sudden movement caused by rough handling of the involved area. Depending on the size of the vessels through which it travels, an embolism may lodge at any of several points. Since veins become larger as they approach the heart, an embolism arising from a thrombus in a leg vein flows easily to the heart and typically gets stuck in a pulmonary artery (pulmonary embolism). An embolism arising from a mitral valve damaged by rheumatic heart disease flows through the left ventricle and aorta and lodges in a smaller artery in the brain, kidney, or other organ. A septic embolism contains infected material from pyogenic bacteria, whereas tumor emboli are groups of cancer cells that have invaded a vein, become detached, and are then carried to the lungs or other organs where they form metastases. Fat emboli are the result of trauma, especially leg fractures, in which marrow fat enters torn peripheral veins and is trapped by the pulmonary circulation. An air embolism refers to bubbles of air introduced into a vein during surgery, trauma, or an improperly administered intravenous injection.

Regardless of its type or source, an embolism blocks the vascular lumen and cuts off the blood supply to the organ or parts supplied by that artery. The effect of an embolism depends on the size of the embolus and on the extent of collateral circulation, which can bring blood to an affected part by an alternate route.

Acute embolic occlusion of an artery most commonly affects the lower extremities. The success of therapy depends on the rapid recognition of the clinical problem and the institution of appropriate treatment. Arteriography is the procedure of choice to confirm the clinical diagnosis and to demonstrate the extent of occlusion, the degree of collateral circulation, and the condition of the distal vessels. Embolic occlusion typically appears as an abrupt termination of the contrast column along with a proximal curved margin reflecting the nonopaque embolus protruding into the contrast-filled lumen (Figure 6-28). In acute occlusion, there is usually little if any evidence of collateral circulation.

Although emergency surgery to remove the embolus (embolectomy) has been the traditional treatment for acute arterial occlusion, the intra-arterial infusion of streptokinase by means of a catheter placed immediately proximal to the occlusion is becoming a more common alternative therapy, especially in patients who are poor surgical risks (Figure

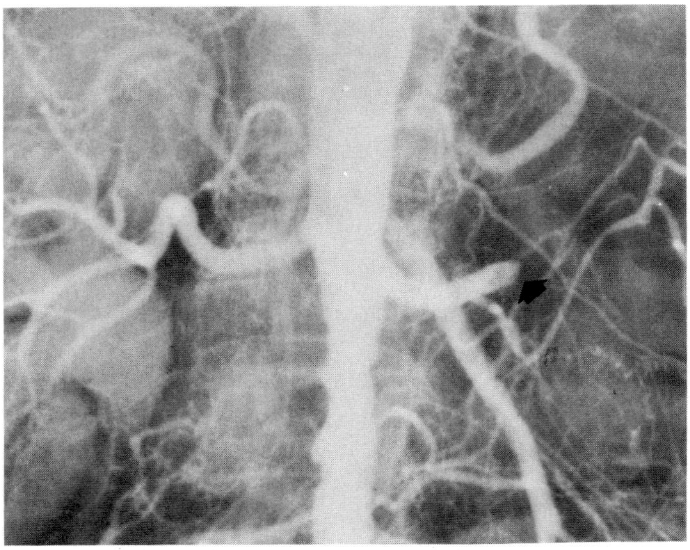

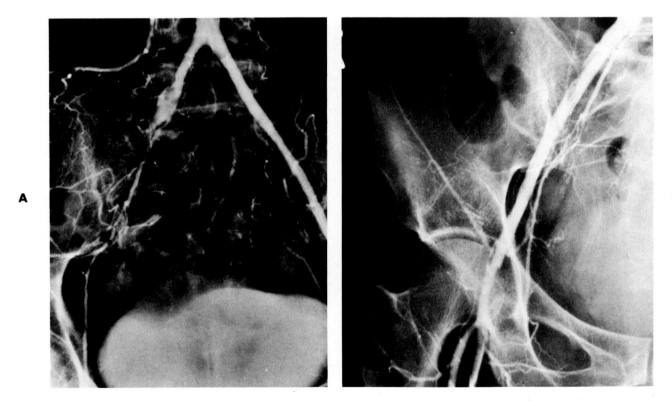

Figure 6-28 Acute embolic occlusion of left renal artery. There is abrupt termination of contrast column *(arrow)*. Notice irregular infrarenal aortic contour, which represents atherosclerotic disease.

Figure 6-29 Streptokinase therapy for acute arterial occlusion. **A,** After angioplasty of right external iliac artery, there was loss of right common femoral pulse. Repeat arteriogram from left femoral approach shows complete occlusion of external iliac artery at its origin. **B,** After 8 hours of streptokinase administration, arteriogram demonstrates lysis of thrombus and reestablishment of lumen. One year after angioplasty, patient had normal femoral pulse and patent artery. (From Katzen BT, van Breda A: *AJR* 136:1171-1178, 1981.)

6-29). The tissue plasminogen activator (TPA) Activase, produced by recombinant DNA technology, has been administered intravenously to lyse thrombi obstructing coronary arteries in the treatment of acute myocardial infarction.

■ Congenital Heart Disease

Left-to-right shunts

The most common congenital cardiac lesions are left-to-right shunts, which permit mixing of blood in the systemic and pulmonary circulations. Because blood is preferentially shunted from the high-pressure systemic circulation to the relatively low-pressure pulmonary circulation, the lungs become overloaded with blood. The magnitude of the shunt depends on the size of the defect and the differences in pressure on both sides of it. An increased load on the heart produces enlargement of specific cardiac chambers, depending on the location of the shunt.

The most common congenital cardiac lesion is **atrial septal defect,** which permits free communication between the two atria. Because the left atrial pressure is usually higher than the pressure in the right atrium, the resulting shunt is from left to right and causes increased pulmonary blood flow and overloading of the right ventricle. This produces a radiographic appearance of enlargement of the right ventricle, right atrium, and the pulmonary outflow tract (Figure 6-30).

In a **ventricular septal defect** the resulting shunt is also from left to right because the left ventricular pressure is usually higher than the pressure in the right ventricle. The shunt causes increased pulmonary blood flow and, consequently, increased pulmonary venous return (Figure 6-31). This leads to diastolic overloading and enlargement of the left atrium and left ventricle. Because shunting occurs primarily in systole and any blood directed to the right ventricle immediately goes into the pulmonary artery, there is no overloading of the right ventricle and no right ventricular enlargement is seen.

The third major type of left-to-right shunt is **patent ductus arteriosus.** The ductus arteriosus is a vessel that extends from the bifurcation of the pulmonary artery to join the aorta just distal to the left subclavian artery. It serves to shunt blood from the pulmonary artery into the systemic circulation during intrauterine life. Persistence of the ductus arteriosus, which normally closes soon after birth, results in a left-to-right shunt. The flow of blood from the higher-pressure aorta to the lower-pressure

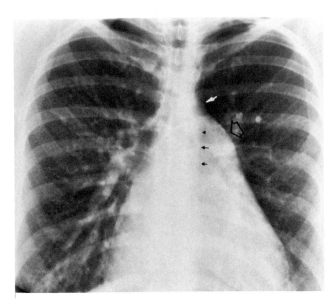

Figure 6-30 Atrial septal defect. Frontal projection of chest demonstrates cardiomegaly along with increase in pulmonary vascularity reflecting left-to-right shunt. Small aortic knob *(white arrow)* and descending aorta *(small arrows)* are dwarfed by enlarged pulmonary outflow tract *(open arrow)*.

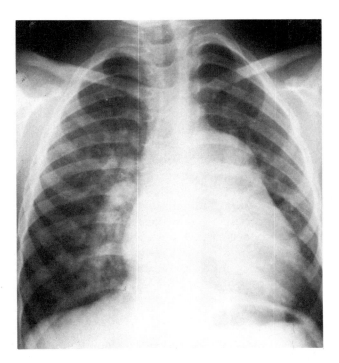

Figure 6-31 Ventricular septal defect. Heart is enlarged and somewhat triangular, and there is increase in pulmonary vascular volume. Pulmonary trunk is very large and overshadows normal-sized aorta, which seems small by comparison. (From Cooley RN, Schreiber MH: *Radiology of the heart and great vessels*, Baltimore, 1978, Williams & Wilkins.)

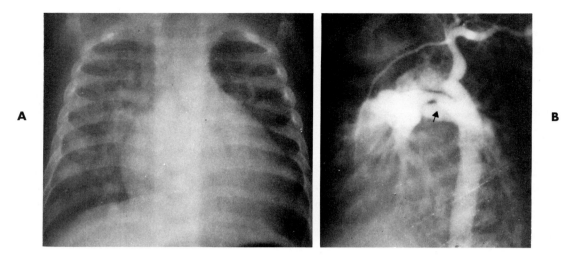

Figure 6-32 Patent ductus arteriosus. **A,** Frontal chest radiograph demonstrates cardiomegaly with enlargement of left atrium, left ventricle, and central pulmonary arteries. There is diffuse increase in pulmonary vascularity. **B,** In another patient, aortogram shows patency of ductus arteriosus *(arrow)*. (From Cooley RN, Schreiber MH: *Radiology of the heart and great vessels,* Baltimore, 1978, Williams & Wilkins.)

pulmonary artery causes increased pulmonary blood flow, and an excess volume of blood is returned to the left atrium and left ventricle. Radiographically, there is enlargement of the left atrium, the left ventricle, and the central pulmonary arteries, along with a diffuse increase in pulmonary vascularity (Figure 6-32). The increased blood flow through the aorta proximal to the shunt produces a prominent aortic knob, in contrast to the small or normal-sized aorta seen in atrial and ventricular septal defects.

All left-to-right shunts can be complicated by the development of pulmonary hypertension (**Eisenmenger's syndrome**). This is caused by increased vascular resistance within the pulmonary arteries related to chronic increased flow through the pulmonary circulation. Pulmonary hypertension appears radiographically as an increased fullness of the central pulmonary arteries with abrupt narrowing and pruning of peripheral vessels (Figure 6-33). The elevation of pulmonary arterial pressure tends to balance or even reverse the left-to-right shunt, thus easing the volume overloading of the heart.

Tetralogy of Fallot

Tetralogy of Fallot is the most common cause of cyanotic congenital heart disease and consists of four (tetra) abnormalities: (1) high ventricular septal defect, (2) pulmonary stenosis, (3) overriding of the aortic orifice above the ventricular defect, and (4) right ventricular hypertrophy. Pulmonary stenosis causes an elevation of pressure in the right ventricle and hypertrophy of that chamber. Because of the

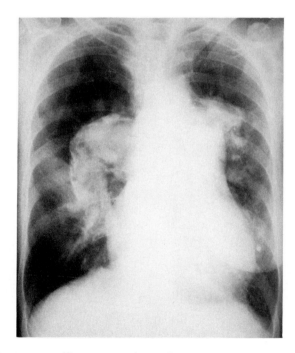

Figure 6-33 Eisenmenger's syndrome in atrial septal defect. There is slight but definite cardiomegaly and great increase in size of pulmonary trunk. Right and left pulmonary artery branches are huge, but peripheral pulmonary vasculature is relatively sparse. Long-standing pulmonary hypertension has produced degenerative changes in walls of pulmonary arteries, which have become densely calcified. (From Cooley RN, Schreiber MH: *Radiology of the heart and great vessels,* Baltimore, 1978, Williams & Wilkins.)

narrow opening of the pulmonary valve, an inadequate amount of blood reaches the lungs to be oxygenated. The ventricular septal defect and the overriding of the aorta produce right-to-left shunting of unoxygenated venous blood into the right ventricle and then into the systemic circulation, thus increasing the degree of cyanosis.

Enlargement of the right ventricle causes upward and lateral displacement of the apex of the heart (Figure 6-34). This results in the classic **coeur en sabot** appearance resembling the curved-toe portion of a wooden shoe. In about one fourth of patients with tetralogy of Fallot the aorta is on the right side.

Coarctation of the aorta

Coarctation refers to a narrowing, or constriction, of the aorta that most commonly occurs just beyond the branching of the blood vessels to the head and arms. Although the blood supply and pressure to the upper extremities is normal, there is decreased blood flow through the constricted area to the abdomen and legs. Classically, the patient has normal blood pressure in the arms but very low blood pressure in the legs.

The relative obstruction of aortic blood flow leads to the progressive development of collateral circula-tion, the enlargement of normally tiny vessels in an attempt to compensate for the inadequate blood supply to the lower portion of the body. This is often seen radiographically as rib notching (usually involving the posterior fourth to eighth ribs) resulting from pressure erosion by dilated and pulsating intercostal collateral vessels, which run along the inferior margins of these ribs (Figure 6-35, A). Notching of the posterior border of the sternum may be produced by dilatation of mammary artery collaterals.

Coarctation of the aorta often causes two bulges in the region of the aortic knob that produce a characteristic figure-3 sign on plain chest radiographs (Figure 6-35, B) and a reverse figure-3 or figure-E impression on the barium-filled esophagus (Figure 6-35, C). The more cephalad bulge represents dilatation of the proximal aorta and the base of the subclavian artery (prestenotic dilatation); the lower bulge reflects poststenotic aortic dilatation.

Aortography can accurately localize the site of obstruction, determine the length of the coarctation, and identify any associated cardiac malformations. More recently, MRI has been used to demonstrate aortic narrowing (Figure 6-36) and to check the appearance of the aorta after corrective surgery.

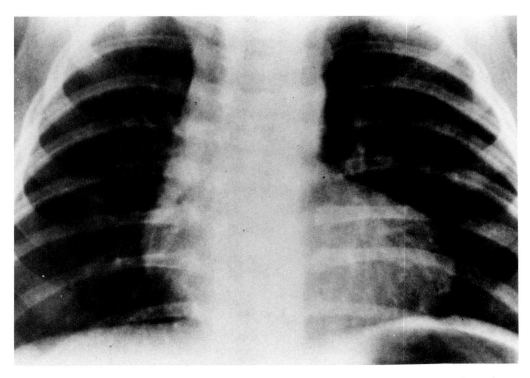

Figure 6-34 Tetralogy of Fallot. Plain chest radiograph demonstrates characteristic lateral displacement and upward tilting of prominent cardiac apex. There is also decreased pulmonary vascularity and flat pulmonary outflow tract.

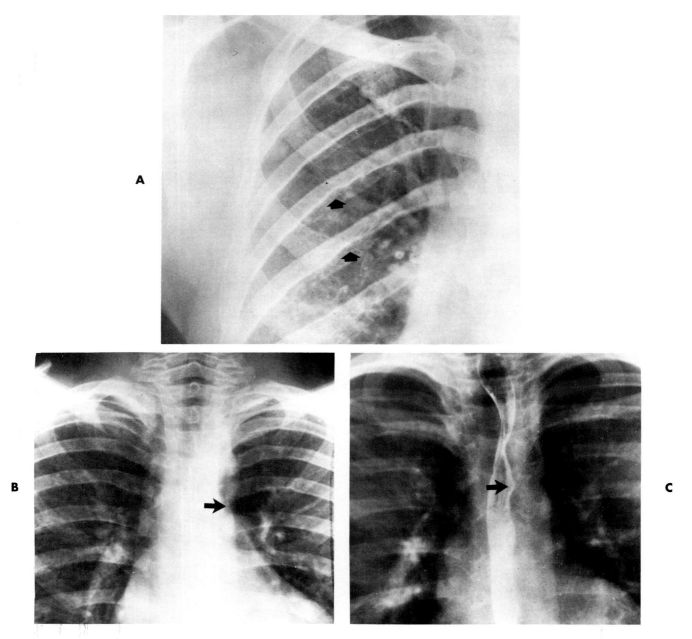

Figure 6-35 Coarctation of aorta. **A,** Rib notching. There is notching of posterior fourth through eighth ribs (arrows point to examples). **B,** Plain chest radiograph demonstrates figure-3 sign (arrow points to center of 3). Upper bulge represents prestenotic dilatation; lower bulge represents poststenotic dilatation. **C,** Esophagram demonstrates reverse figure-3 sign (arrow points to center of reverse figure-3). (From Swischuk LE: *Plain film interpretation in congenital heart disease*, Baltimore, 1979, Williams & Wilkins.)

▪ Rheumatic Heart Disease

Rheumatic fever is an autoimmune disease that results from a reaction of the patient's antibodies against antigens from a previous streptococcal infection. The disease is much less common today because of the frequent use of antibiotics to treat streptococcal throat or ear infections. The symptoms of rheumatic fever (fever, inflamed and painful joints, rash) typically develop several weeks after the streptococcal infection.

The major damage of rheumatic fever is to the valves of the heart, especially the mitral and aortic valves. The allergic response causes inflammation of

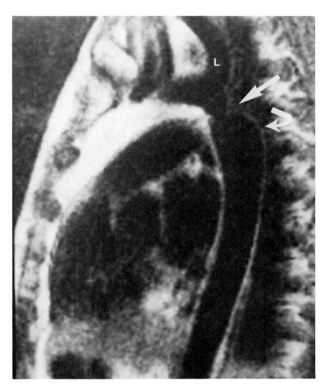

Figure 6-36 Coarctation of aorta. Sagittal magnetic resonance image demonstates coarctation *(straight arrow)* of thoracic aorta with associated poststenotic dilatation of proximal descending thoracic aorta *(curved arrow)*. L, Left subclavian artery.

the valves. Deposits of blood platelets and fibrin from blood flowing over the valve produce small nodules (**vegetations**) along the margin of the valve cusps. The thickened valves may stick together, remaining permanently narrowed (**stenosis**) rather than opening properly when blood flows through the valvular opening. In contrast, fibrous scarring may cause retraction of the valve cusps so that the cusps are unable to meet when the valve tries to close (**insufficiency**). In this case, there is leakage of blood across the valve.

▪ Valvular Disease

The valves of the heart permit blood to flow in only one direction through the heart. When the valve is closed, a heart chamber fills with blood; when the valve opens, blood can move forward and leave the chamber. There are four heart valves. The **tricuspid valve** separates the right atrium and right ventricle, and the **mitral valve** separates the left atrium and left ventricle. The **pulmonary valve** lies between the right ventricle and pulmonary artery, and the **aortic valve** is situated between the left ventricle and the aorta.

The malfunction of a heart valve alters the normal blood flow through the heart. Too small an opening (stenosis) does not permit sufficient blood flow. In contrast, too large an opening or failure of the valve to properly close permits back flow of blood (regurgitation) and the condition of valvular insufficiency. Both stenosis and insufficiency of valves cause heart

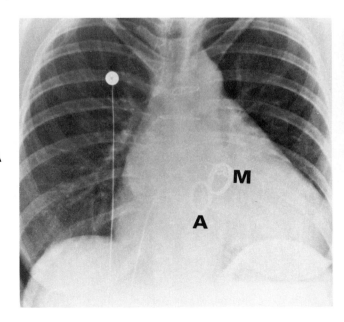
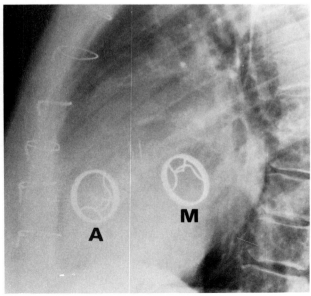

Figure 6-37 Prosthetic aortic and mitral valves. **A,** Frontal and, **B,** lateral projections of chest show anteromedially located prosthetic aortic valve *(A)* and posterolaterally situated prosthetic mitral valve *(M)*.

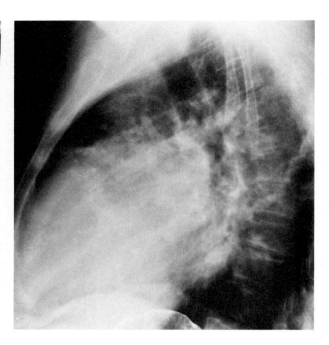

Figure 6-38   Mitral stenosis. **A,** Frontal and, **B,** lateral projections of chest demonstrate cardiomegaly with enlargement of right ventricle and left atrium. Right ventricular enlargement causes obliteration of retrosternal air space, whereas left atrial enlargement produces convexity of upper left border of heart *(arrow).*

murmurs with characteristic sounds that indicate the nature of the defect. Although valvular heart disease used to invariably force a patient to restrict activity and was associated with a limited life-span, surgical reconstruction or replacement of a diseased valve (Figure 6-37) can offer a patient the prospect of a normal life.

Mitral stenosis

Stenosis of the mitral valve, almost always a complication of rheumatic disease, results from diffuse thickening of the valve by fibrous tissue, calcific deposits, or both. The obstruction to blood flow from the left atrium into the left ventricle during diastole causes increased pressure in the left atrium and enlargement of this chamber (Figure 6-38). The enlarged left atrium produces a characteristic anterior impression on and posterior displacement of the barium-filled esophagus that is best seen on lateral and right anterior oblique projections. Other radiographic signs of the left atrial enlargement include posterior displacement of the left main-stem bronchus, widening of the tracheal bifurcation (carina), and a characteristic "double-contour" configuration caused by the projection of the enlarged left atrium through the normal right atrial silhouette. The increased left atrial pressure is transmitted to the

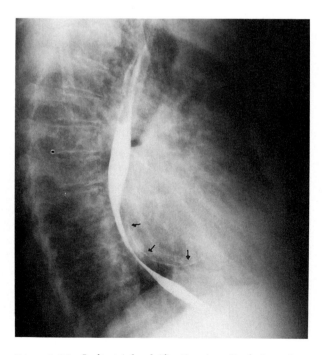

Figure 6-39   Left atrial calcification in mitral stenosis. Lateral projection with barium in esophagus shows enlargement of left atrium and calcification of wall of its chamber *(arrows).* (From Vickers SCW et al: *Radiology* 72:569-575, 1959.)

pulmonary veins and produces the appearance of chronic venous congestion.

Calcification of the mitral valve or left atrial wall (Figure 6-39), best demonstrated by fluoroscopy, can develop in patients with long-standing severe mitral stenosis. A thrombus may form in the dilated left atrium and be the source of emboli to the brain or elsewhere in the systemic circulation.

Echocardiography is the most sensitive and most specific noninvasive method for diagnosing mitral stenosis (Figure 6-40). More recently, MRI has been used to show the abnormal pattern of flow between the left atrium and left ventricle in this condition.

Mitral insufficiency

Although most often caused by rheumatic heart disease, mitral insufficiency may also be caused by rupture of chordae tendineae or by dysfunction of the papillary muscles that are attached to the underside of the valve cusps and normally prevent them from swinging up into the atrium when the ventricles contract. Regurgitation of blood into the left atrium during ventricular systole causes overfilling and dilatation of this chamber (Figure 6-41). In most cases, the left atrium is considerably larger in mitral insufficiency than in mitral stenosis; occasionally, an enormous left atrium can form both the right and left borders of the heart on frontal projections. An increased volume of blood flowing from the dilated left atrium to the left ventricle in diastole increases the left ventricular work load and leads to dilatation and hypertrophy of this chamber. This causes downward displacement of the cardiac apex and rounding of the lower left border of the heart.

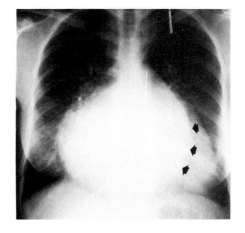

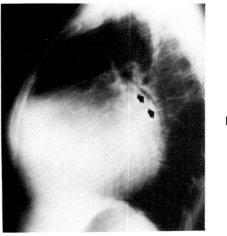

Figure 6-41 Mitral insufficiency. **A,** Frontal and, **B,** lateral projections of chest demonstrate gross cardiomegaly with enlargement of left atrium and left ventricle. Notice striking double-contour configuration *(arrows)* on frontal film and elevation of left main-stem bronchus *(arrows)* on lateral film, characteristic signs of left atrial enlargement.

Aortic stenosis

Aortic stenosis may be caused by rheumatic heart disease, a congenital valvular deformity (especially a bicuspid valve), or a degenerative process of aging (idiopathic calcific stenosis). The obstruction to left ventricular outflow in aortic stenosis increases the work load of the left ventricle. Initially, this results in left ventricular hypertrophy without dilatation that produces only some rounding of the cardiac apex on frontal chest radiographs and slight backward displacement on lateral projections. The overall size of the heart remains within normal limits until left ventricular failure develops. Significant aortic stenosis is usually associated with lateral bulging (poststenotic dilatation) of the ascending aorta caused by the jet of blood forced under high pressure through

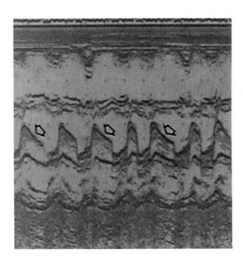

Figure 6-40 Echocardiogram of mitral stenosis. There is thickening of mitral valve with decreased slope *(arrows)*.

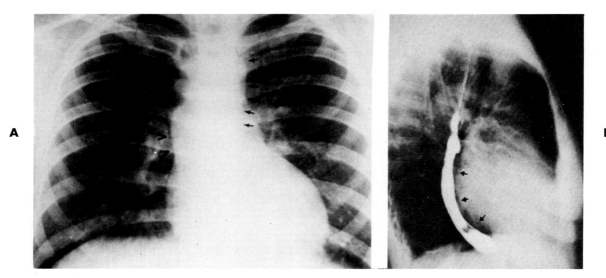

Figure 6-42   Aortic stenosis. **A,** Frontal projection shows downward displacement of cardiac apex with poststenotic dilatation of ascending aorta *(arrowheads).* Aortic knob and descending aorta *(arrows)* are normal. **B,** On lateral projection in another patient, bulging of lower half of posterior cardiac silhouette causes broad indentation on barium-filled esophagus *(arrows).*

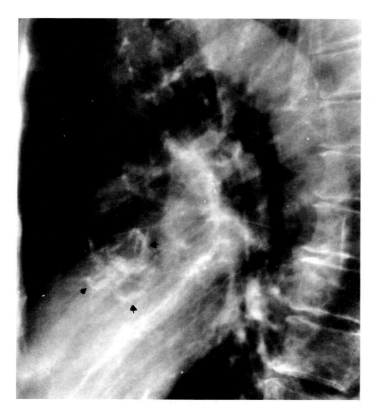

Figure 6-43   Aortic stenosis. Calcification in three leaflets of aortic valve *(arrows).*

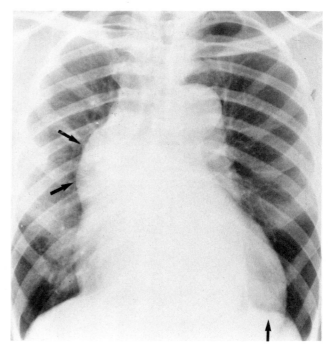

Figure 6-44   Aortic insufficiency. Frontal chest radiograph shows left ventricular enlargement with downward and lateral displacement of cardiac apex. Notice that cardiac shadow extends below dome of left hemidiaphragm *(small arrow).* Ascending aorta is strikingly dilated *(large arrows),* suggestive of some underlying aortic stenosis.

the narrowed valve (Figure 6-42). Aortic valve calcification, best demonstrated on fluoroscopic examination, is a common finding and indicates that the aortic stenosis is severe (Figure 6-43).

Aortic insufficiency

Although most commonly caused by rheumatic heart disease, aortic insufficiency may be attributable to syphilis, infective endocarditis, dissecting aneurysm, or Marfan's syndrome. Reflux of blood from the aorta during diastole causes volume overloading of the left ventricle and dilatation of this chamber. This causes downward, lateral, and posterior displacement of the cardiac apex (Figure 6-44). Pronounced left ventricular dilatation causes relative mitral insufficiency, which leads to left atrial enlargement and signs of pulmonary edema.

Infective endocarditis

Infective endocarditis refers to the development of nodules or vegetations forming on heart valves. Unlike the smaller nodules in rheumatic fever, the vegetations of infective endocarditis are filled with bacteria and tend to break apart easily (friable) to enter the bloodstream and form septic emboli that travel to the brain, kidney, lung, or other vital organs. Emboli lodging in the skin may cause rupture of small blood vessels and characteristic tiny hemorrhagic red spots (petechiae).

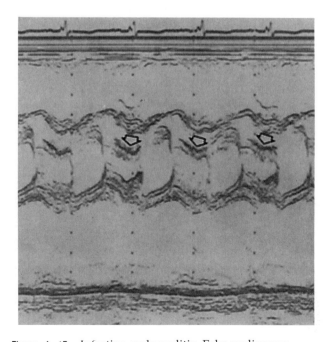

Figure 6-45 Infective endocarditis. Echocardiogram demonstrates vegetations as masses of shaggy echoes producing irregular thickening of aortic valve *(arrows).*

Plain radiography is of little value in patients with infective endocarditis. The cardiac silhouette may be normal or demonstrate evidence of previous valvular heart disease or congestive heart failure. Echocardiography is the only noninvasive procedure that can detect the valvular vegetations that are the hallmark of infective endocarditis. On the echocardiogram, these vegetations appear as masses of shaggy echoes producing an irregular thickening of the affected valves (Figure 6-45).

▪ Pericardial Effusion

Pericardial effusion refers to the accumulation of fluid within the pericardial space surrounding the heart. Echocardiography is the most effective imaging technique for demonstrating pericardial effusions and has largely replaced other methods. As little as 50 ml of fluid can be detected by this modality. On plain chest radiographs, a pericardial effusion causes enlargement of the cardiac silhouette (Figure 6-46). However, at least 200 ml of fluid must be present before a pericardial effusion can be detected by this technique. Rapid enlargement of the cardiac silhouette, especially in the absence of pulmonary vascular engorgement indicating congestive heart failure, is highly suggestive of pericardial effusion.

Angiocardiography, intravenous carbon dioxide injection, and a pericardial tap with air injection have been used in the past to demonstrate pericardial effusion by showing an excessive distance (greater than 5 mm) between the contrast- or air-filled atrium and the outer border of the cardiac silhouette. However, echocardiography has effectively replaced these invasive techniques (Figure 6-47).

Gated MRI (Figure 6-48) shows a pericardial effusion as a region of decreased signal intensity between the myocardium and the fat on the surface of the parietal pericardium (which is usually invisible when it is in direct contact with the heart).

▪ Venous Disease

Deep venous thrombosis

Deep venous thrombosis, which primarily involves the lower extremities, is the major source of potentially fatal pulmonary embolism. Precipitating factors in the development of venous thrombosis include trauma, bacterial infection, prolonged bed rest, and oral contraceptives. At times, deep vein thrombosis may be the earliest symptom of an unsuspected malignancy of the pancreas, lung, or gastrointestinal system.

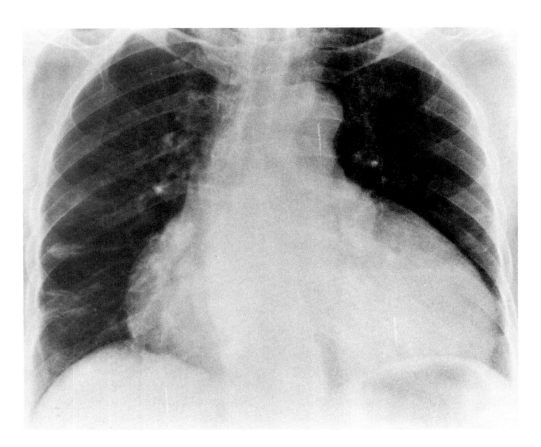

Figure 6-46   Pericardial effusion. Globular enlargement of cardiac silhouette.

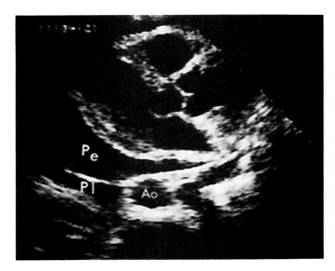

Figure 6-47   Pericardial effusion. Echocardiogram demonstrates both pericardial *(Pe)* and pleural *(Pl)* effusions. Descending aorta *(Ao)* is separated from heart by pericardial effusion. (From Miller SW, Gillam LD: In Eisenberg RL, editor: *Diagnostic imaging: an algorithmic approach,* Philadelphia, 1988, Lippincott.)

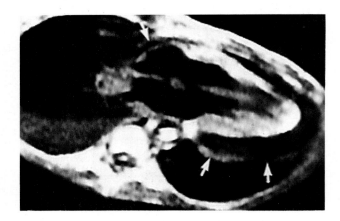

Figure 6-48   Magnetic resonance image of pericardial effusion. Pericardium *(arrows)* is displaced away from heart by huge pericardial effusion that has very little signal intensity. Effect of gravity is seen in posterior location of both pericardial and right pleural effusions. (From Miller SW, Brady TJ, Dinsmore RE, et al: *Radiol Clin North Am* 23:745-764, 1985.)

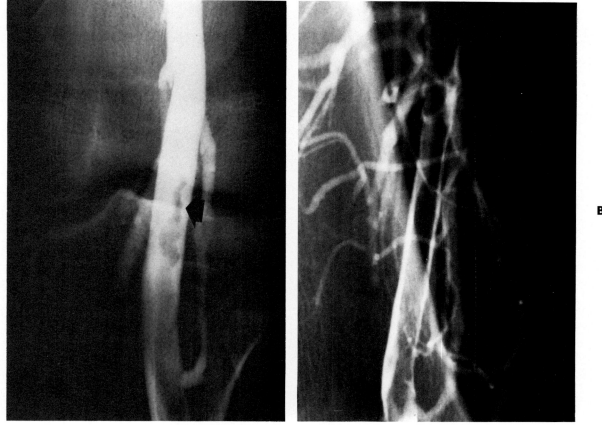

Figure 6-49   Deep vein thrombosis. **A,** Initial contrast venogram demonstrates early nonocclusive thrombus extending from valve cusp. Arrow points to thrombus tail, the portion most likely to embolize. **B,** Subsequent contrast venogram demonstrates growth and proximal extension of thrombus, which has resulted in occlusion of popliteal vein at adductor hiatus. (From Holden RW, Mail JT, Becker GJ: In Eisenberg RL editor: *Diagnostic imaging: an algorithmic approach,* Philadelphia, 1988, Lippincott.)

A precise diagnosis of deep vein thrombosis requires contrast venography, which can demonstrate the major venous channels and their tributaries from the foot to the inferior vena cava. The identification of a constant filling defect, representing the actual thrombus, is conclusive evidence of deep vein thrombosis (Figure 6-49). Venographic findings that are highly suggestive of, though not conclusive for, the diagnosis of deep vein thrombosis include the abrupt ending of the opaque column in a vein, the nonfilling of one or more veins that are normally opacified, and extensive collateral venous circulation.

Because venography is an invasive technique, other modalities have been developed for detecting deep vein thrombosis. Duplex Doppler ultrasound demonstrates changes in the velocity of venous blood flow. It is of special value in showing thrombotic occlusion of major venous pathways in the popliteal and femoral regions. An abnormal Doppler ultrasound examination is not specific for thrombosis, since similar changes in venous blood flow may be caused by congestive heart failure, extensive leg edema, local soft-tissue masses, and decreased inflow of arterial blood into the extremity.

Varicose veins

Varicose veins are dilated, elongated, and tortuous vessels that most commonly involve the superficial veins of the leg just under the skin (Figure 6-50). If the venous dilatation becomes extreme, the valves that normally prevent backflow of blood because of gravity become incompetent and cease to function, thus increasing the volume of blood in these slow-flowing vessels.

Although heredity plays some role in the development of varicose veins, which often run in a

Figure 6-50 Varicose veins. Lower extremity venogram shows multiple tortuous, dilated venous structures.

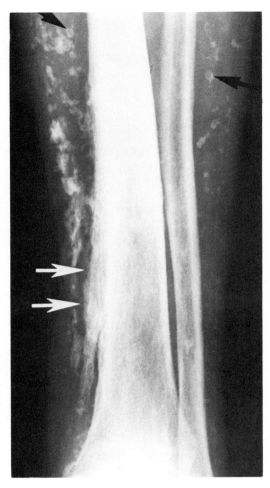

Figure 6-51 Varicose veins. Multiple round and oval calcifications in soft tissues (phleboliths) representing calcified thrombi, some of which have characteristic lucent centers *(black arrows)*. Extensive new bone formation along medial aspect of tibial shaft *(white arrows)* is caused by long-standing venous stasis.

family, the underlying cause is increased pressure in an affected vein. Varicose veins can be an occupational hazard for people who stand or sit for long periods. Normally, the action of leg muscles helps move blood upward toward the heart from one venous valve to the next. If this "milking action" of the muscles is absent, the blood puts pressure on the closed valves and the thin walls of the veins resulting in venous dilatation, incompetence of the valves, and stasis of blood in the stagnant lower extremity veins. Increased pressure on a vein can also be attributable to a pregnant uterus or a pelvic tumor.

Stasis of blood within varicose veins may lead to the development of phleboliths, calcified clots within a vein that appear radiographically as rounded densities that often contain lucent centers (Figure 6-51). Chronic venous stasis may also lead to periosteal new bone formation along the tibial and fibular shafts and development of plaquelike calcifications in the chronically congested subcutaneous tissues. The poor venous flow can lead to the development of superfi-

cial ulcers, and the distended veins can rupture, causing hemorrhage into the surrounding tissues.

Although the diagnosis of varicose veins is primarily based on the clinical observation of the multiple bluish nodules just under the skin, venography is of value in demonstrating the patency of the deep venous system and the degree of collateral circulation from the superficial to the deep veins, especially if there is consideration of surgical intervention (tying off and removing the superficial veins). After the application of a tourniquet to occlude superficial flow, the peripheral injection of contrast material opacifies the deep venous system. Filling of the superficial veins indicates that the perforating veins above the level of the tourniquet are incompetent.

QUESTIONS

1. The heart rate is controlled by the _____ nervous system.
   - A. Psychogenic
   - B. Central
   - C. Peripheral
   - D. Autonomic

2. The _____ valve is located between the left atrium and the left ventricle, whereas the _____ valve is located between the right atrium and right ventricle.
   - I. Tricuspid
   - II. Mitral
   - III. Pulmonary
   - IV. Aortic
   - A. II, I
   - B. III, I
   - C. IV, I
   - D. I, II

3. The general circulation of the body is termed the _____ circulation.
   - A. Pulmonary
   - B. Systemic
   - C. General
   - D. Autonomic

4. The contracting phase of the heart is termed _____ , whereas the relaxation phase is termed _____ .
   - I. Autonomic
   - II. Diastole
   - III. Systemic
   - IV. Systole
   - A. I, III
   - B. II, IV
   - C. II, III
   - D. IV, II

5. Contraction of which chamber of the heart forces oxygenated blood into the aorta?
   - A. Right atrium
   - B. Right ventricle
   - C. Left atrium
   - D. Left ventricle

6. Oxygenated blood reaches the heart muscle by way of the _____ .
   - I. Right coronary artery
   - II. Left coronary artery
   - III. Left coronary vein
   - IV. Right coronary vein
   - A. I, III
   - B. IV, I
   - C. II, I
   - D. II, III

7. The heart has a specialized pacemaker named the _____ .
   - A. Bundle of His
   - B. Sinoatrial node
   - C. Purkinje fibers
   - D. Atrioventricular node

8. Factors that lead to coronary artery disease are _____ .
   - A. Lack of exercise
   - B. Obesity, hypertension
   - C. Smoking, high-cholesterol diet
   - D. All of the above

9. Temporary oxygen insufficiency to the heart muscle causes severe chest pain termed _____ .
   - A. Angina pectoris
   - B. Myocardial occlusion
   - C. Myocardial pectoris
   - D. Angina occlusion

10. Arterial disease caused by fatty deposits on the inner arterial wall is termed _____ .
    - A. Arteriosclerosis
    - B. Myocardial infarction
    - C. Aneurysm
    - D. Myocardial ischemia

11. What radiographic procedure is used to determine the presence of coronary artery disease?
    - A. Angioplasty
    - B. Chest film
    - C. Coronary arteriogram
    - D. CT

12. The procedure of using a balloon to dilate narrowed coronary arteries is named _____ .
    - A. Aortocoronary bypass
    - B. Coronary arteriography
    - C. Percutaneous transluminal angioplasty
    - D. Fluoroscopy

13. The term _____ refers to an inability of the heart to propel blood at a sufficient rate and volume.
    - A. Congestive heart failure
    - B. Pulmonary edema
    - C. Valvular disease
    - D. Valvular stenosis

14. An elevation of the pulmonary venous pressure is the most common cause of _____ .
    - A. Congestive heart failure
    - B. Pulmonary edema
    - C. Valvular disease
    - D. Valvular stenosis

15. The leading cause of strokes and congestive heart failure is _____ .
    - A. Hypertension
    - B. Low blood pressure
    - C. Hypotension
    - D. Cor pulmonale

16. A localized bulging or dilatation of an artery is termed _____ .
    - A. Edema
    - B. Effusion
    - C. Aneurysm
    - D. Fat emboli

17. What is the modality of choice for demonstration of an abdominal aortic aneurysm?
    - A. MRI
    - B. Ultrasonography
    - C. CT
    - D. Plain film radiography

18. A congenital narrowing or constriction of the thoracic aorta is referred to as _____ .
    - A. Embolism
    - B. Plaque
    - C. Coarctation
    - D. Tetralogy

19. The _____ of the heart is the major
    site of damage from rheumatic fever.
    A. Myocardium   C. Septum
    B. Valves   D. Endocardium

20. The most sensitive and specific noninvasive
    method of diagnosing mitral stenosis is
    _____ .
    A. Ultrasonography   C. Cardiac
    B. Echocardiography   arteriography
                          D. CT

21. The accumulation of fluid within the pericardial
    space surrounding the heart is termed
    _____ .
    A. Pericardial   C. Pulmonary edema
       thrombosis   D. Pulmonary effusion
    B. Pericardial effusion

22. The invasive procedure for determining deep
    vein thrombosis is _____ .
    A. Doppler ultrasound C. CT
    B. Venography   D. Arteriography

23. The most accurate screening procedure for as-
    sessing renovascular lesions is
    _____ .
    A. Doppler ultrasound C. CT
    B. Venography   D. Arteriography

24. A potentially life-threatening condition that usu-
    ally begins as a tear in the intima above the
    aortic valve is an _____ .
    A. Aortic stenosis   C. Aortic thrombosis
    B. Aortic coarctation D. Aortic dissection

BIBLIOGRAPHY

Swischuk LE: *Plain film interpretation in congenital heart disease,*
Baltimore, 1979, Williams & Wilkins.

Cooley RN, Schreiber MH: *Radiology of the heart and great vessels,*
Baltimore, 1978, Williams & Wilkins.

CHAPTER 7

Nervous System Disease

- ■ Prerequisite Knowledge

  The student should have a basic knowledge of the anatomy and physiology of the skull and nervous system. In addition, proper learning and understanding of the material will be facilitated if the student has some clinical experience in skull radiography and film evaluation, including a concept of newer imaging modalities (CT, MRI).

- ■ Goals

  To acquaint the student radiographer with the pathophysiology and radiographic manifestations of all of the common and some of the unusual disorders of the skull and nervous system

- ■ Objectives

  1. Understand and be able to define or describe all bold-faced terms in this chapter
  2. Describe the physiology of the nervous system
  3. Identify anatomic structures on both diagrams and radiographs of the skull and nervous system
  4. Be able to describe the various pathologic conditions affecting the skull and nervous system as well as their radiographic manifestations

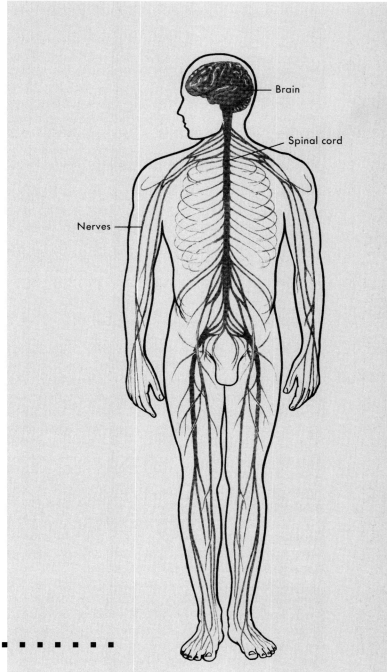

■ ■ ■ ■ ■ ■ **■ Radiographer Notes**

Proper positioning is critical in skull and spine radiography to ensure bilateral symmetry and to permit an evaluation of the complex anatomy and structural relationships. The demonstration of asymmetry or a shift in the normal location of a structure in a patient who is positioned correctly may be indicative of an underlying pathologic condition. Proper positioning and correct angulation of the central ray may allow visualization of otherwise superimposed structures. When evaluating such anatomic areas as the sinuses or facial bones, it is often necessary to place the patient in the erect position (either standing or sitting) and to use a horizontal beam to demonstrate an air-fluid level indicative of underlying inflammatory disease or fracture. If the patient's condition prohibits placement in an erect position, one can demonstrate air-fluid levels only by obtaining a cross-table lateral projection using a horizontal beam with the patient in a dorsal decubitus position.

Exposure factors should produce a scale of contrast that provides for maximal detail (definition), especially when one is imaging vascular structures and subtle changes in bone density such as fractures of the skull or spine. Advanced stages of certain pathologic conditions can result in the need for technical changes to maintain the proper level of penetration, contrast, and visibility of detail (Table 1-1). If contrast material is used, the kVp level must remain in the low to midrange to provide enough radiographic contrast to properly show the contrast-filled vessels.

The administration of radiographic contrast material is an essential component of many examinations of the skull and nervous system. Therefore it is essential that the radiographer be familiar with the use of these agents and be extremely alert to the development of possible allergic reactions. After contrast administration, the radiographer is often left alone in the room with the patient and thus must be able to immediately recognize an allergic reaction to contrast material and be able to initiate and maintain basic life support until advanced life-support personnel have arrived. Depending on departmental policy, it is usually the radiographer's responsibility to assist during resuscitation procedures. Therefore it is essential that the radiographer be familiar with the contents of the emergency cart and be responsible for ensuring that the cart is completely stocked with all appropriate medications.

■ Physiology of the Nervous System

The divisions of the nervous system can be classified by location or by the type of tissue they supply. The **central nervous system** (CNS) consists of the brain and spinal cord. The remaining neural structures, including 12 pairs of cranial nerves, 31 pairs of spinal nerves, autonomic nerves, and ganglia make up the **peripheral nervous system** (PNS). The PNS consists of afferent and efferent neurons. Afferent **(sensory)** neurons conduct impulses from peripheral receptors to the CNS. Efferent **(motor)** neurons conduct impulses away from the CNS to peripheral effectors. The **somatic nervous system** supplies the striated skeletal muscles, whereas the **autonomic nervous system** supplies smooth muscle, cardiac muscle, and glandular epithelial tissue.

The basic unit of the nervous system is the **neuron,** or nerve cell. A neuron consists of a cell body and two types of long threadlike extensions. A single **axon** leads from the nerve cell body, and one or more **dendrites** lead toward it. Axons are insulated by a fatty covering called the **myelin sheath,** which increases the rate of transmission of nervous impulses. Deterioration of this fatty myelin sheath (demyelination) is a characteristic abnormality in multiple sclerosis.

The impulse conduction route to and from the CNS is termed a **reflex arc.** The basic reflex arc consists of an afferent, or sensory, neuron, which conducts impulses to the CNS from the periphery, and an efferent, or motor, neuron, which conducts impulses from the CNS to peripheral effectors (muscles or glandular tissue).

Impulses are passed from one neuron to another at a junction called the **synapse.** Transmission at the synapse is a chemical reaction in which the terminuses of the axon release a neurotransmitter substance that produces an electrical impulse in the dendrites of the next axon. Once the neurotransmitter has accomplished its task, its activity is rapidly terminated so that subsequent impulses can be conducted along this same route.

The largest part of the brain is the **cerebrum,** which consists of two cerebral hemispheres. The surface of the cerebrum is highly convoluted with elevations called **gyri** and shallow grooves called **sulci.** Deeper grooves called fissures divide each cerebral hemisphere into lobes. The outer portion of the cerebrum is termed the **cortex,** which consists of a thin layer of gray matter where the nerve cell bodies are concentrated. The inner area consists of white matter, which is composed of the nerve fiber tracts.

The cerebral cortex is responsible for receiving sensory information from all parts of the body and for triggering impulses that govern all motor activity. Just posterior to the central sulcus, the cerebral cortex has specialized areas to receive and precisely localize sensory information from the PNS. Visual impulses are transmitted to the posterior part of the brain; olfactory (smell) and auditory impulses are received in the lateral parts. The primary motor cortex is just anterior to the central sulcus. Because efferent motor fibers cross over from one side of the body to the other at the level of the medulla and spinal cord, stimulation on one side of the cerebral cortex causes contraction of muscles on the opposite side of the body. The premotor cortex, which lies anterior to the primary motor cortex, controls coordinate movements of muscles by stimulating groups of muscles that work together. This region also contains the portion of the brain responsible for speech, which is usually on the left side in right-handed people. The cerebral cortex also is the site of all higher functions, including memory and creative thought.

The two cerebral hemispheres are connected by a mass of white matter called the **corpus callosum.** These extensive bundles of nerve fibers lie in the midline just above the roofs of the lateral ventricles.

Deep within the white matter are a few islands of gray matter that are collectively called the **basal ganglia.** These structures help control position and automatic movements and consist of the caudate nuclei, globus pallidum, and putamen.

Between the cerebrum and spinal cord lies the brainstem, which is composed (from top down) of the **midbrain** (mesencephalon), **pons,** and **medulla.** In addition to performing sensory, motor, and reflex functions, the brainstem contains the nuclei of the 12 cranial nerves and the vital centers controlling cardiac, vasomotor, and respiratory function. Centers in the medulla are responsible for such nonvital reflexes as vomiting, coughing, sneezing, hiccuping, and swallowing.

The **cerebellum,** the second largest part of the brain, is located just below the posterior portion of the cerebrum. It is composed of two large lateral masses, the cerebellar hemispheres, and a central section **(vermis)** that resembles a worm coiled on itself. The cerebellum acts with the cerebral cortex to produce skilled movements by coordinating the activities of groups of muscles. It coordinates skeletal muscles in maintaining equilibrium and posture by functioning below the level of consciousness to make movements smooth rather than jerky, steady rather than trembling, and efficient and coordinated rather than ineffective and awkward. Therefore cerebellar disease produces such characteristic symptoms as ataxia (muscle incoordination), tremors, and disturbances of gait and equilibrium.

The **diencephalon** lies between the cerebrum and the midbrain. It consists of several structures located around the third ventricle, primarily the thalamus and hypothalamus. The **thalamus** primarily functions as a relay station that receives and processes sensory information of almost all kinds of sensory impulses before sending this information on to the cerebral cortex. The tiny **hypothalamus** is an extremely complex structure that functions as a link between the mind and body and is the site of "pleasure" or "reward" centers for such primary drives as eating, drinking, and mating. It plays a major role in regulating the body's internal environment by coordinating the activities of the autonomic nervous system and secreting the **releasing hormones** that control the secretion of hormones by the anterior and posterior portions of the pituitary gland. The hypothalamus is also important in helping to maintain a normal body temperature and keeping the individual in a waking state.

The spinal cord lies within the vertebral column and extends from its junction with the brainstem at the foramen magnum to approximately the lower border of the first lumbar vertebra. It consists of an inner core of gray matter surrounded by white matter tracts. The basic function of the spinal cord is to conduct impulses up the cord to the brain (ascending tracts) and down the cord from the brain to spinal nerves (descending tracts). It also serves as the center for spinal reflexes, involuntary responses such as the knee jerk (patellar reflex).

The delicate, yet vital, brain and spinal cord are protected by two layers of coverings. The outer bony coverings are the cranial bones of the skull encasing the brain and the vertebrae surrounding the spinal cord. The inner coverings consist of three distinct layers of **meninges.** The innermost layer adhering to the outer surface of the brain and spinal cord is the transparent **pia mater,** and the tough outermost covering is termed the **dura mater.** Between these layers is the delicate, cobweblike **arachnoid membrane.** Inflammation of these three protective layers is called **meningitis.**

Three extensions of the dura mater separate portions of the brain. The **falx cerebri** projects downward into the longitudinal fissure to separate the cerebral hemispheres. Similarly, the **falx cerebelli** separates the two cerebellar hemispheres. The **tentorium cerebelli** forms a tentlike covering over the cerebellum that separates it from the occipital lobe of the cerebrum.

In addition to bony and membranous coverings, the brain and spinal cord are further protected by a cushion of fluid both around them and within them. The ventricles are four spaces within the brain that contain cerebrospinal fluid (CSF). There are two large lateral ventricles, one located in each cerebral hemisphere. The slitlike third ventricle lies between the right and left thalamus. The anterior parts of the lateral ventricles (frontal horns) are connected by a Y-shaped canal that extends downward to open into the upper part of the third ventricle at the foramen of Monro. The fourth ventricle is a diamond-shaped space between the cerebellum posteriorly and the medulla and pons anteriorly. It is continuous inferiorly with the central canal of the spinal cord. The third and fourth ventricles are connected by the aqueduct of Sylvius, a narrow canal that runs through the posterior part of the midbrain.

CSF is formed by filtration of plasma from blood in the choroid plexuses, networks of capillaries that project from the pia mater into the lateral ventricles and into the roofs of the third and fourth ventricles. After flowing through the ventricular system, the fluid circulates in the subarachnoid space around the brain and spinal cord before being absorbed into venous blood through arachnoid villi. Obstruction of CSF circulation results in hydrocephalus.

■ Traumatic Diseases of the Brain

In the patient with head trauma, the purpose of radiographic imaging is to detect a surgically correctable hematoma. Emergency CT has virtually replaced all other radiographic investigations in patients with suspected neurologic dysfunction resulting from head injury. Because the presence or absence of a skull fracture does not correlate with intracranial abnormalities, plain radiographs of the skull are no longer indicated in the patient with head trauma.

Because of medicolegal reasons and the fear of missing a skull fracture, CT scans (and plain skull radiographs) are often overused. The following indications have been established for the use of radiographic procedures in the patient with head trauma:

1. Unexplained focal neurologic signs
2. Unconsciousness (including the unarousable alcoholic)
3. Documented decreasing level of consciousness or progressive mental deterioration

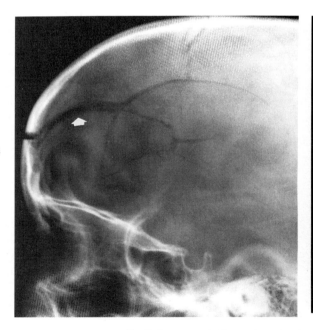 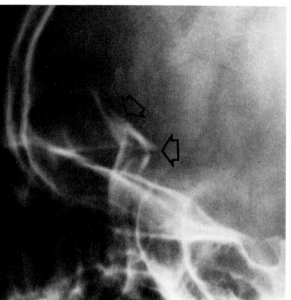

Figure 7-1 Skull fracture. **A,** Lateral projection of skull shows widely separated fracture *(arrow)* extending to star-shaped array of linear fractures. **B,** In another patient, lateral projection shows severely depressed skull fracture *(arrows)*.

4. History of previous craniotomy with shunt tube in place
5. Skull depression or subcutaneous foreign body palpable or identified by a probe through a laceration or puncture wound
6. Hemotympanum or fluid discharge from the ear
7. Discharge of cerebrospinal fluid from the nose
8. Ecchymosis over the mastoid process (Battle's sign)
9. Bilateral orbital ecchymoses (raccoon eyes)

Skull fracture

A linear skull fracture appears on a plain radiograph as a sharp lucent line that is often irregular or jagged and occasionally branches (Figure 7-1). The fracture must be distinguished from suture lines, which generally have serrated edges and tend to be bilateral and symmetric, and vascular grooves, which usually have a smooth curving course and are not as sharp or distinct as a fracture line. The location of a linear skull fracture can indicate possible complications. A fracture that crosses a dural vascular groove may cause vessel laceration leading to an epidural hematoma. A fracture involving the sinuses or mastoid air cells may result in posttraumatic pneumocephalus, with air seen in the ventricles on plain radiographs. A diastatic fracture refers to a linear fracture that intersects a suture and courses along it, causing sutural separation.

More severe trauma, especially if localized to a small area of the skull, may force a fragment of bone to be separated and depressed into the cranial cavity (Figure 7-2). The underlying dura is frequently torn, and there is a relatively high incidence of cerebral parenchymal injury. Depressed fractures are often stellate (star shaped), with multiple fracture lines radiating outward from a central point. When the fracture is viewed en face, the overlap of fragments makes the fracture line appear denser than the normal bone. Tangential views are required to determine the amount of depression.

Fractures limited to the base of the skull are often hidden by the complex basal anatomy and may be very difficult to visualize on plain radiographs. A finding suggestive of a basilar skull fracture is an air-fluid level in the sphenoid sinus seen on an erect or cross-table lateral projection of the skull obtained with a horizontal x-ray beam. CT can demonstrate the presence of blood or fluid in the basilar cisterns and show some basilar skull fractures that are not visible on routine skull radiographs. Potential complications of basal skull fractures include leakage of CSF, meningitis, and damage to the facial nerve or auditory apparatus within the petrous bone.

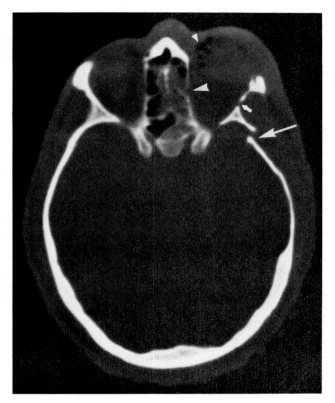

Figure 7-2 Skull fracture. CT bone window image demonstrates depressed temporal fracture *(long arrow)*. Notice also lateral orbital wall fracture *(short arrow)*, medial orbital wall fracture *(large arrowhead)*, and ethmoid opacification caused by hemorrhage. There is also air in orbital soft tissues *(small arrowhead)* resulting from medial fracture into ethmoids. (From Pressman BD: In Eisenberg RL, editor: *Diagnostic imaging: an algorithmic approach*, Philadelphia, 1988, Lippincott.)

It must be emphasized that the presence or absence of a skull fracture does not correlate with intracranial abnormalities. Indeed, serious treatable intracranial hematomas can be present without skull fractures.

Epidural hematoma

Epidural hematomas are caused by acute arterial bleeding and most commonly form over the parietotemporal convexity. Because of a high arterial pressure, epidural hematomas rapidly cause significant mass effect and acute neurologic symptoms. Because the dura is very adherent to the inner table of the skull, an epidural hematoma typically appears as a biconvex (lens-shaped), peripheral high-density lesion (Figure 7-3). There usually is a shift of the midline structures toward the opposite side unless a contralateral balancing hematoma is present. If not promptly recognized, an epidural hematoma can

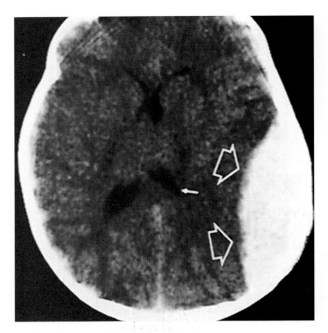

Figure 7-3 Acute epidural hematoma. CT scan of 4-year-old involved in motor vehicle accident shows characteristic lens-shaped epidural hematoma *(open arrows)*. Substantial mass effect associated with hematoma distorts lateral ventricle *(solid arrow)*.

lead to rapid progressive loss of consciousness, dilatation of the ipsilateral pupil, compression of the upper midbrain, and eventually compression of the entire brainstem and death.

Subdural hematoma

Subdural hematomas reflect venous bleeding, most commonly from ruptured veins between the dura and meninges. Symptoms may occur within the first few minutes; however, because of the low pressure of venous bleeding, patients with subdural hematomas tend to have a chronic course with symptoms of headache, agitation, confusion, drowsiness, and gradual neurologic deficits.

An acute subdural hematoma typically appears on CT scans as a peripheral zone of increased density that follows the surface of the brain and has a crescentic shape adjacent to the inner table of the skull (Figure 7-4). There usually is an associated mass effect with displacement of midline structures and obliteration of sulci over the affected hemisphere. The absence of displacement away from the side of a lesion may indicate the not-infrequent presence of bilateral subdural hematomas. On MRI scans, a subdural hematoma is detectable within a few days as an extra-axial mass of high signal intensity representing the accumulation of methemoglobin (Figure 7-5).

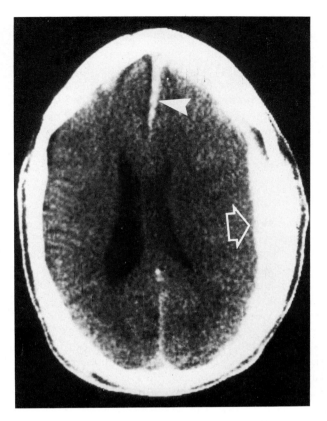

Figure 7-4 Acute subdural hematoma. High-density, crescent-shaped lesion *(arrow)* adjacent to inner table of skull. Hematoma extends into interhemispheric fissure *(arrowhead)*.

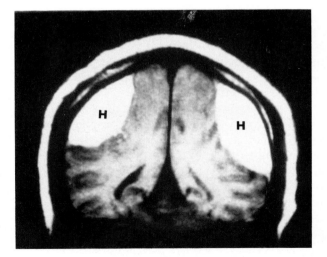

Figure 7-5 Bilateral subdural hematoma. Axial MR image shows high signal intensity of bilateral subdural collections *(H)*.

Serial CT scans demonstrate a gradual decrease in the attenuation value of a subdural hematoma over a period of weeks. With absorption and lysis of the blood clot, the hematoma becomes isodense with normal brain tissue, and the lesion may be identified only because of its mass effect. At this stage, scanning after the administration of contrast material may be of value because of enhancement of the membrane around the subdural hematoma and identification of the cortical veins. MRI scanning of a CT-isodense lesion may show medial displacement of the superficial cerebral veins, an indication of an extracerebral mass, as well as the entire extent of the hematoma over the cerebral convexity. A chronic subdural hematoma has a density similar to that of spinal fluid (Figure 7-6). At times, the small bridging veins associated with a chronic subdural hematoma may bleed and produce the difficult problem of an acute subdural hematoma superimposed on a chronic one.

Cerebral contusion

Cerebral contusion is an injury to brain tissue caused by movement of the brain within the calvarium after blunt trauma to the skull. Contusions occur when

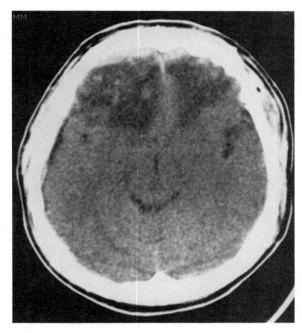

Figure 7-7   Cerebral contusion. CT scan shows small punctate hemorrhages (high density) within extensive areas of edema (low density). (From Pressman BD: In Eisenberg RL, editor: *Diagnostic imaging: an algorithmic approach,* Philadelphia, 1988, Lippincott.)

the brain contacts rough skull surfaces such as the superior orbital roof and petrous ridges. The patient loses consciousness and cannot remember the traumatic event. Cerebral contusions typically appear on CT scans as low-density areas of edema and tissue necrosis, with or without non–homogeneous density zones reflecting multiple small areas of hemorrhage (Figure 7-7). After the administration of intravenous contrast material, contusions generally enhance for several weeks after the injury because of a breakdown of the blood-brain barrier. On MRI scans, the cerebral edema causes high signal intensity on T_2-weighted images; associated areas of hemorrhage may produce high-signal-intensity regions on T_1-weighted scans.

Intracerebral hematoma

Traumatic hemorrhage into the brain parenchyma can result from shearing forces to intraparenchymal arteries, which tend to occur at the junction of the gray and white matter. Injury to the intima of intracranial vessels can cause the development of traumatic aneurysms, which can rupture. On CT scans, an intracerebral hematoma appears as a well-circumscribed, homogeneous, high-density region that usually is surrounded by areas of low-density edema (Figure 7-8). As the blood components

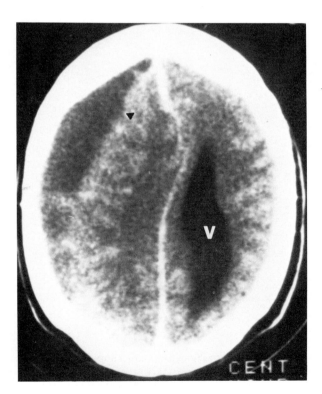

Figure 7-6   Chronic right subdural hematoma. Crescent-shaped, low-density region in right frontoparietal area *(arrows).* Herniation of brain tissue across midline underneath falx is present. *V,* Dilated left lateral ventricle.

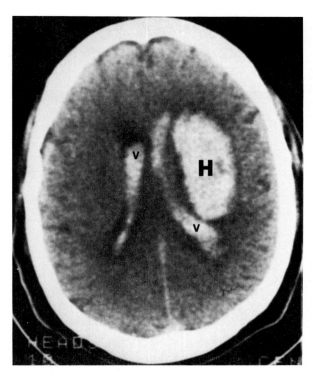

Figure 7-8 Intracerebral hematoma. Large homogeneous high-density area *(H)* with acute bleeding into lateral ventricles *(V)*.

within the hematoma disintegrate, the lesion eventually becomes isodense with normal brain (usually 2 to 4 weeks after injury). On MRI scans, the hematoma has high signal intensity. A chronic hematoma filled with hemosiderin will appear black on T_2-weighted images.

Although most intracerebral hematomas develop immediately after head injury, delayed hemorrhage is common. This is especially frequent after the evacuation of acute subdural hematomas that are compressing (tamponing) potential bleeding sites. Therefore a repeat CT (or MRI) scan is often performed within 48 hours in patients who have undergone decompressive surgery.

Subarachnoid hemorrhage

Injury to surface veins, cerebral parenchyma, or cortical arteries can produce bleeding into the ventricular system. On a CT scan, a subarachnoid hemorrhage appears as increased density within the basilar cisterns, cerebral fissures, and sulci. Identification of the falx cerebri, straight sinus, or superior sagittal sinus on noncontrast CT scans is often considered an indication of subarachnoid blood in the interhemispheric fissure. However, with high-resolution scanners this appearance may be seen in patients with a normal or calcified falx.

Carotid artery injury

The extracerebral carotid arteries can be injured by penetrating trauma to the neck as from gunshot wounds or stabbing. Angiography can demonstrate laceration of the artery or intimal damage, which may result in either dissection or thrombotic occlusion (Figure 7-9). Hyperextension injuries from motor vehicle accidents can cause intimal damage to the carotid or vertebral arteries, which may result in pseudoaneurysm formation. Traumatic arteriovenous fistulas usually arise between the internal carotid artery and the cavernous sinus. In this condition carotid arteriography demonstrates opacification of the cavernous sinus during the arterial phase. Reverse flow from the cavernous sinus may rapidly opacify a greatly dilated ophthalmic vein. The placement of a detachable balloon catheter within the fistula using angiographic guidance may eliminate the need for surgical intervention.

Facial fractures

Although it is padded by overlying skin and fat and the muscles of expression, the face consists of thin and poorly supported bone that can easily break in response to a traumatic force. The purpose of radiographic imaging in the patient with a facial injury is

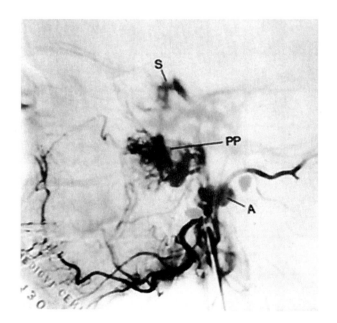

Figure 7-9 Posttraumatic carotid-cavernous fistula. A lateral projection of an external carotid artery angiogram shows a pseudoaneurysm *(A)* and rapid filling of the cavernous sinus *(S)* and pterygoid plexus *(PP)*. There is total interruption of the external carotid artery trunk beyond the takeoff of the facial artery. (From Eisenberg RL: *Diagnostic imaging in surgery*, New York, 1987, McGraw-Hill.)

to demonstrate major disruptions of the facial skeleton and displacement of fracture fragments that will affect the surgical reduction and stabilization of the fracture.

Plain radiographs of the face are usually performed as an initial screening procedure, especially in a severely traumatized patient with substantial injuries to multiple organ systems. Whenever possible, films should be obtained with the patient in the erect position to show any air-fluid levels within the sinuses that could indicate recent hemorrhage and raise the suspicion of an underlying fracture. Complex-motion (pluridirectional) tomography can blur unrelated overlying structures and thus display details of injury that are obscure or only suspected on plain radiographs. CT can demonstrate soft-tissue abnormalities, such as intraorbital or retrobulbar hematomas, that are impossible to detect by conventional means. In addition, bone detail and displacement can be exquisitely demonstrated when CT window and level settings are adjusted to optimize bony structures.

Fractures of the nasal bone are the most common facial fractures. Isolated nasal fractures vary from simple, nondisplaced linear fractures to comminuted lesions with depression of the septum and lateral splaying of the fracture fragments (Figure 7-10). These fractures are best demonstrated on an underexposed (soft-tissue) lateral projection, which also can define interruption of the anterior nasal spine—

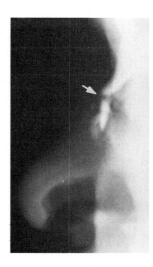

Figure 7-10   Depressed nasal fracture *(arrow).*

the anterior projection of the maxilla at the base of the cartilaginous nasal septum. Most fractures are transverse and tend to depress the distal portion of the nasal bones.

A blowout fracture is caused by a direct blow to the front of the orbit that causes a rapid increase in intraorbital pressure. The fracture occurs in the thinnest, weakest portion of the orbit, which is the orbital floor just above the maxillary sinus. Plain radiographs (modified Waters' method) and thin-section tomography can demonstrate most blowout fractures (Figure 7-11), though CT may be necessary

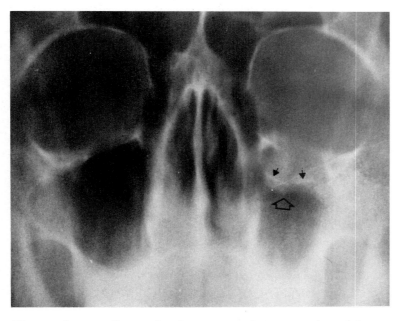

Figure 7-11   Blowout fracture. Conventional tomogram shows comminuted fracture of floor of left orbit with inferior displacement of fracture fragments *(solid arrows).* Notice characteristic soft-tissue shadow *(open arrow)* protruding through floor into superior portion of maxillary sinus.

for better visualization and for detecting entrapment of the extraocular muscles in the upper portion of the adjacent maxillary sinus (Figure 7-12). The fracture segment can be comminuted, with a sagging, hammocklike appearance, or be of the trapdoor variety, with a displaced segment hanging into the antrum by a periosteal hinge. Herniation of orbital fat and extraocular muscles into the fractured orbital floor produces a characteristic soft-tissue shadow protruding through the floor into the superior portion of the maxillary sinus. Opacification of the sinus caused by hemorrhage and mucosal edema is an indirect sign of orbital floor fracture. The presence of air within the orbit (orbital emphysema) indicates that there is a communication with a paranasal sinus, usually the ethmoid, as a result of an associated fracture of the medial wall of the orbit through the lamina papyracea.

The zygomatic arch is vulnerable to a blow from the side of the face, which can produce a fracture with inward displacement of the fragments centrally and outward displacement of the fragments at the zygomatic and temporal ends of the arch (Figure 7-13).

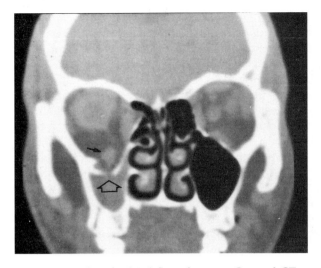

Figure 7-12   CT of orbital floor fracture. Coronal CT scan using bone window shows fractured orbital floor as double-hinged trap door with separation in center (*open arrow*). There is opacification of right maxillary sinus. Notice displacement of inferior rectus muscle (*solid arrow*) in this patient who had limited upward gaze. (Courtesy Kenneth D. Dolan, MD, Iowa City, Ia.)

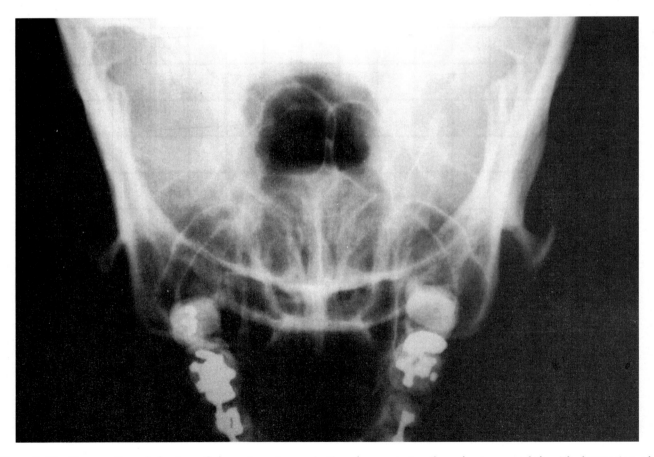

Figure 7-13   Zygomatic arch fracture. Submentovertex projection demonstrates three fractures on left with depression of zygomatic arch. (Courtesy Kenneth D. Dolan, MD, Iowa City, Ia.)

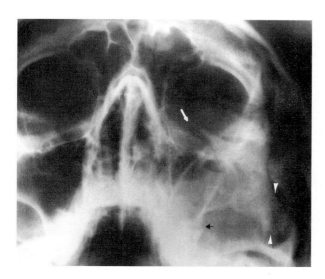

Figure 7-14 Tripod fracture. Interruption of orbital rim *(white arrow),* lateral maxillary fracture *(black arrow),* and undisplaced zygomatic arch fracture *(arrowheads)* are present. (From Dolan K, Jacoby C, Smoker W: *RadioGraphics* 4:576-663, 1984.)

Zygomatic arch fractures are best demonstrated on underexposed films taken in the basal (submentovertex) projection ("jug handle" view).

A tripod fracture consists of fractures of the zygomatic arch and the orbital floor or rim combined with separation of the zygomaticofrontal suture (Figure 7-14). It is so named because it reflects separation of the zygoma from its three principal attachments. The resulting free-floating zygoma may cause facial disfigurement if not diagnosed and properly treated.

The mandible is a prominent, exposed segment of the facial skeleton and is thus a common site for both intentional and accidental trauma. Plain radiographs with oblique views, combined with Panorex tomography, can demonstrate most mandibular fractures (Figure 7-15). The angle of the mandible is the most frequent site of fracture, though fractures can involve any portion of the body and the condylar and coronoid processes. Because the mandible functions essentially as a bony ring, bilateral fractures are common.

LeFort fractures refer to severe injuries in which separation at the fracture site results in the formation of a large, complex detached fragment that is unstable and may have its position altered relative to its site of origin. LeFort fractures involve bilateral and horizontal fractures of the maxillae and are classified as types I, II, or III, depending on the extent of injury (Figure 7-16).

▪ Tumors of the Central Nervous System

Intracranial neoplasms present clinically with seizure disorders or gradual neurologic deficits (difficulty thinking, slow comprehension, weakness, headache). The specific clinical presentation and radiographic appearance depend on the location of the tumor and the site of the subsequent mass effect. MRI is generally considered to be the most sensitive technique for detecting most suspected brain tumors. In general, both the tumor and its surrounding edema have high signal intensity on T_2-weighted images. After the intravenous injection of contrast material, the enhancing tumor usually can

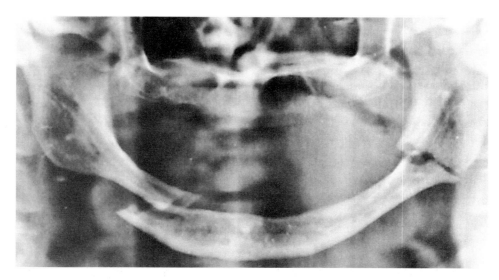

Figure 7-15 Mandibular fracture. Panorex examination in edentulous (without teeth) patient shows fractures of left angle and right body of mandible. (From Rogers LF: *Radiology of skeletal trauma,* New York, 1982, Churchill Livingstone.)

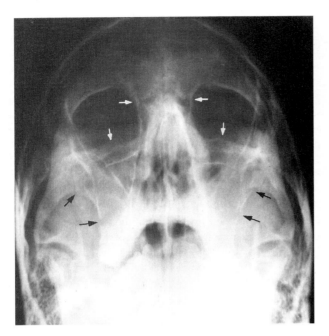

Figure 7-16 LeFort II fracture. Waters's projection shows large separated fragment produced by multiple fractures *(arrows)*. (From Dolan K, Jacoby C, Smoker W: *RadioGraphics* 4:576-663, 1984.)

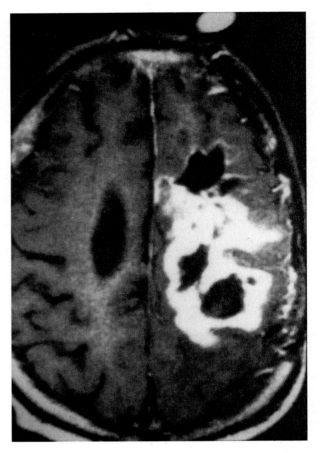

Figure 7-17 Glioblastoma multiforme. Axial T_1-weighted MR scan shows intense contrast enhancement of this complex necrotic mass. (From Eisenberg RL: *Clinical imaging: an atlas of differential diagnosis,* Gaithersburg, Md, 1992, Aspen.)

be distinguished from nonenhancing edema on T_1-weighted scans (Figure 7-17). In addition to its exquisite sensitivity in detecting pathologic alteration of normal tissue constituents, MRI provides excellent delineation of tumor extent and can show associated abnormalities such as hydrocephalus. This modality is of special value in imaging neoplasms of the brainstem and posterior fossa, which may be poorly seen on CT.

CT with contrast enhancement is an excellent examination for evaluating a patient with suspected brain tumor. It is of special value for detecting punctate or larger calcification that cannot be shown by MRI. Although skull radiographs were used in the past to demonstrate tumoral calcification, bone erosion, and displacement of the calcified pineal gland, plain films are no longer indicated, since this information can be more effectively obtained on CT scans.

Before the advent of CT, cerebral arteriography was used to show such evidence of brain tumors as mass effect, contralateral displacement of midline arteries and veins, abnormal vessels with tumor staining, and early venous filling. At present, the major use of arteriography is for precise delineation of the arterial and venous anatomy before surgical therapy and for evaluation of those cases in which a vascular anomaly is a strong consideration in the differential diagnosis of a tumor. Radionuclide brain scans have a relatively high rate of detection of cerebral tumors but are far less specific than CT or MRI.

Glioma

Gliomas are the most common primary brain tumors. They spread by direct extension and can cross from one cerebral hemisphere to the other through connecting white matter tracts such as the corpus callosum. Gliomas have a peak incidence in middle adult life and are infrequent in persons less than 30 years of age.

Glioblastomas are highly malignant lesions that are predominantly cerebral, though similar tumors may occur in the brainstem, cerebellum, or spinal cord. Astrocytomas are slowly growing tumors that have an infiltrative character and can form large cavities or pseudocysts. Favored sites are the cerebrum, cerebellum, thalamus, optic chiasm, and pons.

Less frequent types of gliomas are ependymoma, medulloblastoma, and oligodendrocytoma. Ependy-

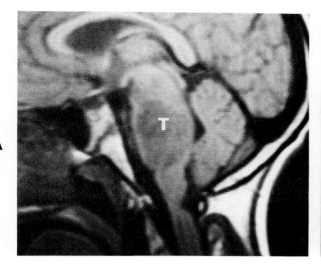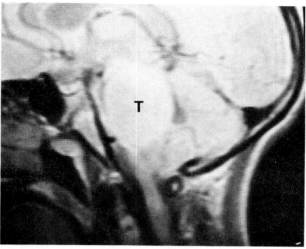

Figure 7-18 Brainstem glioma. Sagittal MR scans show enlargement of brainstem involving pons and midbrain. Notice that various imaging techniques can alter characteristics of tumor (T). On T_1-weighted image, **A,** tumor is gray (low-intensity signal); on T_2-weighted image, **B,** tumor now appears white (high-intensity signal).

momas most commonly arise from the walls of the fourth ventricle, especially in children, and from the lateral ventricles in adults. Medulloblastomas are rapidly growing tumors that develop in the posterior part of the vermis in children and, rarely, in the cerebellar hemisphere in adults. The tumor tends to spread through the subarachnoid space, with metastatic deposits occurring anywhere within the brain or spinal column. Oligodendrocytomas are slow-growing lesions that usually arise in the cerebrum and have a tendency to calcify.

On MRI scans (Figure 7-18), gliomas typically appear as masses of high signal intensity on T_2-weighted images. They may be of low intensity or isointense on T_1-weighted sequences.

On noncontrast CT scans, gliomas most commonly are seen as single, nonhomogeneous masses. Low-grade astrocytomas tend to be low-density lesions (Figure 7-19); glioblastomas most frequently contain areas of both increased and decreased density, though a broad spectrum of CT appearances can occur. Edema is often seen in the adjacent subcortical white matter. After the intravenous injection of contrast material, virtually all gliomas are enhanced, with the most malignant lesions tending to be enhanced to the greatest degree (see Figure 7-17). The most common pattern is an irregular ring of contrast enhancement, representing solid vascularized tumor, surrounding a central low-density area of necrosis. Contrast enhancement also can appear as patches of increased density distributed irregularly throughout a low-density lesion or as

rounded nodules of increased density within the mass.

Meningioma

Meningioma is a benign tumor that arises from arachnoid lining cells and is attached to the dura. The most common sites of meningioma are the

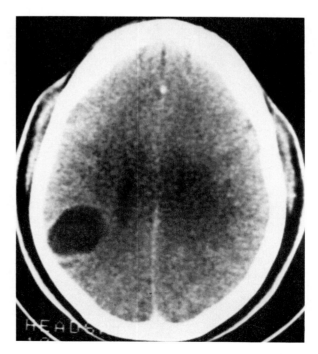

Figure 7-19 Cystic astrocytoma. CT scan shows hypodense mass with thin rim of contrast enhancement.

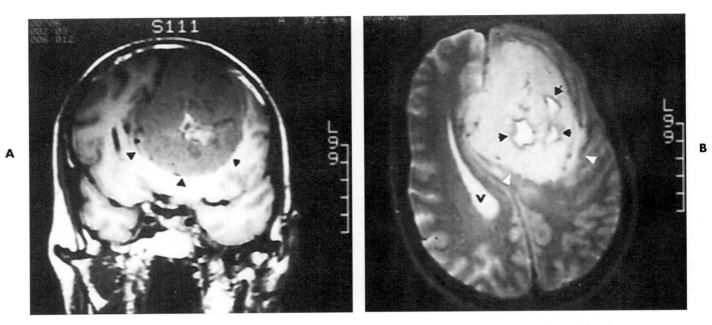

Figure 7-20   Meningioma. Huge mass *(arrowheads)* that appears hypointense on T_1-weighted coronal MR scan, **A,** and hyperintense on T_2-weighted image, **B.** Notice dramatic shift of ventricle *(v)* caused by mass effect of tumor. Arrows point to areas of hemorrhage within neoplasm *(arrowheads).*

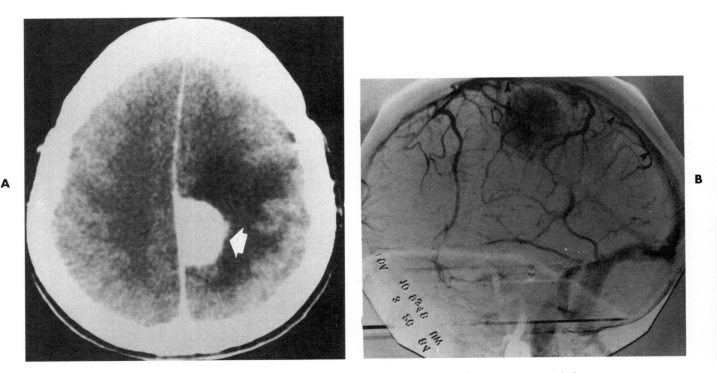

Figure 7-21   Meningioma. **A,** CT scan after intravenous injection of contrast material shows uniformly enhancing mass *(arrow)* with surrounding low-density edema attached to falx. **B,** Venous phase of carotid arteriogram shows characteristic prominent vascular blush *(arrow)* of meningioma. Notice that superior sagittal sinus *(arrowheads)* is patent.

convexity of the calvarium, olfactory groove, tuberculum sellae, parasagittal region, Sylvian fissure, cerebellopontine angle, and spinal canal.

Because meningiomas tend to be isointense with brain on both T_1- and T_2-weighted images, anatomic distortion is the key to the MRI diagnosis (Figure 7-20). A thin rim of low intensity may separate the tumor from adjacent brain. Calcification within a meningioma may produce nonuniform signal or focal signal void. Surrounding edema may make the lesion easier to identify. Just as the detection of meningiomas by CT is facilitated by the use of iodinated contrast material, paramagnetic contrast agents can enhance the detection of meningiomas on MRI.

CT typically shows a meningioma as a rounded, sharply delineated, isodense or hyperdense tumor abutting a dural surface. Calcification often is seen within the mass on noncontrast scans. After the intravenous injection of contrast material, there is intense homogeneous enhancement, which reflects the highly vascular nature of the tumor (Figure 7-21).

Pronounced dilatation of meningeal and diploic vessels, which provide part of the blood supply to the tumor, may produce prominent grooves in the calvarium on plain films of the skull. Calvarial hyperostosis (increased density) may develop because of invasion of the bone by tumor cells that stimulate osteoblastic activity. Dense calcification or granular psammomatous deposits may be seen within the tumor (Figure 7-22).

Arteriography can demonstrate the feeding arteries, which most commonly arise from both the internal and external carotid artery circulation. Preoperative embolization of the external carotid artery supply can decrease the amount of blood loss at surgery.

Acoustic neuroma

Acoustic neuroma is a slowly growing benign tumor that may occur as a solitary lesion or as part of the syndrome of neurofibromatosis. The tumor arises from Schwann cells in the vestibular portion of the auditory (eighth cranial) nerve. It usually originates in the internal auditory canal and extends into the cerebellopontine angle cistern.

MRI scans (T_1-weighted) exquisitely show the tumor as a focal or generalized enlargement of the eighth cranial nerve. This technique can even demonstrate small intracanalicular tumors confined to the internal auditory canal, which may be impossible to show on CT unless contrast material (metrizamide or air) is administered into the ventricular system (Figure 7-23). CT scans demonstrate enlargement and erosion of the internal auditory canal and a uniformly enhancing mass in the cerebellopontine angle (Figure 7-24). Very large tumors may compress the fourth ventricle and lead to the development of hydrocephalus.

Pituitary adenoma

Pituitary adenomas, almost all of which arise in the anterior lobe, constitute more than 10% of all intracranial tumors. Most are nonsecreting **chromophobe adenomas.** As chromophobe tumors enlarge, the

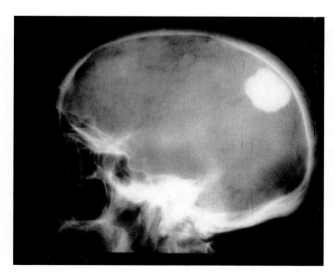

Figure 7-22 Parietal meningioma. Plain skull film shows dense calcification in tumor.

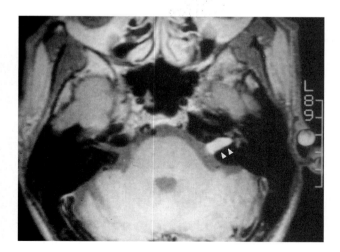

Figure 7-23 Acoustic neuroma. MR scan shows considerable contrast enhancement of the left-sided lesion (*arrowheads*). Notice the normal neural structures on the right. (From Eisenberg RL: *Clinical imaging: an atlas of differential diagnosis,* Gaithersburg, Md, 1992, Aspen.)

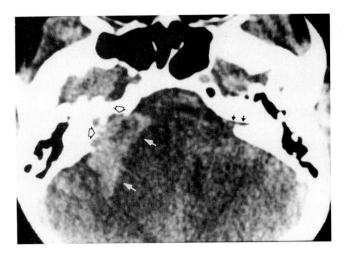

Figure 7-24 Acoustic neuroma. CT scan shows widening and erosion of right internal auditory canal *(open arrows)* associated with large extra-axial mass *(white arrows)* in right cerebellopontine angle. Solid black arrows point to normal internal auditory canal on left.
(From Williams AL, Haughton VM: *Cranial computed tomography,* St Louis, 1985, Mosby.)

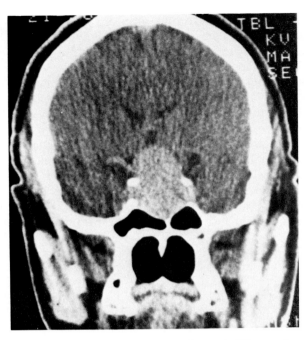

Figure 7-25 Pituitary adenoma. Coronal CT scan shows enhancing mass filling and extending out from pituitary fossa. Notice erosion of base of sella.

adjoining secreting cells within the sella turcica are compressed, leading to diminished secretion and decreased levels of growth hormone, gonadotropins, thyrotropic hormone, and adrenocorticotrophic hormone (ACTH). Large chromophobe adenomas can extend upward to distort the region of the optic chiasm, whereas lateral expansion of tumor can compress the cranial nerves passing within the cavernous sinus.

Hormone-secreting pituitary tumors can cause clinical symptoms even if too small to produce mechanical mass effect. Hypersecretion of growth hormone results in gigantism in adolescents (before the epiphyses have closed) and acromegaly in adults (after the epiphyses have closed). Excess secretion of ACTH by a pituitary tumor results in the hypersecretion of steroid hormones from the adrenal cortex and symptoms of Cushing's disease. Hypersecretion of thyroid-stimulating hormone (TSH) leads to hyperthyroidism; excess secretion of prolactin by a pituitary tumor in women causes the amenorrhea/galactorrhea syndrome.

Thin-section CT and MRI are the examinations of choice in evaluating a patient with a suspected pituitary tumor. After the intravenous administration of contrast material, large pituitary tumors are typically homogeneous and hyperdense with respect to surrounding brain tissue. Most pituitary microadenomas are of lower density than the normal pituitary gland. CT can also demonstrate adjacent bone erosion, tumor extension beyond the con-

fines of the sella, and impression on nearby structures such as the third ventricle, optic nerves, or optic chiasm (Figure 7-25).

Coronal T_1-weighted MRI scans show a microadenoma as a low-intensity focal lesion associated with contralateral deviation of the pituitary stalk and an upwardly convex contour of the gland (Figure 7-26). The intravenous injection of paramagnetic contrast material significantly improves diagnostic sensitivity in patients with tiny secreting pituitary tumors. Immediately after injection, small microadenomas appear hypointense relative to the normally enhancing pituitary gland. On delayed scans, the neoplasm may become hyperintense relative to the normal gland.

Although plain skull radiographs can show enlargement of the sella turcica, erosion of the dorsum sellae, and a double floor resulting from the unequal downward growth of the mass, this imaging modality now is of value only in the incidental detection of sellar enlargement on films taken for other purposes.

Craniopharyngioma

Craniopharyngioma is a benign tumor that contains both cystic and solid components. The lesion usually originates above the sella turcica, depressing the optic chiasm and extending up into the third ventricle. Less commonly, a craniopharyngioma lies

A   **B**

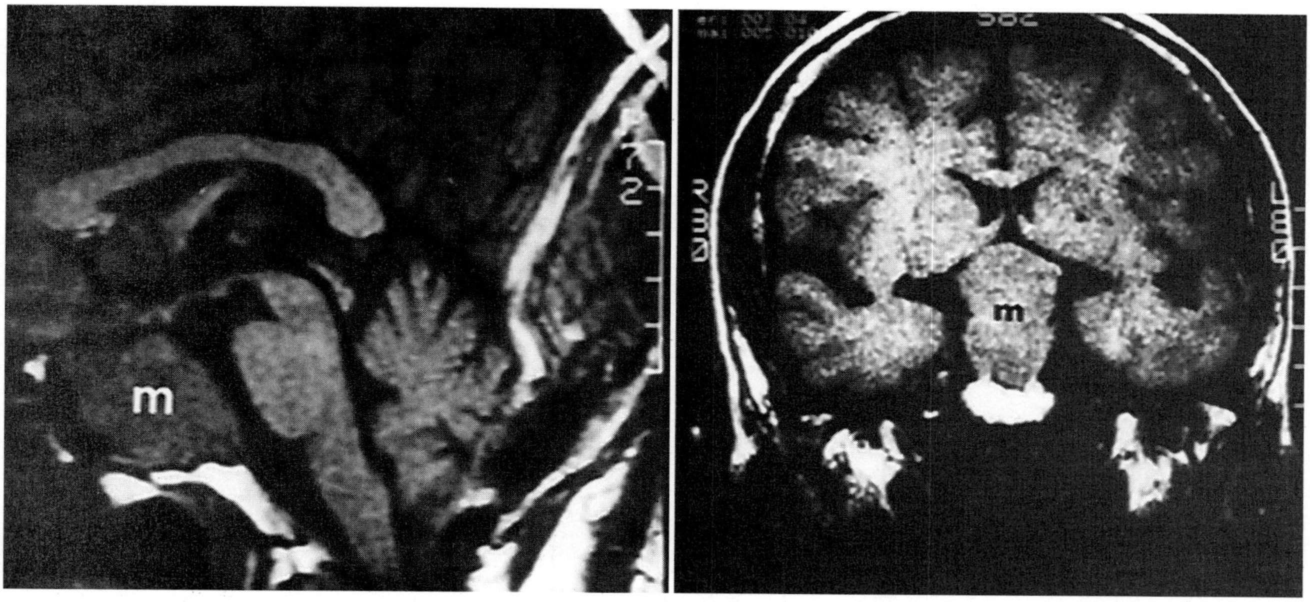

Figure 7-26   Pituitary adenoma. **A,** Sagittal and, **B,** coronal MR scans demonstrate large mass *(m)* that arises from sella turcica and extends upward to fill suprasellar cistern.

within the sella, where it compresses the pituitary gland and may erode adjacent bony walls.

Most craniopharyngiomas have calcification that can be detected on plain skull films or CT scans (Figure 7-27). In cystic lesions, the shell-like calcification lies along the periphery of the tumor; in mixed or solid lesions, the calcification is nodular, amorphous, or cloudlike. CT clearly demonstrates the cystic and solid components of the mass. After the intravenous administration of contrast material, there is variable enhancement, depending on the

type of calcification and the amount of cystic components within the tumor (Figure 7-28). CT can also demonstrate hydrocephalus if the tumor has expanded to obstruct one or both of the foramina of Monro.

The MRI appearance of craniopharyngioma depends on the tissue components of the tumor. Cystic areas have low signal intensity on T_1-weighted scans and high signal intensity on T_2-weighted scans; fat-containing regions have high signal intensity on T_1-weighted images and are of moderate intensity on T_2-weighted scans (Figure 7-29). Large areas of calcification appear dark on all imaging sequences.

Pineal tumors

The most common tumors of the pineal gland are germinomas and teratomas, both of which occur predominantly in males less than 25 years of age and may be associated with precocious puberty.

Sagittal MR scans are ideal for showing pineal tumors, which typically compress the midbrain from above and lift up the splenium of the corpus callosum (Figure 7-30). Although most germinomas are isointense to brain on both T_1- and T_2-weighted images, teratomas may have mixed signal intensity because they contain cystic components and fat.

On CT, germinomas appear as hyperdense or isodense masses that tend to deform or displace the posterior aspect of the third ventricle and often obliterate the quadrigeminal cistern. Punctate calci-

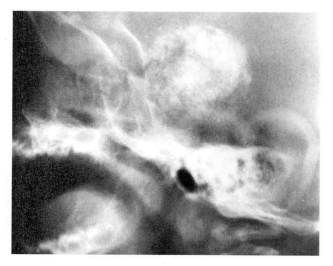

Figure 7-27   Craniopharyngioma. Plain skull radiograph shows large suprasellar calcified mass in child.

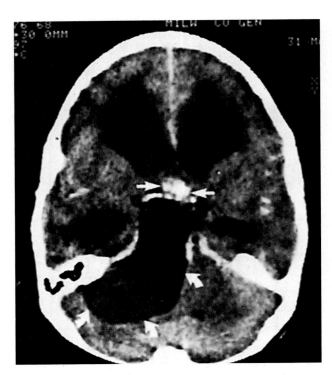

Figure 7-28   Craniopharyngioma. CT scan shows rim-enhancing tumor that contains dense calcification (straight arrows) and large cystic component *(curved arrows)* that extends into posterior fossa. Notice associated hydrocephalus. (From Williams AL, Haughton VM: *Cranial computed tomography,* St Louis, 1985, Mosby.)

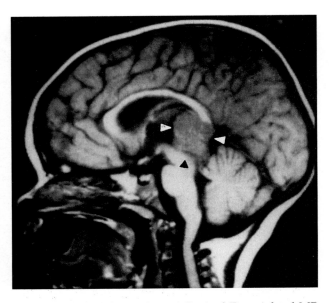

Figure 7-30   Pineal germinoma. Sagittal T_1-weighted MR scan shows a large isointense mass *(arrowheads)* that compresses the midbrain *(arrow)* and elevates the splenium of the corpus callosum. (From Eisenberg RL: *Clinical imaging: an atlas of differential diagnosis,* Gaithersburg, Md, 1992, Aspen.)

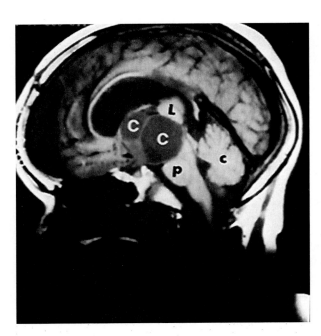

Figure 7-29   Craniopharyngioma. Sagittal MR scan demonstrates large multiloculated suprasellar mass with cystic *(C)* and lipid *(L)* components. *p,* Pons; *c,* cerebellum.

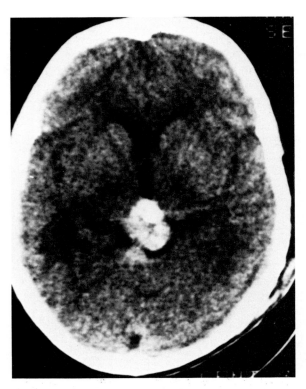

Figure 7-31   Pineal teratoma. Nonenhanced CT scan shows inhomogeneous mass containing large amount of calcification.

fication can often be detected within the mass (Figure 7-31). Intense enhancement of the tumor occurs after the injection of contrast material. Teratomas in the pineal region typically appear as hypodense masses with internal calcification. Occasionally, other formed elements (e.g., teeth) can occur. Contrast enhancement is usually much less pronounced than with germinomas. Large pineal tumors may cause obstructive hydrocephalus with ventricular dilatation.

A small number of tumors with the histologic appearance of pinealomas appear elsewhere in the brain at some distance from the normal pineal gland. These "ectopic pinealomas" generally occur in the anterior aspect of the third ventricle or within the suprasellar cistern. They may produce a clinical triad of bitemporal hemianopsia, hypopituitarism, and diabetes insipidus that simulates a craniopharyngioma.

Chordoma

Chordomas are tumors that arise from remnants of the notochord (the embryonic neural tube). Although any part of the vertebral column and base of the skull can be involved, the most common sites are the clivus and the lower lumbosacral region. The tumors are locally invasive but do not metastasize. Chordomas arising at the base of the skull produce

the striking clinical picture of multiple cranial nerve palsies on one or both sides combined with a retropharyngeal mass and erosion of the clivus.

On plain radiographs, a chordoma tends to be a bulky mass causing ill-defined bone destruction or cortical expansion. Flocculent (fluffy or cloudlike) calcification may develop within a large soft-tissue mass (Figure 7-32, *A*). On CT scans, chordomas at the base of the skull tend to appear as lesions that are slightly denser than brain tissue and often demonstrate moderate contrast enhancement (Figure 7-32, *B*). Sagittal MR scans well demonstrate the clival origin of the mass and its effect on surrounding structures (Figure 7-33).

Metastatic carcinoma

Carcinomas usually reach the brain by hematogenous spread. Infrequently, epithelial malignancies of the nasopharynx can spread into the cranial cavity through neural foramina or by direct invasion through bone. The most common neoplasms that metastasize to the brain arise in the lung and breast. Melanomas, colon carcinomas, and testicular and kidney tumors also cause brain metastases.

On T_2-weighted MRI scans, metastases appear as single or multiple masses of high signal intensity that most commonly are situated at the gray matter–white matter junction (Figure 7-34). Additional le-

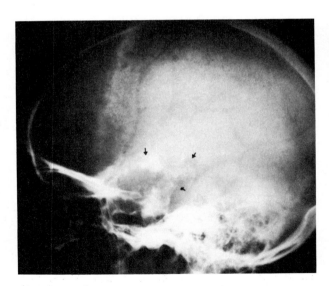
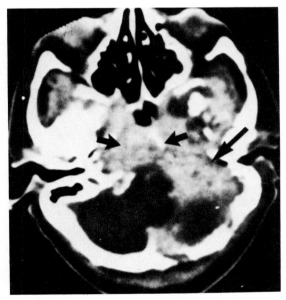

Figure 7-32   Chordoma. **A,** Plain skull radiograph shows dense calcification *(arrows)* within large soft-tissue mass that has an eroded dorsum sellae and upper portion of clivus. **B,** In another patient, CT scan shows enlarging mass with destruction of entire clivus *(short arrows)* and only small bone fragments remaining. Left petrous pyramid is also destroyed *(long arrow)*. (**B** from Levine HL, Kleefield J, Rao KCVG: In Lee SH, Rao KCVG, editors: *Cranial computed tomography,* New York, 1983, McGraw-Hill.)

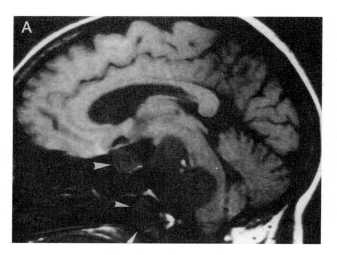

Figure 7-33 Clival chordoma. Sagittal MR scan shows a low-intensity multilobulated mass deforming and displacing the brainstem, destroying the clivus, and extending into the sella turcica *(upper arrowhead)* and nasopharynx *(two lower arrowheads).* (From Bilaniuk LT: *Semin Roentgenol* 25:155-173, 1990.)

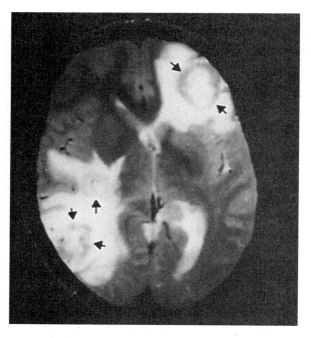

Figure 7-34 Metastases. Axial MR scan demonstrates three large masses *(arrows)* surrounded by extensive high-signal-intensity edema.

sions can often be demonstrated after the injection of a paramagnetic contrast agent. On CT, brain metastases typically appear as multiple enhancing lesions of various sizes with surrounding sizes of low-density edema (Figures 7-35 and 7-36). On noncontrast scans, metastatic deposits may be hypodense, hyperdense, or similar in density to normal brain tissue, depending on such factors as cellular density, tumor neovascularity, and degree of necrosis. In general, metastases from lung, breast, kidney, and colon tend to be hypodense or isodense; hyperdense metastases often reflect hemorrhage or calcification within or adjacent to the tumor.

Single metastatic deposits in the brain may be indistinguishable from primary tumors. However, since primary brain neoplasms are unusual in older patients, single lesions in this population should be suggestive of metastatic disease.

▪ Infections of the Central Nervous System

With the widespread availability of antibiotics, infectious disease of the CNS is now much less common than previously. Nevertheless, bacterial, fungal, viral, or protozoal organisms can infect the brain parenchyma, meningeal linings, and bones of the skull.

Meningitis

Meningitis is an acute inflammation of the pia mater and arachnoid, the membranes covering the brain and spinal cord. Infecting organisms can reach the

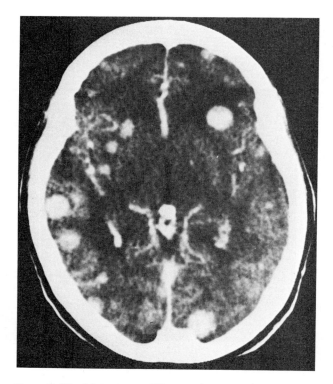

Figure 7-35 Metastases. CT scan shows multiple enhancing masses of various shapes and sizes representing hematogenous metastases from carcinoma of breast.

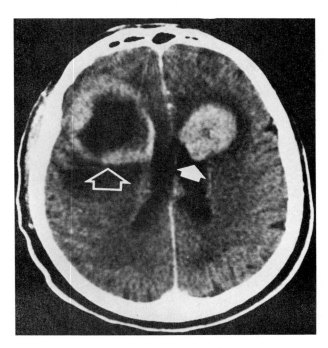

Figure 7-36 Metastases. CT shows enhancing metastases from squamous cell carcinoma of lung that are both ring enhancing *(open arrow)* and solid *(solid arrow).*

meninges from a middle ear, upper respiratory tract, or frontal sinus infection, or they can be spread through the bloodstream from an infection in the lungs or other site. Bacterial meningitis is most commonly caused by *Haemophilus influenzae* in neonates and young children and by meningococci and pneumococci in adolescents and adults. Viral meningitis may be caused by mumps, poliovirus, and occasionally by herpes simplex. A chronic form of meningitis can be caused by tuberculous infection.

Although the meninges initially demonstrate vascular congestion, edema, and minute hemorrhages, the underlying brain remains intact. MR and CT scans are normal during most acute episodes of meningitis and remain normal if appropriate therapy is promptly instituted. If the infection extends to involve the cortex of the brain and the ependymal lining of the ventricles, contrast studies may show characteristic meningeal enhancement in the basal cisterns, interhemispheric fissure, and choroid plexus (Figure 7-37). Diffuse brain swelling may symmetrically compress the lateral and third ventricles. MR and CT are also of value in the early detection of such complications of acute meningitis as arterial or venous vasculitis or thrombosis with infarction, hydrocephalus caused by adhesions or thickening of the arachnoid at the base of the brain, subdural effusion or empyema, and brain abscess.

Although acute bacterial meningitis is best evaluated by MRI or CT, plain films of the sinuses and

skull can demonstrate cranial osteomyelitis, paranasal sinusitis, or a skull fracture as the underlying cause of meningitis. Chest radiographs may show a silent area of pneumonia or a lung abscess.

Encephalitis

Encephalitis is a viral inflammation of the brain and meninges that produces symptoms ranging from mild headache and fever to severe cerebral dysfunction, seizures, and coma. Encephalitis caused by herpes simplex is an often fatal, fulminant process. The earliest and predominant findings in herpetic encephalitis are poorly marginated areas in the temporal lobes that have high signal intensity of T_2-weighted MR images and are of low density on CT. These changes probably represent a combination of tissue necrosis and focal brain edema. A mass effect is common and may be seen as a midline shift or as a focal mass compressing the ventricles or the Sylvian cisterns. Compromise of the blood-brain barrier in areas of rapid, more progressive hemorrhagic necrosis results in a nonhomogeneous pattern of contrast enhancement. Follow-up scans typically demonstrate widespread low-density encephalomalacia involving the temporal and frontal lobes.

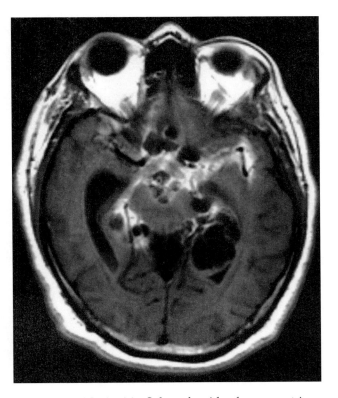

Figure 7-37 Meningitis. Subarachnoid enhancement in the basal cisterns and left sylvian fissure in a patient with cysticercosis. (From Ross MR, Davis DO, Mark AS: *MRI Decisions* 4:24-33, 1990.)

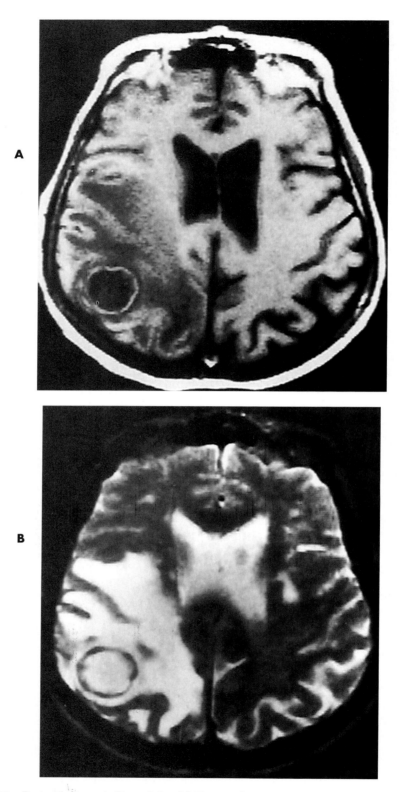

Figure 7-38   Brain abscess. **A,** T_1-weighted MR scan shows a central hypointense necrotic mass with an isointense capsule surrounded by low-signal-intensity edema. **B,** On the T_2-weighted image, the hypointense capsule is highlighted by increased signal centrally and peripherally. (From Edelman RR, Hesselink JR, editors: *Clinical magnetic resonance imaging,* Philadelphia, 1990, Saunders.)

In addition to confirming the clinical diagnosis and excluding the presence of an abscess or tumor, MR and CT are important in the evaluation of herpes simplex encephalitis to indicate the best site for biopsy. A definitive diagnosis of herpes infection is essential before beginning treatment with adenine arabinoside, a chemotherapeutic agent that may be neurotoxic, mutagenic, and carcinogenic.

Brain abscess

Brain abscesses usually are a result of chronic infections of the middle ear, paranasal sinuses, or mastoid air cells or to systemic infections (pneumonia, bacterial endocarditis, osteomyelitis). The most common organisms causing brain abscesses are streptococci. In patients with AIDS, brain abscesses are often caused by unusual organisms such as toxoplasmosis and cryptococcosis.

The earliest sign of brain abscess on MR or CT is an area of abnormal density with poorly defined borders and a mass effect reflecting vascular congestion and edema. Further progression of the inflammatory process leads to cerebral softening, which may undergo necrosis and liquefaction and result in a true abscess. On T_1-weighted MR images, an abscess appears as a hypointense mass with isointense capsule surrounded by low-signal edema (Figure 7-38, A). Both the mass and edema become hyperintense on T_2-weighted images (Figure 7-38, B). After the intravenous administration of contrast material, an oval or circular peripheral ring of contrast enhancement outlines the abscess capsule. Although the wall is usually thin and of uniform thickness, an irregularly thick wall may be seen that mimics the wall of a malignant glioma. Multiple abscesses indicate the possibility of septic emboli from a systemic infection (Figure 7-39).

MR and CT can be used to assess the results of therapy of a brain abscess and to document complications. These modalities can demonstrate the often fatal intraventricular rupture of an abscess and the development of increased intracranial pressure, which may lead to brain herniation.

Plain skull radiographs may show evidence of underlying sinusitis, mastoiditis, or osteomyelitis, though this is better evaluated by CT scanning with bone-window settings. Infection by gas-forming organisms occasionally produces an air-fluid level within the abscess cavity.

Subdural empyema

Subdural empyema is a suppurative process in the space between the inner surface of the dura and the outer surface of the arachnoid. The most common cause of subdural empyema is the spread of infec-

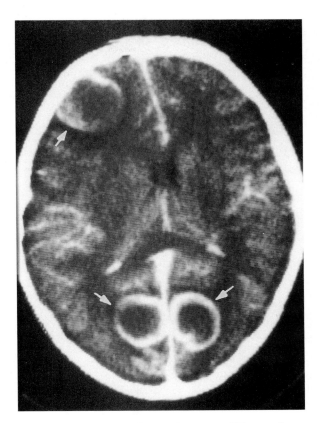

Figure 7-39 Pyogenic brain abscesses. CT scan shows one frontal and two occipital lesions *(arrows)* with relatively thin, uniform rings of enhancement.

tion from the frontal or ethmoid sinuses. Less frequently, subdural empyema may be a result of mastoiditis, middle ear infection, purulent meningitis, penetrating wounds to the skull, craniectomy, or osteomyelitis of the skull. Subdural empyema is often bilateral and is associated with a high mortality even if properly treated. The most common location of a subdural empyema is over the cerebral convexity; the base of the skull is usually spared.

MRI is the procedure of choice in evaluating the patient with suspected subdural empyema. Unlike CT, MR is free from bony artifacts adjacent to the inner table of the skull. In addition, signal characteristics may permit differentiation between benign effusions and infected empyemas. Noncontrast scans demonstrate a crescentic or lentiform (lenslike), extra-axial fluid collection (representing pus) adjacent to the inner border of the skull or the falx (Figure 7-40). There is compression and displacement of the ipsilateral ventricular structures. After the intravenous administration of contrast material, a narrow zone of enhancement of relatively uniform thickness separates the extracerebral collection from the brain surface. MRI can also demonstrate involvement of the adjacent parenchyma by means of retro-

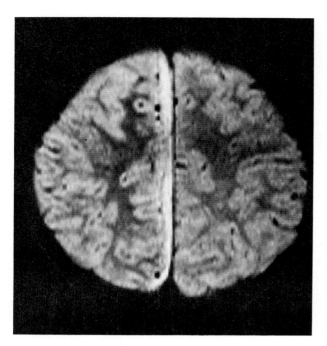

Figure 7-40 Subdural empyema. T_2-weighted MR scan demonstrates high signal intensity of the fluid collections along the falx. (From Stark DD, Bradley WG: *Magnetic resonance imaging*, ed 2, St Louis, 1991, Mosby.)

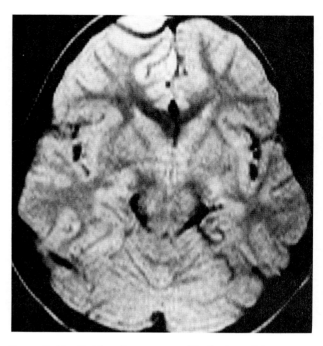

Figure 7-41 Epidural empyema. Black rim of dura delineates the epidural fluid collection in the right frontal region. (From Stark DD, Bradley WG: *Magnetic resonance imaging*, ed 2, St Louis, 1991, Mosby.)

grade thrombophlebitis with resultant infarction or abscess formation, signs associated with a poor prognosis.

Epidural empyema

Epidural empyema (Figure 7-41) is almost invariably associated with osteomyelitis in a cranial bone originating from an infection in the ear or paranasal sinuses. The infectious process is localized outside the dural membrane and beneath the inner table of the skull. The frontal region is most frequently affected because of its close relation to the frontal sinuses and the ease with which the dura can be stripped from the bone.

Noncontrast CT scans demonstrate the epidural infection as a poorly defined area of low density adjacent to the inner table of the skull. An adjacent area of bone destruction or evidence of paranasal sinus or mastoid infection (fluid, soft-tissue thickening) often can be demonstrated on CT or plain skull radiographs. After the intravenous administration of contrast material, the inflamed dural membrane appears as a thickened zone of enhancement on the convex inner side of the lesion. If the collection lies in the midline, the attachment of the falx is displaced inward and separated from the adjacent skull, thus identifying its extradural location.

Osteomyelitis of the skull

Osteomyelitis of the skull is most commonly caused by direct extension of a suppurative process from the paranasal sinuses, mastoid air cells, or scalp. As with osteomyelitis elsewhere in the skeleton, the radiographic changes often develop 1 to 2 weeks after the onset of clinical symptoms and signs.

Acute osteomyelitis first appears radiographically as multiple small, poorly defined areas of lucency (Figure 7-42). Over the next several weeks, the lucencies enlarge and coalesce centrally with an expanding perimeter of small satellite foci. As the infection becomes more chronic (especially with syphilis, tuberculosis, or fungal infections), attempts at bone regeneration produce multiple areas of poorly defined reactive sclerosis.

▪ Vascular Disease of the Central Nervous System

The term **cerebrovascular disease** refers to any process that is caused by an abnormality of the blood vessels or blood supply to the brain. Pathologic processes causing cerebrovascular disease include abnormalities of the vessel wall, occlusion by thrombus or emboli, rupture of blood vessels with subsequent hemorrhage, and decreased cerebral blood flow caused by lowered blood pressure or narrowed

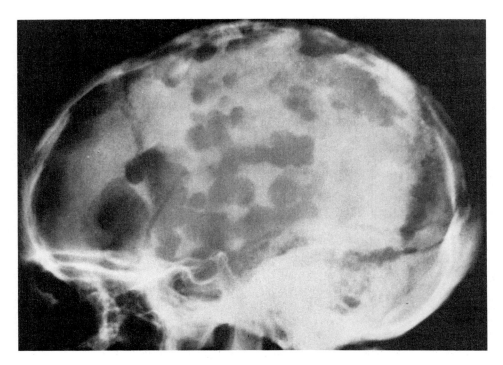

Figure 7-42 Osteomyelitis of skull (blastomycosis). Diffuse areas of osteolytic destruction affect most of calvarium.

lumen caliber. Cerebrovascular diseases include arteriosclerosis, hypertensive hemorrhage, arteritis, aneurysms, and arteriovenous malformations.

The radiographic evaluation of cerebrovascular disease depends on the presenting symptoms and the most likely diagnosis. For ease of classification, patients with cerebrovascular disease can be divided into three categories: completed stroke, transient ischemic attacks (TIAS), and intracranial hemorrhage.

Stroke syndrome

The term **stroke** denotes the sudden and dramatic development of a focal neurologic deficit, which may vary from dense hemiplegia (paralysis on one side of the body) and coma to only a trivial neurologic disorder. The specific neurologic defect depends on the arteries involved. Strokes most commonly involve the circulation of the internal carotid arteries and are seen with symptoms that include acute hemiparesis (weakness of one side of the body) and dysarthria (difficulty speaking).

The purpose of radiographic evaluation in the acute stroke patient is not to confirm the diagnosis of a stroke but to exclude other processes that can simulate the clinical findings (parenchymal hemorrhage, subdural hematoma). Although the abrupt onset of a stroke may permit differentiation from other conditions that have a more gradual onset of symptoms, patients with focal neurologic deficits of various causes may initially be found comatose, so that the history of gradual onset is not elicited. Obviously, it is essential to exclude an intracranial hemorrhage before considering the possibility of treating the stroke patient with anticoagulant therapy.

Noncontrast CT (or MRI, if available) is the examination of choice for the evaluation of the stroke patient. Intravenous contrast material is contraindicated because it is a toxic substance that can cross the disrupted blood-brain barrier in the region of a cerebral infarct and lead to increased edema and a slower recovery for the patient. CT and MRI scans are normal in patients with small infarctions and in the early hours of large infarctions. The initial appearance (8 to 24 hours) of a cerebral infarction is a triangular or wedge-shaped area of hypodensity on CT (Figure 7-43) and high signal on T_2-weighted MRI sequences involving both the cortex and the underlying white matter down to the ventricular surface. The abnormality is confined to the vascular territory of the involved artery. Although little or no mass effect is evident during the first day, progressive edema produces a mass effect that is maximal 7 to 10 days after the acute event. As an infarct ages, brain tissue atrophies, and the adjacent sulci and

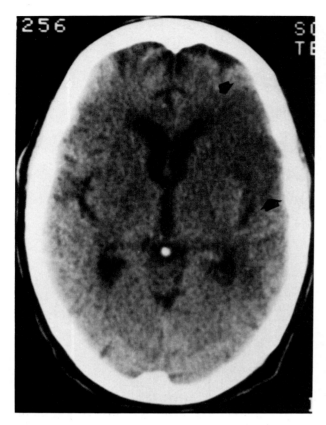

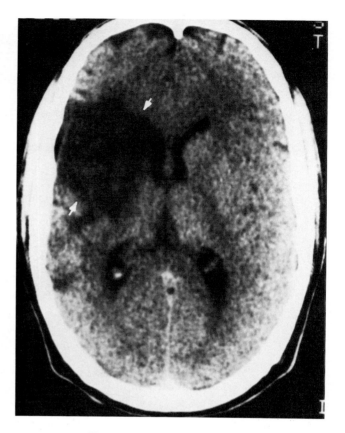

Figure 7-43   Acute left middle cerebral artery infarct. CT scan obtained 20 hours after onset of acute hemiparesis and aphasia shows obliteration of normal sulci *(arrows)* in involved hemisphere. There is low density of gray and white matter in distribution of left middle cerebral artery.

Figure 7-44   Chronic right middle cerebral artery infarct. Low-attenuation region with sharply defined borders *(arrows),* and some dilatation of adjacent ventricle.

ventricular system enlarge (Figure 7-44). In patients with classic stroke symptoms, follow-up CT or MRI scans are not indicated.

Transient ischemic attacks

Transient ischemic attacks (TIAs) present as focal neurologic deficits that completely resolve within 24 hours. They may result from emboli originating from the surface of an arteriosclerotic ulcerated plaque, which causes temporary occlusion of cerebral vessels, or from stenosis of an extracerebral artery, which leads to a reduction in critical blood perfusion. Because almost two thirds of arteriosclerotic strokes are preceded by TIAs and the 5-year cumulative risk of stroke in patients with TIAs may be as high as 50%, accurate diagnosis and appropriate treatment (antiplatelet therapy, anticoagulation therapy, or carotid endarterectomy) are essential.

The most common location of surgically treatable arteriosclerotic disease causing TIAs is the region of the carotid bifurcation in the neck. In patients with an asymptomatic bruit (rumbling noise heard by a

stethoscope) or an unclear history of a TIA, carotid duplex scanning is often the initial screening study (Figure 7-45). This technique combines high-resolution ultrasound imaging and Doppler ultrasound with spectral analysis into a "duplex" unit that avoids many of the problems associated with each of these modalities when used alone. In most cases, carotid duplex scanning can reliably determine whether there is significant disease to warrant more invasive procedures (angiography). Patients with a normal or near-normal carotid duplex scan do not need to undergo more invasive diagnostic procedures for assessment of the carotid bifurcation. Limitations of the usefulness of carotid duplex scanning include its extreme operator dependence and the fact that 10% of patients cannot be successfully imaged with carotid duplex scanning because of anatomic factors (patients with extreme high carotid bifurcations and those with short, thick necks). Using ultrasound techniques, it may be impossible to differentiate patients with a total occlusion of the internal carotid artery from those with a tiny residual lumen. This is an important clinical distinction because patients with even a small remaining

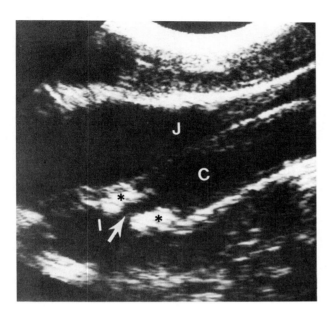

Figure 7-45 Ultrasound of cervical arteriosclerotic occlusive disease. There is severe narrowing *(arrow)* of origin of internal carotid artery *(I)* by densely echogenic arteriosclerotic plaque *(asterisks)*. *C,* Common carotid artery; *J,* jugular vein.

lumen can undergo a successful carotid endarterectomy (surgical removal of atherosclerotic plaque).

Patients with a clear-cut episode of a TIA or a neurologic deficit usually are subjected to an angiographic study for evaluating the carotid arteries. Either intravenous or intra-arterial digital subtraction angiography (DSA) or selective intra-arterial carotid arteriography can be used to demonstrate TIA-producing stenotic or ulcerative lesions that may be amenable to surgical therapy (Figures 7-46 to 7-48). Angiographic evaluation of the aortic arch and vertebral arteries is infrequently indicated in the evaluation of patients with TIAs, both because surgery on the origins of the great vessels and posterior circulation is difficult and not established and also because of the higher morbidity from arch and vertebral angiograms reported in some studies.

Intraparenchymal hemorrhage

Aside from head trauma, the principle cause of intraparenchymal hemorrhage is hypertensive vascular disease. Less frequent causes are rupture of a congenital berry aneurysm or an arteriovenous malformation. Hypertensive hemorrhages result in oval or circular collections that displace the surrounding brain and can cause a significant mass effect. Although they can occur at any location within the brain, hypertensive hemorrhages are most frequent in the basal ganglia, white matter, thalamus, cerebellar hemispheres, and pons. A frequent complication

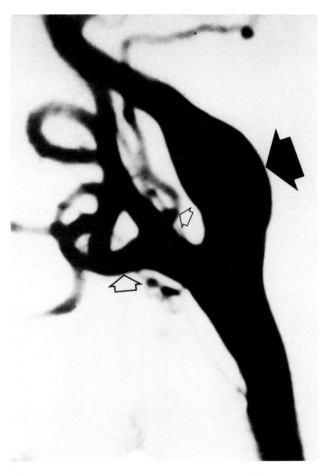

Figure 7-46 Normal carotid artery bifurcation. Common carotid arteriogram shows bulbous origin of internal carotid artery *(solid arrow)* and multiple branches of external carotid artery *(open arrows)*.

is rupture of the hemorrhage into the ventricular system or subarachnoid space. Intraparenchymal hemorrhages resulting from congenital "berry" aneurysms usually are associated with subarachnoid hemorrhage and tend to develop in regions where these congenital vascular anomalies most commonly occur. These include the sylvian fissure (middle cerebral artery) and the midline subfrontal area (anterior communicating artery). Arteriovenous malformations occur throughout the brain and tend to bleed into the white matter.

Patients with a suspected intraparenchymal hemorrhage should be evaluated with MRI or a noncontrast CT scan. A fresh hematoma appears on CT as a homogeneously dense, well-defined lesion with a round to oval configuration (Figure 7-49). Hematomas produce ventricular compression and, when large, considerable midline shift and brain herniation. Steroid therapy, especially in nontraumatic hematomas, usually controls the edema that produces

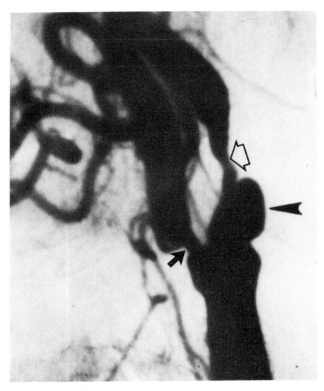

Figure 7-47   Ulceration of internal carotid artery.
Common carotid arteriogram shows ulcerated lesion
(arrowhead) at origin of internal carotid artery with
severe stenosis of internal carotid *(open arrow)* and
external carotid *(black arrow)* arteries.

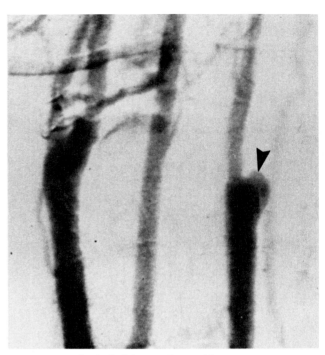

Figure 7-48   Occluded internal carotid artery.
Intravenous digital subtraction angiogram shows
occlusion of left internal carotid artery at its origin
(arrowhead).

much of the mass effect. A hematoma that is not
homogeneously dense is suggestive of hemorrhage
occurring within a tumor, an inflammatory process,
or an infarction. As the hematoma ages, its density
changes. On CT, after passing through an isodense
stage the hematoma becomes hypodense; by 6
months it appears as a well-defined, low-density
region that is often considerably smaller than the
original lesion. Contrast enhancement usually develops about the periphery of a hematoma after 7 to 10
days. On MRI, the high signal intensity within a
hematoma (caused by the conversion of normal
hemoglobin to methemoglobin) arises after a few
days and continues for several months (Figure 7-50).
Once the methemoglobin is completely converted to
paramagnetic hemosiderin, the hematoma has very
low signal intensity on T_2-weighted sequences.

Arteriography is not indicated in patients with
classic hypertensive hematomas. However, arteriography is of value in those patients in whom an
aneurysm or arteriovenous malformation is suspected as the underlying cause of the hematoma. In
patients with a suspected aneurysm, it is important
to determine the number of aneurysms, the aneu-

rysm that has ruptured, the location of the neck of
the aneurysm, and the patency of the circle of Willis.
Statistically, the largest of multiple aneurysms is the
one that has ruptured; it is rare for an aneurysm less
than 5 mm in diameter to rupture. Because an
aneurysm generally ruptures at its apex, an irregular, multiloculated dome is suggestive of a prior
rupture. Spasm in adjacent vessels and adjacent
hematomas also assist in identifying which of several aneurysms has bled.

In patients less than 20 years of age, arteriovenous
malformation is the most common cause of nontraumatic intraparenchymal hemorrhage. On MRI (Figure 7-51), a cerebrovascular malformation appears
as a mass of vascular structures of varying intensity,
depending on whether there is rapid flow (black) or
slow flow (white). On CT, the malformation consists
of an irregular tangle of vessels (best seen after the
intravenous injection of contrast material) and
greatly dilated veins draining from the central
tangle (Figure 7-52, *A*). Arteriography demonstrates
an irregular, racemose tangle of abnormal vessels
that are fed by dilated cerebral or cerebellar arteries
(Figure 7-52, *B*). There is rapid shunting of blood
into dilated, tortuous draining veins. Because of the
often multiple sources of blood flow to an arteriovenous malformation, the arteriographic evaluation

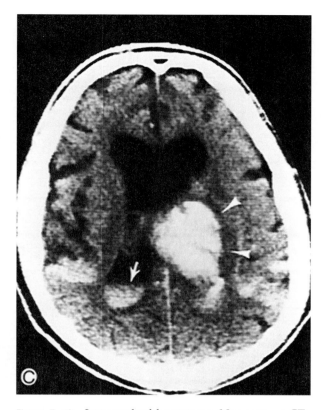

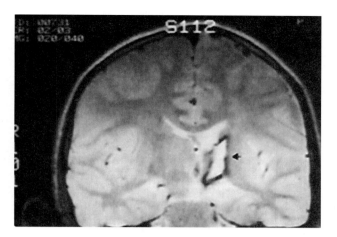

Figure 7-50 Intracerebral hematoma. Coronal T_2-weighted MR scan shows large hematoma in left thalamic region *(arrow)*. Hematoma consists of two portions: central area of increased signal intensity representing methemoglobin, and surrounding area of low signal intensity representing hemosiderin.

Figure 7-49 Intracerebral hematoma. Noncontrast CT scan shows homogeneous, high-density area in left thalamus. Low-density area *(arrowheads)* adjacent to hematoma represents associated ischemia and edema. Hematoma has entered ventricular system, and prominent cerebrospinal fluid–blood level is seen in dependent lateral ventricle *(arrow)*. Such extension of blood into ventricular system is extremely poor prognostic sign. Mass effect caused by hematoma has compressed third ventricle and foramen of Monro and resulted in obstructive enlargement of lateral ventricles. (From Drayer BP: In Rosenberg RN, Heinz ER, editors: *The clinical neurosciences. IV. Neuroradiology,* New York, 1984, Churchill Livingstone.)

should include selective injections of contrast material into both internal and external carotid arteries.

Subarachnoid hemorrhage

A major cause of subarachnoid hemorrhage is rupture of a berry aneurysm (Figure 7-53). Patients with this condition usually have a generalized excruciating headache followed by unconsciousness. The radiographic procedure of choice is a noncontrast CT scan, which can demonstrate high-density blood in the subarachnoid spaces of the basal cisterns in more than 95% of cases. Bleeding may extend into the brain parenchyma adjacent to the aneurysm. Contrast-enhanced CT scans are not indicated in subarachnoid hemorrhage, since the sur-

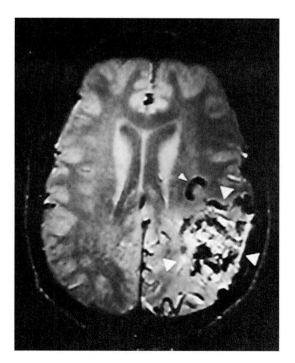

Figure 7-51 Arteriovenous malformation. Axial MR scan shows large left parietal mass *(large arrowheads)* consisting of vascular structures of varying intensity, depending on whether there is rapid flow *(black)* or slow flow *(white)*. Notice greatly dilated vessel *(small arrowhead)* that feeds malformation.

A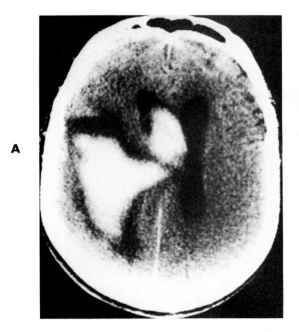

B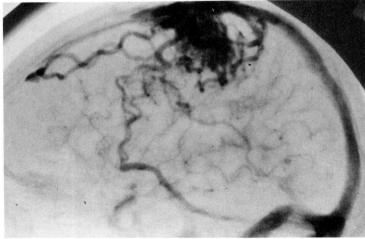

Figure 7-52 Arteriovenous malformation with hemorrhage. **A,** CT scan in 34-year-old comatose man shows high-density hemorrhage in right parietal lobe that extends into ventricular system. **B,** Carotid arteriogram shows dilated blood vessels constituting arteriovenous malformation.

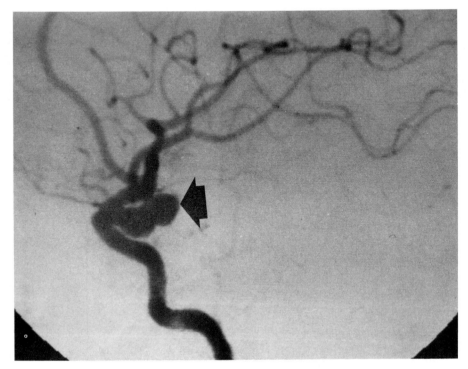

Figure 7-53 Ruptured berry aneurysm. Left carotid arteriogram demonstrates left supraclinoid aneurysm of internal carotid artery. Posterior bulge of aneurysm *(arrow)* represents site of rupture.

geon will not operate for a suspected aneurysm without an angiogram and the patient would thus be exposed to the risk of an excessive load of contrast material.

The timing of angiography in subarachnoid hemorrhage depends on the philosophy of the surgeon. Blood in the subarachnoid space is an irritant that causes vasospasm of the vessels of the circle of Willis and middle cerebral artery. This vasospasm, which can lead to cerebral ischemia and frank infarction, is greatest 3 to 14 days after the acute episode. If emergency surgery within the first 72 hours after the hemorrhage is planned, emergency selective angiography is indicated. If surgical intervention is to be delayed, angiography should be postponed until just before surgery. The most common locations for berry aneurysms are the origins of the posterior cerebral and anterior communicating arteries and the trifurcation of the middle cerebral artery. Because of the 20% incidence of multiple aneurysms, the angiographic procedure should include evaluation of the internal carotid and vertebral arteries bilaterally.

▪ Multiple Sclerosis

Multiple sclerosis is a demyelinating disorder that presents as recurrent attacks of focal neurologic deficits that primarily involve the spinal cord, optic nerves, and central white matter of the brain. The disease has a peak incidence between 20 and 40 years of age, a strong predominance in women, and a clinical course characterized by multiple relapses and remissions. Impairment of nerve conduction caused by the degeneration of myelin sheaths leads to such symptoms as double vision, nystagmus (involuntary, rapid movement of the eyeball in all directions), loss of balance and poor coordination, shaking tremor and muscular weakness, difficulty in speaking clearly, and bladder dysfunction.

MRI is the modality of choice for demonstrating the plaques of demyelinization that are characteristic of multiple sclerosis. The plaques appear as multiple areas of increased signal intensity that primarily involve the periventricular white matter, cerebellum, brainstem, and spinal cord (Figure 7-54). CT shows old inactive disease as well-defined areas of decreased attenuation in the deep white matter and periventricular regions. In the acute phase, CT after the intravenous demonstration of contrast material demonstrates a mixture of nonenhancing focal areas of decreased density (representing old areas of demyelinization) and enhancing regions that represent active foci.

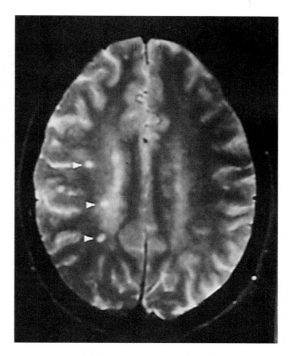

Figure 7-54 Multiple sclerosis. Axial T_2-weighted MR image in 35-year-old woman shows characteristic areas of increased signal intensity (arrowheads) in deep white matter.

▪ Epilepsy and Convulsive Disorders

Epilepsy is a condition in which brain impulses are temporarily disturbed, resulting in a spectrum of symptoms ranging from loss of consciousness for a few seconds to violent seizures (shaking and thrashing movements of all extremities). Although most cases of epilepsy are idiopathic, the disorder can be a result of injury (penetrating or nonpenetrating trauma, depressed skull fracture), birth trauma, or infection.

The mildest type of epilepsy, which primarily occurs in children, is called **petit mal.** This results in brief episodes of loss of consciousness, which may be associated with mild muscular twitching. Petit mal epilepsy usually disappears in young adulthood.

Grand mal epilepsy refers to generalized convulsions associated with the patient falling to the floor, hypersalivating (foaming at the mouth), and losing control of urine and sometimes feces. In many cases an approaching seizure is heralded by an aura, such as a ringing in the ears, a tingling sensation in the fingers, or spots before the eyes. After a seizure, the patient tends to be groggy and unaware of what has happened (postictal state).

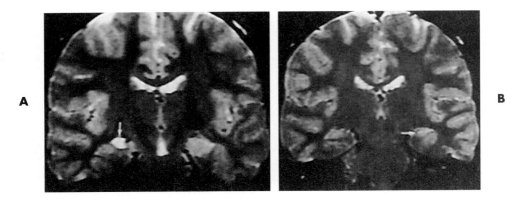

Figure 7-55   Seizure disorder caused by hippocampal sclerosis. **A,** Coronal T_2-weighted Mr scan shows high-intensity signal in the left hippocampal region *(arrow)*. **B,** Normal scan for comparison. (From Bronen RA: *AJR* 159:1165-1174, 1992.)

In the patient who has an acute seizure, the initial effort should be directed toward stabilizing the patient (securing adequate ventilation and perfusion) and stopping the seizure. Subsequently, a careful history, physical examination, and appropriate laboratory studies should be performed to exclude reversible chemical causes of seizures such as hypoglycemia, hyponatremia or hypernatremia, and hypocalcemia or hypercalcemia. If the patient does not respond to routine anticonvulsive treatment, CT may be indicated to search for causes of an acute seizure disorder (e.g., subdural hematoma, intracerebral hematoma), which may be amenable to surgical intervention. These conditions can be adequately assessed with a noncontrast CT scan (see p. 287); plain skull radiographs are not required.

Whenever possible, the radiographic evaluation of a patient with a seizure disorder should be done when the patient is clinically stable. The appropriate procedure is an MR scan to search for an unsuspected brain tumor, arteriovenous malformation, or hippocampal sclerosis (Figure 7-55). Hippocampal sclerosis (mesial temporal sclerosis) refers to neuronal loss and gliosis that occurs in the temporal region. It is the most common cause of seizures that do not respond to medical therapy. Surgical resection of the lesion is associated with a very good outcome. Since most seizure disorders are attributable to small areas of cortical brain injury resulting from trauma or infarction, CT or MRI scans are usually normal. If the MR scan is normal, no further radiographic examination is indicated.

- ### Degenerative Diseases

Normal aging

During normal aging, a gradual loss of neurons results in enlargement of the ventricular system and

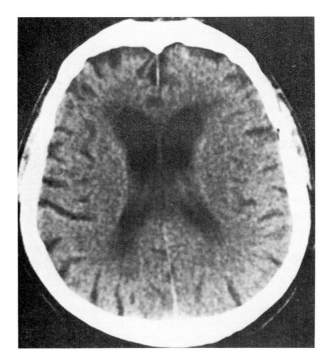

Figure 7-56   Normal aging. CT scan of 70-year-old man shows generalized ventricular dilatation with prominence of sulci over surfaces of cerebral hemisphere.

sulci (Figure 7-56). Demyelination, which is also a part of normal aging, leads to the development of low density in the periventricular regions on CT and high signal intensity on T_2-weighted MR images (Figure 7-57).

Alzheimer's disease

Alzheimer's disease (presenile dementia) is a diffuse form of progressive cerebral atrophy that develops at an earlier age than the senile period. CT and MRI demonstrate nonspecific findings of cerebral atro-

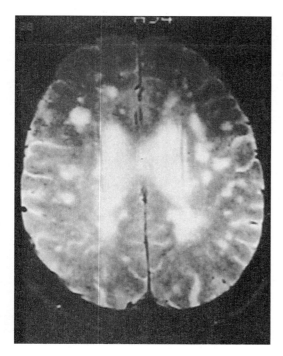

Figure 7-57 Degenerative changes of aging. Axial MR scan demonstrates multiple areas of increased signal intensity around ventricles and in deep white matter, consistent with cerebral ischemia or infarction.

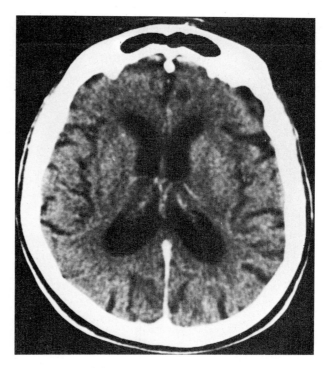

Figure 7-58 Alzheimer's disease. Noncontrast CT scan of 56-year-old woman with progressive dementia shows generalized enlargement of ventricular system and sulci.

phy, including symmetrically enlarged ventricles with prominence of the cortical sulci (Figure 7-58).

Huntington's disease

Huntington's disease is an inherited condition (autosomal dominant) that predominantly involves men and presents in the early to middle adult years with dementia and typical choreiform movements (involuntary movements that are rapid, jerky, and without stop). The pathologic hallmark of Huntington's disease is atrophy of the caudate nucleus and putamen, which produces the typical CT appearance of focal dilatation of the frontal horns and a loss of their normal concave shape (Figure 7-59). Generalized enlargement of the ventricles and dilatation of the cortical sulci can also occur.

Parkinson's disease

Parkinson's disease (shaking palsy) is a progressive degenerative disease characterized by stooped posture, stiffness and slowness of movement, fixed facial expression, and involuntary rhythmic tremor of the limbs that disappears with voluntary movement. A disorder of middle or later life, Parkinson's disease is very gradually progressive and exhibits a prolonged course.

The major degenerative changes in nerve cells in Parkinson's disease occur in the basal ganglia, especially the globus pallidus, substantia nigra, and the fibers of the corpus striatum. The essence of the condition seems to be an enzyme defect that results in an inadequate production of the neuronal transmitter substance, dopamine. The most recent method of treatment is the administration of L-dopa, a substance that is converted to dopamine in the brain. Although this drug therapy does not stop the neuronal degeneration, it dramatically improves both the appearance and behavior of the patient.

CT scans in patients with Parkinson's disease often demonstrate cortical atrophy. However, because this condition is usually seen in older individuals, the ventricular enlargement and prominent cortical sulci found on CT scans may be indistinguishable from that caused by the normal aging process.

Cerebellar atrophy

Isolated atrophy of the cerebellum may represent an inherited disorder, a degenerative disease, or the toxic effect of the prolonged use of such drugs as alcohol and phenytoin (Dilantin) (Figure 7-60).

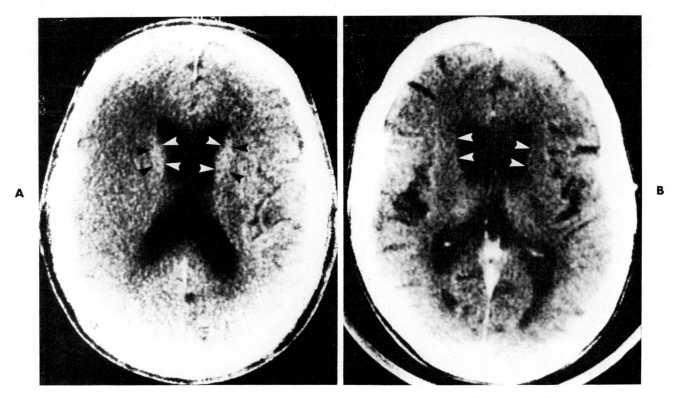

Figure 7-59   Huntington's disease. **A,** CT scan in normal patient shows heads of caudate nucleus *(black arrowheads)* producing normal concavity of frontal horns *(white arrowheads).* **B,** In patient with Huntington's disease, atrophy of caudate nucleus causes characteristic loss of normal concavity *(white arrowheads)* of frontal horns.

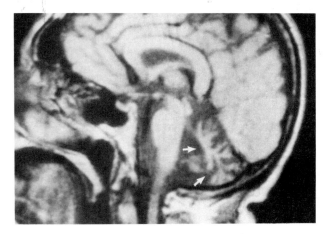

Figure 7-60   Cerebellar atrophy. Sagittal MR scan shows dramatic loss of substance of vermis of cerebellum *(arrows)* in patient with severe alcoholism.

Amyotrophic lateral sclerosis (Lou Gehrig's disease)

In this relentlessly progressive condition of unknown cause, there is widespread selective atrophy and loss of motor nerve cells leading to extensive paralysis and death from respiratory weakness or aspiration pneumonia. Although this disease cannot be diagnosed radiographically, CT, MRI, or myelography is often performed to exclude a spinal malignancy, which could produce a similar clinical appearance.

■ Hydrocephalus

Hydrocephalus refers to dilatation of the ventricular system that is usually associated with increased intracranial pressure. In **noncommunicating** (obstructive) hydrocephalus, there is an obstruction to the flow of CSF somewhere along the ventricular pathways from the lateral ventricles to the outlets of the fourth ventricle. Enlargement of the lateral ventricles with normal-sized third and fourth ventricles indicates an obstruction at the level of the foramina of Monro. This is most commonly attributable to a colloid cyst (Figure 7-61) or suprasellar tumor, especially craniopharyngioma. Enlargement of the lateral and third ventricles with a normal-sized fourth ventricle indicates an obstruction at the level of the aqueduct of Slyvius (Figures 7-62, and 7-63). The most common causes of this appearance are con-

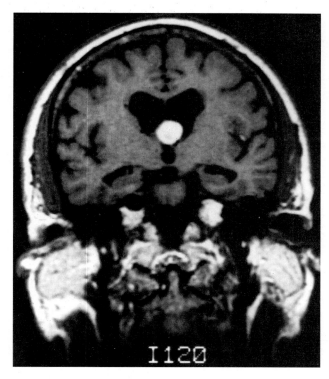

Figure 7-61 Hydrocephalus with obstruction at the level of the foramen of Monro. T_1-weighted MR scan shows a hyperintense colloid cyst *(arrowhead)* causing bilateral enlargement of the frontal horns. (From Johnson CE, Zimmerman RD: *MRI Decisions* 3:2-16, 1989.)

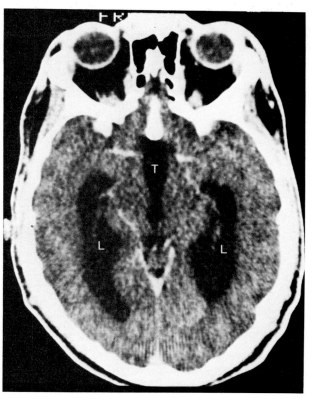

Figure 7-62 Hydrocephalus caused by obstruction at level of aqueduct. Dilatation of lateral *(L)* and third *(T)* ventricles in patient with congenital hydrocephalus. Symptoms of headache and papilledema resolved after ventricular shunting.

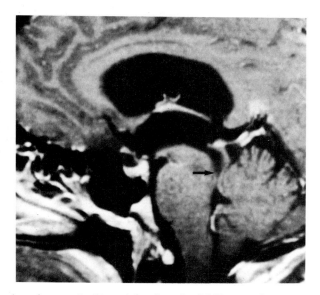

Figure 7-63 Aqueductal stenosis. T_1-weighted sagittal MR scan shows pronounced narrowing of the inferior portion of the aqueduct *(arrow)*. There is flaring of the upper portion of the aqueduct and considerable enlargement of the third and lateral ventricles. Notice that the fourth ventricle is of normal size. (From Stark DD, Bradley WG: *Magnetic resonance imaging,* ed 2, St Louis, 1991, Mosby.)

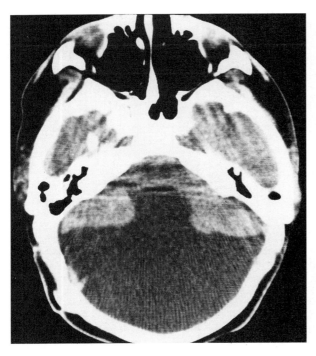

Figure 7-64　Hydrocephalus caused by obstruction at level of outlet of fourth ventricle. Huge low-density cyst (Dandy-Walker cyst) occupies most of enlarged posterior fossa and represents extension of dilated fourth ventricle.

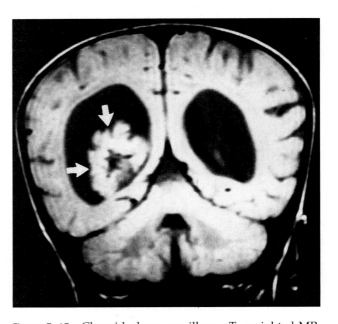

Figure 7-65　Choroid plexus papilloma. T_1-weighted MR scan shows a lobulated isointense mass *(arrows)* in a greatly dilated right lateral ventricle.
(From Eisenberg RL: *Clinical imaging: an atlas of differential diagnosis,* Gaithersburg, Md, 1992, Aspen.)

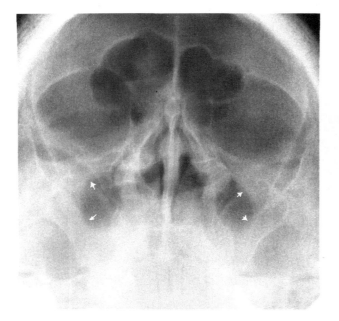

Figure 7-66　Chronic sinusitis. Mucosal thickening appears as soft-tissue density *(arrows)* lining walls of maxillary antra.

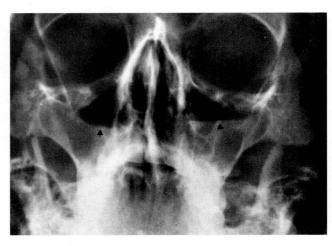

Figure 7-67　Acute sinusitis. There is mucosal thickening involving most of paranasal sinuses and air-fluid levels *(arrows)* in both maxillary antra.

genital aqueduct stenosis or occlusion and neoplasm (pinealoma, teratoma). Enlargement of the entire ventricular system (with the fourth ventricle often dilated out of proportion) indicates an obstruction at the level of the outlet of the fourth ventricle (Figure 7-64), a condition that may reflect congenital atresia, infection, neoplasm, or downward herniation of the cerebellar tonsils through the foramen magnum.

In the much more common **communicating** hydrocephalus, the ventricular fluid passes freely into the extraventricular subarachnoid space. There is generalized ventricular enlargement with normal or absent sulci. Obstruction of the normal CSF pathway distal to the fourth ventricle usually involves the subarachnoid space at the basal cisterns, cerebral convexity, or foramen magnum. Causes include infection (meningitis, empyema), subarachnoid or subdural hemorrhage, congenital anomalies, neoplasm, and dural venous thrombosis. A similar radiographic pattern is seen in **"normal-pressure"** hydrocephalus, a syndrome of gait ataxia, urinary incontinence, and dementia associated with ventricular dilatation and relatively normal CSF pressure.

The diagnosis of dilated ventricles can be easily made by CT or MRI. Ultrasound can show the ventricular dilatation either in utero or after birth as long as the sound waves can traverse the open fontanels.

Generalized enlargement of the ventricular system can also be attributable to the overproduction of CSF by a papilloma (Figure 7-65) or carcinoma arising in the choroid plexus (CSF-secreting vascular tissue in the ventricles). These rare tumors usually occur in the fourth ventricle in adults and the lateral ventricles in children.

Hydrocephalus can often be treated by the placement of a shunt between the dilated ventricles and the heart or the peritoneal cavity. Successful shunting causes a decrease in the intracranial pressure and ventricular size; the latter can be monitored by CT or MRI.

▪ Sinusitis

The paranasal sinuses (maxillary, ethmoid, frontal, and sphenoid) are paired air-filled cavities that are lined with a mucous membrane that is directly continuous with the nasal mucosa. The size and shape of the sinuses vary in different age periods, in different individuals, and on the two sides of the same individual. At birth, the maxillary sinus is only a slitlike space that later expands to fill the maxilla

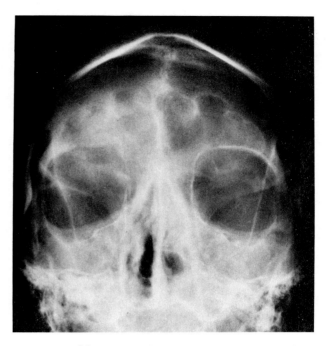

Figure 7-68 Mucormycosis causing pansinusitis with osteomyelitis. Destruction of roof of right orbit and outer margins of right frontal sinus is present.

and is thus responsible for the growth of the face. The ethmoid sinuses can be seen radiographically by 6 years of age, whereas the frontal sinuses usually are not well demonstrated until about 10 years of age. The sphenoid sinuses begin to develop around 2 or 3 years of age and are fully developed by late adolescence.

Viral infection of the upper respiratory tract may lead to obstruction of drainage of the paranasal sinuses and the development of localized pain, tenderness, and fever. Radiographically, acute or chronic sinusitis causes mucosal thickening, which appears as a soft-tissue density lining the walls of the involved sinuses (Figure 7-66). The maxillary antra are most commonly affected and are best visualized on the Waters' projection. An air-fluid level in a sinus is usually considered a manifestation of acute inflammatory disease (Figure 7-67). To demonstrate this finding, it is essential that all sinus films be obtained with the patient erect and with the use of a horizontal beam. The destruction of the bony wall of a sinus is an ominous sign indicating secondary osteomyelitis (Figure 7-68).

QUESTIONS

1. The imaging modality of choice to evaluate patients with suspected neurologic dysfunction caused from head trauma is _____ .
   - A. Ultrasound
   - B. MRI
   - C. CT
   - D. Skull radiographs

2. Arterial bleeding sometimes associated with head trauma can cause _____ hematomas.
   - A. Intracranial
   - B. Subdural
   - C. Epidural
   - D. Acute

3. Venous bleeding sometimes associated with head trauma can cause _____ hematomas.
   - A. Intracranial
   - B. Subdural
   - C. Epidural
   - D. Acute

4. Movement of the brain within the calavarium following blunt trauma to the skull sometimes results in a cerebral _____ .
   - A. Subdural hematoma
   - B. Epidural hematoma
   - C. Acute hematoma
   - D. Contusion

5. Bleeding into the ventricular system caused by injury to surface veins, cerebral parenchyma, or cortical arteries can cause_____ hemorrhage.
   - A. Epidural
   - B. Subdural
   - C. Epiarachnoid
   - D. Subarachnoid

6. Plain radiographs of the facial bones should always be made with the patient in the _____ position if possible.
   - A. Supine
   - B. Erect
   - C. Lateral decubitus
   - D. Anterior

7. The most common primary brain tumor is a _____ .
   - A. Glioma
   - B. Glioblastoma
   - C. Meningioma
   - D. Neurinoma

8. A benign tumor that arises from arachnoid lining cells and is attached the dura is named _____ .
   - A. Glioma
   - B. Glioblastoma
   - C. Meningioma
   - D. Neurinoma

9. The most common neoplasms that metastasize to the brain arise in the _____ and _____ .
   - A. Lung, stomach
   - B. Lung, breast
   - C. Stomach, breast
   - D. Breast, prostate

10. A viral inflammation of the brain and meninges is called _____ .
    - A. Meningitis
    - B. Hydrocephalus
    - C. Encephalitis
    - D. Encephalomalacia

11. The best imaging modality to evaluate brain abscesses is _____ .

12. The two imaging procedures of choice to evaluate the extent of a stroke in the brain are _____ and _____ .

13. The initials *TIA* mean _____ .

14. The imaging modality of choice to demonstrate the plaques of demyelinization that are characteristic of multiple sclerosis is _____ .

15. A condition in which brain impulses are temporarily disturbed, the results of which range from loss of consciousness to violent seizures, is termed _____ .

16. A diffuse form of progressive cerebral atrophy that develops at an earlier age than the senile period is called _____ .

17. A progressive degenerative disease characterized by involuntary tremors of the extremities that disappear with voluntary movement is named _____ .

18. Sinus radiographs should be taken using a _____ beam and with the patient in the _____ position.

19. The pathologic condition that refers to dilatation of the ventricular system and is usually associated with increased intracranial pressure is _____ .

20. If a patient needing facial or sinus radiographs is unable to stand or sit erect, a _____ using a _____ beam may be performed to demonstrate any air or fluid levels that may be present.

_____ 21. Convolutions on the surface of the cerebrum

_____ 22. The basic unit of the nervous system

_____ 23. Combination of 12 pairs of cranial nerves, 31 pairs of spinal nerves, autonomic nerves, and ganglia

_____ 24. Impulse conduction to and from the central nervous system

_____ 25. Entity consisting of the brain and spinal cord

_____ 26. Fatty covering that insulates axons

_____ 27. Junction where impulses are passed from one neuron to another

_____ 28. Part of nervous system that supplies the striated skeletal muscles

_____ 29. Projection leading from the nerve cell body

_____ 30. Part of the nervous system that supplies smooth muscle, cardiac muscle, and glandular epithelial tissue

_____ 31. Shallow grooves on the surface of the cerebrum

_____ 32. Projection leading to a nerve cell body

_____ 33. White matter connecting the two cerebral hemispheres

_____ 34. Midbrain

_____ 35. Transparent covering of the brain and spinal cord

_____ 36. Projects down into the longitudinal fissure to separate the cerebral hemispheres

_____ 37. Slitlike space between the right and left thalami

_____ 38. Inflammation of the protective layers of the brain

_____ 39. Covering over the cerebellum that separates it from the occipital lobe of the cerebrum

_____ 40. Cobweb-like covering of the brain

_____ 41. Diamond-shaped space in front of the cerebellum and behind the medulla and pons

_____ 42. Outermost covering of the brain

_____ 43. Canal connecting the third and fourth ventricles

_____ 44. Result of an obstruction of cerebrospinal spinal fluid

_____ 45. Foramen connecting the third and lateral ventricles

A. Dendrites
B. Dura mater
C. Axon
D. Gyri
E. Monro
F. Pia mater
G. Reflex arc
H. Corpus callosum
I. Synapse
J. Neuron
K. Hydrocephalus
L. Arachnoid
M. Somatic
N. Peripheral nervous system
O. Sulci
P. Myelin sheath
Q. Fourth ventricle
R. Autonomic
S. Falx cerebri
T. CNS
U. Meningitis
V. Mesencephalon
W. Third ventricle
X. Tentorium cerebelli
Y. Aqueduct of Sylvius

BIBLIOGRAPHY

Brant-Zawadzki M, Norman D: _Magnetic resonance imaging of the central nervous system,_ New York, 1987, Raven Press.

Lee SH, Rao KCVG: _Cranial computed tomography and MRI,_ New York, 1992, McGraw-Hill.

Ramsey RG: _Neuroradiology with computed tomography,_ Philadelphia, 1987, Saunders.

Woodruff WW: _Fundamentals of neuroimaging,_ Philadelphia, 1993, Saunders.

CHAPTER 8

Hematopoietic System

■ **Prerequisite Knowledge**

The student should have a basic knowledge of the physiology of the hematopoietic system.

■ **Goals**

To acquaint the student radiographer with the pathophysiology and radiographic manifestations of all the common and some of the unusual disorders of the hematopoietic system.

■ **Objectives**

1. Understand and be able to define or describe all bold-faced terms in this chapter
2. Describe the physiology of the hematopoietic system
3. Identify the basic blood structures on diagrams
4. Be able to describe the various pathologic conditions affecting the hematopoietic system as well as their radiographic manifestations

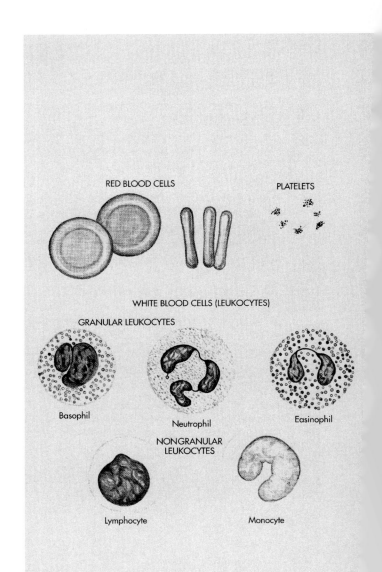

RED BLOOD CELLS   PLATELETS

WHITE BLOOD CELLS (LEUKOCYTES)

GRANULAR LEUKOCYTES

Basophil   Neutrophil   Easinophil

NONGRANULAR LEUKOCYTES

Lymphocyte   Monocyte

■ ■ ■ ■ ■ ■ **■ Radiographer Notes**

Although the hematopoietic system cannot be directly imaged, many blood disorders result in abnormalities that can be demonstrated radiographically. Technical factors may have to be increased or decreased in patients who manifest advanced stages of these diseases (see Table 1-1). The radiographer must be aware of the severe pain experienced by patients undergoing a sickle cell crisis. Patients with advanced leukemia or lymphoma who have an altered immune status may require protective isolation. Because many hematopoietic system diseases cause significant demineralization of bone, the radiographer must be alert to the possibility of pathologic fracture and thus exercise caution when moving and positioning these patients.

■ Diseases of the Blood

Blood and the cells within it are vital to life. An adequate blood supply to all body tissues is necessary to bring oxygen, nutrients, salts, and hormones to the cells and to carry away the waste products of cellular metabolism. The components of blood are also a major defense against infection, toxic substances, and foreign antigens.

Red bone marrow (found in vertebrae and flat bones such as the sternum, ribs, skull, and proximal femurs) and lymph nodes are the blood-forming tissues of the body. Red blood cells (erythrocytes) and platelets (thrombocytes) are made in red bone marrow, whereas white blood cells (leukocytes) are produced in both red marrow and lymphoid tissue.

Erythrocytes are biconcave disks without a nucleus that contain **hemoglobin,** an iron-based protein that carries oxygen from the respiratory tract to the body's tissues. In a normal person, there are 4.5 to 6 million red blood cells in each cubic millimeter of blood. The amount of hemoglobin per deciliter is approximately 14 g in women and 15 g in men.

Leukocytes, or white blood cells, normally number from 5000 to 10,000/mm^3 of blood. Unlike erythrocytes, there are several types of white blood cells. **Neutrophils (polymorphonuclear leukocytes),** which make up 55% to 75% of white blood cells, defend the body against bacteria by ingesting these foreign organisms and destroying them (phagocytosis). The number of polymorphonuclear leukocytes in the blood is enormously increased in acute infections because the bone marrow rapidly releases into the bloodstream the large numbers of these cells kept in reserve. **Eosinophils** (1% to 4%) are red-staining cells whose number greatly increases in allergic and parasitic conditions. The third type of leukocyte is the **basophil** (0% to 1%), which contains granules that stain blue. These three types of cells are formed in the sinusoids of the bone marrow and, as with red blood cells, go through immature stages before the adult form is reached.

Lymphocytes represent about 25% to 40% of white blood cells. They play a major role in the immune system and are involved in the synthesis of antibodies and the production of immunoglobulins.

The final type of white blood cell is the monocyte, which is actively phagocytic and plays an important part in the inflammatory process. **Monocytes** are formed in the bone marrow and represent about 2% to 8% of white blood cells.

Platelets are the smallest blood cells and are essential for blood clotting. Normally, there are about 150,000 to 400,000 platelets in every cubic millimeter of blood.

■ Diseases of Red Blood Cells

Anemia

Anemia refers to a decrease in the amount of oxygen-carrying hemoglobin in the blood. This reduction can be attributable to improper formation of new red blood cells, an increased rate of red blood cell destruction, or a loss of red blood cells as a result of prolonged bleeding. Regardless of the cause, a hemoglobin deficiency makes the anemic person appear pale. This is best appreciated in the mucous membranes of the mouth and conjunctiva and in the nail beds. A decrease in the oxygen-carrying hemoglobin impairs the delivery of an adequate oxygen supply to the cells and tissues, leading to fatigue and muscular weakness and often to shortness of breath on exertion (dyspnea). To meet the body's need for more oxygen, the respiratory rate is increased and the heart beats more rapidly.

Iron deficiency anemia

Iron deficiency is the most common cause of anemia. It most frequently results from chronic blood loss, as from an ulcer, a malignant tumor, or excessive bleeding during menstruation (menorrhagia). Other causes of iron deficiency anemia include inadequate dietary intake of iron and increased iron loss caused by intestinal parasites. Iron deficiency anemia also may develop during pregnancy because the mother's iron supply is depleted by red blood cell development in the fetus.

Hemolytic anemia

The underlying abnormality in hemolytic anemia is a shortened life-span of the red blood cells with resulting hemolysis and the release of hemoglobin into the plasma. Most hemolytic anemias are caused by a hereditary defect that may produce abnormal red cells or abnormal hemoglobin. Less commonly, hemolytic anemia is acquired and related to circulating antibodies from autoimmune or allergic reactions (e.g., drugs such as sulfonamide) or the malaria parasite.

Spherocytosis, sickle cell anemia, and thalassemia are the major hereditary hemolytic anemias. In spherocytosis the erythrocytes have a circular rather than a biconcave shape, making them fragile and susceptible to rupture. In sickle cell anemia, which is generally confined to blacks, the hemoglobin molecule is abnormal and the red cells are crescent or sickle shaped and tend to rupture. A defect in

hemoglobin formation is also responsible for thalassemia, which predominantly occurs in persons living about the Mediterranean, especially those of Italian, Greek, or Sicilian descent.

The breakdown of hemoglobin produces bilirubin, a pigmented substance that is normally detoxified by the liver and converted into bile. The accumulation of large amounts of this orange pigment in the plasma causes the tissues to have a yellow appearance (jaundice).

The hemolytic anemias produce a variety of radiographic abnormalities. Although the radiographic findings are similar in the various types of hemolytic anemia, they tend to be most severe in thalassemia and least prominent in spherocytosis. Extensive marrow hyperplasia, the result of ineffective erythropoiesis and rapid destruction of newly formed red blood cells, causes generalized osteoporosis with pronounced widening of the medullary spaces and thinning of the cortices in long and tubular bones (Figure 8-1). As the fine secondary trabeculae are resorbed, new bone is laid down on the surviving trabeculae, thickening them and producing a coarsened pattern. Normal modeling of long bones does not occur because the expanding marrow flattens or even bulges the normally concave surfaces of the shafts.

In the skull, there is widening of the diploic space and thinning or complete obliteration of the outer table. When the hyperplastic marrow perforates or destroys the outer table, it proliferates under the invisible periosteum, and new bone spicules are laid down perpendicularly to the inner table. This produces the characteristic hair-on-end appearance of vertical striations in a radial pattern (Figure 8-2).

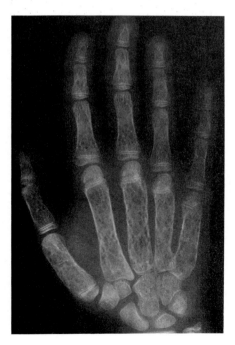

Figure 8-1 Thalassemia. Pronounced widening of medullary spaces with thinning of cortical margins. Notice absence of normal modeling caused by pressure of expanding marrow space. Localized radiolucencies simulating multiple osteolytic lesions represent tumorous collections of hypoplastic marrow.

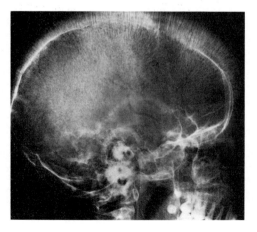

Figure 8-2 Thalassemia. Lateral projection of skull demonstrates hair-on-end appearance. Notice normal appearance of calvarium inferior to internal occipital protuberance, an area in which there is no red marrow, and poor pneumatization of visualized paranasal sinuses.

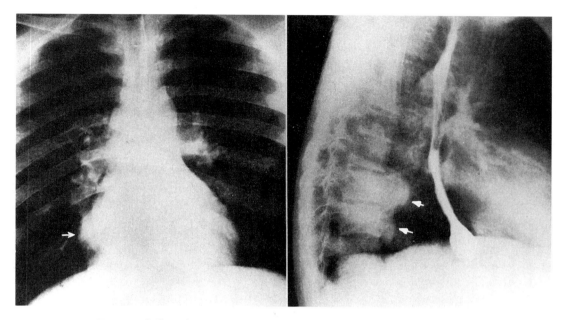

Figure 8-3   Extramedullary hematopoiesis in thalassemia. A lateral projection of chest demonstrates lobulated posterior mediastinal masses of hematopoietic tissue *(arrows)* in lower thoracic region. (From Leight TF: *Radiol Clin North Am* 1:377-393, 1963.)

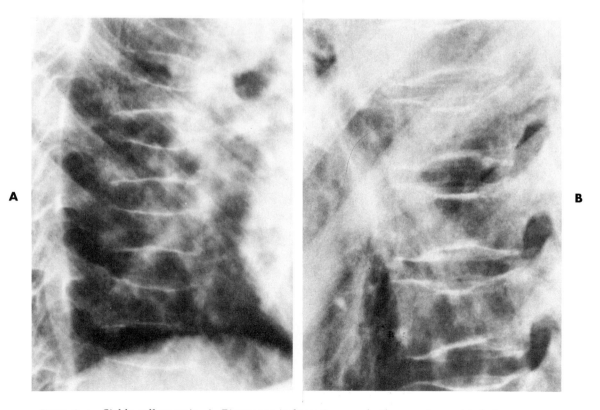

Figure 8-4   Sickle cell anemia. **A,** Biconcave indentations on both superior and inferior margins of soft vertebral bodies produce characteristic fish vertebrae. **B,** Localized steplike central depressions of multiple vertebral end plates.

Extramedullary hematopoiesis is a compensatory mechanism of the reticuloendothelial system (liver, spleen, lymph nodes) in patients with prolonged erythrocyte deficiency resulting from the destruction of red blood cells or the inability of normal blood-forming organs to produce them. Paravertebral collections of hematopoietic tissue may appear on chest radiographs as single or multiple, smooth or lobulated, posterior mediastinal masses that are usually located at the lower thoracic levels (Figure 8-3).

In sickle cell anemia, expansile pressure of the adjacent intervertebral disks produces characteristic biconcave indentations on both the superior and inferior margins of the softened vertebral bodies ("fish vertebrae") (Figure 8-4, *A*). Another typical appearance is the development of localized steplike central depressions of multiple vertebral end plates (Figure 8-4, *B*). This is probably caused by circulatory stasis and ischemia, which retard growth in the central portion of the vertebral cartilaginous growth plate. The periphery of the growth plate, which has a different blood supply, continues to grow at a more normal rate. Bulging of the abnormally shaped red blood cells in sickle cell anemia typically causes focal ischemia and infarction in multiple tissues. Bone infarcts commonly occur in infants and children. These most frequently involve the small bones of the hands and feet, producing an irregular area of bone destruction with overlying periosteal calcification, which may be indistinguishable from osteomyelitis. In older children and adults, bone infarction may initially appear as an ill-defined lucent area that then becomes irregularly calcified. Acute osteomyelitis, often caused by *Salmonella* infection, is a common complication in sickle cell disease. The resulting lytic destruction and periosteal reaction may be extensive, often involving the entire shaft and multiple bones (Figure 8-5). Radiographically, it may be impossible to distinguish between osteomyelitis and bone infarction without infection (Figure 8-6).

Throughout their lives, patients with sickle cell anemia are plagued by recurrent painful crises. These episodes are attributable to recurrent vaso-occlusive phenomena and may appear with explosive suddenness and attack various parts of the

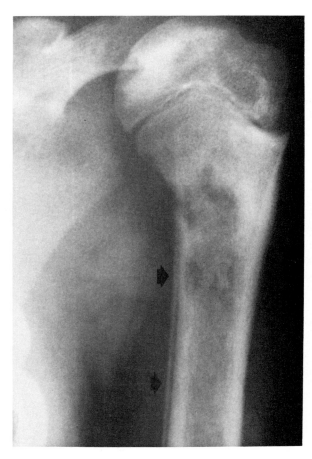

Figure 8-5 Acute osteomyelitis in sickle cell anemia. There is diffuse lytic destruction of proximal humerus along with extensive periosteal reaction *(arrows).*

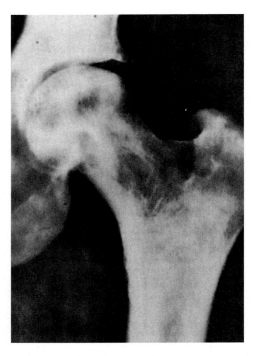

Figure 8-6 Aseptic necrosis of femoral head in sickle cell anemia. Mottled areas of increased and decreased density reflecting osteonecrosis without collapse. Trabeculae in neck and intertrochanteric region are thickened by apposition of new bone. Solid layer of new bone along inner aspect of cortex of femoral shaft causes narrowing of medullary canal. (From Moseley JE: *Semin Roentgenol* 9:169-184, 1984.)

body, especially the abdomen, chest, and joints. It is often difficult to distinguish between a painful sickle crisis and some other type of acute process such as biliary colic, appendicitis, or a perforated viscus. In the extremities, a sickle cell crisis may mimic osteomyelitis or acute arthritis such as gout or rheumatoid arthritis.

The most common extraskeletal abnormality in the hemolytic anemias is cardiomegaly caused by severe anemia and increased cardiac output. The heart has a globular configuration reflecting enlargement of all chambers. Increased pulmonary blood flow produces engorgement of the pulmonary vessels, giving a hypervascular appearance to the lungs. Pulmonary infarction, pulmonary edema and congestive failure, and pneumonia are frequent complications.

Renal abnormalities can be demonstrated by excretory urography in about two thirds of patients with sickle cell disease. A serious complication is renal papillary necrosis, which is probably related to vessel obstruction within the papillae and may produce sinuses or cavity formation within one or more papillae.

Hemolytic anemia of the newborn (erythroblastosis fetalis), can result when the mother is Rh negative and the fetus has Rh-positive blood inherited from the father. Although the fetal and maternal circulations are separate, fetal blood can enter the mother's blood through ruptures in the placenta occurring at delivery. The mother thus becomes sensitized to the Rh factor of the fetus and makes antibodies against it. Any antibodies reaching the fetal blood through the placenta in future pregnancies cause hemolysis of the fetal red blood cells. The severity of the disease ranges from mild anemia with jaundice to fetal death.

Blood testing to determine whether Rh incompatibility exists is now an essential part of prenatal care. If an Rh-negative mother delivers or aborts an Rh-positive infant, she is given a vaccine of Rh immunoglobin within 24 hours to prevent the production of antibodies against the Rh factor.

Megaloblastic anemia

A deficiency of vitamin B_{12} or of folic acid leads to defective DNA synthesis and an anemia in which there is a decreased number of red blood cells, though each cell contains the normal amount of hemoglobin. The most common cause of vitamin B_{12} deficiency is pernicious anemia, in which there is inadequate intrinsic factor secretion related to atrophy of the gastric mucosa. Intrinsic factor acts as a carrier in the small bowel absorption of vitamin B_{12}, which is essential for erythrocyte development. Gastric atrophy is seen radiographically as a tubular stomach with a bald appearance that reflects a decrease or absence of the usually prominent rugal folds (Figure 8-7). It must be emphasized, however, that radiographic findings of atrophic gastritis are

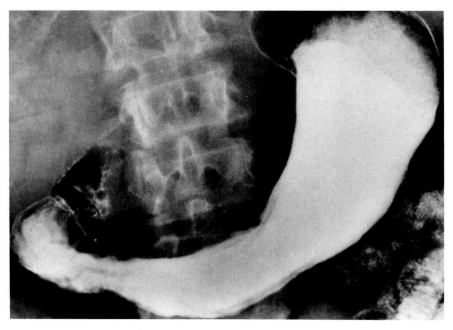

Figure 8-7 Megaloblastic anemia in patient with chronic atrophic gastritis, which presents as tubular stomach with striking decrease in usually prominent rugal folds.

often seen in older persons with no evidence of pernicious anemia.

A deficiency of folic acid (and vitamin B_{12}) may also be related to intestinal malabsorption. This may be related to intestinal parasites or bacterial overproduction, especially in patients with stasis of bowel contents as in blind loop syndrome and multiple jejunal diverticula. Other causes of megaloblastic anemia include a poor diet, such as strict vegetarianism, in which there are no sources of vitamin B_{12}, or long-term alcoholism, in which no folic acid is available.

Aplastic anemia

A generalized failure of the bone marrow to function (aplastic anemia) results in decreased levels of erythrocytes, leukocytes, and platelets. In addition to anemia, the patient cannot fight infection (a white blood cell function) and has a bleeding tendency (platelet depletion). Causes of aplastic anemia include exposure to chemical agents, drugs, or infections or invasion of the bone marrow by cancer. Regular blood transfusions are generally necessary for survival. Bone marrow transplantation is a new technique for treating these patients.

Myelophthisic anemia

Infiltration of bone marrow with tumor cells, or encroachment on marrow cavities caused by cortical thickening, can result in severe anemia and pancytopenia (decreased red and white blood cells and platelets). Tumors may arise from cells that are normally found in the bone marrow (leukemia, lymphoma, myeloma), or the marrow may be invaded by extensive metastases to bone (carcinomas of the breast, prostate, lung, thyroid). Less common causes of marrow replacement include lipid storage disorders (Gaucher's disease), osteopetrosis (marble bones), and myelofibrosis.

Polycythemia
Primary polycythemia (polycythemia vera)

Polycythemia vera is a hematologic disorder characterized by hyperplasia of the bone marrow that results in increased production of erythrocytes, granulocytes, and platelets. The disease is slowly progressive and produces symptoms associated with increased blood volume and viscosity. Cerebrovascular and peripheral vascular insufficiency are common, and many patients give a history of some thrombotic or hemorrhagic event during the course of their disease. There is an increased incidence of peptic ulcer disease, and the excessive cellular proliferation often results in increased levels of uric acid with secondary gout and the formation of urate

stones. The spleen is often massively enlarged and may be seen as a left upper quadrant mass.

Increased blood volume in ploycythemia vera can lead to prominence of the pulmonary vascular shadows, usually without the cardiomegaly associated with the increased pulmonary vascularity that occurs in patients with congenital heart disease (Figure 8-8). Intravascular thrombosis may cause pulmonary infarctions that appear as focal areas of consolidation or as bands of fibrosis.

Secondary polycythemia

Secondary polycythemia may be the result of long-term inadequate oxygen supply in patients with severe chronic pulmonary disease or congenital cyanotic heart disease, or it may develop in persons living at high altitudes. An elevated hemoglobin concentration may also be caused by certain neoplasms (renal cell carcinoma, hepatoma, cerebellar hemangioblastoma) that result in an increased production of erythropoietin, which stimulates red blood cell formation.

Because secondary polycythemia is a compensatory phenomenon, the pulmonary vasculature is normal in appearance and there is no evidence of the disease on chest radiographs. In children with severe secondary polycythemia caused by cyanotic heart disease, the skull may show thickened tables and a hair-on-end appearance similar to the findings in congenital hemolytic anemias.

▪ Diseases of White Blood Cells
Leukemia

Leukemia is a neoplastic proliferation of white blood cells. The two major types of leukemia are named for the site of malignancy. **Myelocytic** leukemia is a cancer of the bone marrow, in which the primitive white blood cells are called "myelocytes." In this condition there is a huge increase in the number of circulating granulocytes with a decreased production of red blood cells and platelets. **Lymphatic** leukemia is a malignancy of the lymph nodes. In this condition the only white blood cells that are dramatically increased are lymphocytes.

Leukemia may be chronic or acute. Acute lymphocytic leukemia, which has an abrupt onset and progresses rapidly, is the most common form in children. Acute myelocytic leukemia is more common in adults. Chronic leukemias run a more prolonged course and may involve either cell type.

Because of the exuberant white cell production, there is generally a decrease in the number of circulating red blood cells and platelets. This results in a typical clinical appearance of weakness, short-

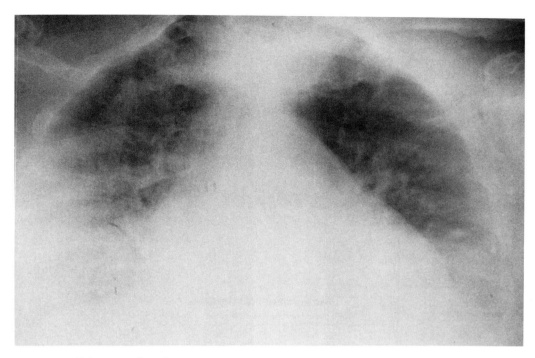

Figure 8-8 Primary polycythemia. Severe hypoventilation caused by profound obesity causes engorgement of pulmonary vessels. Although cardiomegaly is uncommon in polycythemia, in this case it reflects pronounced elevation of diaphragm as result of huge abdominal girth and some underlying cardiac decompensation.

ness of breath, and cardiac palpitations. A decrease in the number of platelets interferes with the blood-clotting mechanism and results in a bleeding tendency. Even though there are more circulating white blood cells than normal, most are immature and thus the patient becomes highly susceptible to infection. Diffuse infiltration of white cells in the spleen and liver may cause massive enlargement of these organs (hepatosplenomegaly).

In childhood leukemia, radiographically detectable skeletal involvement is extremely common as a result of the infiltration of leukemic cells in the marrow. The earliest radiographic sign of disease is usually a transverse radiolucent band at the metaphyseal ends of the long bones, most commonly about the knees, ankles, and wrists (Figure 8-9). Although in infancy this appearance is nonspecific and also occurs with malnutrition or systemic disease, the presence of these transverse lucent metaphyseal bands after 2 years of age is strongly suggestive of acute leukemia.

As the proliferation of neoplastic cells in the marrow becomes more extensive, actual destruction of bone may occur. This may cause patchy lytic lesions, a permeative moth-eaten appearance, or diffuse destruction with cortical erosion (Figure 8-10). A reactive response to proliferating leukemic cells can cause patchy or uniform osteosclerosis; subperiosteal proliferation incites the formation of periosteal new bone. Diffuse skeletal demineralization may result in vertebral compression fractures.

Enlargement of mediastinal and hilar lymph nodes is the most common abnormality on chest radiographs. Diffuse bilateral reticular changes may simulate lymphangitic spread of carcinoma. The nonspecific pulmonary infiltrates seen in patients with acute leukemia are usually attributable to hemorrhage or secondary infection.

The radiographic abnormalities in chronic leukemia are often similar to those in the acute disease, though their frequency and degree may vary. Skeletal changes are much less common and are usually limited to generalized demineralization in the flat bones, where active marrow persists in adulthood. The demonstration of focal areas of destruction, or periosteal new bone formation, indicates probable transformation into an acute phase of the disease.

Hilar and mediastinal adenopathy are common, especially in chronic lymphocytic leukemia. Congestive heart failure commonly results from the associated severe anemia.

Splenomegaly is an almost constant finding in patients with chronic leukemia (Figure 8-11). Leukemic infiltration of the gastrointestinal tract can pro-

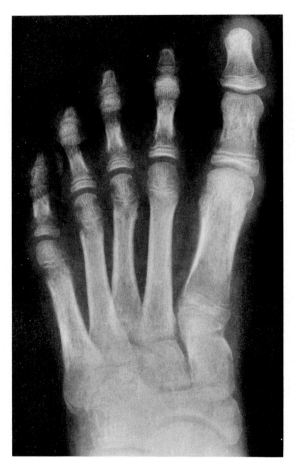

Figure 8-9 Acute leukemia. In addition to radiolucent metaphyseal bands, there is frank bone destruction with cortical erosion involving many metatarsals and proximal phalanges.

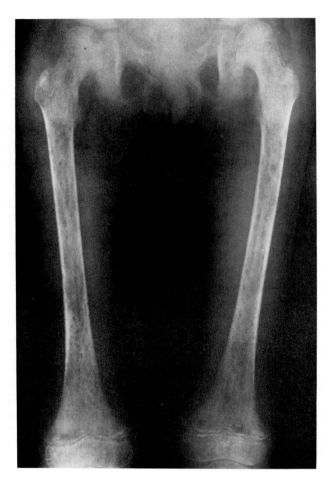

Figure 8-10 Acute leukemia. Proliferation of neoplastic cells in marrow has caused extensive destruction of bone in both femurs.

duce single or multiple intraluminal filling defects or appear as an infiltrative process that may be indistinguishable from carcinoma. Renal infiltration can cause bilateral enlargement of the kidneys. In chronic lymphocytic leukemia, enlargement of retroperitoneal or mesenteric lymph nodes can cause displacement or obstruction of structures in the genitourinary or gastrointestinal tracts.

Lymphoma

Lymphomas are neoplasms of the lymphoreticular system, which includes the lymph nodes, spleen, and the lymphoid tissues of parenchymal organs such as the gastrointestinal tract, lung, or skin. They are usually divided into two major types: Hodgkin's and non-Hodgkin's lymphomas. Ninety percent of cases of Hodgkin's disease originate in the lymph nodes; 10% are of extranodal origin. In contrast, parenchymal organs are more often involved in non-Hodgkin's lymphomas, about 40% of which are

of extranodal origin. Mediastinal lymph node enlargement is the most common radiographic finding in lymphoma (Figure 8-12). It is seen on initial chest radiographs of about half the patients with Hodgkin's disease and about one third of those with non-Hodgkin's lymphoma. Mediastinal lymph node enlargement is usually asymmetric but bilateral. Involvement of anterior mediastinal and retrosternal nodes is common, a major factor in the differential diagnosis from sarcoidosis, which rarely produces radiographically visible enlargement of nodes in the anterior compartment. Calcification may develop in intrathoracic lymph nodes after mediastinal irradiation.

Involvement of the pulmonary parenchyma and pleura usually occurs by direct extension from mediastinal nodes along the lymphatic vessels of the bronchovascular sheaths. Radiographically, this may appear as a coarse interstitial pattern (Figure 8-13), as solitary or multiple ill-defined nodules, or as

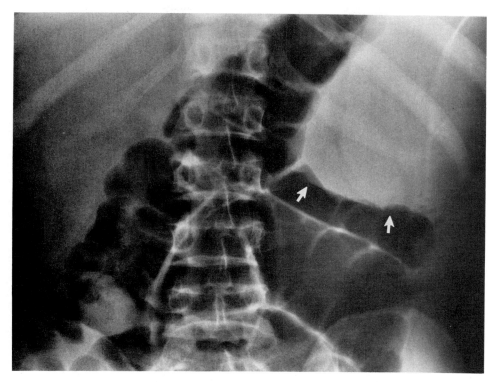

Figure 8-11 Chronic leukemia. Massive splenomegaly causes downward displacement of splenic flexure of colon. Arrow points to inferior margin of spleen.

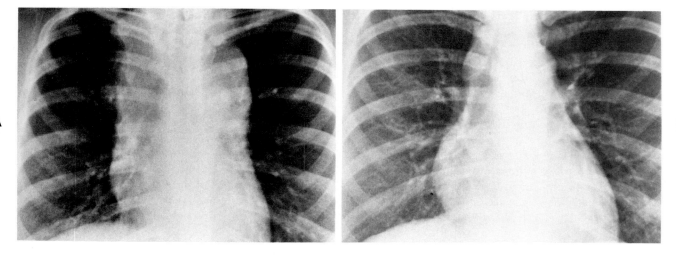

Figure 8-12 Lymphoma. **A,** Initial chest film demonstrates considerable widening of upper half of mediastinum caused by pronounced lymphadenopathy. **B,** After chemotherapy, there is dramatic decrease in width of upper mediastinum.

patchy areas of parenchymal infiltrate that may coalesce to form a large homogeneous mass. At times, it may be difficult to distinguish a superimposed infection after radiation therapy or chemotherapy from the continued spread of lymphomatous tissue. Pleural effusion occurs in up to one third of patients with thoracic lymphoma; extension of the tumor to the pericardium can cause pericardial effusion.

About 5% to 10% of patients with lymphoma have involvement of the gastrointestinal tract, primarily of the stomach and small bowel. Gastric

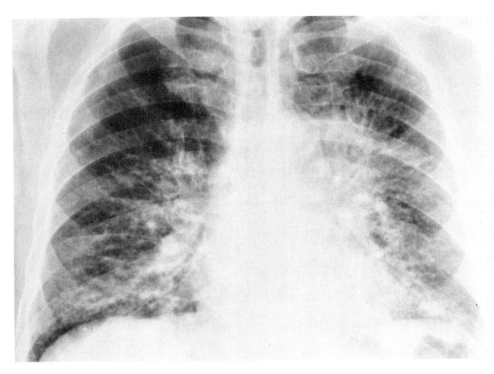

Figure 8-13 Lymphoma. Diffuse reticular and reticulonodular changes causing prominence of interstitial lung markings. Note enlargement of left hilar region.

lymphoma often is seen as a large, bulky polypoid mass, usually irregular and ulcerated, that may be indistinguishable from a carcinoma (Figure 8-14). A multiplicity of malignant ulcers or an aneurysmal appearance of a single huge ulcer (the diameter of which exceeds that of the adjacent gastric lumen) is characteristic of lymphoma. Additional findings suggestive of lymphoma include relative flexibility of the gastric wall, enlargement of the spleen, and associated prominence of retrogastric and other regional lymph nodes that cause extrinsic impressions on the barium-filled stomach. Other manifestations of gastric lymphoma include thickening, distortion, and nodularity of rugal folds (Figure 8-15) and generalized gastric narrowing caused by a severe fibrotic reaction.

Lymphoma can produce virtually any pattern of abnormality in the small bowel. The disease may be localized to a single intestinal segment, be multifocal, or cause diffuse involvement. The major radiographic appearances include irregular thickening of mucosal folds, large ulcerating masses, and multiple intraluminal or intramural filling defects simulating metastatic disease.

Skeletal involvement can be demonstrated in about 15% of patients with lymphoma. Direct extension from adjacent lymph nodes causes bone erosion, especially of the anterior surface of the upper lumbar and lower thoracic spine. Paravertebral soft-tissue masses may occur. The hematogenous spread of lymphoma produces a mottled pattern of destruction and sclerosis, which may simulate metastatic disease. Dense vertebral sclerosis (ivory vertebra) may develop in Hodgkin's disease (Figure 8-16).

Diffuse lymphomatous infiltration may cause renal enlargement with distortion, elongation, and compression of the calyces (Figure 8-17). Single or multiple renal nodules or perirenal masses may displace or distort the kidney. Diffuse retroperitoneal lymphoma can displace the kidneys or ureters and obliterate one or both psoas margins.

Once the diagnosis of lymphoma is made, it is essential to determine the status of the abdominal and pelvic lymph nodes. This is necessary for both the initial staging and treatment planning and for assessing the efficacy of treatment and detecting tumor recurrence.

There is controversy about the best radiographic approach for the staging of a patient with known lymphoma. Although lymphography has long been a most accurate examination for demonstrating lymphomatous involvement of abdominal and pelvic nodes, noninvasive cross-sectional imaging techniques (CT and ultrasound) are now considered by many to be the diagnostic methods of choice. Unlike CT and ultrasound, which rely primarily on an

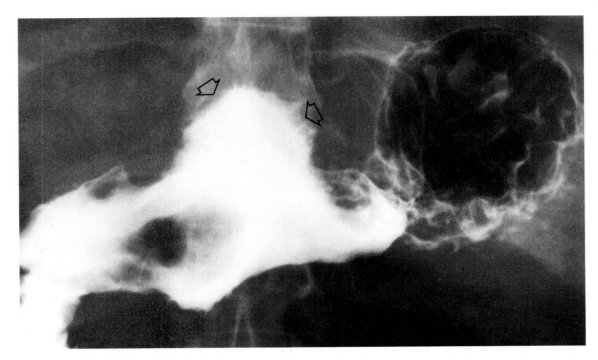

Figure 8-14   Lymphoma presenting as large mass almost filled by huge ulcer *(arrows)*.

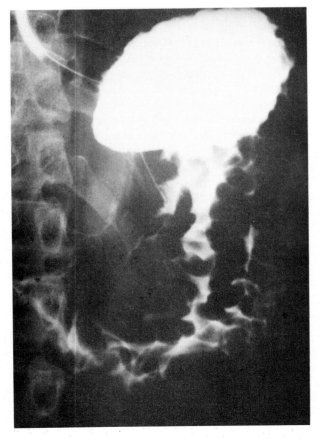

Figure 8-15   Lymphoma of stomach. Notice diffuse thickening, distortion, and nodularity of gastric folds.

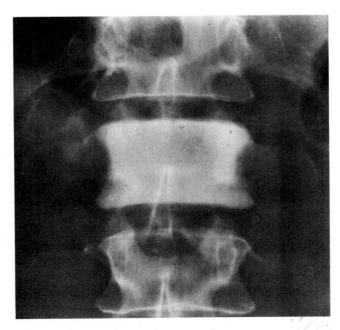

Figure 8-16   Lymphoma. Ivory vertebra.

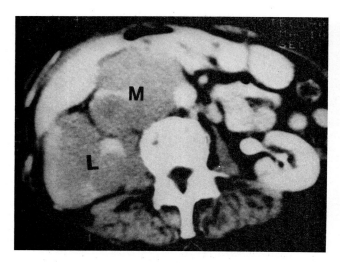

Figure 8-17 Lymphoma. Right kidney is completely replaced by lymphomatous mass *(L)*. Notice extensive involvement of lymph nodes *(M)*.

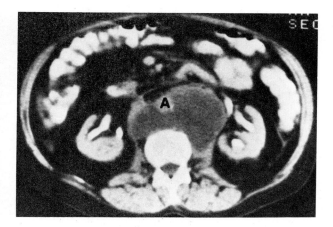

Figure 8-18 Lymphoma. CT scan demonstrates anterior displacement of abdominal aorta *(A)* away from spine caused by lymphomatous involvement of retro-aortic and para-aortic nodes.

increase in node size as a criterion for determining tumor involvement, lymphography can detect microscopic tumor foci and alterations in architecture within normal-sized nodes. It can also distinguish large nodes that contain tumor from similarly enlarged nodes that demonstrate only benign reactive changes. After formal staging procedures, abdominal radiographs can demonstrate retained contrast material within lymph nodes and thus provide an inexpensive and accurate mean for assessing the effect of therapy and detecting relapse. However, lymph nodes in the upper para-aortic, retrocrural, renal hilum, or splenic hilum, porta hepatis, and mesenteric areas cannot be adequately examined by lymphography and require CT or ultrasound (Figure 8-18). CT can also be used to check on the response to treatment, especially since there may be insufficient residual contrast on postlymphography abdominal films to make a diagnosis.

In practice, CT is generally the first procedure used in staging lymphoma patients, especially those with non-Hodgkin's lymphoma, which tends to produce bulky masses in the mesenteric and high retrocrural areas where the contrast material used in lymphography does not reach. An abnormal CT scan eliminates the need for the more invasive lymphography; a normal CT scan obtained at 2 cm intervals can exclude retroperitoneal adenopathy with high confidence. Lymphography is of value primarily in Hodgkin's disease, which infrequently involves the mesenteric nodes, often does not produce bulky masses, and may cause alterations of internal architecture only (which cannot be detected with CT) in normal-sized nodes. Lymphography is also indicated when CT is equivocal because of either a lack of fat or gross-motion artifacts.

Infectious mononucleosis

Mononucleosis is a self-limited viral disease of the lymphoreticular system characterized by vague symptoms of mild fever, fatigue, sore throat, and swollen lymph nodes. It primarily infects young adults and, although often termed the "kissing disease," is not particularly contagious. Blood test show an elevated white cell count with an abnormally high percentage of atypical lymphocytes, which resemble monocytes. The diagnosis is based on the presence of antibodies to the virus in the blood.

Generalized lymphadenopathy and splenomegaly are characteristic clinical and radiographic findings in infectious mononucleosis. Hilar lymph node enlargement, usually bilateral, can be demonstrated in about 15% of cases (Figure 8-19). Pneumonia is a rare complication that can appear as a diffuse reticular pattern indicating interstitial disease or as a patchy, nonspecific air-space consolidation.

■ Diseases of Platelets (Bleeding Disorders)

Blood coagulation (clotting) is a complicated mechanism requiring platelets, calcium, and 12 coenzymes and proteins called **coagulation factors.** A deficiency in quantity or activity of any of these materials may lead to an inability to control hemorrhage or even to spontaneous bleeding.

Hemophilia

Hemophilia is an inherited (sex-linked recessive gene) anomaly of blood coagulation that appears

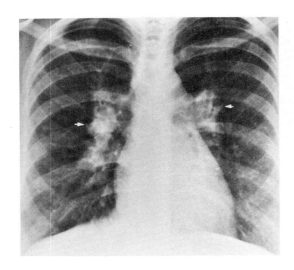
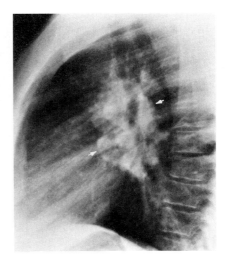

Figure 8-19   Infectious mononucleosis. **A,** Frontal and, **B,** lateral projections of chest demonstrate pronounced enlargement of hilar lymph nodes bilaterally *(arrows).*

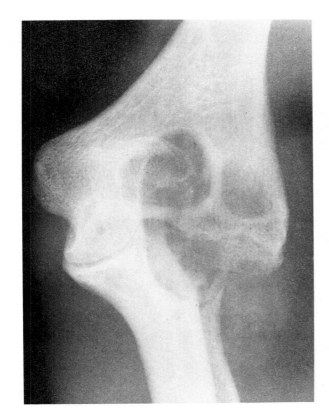

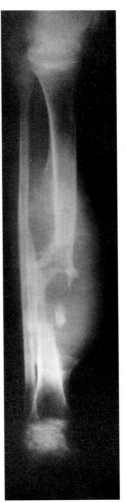

Figure 8-20   Hemophilia. **A,** Large subchondral cysts about elbow. **B,** Destructive, expansile lesion of lower tibial shaft. (From Stoker DJ, Murray RO: *Semin Roentgenol* 9:185-193, 1974.)

clinically only in males. Patients with this disease have a decreased or absent serum concentration of antihemophilic globulin (factor VIII) and suffer a lifelong tendency to spontaneous hemorrhage or severe bleeding from even minor cuts or injuries.

The major radiographic changes in hemophilia are complications of recurrent bleeding into the joints, which most commonly involve the knees, elbows, and ankles. Initially, the hemorrhage produces a generalized nonspecific soft-tissue prominence of the distended joint. Deposition of iron pigment may produce areas of cloudy increased density in the periarticular soft tissues. Although complete resorption of intra-articular blood may leave no residual change, subsequent episodes of bleeding result in synovial hypertrophy. In chronic disease, the hyperplastic synovium causes cartilage destruction and joint space narrowing and often leads to the development of multiple subchondral cysts of varying sizes in the immediate juxta-articular bone (Figure 8-20, *A*). Destruction of articular cartilage and continued use of the damaged joint lead to subchondral sclerosis and collapse, extensive and bizarre spur formation, and often pronounced soft-tissue calcification. Hemorrhage extending into the adjacent bony structures may cause extensive destruction (pseudotumor of hemophilia), which can mimic a malignant tumor (Figure 8-20,*B*).

Repeated joint hemorrhages lead to increased blood flow in the region of the epiphysis and growth plate. These structures may ossify prematurely, become abnormally large, or fuse prematurely with the metaphysis. Increased blood flow and atrophy of bone and muscle that may follow an episode of joint bleeding result in severe osteoporosis. Common signs suggestive, though not pathognomonic, of hemophilia include widening and deepening of the intercondylar notch of the femur (Figure 8-21) and "squaring" of the inferior border of the patella. Asymmetric growth of the distal tibial epiphysis may result in "slanting" of the tibiotalar joint. Hemarthrosis can cause occlusion of epiphyseal vessels and result in avascular necrosis. This most commonly involves the femoral and radial heads, both of which have a totally intracapsular epiphysis and are therefore especially vulnerable to deprivation of their vascular supply from compression by a tense joint effusion.

As in the other bleeding disorders, submucosal bleeding into the wall of the gastrointestinal tract may develop in patients with hemophilia. This most commonly involves the small bowel and produces a short or long segment with regular thickening of folds. In the colon, bleeding may produce the thumbprinting pattern of sharply defined, fingerlike

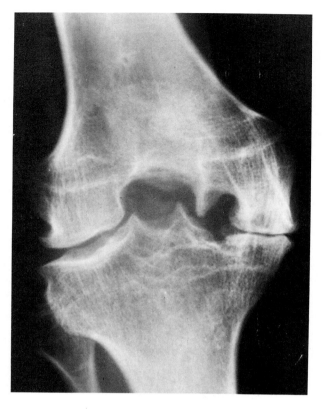

Figure 8-21 Hemophilia. Intercondylar notch is greatly widened, and coarse trabeculae, narrowing of joint space, and hypertrophic spurring can be seen.

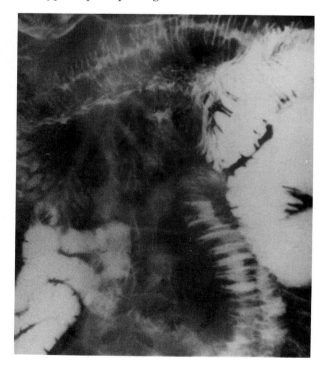

Figure 8-22 Chronic idiopathic thrombocytopenic purpura. Hemorrhage into wall of small bowel causes regular thickening of mucosal folds.

marginal indentations along the contours of the colon wall.

Purpura (thrombocytopenia)

Purpura refers to a deficiency in the number of platelets causing spontaneous hemorrhages in the skin, mucous membranes of the mouth, and internal organs. In the skin, purpura leads to the development of small, flat red spots (petechiae) or larger hemorrhagic areas (ecchymoses).

Acute idiopathic thrombocytopenic purpura typically has the sudden onset of severe purpura 1 to 2 weeks after a sore throat or upper respiratory infection in an otherwise healthy child. In most patients the disorder is self-limited and clears spontaneously within a few weeks. Unlike the acute form, chronic idiopathic thrombocytopenic purpura occurs primarily in young women and has an insidious onset with a relatively long history of easy bruising and

menorrhagia. This condition is generally considered to be an autoimmune disorder, since most patients have a circulating platelet autoantibody that develops without underlying disease or significant exposure to drugs.

Purpura can also be a complication of conditions that suppress the bone marrow (aplastic anemia) or infiltrate the bone marrow with tumor cells (leukemia, lymphoma, myeloma, metastases).

The radiographic changes caused by either acute or chronic idiopathic thrombocytopenic purpura primarily involve the gastrointestinal tract. Hemorrhage into the small bowel produces characteristic uniform, regular thickening of mucosal folds in the affected intestinal segment (Figure 8-22). Splenomegaly is commonly present; splenectomy is often required to remove this important site of platelet destruction and major source of synthesis of platelet antibodies.

QUESTIONS

1. When diseases of the hematopoietic system result in demineralization of bone, the radiographer must be alert to the possibility of
   _____ .
   A. Patient infection   C. Pathologic fracture
   B. Self-infection   D. Syncope

2. Red blood cells are called _____ .
   A. Erythrocytes   C. Thrombocytes
   B. Leukocytes   D. Hemoglobin

3. Platelets are called _____ .
   A. Erythrocytes   C. Thrombocytes
   B. Leukocytes   D. Lymphocytes

4. White blood cells are called _____ .
   A. Erythrocytes   C. Thrombocytes
   B. Leukocytes   D. Paracytes

5. The smallest blood cells, platelets, are essential for what process?
   A. Immunity   C. Carrying oxygen
   B. Clotting   D. Fighting infection

6. Lymphocytes play a major role in the
   _____ system.
   A. Endocrine   C. Immune
   B. Hematopoietic   D. Metabolic

7. The term _____ refers to a decrease in the amount of oxygen-carrying hemoglobin in the blood.
   A. Spherocytosis   C. Anemia
   B. Thalassemia

8. What type of anemia can cause painful bone infarcts and is generally confined to the black race?
   D. Hematopoiesis
   A. Spherocytosis   C. Sickle cell
   B. Thalassemia   D. Salmonella

9. A hematologic disorder characterized by an increase in the production of erythrocytes, granulocytes, and platelets is _____ .
   A. Polycythemia vera C. Sickle cell anemia
   B. Erythrocytosis   D. Hemolytic anemia

10. A cancerous disease of the hematopoietic system characterized by an increase in white blood cells is _____ .
    A. Anemia   C. Leukemia
    B. Thrombocytopenia D. Hemophilia

11. What is the name of an inherited anomaly of blood coagulation?
    A. Sickle cell anemia C. Leukemia
    B. Hemophilia   D. Leukocytosis

12. What pathologic condition refers to a deficiency in the number of platelets resulting in spontaneous hemorrhages in the skin, internal organs, and mucous membranes of the mouth?
    A. Hemophilia   C. Leukemia
    B. Purpura   D. Sickle cell anemia

BIBLIOGRAPHY

Reynolds J: Radiologic manifestations of sickle cell hemoglobulin-opathy, *JAMA* 238:247-250, 1977.

Korsten J et al: Extramedullary hematopoiesis in patients with thalassemia anemia, *Radiology* 95:257-264, 1970.

Stoker DJ, Murray RO: Skeletal changes in hemophilia and other bleeding disorders, *Semin Roentgenol* 9:185-193, 1974.

Pear BL: Skeletal manifestations of the lymphomas and leukemias, *Semin Roentgenol* 9:229-240, 1974.

CHAPTER 9

Endocrine System

■ **Prerequisite Knowledge**

The student should have a basic knowledge of the anatomy and physiology of the endocrine system. In addition, proper learning and understanding of the material will be facilitated if the student has some clinical experience in general radiography and film evaluation, including a concept of the newer imaging modalities (ultrasound, CT, MRI) used to study the various body systems affected by endocrine abnormalities.

■ **Goals**

To acquaint the student radiographer with the pathophysiology and radiographic manifestations of all of the common and some of the unusual disorders of the endocrine system

■ **Objectives**

1. Understand and be able to define or describe all bold-faced terms in this chapter
2. Describe the physiology of the endocrine system
3. Identify anatomic structures on both diagrams and images of the endocrine system
4. Be able to describe the various pathologic conditions affecting the endocrine system as well as their radiographic manifestations

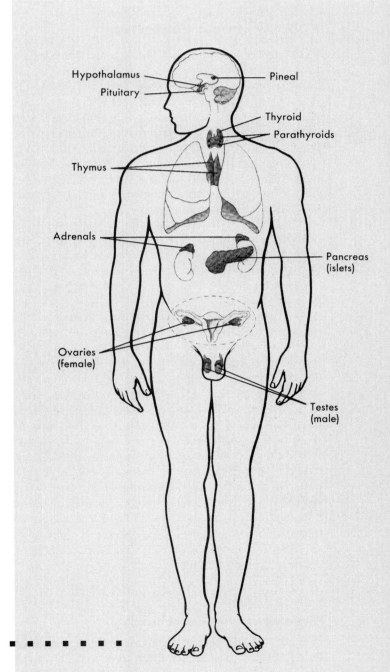

■ Diseases of the Endocrine System

The endocrine system is a biochemical communication network through which several small glands control a broad range of vital body activities. The endocrine glands secrete chemical messengers called "hormones," which circulate in the blood and may affect a single target organ or the entire body. Hormones may be proteins (growth hormone), steroids (cortisone), peptides (antidiuretic hormone), amino acids (thyroxine), or amines (epinephrine). They range from large to small molecules and have chemical structures of varying complexity.

The major endocrine glands are the pituitary, adrenal, thyroid, and parathyroid glands. Inadequate (**hypoactive**) or excess (**hyperactive**) production of hormones from these endocrine glands can give rise to a wide variety of clinical symptoms and radiographic abnormalities.

Because hormones are powerful chemicals, it is essential that their circulating levels be carefully controlled. One type of control is called the "negative feedback mechanism." In this system, an adequate level of a hormone in the blood automatically stops the release of additional hormone (somewhat like a thermostat). As the blood level of the hormone decreases, the gland is stimulated to secrete more of it. Another control mechanism is the production of two different hormones whose actions are opposite to each other. For example, insulin is secreted by the pancreas when the blood glucose level rises. When the blood glucose level falls below normal, a second hormone, glucagon, is secreted by the pancreas to raise the blood glucose. Thus these two hormones are balanced so that a proper blood glucose level is continually maintained.

■ Adrenal Glands

Physiology of the adrenal glands

The adrenal glands are situated at the top of each kidney and consist of an outer cortex and an inner medulla. The adrenal cortex secretes several different types of steroid hormones, which can be divided into three general groups. The **mineralocorticoids** (primarily aldosterone) regulate salt and water balance by causing sodium retention and potassium excretion by the kidneys. The production of aldosterone is primarily regulated by the secretion of renin from specialized cells (juxtaglomerular apparatus) in the kidney. Reduced blood volume (as in hemorrhage) causes low blood pressure, which is detected by the juxtaglomerular apparatus and eventually results in increased aldosterone secretion from the adrenal cortex. **Glucocorticoids** (especially cortisone) regulate carbohydrate metabolism and are under the regulation of ACTH from the anterior pituitary gland. Cortisone also depresses the inflammatory response to almost all forms of injury, thus leading to its use in the treatment of trauma, rheumatoid arthritis, bursitis, and asthma, and as an immunosuppressive agent to help limit rejection after organ transplantation. **Androgens** are sex hormones that tend to masculinize the body, to retain amino acids, and to enhance protein synthesis. It is these hormones that are used both illegally and unwisely by athletes to attempt to increase their body strength.

The adrenal medulla secretes epinephrine (adrenaline) and norepinephrine. These "fight or flight" hormones are secreted in stress situations when additional energy and strength are needed. Epinephrine stimulates heart activity, raises blood pressure, and increases the level of blood glucose. By constricting some blood vessels and dilating others, epinephrine shunts blood to active muscles where oxygen and nutrients are urgently needed.

Diseases of the adrenal cortex
Cushing's syndrome

The excess production of glucocorticoid hormones in Cushing's syndrome may be attributable to generalized bilateral hyperplasia of the adrenal cortex or may be a result of a functioning adrenal or even nonadrenal tumor. It can also be the result of the exogenous administration of cortisone. Excess secretion of glucocorticoid hormones mobilizes lipids and increases their level in the blood. This produces a characteristic obesity that is confined to the trunk of the body and is associated with a round, moon-shaped face and a pathognomonic fat pad that forms behind the shoulders (buffalo hump). Retention of salt and water results in hypertension.

Generalized enlargement of the adrenal glands is best demonstrated by CT, which shows thickening of the wings of the adrenal gland, which appear to have a stellate or Y-shaped configuration in cross section. Ultrasound can also show diffuse adrenal gland enlargement.

Benign and malignant tumors of the adrenal cortex are less common causes of Cushing's syndrome than is nontumorous adrenal hyperfunction. As a general rule, the larger an adrenocortical tumor and the more abrupt the onset of clinical symptoms and signs, the more likely the tumor is to be malignant. However, the differentiation between adenoma and carcinoma may be impossible at the time of histologic examination, and only the clinical course may define the nature of the tumor. On excretory urography with nephrotomography, a left-sided adrenal mass tends to rotate the upper pole of the kidney laterally so that the axis of the kidney no longer parallels the psoas margin. Larger left-sided masses may displace the kidney downward or indent the posterior aspect of the stomach (Figure 9-1). On the right, a mass commonly indents the superior aspect of the right kidney and displaces it downward. CT and ultrasound can demonstrate an adrenal tumor (Figure 9-2). CT is often of more value because the abundance of retroperitoneal fat may prevent an optimal ultrasound examination. Adrenal venography has been widely used to demonstrate adrenal masses and also permits the aspiration of blood samples for assessment of the level of adrenal hormones.

Cushing's syndrome produces radiographic changes in multiple systems. Diffuse osteoporosis causes generalized skeletal demineralization, which may lead to the collapse of vertebral bodies, spontaneous fractures, and aseptic necrosis of the head of the femur or humerus. Widening of the mediastinum as a result of excessive fat deposition sometimes develops in Cushing's syndrome and can be confirmed by CT. Hypercalciuria caused by the elevated steroid levels can lead to renal calculi and nephrocalcinosis.

Imaging of the sella turcica by conventional tomography or by CT is important in the routine assessment of the patient with Cushing's syndrome. Most patients with nontumorous adrenal hyperfunction are found at surgery to have an intrasellar

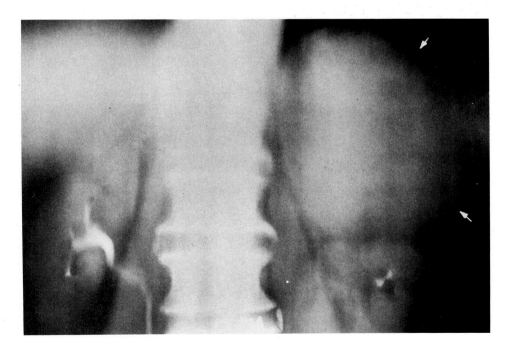

Figure 9-1 Cushing's syndrome caused by large adrenal adenoma. Nephrotomogram demonstrates huge suprarenal mass *(arrows)* causing indentation and downward displacement of left kidney.

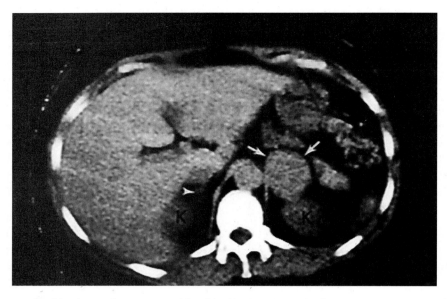

Figure 9-2 Cushing's syndrome caused by functioning cortical adenoma; 4 cm mass in left adrenal gland *(arrows)* is seen posterior to tail of pancreas and anterior to kidney *(K)*. Arrowhead points to normal right adrenal gland. (From Lee JKT, Sagel SS, Stanley RJ, editors: *Computed body tomography,* New York, 1983, Raven Press.)

lesion. It is important to emphasize, however, that small pituitary microadenomas may be present in asymptomatic patients. After adrenal surgery, a pituitary adenoma develops in up to one third of the patients and produces progressive sellar enlargement. For this reason, yearly follow-up sellar tomograms may be indicated after adrenalectomy.

Nonpituitary tumors producing ACTH may cause adrenal hyperfunction and Cushing's syndrome. The most common sites of origin are the lung, thymus, and pancreas; about half of these tumors can be demonstrated on chest radiographs.

Aldosteronism

An overproduction of mineralocorticoid hormones produced by the most superficial layer of the cortex causes retention of sodium and water and abnormal loss of potassium in the urine. This results in hypertension, muscular weakness or paralysis, and excessive thirst (polydypsia). Aldosteronism may be attributable to an adrenocortical adenoma (Conn's syndrome) or to bilateral hyperplasia of the superficial cortical layer. The clinical manifestations of aldosteronism can be cured by the resection of an adenoma but are little affected by the removal of both adrenal glands in the patient with bilateral hyperplasia. Therefore the role of radiographic imaging is to demonstrate the location of adenomas that may be otherwise difficult to detect during exploratory surgery.

Because aldosteronomas are often very small (unlike the large cortical adenomas in patients with Cushing's syndrome), excretory urography with tomography has little usefulness. CT is the major imaging modality and demonstrates the small adrenocortical adenoma as a contour abnormality of the gland (Figure 9-3). Adrenal venography with biochemical assay of a sample of adrenal blood is another important technique for localizing aldosteronomas.

Aldosteronism may also be the result of renin-secreting tumors, renal artery stenosis, malignant hypertension, and bilateral chronic renal disease.

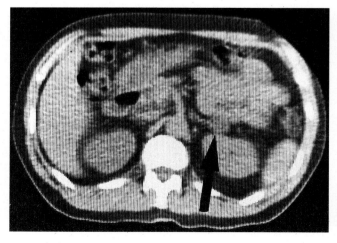

Figure 9-3 Aldosteronoma. Small mass *(arrow)* anterior to left kidney.

Adrenogenital syndrome

The adrenogenital syndrome (adrenal virilism) is caused by the excessive secretion of androgenically active substances by the adrenal gland. In the congenital form, a specific enzyme deficiency that prevents the formation of androgenic hormones causes continuous ACTH stimulation and bilateral hyperplasia. The elevated levels of androgens result in accelerated skeletal maturation along with premature epiphyseal fusion, which may lead to dwarfism.

Most cases of acquired adrenogenital syndrome are caused by adrenocortical tumors, which can be detected by CT (Figure 9-4), ultrasound, or adrenal venography. In women, the tumor causes masculinization with the development of hair on the face (hirsutism). The breasts diminish, the clitoris enlarges, and ovulation and menstruation cease.

Hypoadrenalism

The clinical manifestations of adrenal insufficiency vary from those of a chronic insidious disorder (easy fatigability, anorexia, weakness, weight loss, increased melanin pigmentation) to an acute collapse with hypotension, rapid pulse, vomiting, and diarrhea.

The most common cause of adrenal insufficiency is the excessive administration of steroids. Primary adrenocortical insufficiency (Addison's disease) results from progressive cortical destruction, which must involve more than 90% of the glands before clinical signs of adrenal insufficiency appear. In the past, Addison's disease was usually attributed to tuberculosis; at present most cases reflect idiopathic atrophy, probably on an autoimmune basis. In areas where the disease is endemic, histoplasmosis is an

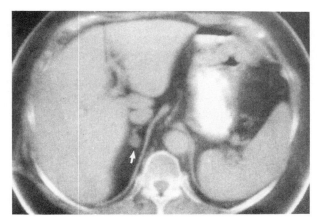

Figure 9-4 Adrenogenital syndrome caused by functioning adrenal carcinoma. Large mass in left upper quadrant *(arrow)* displacing spleen *(S)* anteriorly. Multiple round metastases are present in liver. (From Karstaedt N et al: *Radiology* 129:723-730, 1978.)

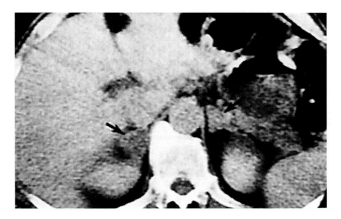

Figure 9-5 Adrenocortical insufficiency caused by disseminated histoplasmosis. CT scan demonstrates bilateral adrenal enlargement *(arrows)*. (From Karstaedt N et al: *Radiology* 129:723-730, 1978.)

occasional cause of adrenal insufficiency (Figure 9-5). Acute inflammatory disease causes generalized enlargement of the adrenal glands, which can be demonstrated by a variety of imaging techniques. Other radiographic findings occasionally seen in patients with adrenal insufficiency include a small heart and calcification of the cartilage of the ear.

Adrenal carcinoma

About half of adrenal carcinomas are functioning tumors that cause Cushing's syndrome, virilization, feminization, or aldosteronism. The tumors grow rapidly and are usually large masses at the time of clinical presentation.

Excretory urography demonstrates an adrenal carcinoma as a nonspecific suprarenal mass that is often lobulated and tends to displace the kidney without evidence of invasion. Ultrasound shows the tumor as a complex mass that may be difficult to separate from an upper pole renal tumor. CT demonstrates an adrenal carcinoma as a large mass that often contains low-density areas resulting from necrosis or prior hemorrhage (Figure 9-6). Because lymphatic and hepatic metastases are common at the time of clinical presentation, CT scans at multiple abdominal levels are necessary to define the extent of the primary tumor and to detect metastases before attempted surgical resection. Extension of the tumor into the renal vein and inferior vena cava can also be detected by CT, especially after the injection of intravenous contrast material, or by MRI (Figure 9-7).

Metastases to the adrenal glands

The adrenal gland is one of the most common sites of metastatic disease. The primary tumors that

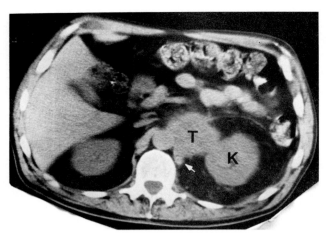

Figure 9-6 Adrenal carcinoma. Large soft-tissue tumor *(T)* invading anteromedial aspect of left kidney *(K)* and left crus of diaphragm *(arrow)*. (Courtesy of Nolan Karstaedt, MD, and Neil Wolfman, MD, Winston-Salem, NC.)

most frequently metastasize to the adrenal gland are carcinomas of the lung and breast; carcinomas of the kidney, ovary, and gastrointestinal tract; and melanomas. Metastatic enlargement of an adrenal gland can cause downward displacement of the kidney with flattening of the upper pole. Ultrasound and CT demonstrate adrenal metastases as solid, soft-tissue masses that vary considerably in size and are frequently bilateral (Figure 9-8). However, the ultrasound and CT patterns are indistinguishable from those of primary malignancies of the gland. There-

fore when a known primary tumor exists elsewhere, it is usually assumed that an adrenal mass is metastatic. If necessary, a needle biopsy using ultrasound guidance may be of value to determine whether the adrenal lesion is primary or metastatic.

Diseases of the adrenal medulla
Pheochromocytoma

A pheochromocytoma is a tumor that most commonly arises in the adrenal medulla and produces an excess of vasopressor substances (epinephrine and norepinephrine), which can cause an uncommon but curable form of hypertension. About 10% of pheochromocytomas are extra-adrenal in origin. About 10% of patients have bilateral tumors, and a similar percentage of pheochromocytomas are malignant.

Because in almost all patients the diagnosis of a pheochromocytoma can be made with biochemical tests, radiographic imaging serves as a confirmatory study and as a means of localizing the tumor. Excretory urography, even with nephrotomography, may be of limited value because the kidney is often not displaced even when an adrenal pheochromocytoma is large.

CT and ultrasound are very useful in the localization of pheochromocytomas. The cross-sectional images not only detail the extent of the adrenal lesion but also define the status of adjacent structures and can demonstrate bilateral or multiple pheochromocytomas, extra-adrenal tumors, and metastases. Pheochromocytomas generally appear as round,

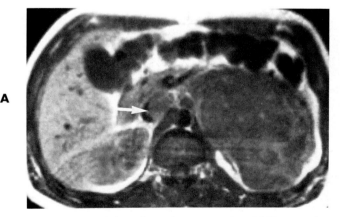
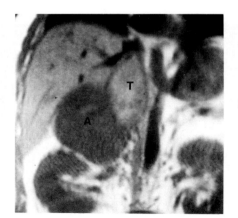

Figure 9-7 Adrenal carcinoma. **A,** Axial MR scan demonstrates a large left adrenal tumor invading the left renal vein and inferior vena cava *(arrows)*. **B,** In another patient, a coronal MR scan shows an adrenal mass *(A)* above the kidney with tumor thrombus of slightly higher signal intensity filling inferior vena cave *(T)*. (From Stark DD, Bradley WG: *Magnetic resonance imaging*, ed 2, St Louis, 1991, Mosby.)

oval, or pear-shaped masses that are slightly less echogenic than liver and kidney parenchyma on ultrasound and have an attenuation value less than these organs on CT (Figure 9-9). MRI can show the relationship of the tumor to surrounding structures in the coronal plane (Figure 9-10).

Most extra-adrenal pheochromocytomas arise in the abdomen (Figure 9-11); a few are found in the chest or neck. The tumor may be located anywhere along the sympathetic nervous system, in the organ of Zuckerkandl, and in chemoreceptor tissues such as the carotid body or the glomus jugulare, in the wall of the urinary bladder, or even in the kidney or ureter. Masses may displace the ureter or kidney or may appear as filling defects in the bladder.

In patients with pheochromocytomas, the arterial injection of contrast material causes a sharp elevation in blood pressure, which must be controlled by α-adrenergic blocking agents. Therefore arteriography is hazardous in these patients.

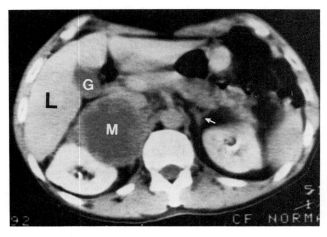

Figure 9-8   Adrenal metastases. Huge irregular low-attenuation mass *(M)* representing adrenal metastasis from oat cell carcinoma of lung. Left adrenal gland *(arrow)* is normal. G, Gallbladder; L, liver.

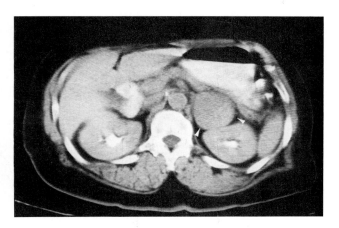

Figure 9-9   Pheochromocytoma. Large pear-shaped mass *(arrows)* anterior to left kidney.

A **B** **C**

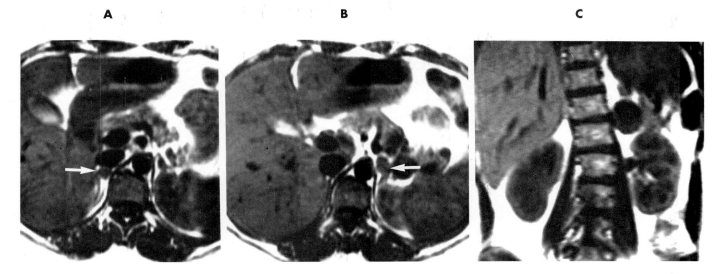

Figure 9-10   Pheochromocytoma. **A** and **B,** Axial MR scans at two levels demonstrate bilateral low-intensity lesions *(arrows).* **C,** Coronal MR scan in a different patient shows a left suprarenal mass. (From Stark DD, Bradley WG: *Magnetic resonance imaging,* ed 2, St. Louis, 1991, Mosby.)

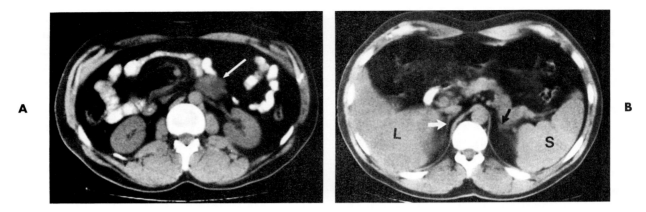

Figure 9-11 Ectopic pheochromocytoma. **A,** Soft-tissue mass *(arrows)* adjacent to aorta and in front of left renal vein. **B,** CT scan taken at higher level demonstrates that both right and left adrenal glands are normal *(arrows)*. *L,* Liver; *S,* spleen. (From Welch TJ et al: *Radiology* 148:501-503, 1983.)

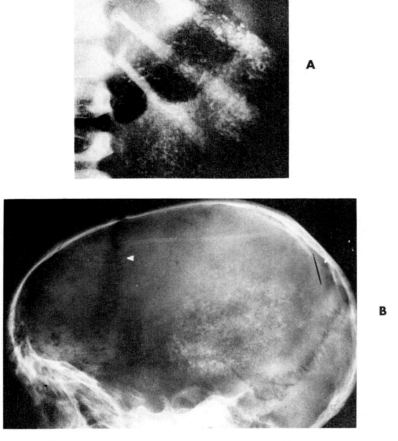

Figure 9-12 Neuroblastoma metastatic to bone. **A,** Plain film of upper abdomen shows diffuse granular calcification within large primary tumor. **B,** Lateral projection of skull shows similar calcifier deposits within metastatic lesion in calvarium. Notice sutural widening *(arrowhead)* consistent with increased intracranial pressure. (From Eisenberg RL: *Diagnostic imaging in surgery,* New York, 1987, McGraw-Hill.)

Neuroblastoma

Neuroblastoma, a tumor of adrenal medullary origin, is the second most common malignancy in children. About 10% of these tumors arise outside the adrenal gland, primarily in sympathetic ganglia in the neck, chest, abdomen, or pelvis. The tumor is highly malignant and tends to attain great size before detection.

Calcification is common in neuroblastoma (occurring in about 50% of cases) in contrast to the relatively infrequent calcification in Wilms' tumor, from which neuroblastoma must be differentiated. Calcification in a neuroblastoma has a fine granular or stippled appearance (Figure 9-12, *A*). Occasionally, there may be a single mass of amorphous calcification. Calcification can also develop in metastases of neuroblastoma in paravertebral lymph nodes and liver.

Excretory urography usually demonstrates downward and lateral renal displacement by the tumor mass (Figure 9-13). Neuroblastoma tends to cause the entire kidney and its collecting system to be displaced as a unit, unlike Wilms' tumor, which has an intrarenal origin and thus tends to distort and widen the pelvocalyceal system.

Because of its non-ionizing character, ultrasound is a superb modality for evaluating abdominal masses in children. A neuroblastoma appears as a solid or semisolid mass that is separate from the kidney. The tumor is often diffusely highly echogenic, probably because of necrosis and hemorrhage. CT can show evidence of tumor spread to lymph nodes and the sympathetic chain, widening of the paravertebral stripe (also seen on plain films) (Figure 9-14), and metastases to the liver and chest. This modality can also be used to assess the response to treatment.

Metastases to bone, liver, and lungs are common in neuroblastoma. Metastases to the skull typically cause spreading of cranial sutures because of plaques of tumor tissue growing along the surface of the brain. Bone destruction leads to a granular pattern of osteoporosis that is often associated with thin whiskerlike calcifications coursing outward and inward from the tables of the skull (Figure 9-12, *B*). Metastases in long tubular bones are often multiple and relatively symmetric and present a permeative destructive pattern.

Neuroblastomas arising in the chest appear as posterior mediastinal masses. Metastases to the chest most commonly cause asymmetric enlargement of mediastinal nodes; metastases to the pulmonary parenchyma are infrequent.

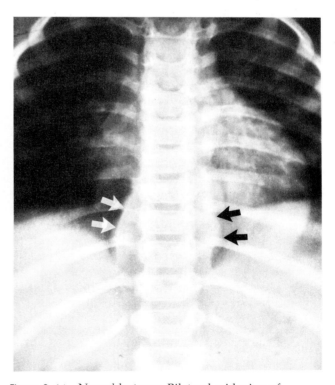

Figure 9-14 Neuroblastoma. Bilateral widening of paravertebral stripes *(arrows)* represents metastatic deposits. (From Friedland GW et al: *Uroradiology: an integrated approach,* New York, 1983, Churchill Livingstone.)

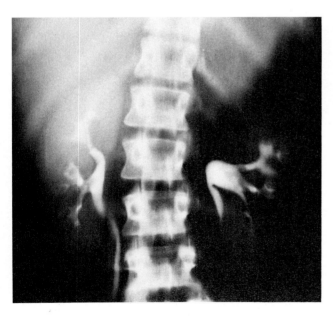

Figure 9-13 Neuroblastoma. Nephrotomogram demonstrates downward and lateral displacement of upper pole of left kidney.

■ Pituitary Gland

The pituitary gland is often called the "master gland" because the many hormones it secretes control the level of most glandular activity throughout the body. The hormone secretion of the pituitary gland itself is controlled by the hypothalamus.

The pituitary is a tiny gland about the size of a pea that is suspended from the base of the brain by a slender stalk (infundibulum) and is situated in the bony depression of the sella turcica. It is divided into anterior and posterior portions, each of which secretes different hormones.

The anterior lobe of the pituitary gland secretes growth hormone, thyroid-stimulating hormone (TSH), adrenocorticotropic hormone (ACTH), and a group of hormones that affect the sex organs, or gonads. These gonadotropins include follicle-stimulating hormone (FSH) and luteinizing hormone (LH), which regulate the menstrual cycle and secretion of male and female sex hormones, and prolactin, which stimulates the production of milk during pregnancy and after delivery.

Growth hormone affects all parts of the body by promoting the growth and development of the tissues. Before puberty, it stimulates the growth of long bones (increasing the child's height) and the size of such organs as the liver, heart, and kidneys. After adolescence, growth hormone is secreted in lesser amounts but continues to function in promoting tissue replacement and repair. TSH controls the secretion of thyroid hormone, which regulates the body's metabolism (production and use of energy). ACTH controls the level of activity of the adrenal cortex.

The posterior lobe of the pituitary gland (neurohypophysis) produces two hormones: vasopressin (antidiuretic hormone) and oxytocin. Antidiuretic hormone (ADH) increases the rate of reabsorption of water and electrolytes by the renal tubules, thus decreasing the output of urine and protecting the individual from excessive water loss. Oxytocin causes contraction of smooth muscle, especially in the uterus, and thus strengthens contractions during labor and helps to prevent hemorrhage after delivery.

Diseases of the pituitary gland
Hyperpituitarism

Hyperpituitarism results from an excess of growth hormone produced by a tumor (Figures 7-25 and 7-26) or generalized hyperplasia of the anterior lobe of the pituitary gland. The development of this condition before enchondral bone growth has ceased results in **gigantism;** hyperpituitarism beginning after bone growth has stopped produces **acromegaly.**

Generalized overgrowth of all the body tissues is the underlying abnormality in acromegaly. Although the long bones can no longer grow because the epiphyses are closed, the bones of the hands, feet, and face enlarge, and there is excessive growth of soft tissues. Proliferation of cartilage may cause joint space widening, especially of the metacarpophalangeal and hip joints. The slight increase in length of each of the seven articular cartilages for each digit leads to perceptible lengthening of the fingers. Overgrowth of the tips of the distal phalanges produces thick bony tufts with pointed lateral margins. The associated hypertrophy of the soft tissues produces the characteristic square, spade-shaped hand of acromegaly. Degenerative changes develop early and are associated with prominent hypertrophic spurring. Unlike typical osteoarthritis, acromegaly results in joint spaces that remain normal or are even widened.

Thickening of the heel pads (the soft tissue inferior to the plantar aspect of the calcaneus) to greater than 23 mm is highly suggestive of acromegaly (Figure 9-15). However, a similar appearance may also be seen in patients with obesity, myxedema, or generalized edema.

The bones of the skull become thickened and have increased density, often with obliteration of the diploic space. This bone thickening is especially prominent in the frontal and occipital regions, leading to characteristic frontal bossing and enlargement of the occipital protuberance. The paranasal sinuses

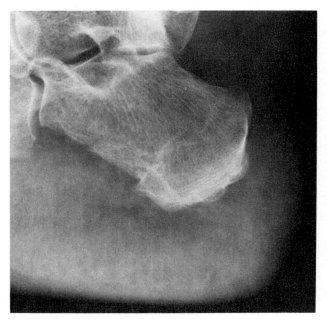

Figure 9-15   Acromegaly. Prominent thickening of heel pad, which measured 32 mm on original radiograph.

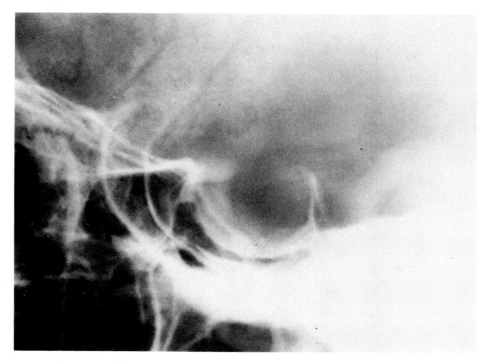

Figure 9-16 Pituitary adenoma causing acromegaly. Ballooning of sella turcica with downward displacement of floor.

(especially the frontal) become enlarged, and the mastoid processes are usually overpneumatized. Lengthening of the mandible and an increased mandibular angle produce prognathism, one of the typical clinical features of acromegaly. Thickening of the tongue may lead to slurred speech. Pituitary enlargement causes expansion and erosion of the sella turcica (Figure 9-16).

In the spine, hypertrophy of cartilage causes an increased width of the intervertebral disk spaces. An increase in the size of the vertebral bodies is best seen on lateral projections. Hypertrophy of soft tissues may produce an increased concavity of the posterior aspect of the vertebral bodies (scalloping) that is most prominent in the lumbar spine (Figure 9-17).

Extraskeletal manifestations of acromegaly include visceral enlargement, especially of the heart and kidney, enlargement of the tongue, and calcification of cartilage in the pinna of the ear.

Gigantism is manifested as an excessively large skeleton. If hypersecretion of growth hormone continues after epiphyseal closure, the soft tissue and bony changes of acromegaly are superimposed.

Hypopituitarism

Because the pituitary gland controls the level of secretion of gonadal and thyroid hormones and the production of growth hormone, decreased function

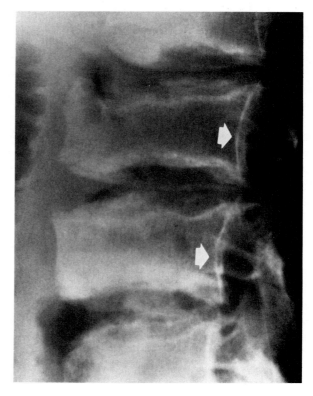

Figure 9-17 Acromegaly. Posterior scalloping *(arrows)* associated with enlargement of vertebral bodies (especially in anteroposterior dimension).

of the pituitary gland causes profound generalized disturbances in bone growth and maturation. In children, hypopituitarism typically leads to a type of dwarfism in which the delayed appearance of epiphyseal centers causes the failure of bones to grow normally in length or width. This results in a person who is small in stature and sexually immature, though well-proportional and of normal mentality. In many patients there is a delay in the eruption of the teeth, which tend to become impacted because their size is not affected. The arrest in the growth of the skeleton occurs during childhood, when the cranial vault is proportionally greater in relation to the facial bones than in the adult. Since this discrepancy remains into adulthood in hypopituitary dwarfism, the relatively large skull may be mistakenly believed to result from hydrocephaly.

Hypopituitarism occurring after adolescence results in hypofunction of the thyroid gland, adrenal glands, and gonads but usually causes few radiologic findings. The heart and kidneys are often small, and calcification or ossification may develop in the articular cartilages.

Diabetes insipidus

The impaired ability of the kidneys to conserve water in diabetes insipidus results from low blood levels of antidiuretic hormone reflecting deficient vasopressin release by the posterior lobe of the pituitary gland in response to normal physiologic stimuli. In response to excessive water loss in the urine (polyuria), the body compensates by developing an insatiable thirst (polydypsia). Severe polyuria can lead to massive dilatation of the renal pelves, calyces, and ureters. This probably represents a compensatory alteration to accommodate the huge volume of excreted urine.

It must be stressed that diabetes insipidus is completely unrelated to diabetes mellitus.

▪ Thyroid Gland

The thyroid is a butterfly-shaped gland located in the neck at the level of the larynx. It consists of two lobes, one on each side of the trachea, and a connecting strip (isthmus) that runs anterior to the trachea and connects the lower portions of the two lobes. The thyroid lies just below the Adam's apple, the protrusion formed by the cricoid cartilage of the larynx. Microscopically, the thyroid gland consists of innumerable follicles surrounding a central core of colloid, the storage form of the active material known as thyroxine, which is the only natural iodine-containing substance in the body.

The thyroid gland picks up iodine from the bloodstream and combines it with the amino acid tyrosine to synthesize thyroid hormones, which are stored in the gland until released into the bloodstream when stimulated by TSH from the anterior lobe of the pituitary gland. The active hormone, **thyroxine,** is a small molecule that may contain either three iodine molecules (T_3) or four iodine molecules (T_4). These substances stimulate the rate of cellular metabolism in response to the body's need for increased energy production. The increased cellular metabolism requires additional oxygen circulated to the cells and the removal of waste materials, both of which require increased blood flow and greater cardiac output. The increased demand for oxygen stimulates the respiratory center and results in a faster rate and greater depth of breathing. Increased cellular metabolism produces heat, which is dissipated by perspiration and by increased blood flow through dilated vessels in the skin, giving the person a flushed appearance. Thyroid hormone also increases the secretion of digestive juices and the movement of ingested material through the intestinal tract.

The release of thyroid hormone is controlled by thyroid-stimulating hormone (TSH), which is secreted by the anterior lobe of the pituitary gland. This process is a negative feedback mechanism, in which a high blood level of thyroxine inhibits the anterior pituitary and TSH release, whereas a low level of thyroxine forces the anterior pituitary to release TSH again.

Diseases of the thyroid gland
Radioactive iodine scanning

Scanning after the administration of radioactive iodine is the major imaging modality for demonstrating both functioning and nonfunctioning thyroid tissue. This technique is used to localize palpable nodules, to determine the function of nodules, to detect nonpalpable lesions (especially in patients with a history of neck irradiation), and to evaluate the extent of residual tissue after surgical or radioisotopic thyroid ablation. Radionuclide scanning may be combined with uptake, stimulation, or suppression techniques to better characterize thyroid lesions.

The distribution of radioactivity is uniform throughout the normal thyroid gland (Figure 9-18). Diffuse thyroid enlargement without hyperthyroidism most frequently represents a multinodular goiter of Hashimoto's thyroiditis. In a patient with hyperthyroidism, diffuse thyroid enlargement is suggestive of Graves' disease.

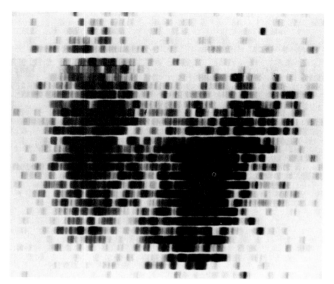

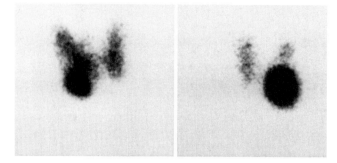

Figure 9-19 Hyperfunctioning (hot) nodules in two patients. Notice variable amount of suppression of remainder of thyroid gland. (From Palmer EL, Scott JA, Strauss HW: *Practical nuclear medicine,* Philadelphia, 1992, Saunders.)

Figure 9-18 Normal radioactive iodine scan. Uniform distribution of nuclide activity throughout thyroid gland. (From Palmer EL, Scott JA, Strauss HW: *Practical nuclear medicine,* Philadelphia, 1992, Saunders.)

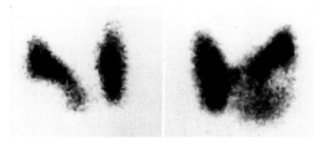

Figure 9-20 Nonfunctioning (cold) nodules in two patients.

Masses within the thyroid gland appear as hyperfunctioning ("hot") or poorly functioning ("cold") nodules. A hot nodule demonstrates increased radionuclide uptake compared with surrounding thyroid tissue (Figure 9-19). These hot nodules usually represent autonomously functioning thyroid tissue and are rarely malignant, though malignancy is sometimes reported elsewhere in the same gland. Large hyperfunctioning nodules may completely suppress the remaining thyroid tissue so that only the nodule itself is visualized. An autonomous nodule may eventually develop central hemorrhage or cystic change and evolve into a nonfunctioning (cold) nodule.

Cold thyroid nodules contain less radionuclide per unit tissue mass than adjacent normal thyroid tissue (Figure 9-20). Most cold nodules represent poorly functioning adenomas. Thyroid cysts, carcinoma, and thyroiditis can also produce this appearance. In a young patient the absence of uptake in the region of a solitary cold thyroid nodule is associated with a 10% to 25% probability that the nodule is malignant. Although ultrasound can distinguish a thyroid cyst from the other causes of cold nodules, this modality is of little value in further characterizing noncystic thyroid masses.

Hyperthyroidism

Hyperthyroidism results from the excessive production of thyroid hormone, either from the entire gland (Graves' disease) or from one or more func-

tioning adenomas. Graves' disease is a relatively common disorder that most often develops in the third and fourth decades and has a strong female predominance. The major clinical symptoms include nervousness, emotional lability, an inability to sleep, tremors, rapid pulse rate (tachycardia), palpitations, excessive sweating, and heat intolerance. Weight loss is frequent, usually despite an increased appetite. A characteristic physical finding is exophthalmos, outward protrusion of the eyeball caused by edema in the tissue behind the eyes.

Radioactive iodine scans in patients with Graves' disease typically demonstrate diffuse enlargement of the thyroid gland with increased radioiodine uptake (Figure 9-21). In severe disease, high-output cardiac failure may develop along with generalized cardiomegaly and pulmonary congestion. Unilateral or bilateral exophthalmos as a result of Graves' disease can be demonstrated by CT as thickening of the extraocular muscles.

Hypothyroidism

Hypothyroidism can result from any structural or functional abnormality that leads to an insufficient synthesis of thyroid hormone. Hypothyroidism dat-

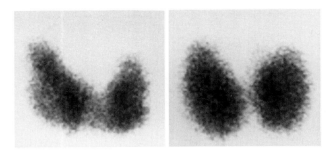

Figure 9-21 Hyperthyroidism. Radionuclide scans in two patients with Graves' disease show symmetrically enlarged thyroid glands with homogeneous increased iodine uptake.

ing from birth (cretinism) results in multiple developmental abnormalities. Children with cretinism typically have a short stature; coarse features with a protruding tongue, a broad, flattened nose, and widely set eyes; sparse hair; dry skin; and a protuberant abdomen with an umbilical hernia. The major radiographic abnormalities include a delay in the appearance and subsequent growth of ossification centers and retarded bone age. Skull changes are common and include an increase in the thickness of the cranial vault, underpneumatization of the sinuses and mastoid air cells, widened sutures with delayed closure, and a delay in the development and eruption of the teeth (Figure 9-22). Adult hypothyroidism has an insidious onset with nonspecific symptoms including lethargy, somnolence (sleeping up to 16 hours a day), constipation, cold intolerance, slowing of intellectual and motor activity, and weight gain despite a decreased appetite. Dry skin, stiff aching muscles, and a deepening voice with hoarseness often occur. The facial features are thickened, and there is a doughy thickening of the skin (myxedema). Radiographically, the heart is typically enlarged because of pericardial effusion. Soft-tissue thickening is often seen on films of the extremities, and adynamic ileus is a common finding on abdominal radiographs.

Goiter

A goiter is an enlargement of the thyroid gland that does not result from an inflammatory or neoplastic process and is not initially associated with hyperthyroidism or myxedema. Simple (nontoxic) goiter results when one or more factors impair the capacity of the thyroid gland in the basal state to secrete the quantities of active hormones necessary to meet the needs of the body. Because the blood level of thyroid hormone is low, there is nothing to inhibit the anterior pituitary, which continues to secrete thyroid-stimulating hormone, which causes the thyroid gland to enlarge. In most cases, there is a

sufficient increase in both the functioning thyroid mass and the cellular activity to overcome the mild or moderate impairment of hormone synthesis, permitting the patient to remain metabolically normal though goitrous. On a radioactive iodine scan, a

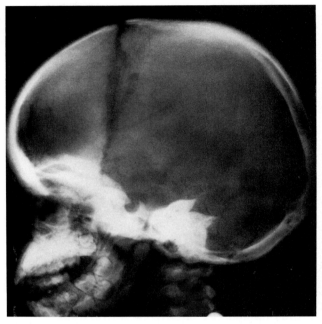

Figure 9-22 Cretinism. Lateral projection of skull shows increased density at base, small underdeveloped sinuses, and hypoplasia of teeth with delayed eruption. Retardation of facial maturation makes face appear small relative to size of calvarium.

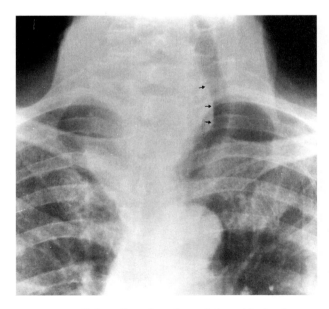

Figure 9-23 Goiter. Greatly enlarged thyroid gland appears as soft-tissue mass impressing trachea (*arrows*) and displacing it to left.

nontoxic goiter usually appears as symmetric or asymmetric enlargement of the thyroid gland. Plain radiographs and esophagrams often show the enlarged thyroid gland impressing or displacing the trachea and esophagus (Figure 9-23).

Although goiters were once common in endemic areas in which there was insufficient iodine in the diet, this is now a rare cause because of the commercial addition of iodine to salt and bread.

Toxic multinodular goiter may be a consequence of long-standing nontoxic goiter. In this condition, one or more areas of the gland become independent of TSH stimulation. Radioactive iodine scans most commonly show accumulation of iodine diffusely but in patchy foci throughout the gland (Figure 9-24). Another pattern consists of iodine accumulation in one or more discrete nodules within the gland, with the remainder of the gland being essentially nonfunctional.

Tumors of the thyroid gland

Benign thyroid adenomas are encapsulated tumors that vary greatly in size and usually compress adjacent tissue. They may be located within the neck, where they tend to cause deviation or compression of the trachea, or they may extend substernally and appear as masses in the superior portion of the anterior mediastinum. Calcification may develop within the mass (Figure 9-25). Thyroid adenomas can appear as hot or cold nodules, depending on their functional capacity.

The three major types of thyroid carcinomas are papillary, follicular, and medullary. Papillary carcinoma, the most common type, has peaks of incidence occurring in adolescence and young adulthood and again in later life. The tumor is usually slow-growing, and it typically spreads to regional lymph nodes, where it may remain silent for many years. Metastases to the lungs often cause only mild, nonspecific thickening of bronchovascular markings, though the metastases may also appear as miliary and nodular densities that predominantly involve the lower lobes.

Follicular carcinoma has a histologic appearance that closely mimics normal thyroid tissue. The tumor usually undergoes early hematogenous spread, especially to the lung and bone. Skeletal metastases, which may be the initial presentation, tend to produce entirely lytic, expansile destruction that extends into the soft tissues and is associated with little or no periosteal reaction.

Medullary carcinoma is the least common type of thyroid malignancy. At least 10% of the cases are familial, most often appearing as a component of a syndrome in which there are multiple endocrine tumors. Dense, amorphous calcifications can often be seen within the tumor.

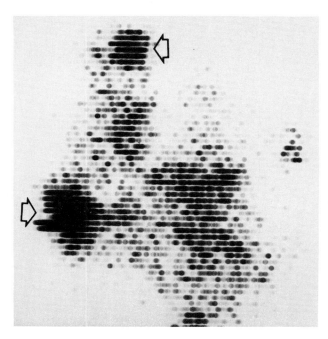

Figure 9-24 Toxic multinodular goiter. Radioactive iodine scan shows patchy uptake of nuclide and several hot nodules *(arrows)* within enlarged gland.

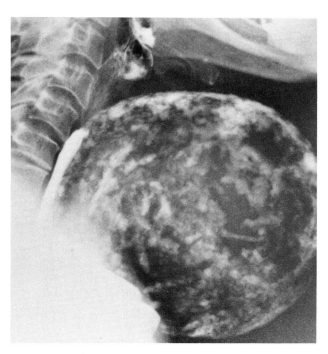

Figure 9-25 Thyroid adenoma. Lateral projection of neck shows huge calcified thyroid mass.

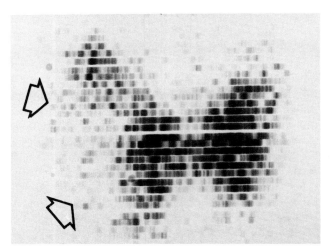

Figure 9-26 Thyroid carcinoma. Radioactive iodine scan shows solitary cold nodule *(arrows)* that correspond to patient's palpable mass.

On radioactive iodine scans, thyroid carcinoma usually appears as a solitary cold nodule that corresponds to a palpable mass (Figure 9-26). A nodule that is functioning (hot) can essentially be excluded from a diagnosis of thyroid carcinoma.

There is a substantially increased risk of thyroid cancer in persons with a history of therapeutic neck irradiation in childhood. In the past such radiation was used for benign disease such as enlargement of the tonsils, adenoids, and thymus; middle ear disease; and a variety of skin disorders, including acne.

▪ Parathyroid Glands

The parathyroids are four tiny glands, two on each side, that lie behind the upper and lower poles of the thyroid gland. They secrete **parathormone,** which is responsible for regulating the blood levels of calcium and phosphate. Parathormone raises a low serum calcium level by three mechanisms. It increases the amount of calcium absorbed from the intestinal tract by interaction with ingested vitamin D. The hormone prevents a loss of calcium through the kidneys and releases calcium from bones by stimulating osteoclastic activity. The parathyroid glands also secrete calcitonin, which decreases the serum calcium level and appears to play a role analogous to that of glucagon in the pancreas.

Diseases of the parathyroid glands
Hyperparathyroidism

Excessive secretion of parathormone leads to a generalized disorder of calcium, phosphate, and bone metabolism that results in elevated serum levels of calcium and phosphate. Primary hyperpar-

athyroidism may be caused by a discrete adenoma or carcinoma or by generalized hyperplasia of all glands. Other causes include nonparathyroid tumors that secrete a parathormone-like substance and the familial syndrome of multiple endocrine neoplasia. Secondary hyperparathyroidism occurs more frequently than the primary form and is most often attributable to chronic renal failure. Tertiary hyperparathyroidism refers to the development of autonomous functioning parathyroid glands in patients who demonstrate progressive bone disease in the presence of biochemical and clinically controlled renal disease.

The radiographic findings of primary and secondary hyperparathyroidism are similar, except that in the secondary form brown tumors (focal areas of bone destruction) are rare and osteosclerosis is more

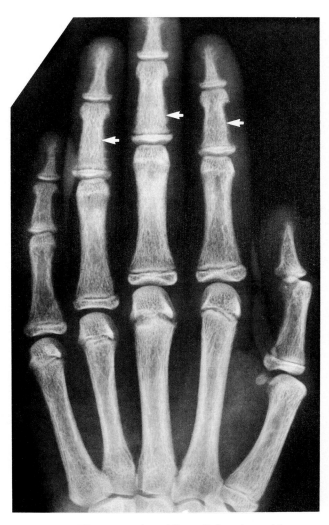

Figure 9-27 Hyperparathyroidism. Subperiosteal bone resorption that predominantly involves radial margins of middle phalanges of second, third, and fourth digits *(arrows).* Notice also resorption of terminal tufts.

common. The earliest change is subperiosteal bone resorption, which particularly involves the radial margins of the middle phalanges (Figure 9-27), the distal clavicles (Figure 9-28), and the medial aspect of the upper third of the tibias. Loss of normal cortical definition is followed by an irregularly lacy resorption, with the endosteal margin initially remaining intact. Erosions of the terminal tufts of the fingers and loss of the lamina dura of the teeth often occur, though these are nonspecific findings that also are seen in other conditions.

Generalized loss of bone density may produce a ground-glass appearance. So-called brown tumors may become large and expansile and even simulate a malignant process (Figure 9-29). Pathologic fractures may lead to bizarre deformities. Irregular demineralization of the calvarium produces the characteristic salt-and-pepper skull (Figure 9-30).

A generalized increase in bone density (osteosclerosis) may develop in patients with hyperparathyroidism, especially when it is a result of renal failure. Thick bands of increased density adjacent to the superior and inferior margins of vertebral bodies produce the characteristic "rugger-jersey" spine (Figure 9-31).

Soft-tissue calcification is common, especially in secondary hyperparathyroidism. Calcific deposits may develop in vessels, articular cartilages, menisci, joint capsules, and periarticular tissues (Figure 9-32). Elevated serum calcium and decreased excretion of calcium in the urine may result in nephrocalcinosis and urinary tract stones. An increased incidence of pancreatic calculi and pancreatitis, peptic ulcer, and gallstones also has been reported in patients with hyperparathyroidism.

The preoperative localization of a functioning parathyroid adenoma has long been a difficult radiographic problem. In many cases preoperative parathyroid localization is not required, since in patients who have not had previous neck surgery a standard bilateral neck dissection by an experienced parathyroid surgeon can be expected to have a 95% success rate in controlling hyperparathyroidism. Plain radiographs and barium studies are of virtually no value unless the tumor is huge.

The major role of sophisticated imaging modalities in localization of functioning parathyroid adenomas is in patients who remain hypercalcemic, or in whom hypercalcemia recurs, after neck surgery for hyperparathyroidism. In these patients, normal

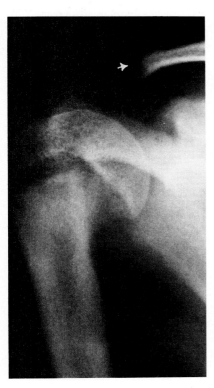

Figure 9-28 Hyperparathyroidism. Characteristic erosion of distal clavicle *(arrow)*. Metaphyseal subperiosteal resorption beneath proximal humeral head has led to pathologic fracture with slippage of humeral head.

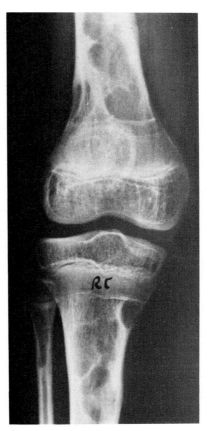

Figure 9-29 Hyperparathyroidism. Brown tumors produce multiple lytic lesions about knee.

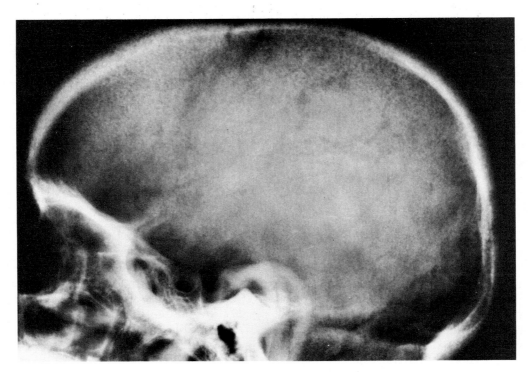

Figure 9-30   Hyperparathyroidism. Characteristic salt-and-pepper skull.

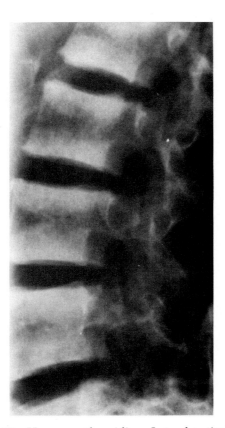

Figure 9-31   Hyperparathyroidism. Lateral projection of lumbar spine demonstrates osteosclerosis of superior and inferior margins of vertebral bodies (rugger-jersey spine).

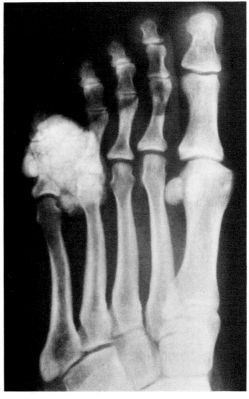

Figure 9-32   Hyperparathyroidism. Dense mass of tumoral calcification in joint capsules and periarticular soft tissues on lateral aspect of foot in patient with chronic renal disease.

anatomic relations are disturbed, landmarks may be absent, and scarring and adhesions distort the field and complicate the surgical technique. The illusive parathyroid tumor is also more likely to be situated in an ectopic position (Figure 9-33). Thus the success rate for parathyroid re-exploration is less than 65%.

Ultrasound, radionuclide scanning, CT, and MRI are complementary modalities for investigating the patient with hypercalcemia after parathyroid surgery. If these techniques fail to demonstrate a lesion, arteriography and venography with venous sampling may be performed for localization.

Preoperative fine-needle aspiration biopsy using ultrasound or CT guidance can increase the specificity in localizing and confirming the exact site of a parathyroid adenoma, especially in patients who have undergone previous neck dissection. When a successful aspiration biopsy of the neck shows the presence of parathyroid cells, there is no doubt that abnormal parathyroid tissue is situated at this site, and this eliminates the need for extensive surgical dissection.

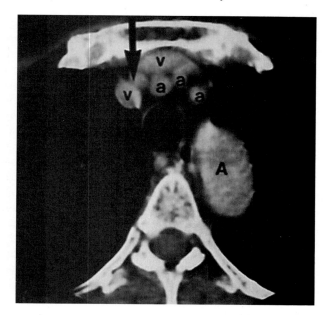

Figure 9-33   Ectopic parathyroid adenoma. CT scan shows small soft-tissue mass *(arrow)* in anterior mediastinum. *A,* Aorta; *a,* three major branches of aorta (from patient's right to left, brachiocephalic, left carotid, and left subclavian arteries); *v,* right and left brachiocephalic veins. (From Stark DD et al: *Radiology* 148:297-303, 1983.)

Hypoparathyroidism

Hypoparathyroidism usually results from injury or accidental removal of the glands during thyroidectomy and is not associated with any significant radiographic abnormalities. In the less common primary type of hypoparathyroidism, the major radiographic finding on plain skull radiographs or CT of the skull is cerebral calcification, especially involving the basal ganglia (Figure 9-34), dentate nuclei of the cerebellum, and choroid plexus. A pattern of increased density may develop in the long bones, usually localized to the metaphyseal area.

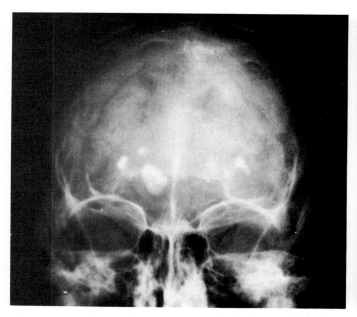

A

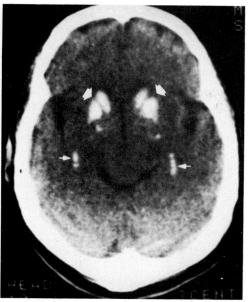

B

Figure 9-34   Hypoparathyroidism. **A,** Frontal projection of skull demonstrates calcification in basal ganglia bilaterally. **B,** CT scan shows characteristic bilateral calcification in basal ganglia *(broad arrows).* Notice also small calcific deposits in tail of caudate nuclei *(thin arrows).*

Clinically, hypoparathyroidism causes sustained muscular contraction (tetany), muscle cramps in hands and feet, and numbness and tingling of the extremities. Spasm of laryngeal muscles can cause fatal obstruction of the respiratory tract.

Pseudohypoparathyroidism and pseudopseudohypoparathyroidism

Pseudohypoparathyroidism is a hereditary disorder in which there is failure of normal end-organ response to normal levels of circulating parathyroid hormone. Most patients are obese and have short stature, with round faces, opacities in the cornea or lens of the eye, short fingers, and mental retardation. The most common radiographic abnormality is shortening of the tubular bones of the hands and feet (especially the fourth and fifth metacarpals) (see Figure 1-2) and calcific or bony deposits in the skin or subcutaneous tissues. An appearance similar to rickets may develop. As in idiopathic hypoparathyroidism, calcification is often found in the brain, especially the basal ganglia.

Pseudopseudohypoparathyroidism refers to the presence of similar skeletal anomalies in other members of the patient's family in the absence of biochemical disturbances.

▪ Diabetes Mellitus

Diabetes mellitus is a common endocrine disorder in which beta cells in the islets of Langerhans in the pancreas fail to secrete insulin, or target cells throughout the body fail to respond to this hormone. A lack of insulin prevents glucose from entering the cells, thus depriving the cells of their major nutrient for the production of energy. The blood glucose level increases **(hyperglycemia)**.

The severity and age of onset of diabetes varies. Juvenile-onset diabetes, which develops in childhood, and insulin-dependent diabetes require the patient to undergo daily insulin injections. Non–insulin dependent diabetes, which tends to develop later in life, is less severe and can often be controlled by diet alone. The precise cause of diabetes is unknown, though it is generally considered that heredity is an important factor.

Polyuria (excessive urination) and polydypsia (drinking large quantities of liquid) are common manifestations of diabetes. The large amount of sugar filtered through the kidneys exceeds the amount that the renal tubules can absorb. This leads to the excretion of glucose in the urine (glycosuria), which is a major sign of diabetes.

Glucose is the major fuel of the body. However, since glucose cannot enter the cells without the action of insulin, diabetic patients are forced to metabolize a large amount of fat. This produces a large number of fatty acids and ketone bodies, which can be detected in the urine. Production of fatty acids lowers the body's pH (acidosis). Severe acidosis and dehydration in a diabetic patient who fails to take enough insulin or eats a high-sugar diet can lead to diabetic coma, which may be fatal if not treated rapidly with fluids and a large dose of insulin.

A major complication of diabetes is the deposition of lipids within the walls of blood vessels (atherosclerosis). This causes arterial narrowing and even occlusion, resulting in myocardial infarction (coronary artery), stroke (carotid artery), or gangrene (peripheral artery). Excess glucose in tissues provides an excellent bacterial culture medium and leads to the frequent development of infections, which tend to heal poorly because of the generally poor circulation in diabetic patients. The kidneys are always affected by long-standing diabetes, and kidney failure is frequently the cause of death. Another complication is narrowing and rupture of minute retinal blood vessels, which may lead to blindness.

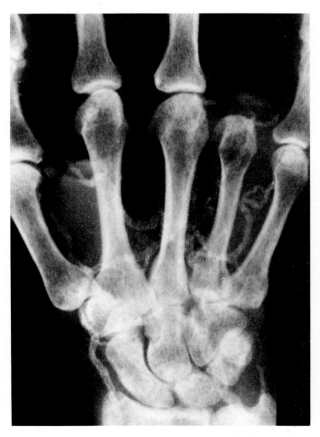

Figure 9-35 Diabetes mellitus. Typical calcification in moderate-sized vessels of hand and wrist. Notice prior surgical resection of phalanges of fourth digit.

Poor circulation to the nervous system may produce intractable pain, tingling sensations, loss of feeling, and paralysis.

A patient with diabetes must also be wary of developing insulin shock (hypoglycemic shock), which results from too much insulin, not enough food, or excessive exercise. The patient feels light-headed and faint, trembles, and begins to perspire. In the radiology department this may occur in diabetic patients who have not eaten or drunk before gastrointestinal examination or other special procedures. It is essential that this condition be rapidly recognized and sugar given, usually in the form of orange juice or candy.

Diabetes mellitus produces a variety of radiographic findings that involve multiple organ systems. Atherosclerotic disease and subsequent ischemia involving the coronary, extracerebral, and peripheral circulations occur earlier and are more extensive in diabetics, especially those who smoke. Calcifications in peripheral vessels, especially those of the hands and feet, are virtually pathognomonic of the disease (Figure 9-35). Men with diabetes may demonstrate characteristic calcification of the vas deferens, which appears as bilaterally symmetric parallel tubular densities that run medially and caudally to enter the medial aspect of the seminal vesicles at the base of the prostate gland (Figure 9-36).

Diabetic persons have an increased susceptibility to infection; this especially affects the feet and may lead to severe osteomyelitis, which produces bone destruction without periosteal reaction. Diabetic neuropathy with gait abnormalities and the loss of deep pain sensation may lead to repeated trauma on an unstable joint. Degeneration of cartilage, recurrent fracture and fragmentation of subchondral bone, soft-tissue debris, and considerable proliferation of adjacent bone can lead to total disorganization of the joint (Charcot, or neuropathic, joint) (Figure 9-37). Vascular disease with diminished blood supply can lead to gas gangrene, in which bubbles or streaks of gas develop in the subcutaneous or deeper tissues (Figure 9-38).

Diabetic neuropathy often causes radiographically evident abnormalities in the gastrointestinal tract. Findings include decreased primary peristalsis and tertiary contractions in the esophagus, delayed gastric emptying, and dilatation of the small bowel. Emphysematous cholecystitis with gas in the lumen and wall of the gallbladder (see Figure 4-80) is a severe complication that occurs almost exclusively in diabetic patients.

Renal disease is a common complication and a leading cause of death in persons with diabetes. Acute and chronic pyelonephritis, renal papillary necrosis, and cystitis often occur. Diabetic neuropathy can cause dilatation and atony of the bladder with incomplete emptying.

Mucormycosis infection is a devastating fungal disease that occurs virtually only in uncontrolled diabetics. It usually originates in the nose and paranasal sinuses, from which it can extend to destroy the walls of the sinus and invade the substance of the brain. Pulmonary mucormycosis is a progressive severe pneumonia that is widespread and confluent and often cavitates (Figure 9-39).

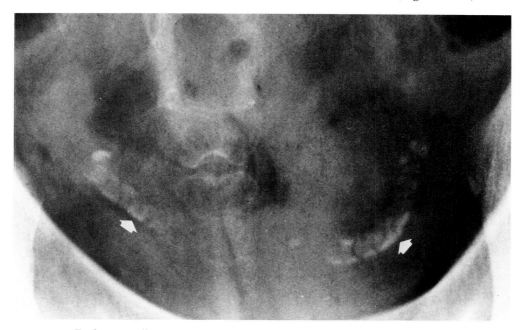

Figure 9-36   Diabetes mellitus. Bilateral calcification of vas deferens.

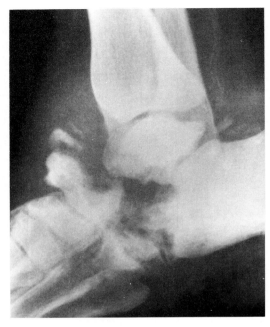

Figure 9-37 Neuropathic joint in diabetes mellitus. Severe destructive changes with calcific debris about intertarsal joints. Notice characteristic vascular calcification posterior to ankle joint.

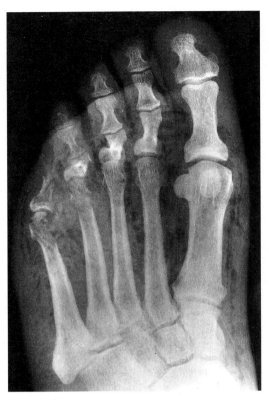

Figure 9-38 Diabetic gangrene. Diffuse destruction of phalanges and metatarsal head of fifth digit. Notice large amount of gas in soft tissues of foot.

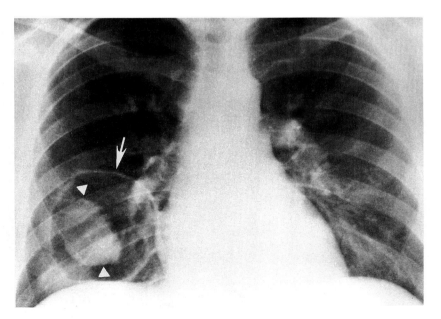

Figure 9-39 Mucormycosis in diabetic patient. Large thin-walled cavity *(arrow)* containing smooth, elliptical, homogeneous mass *(arrowheads)* representing fungus ball.

QUESTIONS

1. What organ in the body is responsible for the release of insulin?
   A. Speen
   B. Liver
   C. Pancreas
   D. Small intestine

2. What organ in the body is responsible for the release of glucagon?
   A. Spleen
   B. Liver
   C. Pancreas
   D. Small intestine

3. The _____ glands secrete several types of steroid hormones and lie above each kidney.
   A. Adrenal
   B. Pituitary
   C. Pineal
   D. Thymus

4. What hormone has the ability to constrict some blood vessels while dilating others to shunt blood to active muscles where oxygen and nutrients are needed?
   A. Androgen
   B. Epinephrine
   C. Glucocorticoids
   D. Aldosterone

5. What hormones are known as the "fight or flight" hormones?
   A. Androgen; epinephrine
   B. Adrenaline; norepinephrine
   C. Glucocorticoid; adrenaline
   D. Androgen; glucocorticoid

6. Enlargement of the adrenal glands is best demonstrated by what diagnostic modality?
   A. Ultrasound
   B. MRI
   C. CT
   D. Plain film radiography

7. What pathologic condition is characterized by obesity of the trunk of the body, a fat pad behind the shoulders, and a moon-shaped face?
   A. Conn's syndrome
   B. Cushing's syndrome
   C. Adrenogenital syndrome
   D. Addison's syndrome

8. One complication of Cushing's syndrome that radiographers must be cautious of is _____ .
   A. Buffalo hump
   B. Spontaneous fractures
   C. Hypercalciuria
   D. Sella erosion

9. Excessive administration of _____ is the most common cause of adrenal insufficiency.
   A. Adrenalin
   B. Aldosterone
   C. Steroids
   D. ACTH

10. The second most common malignancy in children is _____ .
    A. Pheochromocytoma
    B. Neuroblastoma
    C. Wilms' tumor
    D. Adenoma

11. The _____ controls the hormone secretion of the pituitary gland.
    A. Cerebellum
    B. Pons
    C. Medulla oblongata
    D. Hypothalamus

12. Enlargement of the hands, feet, and face is characteristic of what pathologic condition?
    A. Adenoma
    B. Acromegaly
    C. Gigantism
    D. None of the above

13. A pea-sized gland suspended from the base of the brain, sometimes referred to as the "master gland," is called the _____ .
    A. Thymus
    B. Pineal
    C. Pituitary
    D. Pinna

14. What is the name for the butterfly-shaped gland located at the level of the larynx?
    A. Thymus
    B. Thyroid
    C. Pituitary
    D. Pineal

15. Thyroid tissue is best demonstrated by what imaging modality?
    A. CT
    B. Radionuclide imaging
    C. Ultrasound
    D. Plain film radiography

16. Insufficient synthesis of thyroid hormone can lead to what pathologic condition?
    A. Hyperthyroidism
    B. Hypothyroidism
    C. Exophthalmos
    D. Graves' disease

17. What is the name for an enlargement of the thyroid gland that does not result from an inflammatory or neoplastic process?
    A. Exophthalmos
    B. Goiter
    C. Myxedema
    D. Skin thickening

18. There is a significant increased risk of thyroid cancer in people who received _____ .
    A. Neck radiation in childhood
    B. Steroid therapy in childhood
    C. Chest radiographs in childhood
    D. Skull radiographs in childhood

19. If beta cells in the islets of Langerhans fail to secrete insulin, what pathologic condition results?
    A. Goiter
    B. Exophthalmos
    C. Diabetes
    D. Hypothyroidism

20. A diabetic patient who receives insulin before reporting to the radiology department for an upper gastrointestinal study should be monitored by the radiographer for any signs of developing _____ .
    A. Ketoacidosis
    B. Hypoglycemic shock
    C. Acidosis
    D. Hyperglycemic shock

21. The most common complication and leading cause of death in diabetic patients is _____ .
    A. Hypoglycemia
    B. Hyperglycemia
    C. Pancreatic disease
    D. Renal disease

BIBLIOGRAPHY

Beck RE: Roentgen findings in the complications of diabetes mellitus, *Am J Roentgenol* 82:887-896, 1959.

LeMay M: The radiologic diagnosis of pituitary disease, *Radiol Clin North Am* 5:303-315, 1967.

Mitty HA, Yeh HC: *Radiology of the adrenals with sonography and CT*, Philadelphia, 1982, Saunders.

Sandler MP, Patton JA, Partain CL: *Thyroid and parathyroid imaging*, Norwalk, 1986, Appleton-Century-Crofts.

CHAPTER 10

Reproductive System

■ **Prerequisite Knowledge**

The student should have a basic knowledge of the anatomy and physiology of the reproductive system. In addition, proper learning and understanding of the material will be facilitated if the student has some clinical experience in reproductive system radiography and film evaluation.

■ **Goals**

To acquaint the student radiographer with the pathophysiology and radiographic manifestations of all of the common and some of the unusual disorders of the reproductive system.

■ **Objectives**

1. Understand and be able to define or describe all bold-faced terms in this chapter
2. Describe the physiology of the reproductive system
3. Identify anatomic structures on both diagrams and radiographs of the reproductive system
4. Be able to describe the various pathologic conditions affecting the reproductive system as well as their radiographic manifestations
5. Be familiar with the changes in technical factors required for obtaining optimal quality radiographs

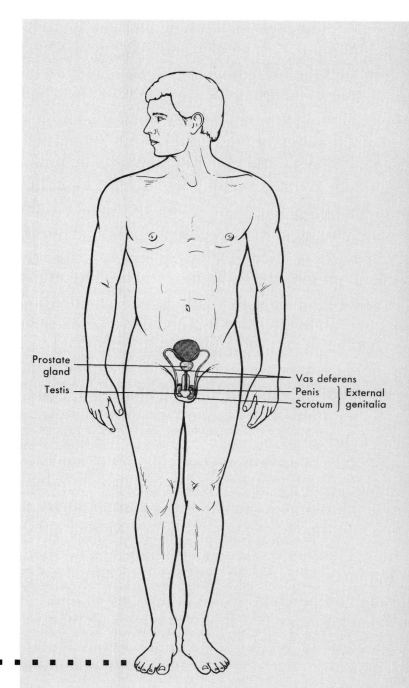

Prostate gland

Testis

Vas deferens

Penis ⎱ External
Scrotum ⎰ genitalia

■ Radiographer Notes

Because of its nonionizing character, ultrasound has become the major modality for imaging both the male and female reproductive systems. CT and MRI are used for staging malignant tumors, and radionuclide studies are used to differentiate testicular torsion from epididymitis.

Conventional plain film radiography is virtually never indicated for disorders of the pregnant patient. The once common pelvimetry and gravid uterus examinations have been almost completely replaced by nonionizing ultrasound imaging. The two radiographic studies of the female reproductive system that are in current use are hysterosalpingography and mammography. Hysterosalpingography, which is performed by use of fluoroscopic guidance, evaluates the patency (openness) of the fallopian tubes. Plain radiographs are obtained only to provide a permanent record. Mammography requires dedicated equipment and a specially trained radiographer. Properly performed mammograms can detect very early breast cancer before it is symptomatic, thus decreasing the incidence of metastases and greatly improving patient survival rates. However, mammograms performed by poorly trained radiographers or on inadequate equipment may fail to demonstrate early lesions and condemn an otherwise curable woman to unnecessary suffering and even death.

It is essential that the radiographer attempt to put the patient at ease when performing an examination of the reproductive system. Although these procedures are not actually painful, they may at times be uncomfortable and are frequently embarrassing for the patient. A good professional attitude goes a long way in reassuring the patient and making these examinations as comfortable as possible.

■ Inflammatory Disease

Syphilis

Syphilis is a chronic sexually transmitted systemic infection caused by the spirochete *Treponema pallidum*. The baby of an infected mother may be born with congenital syphilis. In the primary stage of infection, a chancre, or ulceration, develops on the genitals (usually the vulva of the female and the penis of the male). If untreated with antibiotics, the second phase of the disease appears as a nonitching rash that affects any part of the body. At this stage, the patient is still infectious but can be successfully treated with antibiotics. If still untreated, the disease may become dormant for many years before the development of the most serious, or tertiary, phase of the disease in which radiographic abnormalities become apparent.

Cardiovascular syphilis primarily involves the ascending aorta, which may become aneurysmally dilated and often demonstrates linear calcification of the wall (Figure 10-1). Syphilitic aortitis often involves the aortic valvular ring and produces aortic regurgitation with enlargement of the left ventricle.

Syphilitic involvement of the skeletal system most commonly produces radiographic findings of chronic osteomyelitis, which usually affects the long bones and skull. The destruction of bone incites a prominent periosteal reaction, and dense sclerosis is the most outstanding feature (Figure 10-2). Syphilis is a major cause of neuropathic joint disease (Char-

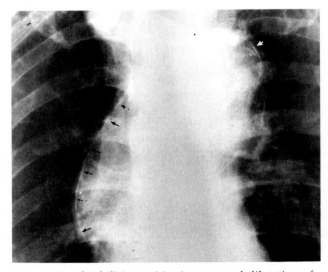

Figure 10-1 Syphilitic aortitis. Aneurysmal dilatation of ascending aorta with extensive linear calcification of wall *(black arrows)*. Some calcification is also seen in distal aortic arch *(white arrow)*.

cot joint), in which bone resorption and total disorganization of the joint are associated with calcific and bony debris (Figure 10-3).

Syphilitic lesions developing in the cerebral cortex can cause mental disorders, deafness, and blindness. Diffuse thickening of the gastric wall can cause narrowing of the lumen indistinguishable from carcinoma.

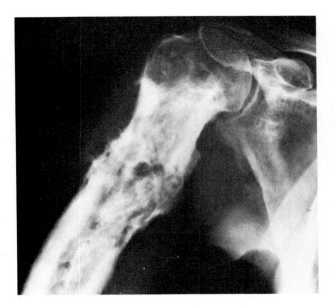

Figure 10-2 Syphilitic osteomyelitis. Diffuse lytic destruction of proximal humerus with reactive sclerosis and periosteal new bone formation.

Multiple bone abnormalities can occur in infants with congenital syphilis who are born to infected mothers (Figure 10-4). Mental retardation, deafness, and blindness are common complications.

Gonorrhea

Gonorrhea is a bacterial infection that is one of the most common and widespread of the venereal diseases. Symptoms usually occur a few days after infection. An acute urethritis with copious discharge of pus develops in men. Women may be asymptomatic or have minimal symptoms of urethral or cervical inflammation. Gonorrhea usually responds rapidly to antibiotic therapy, but if untreated the inflammation may become chronic, spread upward, and produce fibrosis leading to urethral stricture in men (Figure 10-5) and pelvic inflammatory disease in women. A serious complication is fibrous scarring of the fallopian tubes that may result in sterility or an ectopic pregnancy.

Gonorrheal infection can cause septic arthritis leading to articular erosion and joint space narrowing.

Male Reproductive System

▪ Physiology of the Male Reproductive System

The major function of the male reproductive system is the formation of sperm **(spermatogenesis),** which begins at about 13 years of age and continues throughout life. Under the influence of follicle-

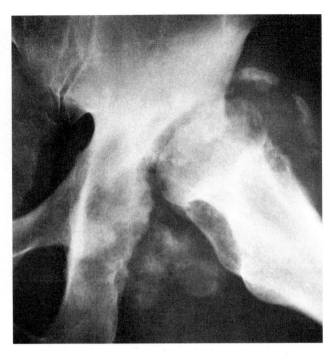

Figure 10-3 Neuropathic joint disease in syphilis. Joint fragmentation, sclerosis, and calcific debris about hip.

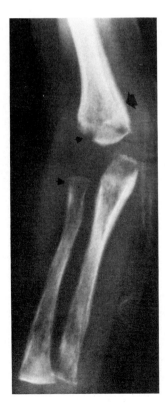

Figure 10-4 Congenital syphilis. Transverse bands of decreased density across metaphyses *(small arrows)* associated with patchy areas of bone destruction in diaphyses. There is solid periosteal new bone formation *(large arrow),* which is best seen about distal humerus.

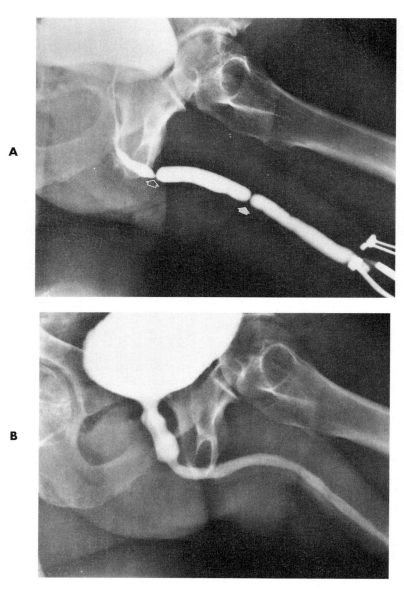

Figure 10-5 Gonococcal urethral stricture. **A,** Initial retrograde urethrogram shows diffuse stricture of bulbar urethra and high-grade stenoses in anterior *(solid arrow)* and posterior *(open arrow)* portions of urethra. **B,** After balloon dilatation, voiding urethrogram shows considerable improvement in appearance of urethra. (From Russinovich NAE et al: *Urol Radiol* 2:33-37, 1980.)

stimulating hormone (FSH) secreted by the anterior lobe of the pituitary gland, the seminiferous tubules of the testes are stimulated to produce the male germ cells called spermatozoa. In addition to sperm cell production the testes secrete the male hormone **testosterone.** This substance stimulates the development and activity of the accessory sex organs (prostate, seminal vesicles) and is responsible for adult male sexual behavior. Testosterone causes the typically male changes that occur at puberty, including the development of facial and body hair and alterations in the larynx that result in a deepened voice.

Testosterone also helps regulate metabolism by promoting growth of skeletal muscles and is thus responsible for the greater male muscular development and strength.

The final maturation of sperm occurs in the **epididymis,** a tightly coiled tube enclosed in a fibrous casing. The sperm spend about 1 to 3 weeks in this segment of the duct system, where they become motile and capable of fertilizing an ovum. The tail of the epididymis leads into the **vas deferens,** a muscular tube that passes through the inguinal canal as part of the spermatic cord and joins the duct from the **seminal vesicle** to form the ejaculatory duct. Depending on the degree of sexual activity and frequency of ejaculation, sperm may remain in the vas deferens up to 1 month with no loss of fertility. Severing of the vas deferens **(vasectomy)** is an operation performed to make a man sterile. Vasectomy interrupts the route from the epididymis to the remainder of the genital tract.

The **seminal vesicles** lie on the posterior aspect of the base of the bladder and secrete a thick liquid that is rich in fructose, a simple sugar that serves as an energy source for sperm motility after ejaculation. The seminal vesicles also secrete prostaglandin, which increases uterine contractions in the woman and helps propel the sperm toward the fallopian tubes.

The **prostate gland** lies just below the bladder and surrounds the urethra. It secretes a thin alkaline substance that constitutes the major portion of the seminal fluid volume. The alkalinity of this material is essential to sperm motility, which would otherwise be inhibited by the highly acidic vaginal secretions.

Intense sexual stimulation causes peristaltic contractions in the walls of the epididymis and vas deferens, propelling sperm into the urethra. At the same time, the seminal vesicles and prostate gland release their secretions, which mix with the mucous secretion of the bulbourethral glands to form semen. The ejaculation of semen occurs when intense muscular contractions of erectile tissue cause the semen to be expressed through the urethral opening.

Male fertility is related not only to the number of sperm ejaculated but also to their size, shape, and motility. Although only one sperm fertilizes an ovum, millions of sperm seem to be necessary for fertilization to occur. Indeed, it is estimated that sterility may result when the sperm count falls below about 50 million/ml of semen.

■ Benign Prostatic Hyperplasia

Enlargement of the prostate gland is common in men over 60 years of age and may be detected on a digital rectal examination. The enlargement is probably related to a disturbance of hormone secretions from the sex glands that occurs as the period of reproductive activity declines. The major effect of prostatic enlargement is an inability to empty the bladder completely, leading to partial urinary tract obstruction, bilateral ureteral dilatation, and hydronephrosis. On excretory urography, the enlarged prostate typically produces elevation and a smooth impression on the floor of the contrast-filled bladder (Figure 10-6). Elevation of the insertion of the ure-

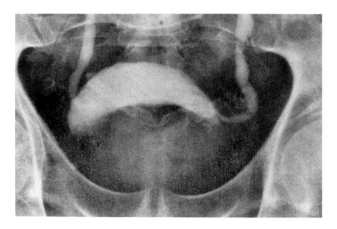

Figure 10-6   Benign prostatic hyperplasia. Large, smooth filling defect at base of bladder. Notice fish-hook appearance of distal ureters and calcification in vas deferens.

ters on the trigone of the bladder produces a characteristic J-shaped or "fish-hook" appearance of the distal ureters. Residual urine in the bladder provides a growth medium for bacterial infection, which produces cystitis; the infection may ascend from the bladder to the kidney, resulting in pyelonephritis.

On MRI, benign prostatic hyperplasia causes a diffuse or nodular area of homogeneous low intensity on T_1-weighted images and an inhomogeneous, mixed intermediate-high signal intensity on T_2-weighted images (Figure 10-7). Focal enlargement is often accentuated by a pseudocapsule, representing compression of adjacent tissue visualized as a low-intensity rim. Diffuse enlargement shows similar intensity changes, though the pseudocapsule is not present. Unfortunately, the intensity of benign prostatic hyperplasia may often be similar to that of the normal prostate or a region of prostatitis.

Surgical resection of the prostate (transurethral resection, or TUR) can relieve the obstructive symptoms.

■ Carcinoma of the Prostate Gland

Carcinoma of the prostate gland is the second most common malignancy in men. The disease is rare before 50 years of age, and the incidence increases with advancing age. The tumor can be slow growing and asymptomatic for long periods or can behave aggressively with extensive metastases.

Carcinoma of the prostate is best detected by palpation of a hard, nodular, and irregular mass on a routine rectal examination. Radiographically, carcinoma of the prostate often elevates and impresses the floor of the contrast-filled bladder. Unlike the smooth contour in benign prostatic hyperplasia, in

A

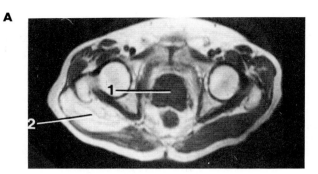

B

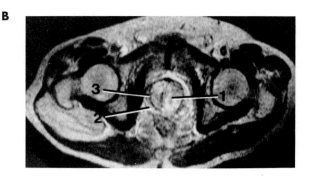

Figure 10-7　Benign prostatic hyperplasia. **A,** T_1-weighted magnetic resonance image shows prostatic enlargement of homogeneous low intensity. Notice high signal intensity of large lipoma *(2)* in right gluteal region. **B,** On T_2-weighted image, intermediate signal of enlarged transitional zone *(1)* shows increased inhomogeneity and is separated from high-signal-intensity peripheral zone *(2)* by low-intensity rim of pseudocapsule. (From McCarthy S, Fritzsche PJ: In Stark DD, Bradley WG, editors: *Magnetic resonance imaging,* St. Louis, 1988, Mosby.)

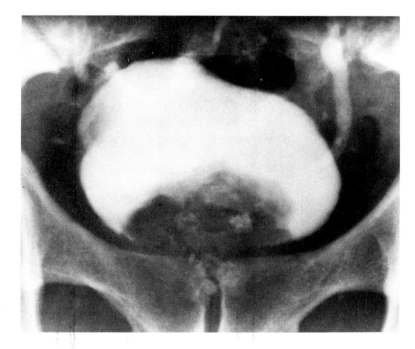

Figure 10-8　Carcinoma of prostate. Large irregular mass that elevates and impresses floor of contrast-filled bladder.

carcinoma the impression on the bladder floor is usually more irregular (Figure 10-8). Bladder neck obstruction, infiltration of the trigone, or invasive obstruction of the ureters above the bladder may produce obstruction of the upper urinary tract.

Ultrasound performed by means of a probe inserted into the rectum is a new technique for detecting carcinoma of the prostate (Figure 10-9). The normal prostate has a generally homogeneous appearance with a moderate echo pattern. Early studies indicated that prostatic carcinoma appeared as hyperechoic areas. However, with the development of newer and higher frequency transducers, many carcinomas appear as areas of low echogenicity within the prostate. Up to 40% of carcinomas are isoechoic with normal prostate tissue and thus cannot be visualized on ultrasound. The most recent studies have concluded that the wide range of sonographic patterns in carcinoma indicates that ultrasound cannot reliably differentiate prostatic malignancy from benign disease.

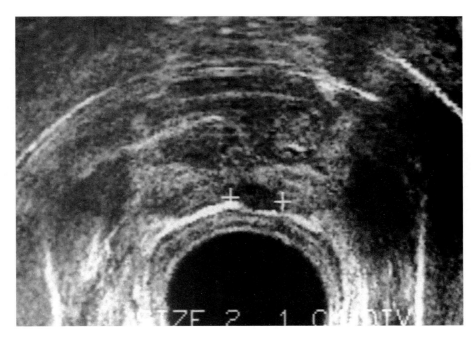

Figure 10-9   Cancer of prostate. Transrectal ultrasound demonstrates hypoechoic mass (between cursors).

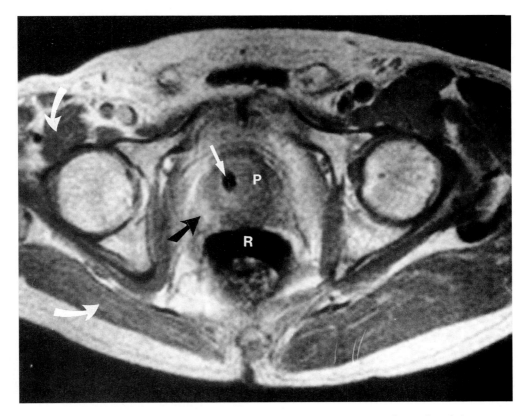

Figure 10-10   Carcinoma of prostate. Axial magnetic resonance image through pelvis demonstrates abnormal area of increased signal intensity *(black arrow)* within prostate gland *(P)*. Foley catheter is in place *(straight white arrow)*, and rectum *(R)* contains air and feces. Notice decreased size of pelvic musculature on right *(curved white arrows)* in this patient with above-knee amputation.

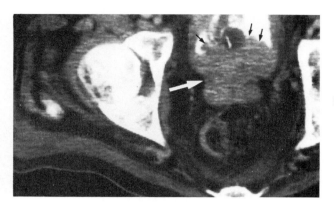

Figure 10-11   Metastatic carcinoma of prostate gland. **A,** CT scan shows prostatic carcinoma *(p)* invading wall of bladder *(arrow)* and seminal vesicles *(v).* **B,** In another patient, CT scan shows prostatic carcinoma involving bladder *(black arrows)* and seminal vesicles. Normal sharp angle between seminal vesicles and prostate is lost *(white arrow).* (From Thoeni RF: In Moss AA, Gamsu G, Genant HK, editors: *Computed tomography of the body,* Philadelphia, 1983, Saunders.)

MRI can superbly delineate the prostate, seminal vesicles, and surrounding organs to provide accurate staging of pelvic neoplasms. When the spin echo technique is used, the central and peripheral zones of the prostate are well demonstrated and distinctly separate from the surrounding levator ani muscles. In the sagittal plane the relation of the prostate to the bladder, rectum, and seminal vesicles is clearly shown. Prostatic carcinoma is best demonstrated on long TR images, where it appears as disruption of the normally uniform high signal intensity of the peripheral zone of the prostate (Figure 10-10). However, there is much controversy whether MRI is reliable for detection and diagnosis of prostate cancer. It has been demonstrated that a normal appearing prostate gland on MRI does not exclude the presence of a neoplasm. In addition, inhomogeneity of the gland is a common nonspecific finding that also can be seen in patients with adenoma or prostatitis.

Carcinoma of the prostate may spread by direct extension or by way of the lymphatics or the bloodstream. Spread of carcinoma of the prostate to the rectum can produce a large, smooth, concave pressure defect, a fungating ulcerated mass simulating primary rectal carcinoma, or a long, asymmetric annular stricture. Both ultrasound and CT may aid in defining extension of tumor into the bladder and seminal vesicles and in detecting metastases in enlarged lymph nodes (Figure 10-11).

The most common hematogenous metastases are to bone. They primarily involve the pelvis, thoracolumbar spine, femurs, and ribs. These lesions are most commonly osteoblastic and appear as multiple rounded foci of sclerotic density (Figure 10-12) or, occasionally, diffuse sclerosis involving an entire bone ("ivory vertebra"). Patients with bony metastases usually have strikingly elevated levels of serum acid phosphatase. Because significant bone destruction or bone reaction must occur before a lesion can be detected on plain radiographs, the radionuclide bone scan is the best screening technique for detection of asymptomatic skeletal metastases in patients with carcinoma of the prostate. However, since the radionuclide scan is very sensitive but not specific and may show increased uptake in multiple disorders of the bone, conventional radiography of the affected site should be performed when a positive scan is obtained.

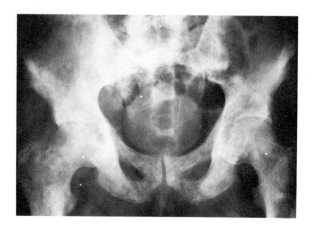

Figure 10-12   Metastatic carcinoma of prostate. Diffuse osteoblastic metastases involving bones about pelvis.

▪ Undescended Testis (Cryptorchidism)

Near the end of gestation, the testis normally migrates from its intra-abdominal position through the inguinal canal into the scrotal sac. If one of the testicles cannot be palpated within the scrotum, it is important to determine whether this represents an absent testis or an ectopic position of the testis. The rate of malignancy is up to 40 times higher in the undescended (intra-abdominal) than in the descended testicle. Because of this extremely high rate of malignancy, the diagnosis of undescended testis

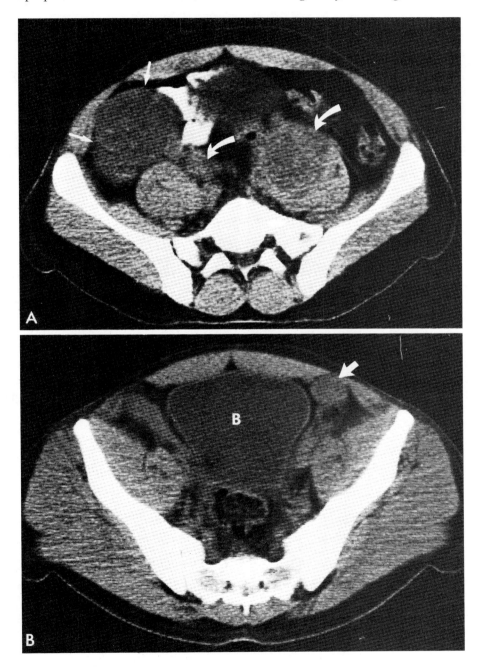

Figure 10-13 Malignant neoplasms developing in one of bilateral undescended testes. **A,** Undescended right testis is enlarged by carcinoma *(straight arrows)*. Tumor has metastasized to lymph nodes *(curved arrows)*, which are enlarged. **B,** Nontumorous intra-abdominal left testis *(arrow)* appears as smaller, rounded structure adjacent to bladder *(B)*. (From Jeffrey RB: In Moss AA, Gamsu G, Genant HK, editors: *Computed tomography of the body*, Philadelphia, 1983, Saunders.)

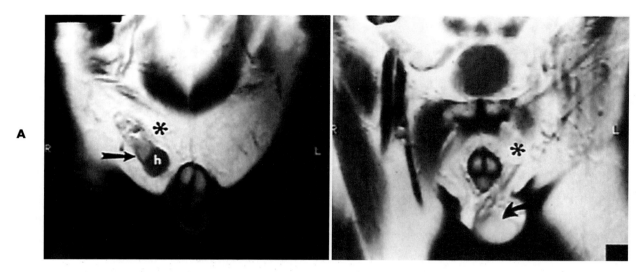

Figure 10-14   Atrophic undescended testis. **A,** Coronal magnetic resonance scan shows small, intermediate-signal-intensity testis *(arrow)* associated with low-signal-intensity hydrocele *(h)*. Intensity of testis is low compared with that of fat (*). **B,** Image slightly posterior to **A** shows normally descended contralateral testis *(curved arrow)*, which has high signal intensity similar to that of fat (*). (From Fritzsche PJ, et al: *Radiology* 164:169-173, 1987.)

usually leads to orchiopexy (surgical fixation of an undescended testis in the scrotum) in patients younger than 10 years of age and orchiectomy (surgical removal) in those seen after puberty.

In the absence of a palpable testicle, ultrasound is usually used as a screening technique. This modality carries no radiation risk and has a high diagnostic accuracy in demonstrating undescended testicles that are located in the inguinal canal. However, sonography is not successful in detecting ectopic testicles in the pelvis or abdomen. If ultrasound fails to demonstrate an undescended testis, MRI or CT is indicated (Figure 10-13 and 10-14).

▪ Testicular Torsion and Epididymitis

Testicular torsion refers to the twisting of the gonad on its pedicle, which leads to the compromise of circulation and the sudden onset of severe scrotal pain. Although primarily a clinical diagnosis, the scrotal pain and swelling of testicular torsion may be difficult to distinguish from that caused by inflammation of the epididymis (epididymitis). In such cases, Doppler ultrasound or radionuclide studies are of value.

Doppler ultrasound demonstrates the presence of intratesticular arterial pulsations. In testicular torsion the arterial perfusion is diminished or absent, whereas in epididymitis there is increased blood flow. Similarly, the radionuclide angiogram shows that isotope activity on the twisted side is either slightly decreased or at the normal, barely percep-

tible level. On the uninvolved side, the perfusion should be normal. When compared with the decreased activity on the involved side, the perfusion appears increased. Static nuclear scans demonstrate a rounded, cold area replacing the testicle in patients with torsion (Figure 10-15) but are a hot area in those with epididymitis (Figure 10-16).

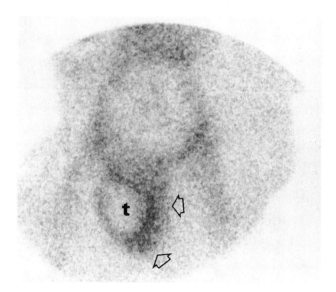

Figure 10-15   Testicular torsion. Severe diminished arterial perfusion causes testicle to appear as rounded, cold area *(t)* on radionuclide scan. Surrounding rim of increased activity represents blood supply to scrotal sac *(arrows)*.

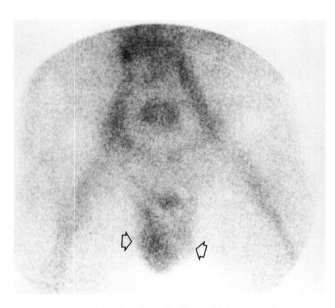

Figure 10-16   Epididymitis. Radionuclide scan shows high isotope uptake in region of testicle *(arrows)* caused by increased blood flow.

▪ Testicular Tumors

Testicular tumors are the most common neoplasms in men between 20 and 35 years of age. Almost all testicular tumors are malignant, and they tend to metastasize to the lymphatics that follow the course of the testicular arteries and veins and drain into para-aortic lymph nodes at the level of the kidneys.

There are two major types of testicular tumor. Seminomas arise from the seminiferous tubules, whereas teratomas arise from a primitive germ cell and consist of a variety of tissues. Seminomas are radiosensitive, and early diagnosis and irradiation have resulted in many cures.

Testicular tumors are best diagnosed on ultrasound examination. The normal testis has a homogeneous, medium-level echogenicity. A localized testicular tumor appears as a circumscribed mass with either increased or decreased echogenicity in an otherwise uniform testicular echo structure (Figure 10-17). Testicular tumors also can be detected on MRI (Figure 10-18).

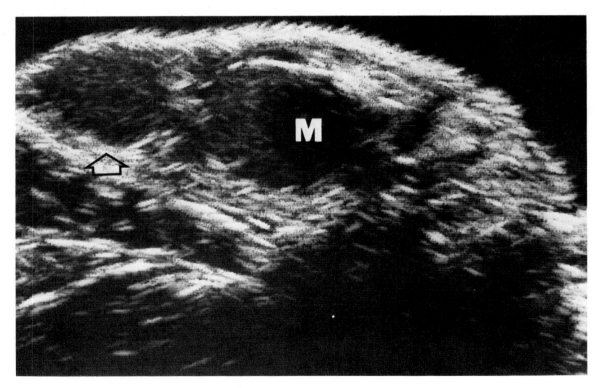

Figure 10-17   Testicular carcinoma. Transverse sonogram shows predominantly sonolucent mass *(M)* within enlarged left testis. Right testis *(arrow)* is normal. (*Courtesy Robert Mevorach, MD*, Rochester, NY.)

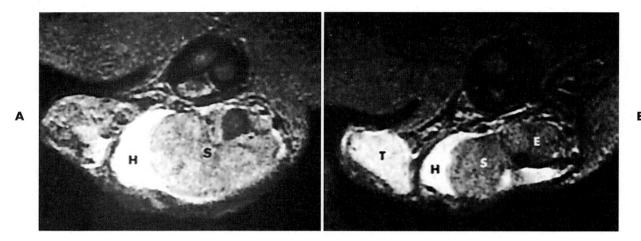

Figure 10-18   Testicular seminoma. **A,** T$_2$-weighted magnetic resonance scan shows that seminoma *(S)* in left testis has inhomogeneous signal with pronounced difference in contrast from adjacent hydrocele *(H)*. **B,** Inhomogeneous intermediate signal of intratesticular tumor *(S)* extends into epididymis *(E)*. Notice that normal contralateral testis *(T)* has much higher signal intensity. (From Baker LL et al: *Radiology* 163:93-98, 1987.)

Lymphatic metastases from testicular tumors typically occur at the level of the renal hilum (where the gonadal veins drain) and are best detected by CT (Figure 10-19). This modality also can detect spread of tumor to the lung or liver.

Female Reproductive System

▪ **Physiology of the Female Reproductive System**

The ovaries are the equivalent of the testes in the male and are responsible for the production of ova and the secretion of female hormones. A woman's reproductive life begins with the onset of menstruation, the **menarche,** which generally occurs between 11 and 15 years of age. Once each month, on about the first day of menstruation, several primitive graafian follicles and their enclosed ova begin to grow and develop and the follicular cells start to secrete **estrogen.** In most cycles, only one follicle matures and migrates to the surface of the ovary, where it ruptures and expels the mature ovum into the pelvic cavity **(ovulation).**

After the release of the ovum, the remaining cells of the ruptured follicle enlarge and a golden-colored pigment (lutein) becomes deposited in their cytoplasm. This **corpus luteum** continues to grow for 7 to 8 days and secretes **progesterone** in increasing amounts. If fertilization of the ovum has not occurred, the size and secretions of the corpus luteum gradually diminish until the nonfunctional structure is reduced to a white scar (corpus albicans) that

moves into the central portion of the ovary and eventually disappears. If fertilization does occur, however, the corpus luteum remains intact throughout pregnancy.

The cyclic changes in the ovaries are controlled by a variety of substances secreted by the anterior pituitary gland. Growth of the primitive graafian follicles and ova and the secretion of estrogen are controlled by follicle-stimulating hormone (FSH), whereas follicular rupture, expulsion of its ripe ovum, and the secretion of progesterone are under the control of luteinizing hormone (LH).

The fallopian tubes serve as ducts for the ovaries, even though they are not directly attached to them. The union of an ovum and a spermatozoon (fertilization) normally occurs in the fallopian tubes. About 1 day later, the resulting embryo reaches the uterus, where it begins to implant itself in the endometrium. Occasionally, implantation occurs in the fallopian tube or pelvic cavity instead of in the uterus, resulting in an **ectopic pregnancy.** Within 10 days, there is the earliest development of the placenta, which is derived in part from both the developing embryo and from maternal tissues and serves to nourish the fetus and anchor it to the uterus. Although they are closely related, maternal and fetal blood do not mix, and the exchange of nutrients occurs across the important fetal membrane termed the **chorion.**

The menstrual cycle refers to the changes in the endometrium of the uterus that occur in women throughout the childbearing years. Each cycle lasts about 28 days and is divided into three phases: proliferative, secretory, and menstrual. Although the

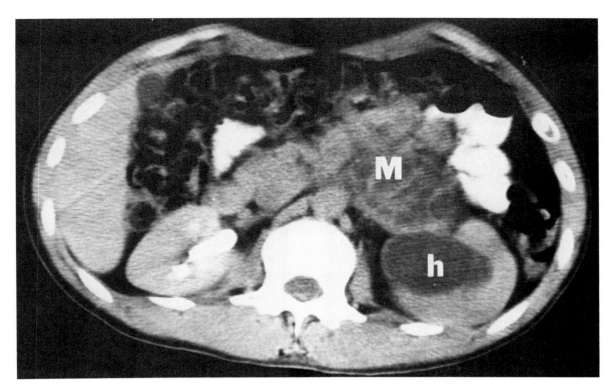

Figure 10-19   Metastatic testicular seminoma. CT scan through level of kidneys shows diffuse
nodal metastases *(M)* containing characteristic low-attenuation areas. Extrinsic pressure on
lower left ureter has caused severe hydronephrosis with dilatation of renal pelvis *(h)*.

first day of menstruation is normally considered as
the first day of the cycle, for ease of description the
menstrual phase will be described last.

The **proliferative,** or **postmenstrual,** phase occurs
between the end of the menses and ovulation. Production of estrogen by ovarian follicular cells under
the influence of FSH causes proliferation of the
endometrium of the uterus. In a typical 28-day
cycle, the proliferative phase usually includes cycle
days 6 to 13 or 14. However, there is far more
variability in the length of this phase than in the
others.

The **secretory,** or **postovulatory,** phase occurs
between ovulation and the onset of the menses. The
high level of estrogen in the blood after ovulation
inhibits the secretion of FSH, and the anterior lobe of
the pituitary gland begins to secrete LH. This stimulates the corpus luteum to produce the hormone
progesterone, which stimulates a further increase in
the thickness of the endometrium and prepares the
uterus for implantation of the ovum should fertilization occur. The length of the secretory phase is fairly
constant and usually lasts 14 days.

If fertilization of the ovum does not occur, the
high level of progesterone in the blood inhibits the

secretion of LH so that the corpus luteum begins to
degenerate and ceases to produce progesterone. As
the superficial layers of the hypertrophied endometrium begin to break down, denuded bleeding
areas are exposed. The flow of blood, mucus, and
sloughed endometrium from the uterus is called the
menstrual flow. This **menstrual** phase of the cycle
lasts about 4 to 6 days, until the low level of
progesterone causes the pituitary gland to again
secrete FSH and a new menstrual cycle begins. Of
course, if the ovum is fertilized, the corpus luteum
does not degenerate and the endometrium remains
intact throughout pregnancy.

The reproductive years terminate with the cessa-
tion of menstrual periods **(menopause),** which usually begins in the late 40s or early 50s.

▪ Pelvic Inflammatory Disease

Inflammation of the pelvic reproductive organs is
usually the result of venereal disease (especially
gonorrhea) in women of childbearing age. It can also
develop from an unsterile abortion or delivery or be
a complication of intrauterine devices. If pelvic inflammatory disease is not promptly and adequately

treated, spread of infection to the fallopian tubes may cause fibrous adhesions that obstruct the inner portion near the uterus. If the outer ends of the tubes remain open, the spill of purulent material can lead to peritonitis and the formation of a pelvic abscess. More commonly, the outer ends close and the fallopian tubes fill with pus **(pyosalpinx).** After antibiotic therapy, the infection subsides and the tubes may remain filled with a watery fluid **(hydro-salpinx).** Obstruction of the fallopian tubes can result in infertility or ectopic pregnancy. Spread of infection to involve the ovaries can produce tubo-ovarian abscesses, which are usually bilateral.

Ultrasound is the imaging procedure of choice for detecting pelvic inflammatory disease and pelvic abscesses. The fluid-filled urinary bladder provides an excellent acoustic window and permits confusing loops of small bowel to be displaced out of the pelvis. Pyosalpinx and tubo-ovarian abscesses typically are seen as tubular adnexal masses that are sonolucent and compatible with fluid collections (Figure 10-20). However, abscesses may also have thick and irregular, or "shaggy," walls or may contain echoes or fluid levels representing the layering of purulent debris (Figure 10-21).

The status of the fallopian tubes can be assessed radiographically by hysterosalpingography, in which

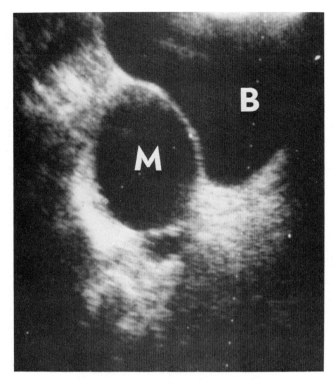

Figure 10-20 Tubo-ovarian abscess. Ultrasound demonstrates large sonolucent mass *(M)* posterior to bladder *(B).*

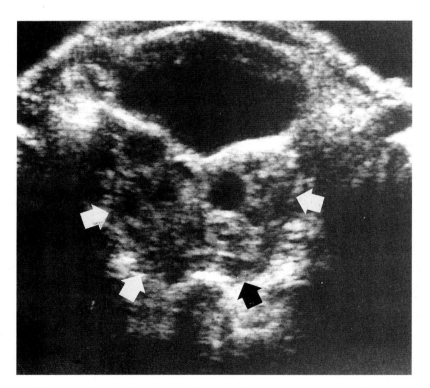

Figure 10-21 Chronic pelvic inflammatory disease. Transverse sonogram demonstrates large, complex cystic and echogenic masses *(arrows)* posterior to echo-free bladder. (From Callen PW, editor: *Ultrasonography in obstetrics and gynecology,* Philadelphia, 1983, Saunders.)

the uterine cavity and fallopian tubes are opacified after the injection of contrast material into the uterus. In the normal woman with patent fallopian tubes, contrast material extravasating into the pelvic peritoneal cavity outlines the peritoneal surfaces and often loops of bowel within the pelvis (Figure 10-22). If the fallopian tubes are occluded by fibrosis from pelvic inflammatory disease or developmental anomalies, there is no evidence of the contrast material reaching the peritoneal cavity (Figure 10-23).

Plain abdominal or pelvic radiographs are of little value in detecting pelvic inflammatory disease and pelvic abscesses. Abnormal gas collections can be masked by fecal material in the rectum and in loops of small bowel.

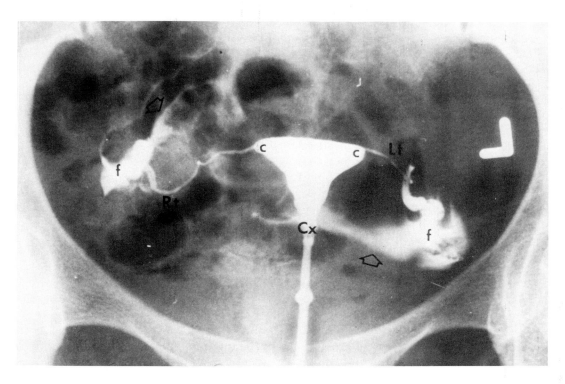

Figure 10-22 Normal hysterosalpingogram. Arrows point to bilateral spill of contrast material into peritoneal cavity. *Cx,* Internal cervical os; *c,* cornua of uterus; *RT* and *LT,* right and left fallopian tubes; *f,* fimbriated portion. (From Yune HJ et al: *AJR* 122:642-651, 1974.)

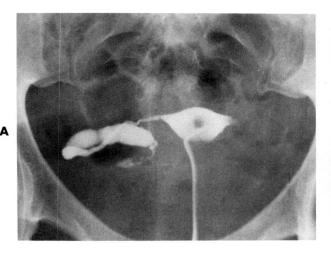
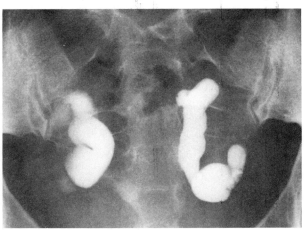

Figure 10-23 Hydrosalpinx. **A,** Unilateral and, **B,** bilateral gross dilatation of fallopian tubes without evidence of free spill of contrast material into peritoneal cavity.

▪ Cysts and Tumors

Ovarian cysts and tumors

Physiologic ovarian cysts are most common in the female infant and in women of childbearing age. They include follicular cysts (unruptured, enlarged follicles) and corpus luteum cysts, which occur after continued hemorrhage or lack of resolution of the corpus luteum. On ultrasound, cysts appear as rounded, anechoic adnexal masses.

The most common malignancies involving the ovaries are metastatic tumors, which primarily arise from carcinomas of the breast, colon, and stomach. They are frequently bilateral and often asymptomatic.

Primary cystadenocarcinoma of the ovary often contains psammomatous bodies, depositions of calcium carbonate located in the fibrous stroma of the tumor that can be detected on plain abdominal radiographs. These psammomatous calcifications appear as scattered, fine amorphous shadows that are barely denser than the normal soft tissues and can therefore be easily missed unless they are extensive (Figure 10-24). On ultrasound examination, cystadenocarcinoma typically appears as a large cystic mass with internal septa. It may be difficult to distinguish cystadenocarcinoma from cystadenoma, its benign counterpart (Figure 10-25). The more solid and irregular the areas within the mass on ultrasound, the more likely it represents a malignant tumor. In addition, the association of ascites with an ovarian mass is strongly suggestive of underlying malignancy.

Ovarian carcinomas usually spread by implanting widely on the omental and peritoneal surfaces. This can produce the characteristic CT appearance of an "omental cake," an irregular sheet of soft-tissue densities beneath the anterior abdominal wall (Figure 10-26). CT also is of value in detecting tumor adherence to bowel, ureteral involvement, and retroperitoneal adenopathy.

Dermoid cyst (teratoma)

A dermoid cyst, the most common type of germ cell tumor, contains skin, hair, teeth, and fatty elements, all of which typically derive from ectodermal tissue. They are of no clinical significance unless they grow so large that they produce symptoms by compressing adjacent structures. About half of all ovarian dermoid cysts contain some calcification. This is usually in the form of a partially or completely formed tooth (Figure 10-27); less frequently, the wall of the cyst is partially calcified. The characteristic calcification combined with the relative radiolucency of the lipid material within the lesion is pathognomonic of an ovarian dermoid cyst.

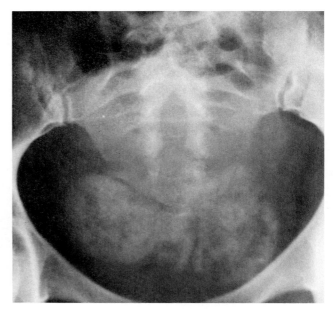

Figure 10-24   Psammomatous calcifications. Diffuse, ill-defined collections of granular amorphous calcification are visible within this cystadenocarcinoma of ovary. (From Eisenberg RL: *Diagnostic imaging in surgery,* New York, 1987, McGraw-Hill.)

The most common ultrasound appearance of a dermoid cyst is a complex, primarily solid mass containing high-level echoes arising from hair or calcification within the mass (Figure 10-28). The highly echogenic nature of these masses may make it difficult to delineate the lesion completely or to distinguish it from surrounding gas-containing loops of bowel.

Uterine fibroids

Fibroids (leiomyomas) of the uterus are benign smooth-muscle tumors that are very common, often multiple, and vary greatly in size. Growth of fibroid tumors is stimulated by estrogen. They develop only during the reproductive years and tend to shrink after menopause. Abnormal bleeding between periods or excessively heavy menstrual flow is the most common symptom. Large tumors may project from the uterus to put pressure on surrounding organs and cause pelvic pain. They also can interfere with delivery or, if on a stalk (pedunculated), protrude into the vagina.

Uterine fibroids are by far the most common calcified lesions of the female genital tract. They have a characteristic mottled, mulberry, or popcorn type of calcification and appear on plain abdominal radiographs as smooth or lobulated nodules with a stippled or whorled appearance. A very large calcified fibroid occasionally occupies the entire pelvis or

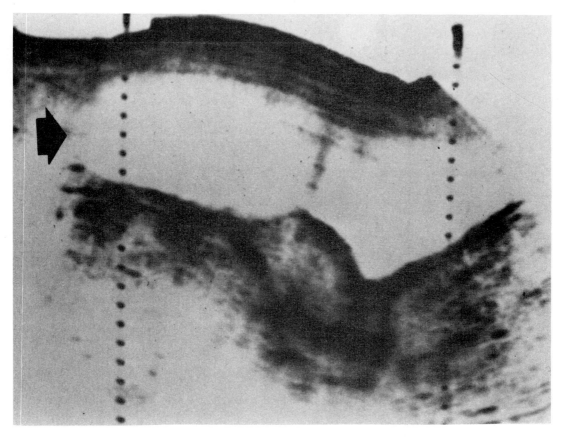

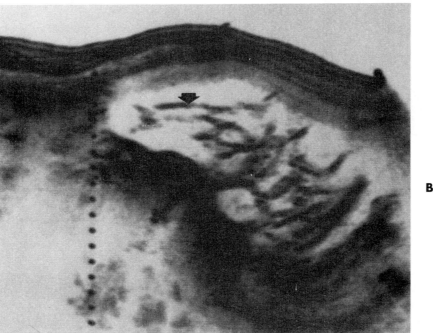

Figure 10-25   Cystadenoma. **A,** Longitudinal sonogram in asymptomatic girl demonstrates large, sonolucent, completely cystic mass *(arrow).* **B,** In another patient, longitudinal sonogram demonstrates complex, predominantly cystic mass containing several thin and well-defined septations *(arrow).*   (From Callen PW, editor: *Ultrasonography in obstetrics and gynecology,* Philadelphia, 1983, Saunders.)

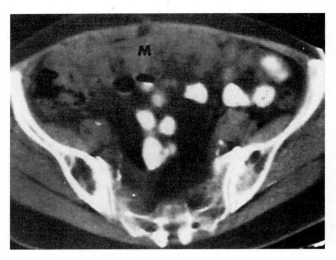

Figure 10-26　Omental cake. Metastases *(M)* resulting from cystadenocarcinoma of ovary cause irregular sheet of soft-tissue densities beneath anterior abdominal wall that posteriorly displaces adjacent contrast-filled bowel loops. (From Lee JKT, Sagel SS, Stanley RJ, editors: *Computed body tomography,* New York, 1983, Raven Press.)

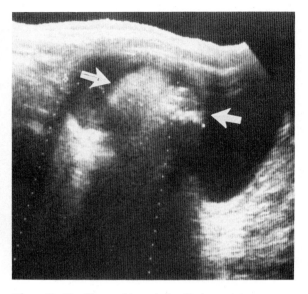

Figure 10-28　Dermoid cyst. Sagittal sonogram demonstrates only near wall of dermoid because of acoustic shadowing from hairball *(arrows)*, producing so-called tip of iceberg sign. (From Eisenberg R: *Altas of sign in radiology,* Philadelphia, 1984, Lippincott.)

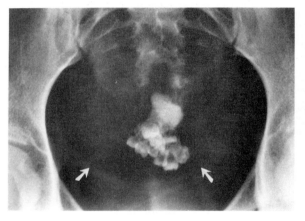

Figure 10-27　Dermoid cyst containing multiple well-formed teeth. Notice relative lucency of mass *(arrows)*, which is composed largely of fatty tissue.

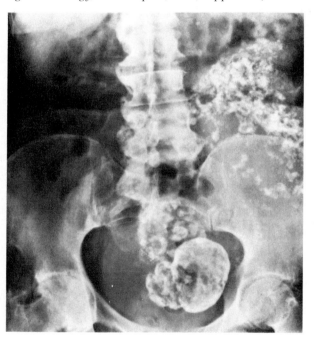

Figure 10-29　Calcified uterine fibroid. Calcified mass extends well beyond confines of pelvis.

even extends out of the pelvis to lie in the lower abdomen (Figure 10-29).

During excretory urography, persistent uterine opacification is often seen in patients with an underlying uterine fibroid tumor (Figure 10-30). The tumor typically presses on the fundus of the bladder, causing a lobulated extrinsic impression that differs from the smooth impression usually seen with ovarian cysts. Extension of a fibroid into the adjacent tissues (parametrium) may cause medial displacement of the pelvic ureter or ureteral compression leading to hydronephrosis.

The classic ultrasound appearance of a uterine fibroid is a hypoechoic, solid contour-deforming mass in an enlarged, inhomogeneous uterus (Figure 10-31). Fatty degeneration and calcification cause focal increased echogenicity; the calcification may

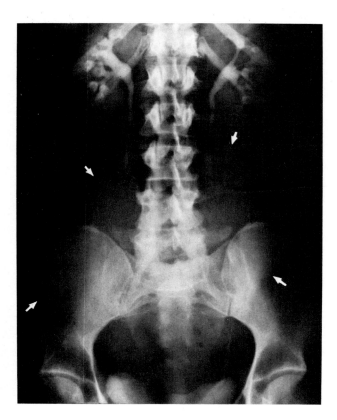

Figure 10-30 Uterine fibroid. Excretory urogram demonstrates persistent dense opacification of huge uterine leiomyoma *(arrows)*.

result in acoustic shadowing. A subserosal fibroid projecting from the uterus but attached to it by a large stalk may occasionally simulate an adnexal mass or ovarian tumor.

Endometrial carcinoma

Adenocarcinoma of the endometrium is the predominant neoplasm of the uterine body and is the most common invasive gynecologic neoplasm. It usually occurs in postmenopausal women, especially those who have never had children. Most patients are seen clinically with postmenopausal bleeding.

Excretory urography may demonstrate an enlarged uterus impressing or invading the posterior wall and fundus of the bladder. The typical ultrasound appearance of endometrial carcinoma is an enlarged uterus with irregular areas of low-level echoes and bizarre clusters of high-intensity echoes (Figure 10-32). Unless evidence of local invasion can be demonstrated, the ultrasound findings are indistinguishable from those of fibroid tumors, which often occur in patients with endometrial carcinoma. CT demonstrates focal or diffuse enlargement of the body of the uterus (Figure 10-33). This modality is especially useful in detecting clinically unsuspected omental and nodal metastases in patients with advanced disease, as well as in evaluating patients with suspected neoplastic recurrence and in check-

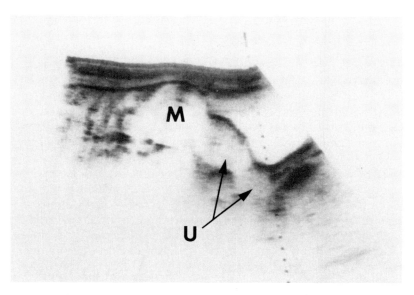

Figure 10-31 Uterine fibroid. Longitudinal sonogram demonstrates pedunculated leiomyoma as hypoechoic mass *(M)* projecting from fundus of uterus *(U)*. Decreased sound transmission through mass indicates its solid nature. (From Callen PW, editor: *Ultrasonography in obstetrics and gynecology,* Philadelphia, 1983, Saunders.)

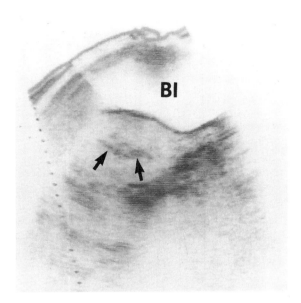

Figure 10-32   Endometrial carcinoma. Longitudinal sonogram shows uterus to be enlarged and bulbous. There are clusters of high-amplitude echoes *(arrows)* in region of central cavity echo. *Bl,* Bladder. (From Gross BH et al: *AJR* 141:765-773, 1983.)

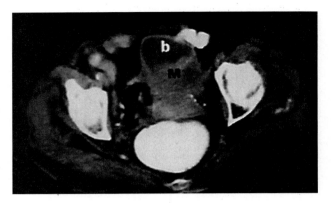

Figure 10-33   Bladder invasion by endometrial carcinoma. CT scan shows mass *(M)* obliterating fat planes between bladder *(b)* and uterus. Urine within bladder outlines thickening of posterior bladder wall. (From Gross BH, et al: *AJR* 141:765-773, 1983.)

ing the response to chemotherapy or radiation treatment.

MRI allows differentiation of the endometrium (inner lining) from the myometrium (muscle layer) of the uterus and has been shown to be useful in demonstrating focal or diffuse endometrial tumors (Figure 10-34). The excellent contrast resolution of this technique may allow determination of the depth of myometrial invasion.

Endometriosis

Endometriosis is the presence of normal appearing endometrium in sites other than their normal location inside the uterus. Although tissues next to the uterus (ovaries, uterine ligaments, rectovaginal septum, pelvic peritoneum) are most frequently involved in endometriosis, the gastrointestinal and urinary tracts can also be affected. Current theories of the cause of endometriosis include (1) reflux of endometrial fragments backward through the fallopian tubes during menstruation with implantation in the pelvis; (2) transformation of multipotential cells in the abdomen and pelvis; (3) implantation of endometrial fragments during surgery or delivery; and (4) spread of endometrial tissue by way of the bloodstream or lymphatic system.

Even though the endometrial tissue lies outside the uterus, it still responds to hormonal changes and undergoes a proliferative and secretory phase along with sloughing and subsequent bleeding. Thus an endometrial implant within a closed space can continue to grow with each menstrual cycle (Figure 10-35). Clinical symptoms include abnormal bleeding, painful menstruation (dysmenorrhea), and pain during sexual intercourse (dyspareunia). Because endometriosis is usually clinically apparent only when ovarian function is active, most women who are symptomatic for endometriosis are between 20 and 45 years of age.

Endometriosis involving the urinary tract most commonly produces ureteral obstruction below the level of the pelvis brim. The condition mimics a ureteral tumor and may appear as an intraluminal mass or stricture or as a smooth, rounded, or multilobular filling defect in the bladder. In the gastrointestinal tract, endometriosis primarily affects those segments that are situated in the pelvis (especially the rectosigmoid colon). It typically causes abdominal cramps and diarrhea during the menstrual period and may appear as single or multiple masses in the colon (Figure 10-36). Repeated shedding of endometrial tissue and blood into the peritoneal cavity can lead to the development of dense adhesive bands causing small bowel obstruction.

A rare complication of endometriosis with intrathoracic implants of endometrial tissue is recurrent catamenial pneumothorax, which is usually right sided and occurs during menstrual flow.

Carcinoma of the cervix

Carcinoma of the cervix is the second most common form of cancer in women. Development of the tumor appears to be related to chronic irritation, infection, and poor hygiene, and there is a higher incidence in

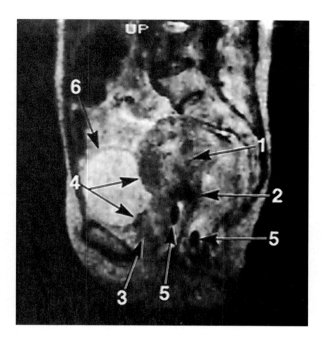

Figure 10-34   Endometrial carcinoma. Sagittal T$_2$-weighted magnetic resonance scan shows extensive tumor of mixed signal intensity *(1)* that has invaded endocervix and permits identification only of ectocervix *(2)*. Tumor has extended interiorly along serosal surface of uterus into vesicovaginal septum *(3)* and bladder wall *(4)*. Low-intensity foci in vagina represent radiotherapy implants *(5)*. Notice normal urinary bladder wall superiorly *(6)*. (From Lupetin AR: In Stark DD, Bradley WG, editors: *Magnetic resonance imaging*, St Louis, 1988, Mosby.)

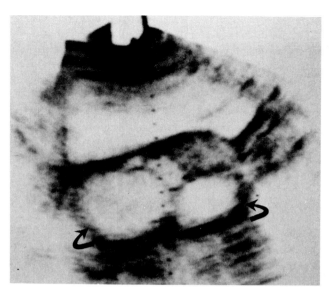

Figure 10-35   Endometrioma. Several sonolucent masses *(arrows)* simulating multiple follicular cysts arising from ovary. (From Callen PW, editor: *Ultrasonography in obstetrics and gynecology*, Philadelphia, 1983, Saunders.)

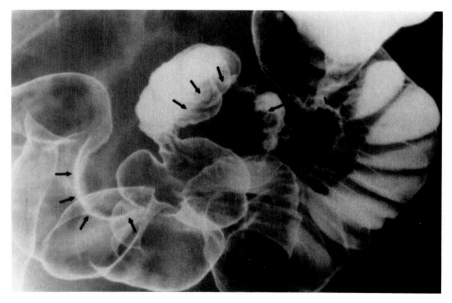

Figure 10-36   Endometriosis. Three separate endometrial implants *(arrows* and *arrowheads)* are seen in sigmoid colon. Most distal lesion has smooth interface with bowel wall, indicating no intramural invasion. The two more proximal lesions have irregular borders, indicating intramural or submucosal invasion. (From Gedgaudas RK, et al: *Radiology* 146:609-616, 1983.)

women who have begun sexual activity at an early age and have had multiple sexual partners. The development of the Pap smear examination has permitted detection of cervical carcinoma at a very early stage (carcinoma in situ) when it has not yet invaded the underlying tissues and is surgically curable. Widespread cervical cancer becomes inoperable, and radiation therapy is the usual treatment.

At the time of the initial staging, one third of patients have unilateral or bilateral hydronephrosis that can be demonstrated by excretory urography or ultrasound. Indeed, the most common cause of death in patients with carcinoma of the cervix is impairment of renal function caused by ureteral obstruction. Extension of the tumor to the bladder may cause an irregular filling defect; direct infiltration of the perirectal tissues may produce irregular narrowing of the rectosigmoid colon and widening of the retrorectal space. Distant metastases to the skeleton or lungs are uncommon, even in patients with advanced disease.

Ultrasound usually demonstrates a cervical carcinoma as a solid mass behind the bladder (Figure 10-37). CT is more accurate in detecting pelvic sidewall invasion and therefore is usually the initial staging procedure in patients in whom there is a clinical suspicion of advanced disease (Figures 10-38 and 10-39). This modality is also the procedure of choice for monitoring tumor response to treatment and for assessing suspected recurrence.

MRI can permit the cervix to be distinguished from the uterus and vagina and is thus of value in detecting and staging cervical carcinoma (Figures 10-40 and 10-41).

After radiation therapy for carcinoma of the cervix (and other types of pelvic carcinoma), it may be difficult to distinguish chronic rectal narrowing and widening of the retrorectal space caused by radiation effects from that caused by recurrence of tumor. Radiation therapy can also lead to the development of fibrous inflammatory adhesions between loops of

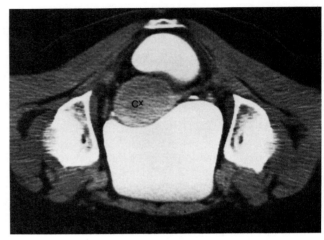

Figure 10-38   Carcinoma of cervix. CT scan demonstrates inhomogeneity of enlarged cervix *(Cx)* without evidence of bladder invasion. (From Gross BH et al: *AJR* 141:765-773, 1983.)

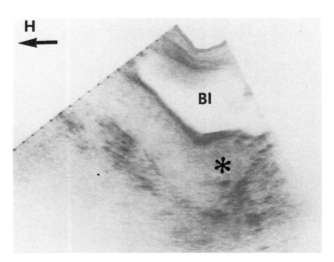

Figure 10-37   Carcinoma of cervix. Sonogram demonstrates solid, echogenic mass *(asterisk)* lying behind bladder *(Bl)* that is indistinguishable from benign cervical myoma. (From Callen PW, editor: *Ultrasonography in obstetrics and gynecology,* Philadelphia, 1983, Saunders.)

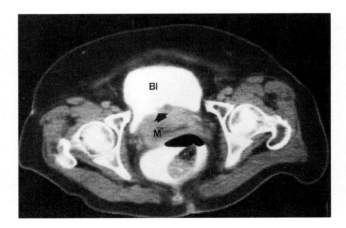

Figure 10-39   Bladder invasion by carcinoma of cervix. CT scan shows irregularity *(arrow)* of posterior margin of contrast-filled urinary bladder *(Bl)* and adjacent inhomogeneous cervical mass *(M).* (From Callen PW, editor: *Ultrasonography in obstetrics and gynecology,* Philadelphia, 1983, Saunders.)

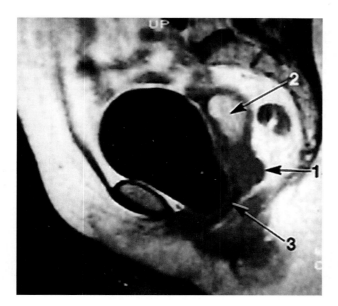

Figure 10-40   Cervical carcinoma. On this sagittal T_1-weighted magnetic resonance scan, posterior cervical lobulation *(1)* is the only primary sign of infiltrating cervical neoplasm. Notice considerable widening of central uterine high-intensity zone *(2)* caused by accumulation of menstrual products in endometrial canal resulting from tumor occlusion of endocervical canal. Urine *(3)* within vagina produces low signal intensity on this imaging sequence. (From Lupetin AR: In Stark DD, Bradley WG, editors: *Magnetic resonance imaging,* St Louis, 1988, Mosby.)

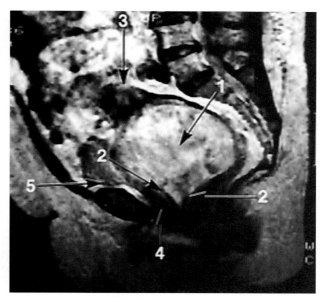

Figure 10-41   Carcinoma of cervix. Sagittal T_2-weighted magnetic resonance image shows bulky cervical neoplasm *(1)* with mottled high signal intensity. Lesion has invaded upper third of vaginal stroma *(2)* anteriorly and posteriorly but has spared uterus *(3)*. Urethra *(4)* and urinary bladder *(5)* are anteriorly displaced by tumor. (From Lupetin AR: In Stark DD, Bradley WG, editors: *Magnetic resonance imaging,* St Louis, 1988, Mosby.)

bowel and the bladder, resulting in the development of fistulas between bowel loops (enteric-enteric) and between a bowel loop and the urinary bladder (enteric-vesical).

▪ Breast Cancer

Breast cancer is the most common malignancy among women. Current surgical and radiation therapy techniques provide highly effective treatment, but only if the cancers are detected when localized to the breast itself. Unfortunately, most breast tumors are discovered accidentally rather than in the course of regular survey examinations. By this time, the majority have spread either to regional lymph nodes or systemically, accounting for the current high mortality (about 50%) that makes breast cancer the leading cause of cancer death in women.

Periodic careful physical examination of the breast, done either by a trained health professional or by the patient herself, will discover cancers that are small and more likely to be localized. Even smaller, nonpalpable, and potentially more curable lesions can be detected by mammography, a radio-graphic examination that is by far the most effective breast diagnostic procedure. Indeed, routine mammography combined with physical examination is the only approach currently available that promises to significantly reduce breast cancer mortality.

The two major radiographic techniques for diagnosing breast cancer are screen-film mammography and xeromammography. Screen-film imaging uses a specially designed x-ray screen that permits the proper exposure of film by many fewer x rays than would be otherwise necessary. This produces a conventional black-and-white image at a very low radiation dose. Xeromammography is an adaptation of the standard xerographic photocopying process; the blue-and-white x-ray images are made on paper rather than on film.

Almost all breast cancers are seen mammographically as a tumor mass or clustered calcifications, or both. Either feature, when clearly demonstrated, is so suspicious of malignancy as to require prompt biopsy whether the lesion is palpable or not. Secondary changes of breast carcinoma include skin thickening and nipple retraction. Magnification imaging and compression techniques greatly improve the diagnostic value of the image.

The typical malignant tumor mass is poorly defined, has irregular margins, and demonstrates numerous fine linear strands or spicules radiating out from the mass (Figure 10-42). This appearance is characteristic but not diagnostic of malignancy and is in stark contrast to the typical mammographic picture of a benign mass, which has well-defined, smooth margins and a round, oval, or gently lobulated contour (Figure 10-43).

Clustered calcifications in breast cancer are typically numerous, very small, and localized to one segment of the breast. They demonstrate a wide variety of shapes, including fine linear, curvilinear, and branching forms (Figure 10-44). Although only about half of breast cancers present mammographically as clusters of calcifications, typical calcifications are seen in many of the nonpalpable intraductal cancers that often do not form mass lesions and may otherwise escape detection.

Ultrasound can differentiate a benign cyst from a solid mass and thus substantially reduces the number of biopsies done for benign cysts (Figure 10-45). However, ultrasound is of limited value in detecting nonpalpable cancers, particularly those that present

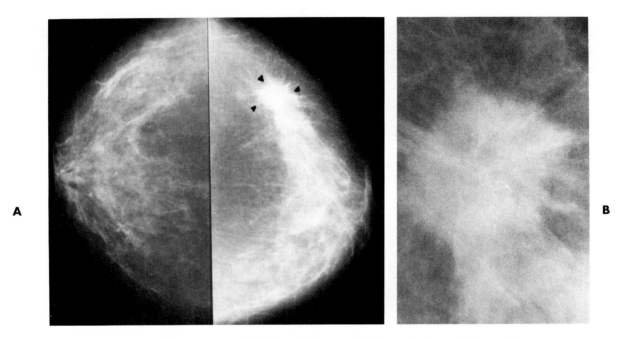

Figure 10-42 Breast cancer. **A,** Full and, **B,** magnified coned views of breast demonstrate ill-defined, irregular mass with radiating spicules *(arrowheads).*

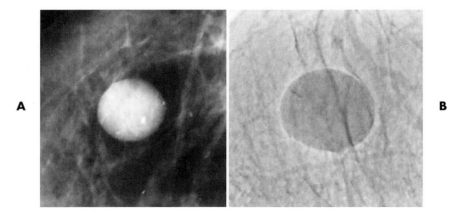

Figure 10-43 Benign breast masses. **A,** Screen-film mammogram demonstrates smooth, round fibroadenoma with clearly defined margins. **B,** Xeromammogram demonstrates smooth contour and sharply defined margins of benign cyst.

with calcifications alone, and thus it cannot substitute for mammography as a standard examination.

Although relatively infrequent, breast cancer also can develop in men.

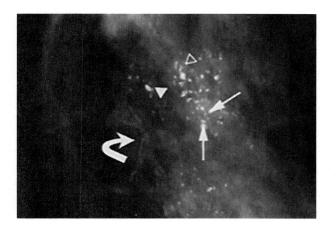

Figure 10-44 Malignant calcifications in breast cancer. Numerous tiny calcific particles with linear *(arrows)*, curvilinear *(solid arrowhead)*, and branching *(open arrowhead)* forms characteristic of malignancy. Notice benign calcification in arterial wall, which is easily recognized by its large size and tubular distribution *(curved arrow)*.

Benign breast disease

Fibrocystic disease of the breast is a common benign condition occurring in about 20% of premenopausal women. It is usually bilateral with cysts of various sizes distributed throughout breasts that also contain an increased amount of fibrous tissue.

A fibroadenoma is the most common benign breast tumor. It generally appears as a smooth, well-circumscribed mass with no invasion of surrounding tissue (Figure 10-43, *A*). Ultrasound permits differentiation of a solid fibroadenoma from a fluid-filled breast cyst.

▪ Imaging in Pregnancy

Because of its noninvasive and nonionizing character, ultrasound is the modality of choice in the evaluation of possible complications of pregnancy. A major role of this modality is to assess the gestational age, a measurement that is often highly inaccurate when based on the data of the last menstrual period. A knowledge of the true gestational age may be critically important for obstetric decisions, since the length of pregnancy is a major factor in interpreting the graphs that indicate the status of the fetus. Measurements of fetal age by ultrasound in-

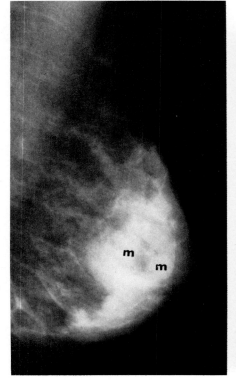

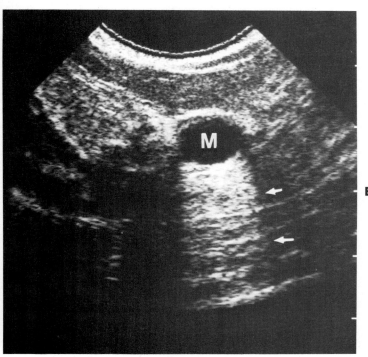

Figure 10-45 Sonography in breast disease. **A,** Mammogram shows several rounded masses *(m)* that could be solid or cystic in breast that is very dense anteriorly. **B,** Sonogram clearly shows that largest mass *(M)* is cystic, since it contains no internal echoes and shows considerable posterior enhancement *(arrows)*.

clude the longest biparietal diameter (BPD), the crown-rump length, and the length of the fetal femur. The BPD is measured from the outer margin of the skull on one side to the inner margin on the other side at the level of the thalami (Figure 10-46). A single measurement of the biparietal diameter has its greatest accuracy between 12 and 26 weeks; after this time, the size of the head and thus the BPD may be affected by a growth disturbance. The crown-

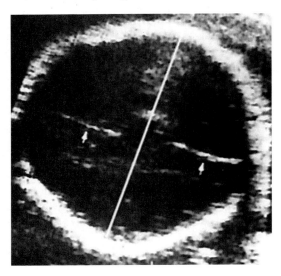

Figure 10-46 Biparietal diameter in 28-week fetus. White line indicates biparietal diameter, which is measured from outer margin of skull on one side to inner margin on other side. Arrows point to midline falx.

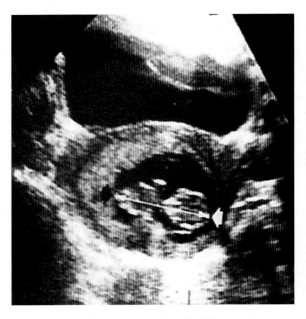

Figure 10-47 Crown-rump length. Distance between tip of head (*white arrow*) and bottom of fetal trunk (*black arrow*) measures 42 mm, equivalent to gestational age of approximately 11 weeks.

rump length refers to the distance between the tip of the head and the bottom of the fetal trunk (Figure 10-47). This measurement is highly accurate in assessing gestational age in early pregnancy (less than 11 weeks).

An early diagnosis of multiple pregnancies can be made by ultrasound (Figure 10-48). This is essential so that therapeutic measures can be taken to reduce the high complication rate associated with twin (or more) pregnancies.

Ultrasound can be used to detect abnormalities in the volume of amniotic fluid, which is often associated with underlying fetal anomalies. **Polyhydramnios** represents the excessive accumulation of amniotic fluid that may be caused by maternal disorders such as diabetes mellitus and Rh isoimmunization (Figure 10-49). Polyhydramnios is also caused by fetal abnormalities, especially those related to the central nervous system, the gastrointestinal tract, the circulatory system, and dwarfism. **Oligohydramnios** refers to a very small volume of amniotic fluid.

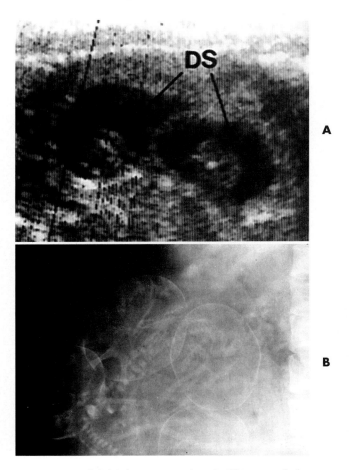

Figure 10-48 Multiple pregnancies. **A,** Ultrasound shows twin pregnancy. *DS,* Desidual sac. **B,** Lateral abdominal radiograph of woman with quadruplets clearly shows four separate fetal skulls and spines.

This condition primarily results from fetal urinary tract disorders such as renal aplasia, renal dysplasia, and urethral obstruction. Oligohydramnios is also associated with intrauterine growth retardation.

Clinically significant errors of morphologic development occur in up to 5% of all children. The in utero detection of these anomalies by ultrasound may permit in utero medical or surgical therapy, provide an indication for termination of the pregnancy, or influence the mode of delivery. Although a detailed description of the rapidly expanding field of prenatal sonography is beyond the scope of this book, some of the abnormalities that can be detected, and often treated, in utero are osseous (bony) and neural anomalies of the fetal cranium and spine, gastrointestinal atresias and developmental cysts, cystic and obstructive lesions of the genitourinary tract, and congenital cardiac diseases (Figures 10-50 to 10-52).

Because ultrasound examinations can demonstrate the fetus and placenta with no apparent risk to the mother or unborn child, ultrasonography is unquestionably the imaging study of choice for evaluating the gravid (pregnant) woman. In extremely rare instances, there may be justification for performing radiographic pelvimetry to demonstrate the architecture of the maternal pelvis and to compare the size of the fetal head with the size of the maternal bony pelvic outlet to determine whether the pelvic diameters are adequate for normal delivery or a cesarean section will be required. In almost all cases, however, the combination of careful clinical evaluation and ultrasonography is sufficient to make these decisions without the need to resort to radiographic pelvimetry and its high radiation dose. There is absolutely no indication ever to perform fetography, the radiographic demonstration of the fetus in utero. Ultrasound can provide far better diagnostic information and is not associated with the danger of producing radiation-induced fetal malformations.

Ectopic pregnancy

Although ectopic pregnancy is a life-threatening condition, responsible for up to one fourth of mater-

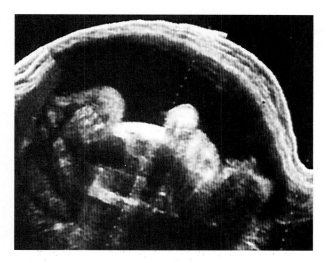

Figure 10-49 Polyhydramnios. Excessive accumulation of amniotic fluid surrounds fetus in mother with diabetes mellitus.

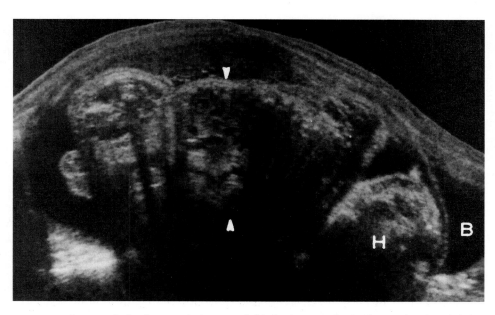

Figure 10-50 Anencephaly. Long-axis image of third-trimester fetus shows that head *(H)* is irregularly shaped, echogenic, and much smaller than body *(arrowheads)*. B, Maternal bladder. (From Pasto ME, Kurtz AM: *Semin Ultrasound CT MR* 5:170-193, 1984.)

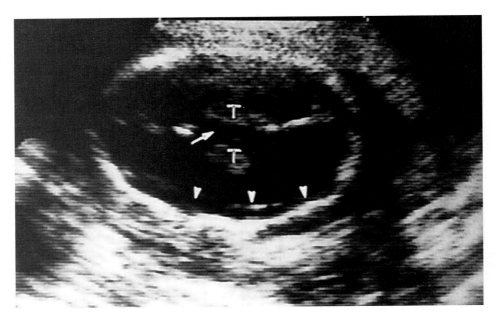

Figure 10-51   Severe hydrocephalus resulting from aqueductal stenosis. Transaxial projection demonstrates greatly dilated lateral ventricles and dilated third ventricle *(arrow)* between thalami *(T).* Arrowheads show extremely thin residual cerebral cortex. (From Pasto ME, Kurtz AM: *Semin Ultrasound CT MR* 5:170-193, 1984.)

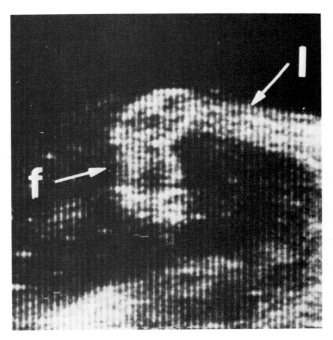

Figure 10-52   Clubfoot. Prenatal ultrasound scan shows that foot *(f)* is at right angle to leg. (From Jeanty P, Romero R: *Semin Ultrasound CT MR* 5:253-268, 1984.)

nal deaths, the diagnosis is missed by the initial examining physician in up to three fourths of the cases. More than 95% of ectopic pregnancies occur within the fallopian tubes, and more than half the patients with this complication of pregnancy have a history or pathologic evidence of pelvic inflammatory disease. Ectopic pregnancies are often associated with urine or plasma levels of human chorionic gonadotropin (HCG) that are substantially lower for the expected date of gestation than those in patients with normal intrauterine pregnancies.

Ultrasound is the major imaging modality for diagnosing ectopic pregnancy. The classic appearance consists of an enlarged uterus that does not contain a gestational sac and is associated with an irregular adnexal mass, an "ectopic fetal head," or fluid in the cul-de-sac (Figure 10-53). The unequivocal demonstration of an intrauterine pregnancy virtually excludes an ectopic pregnancy, since the incidence of coexisting ectopic and intrauterine pregnancies is only one in 30,000.

Trophoblastic disease

Trophoblastic disease refers to a spectrum of pregnancy-related disorders ranging from benign hydatidiform mole to the more malignant and frequently metastatic choriocarcinoma. A hydatidiform mole typically appears on ultrasound as a large, soft-tissue mass of placental (trophoblastic) tissue filling the uterine cavity and containing low-to-moderate amplitude echoes (Figure 10-54). No evidence of a developing fetus exists.

About half of choriocarcinomas follow pregnancies complicated by hydatidiform mole. The remainder occur after spontaneous abortion, ectopic pregnancy, or normal deliveries. On ultrasound, choriocarcinoma resembles benign hydatidiform mole and usually appears as a large complex mass in the expected position of the uterus. Choriocarcinoma tends to metastasize to the lungs, where it typically produces multiple large masses that rapidly regress once appropriate chemotherapy is instituted.

▪ Female Infertility

The major radiographic procedure for evaluating infertile women is hysterosalpingography, in which the uterine cavity and fallopian tubes are opacified after the injection of contrast material into the uterus. In the normal woman with patent fallopian

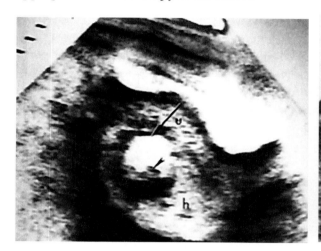
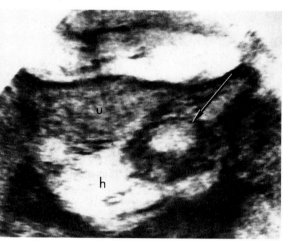

Figure 10-53 Ectopic pregnancy. **A,** Sagittal and, **B,** transverse sonograms show extrauterine gestational sac *(arrow)* on left with fetus within it *(arrowhead)*. Notice complex cystic mass *(h)*, which represents hematoma, in cul-de-sac. No fetal heart activity was noted. *u,* Uterus. (From Spirt BA et al: *RadioGraphics* 4:821-848, 1984.)

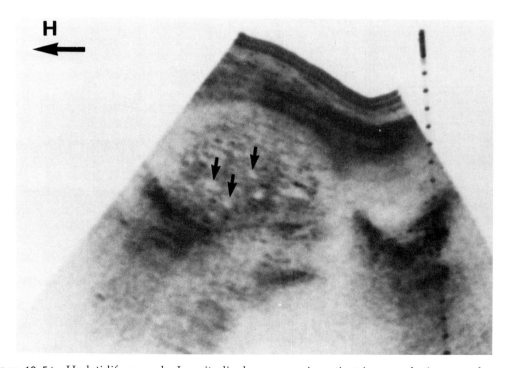

Figure 10-54 Hydatidiform mole. Longitudinal sonogram in patient in second trimester of pregnancy demonstrates large, moderately echogenic mass filling central uterine cavity. Notice numerous small cystic spaces *(arrows)* that represent greatly hydropic chorionic villi. (From Callen PW, editor: *Ultrasonography in obstetrics and gynecology,* Philadelphia, 1983, Saunders.)

tubes, contrast material extravasating into the pelvic peritoneal cavity outlines the peritoneal surfaces and often loops of bowel within the pelvis (Figure 10-22). Developmental anomalies or fibrosis from pelvic inflammatory disease may cause occlusion of one or both of the fallopian tubes; in such cases, there is no evidence of the contrast material's reaching the peritoneal cavity (Figure 10-23). In addition to assessing tubal patency, hysterosalpingography can also demonstrate uterine abnormalities contributing to infertility, such as intrauterine fibroids, severe uterine flexion or retroversion, and other congenital and acquired malformations.

In female infertility patients receiving ovulation-induction agents, ultrasound can be used to monitor maturation of the ovarian follicles. Low-level internal echoes in mature ovarian follicles appear to be a prognostic indicator of fertility. They may represent a periovulatory state, which is an appropriate time for artificial insemination or in vitro fertilization. Ultrasound can also demonstrate the characteristic bilateral multicystic ovarian enlargement in the ovarian hyperstimulation syndrome, which may develop in women receiving menotropin (Pergonal) therapy for infertility.

QUESTIONS

1. Why has ultrasound become the major imaging modality for both the male and female reproductive systems?

2. In addition to ultrasound, what are the main radiographic studies currently used for the female reproductive system?

3. The formation of sperm is known as _____ .

4. What male hormone helps to regulate metabolism by promoting growth of skeletal muscles and is considered responsible for the greater degree of muscle development in males?

5. Severing of the vas deferens to create sterility is termed _____ .

6. The second most common cause of malignancy in men is _____ .

7. What imaging modality for demonstrating the prostate gland uses a probe inserted into the rectum?

8. Ultrasound studies of the prostate gland *cannot* always determine the malignant or benign status of prostatic disease.   TRUE   FALSE

9. Prostatic carcinoma can often spread through the bloodstream to the bone and can sometimes cause sclerosis of an entire vertebra. This pathologic condition is termed _____ .

10. What screening technique is usually employed to identify the location of an undescended testicle?

11. What is the term used to describe the twisting of the male gonad on its pedicle?

12. The most common neoplasms in men between 20 and 35 years of age are _____ tumors that tend to metastasize through the _____ system.

13. The rupture and expulsion of the mature ovum into the pelvic cavity is termed _____ .

14. A pregnancy that occurs in a fallopian tube or in the pelvic cavity is termed _____ .

15. What is the name of the radiographic procedure used to demonstrate the patency or status of the fallopian tubes?

16. Untreated _____ can lead to cerebral cortical lesions causing mental disorders and involvement of the skeletal system and affects infants born to infected mothers.

17. The most common type of germ cell tumor, often containing teeth, hair, and fatty material, is called a _____ .

18. Leiomyomas, more commonly referred to as _____ , are benign smooth-muscle tumors of the uterus.

19. The most common malignancy among women occurs in the _____ .

20. The second most common form of cancer in women is _____ .

BIBLIOGRAPHY

Callen PW: *Ultrasonography in obstetrics and gynecology*, Philadelphia, 1992, Saunders.

de Paredes ES: *Atlas of film-screen mammogram*, Baltimore, 1992, Williams & Wilkins.

Sanders RC, James AE: *Ultrasonography in obstetrics and gynecology*, Norwalk, 1992, Appleton-Century-Crofts.

Tabar L, Dean PB: *Teaching atlas of mammography*, ed 2, New York, 1985, Thieme.

CHAPTER 11

Miscellaneous Diseases

■ **Prerequisite Knowledge**

The student should have a basic understanding of the physiology of the various body systems. In addition, the proper learning and understanding of the material will be facilitated if the student has some clinical experience in general radiography.

■ **Goals**

To acquaint the student with the pathophysiology and radiographic manifestations of both common and unusual disorders caused by vitamin deficiencies and some disease processes that do not fit neatly into a single body system, and to understand the use, positioning, and complications of various tubes, catheters, and wires in the chest.

■ **Objectives**

1. Describe nutritional disorders and their possible relationship to disorders of other organs
2. Be able to define terminology relating to nutritional disorders
3. Be able to describe the pathologic conditions caused by various vitamin deficiencies
4. Be able to describe the pathologic conditions associated with sarcoidosis
5. Be able to describe the pathologic conditions associated with muscular dystrophy
6. Be able to describe the pathologic conditions associated with melanoma
7. Be able to describe the pathologic conditions associated with systemic lupus erythematosus
8. Be able to describe the correct location for an endotracheal tube, central venous catheter, Swan-Ganz catheter, and transvenous cardiac pacemaker
9. Be able to state the most common complications involved with improper placement of the aforementioned catheters and how chest radiography plays an important role in the diagnosis of these complications

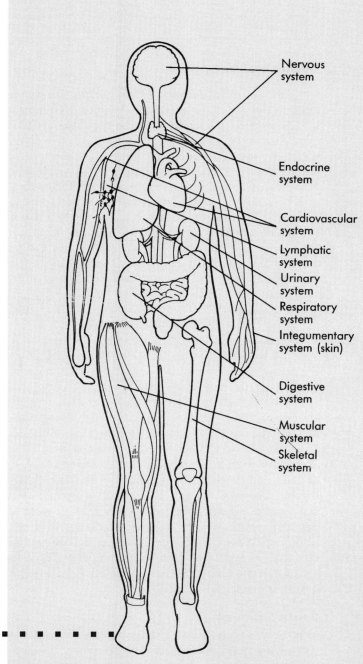

Nervous system

Endocrine system

Cardiovascular system

Lymphatic system

Urinary system

Respiratory system

Integumentary system (skin)

Digestive system

Muscular system

Skeletal system

■ Radiographer Notes

Radiography of patients with various nutritional diseases can be challenging because of the many effects these diseases have on all body systems. Some produce deformities; others can cause mental disorders. Obese patients can present unique problems in positioning or setting radiographic techniques. The radiographer must be especially empathetic when dealing with these patients, who often are embarrassed because of their size and thus difficult to deal with. Patients with melanoma that has already metastasized or those who are facing extensive surgical intervention are usually very depressed and sometimes require special handling. The manifestations of systemic lupus erythematosus cause considerable discomfort for the patient. Patients with muscular dystrophy can be easily agitated and are usually frustrated at their inability to control themselves. In general, patients suffering from the various diseases in the miscellaneous category can be very demanding and require considerable patience on the part of the radiographer.

■ Nutritional Diseases

Disorders of nutrition range from malnutrition and vitamin deficiency to obesity and hypervitaminosis. In addition to inadequate intake, nutritional deficiency may be related to disorders of the liver, pancreas, and gastrointestinal tract that result in an inability of the body to digest and properly use proteins, carbohydrates, and lipids. In diabetes mellitus the absence of insulin prevents entry of glucose into the cells and thus deprives the body of its major source of energy. Abnormalities of the pancreas, liver, and gastrointestinal tract causing nutritional disease are discussed elsewhere; this section deals with diseases caused by vitamin deficiency, malnutrition, and obesity.

Vitamin deficiencies

Vitamins are an essential part of the enzymatic systems that are vital to the cellular metabolism of the body. Vitamins are formed (synthesized) only by plants, not by animals. Therefore man's supply of vitamins comes directly from eating fruits and vegetables or from animals (including fish) that have eaten plants and have stored the vitamins. Vitamins are generally divided into two categories: fat soluble and water soluble. The fat-soluble vitamins (A, D, E, and K) can be stored within body tissues. Water-soluble vitamins (B and C) cannot be stored and must be a regular part of the diet to prevent a deficiency. The major B vitamins include thiamine, riboflavin, niacin, pantothenic acid, cobalamin (vitamin B_{12}), and folic acid. Vitamin deficiency diseases are rare in the United States but are all too prevalent in underdeveloped countries.

Beriberi (thiamine)

Beriberi results from a deficiency in thiamine, a co-enzyme that is essential for carbohydrate metabolism. It primarily occurs in rice-eating countries such as China, in which the main staple is polished rice that has had the vitamin-containing skin and germ removed. Initially, peripheral vasodilatation in beriberi causes increased cardiac output, which then produces a generalized enlargement of the cardiac silhouette and increased pulmonary vascular markings. With progression of disease, the myocardium becomes edematous and flabby and cannot function properly, leading to congestive heart failure and generalized edema (Figure 11-1). Noninflammatory degeneration of myelin sheaths caused by thiamine deficiency produces a peripheral neuropathy characterized by weakness of the limbs and a "pins and needles" sensation in the extremities.

Pellagra (niacin)

Pellagra is caused by a deficiency of niacin and is characterized by reddening and scaling of the skin

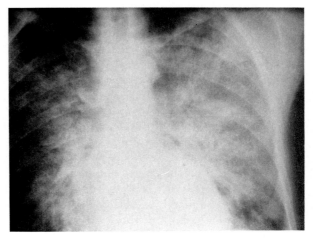

Figure 11-1 Beriberi. Diffuse pulmonary edema caused by severe high-output heart failure.

on exposed parts of the body, vomiting and severe diarrhea, and nervous and mental disorders (ranging from chronic depression to violent, irrational behavior).

Scurvy (vitamin C)

The deficiency of ascorbic acid (vitamin C) in scurvy leads to an inability of the supporting tissues to produce and maintain vascular endothelium and the cementing substances that hold epithelial cells together (collagen, osteoid, dentin). Scurvy was classically a disease of sailors and explorers deprived of fresh fruit and vegetables containing vitamin C.

Weakening of capillary walls in scurvy often results in bleeding into the skin, joints, and internal organs. The gums are especially affected and bleed easily. The open lesions provide an entry for bacteria, leading to necrosis of gum tissue and tooth loosening and loss. Impaired synthesis of collagen leads to poor and delayed wound healing.

In children, disordered chondroblastic and osteoblastic activity cause radiographic bone changes that are most prevalent where growth is normally most rapid (especially about the knee and wrist). The bones are generally osteoporotic with blurring or disappearance of trabecular markings and severe cortical thinning. Widening and increased density of the zone of provisional calcification produce the characteristic "white line" of scurvy (Figure 11-2). A relatively lucent osteoporotic zone forms on the diaphyseal side of the white line. This osteoporotic zone is easily fractured, permitting the dense bone to become impacted on the shaft and jut laterally beyond it, thus giving rise to characteristic marginal spur formation (Pelken's spur). The epiphyseal ossification centers are demineralized and surrounded by dense, sharply demarcated rings of calcification (Wimberger's sign of scurvy). If epiphyseal dislocations have not occurred, the appearance of the skeletal structures usually returns to normal after appropriate therapy.

Subperiosteal hemorrhage often occurs along the shafts of the long bones. Calcification of the elevated periosteum and underlying hematoma is a radiographic sign of healing.

Vitamin D (rickets)

Rickets is a bone disease of young children in which a lack of vitamin D leads to decreased absorption of calcium from the gastrointestinal tract, resulting in weak, deformed bones. In adults, lack of vitamin D causes generalized softening of bones (osteomalacia). The radiographic findings of rickets and osteomalacia are found in Chapter 3.

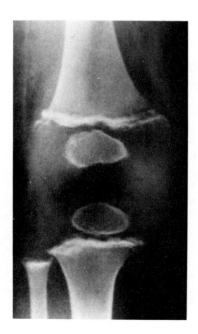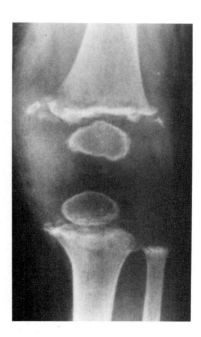

Figure 11-2 Scurvy. Frontal projections of both knees demonstrate widening and increased density of zone of provisional calcification, producing characteristic white line of scurvy. Notice also submetaphyseal zone of lucency and characteristic marginal spur formation (Pelken's spur). Epiphyseal ossification centers are surrounded by dense, sharply demarcated ring of calcification (Wimberger's sign). From Eisenberg R: *Atlas of signs in radiology,* Philadelphia, 1984, Lippincott.)

Vitamin A

Vitamin A is essential for vision because it is a vital component of the pigment that absorbs light in the rods of the retina. A lack of vitamin A results in night blindness, an inability to see in dim light. Vitamin A also is important for maintaining the integrity of mucous membranes lining the respiratory, gastrointestinal, and urogenital tracts. A lack of vitamin A makes these membranes dry and susceptible to cracking, permitting infectious organisms to enter the underlying tissues.

Vitamin A is derived from carotene, a yellow plant pigment that is converted into vitamin A by the liver. Good sources of vitamin A include dairy products, egg yolks, and vegetables such as carrots.

Vitamin K

Vitamin K is necessary for the formation of prothrombin, an essential ingredient in the blood-clotting mechanism. It is primarily found in green leafy vegetables. A deficiency of vitamin K results in excessive bleeding.

Hypervitaminosis

Chronic excessive intake of vitamin A produces a syndrome characterized by bone and joint pain, hair loss, itching, anorexia, dryness and fissuring of the lips, hepatosplenomegaly, and yellow tinting of the skin. This condition usually affects young children, who become irritable and fail to gain weight.

Excess vitamin D causes too much calcium to be absorbed from the gastrointestinal tract. The resulting hypercalcemia leads to the deposition of calcium in the kidney, heart, lungs, and wall of the stomach (Figure 11-3).

Protein-calorie malnutrition (kwashiorkor)

Severe protein-calorie malnutrition (kwashiorkor) affects millions of young children in developing countries and produces abnormalities involving the gastrointestinal tract and nervous system. Fatty replacement of liver tissue and resulting decreased levels of albumin lead to diffuse edema and ascites and the characteristic clinical appearance of a considerably protuberant abdomen. Damage to the pancreas and intestinal mucosa prevents proper digestion and absorption of nutrients. Retarded bone growth with thinned cortices usually occurs. Atrophy of the thymus gland and lymphoid tissues diminish the child's resistance to infection from organisms that enter the body through skin lesions and the damaged mucous membranes of the gastrointestinal tract. Mental development is also impaired, and brain atrophy can be demonstrated radiographically.

Obesity

Obesity refers to an excess of adipose (fatty) tissue that develops when the caloric intake (food) consistently exceeds the amount of calories required by the

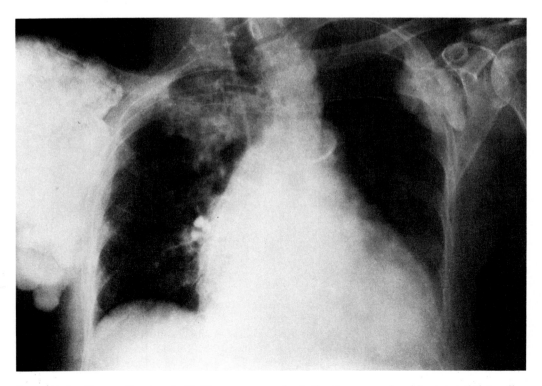

Figure 11-3   Hypervitaminosis D. Huge masses of calcification near shoulder joints bilaterally.

body to perform its daily activities. It may be related simply to personal habits of excessive eating combined with a lack of activity or may be a result of such conditions as hypothyroidism, Cushing's disease, insulinoma, and hypothalamic disorders.

Excess adipose tissue can cause displacement of normal abdominal structures, producing such radiographic patterns as widening of the retrogastric (Figure 11-4) and retrorectal spaces. An extreme increase in the intra-abdominal volume causes diffuse elevation of the diaphragm with a relatively transverse position of the heart (simulating cardiomegaly), prominence of pulmonary markings, and atelectatic changes at the lung bases. In the most severe form of obesity (pickwickian syndrome), the excursion of the diaphragm is limited and the lungs can barely expand with breathing. This results in profound hypoventilation, hypoxia, retention of carbon dioxide, secondary polycythemia, and pulmonary hypertension with right heart failure. An excessive deposition of fatty tissue can also appear radiographically as widening of the mediastinum and prominence of the pericardial fat pads.

Patients with morbid obesity may undergo surgical procedures in an attempt to lose large amounts of weight. Gastric restrictive operations attempt to limit gastric capacity and restrict gastric outflow, thus making the patient feel full after a small meal. This causes the patient to limit his or her oral intake and results in weight control. The major procedure is a gastroplasty, in which a small upper gastric remnant is connected to a larger

lower gastric pouch by a narrow channel. Complications of gastric restrictive procedures can occur in the early and late postoperative periods and include leakage, perforation, widening of the channel, and obstruction.

▪ Lead Poisoning

Lead poisoning results from the ingestion of lead-containing materials (especially paint) or from the occupational inhalation of lead fumes. In children, because lead and calcium are used interchangeably by bone, high concentrations of lead are deposited in the most rapidly growing portions of the skeleton, especially the metaphyses at the distal ends of the femur. This results in classic lead lines, dense transverse bands extending across the metaphyses of the long bones and along the margins of flat bones such as the iliac crest (Figure 11-5). In young children who eat lead-containing paint (pica), plain abdominal radiographs may show extensive mottled opacities, which are suggestive of intestinal barium, even though no contrast material has been administered (Figure 11-6).

▪ Sarcoidosis

Sarcoidosis is a multisystem granulomatous disease of unknown cause that is most often detected in young adults. Women are affected slightly more often than men, and the disease is far more prevalent among blacks than whites.

Figure 11-4 Obesity. Enlargement of retrogastric space caused by massive deposition of fatty tissue.

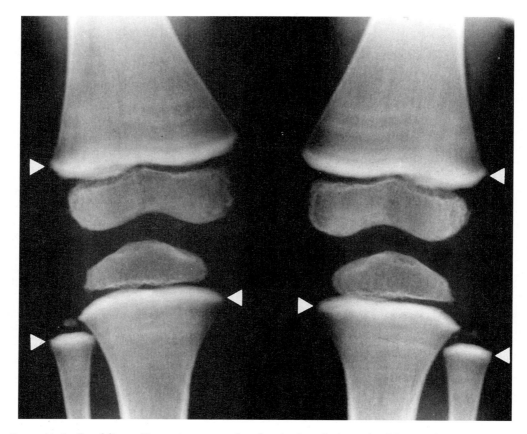

Figure 11-5 Lead lines. Dense transverse bands of sclerosis *(arrowheads)* extend across the metaphyses of the distal femurs and the proximal tibias and fibulas. (From Eisenberg RL: *Diagnostic imaging in internal medicine,* New York, 1985, McGraw-Hill.)

Figure 11-6 Pica. Large amounts of lead-containing material ingested by a young child who had received no contrast material. (From Eisenberg RL: *Gastrointestinal radiology: a pattern approach,* Philadelphia, 1990, Lippincott.)

Ninety percent of patients with sarcoidosis have radiographic evidence of thoracic involvement. Indeed, in most cases the presence of the disease is first identified on a screening chest radiograph of an asymptomatic individual.

Bilateral, symmetric hilar lymph node enlargement, with or without diffuse parenchymal disease, is the classic radiographic abnormality in sarcoidosis. There is also usually enlargement of the right paratracheal nodes, producing the typical 1-2-3 pattern (Figure 11-7). Conventional tomography frequently reveals additional enlargement of the left paratracheal nodes, which usually cannot be seen on routine frontal radiographs because they are obscured by the superimposed aorta and brachiocephalic vessels. Unilateral hilar enlargement, which is a common manifestation of primary tuberculosis or lymphoma, is rare in sarcoidosis.

Diffuse pulmonary disease develops in most patients with sarcoidosis. Although hilar and mediastinal adenopathy is often associated, there tends to

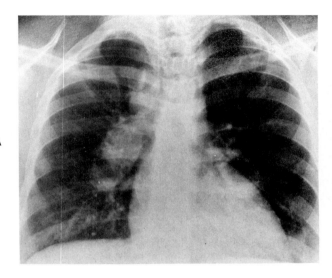

A

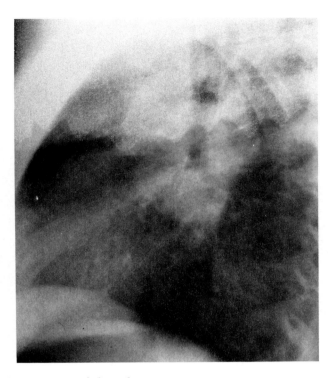

Figure 11-7   Sarcoidosis. **A,** Frontal and, **B,** lateral projections of chest demonstrate enlargement of right hilar, left hilar, and right paratracheal lymph nodes, producing classic 1-2-3 pattern of adenopathy. (From Eisenberg R: *Atlas of signs in radiology,* Philadelphia, 1984, Lippincott.)

be an inverse relationship between the degree of adenopathy and the extent of parenchymal disease, with the latter increasing while the adenopathy regresses. The most common appearance is a diffuse interstitial pattern that is widely distributed throughout both lungs (Figure 11-8). The alveolar pattern appears as ill-defined densities that may be discrete or may coalesce into large areas of consolidation. This pattern resembles an acute inflammatory process and may contain an air bronchogram. Infrequently, large, dense, round lesions may simulate metastatic malignancy.

Although the pulmonary lesions usually regress spontaneously or after steroid therapy, irreversible pulmonary changes develop in up to 20% of the cases. Coarse scarring is seen as irregular linear strands extending outward from the hilum toward the periphery, often associated with bulla formation (Figure 11-9). Severe fibrosis and emphysema can cause pulmonary hypertension and right-sided heart failure.

The skeletal lesions in sarcoidosis primarily involve the small bones of the hands and feet. Granulomatous infiltration can cause destruction of the fine trabeculae, producing a mottled to lacelike,

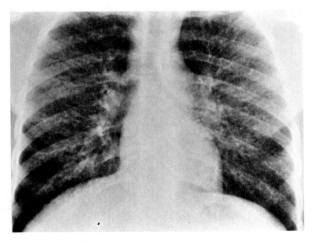

Figure 11-8   Sarcoidosis. Diffuse coarse interstitial pattern.

coarsely trabeculated pattern. Lytic destruction can produce sharply circumscribed, punched-out areas of lucency (Figure 11-10). About 10% of patients with sarcoidosis have elevated levels of serum calcium, which may lead to nephrocalcinosis. Sarcoid involvement of the stomach can produce discrete masses or generalized luminal narrowing that predominantly involves the antrum.

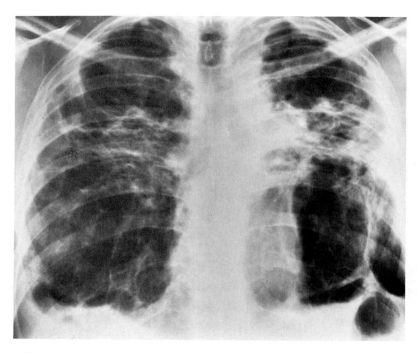

Figure 11-9 Sarcoidosis. In end-stage disease, there is severe fibrous scarring, bleb formation, and emphysema.

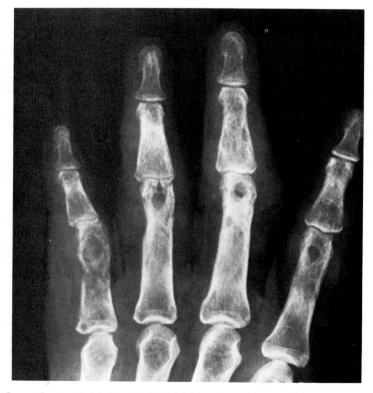

Figure 11-10 Sarcoidosis. Multiple osteolytic lesions throughout phalanges, producing typical punched-out appearance. Apparent air density in soft tissues in photographic artifact.

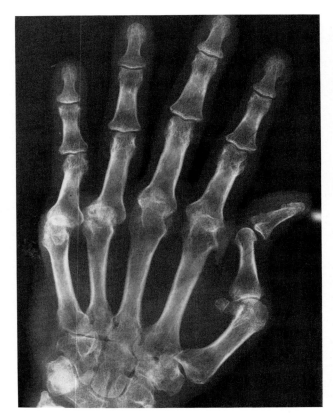 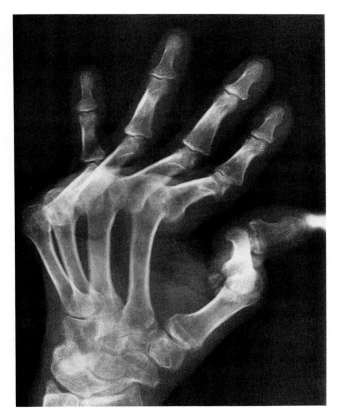

Figure 11-11 Systemic lupus erythematosus. Frontal and oblique projections of hand show subluxation of phalanges at metacarpal articulations and hyperextension deformities of proximal interphalangeal joints. Notice absence of erosive changes. (From Brown JC, Forrester DM: In Eisenberg RL, Amberg JR, editors: *Critical diagnostic pathways in radiology: an algorithmic approach,* Philadelphia, 1981, Lippincott.)

▪ Systemic Lupus Erythematosus

Systemic lupus erythematosus is a connective tissue disorder that primarily involves young or middle-aged women and most likely represents an immune-complex disease. The presentation and course of the disease are highly variable. Characteristic findings include a butterfly-shaped rash over the nose and cheeks and extreme sensitivity of the skin to sunlight.

Pain in multiple muscles and joints is the most frequent clinical complaint in patients with systemic lupus erythematosus. A characteristic finding is subluxations and malalignment of joints in the absence of erosions (Figure 11-11). Cardiopulmonary abnormalities also frequently develop. Pleural effusions, usually bilateral and small but occasionally massive, occur in about half of the patients (Figure 11-12). Enlargement of the cardiac silhouette is generally the result of pericarditis and pericardial effusion.

Although kidney involvement, often leading to renal failure, is one of the most serious manifesta-

tions of systemic lupus erythematosus, no specific urographic findings are seen. Enlargement of the liver, spleen, and lymph nodes occurs in about one fourth of patients. In the gastrointestinal system, a necrotizing inflammation of blood vessels can result in massive bleeding, multiple infarctions, and bowel perforation.

Many of the radiographic manifestations of systemic lupus erythematosus tend to disappear during spontaneous remissions or after steroid therapy.

▪ Melanoma

Melanoma is an extremely malignant skin cancer that metastasizes widely throughout the body. The tumor develops from a benign mole (nevus), which changes size and color and becomes itchy and sore.

Metastases from malignant melanoma frequently involve the gastrointestinal tract, usually sparing the large bowel. They are typically well-circumscribed, round or oval nodules that may develop central

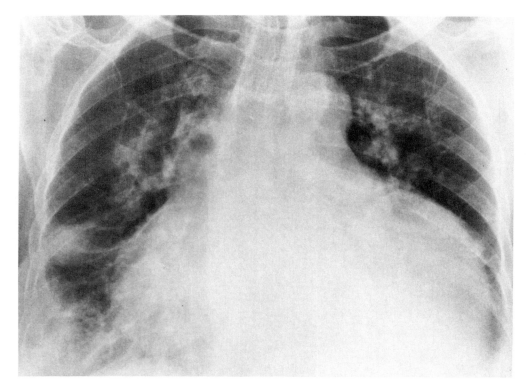

Figure 11-12 Systemic lupus erythematosus. Bilateral pleural effusions, more pronounced on right, with some streaks of basilar atelectasis. Massive cardiomegaly is attributable to combination of pericarditis and pericardial effusion.

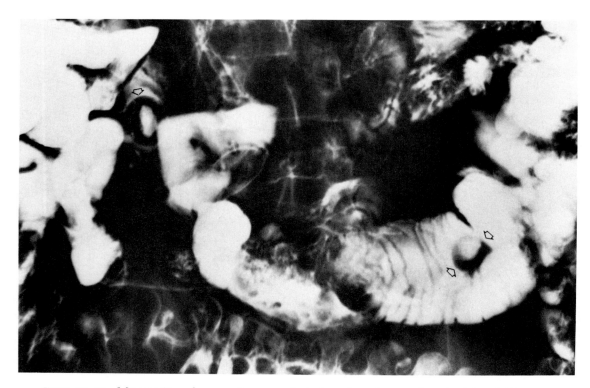

Figure 11-13 Metastatic melanoma. Large central ulcerations in two sharply defined filling defects in small bowel *(arrows)*.

necrosis and ulceration to produce a dense, barium-filled central crater surrounded by a sharply margin-ated nodular mass (bull's-eye, or target, lesion) (Figure 11-13). Gastrointestinal metastases can be the first clinical manifestation of metastatic melanoma; at times it can be impossible to identify the primary tumor site.

Metastatic melanoma can also produce multiple nodules in the lung and destructive bone lesions with neither new bone formation nor reactive sclerosis.

▪ Muscular Dystrophy

Muscular dystrophy refers to a group of chronic inherited conditions in which there is replacement of muscle by fat leading to generalized weakness and eventually death caused by respiratory muscle failure or pneumonia. On radiographs of the extremities, the extensive accumulation of fat within the remaining muscle bundles produces a fine striated, or striped, appearance (Figure 11-14). Because most of the muscle tissue is replaced by fat, the fascial sheath bounding the muscles may stand out as a thin shadow or increased density as it is visualized on edge. Decreased muscular tone can lead to osteoporosis, bone atrophy with cortical thinning, scoliosis, and joint contractures.

An abnormal swallowing mechanism in muscular dystrophy can result in the failure to clear barium adequately from the pharynx; this may lead to tracheal aspiration and nasal regurgitation of contrast material (or other ingested substances).

▪ Internal Devices

Endotracheal tube

A chest radiograph should always be obtained immediately after endotracheal intubation to ensure proper positioning because clinical evaluation (bilateral breath sounds, symmetric thoracic expansion, palpation of the tube in the sternal notch) does not allow detection of the majority of malpositioned tubes. Daily radiographs are usually taken to make certain that the tube has not been inadvertently displaced by the weight of the respirator apparatus, by the patient's coughing, or by other unforeseen events. In addition, this permits prompt detection of complications of intubation and barotrauma (positive-pressure breathing) such as pneumothorax and pneumomediastinum.

The relation between the tip of the tube and the carina (tracheal bifurcation) must be carefully assessed. When the head and neck are in a neutral position, the endotracheal tube tip ideally should be

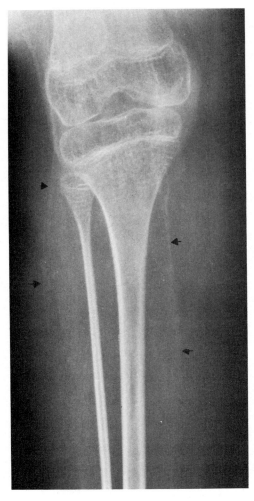

Figure 11-14 Muscular dystrophy. Thin, demineralized bones of lower leg. Increased lucency, representing fatty infiltration in muscle bundles, makes fascial sheaths appear as thin shadows of increased density *(arrows)* surrounded by fat.

about 5 to 7 cm above the carina (Figure 11-15). With flexion and extension of the neck, the tip of the tube will move about 2 cm caudally and cranially respectively.

About 10% to 20% of endotracheal tubes require repositioning after insertion. A tube positioned too low usually extends into the right main-stem bronchus, where it eventually leads to atelectasis of the left lung (see Figure 2-50). A tube positioned excessively high or in the esophagus causes the inspired air to enter the stomach, causing severe gastric dilatation and a high likelihood of regurgitation of gastric contents and aspiration pneumonia.

Central venous catheters

Central venous catheters inserted into the subclavian vein or a more peripheral vein in the upper

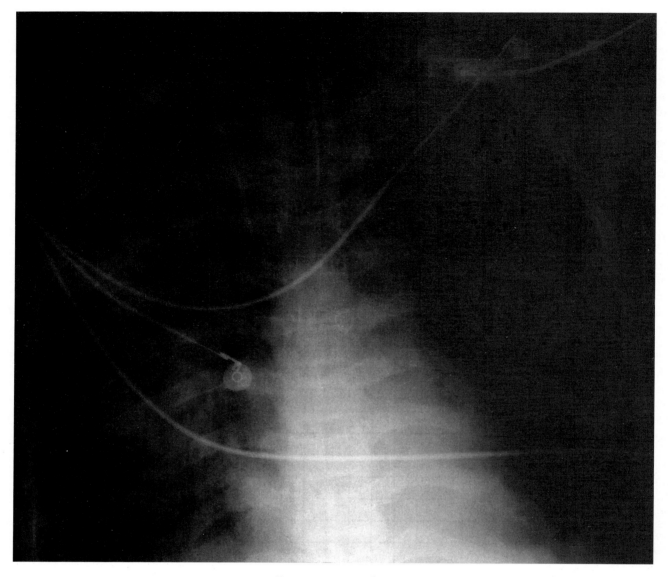

Figure 11-15   Proper position of endotracheal tube.

extremity are extremely useful for measurement of the central venous pressure (CVP) and for providing a conduit for the rapid infusion of fluid or chronic hyperalimentation. So that the CVP may be correctly measured, the catheter must be located within the true central venous system, beyond all the valves, which interfere with direct transmission of right atrial pressure to the catheter. The optimal location is where the brachiocephalic veins join to form the superior vena cava (medial to the anterior border of the first rib on chest radiographs) or within the superior vena cava itself.

Because up to one third of CVP catheters are incorrectly placed at the time of initial insertion, correct positioning of the catheter should be confirmed by a chest radiograph. The most common

aberrant location of a CVP catheter is the internal jugular vein (Figure 11-16). CVP catheters that extend to the right atrium are associated with an increased risk of cardiac arrhythmias and even perforation. Extension of the catheter into the hepatic veins may permit the infusion of potentially toxic substances (some antibiotics and hypertonic alimentation solutions) directly into the liver. Because CVP catheters may change position after initial placement because of patient motion or medical manipulation, periodic radiographic confirmation of the catheter position is often recommended.

The anatomy of the subclavian region may lead to complications when a central catheter is introduced via the subclavian vein. Because the pleura covering the apex of the lung lies just deep to the subclavian vein, a pneumothorax may develop. Since this may be difficult to detect clinically, a chest radiograph (if possible, with the patient in an upright position in expiration) should be obtained whenever insertion of a subclavian catheter has been attempted. Another complication is perivascular CVP placement, which may result in ectopic infusion of fluid into the mediastinum or pleural space. This diagnosis should be suggested if there is rapid development of mediastinal widening or pleural effusion after CVP catheter insertion (Figure 11-17). Other complications include inadvertent puncture of the subclavian artery, air embolism, and injury to the phrenic nerve.

Catheter breakage and embolization can result from laceration of the catheter by the needle used to insert it, fracture at a point of stress, or detachment of the catheter from its hub. The catheter fragment may lodge in the vena cava, in the right side of the heart, or in branches of the pulmonary artery (Figure 11-18), and result in thrombosis, infection, or perforation.

Swan-Ganz catheters

The flow-directed Swan-Ganz catheter consists of a central channel for measuring pulmonary capillary wedge (PCW) pressure and a second, smaller channel connected to an inflatable balloon at the catheter tip. Cardiac output and central venous pressure can also be measured by use of this catheter. It can be inserted at the bedside and floated to the pulmonary artery without the need for fluoroscopic monitoring.

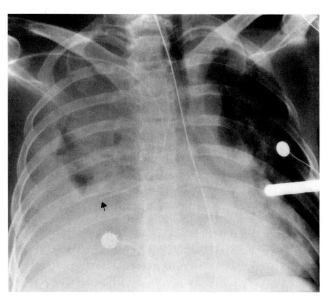

Figure 11-17 Central venous pressure catheter with its tip in the pleural space. A right subclavian catheter, which was introduced for total parenteral nutrition, perforated the superior vena cava and eroded into the right pleural space. Notice the tip of the catheter projecting beyond the right border of the mediastinum *(arrow)*. The direct infusion of parenteral fluid into the pleural space has led to a large right hydrothorax. (From Eisenberg RL: *Diagnostic imaging in internal medicine*, New York, 1985, McGraw-Hill.)

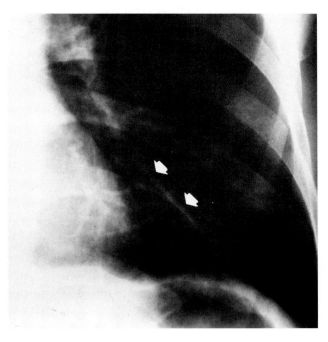

Figure 11-18 Broken central venous pressure catheter. The sheared-off portion of the catheter *(arrow)* is located in the left lower lobe. (From Eisenberg RL: *Diagnostic imaging in internal medicine*, New York, 1985, McGraw-Hill.)

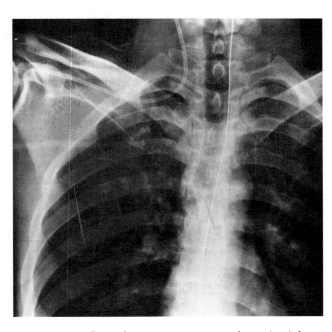

Figure 11-16 Central venous pressure catheter in right internal jugular vein. (From Dunbar RD: *Radiol Clin North Am* 22:699-722, 1984.)

Ideally, the catheter is positioned so that it lies within the right or left main pulmonary artery. Inflating the balloon causes the catheter to float downstream into a wedge position; deflating the balloon permits the catheter to recoil into the central pulmonary artery. Unlike standard intravenous catheters, the Swan-Ganz catheter has a characteristic radiopaque strip down its center.

The most common complication associated with the use of a Swan-Ganz catheter is pulmonary infarction distal to the catheter tip. Infarction may result from occlusion of a pulmonary artery by the catheter itself (if it is wedged in a too-peripheral vessel) or from clot formation in or about the catheter. The pulmonary infarction appears as a patchy air-space consolidation involving the area of the lung supplied by the pulmonary artery in which the catheter lies. The appropriate treatment is simple removal of the Swan-Ganz catheter; systemic heparinization is not required once this source of emboli or obstruction has been removed.

Transvenous cardiac pacemakers

Transvenous endocardial pacing is the method of choice for maintaining cardiac rhythm in patients with heart block or bradyarrythmias. Radiographic evaluation plays an important role in the initial placement of a pacemaker as well as in the detection of any subsequent complications. An overexposed film can demonstrate both the generator (for permanent pacemakers) and the course of the electrodes.

Ideally, the tip of the pacemaker should be positioned at the apex of the right ventricle. One common aberrant location is the coronary sinus. On a frontal radiograph, the tip often appears to be well positioned. A lateral projection is required to show that the tip is directly posteriorly in the coronary sinus, rather than in its proper position anteriorly in the right ventricle.

Although electrode fractures have become less common because of the development of new alloys, they are still a significant cause of pacing failure (Figure 11-19). The usual sites of fracture are near the pulse generator, at sharp bends in the wires, and at the point where the electrodes are inserted into the epicardium. Although most electrode fractures are easily detected on routine chest radiographs, some subtle fractures may be demonstrated only on oblique views or at fluoroscopy.

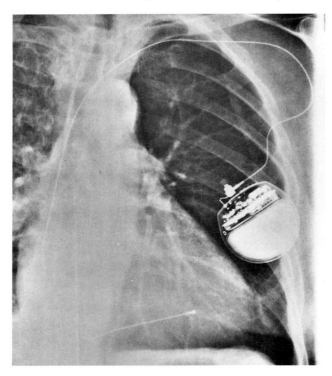

Figure 11-19 Pacemaker tip in coronary sinus. On the frontal projection, the tip of the electrode is angled slightly superiorly, traversing the heart in a higher plane than when it is located in the right ventricle. (From Dunbar RD: *Radiol Clin North Am* 22:699-722, 1984.)

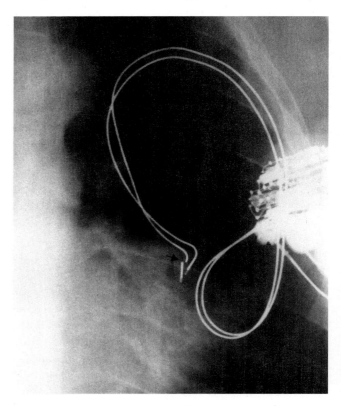

Figure 11-20 Fracture of a cardiac pacemaker wire *(arrow).* (From Eisenberg RL: *Diagnostic imaging in internal medicine,* New York, 1985, McGraw-Hill.)

Perforation of the myocardium by an intravenous electrode usually occurs at the time of insertion or during the first few days thereafter. Perforation should be suspected when the pacemaker fails to sense or elicit a ventricular response. Plain radiographs show the electrode tip lying outside the right ventricular cavity (Figure 11-20).

QUESTIONS

1. A vitamin C deficiency that was, years ago, common among sailors because of their lack of fresh fruit and vegetables is termed _____ .

2. _____ is a vitamin deficiency disease that occurs primarily in countries in which polished rice is the main staple.

3. A deficiency of niacin, characterized by reddening and scaling of exposed skin, vomiting, diarrhea, and nervous and mental disorders is termed _____ .

4. A bone disease of young children who have been deprived of adequate vitamin D is termed _____ .

5. Vitamin _____ is necessary in the bloodclotting mechanism.

6. A lack of vitamin _____ can result in night blindness.

7. When caloric intake consistently exceeds the amount needed for the body to function, _____ occurs.

8. A granulomatous disease of unknown origin that usually affects women more than men and blacks more than whites and whose presence is most often identified on screening chest radiographs is _____ .

9. A disease of young to middle-aged women, which is most likely an immune-complex disease, can affect several systems of the body and is characterized by a butterfly-shaped rash across the nose and cheeks is _____ .

10. A very malignant form of skin cancer, capable of metastasizing throughout the body, is _____ .

11. An inherited muscular disease characterized by severe weakness and eventual death from respiratory muscle failure or pneumonia is _____ .

12. The radiographer should be very alert to the possibility of _____ in patients with muscular dystrophy who lack normal swallowing ability.

13. Two common complications of intubation and barotrauma are _____ and _____ .

14. A common catheter used to measure cardiac output and central venous pressure is the _____ .

15. The optimal location for a central venous catheter is where the brachiocephalic veins join to form the _____ .

16. An overexposed radiograph is often requested for visualizing transvenous endocardiac pacers to demonstrate both the _____ and the _____ .

17. The most common complication associated with the Swan-Ganz catheter is _____ distal to the catheter tip.

18. Briefly describe why a lateral chest radiograph is very important in determining the correct position of the tip of the electrode of a transvenous cardiac pacer.

BIBLIOGRAPHY

Goodman LR, Putman C: *Critical care imaging,* Philadelphia 1991, Saunders.

Juhl JH, Crummy AB: *Essentials of radiologic imaging,* Philadelphia, 1987, Lippincott.

Kirks DR, McCormick VD, Greenspan RH: Pulmonary sarcoidosis, Am J Roentgenol 117:777-786, 1973.

Lubowitz R, Schumacher HR: Articular manifestations of systemic lupus erythematosus, Ann Intern Med 74:911-921, 1974.

GLOSSARY

achalasia Failure of the lower esophageal sphincter to relax because of absence or destruction of cells in the myenteric nerve plexus, which results in difficulty swallowing

adenopathy Enlargement of the lymphatic glands

adnexal Pertaining to the uterine appendages (ovaries, fallopian tubes, and ligaments)

amorphous Without shape or definite form

anechoic Not containing internal echoes (on ultrasound)

ankylosis Immobility and consolidation of a joint caused by disease, injury, or surgical procedure

anticoagulant Substance that suppresses or delays coagulation of the blood

arteriorvenous malformation Abnormal communication between an artery and vein

ascites Accumulation of fluid in the abdominal cavity

atresia Congenital absence or closure of a normal body orifice or tubular organ

Bence Jones protein Abnormal substance typically found in the blood of patients with multiple myeloma

bougienage Passage of an instrument through a tubular structure to increase its caliber (as in the treatment of a stricture of the esophagus)

bulla Large air-containing space

callus Formation of new bone that reunites the parts about a fracture

caseation Form of necrosis in which the tissue is changed into a dry, amorphous mass resembling cheese

catamenial Pertaining to menstruation

cavitation Formation of cavities, as in pulmonary tuberculosis or neoplasm

chondroblastic Forming cartilaginous tissue

chordae tendineae Thin cords that connect each cusp of the two atrioventricular valves to papillary muscles in the heart ventricles

coalesce To merge into a single mass

colic Intermittent abdominal pain that fluctuates corresponding to smooth muscle peristalsis

collaterals Blood vessels that develop or enlarge to provide an alternative route around an obstruction

congenital Existing at birth

conjunctivitis Inflammation of the delicate membrane that lines the eyelids and covers the exposed surface of sclera (white part) of the eye

contracture Shortening or shrinkage of a muscle or tendon resulting in persistent flexion or distortion at a joint

cortex Outer portion of a bone or internal organ (kidney, adrenal gland, brain)

curvilinear Having a curved configuration

de novo From the beginning; anew

demarcate To set or mark the limits of

diaphysis Shaft of a long bone

diploic space Loose osseous tissue between the two tables of the skull

dysphagia Difficulty swallowing

dysplasia Disordered growth or faulty development of various tissues or body parts

dyspnea Shortness of breath

effaced Wiped out or obliterated

embolus Any foreign matter, such as a blood clot or an air bubble, carried in the bloodstream

emphysema Pathologic accumulation of air in tissues or organs (especially applied to a disease of the lungs)

endemic Native to a particular country, nation, or region

endogenous Originating from within the body

engorgement Congestion of a blood vessel or tissue with blood or other fluid

epiphysis End of a long bone that at first is separated from the main part by cartilage but later fuses with it by ossification

erythropoietin Substance(s) serving as the humoral regulator of red blood cell formation

etiology The study of disease causes; do not use as a synonym for "cause"

exacerbation Increase in the severity of a disease or any of its symptoms

exogenous Arising from outside the body

exophthalmos Abnormal protrusion of the eyeball

extramedullary hematopoiesis Formation of red blood cells outside of the bone marrow

exudate Material such as fluid, cells, or cellular debris that has escaped from blood vessels and has been deposited in tissues or on tissue surfaces, usually as a result of inflammation

fecalith Intestinal stone formed around a center of fecal material

fibrin Essential portion of a blood clot

fibrinolysis Breaking up of a blood clot

fistula Abnormal connection, usually between two internal organs or from an internal organ to the surface of the body

focal Localized

fusiform Spindle shaped

Gram method Technique for staining microorganisms

granuloma Tumorlike mass of tissue caused by a chronic inflammatory process

Heberden's nodes Small, hard nodules at the distal interphalanageal joints of the fingers produced by calcific spurs of the articular cartilage and associated with osteoarthritis

hematogenous Spread by means of the blood stream

hemodynamic Pertaining to the movements involved in the circulation of the blood

hemoptysis Coughing up blood or bloodstained sputum

homogeneous Composed of material of similar or identical structure or quality

hydrocephalus Enlargement of the head because of an abnormal increase in fluid within the ventricular system

hyperlucency Overly black appearance on a radiograph

hyperplasia Abnormal increase in the number of cells composing a tissue or organ

hypertension High blood pressure

hypotension Low blood pressure

hypoxia Deficiency (lack) of oxygen

iatrogenic Resulting from the activity of physicians

indolent Causing little or no pain; slow to heal

infarction Death of tissue because of interruption of the normal blood supply

infundibula Thin passages connecting the calyces to the renal pelvis

inguinal Pertaining to the groin

insidious Developing in a slow or not apparent manner; more dangerous than seems evident, as in an insidious disease

intima Innermost layer of an organ or blood vessel

intraluminal Within the empty space (lumen) of a hollow viscus

intramural Within the wall of an organ

intrinsic Belonging to the real nature of a thing

ischemia Lack of blood supply in an organ or tissue

juxta-articular Adjacent to a joint

kyphosis Anterior convexity in the curvature of the thoracic spine, sacrum, and coccyx, as viewed from the side

leukocytosis Abnormal amount of white blood cells in the blood

lipoma Tumor composed of fat

lordosis Anterior concavity in the curvature of the lumbar and cervical spine, as viewed from the side

lymphangitic Spread by means of the lymphatic system

lymphoma Neoplastic disorder of lymphoid tissue

lytic Destructive

malaise Vague feeling of physical discomfort or uneasiness, as early in an illness

matrix Basic material from which a thing develops

medulla Inner substance of a bone (bone marrow) or an internal organ (kidney, adrenal gland)

mesentery Peritoneal folds attaching the small and large bowel to the back wall of the peritoneal cavity

mesothelioma Tumor developing from the surface of the pleura, pericardium, or peritoneum

metaphysis Wider part at the end of the shaft of a long bone, adjacent to the epiphyseal plate; located between the epiphysis and the diaphysis

monoclonal immunoglobulin Antibodies that are formed against a specific cell type

Morgagni hernia Protrusion of abdominal contents into the anterior and lateral aspects of the thoracic cavity

morphologic Pertaining to the form and structure of an organ

multilocular Having many cells or compartments

mycoplasma Colloquial usage for any of a genus of tiny microorganisms, smaller than bacteria but larger than viruses, that appear to be the causative agents of many diseases

myxedema Puffy thickening of the skin with slowing down of physical and mental activity caused by failure of the thyroid gland

necrosis Death of tissue

necrotic Dead or decayed

neoplasm Any new and abnormal growth, especially when the growth is uncontrolled and progressive

nephrocalcinosis Calcium deposits within the substance of the kidney

neurogenic Originating in the nervous system

nidus Focal point, especially of a stone or inflammatory process

oligemia Decreased blood flow

osteoblastic Forming bony tissue

osteoclastic Destroying bone

osteolytic Destroying bone

palpitations Rapid or fluttering beating of the heart, of which one is aware

paradoxical Seemingly contradictory or unbelievable, but which may actually be true in fact

parenchyma Essential elements of an organ

pathognomonic Specially distinctive or characteristic of a disease or pathologic condition

pedunculated Having a stalk (pedicle)

periphery Outside or away from the central portion of a structure

peristalsis Wormlike movement by which the alimentary canal or other tubular organ propels its contents

permeative Diffusely spreading through or penetrating a substance, tissue, or organ, as by a disease process such as cancer

pinna Cartilaginous lower projecting portion of the external ear

pneumococcus Type of gram-positive bacteria

pneumoperitoneum Presence of free gas in the peritoneal cavity

postpartum After childbirth

proliferate To multiply rapidly, increase profusely

punctate Marked with dots or tiny spots

rudimentary Imperfectly developed

sclerosis Conversion of a portion of bone into an ivory-like, densely opaque mass; an abnormal hardening of body tissues or parts, especially of the walls of arteries

sequestrum Piece of dead bone that has become separated from the surrounding healthy bone

serosa Outer layer of a viscus (especially in the alimentary tract)

shock Acute peripheral circulatory failure

silhouette (cardiac) Outer border of the heart, seen against the radiolucent lungs

spirochete Spiral type of bacterium of the genus *Spirochaeta*

staging Determination of the amount of spread of a neoplasm, necessary to select appropriate therapy and to predict the future course of a disease

stasis Stagnation of some fluid in the body (as of blood in veins); reduced peristalsis of the intestines resulting in the retention of feces

subchondral Just beneath the articular margin

subluxation Incomplete or partial dislocation

telangiectasia Vascular lesion formed by dilatation of a group of small blood vessels

teratoma Neoplasm composed to various kinds of embryonic tissue

thymoma Tumor originating from the thymus gland

tortuous Full of twists, turns, or curves

trabecula Supporting or anchoring strands of connective tissue within body structures

triradiate Radiating in three directions

trophoblastic Relating to the layer by which the fertilized ovum is attached to the uterine wall and from which the developing embryo receives its nourishment

urate Salt of uric acid

valvulae conniventes Circular folds of the small bowel

vasculitis Inflammation of a vessel

virus One of a group of minute infectious agents characterized by a lack of independent metabolism and by the ability to reproduce only within living host cells

viscous Thick, sticky

viscus Any large internal organ, especially in the abdomen

APPENDIX A

Prefixes/Suffixes/Roots

Prefix/Suffix/Root	Meaning	Example
a-, ab-	away from	abduction
a-, an-	without; not	asymmetric, anencephalic
ad-	toward	adduction
-algia	pain	arthralgia
ana-	up, back again	anaplastic
ante-	before, in front of	antecubital
anti-, ant-	against	antibody, antitoxin
auto-	self	autoimmune
bi-	two	bilateral, bidirectional
-blast	budding	osteoblast
cardi-	heart	cardiology, cardiac; pericardium
caudal	tail	caudal
cephal-	head	cephalic; hydrocephaly
chondro-	cartilage	chondroma, chondrosarcoma
-clast	destroyer, breaker	osteoclast
contra-	opposite	contralateral
crani-	skull	cranium, cranial
cyano-	dark blue	cyanotic
cyto-	cell	cytoplasm; erythrocyte, leukocyte
-dactyl-	finger, toe	polydactyly, arachnodactyly
deci-	tenth	decimal

derm-	skin	dermatology; epidermis
dys-	bad; difficult	dysplasia, dysuria
ecto-	outside of	ectoderm, ectopic
endo-, ento-	within	endoderm, endometrium
erythr-	red	erythrocyte
gastr-	stomach	gastric
-genic	causing	carcinogenic, pathogenic
gyn-, gyneco-	woman	gynecology
hem-, haem-	blood	hemorrhage, hemolytic
hemi-	half	hemisphere, hemidiaphragm
hetero-	different	heterogeneous
homo-	same	homogeneous
hyper-	over; excessively	hyperthyroidism, hypertension, hyperintense
hypo-	under; too little	hypothyroidism, hypotension, hypointense
iatro-	healer, healing	iatrogenic; psychiatry
infra-	below	infratemporal
intra-	within	intramural, intradermal
ipsi-	same	ipsilateral
iso-	equal	isointense
-itis	inflammation	appendicitis, diverticulitis
juxta-	near, next to	juxta-articular
kilo-	thousand	kilogram
leuko-, leuco-	white	leukocyte, leukemia
lipo-	fat	lipoma, liposarcoma
-lysis, -lytic	dissolve	lytic, osteolytic
macro-	large	macroadenoma
magn-	great, large	magnify, magnum (foramen)
mal-	bad, ill	malunion, malalignment
mega-, megalo-	large	megadose
melan-	black	melanoma, melanin
micro-	small	microscope, microadenoma, microcirculation
milli-	thousandth	milligram, milliliter
mono-	one	monostotic, monoclonal
multi-	many	multilocular, multifaceted
myelo-	marrow	myelogram; osteomyelitis
myo-	muscle	myoma, myostitis
necro-	dead	necrosis
neo-	new	neovascularity, neoplasm
non-	not	nonunion, nonviable
ocul-	eye	ocular, oculomotor [nerve]
oligo-	few	oligemia
-ology	study of	radiology, pathology
onco-	tumor	oncology
ophthalm-	eye	ophthalmology
-osis	condition of	diverticulosis
osteo-	bone	osteomyelitis, osteosarcoma
pan-	all	pansinusitis, pancytopenia
par-, para-	beside	para-aortic, paravertebral
patho-	disease	pathology; adenopathy
peri-	around	periarticular, periventricular, pericardium
plasm-, plast-	shape, form	neoplasm; anaplastic
pleur-	rib; side	pleural, pleurisy
pneumo-	air, breath	pneumothorax, pneumonia
poly-	many	polycystic, polyostotic
post-	after, later; behind	posttraumatic, postsurgical, postoperative
pre-	before	premenstrual, prepontine
pseudo-	false	pseudotumor, pseudopolyp
psych-	mind, spirit	psychiatry, psychology
re-	again, anew	reoperate, recalcify
retro-	backward; behind	retroperitoneum
-rrhea	flow, gush	diarrhea
schizo-	split	schizophrenia
sclero-	hard	sclerotic; atherosclerosis
semi-	half	semicircular
sub-	under, below	suborbital, subphrenic, subhepatic

super-, supra-	above; more than	suprarenal; supraorbital
syn-, sym-	with, together	synthesis, symmetric
tachy-	fast	tachycardia
techn-	art, skill	technology, technique
terti-	third	tertiary
tetra-	four	tetralogy [of Fallot]
thermo-	heat	thermometer
tomo-, -tome	cut	tomography; microtome
trans-	across	transverse [colon], transvenous [pacer]
tri-	three	trimalleolar, trisomy
ultra-	beyond	ultrasound
uni-	one	unilateral

Appendix B

Laboratory Tests

↑ Acid phosphatase	Prostate cancer, metastatic to bone
↑ Alkaline phosphatase	Liver disease; Paget's disease; bone tumor
↑ Amylase	Pancreatitis
↑ Bilirubin	Liver disease
↑ Calcium	Hyperparathyroidism, bone destruction
↑ Cholesterol	Tendency toward atherosclerosis
↑ Creatinine phosphokinase (CPK)	Myocardial infarction; pulmonary infarction
↑ Creatinine	Kidney disease
↑ Glucose	Diabetes mellitus; Cushing's syndrome; glucagonsecreting pancreatic tumor
↑ Lactic dehydrogenase (LDH)	Myocardial infarction; pulmonary infarction; liver disease
↑ Total protein	Dehydration; immunoglobinopathy
↑ Serum glutamic oxaloacetic transaminase (SGOT)	Liver disease
↑ Serum glutamic pyruvic transaminase (SGPT)	Myocardial infarction; liver disease
↑ Blood urea nitrogen (BUN)	Kidney disease
↑ Uric acid	Gout; antidiuretic therapy
↓ Calcium	Hypoparathyroidism; malabsorption; osteomalacia/rickets
↓ Total protein	Chronic liver disease; malnutrition; nephrotic syndrome
↓ Cholesterol	Malnutrition; liver disease
↓ Glucose	Insulin-secreting pancreatic tumor; liver disease; hypopituitarism

Appendix C

Chapter 1 Key:

1. edema
2. phagocytosis
3. keloid
4. suppurative
5. ischemia
6. infarct
7. hemotoma
8. atrophy
9. neoplasia
10. adenoma
11. F
12. I
13. Q
14. B
15. J

16. O
17. T
18. P
19. C
20. G
21. D
22. J
23. E
24. N
25. L
26. K
27. S
28. A
29. R
30. M

Chapter 2 Key:

1. patient inhales, then exhales, then inhales again to full inspiration
2. alveoli
3. pleura (visceral)
4. lung abscess
5. bronchography
6. emphysema
7. silicosis, asbestosis, coal workers' pneumoconiosis
8. pulmonary arteriovenous fistula
9. hyaline membrane disease
10. tension pneumothorax
11. empyema
12. diaphragm
13. to demonstrate air fluid levels
14. B
15. H H
    H H
    E H
    E H
    H H

16. low-pressure, low-resistance system through which oxygen enters and carbon dioxide is removed
17. high-pressure systemic circulation by which oxygenated blood is supplied to nourish the lung tissue
18. parietal pleura
19. pneumonia
20. coughing, droplets
21. pneumothorax
22. emphysema
23. pneumoconiosis
24. septic embolism
25. cystic fibrosis
26. atelectasis
27. subcutaneous emphysema
28. expiration, lateral decubitus
29. tracheoesophageal fistula
30. C
31. lateral decubitus
32. mediastinal emphysema (pneumomediastinum)
33. C

Chapter 3 Key:

1. B
2. A
3. D
4. D
5. B
6. A
7. B
8. A
9. B
10. C
11. A
12. D
13. B
14. D
15. C

16. B
17. C
18. B
19. D
20. B
21. C
22. A
23. C
24. D
25. B
26. B
27. H   H
    H (initially) / E (later) E
    E   E
    E   H

Chapter 4 Key:

1. B
2. C
3. A
4. B
5. C
6. A
7. B
8. D
9. C
10. C
11. C
12. B
13. B

14. D
15. D
16. A
17. B
18. A
19. D
20. B
21. B
22. D
23. B
24. C
25. A

Chapter 5 Key:

1. C
2. D
3. B
4. A
5. C

6. D
7. C
8. D
9. C
10. A

Chapter 6 Key:

1. D
2. A
3. B
4. D
5. D
6. C
7. B
8. D
9. A
10. A
11. C
12. C

13. A
14. B
15. A
16. C
17. B
18. C
19. B
20. B
21. B
22. B
23. D
24. D

Chapter 7 Key:

1. C
2. C
3. B
4. D
5. D
6. B
7. A
8. C
9. B
10. C
11. CT
12. CT, MRI
13. transient ischemic attack
14. MRI
15. epilepsy
16. Alzheimer's disease
17. Parkinson's disease
18. horizontal, erect
19. hydrocephalus
20. cross-table lateral, horizontal
21. D
22. J
23. N

24. G
25. T
26. P
27. I
28. M
29. C
30. R
31. O
32. A
33. H
34. V
35. F
36. S
37. W
38. U
39. X
40. L
41. Q
42. B
43. Y
44. K
45. E

Chapter 8 Key:

1. C
2. A
3. C
4. B
5. B
6. C

7. C
8. C
9. A
10. C
11. B
12. B

Chapter 9 Key:

1. C
2. C
3. A
4. B
5. B
6. C
7. B
8. B
9. C
10. B
11. D
12. B
13. C
14. B
15. B
16. B
17. B
18. A
19. C
20. B
21. D

Chapter 10 Key:

1. nonionizing
2. hysterosalpingography, mammography
3. spermatogenesis
4. testosterone
5. vasectomy
6. cancer of the prostate
7. ultrasound
8. T
9. ivory vertebra
10. ultrasound
11. testicular torsion
12. testicular, lymphatic
13. ovulation
14. ectopic
15. hysterosalpingography
16. syphilis
17. dermoid/teratoma
18. fibroids
19. breast
20. carcinoma of the cervix

Chapter 11 Key:

1. scurvy
2. beriberi
3. pellagra
4. rickets
5. K
6. A
7. obesity
8. sarcoidosis
9. systemic lupus erythematosus
10. melanoma
11. muscular dystrophy
12. aspiration
13. pneumothorax, pneumomediastinum
14. Swan-Ganz
15. superior vena cava
16. generator, electrodes
17. infarction
18. The AP and PA radiograph may show the tip appearing in the correct position, whereas a lateral is needed to assure proper position of the tip in the anterior portion of the right ventricle.

Index